I0125989

# THE "FEDERAL" RESERVE CONSPIRACY
# &
# ROCKEFELLERS

## THEIR "GOLD CORNER"

By Emanuel M. Josephson

*Author of*
THE BLACKED-OUT HISTORY SERIES
    Rockefeller "Internationalist"
    The Truth About Rockefeller, "Public Enemy No. 1"
    Strange Death of F. D. Roosevelt
    Roosevelt's Communist Manifesto
    Rackets, Social Service & Medical
    Your Life Is Their Toy
    Merchants In Medicine
    Unheeded Teachings of Jesus, Or Christ Rejected
* * * * * *

    Nearsightedness Is Preventable
    Glaucoma & Its Medical Treatment
    Breathe Deeply & Avoid Colds
    The Thymus, Manganese & Myasthenia Gravis

CHEDNEY PRESS
230 E. 61 St.        New York City, N.Y. 10021

ISBN: 978-2-925369-96-7
Printed in the USA.

## CONTENTS

This is the story of the true-to-life prototype of Ian Fleming's *Goldfinger*. The truth, in this instance, is stranger, more menacing and frightening than fiction. The key characters are not as ostentatious in their criminalty. They are far more ruthless, though cowardly, gangsters. They pose as "philanthropists" and are unsuspected. They use the U.S. and other governments, their dis-"United" Nations, and kings and queens as pawns in their game. Millions of humans have been slaughtered in an endless series of wars they have engineered to expand their Empire and increase their loot. Their grandiose objective is "internationalist," "One World" dictatorship, genocide and enslavement of mankind.

An honest Supreme Court, not yet "packed" by them, ruled in its 1911 Standard Oil Co. dissolution decree:

> *"For the safety of the Republic we now decree that the dangerous conspiracy must be ended by November 15 (1911)."*

They "thumbed their noses" at the Court. They were then developing a far vaster and more devastating conspiracy: the first of a series of World Wars, a "Federal" Reserve conspiracy, a Federal income tax and a worldwide "Gold Corner" that would make possible instant, global looting. Entirely unsuspected, except by a few astute observers, they cunningly and patiently wove a web in which they have entrapped mankind. They have succeeded in undermining our Republic and betraying our nation. Their shrewd kinsman, ex-President Harry Shippe Truman, accused them, fortunately for us, of plotting our defeat in World War II, on the floor of the Senate, on March 27, 1942, in the words:

> "Even after we were in the war, Standard Oil of New Jersey was putting forth every effort of which it was capable to protect the control of the German government over vital war materiel. As Patrick Henry said: 'If that is treason (and it certainly is treason) then make the most of it.' *Yes it is treason.* You can not translate it in any other way." (15:3)

Liberty Lobby has stated that the trading of the conspirators in the lives of our soldiers in Vietnam and elsewhere escapes the charge of treason, and capital punishment, only because of the technicality that war has not been declared. (414)

On January 15, 1967, Rockefellers announced that they were joining their agent, Cyrus Eaton Jr. in financing the industry and commerce of our enemy, Soviet Russia, who make no secret of their supplying the North Vietnamese with arms and munitions to slaughter our GIs. The Daily News (N.Y.) sardonically commented editorially: "...it would be sad to see some Rockefeller or some Eaton marched off to the jug for having accidentally sold strategic goods to enemy nations." (411) At the time of the announcement of the deal, Kosygin proclaimed that Russia planned to increase the volume of arms and munitions it was supplying our foes in Vietnam. One year later numerous huge tanks and jet planes of the design, supplied by Soviet Russia with "foreign aid" money furnished by American taxpayers through Rockefeller and Eaton, began to mow down

## KHRUSHCHEV MEETS HIS ROCKEFELLER MASTER

Gov. Nelson Rockefeller Visits Khrushchev's Quarters At Waldorf Astoria Tower; And Cordially And Comradely Greets Him. False Headlines Say That They Met "For The First Time" and "As Total Strangers". Khrushchev Boasts That He Receives Secret Codes, Money And All "Secret" Reports From Rockefeller Dominated CIA Quislings. (World Wide News) our GIs by the thousands in Vietnam in the 1968 Tet New Year Communist offensive. There could be no doubt that the "philanthropist" internationalists had given aid and comfort to our enemies in time of war. The Constitution states that to "give aid and comfort to the enemy" is treason, whether in peace or war. But who dares charge the conspirators with treason, or see them "marched off to the jug?" Do not our GIs and all of us live at their "tender mercy?" Should we not render obeisance to our "beneficent benefactors" who have granted us the privilege of laying down our lives and our fortunes to serve their Vietnamese and Soviet interests, and let them "draft" themselves to rule us as dictator Presidents?

Our military reverses in Vietnam have aggravated the financial crisis, both of them engineered by the conspirators. It has helped the conspirators materially in hastening the culmination of their "Gold Corner," through the agency of their private stock corporation, the fraudulent "Federal" Reserve. That has enabled them to transfer the gold looted from us during their "New" Deal, to their "foreign" accounts. Since in years gone by, they have designedly and purposefully tied the value of the dollar to gold, our Treasury is once again threatened by them with "insolvency" and our dollars with worthlessness; and as a consequence many of our people face wiping out of savings, pensions insurance and other forms of liquid wealth, and ruin. And duped by the scorn of the concept of "conspiracy" and treason created by the conspirators through their numerous propagandists paid and voluntary, most folks are bewildered and face the affair with a feeling of helplessness.

It is the purpose of this eighth volume in my *Blacked Out History* series to alert the nation to the fact that by simple, legal and just measures the conspirators can be thwarted, our Treasury restored to complete and impregnable solvency, our Republic, the dollar and our public and private fortunes saved. The measures we must adopt and the actions we must take to effect this rescue, are the subjects of the last several chapters of this book.

Limitations of space have precluded the inclusion of much background material that is beyond its scope but essential for a full understanding of the subject. For this information the reader is referred to other books of the series listed on the title page, especially *The Truth About Rockefeller*, "*Public Enemy No. 1*," *Studies in Criminal Psychopathy*, and *Rockefeller "Internationalist."*

The presentation herein is largely based on statements of the conspirators and their pressagents. The numbers in parentheses indicate references listed in the bibliography; and numbers following colons refer to pages.

Bear in mind that the conspiracy can be frustrated completely, even at this stage, and our Republic and fortunes saved, if we act promptly and *if there can be found in Congress a sufficient number of uncorrupted patriots intelligently interested in saving the their own fortunes, ours and the nation.*

I hope that the reader will be guided by insight into the truth and will be as successful as I in anticipating future schemes and developments and adopting protective measures.

# CHAPTER I
## THE ULTIMATE "POWER OF THE PURSE":
## THE ISSUE OF MONEY

Human experience teaches the power of the purse. One may well wonder if it is not Almighty.

Few of the power-mad characters of history who have sought to rule their fellows and to build empires have failed to grab the wealth of lands on which they have design, and usurp the power of purse over those whom they seek to subjugate. This is true even of those who have been more motivated by the lust for power than by simple thievery and brigandage. For money is the lifeblood of commerce and industry. In the form of either cash or credit, money enables the expansion of a nation's economy beyond the narrow limits of crude barter. Since commerce and industry are the livelihoods of nations and their peoples, the control of money is the obvious key to the control of nations and the world.

From time immemorial, rulers of lands have seized and retained control of their monetary systems. The issuance of coins and the control of currency have been cherished throughout the ages as the prime source of wealth, might and power. Roman emperors, for instance, proudly stamped their images on their coins as an expression of their power; and manipulated the content of those coins for their personal profit.

Rome's successor, the Holy Roman Empire, dissimulated its interest in money and its power. This was in accord with its professed tenets of Nazarene, theistic Communism. Under ecclesiastic, Canon Law, even profits in business transactions were decreed to be the cardinal sin and capital offence of "usury". As late as the sixteenth century, one hundred Christian business men who held no Papal dispensation, were burned at the stake in Geneva, as a penalty under Church law, for making profits in their business transactions. Title to all wealth as well as to the persons and lives of all the earth are claimed by the Church, on the ground that their ownership is divinely vested in the Pope as the vicar of Jesus Christ on earth. Thus theistic, Nazarene Communism, and the "modern" religion that goes by the name of Communism and is supposedly atheist, both are basically super-capitalist and both mask their avid grab for money and wealth. Title to all wealth was vested in the Church and in its champion "knights," who at the same time assumed the role of so-called "protectors," much like the present-day "labor leaders," of their vassals whom they mercilessly enslaved and looted.

Both Churchmen and lay knights used the despised Jews for the conduct of their usurious financial operations, in order to avoid "sinning" and the death penalty that it involved. The Jews proved very useful and handy for that purpose. Their use was justified by their "Christian" masters in a manner that they were taught by their faith was incontrovertible. Jews were damned and doomed by their faith and their failure to accept the divinity of Jesus and the perversion of His teachings by the Jewish merchant, Saul of Tarsus, alias St. Paul, opined the Churchmen; and therefore it was a "good work" to hasten them to their damnation. This they did by forcing their Jewish serfs

3

to engage, as their pawns, in the "sin" and crime of "usury" by which was meant the charging of interest as well as loan-sharking and engaging in profitable commerce, for their Christian, ecclesiastical bosses.

Often the Churchmen barred the Jews, by their orders and laws, from engaging in any other vocation than those to which the stigma of usury was attached, especially loan-sharking, as their agents. This was a particularly advantageous setup for the Churchmen. For if the Jew was merciful and failed to extract from the victims everything that they possessed, "the last drop of blood", he was burned at the stake as a "heretic". On the other hand, if the Jew mercilessly followed orders of his priestly boss, was honest with his boss and amassed a fortune for him and for himself, there was nothing to bar his Christian master from exercising his cupidity and robbing his faithful loan-shark by charging him with the "sin" of usury, confiscating the fortune that he had made in his service, and with great hypocritic show of "piety," burn him at the stake—"to insure his salvation."

The victorious Lombard invaders of the Holy Roman Empire changed the financial situation in much the same manner as have the latter-day Maffia extortioners and blackmailers. Seizing control of the Church, they gave themselves "dispensation" to disregard the Canon Law on usury. They openly engaged in it from the very steps of the Vatican.

Dispensation from the Canon on Usury was subsequently granted by the Vatican, in the 15th century, to the German Fuggers, the Rockefellers of that era. Their profits from commerce, usury and the sale of Papal dispensations, as agents of the Vatican, grew rapidly, as did their "payoff" to the Church. They were heaped with Papal honors. But their grasping greed and merciless loan-sharking earned for them distrust and terror. When one of their number was elevated to the rank of Cardinal, the Churchmen feared that the Fuggers would reach out and steal the Vatican itself. They then decided that their Jewish pawns were more completely at their mercy, more amenable and safer.

Trusteeship of the fortune of one of the wealthiest Christian rulers of Europe whose confidence had been earned by honest and trustworthy dealings, during the Napoleonic wars, is the source of the wealth and influence that the Rothschilds acquired in the first decades of the 19th century. Subsequently, after making a large loan to the hard-pressed Vatican, that no Christian would consider making, they became the fiscal agents of the Vatican, received Papal decorations and preferments, and enforced the policies dictated by the Church. It was largely in this sense that they were "international bankers". And the policies dictated by them were in effect the policies dictated by the Church. They enforced those policies through their establishments in many lands.

An amusing story is told of the earliest relations of the Rothschilds with the Vatican. The Vatican found itself short of ready cash after almost half a century of war waged on it for the Jesuit Order by one of its unordained members, Adam Weishaupt, to avenge its abolition, in 1773, as "immoral and a menace to the Church and the Faith" by short-lived Pope Clement XIV in his Papal breve *Dominus Ac Redemptor*. Weishaupt and his fellow Jesuits cut off the income to the Vatican by launching and leading the French Revolution; by directing Napoleon's conquest of Catholic Europe; by the revolt against the Church led by such priests as Father Hidalgo, in Mexico and Latin America; by eventually having Napoleon throw Pope Pius VII in jail at Avignon until he agreed, as the price for his release, to reestablish the Jesuit Order. This Jesuit war on the Vatican was terminated by the Congress of Vienna and by the secret, 1822, Treaty of Verona. (72:8 ;73)

The Jesuits thus so completely impaired the credit of the Vatican that no Christian banker would entrust it with a loan of needed funds. Only the nouveau riche Jewish upstarts, who had made their fortune in the latter part of the Napoleonic wars, the Rothschilds, would trust the Church with urgently needed 5 million pounds.

Pope Gregory XVI was so grateful to the Rothschilds that he conferred on Kalman Rothschild a Papal decoration. In deference to the Jewish faith of the philanthropic banker, the usual cross in the decoration was replaced by a Star of David. Rothschild was incensed at this discriminatory gesture. He demanded, and was awarded, the decoration with a cross. Ever since, the Rothschilds have been the fiscal agents of the Vatican.

The Rothschilds sought to extend their financial and political dominion to the United States, for themselves primarily to serve the interests of their Vatican masters. The Vatican's interest in the U.S. Republic was clearly revealed in the Treaty of Verona, in which the Jesuit Order pledged itself, as the price of its reestablishment, to destroy the "works of Satan" that it had accomplished in setting up, by revolts, representative governments such as republics and so-called "democracies". (72:8) Senator Robert Owen pointed out, in the Senate, that the prime target to which the Vatican and the "Holy Alliance" directed the subversive and destructive activities of the Society of Jesus is the United States (73), as well as other republics of the Western Hemisphere. (72:10) This plot, he related, was the target at which the Monroe Doctrine was directed.

The Rothschild-Vatican cabal unsuccessfully attempted to gain control over the power of the purse in the U.S. through the First and the Second Bank of the United States. They were established under the emergency powers granted the President by the Constitution, as temporary institutions to tide the country through the periods of financial stress occasioned by the Revolutionary and 1812 Wars. But the conspirators failed in their efforts to fasten their hold on the nation's power of the purse through establishment of a privately controlled central bank of permanent character. They were doomed to failure by the stumbling block of fear of a banking monopoly, and by the deliberate barrier against central banking and Federal control and issue of currency that had been embodied in the Constitution for reasons that will be related.

"Give me control of a nation's money, and I care not who rules it," is an age-old adage, the origination of which is attributed to Amshel Mayer Rothschild. It is a trite expression of the power of the purse that he might well have learned as a familiar nursery rhyme.

Few of the plotters who have conspired to enslave and rule mankind plotted more studied use of the control of money and wealth than did the founders of modern-day Communism: Jesuit Adam Weishaupt, alias Spartacus, and his disciple, Moses Mordecai Marx Levy, alias (Heinrich) Karl Marx. They proposed for the purpose of sneakily stealing control of the world and of looting everyone, three basic measures: First, their control, as rulers, of money and banking. Second, a progressive income tax that would be perverted into a capital tax. Third, a confiscatory inheritance tax. The manner in which this conspiracy has been imposed on the nation is our theme.

## CHAPTER II
## AMERICAN COLONIES' STRUGGLE WITH
## THE BOARD OF TRADE

The American colonists had a long and unfortunate experience with the use of money as a medium of control and looting, at the hands of the British Board of Trade. The function of the Board was to provide steadily increasing revenue for themselves and the King. Its personnel included no Lombards or Jewish moneylenders. The Board was composed of agents of the King, and included, with members of the Privy Council, the Archbishop of Canterbury who represented the Church of England. Shylock could not have been harder in the treatment of the colonists than the Board members in their effort to squeeze the last drop of blood, the last farthing, out of the colonial subjects.

One of the principal devices adopted by these dignitaries of Church and State in their colonial extortion scheme was monetary control. The colonies were denied credit and were required to pay levied taxes and make payment for imports with either metallic coins or other currency of the realm. Since the colonies then produced no gold or silver, and had to import most of their needs, they were soon drained of both of those forms of payment. Money acceptable to the Board of Trade became the scarcest of all commodities. And that scarcity, in turn, depreciated the value of all other commodities. The only alternative left to the colonists was the highly inconvenient and disadvantageous process of barter.

Benjamin Franklin described the depression that resulted, in his tract entitled *A Modest Enquiry Into The Nature And Necessity Of A Paper Currency (71)*. He reported that New England began to issue colonial paper money in 1696. (68:207) Also Massachussetts, with characteristic Yankee ingenuity and sound common sense, had issued bills of credit to landowners that were secured by mortgages on their land. These notes bore interest which became a sound public revenue. (69:262)

The representatives of the Crown on the Board of Trade were displeased and alarmed by the issuance of paper money by the Colonies because it meant an escape from their control and looting through the

6

power of the purse. An attempt was made by the Board to retrieve this control by the issuance, in 1720, of an order to the governors of the Colonies that made emission of so-called Bills of Credit by the Colonists subject to the King's pleasure. (69:262) Pennsylvania disregarded that order and issued paper money, as did also New York and New Jersey. Pennsylvania also made loans to new colonists that bore a low rate of interest and were repayable in instalments.

In March, 1751, the Board of Trade presented Parliament with a Restraining Act which barred the Colonies by law, from issuing paper money, letters of credit, that gave the King's orders the validity of formal law. (69:367) The Board was determined to make restriction of the supply of money in the Colonies, a constantly more profitable venture. The pressure of the Lords of the Board of Trade resulted in severe depreciation of colonial currency in international trade, effected by repressive measures and denial of customary rights. (69:370) This was accentuated by the determination of the Trade Lords to extract more revenue from the Colonies at the time of the French-Indian War.

The basic cause of the Revolutionary War was the persistent effort of the Board of Trade to profitably maintain the power of purse over the Colonies. This stimulated in the Colonies the quest for independence, which came to a head when their representatives assembled in Albany to deal with the Indian tribes. There, at the urging of Benjamin Franklin, they carried out the plan that had been advanced originally as early as 1697, by William Penn: a Confederacy of the Colonies that would regulate commerce on the American continent. (69:388)

On July 10, 1754, a Constitution for a perpetual Confederacy and Union was adopted by the assembled representatives of the Colonies. Among the articles incorporated in the Constitution was one that provided for the issuance by the Colonies, on their joint order only, of paper money. (69:385) This had been long advocated by Franklin. In March 1755, the Pennsylvania Assembly borrowed money and issued bills of credit without authorization of either King or Governor.

It fell to the lot of Franklin to reply to a statement made by Lord Hillborough on behalf of the Board of Trade, that undertook to justify restraint of issuance of bills of credit by the Colonies, and to reply to its February 9, 1764 Report. The Report alleged that it was essential that "every medium of trade should have an intrinsic value... Gold and silver are therefore the fittest for this medium..."; and that permitting the issuance of paper money "ruins...the Colonies". Franklin replied to the contrary, that paper money that served as a medium of exchange and credit had made possible the growth of the Colonies and their trade, that had profited England by providing greater facility and convenience in trade than does barter, and was the only alternative in face of the shortage of British coins. He noted that the wealthy, presumably Tory, elements among the Colonists who profited from the money shortage as bankers and moneylenders and regarded the issuance of paper money by the Colonies as a dilution of their control of wealth, had also opposed the issuance of paper money. (70:164; 68:206)

The experience of the Colonists with the efforts of the Board of

7

Trade to use money as a medium of control and a device for extortion, that drove them to eventual rebellion and revolt, could be expected to make them fearful of extending to any agency the power of issuing bills of credit and paper money. They realized too well from their fresh experiences, that the delegation of this power could ultimately lead to the menace of dictatorship and subjection. This explains why the Constitution of the United States denies the Federal government the power to issue currency other than coins, or to set up or charter banks. These powers were jealously guarded for themselves by the States and retained by them as States Rights.

## CHAPTER III
## THE CONSTITUTION DENIES CONGRESS THE RIGHT TO ISSUE MONEY.
## CONTROL OF CONGRESS IS RESTRICTED TO COINAGE.

The authors of the Constitution firmly held in mind the dread experience that the Colonies had had with the Board of Trade vested with the power of the purse and its control of the issuance of monetary notes. They were confronted, also, with violent opposition against Federal involvement in banking and finance by the vested money and banking interests, comprised largely of the Tory element that had collaborated with the Board of Trade prior to the Revolution. For the purpose of usurping continued control of money and banking, that element undertook to block the signing of the Constitution by their respective States, if control of those function were taken away from them.

The Articles of Confederation provided, in Article IX:

"The United States in Congress assembled, shall have the sole and exclusive right and power of regulating the alloy and value of *coin* struck by their own authority, *or by that of the respective States...*"

As a result of the vigorous fight waged by the Tory bankers, the same limitation of the Federal Government to the issue and control of coins, only, was embodied in the Constitution, in

"Section 8. Legislative Powers of Congress.

"Congress shall have the power

"5. To *coin* money; to regulate the value thereof..."

This was supplemented by restriction of the powers of the States, which further clarifies the intent of the framers of the Constitution, as follows:

"Section 10. Prohibition upon the States

"5. No State shall..make anything but gold and silver *coin* a tender in payment of debts..."

8

## MADISON'S "FEDERALIST" LETTER EXPLAINS
## BARRING CONGRESS NOTE ISSUE

The strength of the opposition even to the delegation to Congress and the Federal Government of these very limited monetary provisions is indicated by the arguments advanced in their favor by James Madison in *The Federalist*, No. XLIII, as follows:

"The right of coining money, which is here taken away from the States, was left in their hands by the Confederation as a concurrent right with that of Congress, under an exception in favor of the exclusive right of Congress to regulate the alloy and value. In this instance also, the new provision is an improvement on the old. While the alloy and value depend on the general authority, a right of coinage in the particular States could have no other effect than to multiply expensive mints, and diversify the forms and weights of the circulating pieces. The latter inconveniency defeats one purpose for which the power was originally submitted to the federal head; and as far as the former might prevent an inconvenient remittance of gold and silver to the central mint for recoinage, the end can be attained by local mints established under the general authority.

"The extension of the prohibition of bills of credit must give pleasure to every citizen, in proportion to his love of justice and his knowledge of the true springs of public prosperity. The loss which America has sustained since the peace, from the pestilent effects of paper money on the necessary confidence between man and man, on the necessary confidence in the public councils, on the industry and morals of the people, and on the character of republican government, constitutes an enormous debt against the States chargeable with unadvised measure, which must long remain unsatisfied; or rather an accumulation of guilt, which can be expiated no otherwise than by voluntary sacrifice on the altar of justice, of the power which has been the instrument of it. In addition to these persuasive considerations, it may be observed that the same reasons which show the necessity of denying to the States the power of regulating coin prove with equal force that *they ought not be at liberty to substitute a paper medium in place of coin.* Had every State a right to regulate the value of its coin, there might be as many different currencies as States, and thus the intercourse among them would be impeded; retrospective alterations in its value might be made, and thus the citizens of other States be injured, and animosities be kindled among the States themselves. The subjects of foreign powers might suffer from the same cause, and hence the Union be discredited and embroiled by the indiscretion of a single member. No one of these mischiefs is less incident to a power in the States to emit paper money, than to coin gold or silver. The power to make anything but gold and silver a tender in payment of debts, is withdrawn from the States, on the same principle with that of issuing paper currency."

There is a curious and highly significant omission in Madison's presentation of the case for paper money. He makes no mention of such money, paper notes issued by the State of Massachussetts Bay, which is the only money ever issued in the history of our country, up to that time and ever since, that was redeemed at the exact value, in purchasing power, as when it was issued. The credit of the States had been destroyed in the course of the Revolutionary War by the issue of fiat currency that became worthless directly after their issue. They gave rise to the expression: "Not worth a Continental".

Soldiers and veterans who had received no other pay or subsistence than the worthless Continentals, returned in numbers from the War and demanded emolument in money that had value and purchasing power. They constituted a threat to the political powers. The shrewd Yankee politicians and bankers put their heads together to figure out some way to restore the credit of the State so that they could borrow money enough to meet its obligations. Necessity proved to be the mother of invention. They recognized that the basic, and often the sole, value of money is its acceptance in exchange for the necessities of life; and that the only valid and ultimate base for money is raw materials of the necessities of life.

The shrewd Yankee politicians, to restore confidence in the credit of the Colony that would enable them to borrow money to pay its debts, issued, in 1780, promissory notes, the value of which was defined in terms of specific quantities of the necessities of life: sheep wool, sole leather, beef and corn. The lenders were thus assured that the currency in which they were repaid in 1784 would purchase as much of those necessities as that which they had loaned. In the meantime the affairs of the State of Massachussetts Bay had prospered in contrast with the depression that prevailed among their neighbors.

For the usurers, moneylenders and bankers, this honest currency presented a sad dilemma. They had to be content with an honest living; and they did not prosper, as is their wont, while victimizing the community. They could not swindle the community by juggling its power of the purse, by speculative manipulation of the value of necessities of life by creating shortages of money and credit. As is usual under these circumstances, they were chagrinned and enraged to see their financial loot dwindle, while the community prospered. For them, this was an "alarming development" and "an intolerable situation". And they resolved that it must be stopped.

The only uniformly loyal moneyed group were the Jewish refugee group fleeing from the Inquisition that had followed them to Brazil, who had settled in Philadelphia. They so highly cherished the freedom that they had found there that some of them had turned over their entire fortunes to finance the Revolution. They were members of the group that are buried in the Jewish Cemetery of the Mikveh Israel Congregation in Philadelphia, at Ninth and Spruce Streets, that has been made a national monument. It included Haym Salomon (who unstintingly gave his entire fortune to the Revolutionary cause and was never repaid a farthing of it), Samuel Hays (the ancestor of a many distinguished servants of our Republic), Philip Moses Russel (a Revolutionary War surgeon and reputed ancestor of the Senator from Georgia), Michael Gratz (in whose grocery Thomas Jefferson is reported to have drafted the Declaration of Independence), and Manuel Josephson, among others. (187) Their loyalty contrasted sharply with the attitude of another group of Brazilian Jewish refugees who migrated to New York, including some of the van Rosenvelts (now

10

known as Roosevelts) who became ringleaders of the Illuminist Communist conspiracy in Revolutionary days, (7;188) and became identified with the Tory moneylenders and merchants.

When the Tory moneylenders and bankers were granted amnesty, they promptly began to assert their power by threatening to bar acceptance of the Constitution by their respective States unless the control of currency, credit and banking was left in their hands. Miner, in his *Ratification Of The Constitution By The State Of New York,* points out:

"This ever-widening breach (between Tories and patriots) was emphasized still more by a third great question, that of paper money. This had been more or less of a moot point throughout the whole of the colonial period...In general, in New York, on the side of paper money were to be found the city's shopkeepers, country merchants, manufacturers and the debtor class, while ranged in opposition were the merchants, importers, moneyed men and creditors...Thus from 1783 to 1787, there was a slow but steady separation into two great camps of opinion...and the appearance of the new Constitution found both sides fully organized, conscious of each other's strength..." (189:47f)

The person who bore the brunt of the task of effecting a compromise that would make the Constitution acceptable on this score was the son of the Jewish West Indies planter, John Michael Levine, by the mulatto, Rachel Faucitt, his unfaithful wife. He was Washington's trusted aide-de-camp, the Hebrew school trained Alexander Hamilton, whom his descendants prefer to stigmatize as a "bastard" rather than acknowledge his Negro and Jewish ancestry. (190;7:79f)

Acceptance of the Constitution by New York, Massachusetts and other key States was attained only by yielding to the combined forces of the moneylenders and of the citizenry fearful of centralized monetary power dictatorship. The Federal government was denied the right to set up a banking system or to issue currency other than coins of gold and silver. Issuance of other currency was reserved for usurpation by private bankers.

The consequences of the denial of the basic power of the purse to Congress by the Constitution has proved enormously costly and oft disastrous to the nation. It has made financial history of our country an unending series of swindles, booms and depressions, with huge fortunes attained by thievery, fraud and crime, on one hand; and on the other, widespread improverishment resulting from periodic speculative manipulations of money, credit, prices and employment that too often has robbed the industrious of the fruits of their labor, and contrived depressions that rob many of the opportunity to work and earn a living, while wiping out their savings. It has given us an economy that is the antithesis of true capitalism.

This major defect in our Constitution has barred the way for many to freedom to earn a living, without which "freedom of life, liberty and pursuit of happiness" is non-existent despite the Declaration of Independence. Aggravated by the Illuminist-Marxist-Socialist-Communist concept of enhancing the value of human labor by maintaining an artificial scarcity through labor unionism, it has made impossible the realization of the blueprint of our Republic as a social organization insuring a maximal preservation of human freedom

11

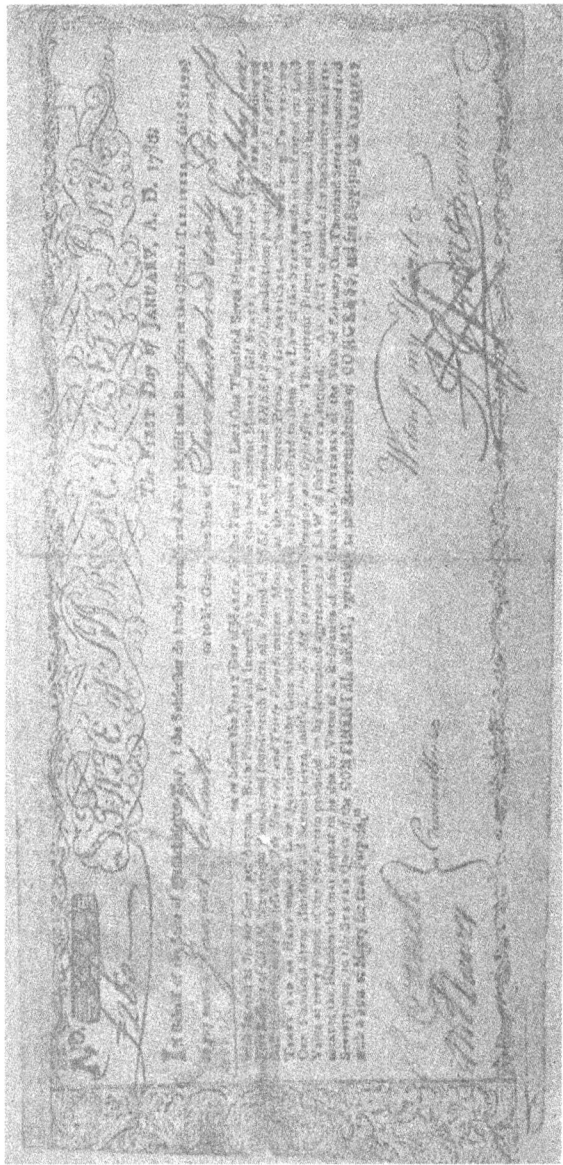

## COMMODITY BASED CURRENCY NOTE
## OF STATE OF MASSACHUSETTS BAY

This is the only currency note in American history redeemed at the same purchasing power as when issued. Its value was defined in terms of Corn, Beef, Sheepswool and Sole Leather, raw materials of the necessities of life, purchasable for the sum at the time of issue. It is the prototype of sound, uninflatable money of stable pur- chasing power. This shrewd Yankee politicians, forced to invent by the necessity of raising money to maintain themselves in power, adopted the only sound base for stable money, an array of commodities that are the raw materials of the necessities of life.

compatible with the maintenance of law and order.

The issuance of currency, other than coins, in amount requisite for the needs of our growing nation was left in the hands of private banks, moneylenders and assorted usurers, to supply if and when it suited their benign or malevolent purposes. They plied their trade with complete ruthlessness, except in some rare instances. Supposedly controlled by local authorities, they issued currency that too often was proved worthless by bankruptcies; accepted deposits that, as often as not, were wiped out by defalcations and conversion of funds that led to bank closures; and preyed on the communities with relative impunity.

The closing of the banks periodically bankrupted their depositors, causing widespread improverishment. Normal cycles of production and industry have been intensified and deepened by the ruthless operations of many of these private banks operated by powerful conspirators engaged in the racket of manipulation of money and finance.

The record justifies the cynical remark of the monetary expert, Franz Pick, that currency is a device for systematically looting people and nations. (19) Unfortunately, under our present system, those who dominate banking and finance too frequently rank as top level racketeers and brigands; and their activities have been disastrous for the nation.

## CHAPTER IV
### "GOLD STANDARD" ORIGIN

It is generally assumed that the use of gold as a standard of value dates back to the origins of history. This assumption is entirely false. It is true that gold has been held in high value by peoples throughout cognate history. The reason for this is obvious. Gold is one of the few metals that is found in uncombined state in nature, that is stable, nontarnishing and soft, ductile, malleable and readily workable by primitive technology. This, plus its rarity, gave it extraordinary value in the ages when metallurgy was an undeveloped art and science.

The exchange value of gold, however, was not fixed until the 19th century in the latter part of the Napoleonic era. Gold was exchanged on the marketplace, like any other commodity, solely on the basis of its relative supply and demand; and its price fluctuated widely, even when it was put in the form of coins of various lands.

The immediate occasion for fixing the value of gold, as a "standard" of value, was England's fear of an invasion by Napoleon. For the purpose of diverting Napoleon from crossing the Channel, England entered into alliances with Continental powers; and induced them to attack Napoleon's flanks, thus compelling diversion of his

12

forces from the Channel. For this purpose, the English paid their allies. Payment was made by emissaries carrying bags of metallic coins, gold, silver and base metallic, in the early part of the war. These payments involved large losses for the English, because of various mishaps. In some instances, the emissaries were waylaid and robbed, or captured. In other instances they developed "sticky fingers" and absconded with the money. But the most serious losses were those caused by the effect of the arrival of the coins in large volume which caused the moneychangers to lower their rate of exchange for local currency needed for paying the soldiers and other mercenaries. The British were distressed, repeatedly, with the experience of the payments being rendered inadequate because of the losses caused by drop in the exchange rates.

## PARLIAMENT ASKED BANK OF ENGLAND FOR SOLUTION OF EXCHANGE PROBLEM

Parliament sought some method of eliminating the losses caused by the instability in the value of money caused by fluctuating exchange rates in the countries to which it was shipped. After lengthy hearings on the matter, there was drafted and forwarded to Parliament the *Bullion Report Of June 8, 1810*. This was the basis for the plan to give gold an arbitrary but fixed value, alone among the commodities, and a fixed exchange value in terms of foreign currencies. That is now known as the "Gold Standard". (45)

The rationale of the British originators of the "Gold Standard" was simple. The Napoleonic wars and the French Revolution that had preceded it, had resulted in a flight of wealth and capital, for safekeeping, to England. A large part of this wealth was gold. As a result, England was the world's largest holder of gold. The British plan was to offer support to the currencies of the Continental allies with the gold hoard, and establish a fixed rate of exchange of their local currencies, for gold, thus stabilizing their value. This offer had a strong appeal to the Continental powers that trembled before Napoleon's threats.

## TRUE PURPOSE OF BRITISH "GOLD STANDARD" SCHEME.

England succeeded in inducing her allies to agree to accept a fixed value for gold, the "Gold Standard"; and a fixed gold content for their coins, which would determine their rate of exchange. This served a number of designed purposes, including:

First: It enabled England to transfer a fixed weight of gold to her allies and mercenaries to discharge obligations without any loss in exchange.

Second: It made the Continental allies dependent upon England's gold holdings for the maintenance of their national solvency. Those holdings had been greatly increased by the flight of gold to England from the Continent; by payment in gold for materiel and supplies furnished by the British to the Continental powers; and by other devices.

Third: The Continental powers allied with England were forced by the "Gold Standard" device to accept British dictation.

Fourth: With the help of British bankers, including the Barings and the Rothschilds, who had correspondents behind the French lines and in various Continental countries, it was possible for England to transfer gold by draft, and avoid the losses by theft, absconding and enemy seizure.

13

An interesting sidelight on the origin of the "Gold Standard" is offered by the role played unwittingly by Prince William of Hesse-Hanau, the royal usurer. Fearing seizure of his fortune by Napoleon, he entrusted it to the safekeeping of the Rothschilds who managed their trust so well that the Prince's fortune emerged from the war greatly enhanced. In the process the Rothschilds laid the foundation of their fortune. Subsequently, the Grand Duke of Hesse created his mistress and morganatic wife of Jewish origin the Countess, and, subsequently the Princess, of Battenberg, now known as Mountbatten. Their offspring married into the British and other royal families of Europe, and introduced into them the hemophiliac strain. Later intermarriages introduced the Rothschild strain into royalty.

From its very inception, the "Gold Standard" was designed and served more importantly as a medium of control than as a medium of exchange. The "Gold Standard" became the prime device for manipulation and looting of nations and for perpetrations of frauds on gigantic scales.

### GOLD HAD LOST MUCH OF ITS UNIQUE TECHNICAL VALUE WHEN ADOPTED AS "STANDARD"

It is the height of irony that at the very time that gold became enshrined as a standard and was imposed on the world as a determinant of all other values, it had begun to lose much of the unique technologic value it possessed as metal. For at that very time the Bessemer steel process had solved the problem of the technology of working of steel and of hard, rigid metals that are far superior to gold for many of its former uses.

### TRADE FORCED THE ADOPTION OF GOLD AS CURRENCY ON THE U.S.A.

The dollar originally was made, at the instance of Alexander Hamilton, the basis for the currency of the United States, an exact counterpart of the widely used Spanish silver coins, "pieces of eight" (*reales*), that were widely used in trade. The Mint Act, of April 2, 1792, defined the dollar as a coin with the content of 317¼ grains of pure silver. Thus silver became the real base of our currency, as it was also the original base of the currency of England, the pound sterling.

With the imposition of the "Gold Standard" on its Empire and on Europe, it became necessary for all lands that traded with England, and they all did, to scramble to secure gold to make payment for imported goods. It is amusing to consider that the sections of the world that followed England in acceptance of the "Gold Standard", are known as the "Sterling" area.

Since the bulk of the trade of the newly formed United States was with Europe and the "Sterling" area, American finance became largely a matter of gold speculation and manipulation in gold. Silver was relegated to a secondary status and served as money primarily in the trade with the Far East countries that were on a silver standard. For trade with them, special "Trade Dollars" were minted. And they became one of the most widely used media of exchange in that part of the world.

It was only secondarily that the dollar was defined in terms of their exchange value in gold at the then prevailing market price. The dollar was given a content of 23¾ grains of gold.

14

## CHAPTER V
## SUPREME COURT SUSTAINED EVASIONS OF
## CONSTITUTION ON MONEY ISSUE

An exception written into the Constitution made it possible for the Federal government to issue currency and establish banks in national emergencies and war, under emergency powers granted the President. In the early days of the Republic, these powers were exercised in real emergencies created by the Revolution and the war of 1812, when private banking was unable to cope with the financial situation and the very existence of the nation was threatened. Following the Revolutionary War, the bankers and moneylenders found that they had bitten off more than they could chew, in usurping the power to issue money and establish banks. They were delighted to have the Federal government use the emergency powers granted by the Constitution to bail them out and supply them with money and credit.

## FIRST BANK OF THE U.S. RESCUED NATION'S BANKERS
## IN REVOLUTIONARY WAR EMERGENCY

The First Bank Of The U.S. was the first entry of the Federal government into the field of money and banking under the emergency powers granted by the Constitution. Private bankers were unable to provide the funds for the payment of war debts, were overextended and clamored for the government to come to their rescue. Pres. Washington had misgivings in the matter, but the emergency was so threatening to the survival of the Republic that he set them aside.

The Federal Government subscribed $2 million for a fifth of the capital stock of the Bank. Operating under the guidance of Secretary of the Treasury, Alexander Hamilton, it was honestly and well managed; and he exercised a salutary controlling influence over the State-chartered private banks, restoring their solvency. But as the emergency cleared up, the private bankers chafed at honest guidance and control and resented the barrier which it set up to looting the public. When the Bank's charter came up for renewal, they fought it bitterly but successfully and forced its profitable liquidation.

## "WILDCAT" STATE BANK FRAUDS & 1812 WAR MADE
## 2ND BANK OF U.S. URGENT NECESSITY.

The shutdown of the First Bank of the U.S. and the end of limited control exercised by Hamilton over State banks, was followed by a fraud-ridden half decade (1811-1816) of swindling of the nation by 'wildcat" banks that issued uncontrolled volumes of currency that far exceeded their assets and that they had no honest intention of redeeming in specie. During the period, the volume of notes they issued rose from $23 million to $100 million. The Government deposits in

15

them were wiped out by their failures, in the amount of more than $5 million. As a consequence, Washington was unable to meet its 1812 War obligations and was forced to borrow on the basis of notes that depreciated rapidly, as a result of the Government's impaired credit. The emergency forced the Government, once again, as has become quite customary, to step into the situation to bail out the bankers and usurers, and charter and finance the Second Bank of the U.S.

Unfortunately, the Second Bank at its start lacked the honest, patriotic management of Alexander Hamilton. He had been assassinated by his rival and political opponent whom he had challenged to a duel to avenge an insult offered him by Aaron Burr in the form of derogatory comments on his Jewish and Negro origins.

The Bank lacked specie and capital, in the early years of its existence, 1817-1823, because of failure of stockholders to pay in full the instalments on their stock, and speculation and other irregularities on the part of its officers. Nicholas Biddle's election, as the Bank's third president, brought about as a result of a panic precipitated by its mismanagement, was followed by a measure of success comparable with that of the First Bank. But political activities of Biddle and other Bank officers aroused the antagonism of Pres. Andrew Jackson who, unfortunately for the finances of the nation, vetoed the charter for a Third Bank of the U.S. that had been passed by Congress, after having withdrawn all Government deposits in the Bank in 1833.

### "WILDCAT" STATE BANK FRAUDS & SWINDLES DOMINATED NATION FROM 1836 TO 1863.

The period following the shutdown of the Second Bank of the U.S., between 1836 and 1863, was an era of bank frauds and swindles by so-called "wildcat" banks. Though the extent of the fraud was not comparable in amount with that involved in the current "Federal" Reserve frauds, its mode of perpetration was more flamboyant and colorful. The term "wildcat" was applied to these banks because they were generally set up in remote sections where one might expect to find wildcats, but few or no humans. This was intended to make the conversion of the notes issued by the banks into specie difficult, if not impossible.

Political influence in chartering banks was replaced by uniform regulations set up in the so-called "Free Banking Act" first adopted in New York State. The banks were too often entirely "free". The stock of the banks was issued free of charge to the stockholders. And they were generally "free" of all capital assets. Often if and when a victim sought to redeem the banks' notes in specie which they did not possess, they would go out of business, bankrupt. During this period the number of State chartered banks rose from 506, in 1834, to 1601 in 1861; and their note issues rose from $95 million to $202 million. (192:417—8)

### GOVERNMENT MOVED TO PROTECT ITSELF FROM LOSSES BY BANK FRAUDS.

The Federal and State governments were forced to act to protect themselves from bank frauds and failures. The Federal Government established, in 1840 and 1846, the Independent Treasury System, as a division of the Treasury, to serve as a depositary for Government funds. Complying with the Constitutional provisions, its principal dealing were in legal tender, specie, gold and silver, "hard money". It remained in operation as the exclusive depository of the Government, until, during the Civil War, the National Banking System was established under the war emergency powers of the Constitution.

Indiana's Hoosiers established the first sound State banking system designed to protect it and its citizenry, the Indiana State Bank. It was a State-wide monopoly of banking, patterned after the First Bank of the U.S. but improving on its setup by requiring that all of its stock must be paid for in specie. The State subscribed to more than half of the Bank's stock, and insured honest management. Established in 1834, it operated successfully until its charter expired in 1859. A similar State banking monopoly was established in Ohio, in 1845.

## CIVIL WAR EMERGENCY GAVE RISE TO GREENBACKS & NATIONAL BANKING SYSTEM

The chaos created by "wildcat" banking resulted in placing in circulation in the country about 7,000 different currency issues, most of which were irredeemable and of dubious or no value; and about 5,000 note issues that were totally fraudulent. Financing of the war by the Union was impossible under this situation, either domestically or by foreign loan. Once again it became obvious that a central banking system controlled by the Government, such as is barred by the Constitution, except in national emergency was essential for national survival.

At syndicate of New York, Boston and Philadelphia banks undertook to make a loan to the Government of $50 million, in 1861, to tide it over. And they agreed to underwrite two more issues of $50 million each, in the future. Treasury Secretary Chase, however, made it impossible for the banks to carry out their agreement by demanding that they deliver the first loan to the Treasury in specie, in silver and gold coins, instead permitting them to hold the funds subject to Government check drafts. This resulted in depleting the banks of their reserves and forced them to suspend specie payment. Shortly thereafter, the Treasury itself was forced to suspend redemption of government-issued money.

Congress was then induced by Secretary of the Treasury, Salmon P. Chase, to authorize the issue of $150 million of United States notes that came to be known as "greenbacks"; and to declare the greenbacks legal tender for all public and private debts except custom duties and payment of interest on public debts. The original bill, passed by Congress on February 25, 1862, made the greenbacks convertible into 6% twenty-five year bonds. The same provision was incorporated in the Act of Congress providing for the issuance of another $150 million greenbacks, in July 1862. The conversion privilege was repudiated, however in the third Act of March 3, 1863, providing for the issue of another $150 million greenbacks.

After the close of the War, in 1866, Congress authorized redemption of limited amounts of the $1,540 million greenbacks issued. But this redemption was suspended in the following year. The Resumption Act of 1875 provided for continued redemption of the greenbacks after January 1, 1879. This and the subsequent provision of $150 million in gold for redemption of outstanding greenbacks provided in the Gold Standard Act of 1900 did eventually raise their market value to par. This afforded informed parties a chance to profit hugely from the rise in value, of the highly depreciated greenbacks.

For the purpose of making possible the financing of the Civil War, the National Banking Act was passed by Congress in 1863 and amended in the two following years, once again providing centralized banking under Federal control in war emergency, under the powers granted by the Constitution. The chartering of the banks, under this Act, was controlled by a newly created official of the Treasury, the Comptroller of the Currency, who was given the power to supervise and examine them. The Act provided for full payment for capital stock, and the setting up of a surplus of 20% of the paid-in capital.

The banks were required to purchase Government bonds with one third of their capital, in the minimum amount of $30,000, and deposit them in the Treasury. Against them, they were permitted to issue notes to the extent of 90% of the deposited bonds. Thus they held the bonds on a 10% margin, and collected the interest on them in full. Each of the banks was required to accept the notes of every other bank in the system at full face value; and all of the issue, up to a maximum of $300 million was guaranteed by the Government. Originally the banks were required to maintain reserves in cash in their vaults against both their deposits and their notes. At a later date, the cash reserve against the notes was dropped and instead the banks issuing notes were required to contribute to a 5% bond redemption fund maintained by the Treasury.

The banks were made depositories of Treasury for Government funds other than custom duties, provided that they deposited adequate collateral in the Treasury. They were barred from making loans on real estate, from undertaking trust functions, from loaning any one borrower more than 10% of their capital and surplus, and were taxed ½% on their average note circulation and ¼% on their capital not invested in government bonds. The most irksome restriction from the viewpoint of the bankers was barring of usury and the limitation of interest charges.

The National Banks thus provided a captive market for Government bonds. This market was materially widened when, in July 1866, the Federal Government taxed the State-chartered banks 10% per annum on their note issues as contrasted with ½% tax on the National Bank issues. Then as ever since, bankers cherished the profits involved in the bank note issue swindle. And many State-chartered banks flocked into the National Bank setup.

## SUPREME COURT PERVERTS CONSTITUTION & EXTENDS CHARTERS BEYOND EMERGENCIES

The Supreme Court has rolled up a long and shameful record of perverting, and supporting defiance of, the Constitution by the banking conspirators, by a series of decisions regarding extension or perpetuation of Federal chartering of banks beyond periods of real or engineered emergencies. On each occasion when the emergency powers extended by the Constitution were exercised, the moneylenders, usurers and bankers instituted suits to preserve their banking and monetary monopolies and to prevent the Government assuming those functions for a period longer than was necessary to bail them out. There is reason to believe that on more than one occasion, a treasonous desire to destroy or betray our Republic was involved in these suits.

## MCCULLOUGH V. MARYLAND: MARSHALL'S
## DOCTRINE OF "IMPLIED POWERS"

Chief Justice John Marshall, in 1819, handed down the decision in the earliest case dealing with the power of the Federal Government, including its right to charter a national bank, only in times of emergency under the powers granted it under the Constitution. He upheld the power of the Federal Government to set up a national bank under what he ruled was "the implied powers" involved in the powers specifically granted it by the States.

This ruling of the Court violated the express intent of the framers of the Constitution. The Constitution clearly specifies that all powers not expressly granted to the Federal Government were reserved by the States. The decision represented one of the earliest arrogations of legislative powers by the Supreme Court, in violation of the Constitution; and it set a precedent that has been followed by the Court much too often for the safety of our Republic.

## CIVIL WAR FINANCING: HEPBURN V. GRISWOLD &
## "THE LEGAL TENDER CASES"

When the debacle of the State banks at the outset of the Civil War forced the establishment of the National Banks and the issue of greenbacks under the Legal Tender Act (February 25, 1862), Secretary of the Treasury, Salmon P. Chase (after whom Chase National Bank was named) succeeded in convincing Congress that it must make the greenbacks issued by the Treasury legal tender for the payment of public debts. In 1864, Chase was appointed Chief Justice of the Supreme Court, to succeed Justice Taney, by Pres. Lincoln.

Following Lincoln's assassination, Chase shamelessly dragged the Supreme Court into politics in his quest for the Presidential nomination, as successor of Pres. Johnson. Like his successor, Chief Justice Earl Warren, he assiduously courted the vote of the criminal elements and the Negroes, and added shamefully to the dishonorable, ugly picture of the so-called "Reconstruction" Era. He toured the South and addressed himself exclusively to the freed Negroes whom he had made a career of championing, as a so-called "Liberal," Radical or Red. And he shunned the Southern whites. (193:55f).

Chief Justice Chase, though he had induced Congress to make greenbacks legal tender, seven years later in 1869, ruled in the case of Hepburn v. Griswold (195) that the Legal Tender Act, that he had sponsored, as Secretary of the Treasury, was un-Constitutional. In effect, he and his associates on the bench, ruled that the emergency power granted by the Constitution to the Federal Government, was un-Constitutional.

Chase was too well versed in national finances to be ignorant of the consequences of the decision that he wrote, and the effect it would have on the price of gold. The decision laid the foundation for the "Gold Corner" that a swindler named Gold, who adopted the alias Jay Gould, staged with the bribed support of Pres. Ulysses S. Grant. It netted those involved more than $30 million, bankrupted a large part of American business and industry, and precipitated a panic. In view of his malodorous record, it is hard to believe that Chase did not share in the loot.

The financial situation became so critical as a consequence of the

Gould-Grant "Gold Corner", that it became imperative that the Constitutionality of the Legal Tender Act be affirmed by the Court reversing itself. This was done by the Supreme Court, two years later, in 1871, with Chase sitting as Chief Justice, in the so-called "Legal Tender Cases": Knox v. Lee, and Parker v. Davis. (196) The cases were heard by the Court at the request of Attorney General Ebenezer Rockwood Hoar, whose nomination to the Court by Pres. Grant had been turned down by the Senate when it ratified the appointment of Secretary of War Edwin Stanton who was widely and justifiably suspected of involvement in the assassination of Lincoln. (72)

The two nominations had been made possible by a law passed by Congress in 1866, which barred Pres. Johnson who was hated by the Radicals, as the Communists were then termed, and their ecclesiastic supporters, because he would not help them destroy our Republic. The law barred Pres. Johnson from filling three vacancies on the Supreme Court bench. Pres. Grant conveniently accomplished the reversal of the earlier decision barring the use of greenbacks as legal tender, by "packing" the Court with Justices known to be in favor of reversal of the decision. (197:170f). In this "packing" of the Supreme Court Pres. Grant was more successful than his cousin, Pres. F.D. Roosevelt, (7:241) who attempted it.

## ROTHSCHILD'S ACTIVITIES IN CIVIL WAR FINANCING

Many myths have circulated about the "malevolent conspiracy" that was supposed to have been conducted by the Jewish "international bankers" during the Civil War. One of the most absurd is the myth that Lincoln's death was motivated by his supposed initiative in issuing the greenbacks and making them legal tender, thereby incensing "international bankers." As has been related, greenbacks were authorized and made legal tender by an act of Congress, and not by Lincoln. They were made necessary not by "international bankers," but by the swindling domestic bankers who operated "wildcat" banks and defrauded both the public and the Government. The "villain" in the Government who was responsible for inducing Congress to make greenbacks legal tender, was not Lincoln, but was his Secretary of the Treasury Chase.

## WHO PLOTTED LINCOLN'S ASSASSINATION & CARRIED IT OUT

The scoundrels who plotted the Civil War and the assassination of Lincoln, the Radicals and their ecclesiastic masterminds, and their motives were fully exposed in the trial of the Jesuit-trained conspirator, John Surratt. (168); by Father Chiniquy, in his book *Fifty Years In The Church Of Rome* (199:492f); and by Burke McCarty, in her *Suppressed Truth About The Assassination Of Abraham Lincoln* (72).

## TRUTH ABOUT "INTERNATIONAL BANKERS"

The truth about the role of the "international bankers" on both sides in the Civil War was honestly attested by W.W. Murphy, an Irishman who can not be accused of being biased in favor of the Jews, American consul-general at Frankfort at that time, in a letter to the editor of *Harper's Weekly*, in which he stated:

"You do a great injustice to the eminent firm of Rothschilds here...the firm of M.M. Rothschild & Son are opposed to slavery and in favor of the Union. *A converted Jew*, Erlanger, has taken

20

a rebel loan of three million pounds and lives in this city; and Baron Rothschild informed me that all Germany condemned this act of lending money to a slave-holding government, and that so great was public opinion against it that Erlanger & Son dared not offer it on the Frankfort Bourse." (200:10)

In short, the truth was that it was a Catholic international banker, Erlanger, whose son was married to the daughter of Senator Slidell, of Louisiana in the Catholic Church, who sought to further the activities of the Society of Jesus in undermining the Union.

## ROTHSCHILD "INTERNATIONAL BANKER" MYTHS

The myth that the Rothschilds played a malign role in the Civil War is no more truthful than the fable of the role which some dishonest bigots assign to them in the American Revolutionary War, before they had made their fortune and existed as a banking firm. *The Economist,* a London publication, reported that Nathan Rothschild arrived in London, in 1804, with a total capital of $56,000; and that his fortune was made in the few days following the Battle of Waterloo, after June 18, 1915. (201)

The capital that Rothschild possessed two decades after the end of the Revolutionary War would have been of no significance as compared with the Revolutionary War needs. A far wealthier, Philadelphia Jewish banker and broker, Haym Solomon (member of the group buried in the National Monument there, to which reference has been made) loaned Gen. George Washington his entire fortune, a quarter of a million dollars in specie, for the Army camped at Valley Forge to provide for them during the winter. He advanced the money to Washington on a note signed by him as Commander-in-Chief of the Army, when no other person would trust him, with assurance that it would be honored by Congress. Though he thereby saved the Army and made possible the success of the Revolution, Haym Solomon and his family have never been repaid a penny of that loan to this day. But at the time, the Rothschilds had not the proverbial "pot or window," to bolster the myth of the bigots who prefer not to mention Solomon.

When the Rothschilds decided to establish a branch of the firm in New York, in 1837, they entrusted the task to their German, Jewish kinsman and employee, August Schoenberg, who adopted the French translation of his name, August Belmont. Belmont promptly became a naturalized citizen and took an active part in American affairs. From 1853 to 1857, he served as American Minister at Hague. An active Democrat since 1844, he was chairman of the Democratic National Committee. His marriage to the daughter of Commodore Matthew C. Perry and niece of Sen. John Slidell, made him a kinsman by marriage of the apostate Erlanger, and lent false color to the rumors of his support of the rebels. But it is a matter of record that his loyalty and support, both moral and financial, of the Union gave it the unswerving and dedicated service of the Rothschilds, despite division of their interests abroad and sympathies of some of them for the South. (200)

There was none of the blatant fraud in the dealings of the Rothschild interests with the Union that characterized those of other banking and commercial native American interests. Banker John P. Morgan, for example, swindled the Government out of huge sums by selling back to it, at enormous profits, worthless and condemned rifles

21

that he had arranged to purchase from it for that purpose. Nor was there any defrauding of the Government by the Rothschilds by defaulting on payment to the Government of moneys deposited with their firm, as in the instance of the "wildcat" banks. Nevertheless, there has been directed against the Rothschilds a constant stream of calumny that has two prime purposes: one, is the efforts of vicious and malign conspirators to divert attention from their criminal activities by propaganda directed by them, and their paid or subsidized agents, against others, especially such easy targets as the Rothschilds, who have adopted a policy of disregarding false attacks on them; and second, are the spewings of anti-Semitic propagandists who have not the slightest regard for the truth, that have ready acceptance among similarly bigoted folk. They usually are subsidized by the conspirators to serve their purposes.

Among the more widespread disseminated false propaganda against the Rothschilds belying their services to the Union during the Civil War are:

Ezra Pound's charge that "the United States were sold to the Rothschilds in 1863." (204:13; 205:5)

Willis P. Overholser's forgery of letters between the Rothschilds and a non-existent and mythical firm of "Ikleheimer, Morton & Vandergould" respecting the establishment of a National Banking System. (203:46)

Father Charles E. Coughlin's charges published in an article in his magazine *Social Justice*, entitled *Abraham Lincoln & Rothschilds*, in the issue of February 12, 1940, in which he alleged that the Civil War was plotted by the Rothschilds to secure "financial domination" of the U.S. and that the assassination of Lincoln was a part of that scheme.

Fr. Coughlin was well aware of the falsity of his statements. His opening radio broadcast in his "Social Justice" campaign embodied a garbled version of data presented by this author in magazine article published in March, 1933, entitled *The Gold Standard Myth*. Much of that article was incorporated in Fr. Coughlin's broadcast, verbatim, but garbled with the "gold index" doubletalk of Prof. Irving Fisher, and religion. This author's article named the Rockefellers as the master banking and monetary conspirators who had engineered the depression then under way. This material was included in Coughlin's broadcast. (206)

Shortly after the broadcast, Fr. Coughlin was approached by one of the agents of the conspirators with a "proposition." If he would refrain from ever again mentioning the Rockefeller name, the report related, and blame instead the "international bankers" and the Rothschilds, he would be handsomely subsidized by the conspirators through a speculation in 100,000 ounces of silver.

A subsequent Congressional investigation revealed that Fr. Coughlin and his outfit, the Radio League, had profited from speculation in silver, in the company of a large group of the conspirators' associates who had been given advance, inside information on their plans for manipulating the market price of silver. Coughlin's speculative "payoff" was made in the name of his League secretary, Miss Amy Collins. (97:187) The Rockefeller name was never again mentioned in the subsequent years of broadcasting of Fr. Coughlin's campaign. Instead, he laid the blame for all of the nation's and the world's financial ills on the "Jewish international bankers" and the Rothschilds.

Father Coughlin could hardly have been ignorant of the role of his Church in the precipitation of the Civil War and the simultaneous invasion of Mexico by Maximilian, who had been crowned as its Emperor by the Pope, at the Vatican, at the head of an army largely financed by the Church. He could not have been ignorant of the terms for reestablishment of the Jesuit order that were embodied in the agreement of the "Holly Alliance" at the Congress of Vienna, and incorporated in 1822 in the Treaty of Verona. (72:8) The Treaty, as has been related, pledged its signatories to destroy the "work of Satan" in the form of representative government, and replace it with the only form of government approved by the Church, rule by "divine right" as dictated by the Vatican. He could not have been ignorant of the well-known fact that the missionary society known as the St. Leopold Society had been established for the purpose of carrying out this plot in the United States. (72:22) Nor could he have been ignorant of the role of the Jesuits in Lincoln's assassination that had been completely exposed in the trial of John Surratt (168), the works of Father Chiniquy (199) and of Burke McCarty (72), his co-religionists. Nor could he have been ignorant of the plan of the Vatican, in 1866, to flee from the menacing Italian insurrection to the United States that the Church still hoped to "reclaim" in spite of the failure of the Maximilian deal with Confederate President Jefferson Davis. (72:55) The plan of the Vatican was well known in Church circles.

During the recent visit of Pope Paul VI to the U.N., Bishop Fulton Sheen, who acted as radio and television commentator, related the story in his broadcast. He did not explain that the plan was dropped as a result of the outraging of American public opinion by the role played by the Church in the Lincoln assassination that was exposed in the Surratt trial.

The Military Order of the Loyal Legion, whose membership is composed of descendants of Civil War Officers, reprinted in the June 1959 issue of their *Bulletin,* the falsified Fr. Coughlin myth accusing the Rothschilds of plotting Lincoln's assassination. An amusing aspect of the publication is the fact that it had the "warm endorsement" of Gen. U.S. Grant III, kinsman of Jewish immigrant van Rosenvelt (or Rosenfeld) whose descendants we now know as Roosevelts. (7:80) His grandfther, Pres. Grant was the closest relative of Pres. Franklin D. Roosevelt among the numerous kinsmen of the Roosevelts who have occupied the Presidency. (7:24f) He was chairman of the Civil War Centennial Commission. It is indeed ironic that a descendant of the accomplice of Gould in the most shameful looting of the nation should seek to thus "alibi" his ancestor!

## AUTHOR'S MOTIVE IN ELICITING THE TRUTH ABOUT ROTHSCHILDS' ROLE

In view of the fact that agents of the conspirators have falsely charged this author with serving the Rothschild interests in eliciting the truth about their role in our history, and of so doing because of religious bias, the following is related to refute those false charges. The author's only faith rests on the Golden Rule and the Constitution of the U.S that, in its unperverted form, he regards as the most perfect blueprint of human organization for the maximum preservation of human freedom. That is his only "bias." He accepts literally the law that makes persons who shield malefactors and traitors, or seek to create diversions for them, post facto accomplices. They should be regarded as even more criminal and traitorous than the perpetrators themselves.

Since the conspirators and their traitorous agents have used the Rothschild myth for the purpose of diverting the odium and onus of their crimes from themselves, he regards it as his duty to expose their nefarious, subversive and treasonous acts and libels. These bogus, prostituted, self-styled "patriots" have succeeded either in establishing fake "conservative" or "patriotic" organizations, controlled "opposition," with the help of the conspirators, or in taking over organizations established by loyal Americans and converting them into the traitors' fake opposition. If our Republic is destroyed, those wolves in sheep's clothes can claim most of the credit for it as due to their success in diverting and duping the multitude of naive, guileless and gullible patriots.

This author is willing to risk the false, malicious and libelous attacks directed against him by these fake "patriots" and so-called "conservatives," in the hope that his report of the truth may penetrate the barrage of false propaganda and serve to frustrate the conspirators, restore the Constitution as our basic law, and create and preserve the Republic which it was designed to establish. And he seeks to stress the view that their treason is all the more vicious and contemptible in its appeal to religious bigotry that is involved in their attributing the acts of their patrons to the Rothschilds and the "international bankers."

CHAPTER VI
PRES. GRANT SET DYNASTIC PRECEDENT: THE
GOULD-GRANT "GOLD CORNER"

The viciously and criminally corrupt and venal Grant Administration took its tone from the bibulous character at its head. Insobriety did not affect his ability as a forceful fighter and military leader. This is reflected in Pres. Lincoln's reply to a report that Gen. Grant drank heavily during his campaign, which was to the effect that if he knew what brand of liquor Grant drank to keep in his fighting mood, he would send kegs of it to other Army leaders. This expressed recognition of the fact that for many characters, drunkenness elicits reckless pugnacity. However, the boon companions and lusty associates that the drunkard acquires are seldom noted for moral rectitude, principle or superior intelligence.

The scoundrels with whom Pres. Grant "did business" in engineering the "Gold Corner", Jay Gould and Jim Fisk, were no exception to this rule. And the President's brother-in-law, Abel Rathbone Corbin (who had married his middle-aged sister Jenny) was no less a scoundrel; a lobbyist, shady manipulator and "pious Methodist churchman," he had been soundly trounced by a Congressional committee. Corbin made a deal with Gould to "fix" Grant in return for $100,000, half of which was reported to have been paid over to his sister-in-law, Mrs. Grant. This outstanding corruption was never matched until more than a half century later, when Grant's cousin and closest relative among more than a dozen Presidents, Franklin Delano Roosevelt, (7:8f) served as a pawn in an even more thievish and fraudulent gold swindle, thievery and brigandage, that will be related in a later chapter. It is the basis of the vastly greater, world-wide "Gold Corner" now in progress, of the earlier consequence of which the nation and the world are now suffering.

## GOULD & FISK PROVED TOP-NOTCH SWINDLERS & CRIMINAL "GENIUSES"

Before Pres. Grant had joined them in their criminal conspiracy through the agency of his kin, both Gould and Fisk had earned for themselves nationwide reputations as swindlers. By their outstanding criminal "genius" and "achievements," they were deemed qualified to take their places beside the nation's chief executive.

Jay Gould, a New York clerk, surveyor, pamphleteer and mouse trap inventor, had launched his career of crime by diverting the funds of his wealthy partner, Charles Leupp, with whom he engaged in the tannery business. Ruined partner Leupp committed suicide. Gould went on to greener fields in New York City, where he evaded Civil War military service, set himself up in stock brokerage business and speculated in railroads.

Jim Fisk, Vermont Yankee, circus roustabout, peddler, war profiteer, bootlegger, smuggler and draft dodger, started his career as a trustworthy merchant and showed a measure of principle and honesty of which Gould was devoid. Late in 1864, he opened a brokerage office with his funds derived from wartime profiteering as a partner of Eben Jordan, of Jordan, Marsh & Co. Within six months, his speculation almost had wiped out his capital. He recouped his fortune by the same device that had enabled the Rothschilds to make their fortune after Waterloo,—by taking advantage of advances in communication. Whereas Rothschilds had used pigeons and fast couriers, Fisk used the telegraph. He formed a syndicate that arranged to reach the London market two days ahead of news of the Confederate defeat, and sold short $5 million of Confederate bonds, making a "killing" in their drop from 80 to 22. With those profits, he bought and developed the Goulding patent for improvements in textile weaving. He then extended his activities in the stock market by entering into association with the most notorious stock market manipulator, crook and swindler, the psalm-singing, Bible-thumping Methodist founder of the Drew Theological Seminary, Daniel Drew. (74)

Gould and Fisk joined up with Drew, and later with Commodore Vanderbilt, John Eldridge and Boss Tweed, in mercilessly looting the Erie Railroad, its stockholders and the public of tens of millions of dollars. Their swindle, that involved a wide assortment of crimes, was the outstanding fraud, up to that time, in the history of what is

25

misnamed "American finance".

Gould and Fisk, after evading prosecution for their crimes by various devices and by agreeing to split the loot with their partners, emerged as President and Comptroller of the Erie Railroad. They continued to loot the road and the public of many more millions in those positions. (74)

Gould's insatiable lust for loot was merely whetted by the millions that he stole in the Erie swindle. It provided him with the capital for his "Gold Corner." The ground for it had been prepared by the challenge of greenbacks as legal tender, that met with the approval of the Supreme Court and its Chief Justice Chase who could hardly be judged to be sufficiently principled not to enter into such a conspiracy. The collaboration of Pres. Grant had been assured by the bribed collaboration of his brother-in-law, Corbin, and reputedly of Mrs. Grant as sharer in the bribe. Grant's collaboration was absolutely essential for the success of the swindle. For only he could assure Gould that none of the $100 million in gold that the Government held in the Treasury would be released to increase the floating supply of $15 million, that Gould planned to "corner," and defeat the plot.

## PRES. GRANT GAVE CONVINCING PERSONAL SUPPORT TO CROOKS, GOULD & FISK

Pres. Grant left no stone unturned to publicize ostentatiously his support of Gould and Fisk. On June 15, 1869, he accepted Fisk's invitation to sail to the Boston Peace Jubilee on Fisk's steamer, the Providence. Intensive publicity of the event was doubly insured by Pres. Grant's ride from the Corbin residence to the Chamber Street pier at which the Providence was docked, in the center of a circuslike parade led by Fisk, with a military escort.

On the following day, in Boston, the scoundrels, Gould and Fisk, were prominent in the escort of Pres. Grant as he entered the Boston Coliseum. Fisk was bedecked in the absurdly ostentatious outfit of "Admiral" that he affected, while Gould was content to remain in the background, less conspicuous. (74)

On the return of the party to New York, on June 18, Pres. Grant, with his wife, sister and brother-in-law, occupied Fisk's proscenium box at his Fifth Avenue Theatre. The public had no occasion to question that Pres. Grant was an intimate associate of these thievish scoundrels, and lent his approval and support to their crimes. This was more amply confirmed, shortly thereafter, when Pres. Grant appointed his kinsman, Robert B. Catherwood, to the post of Assistant United States Treasurer in New York control of which was essential for the conspirators. When Catherwood discovered that he was expected to play a key role in the swindle, his honesty impelled him to resign. Directly thereafter, Pres. Grant appointed to the post a pliable and unprincipled character, Gen. Daniel Butterfield, who gleefully joined in the conspiracy—for a consideration.

## GOULD'S "GOLD CORNER" PLOT.

Gould's deeply laid plan and plot rested on the role of the "Gold Standard" and the status of gold as the only legal tender. During the Civil War, the scramble to purchase gold for the payment of taxes and duties to the Government, and of other domestic and foreign obligations, had raised its price 141%, from five ounces for $100 to five ounces for $241. When greenbacks were made legal tender, by Congress at the instance of Treasury Secretary Chase, the price of gold dropped steadily. In the Spring of 1869, Gould was able to purchase $7 million of gold at five ounces for $131. This was almost half of the $15 million of gold that was in circulation in the country.

When Gould had reached into the White House and secured the collaboration of Pres. Grant in withholding from circulation the $100 million of gold held by the Treasury, and gold was once again restored to the status of the sole legal tender by Chief Justice Chase's Supreme Court decision, he expected to boost the price of gold rapidly. But it scarcely budged. The *New York Times* was impressed into service. Simultaneously with a visit of Pres. Grant to New York City, on August 25, 1869, the *Times* published, as an editorial, an article designed to boost the price of gold that had been written by Gould's agent, Grant's brother-in-law, Corbin. It proclaimed it to be the policy of the Grant Administration not to release any of the Treasury's gold for several months.

In gratitude for this support and payment, Gould bought for the account of Mrs. Corbin $1.5 million of gold, and an equal amount for Assistant Secretary of the Treasury, Gen. Butterfield (after lending him $10,000) with the assurance that they would be given the profits which would amount to $15,000 for each penny rise in the price of gold. Gould also purchased, subsequently and on the same terms, half a million in gold for Pres. Grant's close friend and secretary, Gen. Horace Porter. But the price of gold rose to a little above $137, and then sagged. (74)

### GRANT ROSE TO GOULD'S RESCUE & HELPED HIM TRAP FISK

Gould and his confederates were frantic about the failure of the gold price to rise. On September 15, Pres. Grant left for Pennsylvania, with the compliments of Gould, in the private car of the Erie directors. This helped influence Fisk, who had hitherto refused to join Gould in his "Gold Corner," to reconsider. The decision was materially influenced by Gould's assurance given him that Pres. Grant and his entourage were partners in the plot; and that Mrs. Grant already had been given a $25,000 advance on the profits thereof. By September 17, Fisk had purchased more than $8 million of gold. Steady purchasing by Gould and Fisk had raised the gold price to $141 by September 23. This created a financial panic that bankrupted numerous firms. Tremendous pressure was brought on the Government to release its gold to break the "corner."

### PRES. GRANT YIELDED TO PRESSURE. ORDERED "CORNER" ENDED.

Public pressure on Pres. Grant rose so high that he flinched and "turned yellow." Through brother-in-law Corbin, he apprised Gould that he planned to release Treasury gold, thereby breaking the "corner." Gould withheld this information from his partner, Fisk, whom he encouraged to continue his wild and steady buying of gold. In the meanwhile, Gould sold his gold, unloading much of it on Fisk.

On Friday, September 24, the *New York Times* published an editorial exposing the plot and Pres. Grant's complicity in it, as talked of freely" by its "engineers." It related:

"They not only bulled gold with a will, but talked freely of

27

the warrant they had from Washington that the government would not interfere with them."

This editorial brought additional pressure to bear on Grant to release Treasury gold. And it insured Gould added profits derived from "selling gold short." Meanwhile, Fisk bought the gold that was being unloaded by Gould, his doublecrossing "partner." The price of gold reached $164 by 11:30 A.M., when Pres. Grant's order to Secretary of the Treasury Boutwell to release $4 million in gold reached Assistant Treasurer Butterfield in New York. After he sold gold "short" on his account, he sent word to Gould about the Treasury release twenty five minutes before he made the information public, so as to enable him to more fully profit from the advance information. Within a half hour after publication of the news, the price of gold dropped to $135.

## "BLACK FRIDAY" PANIC

On what came to be known as "Black Friday," September 24, 1869, numerous firms and persons, including half of Wall Street, it was estimated, were bankrupted; and the nation was thrown into panic and depression, much in the same manner as was brought about in 1929, by the same "Gold Corner" device. Gould emerged from the swindle with a profit of $11 million, and unsuspected by the public as its author. When interviewed by a reporter of the New York Sun, he hypocritically moaned, in the manner that has become customary among the conspirators:

"I regret very much the depression in financial circles, *but I predicted it long ago. I was in no way instrumental in producing the panic," he lied.*

## CONGRESS, AS CUSTOMARY, "WHITEWASHED"
## THE CULPRITS

Cowardly Gould craftily managed to shift the blame and public hatred and bitterness over the situation to his doublecrossed tool, Fisk, making him the goat. Fisk never suspected or blamed his "partner," Gould; but held his associates, Pres. Grant and his brother-in-law, Corbin, responsible for not blocking the release of Treasury gold. With the aid of a batch of crooked injunctions handed down by corrupt Tammany judges, Barnard and Cardozo, Fisk arranged to come out a winner by repudiating his purchases, claiming he had bought the gold for the account of William Belden, one of his dummy broker agents. Fisk claimed to have won $9 million dollars but bemoaned as a "loss" the additional $6 million that he missed. Belden went into bankruptcy, with the result that those who had sold the gold could not collect. This was a favorite trick of Drew's that came to be known as "squatting."

In the spirit of lese majeste that has been conveniently adopted to spare crooked, corrupt and criminal Presidents from exposure of their crimes, Pres. Grant got off with relative impunity and undisclosed benefits. The coverup was absolutely essential for his Party and was most carefully managed by its members in Congress and by a venal press.

An investigation by the House Banking and Finance Committee under the chairmanship of Congressman James Garfield, who was later rewarded for his role in the coverup with the Party's Presidential nomination, completely whitewashed Pres. Grant and all persons involved, except Assistant Treasurer Butterfield who was exposed as having gained a mere $500,000 in loot, and was forced to resign. Thus shielded Pres. Grant and his Administration proceeded to perpetrate many other scandalous swindles.

Gould's control of the Erie Railroad that had been gained by fraud and swindling, proved to be a point of contact with another rising racketeer who operated in bootlegging Harkness's unstamped whiskey to Civil War soldiers and in the field of oil, John D. Rockefeller. Their dealings in oil transportation, however were not always friendly. Gould's successful "Gold Corner" inspired John D. to stage repeated relatively smaller "Gold Corners" in the course of the next half century, as will be related. And in the following decades cordial cooperation of the Rockefeller and Gould interests were effected by George Jay Gould. (77:293f)

CHAPTER VII
## JOHN D. WIDENED THE RANGE OF ROCKEFELLER CRIMES TO INCLUDE "GOLD CORNERS"

The notoriety and "glory" of rigging of "gold corners" were shared by Gould, Fisk and Grant. But John D. Rockefeller, following in their footsteps while skulking behind the scenes and lurking in the shadows, derived infinitely greater loot from numerous repetitions of "gold corners" in the following half century. Entirely unpublicized and unsuspected he repeatedly threw the nation into panic and depression whenever it suited his thievish purposes to do so. And the loot which he amassed through his brigandage far exceeded the ten or twenty million dollars that Gould, Fisk and their partners in the Grant Administration had garnered on "Black Friday."

John D. was an apt pupil in crime. His criminality was truly hereditary. And his natural, inherited aptitude was highly sharpened by the Fagin-like training that he had received at the hand of his father, "Doc" William Avery Rockefeller. To this John D. proudly attested in a book that was published in his name, entitled *Random Reminiscences*, in the following words:

> "To my father I owe a great debt in that he himself trained me in practical ways. He was engaged in different enterprises; he used to tell me about these things, explaining their significance; and he taught me the principles and methods of business."(16:33)

"The many different enterprises" in which "Doc" Bill engaged covered the entire range of vicious crimes. In the official biography of John D. that was authorized by the family and written for them by Allan Nevins on the basis of their records, they acknowledge that he was a horse thief, a swindler, a bigamist and a rapist. (77)) These

29

"enterprises" they could not deny, because the court records of them are still available. This author has cited, in his work *The Truth About Rockefeller*, the rape indictment, of which this author has the sole surviving copy certified by the court clerk, against William A. Rockefeller, who, it charges:

"...violently and feloniously did make an assault on her the said Anne Vanderbeak then and there violently and against her will did ravish and carnally know (her)..." (79:8;77:I:52)

"Doc" Bill, a quack patent medicine vendor prowled about the country with his show, selling crude petroleum oil as a guaranteed cure for cancer and all other ills of man and beast, preying on the gullible; but carefully avoiding visiting the same town twice. Numerous criminal indictments still stand against him, as a tribute to his felonious "talents," in the court records of the communities in which he plied his arts. There is no record, however, of his apprehension, trial or imprisonment. This he owed to the facilities that the wilderness that was early America offered fugitives from justice; and not, as the case of his descendants, to the control of the law and of the government.

An art which "Doc" Bill held in highest regard was swindling. But scarcely less highly did he hold loan sharking which had the advantage of not being entirely outside the law, if practised without violence. In accord with his "sterling" character, "Doc" Bill did not "sully" his bigamous record by providing for any of his families. But, he boasted to his cronies that he made amends for his failure to provide for them by the Fagin-like training which he gave his offspring who undertook to help their mother provide for them by doing chores for their neighbors and earning some pennies. He crowed:

"I cheat my boys every time I get a chance. I want to make 'em sharp. I trade with the boys and skin 'em and just beat 'em every time I can. I want to make 'em sharp." (77:I:93)

When the fugitive quack "Doc" Bill, sneaked home after Saturday midnight when he could not be served a summons, under the law, once or twice a year to provide his wife with another offspring to divert her, he would swindle the boys of the pennies that they had earned. These were "the principles and methods of business" to which his eldest offspring, John D. referred. (16:33) No scheme, he taught, was too crooked, no crime too vicious or sordid, if the loot was rich. And he made it the traditional training of his descendants.

It was "Doc" Bill's dedication to loan sharking that divested him of the control of the company that first successfully drilled for oil in the U.S.A. He had made usurious loans to the officers of the Pennsylvania Rock Oil Co. that gave him control. He ordered that the name of the company be changed to Seneca Oil Co. to correspond with the "Seneca Indian Oil" which he peddled. He was about to take complete possession of the company when the officers discovered that the name, Dr. Levingston, under which he had made the loan was an alias for "Doc" Bill Rockefeller who was a fugitive from justice in New York. With this information, the victims were able to force out loan shark Rockefeller.

And outstanding trait of "Doc" Rockefeller, inherited by his descendants, was singleness of purpose in criminality. Once he had set himself any criminal objective nothing could swerve him from it. He launched his offspring, a "chip off the old block," in the oil business, in which he himself was blackballed because of his loan sharking and criminal record. To overcome that bar to credit and financial rating, he advised John D. to use religiosity, instilled in him by his mother, as a studied, ostentatious pose; and to join a church as the most effective measure for establishing a credit rating.

"Doc" Bill loaned his son, John D., who was in effect his deputy, the money for his business on his usual usurious terms. He did, however, stand by him, in Cleveland, to guide his activities. He instilled in him the ambition not to be outdone by anyone in his enterprises, no matter how criminal they might be; and to seek to attain ever higher levels of sharpness and criminality. Thus originated the tradition of the Rockefeller Dynasty that each generation must undertake to outstrip its antecedent in brigandage and thievery, and to ever "refine" and "improve" on their "talents". The Rockefeller Brothers stress this in the instructions that they give their biographers, sardonically alleging their efforts are aimed at "serving mankind."

John D. was an apt pupil. But under the guidance of his father, he replaced lusty criminality with sneaky, undercover thievery and loan-sharking that stopped at no crime and regarded none as too low and vicious, if it yielded ample loot. He masked his criminal activities with a Uriah Heepish cloak of religiosity.

## CHAPTER VIII
## ROCKEFELLER RIGS THE "GOLD STANDARD" FOR U.S.

William Manchester, in his campaign biography entitled *A Rockefeller Family Portrait* (55:80), boasts, on their behalf, of John D.'s practise of shunning honest and above-board dealings. He relates how Rockefeller made a practise of falsely pretending to compete with, or to oppose, ventures that he secretly owned and controlled; and how he used those rigged enterprises as "Trojan horses" to trap and betray those whom he sought to destroy.

Crafty duplicity and sly, ruthless, perverted, criminal cunning were the traits of which "Doc" Bill and his pupil, John D. were proudest. Their descendants, in the main, have followed in their footsteps. With more polish, they have learned to dissemble and to adopt, in public, a sanctimonious pose of "benevolence" and "philanthropy," and a pretended interest in public welfare. Their admiration, however, of the raw criminality of their ancestors emerges in every account that they have had written and published by their publicity men. Thus Manchester expressed their glory in the achievements of John D. in the passage:

31

"For a long time the public did not realize how powerful he (John D.) was because he kept insisting that he was battling firms that he secretly owned outright. His real rivals were forever discovering that their most trusted officers were in his pocket." (55:80)

It fully explains the statement of John D., in the book *Random Reminiscences:*

"The Standard Oil Company does not own or control 'a chain of banks,' nor has it any interest directly or indirectly in any bank. Its relations are confined to the functions of ordinary banking, such as other depositors have. It buys and sells its own exchange; and these have made its bills of exchange acceptable all over the world." (16:94)

This statement echoed the false testimony given by Rockefeller before a Congressional committee investigating his activities, prepared by his lawyers is as ambigious as one might expect of the son of slippery "Doc" Bill. It must be viewed in the light of the Rockefeller tradition of systematic use in their dealings of deceit, trickery, and treachery masked under a sham of religiosity and "philanthropy"; and of the tradition of the medicine show and country fair, of using "shills" for the purpose of trapping victims and diverting them while plucking and looting them and picking their pockets.

ROCKEFELLER GOLD OPERATIONS & PERIODIC "CORNERS"

John D's denial of banking interests was false, both as regards to himself and the Standard Oil Co. In his management of Standard Oil and its subsidiaries, he had kept free of any outside banking control by operating it as a bank and making it financially independent. He had learned from the gold manipulators of the Civil War and Gould's "Gold Corner," the advantages of maintaining a dominant position in the gold market. Periodically he resorted to the device of stripping the Treasury of its gold holdings precipitating panics, and threatening national insolvency. Then when he had attained his predatory objectives, he assumed his customary, sham "philanthropic" pose, and loaned the Treasury some of the gold that he had withdrawn.

Allan Nevins, in his authorized biography, reported that John D. Rockefeller, through his Standard Oil Co. and National City Bank, in 1894 supplied, the Treasury with twenty million in gold to restore gold payments and its solvency, in one of the series of annual panics precipitated by the gold withdrawals. (77:II:440) Nevins belied Rockefeller's testimony before the Congressional committee with a quote from John Moody, who stated that the Standard Oil Co.

"...was really a bank of the most gigantic character—a bank within an industry...continually lending vast sums of money to needy borrowers ...just as other great banks were doing."

He related that the Company was known in financial circles as the "Standard Oil Bank." (77:II:439)

Nevins reported (77:II:44) that by the turn of the century banking had taken over control of industry instead of merely serving it. John D., despite his sneaky dissembling and false denials, was the real leader in setting up a monopolistic control of banking and national finance though he posed as "being retired." The nature of his "retirement," more than two decades later, is reported by John K.

Winkler in his *John D. A Portrait,* as follows:

"While the papers are speculating upon the health of a great diplomat or the possible overthrow of a government, he has already been informed of the latest developments, through direct wires leading from Pocantico Hills to Standard Oil offices and, indirectly, to remote places of the earth. There are over a hundred telephones at Pocantico..." (3:234)

Battling for world financial control with J. P. Morgan & Co., the Rockefeller-Standard Oil crowd joined forces with other antagonists of Morgan who included Kuhn Loeb & Co. and E. H. Harriman, in the reorganization of the Union Pacific and the Southern Pacific railroads. They roundly defeated Morgan, and backed Hill, in the 1901 "corner" of Union Pacific Railroad stock, in a battle for control of that road.

John D. Rockefeller and his associates were the principal manipulators of the gold and monetary market in the final decades of the 19th century. By gangsterism, brigandage and thievery, he had attained wealth enough to control the available supply of gold. He had appropriated, principally by foul means, the bulk of the petroleum industry of the Western Hemisphere and molded it into a gigantic monopoly, or Trust. At the same time, he had forced his way, by hook or crook, into Trusts that had been engineered by J. P. Morgan and his associates in a wide array of industries during the period that the latter's agent, Pres. Theodore Roosevelt, pretended to engage in "Trust busting." He participated with Sen. Nelson Aldrich (grandfather and namesake of Nelson Rockefeller) the Dukes and Thomas Fortune Ryan in setting up the Tobacco Trust. With the Guggenheims, he participated in setting up a world-wide Rubber Trust and a Non-Ferrous Metal Trust. The key market operator for the Rockefellers and their fellow conspirators in these schemes was their agent, Bernard Baruch.

John D. forced his way into the organization of the Steel Trust by his control of the Mesabi Range. This he had obtained by defrauding the owners, the Merritt brothers with the assistance of the Baptist minister, Reverend Frederick T. Gates who by this larceny won Rockefeller's frank admiration and appointment as his "almoner." (78:79;77:II:336f)

## ROCKEFELLERS SEEK "SECURITY"
## FOR THEMSELVES ONLY

Despite his immense loot, Rockefeller lived in fear of poverty. And he instilled his mania into his offspring in such intense degree that his fear of poverty has become a fixed, paranoid characteristic of the Dynasty. (79) Rockefeller yearned, above all things, for "security" for himself in his piracy. This meant to him that he must loot and despoil everyone, enslave the world and rob everyone else of their possessions and security in order to make sure that no one more ruthless and criminal than himself could arise and rob him of his loot. Like an ugly, monstrous spider, John D. sat in the midst of a vast web of conspiracy in which he had entrapped the U.S.A. and the rest of the world, ready to pounce on and devour his victims, mankind.

His grandiose plan was to found a Dynasty that would rule, loot and despoil the world, in perpetuo. The first step in this super-Macchiavellian plot was a program of merciless looting and absolute sub-

33

jugation of the U.S.A. for use by the Dynasty to establish a world dictatorship, "One (Rockefeller) World."

To mask this plot, Rockefeller was counselled by his advisers that he must adopt a pose of "philanthropist." (15:69f) This is a traditional pose recommended for would-be dictators and tyrants, as the road to power by way of duping the moronic elements of the populace adopted by the Illuminist-Communist, Jesuit conspirator, Adam Weishaupt, alias Spartacus, and by his disciple, Moses Mordecai Marx Levy, alias (Heinrich) Karl Marx. It is a device that disarms the morons, imbeciles and idiots, because of the larceny that lurks in men's hearts, from which springs the hope of getting something for nothing.

Under the disarming mask of bogus "philanthropy," Rockefeller undertook to impose on the U.S.A. every phase of the Weishaupt-Marx Illuminist-Socialist-Communist conspiracy, in which they recognized the most effective brand of "instant looting" of whole peoples and nations. It is the only device by which whole lands and their peoples can be enslaved and looted, overnight.

## ROCKEFELLERS PROMOTE COMMUNISM BY "BRAINWASHING" THRU FOUNDATIONS.

As the first step toward the conspiratorial goal of totalitarianism, the Rockefellers followed the Weishauptian precepts and reached out for control of the "minds" of the people through control of education by their bogus "philanthropy," the General Education Board. They have so low an opinion of the public's mentality (seemingly justified—they call them "peasants" among themselves) that they made no effort to hide their conspiratorial purpose. In the Rockefeller-Gates *Occasional Letter No 1*, issued in 1904, they openly stated that the purpose of their G. E. B. was to brainwash the nation, through education and all media of mass-communication, into subjection to their dictates. Paraphrasing Weishaupt, they wrote: (15:125f; 29:17)

"In our dreams we have limitless resources (the pocketbooks of the nation) and the people yield themselves with perfect docility to our molding hands. The present educational conventions fade from our minds (the 3 R's, morality and ethics) and *we work our own good will* (tax looting, regimentation and war) upon a grateful and responsive rural folk (peasants)."

## GRAND DUKE ALEXANDER ESPIED U.S.A AS "ROCKEFELLER'S EMPIRE," IN 1913.

Rockefellers' success in accomplishing the subversion of our people and government was so rapid and complete that by 1913 the situation was perfectly obvious to intelligent visitors from abroad. Grand Duke Alexander, of Russia, visited our country in that year, after an absence of twenty years. He relates in his autobiography entitled *Once A Grand Duke:*

"The rustic republic of Jefferson was rapidly giving way to the *Empire Of The Rockefellers,* but the average mentality of the man-on-the-street had not caught up with this new order of things ..." (80:242)

Proof that it was not only Americans who were myopic can be discerned in the failure of the Grand Duke to realize that it was the Rockefellers who had financed Lenin and Trotzky in the overthrow of the Czarist regime in Russia, through their agent and banker, Jacob Schiff.

34

The financing of upheavals and revolutions around the world has been a policy that has been persistently pursued by the conspirators through their foundations. Highly successful has been the Rockefeller financing of the British aspect of the Weishaupt-Marx conspiracy, the Fabian Society, in destroying the British Empire as a rival for world control. Lord Beveridge published in his *Power & Influence* (2:199) John D. Rockefeller's letter, dated January 14, 1927, in which he personally undertook to finance the purchase of a site for that hotbed of Communism, the London School of Economics & Political Science, which has ably served them in destroying the Empire.

## ROCKEFELLER AGENT SUCCESSFULLY PROPAGANDIZED "GOLD STANDARD" FOR U.S.

Rockefeller's first move in attaining "security" for himself was effecting the imposition of the so-called "Gold Standard" on the nation. His obvious purpose was to insure himself and his gang "security" in their periodic and systematic looting of the nation by gold manipulations and "corners." The immediate, urgent, impetus for this action rose from the silver situation at the turn of the century.

The volume of silver that was being produced, in contrast with the limited production of gold, rose constantly and rapidly. Much of it is a by-product of the mining and refining of base metals. The mining industry had difficulty in finding a ready industrial market for the rising silver production. It sought a solution for this problem in increased coinage of silver by the Federal government. To avert the speculative pressure of a "supply and demand" market, the silver interests endeavored to restore silver to the status of legal tender at a fixed value relative to gold.

This plan was propagandized on behalf of the silver interests by "Coin" Harvey in his book *Coin's Financial School* (81). Supported by the mining interests and their spokesman, William Jennings Bryan, the perennial Presidential candidate, and the Democratic Party, it received wide acclaim. Harvey's book swept the country as a best seller, with a phenomenal sale of six hundred thousand copies. The situation was quite alarming for the gold manipulators.

Rockefeller reacted with vigor. J. Laurence Laughlin, Professor of Political Economy of Rockefeller's University of Chicago, was employed and assigned the task of defeating the silver advocates by counter-propaganda rapidly disseminated, through their controlled press, as professional "wisdom and erudition." This propaganda device is the standard practise of the conspirators, aided by menagerie of professorial "trained seals" who are ever ready to sell their talents. They remind one of the courtesan who eagerly peddles her "favors" with a bed that she carries on her back.

Professor Laughlin related in his autobiographic, documented confession that he published under the title *The Federal Reserve Act: Its Origin & Its Problems:*

"Through H. H. Kohlsatt, articles were daily written by me for his editorial page in the *Times-Herald* of fifteen hundred words each, devoted to the fallacies of Harvey's book. In three months we had stopped the sale of this book." (1:3)

Rockefeller feared that the flood of silver would mean a halt to their power to swindle the nation by the creation of panics brought about by "Gold Corners."

The next step in the conspiracy was to call a convention of their associates and agents in Indianapolis, the so-called Monetary Convention of 1897. Its ostensible and announced purpose was the appointment of a "non-partisan" committee to "study" the monetary situation and bring in an "unbiassed" report, that was rigged by them in advance, to serve their purposes. Rockefeller's agent. Prof. Laughlin, frankly relates:

"...I was instructed to prepare this report...There followed from it the introduction of the bill which became the ("Gold Standard") act of March 14, 1900. *The Law Practically Ended The Anxiety About The Possibility Of A Silver Standard.*" (1:3)

## "GOLD STANDARD" ACT WAS A FRAUD PERPETRATED ON THE NATION

The "Gold Standard" Act is conceptually based on the obviously false premise that gold is the only indispensible necessity of life requisite for our survival as individuals and as a nation; that we can not feed, clothe, shelter or defend ourselves without gold; and that therefore we undertake, as a nation, to stabilize the monetary value of gold. No other premise could justify warping the national effort and economy by straightjacketing it within the bounds of the value of one of its scarcest commodities. The falsity of the premise implied in the Act makes it obvious that its motivation was false.

The malign motivation of the Act is verified by its content. Only a fraction of the money under the terms of the Act is redeemable in gold. Two and a half dollar gold notes were issued for every dollar in the gold base. The "justification" that its sponsors gave for this obvious fraud has been that not all holders of gold certificates will, under ordinary circumstances, demand redemption in gold and the shortage will not be discovered. This situation is no less fraudulent than the "kiting" of cheeks by the individual who issues $250.00 in checks for the $100.00 that he has in the bank.

## CHAPTER IX
## RIGGED 1907 PANIC USED AS PRETEXT FOR XVITH AMENDMENT & "FEDERAL" RESERVE

The monetary stringency that their "Gold Standard" Act facilitated, enabled the Rockefeller conspirators to precipitate the panic of 1907 as an act of vengeance for the fining of their Standard Oil Co. twenty-nine millions dollars by Judge Kenesaw Landis, for their criminal, racketeering. (15:163) The panic that they precipitated, in turn, was used by them as a pretext for carrying out two of the basic plots conceived by the Weishaupt-Marx Illuminist-Communist conspirators as features of their program for a super-capitalistic world dictatorship: control of money and credit by a central banking system, and control of wealth through progressively more confiscatory income and capital taxes.

## GOV. NELSON ROCKEFELLER'S GRANDFATHER, SEN. ALDRICH GAVE US INCOME TAX.

The two fundamental measures for carrying out the conspiracy were introduced in Congress by the grandfather and namesake of Gov. Nelson Aldrich Rockefeller, the Republican boss of Congress, Sen. Nelson Adrich. He introduced the bill that was craftily designed to destroy one of the most important checks incorporated in the Constitution to limit the power of the Federal Government: barring direct taxation, limiting it to taxation by apportionment among the States. The XVIth Amendment nullifies this basic feature of the Constitution, and permits direct Federal taxation without regard to apportionment. The amendment is the basis of a structure of laws, rules, regulations, bureaucratic edicts and decisions by corrupted courts, that has enabled the conspirators to gain, complete and unlimited control of the wealth of the citizenry and the nation. It has, in effect, converted the government into their agency for unrestricted looting of the nation, for espionage into the private affairs of all but the privileged, and for nullification of the protection of the Constitution and the Bill of Rights. It compels one to give evidence against oneself, to submit to star chamber trials by bureaucrats, to submit to search without warrant, and nullifies the principle that one is innocent until proved guilty. It has made resistance to looting by the conspirators and their political agents the most heinous and unpardonable crime. By numerous provisions especially written for themselves, the conspirators have virtually exempted themselves from taxation; and have sluiced off into their own purses the loot that they use the Government to extort from the rest of the nation. In short, the conspirators have invented for themselves a "perfect crime".

The Illuminist-Communist "progressive income tax" device was the objective of our so-called "liberals", or Reds, since the founding of our Republic. Whenever they had succeeded in placing income tax laws on the statute books, they were promptly declared un-Constitutional by honest Justices on the Supreme Court bench, as in the Pollock case (1895). But the "liberal" termites persisted in their efforts. The Republican campaign literature in 1894 stated: "In this country an income tax of any sort is odious . . ."

The "liberal" Democrats persisted in their efforts to impose their Red, Federal income tax scheme. Cordell Hull, a young Congressman from Tennessee, assumed the leadership of the campaign of the Democrats for adoption of the tax in the 60th Congress. He wrote: "...I introduced on December 19, 1907, a comprehensive income tax bill." He stated that he did so in spite of the certainty that "income taxation could not be enacted except through a Constitutional amendment." (23:48) He added "...we had a reconstituted (Ed. packed) Court that might be more favorably inclined toward the principle." (23:49)

Wily, vulpine John D. Rockefeller and his more covertly, timidly but no less viciously crafty heir, John D. Jr., shrewdly recognized the thievish character of the Weishaupt-Marx Communist "progressive income tax" scheme. They cautiously avoided openly joining forces with the "liberal" Democrats in demanding its adoption. They employed their usual trick of pretending to oppose the very measure that they were promoting. They posed as "tried and trusted" Republicans. But undercover, they split the Republicans by financing, through their agents, their avowed enemy, ex-President Theodore Roosevelt, and his Bull Moose "liberals", or "moderates", who joined the Democrats in putting over the subversive XVIth Amendment.

The conspirators' tactics were ably seconded by their in-law, Sen. Nelson Aldrich. As Republican leader, he duped the Party into support of the subversive, un-Constitutional XVIth Amendment. With the treachery that characterizes all of the conspirators' activities, he represented to his followers that the Amendment to the Constitution was un-Constitutional, and therefore would defeat itself. This treachery was aptly described by Cordell Hull as follows:

". . . the Old Guard crowd in charge of the Senate under the leadership of Senator Aldrich saw there was a real chance of the provision being approved. They decided that they would give an appearance of acquiescing in income tax and at the same time kill it by substituting for the provision a proposed constitutional amendment." (23:60)

For the purpose of insuring Republican approval of the provision, Sen. Aldrich introduced it as an amendment to the Republican sponsored Payne-Aldrich Tariff Bill.

## SEN. ALDRICH WIDENED CONSPIRATORS' BRIGANDAGE: SPONSORED "FEDERAL" RESERVE ACT

Looting the people of what little might be left in their purses by the income tax, and seizing absolute control of the national and international power of the purse were the purposes of the conspirators' "Federal" Reserve conspiracy. The stage for it also was set by their 1907 panic.

The "Federal" Reserve conspiracy also was launched by Rockefeller's in-law, Sen. Nelson Aldrich. The Aldrich-Vreeland Bill was represented to the nation as a "solution" of the problems of the depression. Flaunting the recommendations of the House Banking Committee, it was pushed through Congress on May 30, 1908, by the joint efforts of Sen. Aldrich in the Senate, and of autocratic Speaker Cannon in the House. The bill authorized the private national banks to form local, so-called "national currency associations" that could obtain currency from the Comptroller of the Currency on the basis of securities that were otherwise not acceptable for the purpose. The notes were known as the "Aldrich-Vreeland notes". The "sleeper" in the bill was a provision for creation of a "National Monetary Commission" for further "study" of the currency and banking problem. The conspirators' agent, Prof. Laughlin reported that he drafted a report for their American Bankers Association supporting this phase of the plot. (1:5)

## "NATIONAL MONETARY COMMISSION" WAS SEN. ALDRICH, ROCKEFELLER IN-LAW

The so-called "National Monetary Commission" created under this provision of the Aldrich-Vreeland Bill, was in effect Rockefeller's in-law, Sen. Aldrich himself and virtually alone. Laughlin reported:

"The work was really carried out by Sen. Aldrich himself, with the aid of the Secretary, A. Piatt Andrew". (1:5)

Though the "Commission" was supposed to consist of nine members each, from the Senate and the House, like all Rockefeller "Committees" it reflected only the views of the conspirators. They were free to use Congress to promote their banking and monetary conspiracy, entirely unhampered by any restriction or control other than the will of their in-law, Sen. Aldrich. The tragic irony of the situation was that the conspirators pretended that they were preparing a solution for the situation that they themselves had deliberately created by restriction of currency and credit available to the nation through their gold manipulations that they could instantly remedy by releasing gold, if they so desired.

### SENATOR NELSON ALDRICH, "PHILANTHROPIST"

Sen. Aldrich was no banker. But he had done right well for himself as a skinflint, New England usurer, so-called "humanitarian" and "philanthropist. His "genius" matched that of the Rockefellers. He had also done right well for himself as political boss. He joined Rockefeller, Duke and Ryan in creating the Tobacco Trust, with the help of their agent and market manipulator, Bernard Baruch. After the Trust got under way, he displayed the characteristic "benevolence" and "philanthropy" of his breed.

Sen. Aldrich, political boss of Rhode Island, "benignly" let the schoolchildren of Rhode Island enjoy the "blessings" of tobacco that he marketed. Smoking rooms were provided in all the public schools. And youngsters were taught and encouraged to start to smoke at the age of eight years. This "benevolence" characterizes the "philanthropy" of the conspirators.

Senator Aldrich's grandchildren, the Rockefeller brothers, still enjoy the revenues derived from this ancestral "philanthropy." But they know better than to smoke his tobacco. His namesake, Nelson Aldrich Rockefeller, has preserved for posterity many of the "noble" traits of his ancestor. Judging by the current intensive propaganda drive against cigarettes in all the media of mass communication controlled by them, the Senator's descendants may well outstrip their ancestors by effecting thereby a sole and absolute monopoly of the cigarette and tobacco market by driving out all competition in an operation that matches their takeover of the liquor industry through their prohibition campaign.

Loughlin reported that

". . . Mr. Aldrich's chief interest centered in provisions on control (Ed. of currency) . . ." (1:16)

Developments indicate that though he was perfectly willing to provide his conspirator in-laws with the control of currency that they sought, he did not trust them sufficiently to give them also the control of credit that they demanded. He was too well aware of the brigand character of the "philanthropists" to trust them with the control of his credit and that of the nation. He was too well aware of the mythical character of "honor among thieves."

Sen. Aldrich made a pretense of "investigating" and "studying" the central banking systems of Europe in brief junkets made as chairman of his National Monetary Commission in the company of his secretary. European lands had long had central banking, whereas the

U.S. had had none since the Second Bank of the U.S. had been denied a renewal of its charter.

## PAUL WARBURG: ROCKEFELLERS' GERMAN AGENT & CENTRAL BANKER

Shortly after the enactment of the Gold Standard Act, the conspirators, with characteristic long-range plotting, had imported, in 1900, a man who was to serve them in double capacity as central banking expert and German agent, Paul Warburg. Warburg's brother was chief of espionage and intelligence of Germany and in an unexcelled position to effect contact of the conspirators with Kaiser Wilhelm when it would be desired by them. As son of M. M. Warburg, of the Hamburg firm that were correspondents of the Rothschilds, Paul Warburg had had extensive experience with central banking. The firm was also affiliated with one of the American correspondents of the Rothschilds, that shared their business with J. P. Morgan & Co., Kuhn Loeb & Co. The Rothschild correspondents had ingratiated themselves with Rockefeller, who distrusted Wall Street and Morgan, by arranging to finance his Standard Oil and other companies, with moneys derived from their chief competitor, the Royal Dutch Company that was controlled, jointly with the British and Dutch crowns, by the Rothschild-Sassoon-Isaacs-Samuel group. In this treachery, the Warburg firm had collaborated.

Paul M. Warburg, and his brother Felix, were given partnerships in the Kuhn Loeb firm that netted each of them an annual income of $500 million. For this wage he did no banking. His assigned task was propagandizing on behalf of the conspirators their central banking plot to overcome the traditional American aversion to central banking and banking monopoly.

Paul Warburg was personally repugnant to the Rockefeller-Aldrich clan. Almost a caricature of the German, more Prussian than Jew, argumentative, opinionated, conceited and pedantic, he was fond of displaying his learning in long speeches in his thick, guttural accent. He was certainly not a character that they would welcome in their clubs in spite of his wealth. Their contempt for him was especially vigorously voiced by his closest collaborator, Sen. Aldrich, whose vanity he offended. But the conspirators dared not let their contempt obtrude too forcibly, because the "oaf" was valuable to them. They were dependent on his know-how and skill in central banking and also on his capacity as German agent.

Nationwide publicity was given the scheme drawn up by Paul Warburg in collaboration with Sen. Aldrich. It was labelled the "United Reserve Bank." It was a blueprint of a thinly masked central bank for the control of currency. He presented his scheme before the Financial Forum and it was published in full, on March 24, 1910, in the conspirators' official organ, the *New York Times*. The conspirators rejected this Aldrich-Warburg scheme because it would not give them control of credit as well as of currency.

Laughlin presented before the conspirators' agency, the Academy of Political Science, Columbia University, on November 12, 1910, the scheme that they required to give them absolute control of both currency and credit. (1:18) It was subsequently published in the December 1910 issue of their *Journal of Political Economy* under the title *Bank Notes & Lending Power*. (1:375f; 82:777f) The conspirators' direction of this program is clearly indicated by Laughlin in his words:

"This proposal of mine fell in with the plans *intended to be developed...*" (1:14)

The use by the conspirators of one set of their agents, Laughlin and his associates, to connive the defeat of another group of their pawns, in-law Aldrich and Warburg, is as characteristic of Rockefeller treachery and double-dealing as are the dealings with their Red agents. And it is a source of great pride to them.

## THE JEKYLL ISLAND RUSE

The Jekyll Island conference was another such crafty device used by the conspirators to discredit the Aldrich-Warburg bill. Supposedly a carefully-guarded secret, their tightly-controlled and censored press broadcast it as a "leak" in the monetary conspiracy. Laughlin relates

"The names of the men who went to Jekyll Island were not given to the public, for the reason that it might have been supposed to have been a scheme proposed by Wall Street interests, with the intention, if the act were passed, of finally controlling the organization." (1:16)

What the public was not informed was that the reason for holding the conference of Jekyll Island was that a Wall Street group headed by Rockefeller and Morgan were members of an ultra-exclusive and highly-"restricted" club that own the island. They also control the adjoining Sea Island, and St. Simon Island, where the Rockefeller conspirators held, at a later date, one of their nefarious Bilderberg conferences. Rockefellers owned a mansion on the island that later, when they tired of paying taxes on it, they gave to the State of Georgia as a museum. It is reported that some of the sessions of the inner ring of conferees were held in the Rockefeller mansion. The museum might well be regarded as a memorial to Rockefellers' greatest swindle.

Among the Jekyll Island conferees were the following:

*Representing Rockefeller interests:*

Sen. Nelson Aldrich, betrayed and double-crossed Rockefeller in-law.

Frank A. Vanderlip, President of Rockefeller's National City Bank. (N. Y.).

Paul Moritz Warburg, Rockefeller banking propagandist and German agent.

*Representing the Morgan interests:*

Henry P. Davison, senior partner of J. P. Morgan & Co.

Charles D. Norton, President of the First National Bank (N. Y.).

*Rockefeller-Morgan liaison agent:*

Benjamin Strong, Morgan lieutenant. (Bessie Rockefeller married a Strong. Strong is reported to have been a companion of Warburg's.

As the conspirators hoped and planned, the story of the Jekyll Island conference, that had been "leaked" by them, intensified the antagonism that they stirred up against Sen. Aldrich, personally, and the opposition to his bill which they were intent on defeating. With characteristic ruthlessness, their strategy was ousting Aldrich and the Republicans and turning over control of the Government to Democratic agents of theirs. This was facilitated by their vengeful success in delivering the House to the Democrats in the next election following the judgement against them handed down by Judge Landis and the $29,000,000 fine imposed by him on their Standard Oil Co.

41

## ROCKEFELLER HOME ON JEKYLL ISLAND IN WHICH "FEDERAL" RESERVE CONSPIRACY WAS PLOTTED

The meeting at which the fraudulent "Federal" Reserve plot was deliberately "leaked" to the press was held on Jekyll Island that was owned by a "highly restricted" private club of financial brigands, including the Morgans and the Rockefellers. They owned homes on the island, of which the above is a specimen. Discussions on the "F"R plot were held in these homes and in the club. The true reason for holding the conference at this notorious Wall Street manipulators' club was to discredit and defeat the bill drawn up by Paul Warburg for introduction by Rockefellers' in-law, Sen. Nelson Aldrich, because it was not crooked enough to satisfy the demands of John D. the First for the control and manipulation of both money and credit of the nation and of our wealth. After the conspirators ousted Aldrich and the Republicans, Pres. Wilson forced the crooked bill through Congress. The Rockefeller home was given Georgia as a museum to avoid taxes and as a monument to the "F"R, the greatest fraud in history.

## ALDRICH-WARBURG CLIQUE & BILL SCRAPPED BY ROCKEFELLER CONSPIRATORS

Rockefeller's agent, Prof. Laughlin, made clear the purpose and success of the treachery, and no effort was made to hide their intent.

". . . I told him (Warburg) . . . the political difficulties found in Congress to pass a bill closely associated with the name of Aldrich . . . (1:43) Consequently it was suggested that a bill when perfected should not be associated with Senator Aldrich's name. . . . Such a suggestion, however, brought to the surface how strongly Mr. Aldrich and his friends were personally interested in having credit for this currency legislation. Mr. Warburg . . . objected strongly. (1:44)

"The Republican forces overstayed their time; and with the change of political power to the Democrats in the House, in June, 1911, the Republican Aldrich bill ceased to be possible legislation." (1:55)

Laughlin made it quite clear that Rockefellers' success in replacing the Republicans with a Democratic regime implied a welcome riddance of the "nuisance" of the less thievish Aldrich-Warburg bill.

Sen. Aldrich personally, however, was amusingly unsuspecting of the doublecross which his Rockefeller kinsmen and their agents were giving him. Laughlin quotes in full the letter which Aldrich sent him, in which he listed the Senators who could be "reached", "pressured" or bribed to vote for his bill, directing him to do so. In the letter dated June 13, 1911, Aldrich advised:

"I will say that the Democrats *to be reached* in the Senate are of course, first perhaps, Senator Bailey, who I think is inclined to be all right. . . . We ought to be able *to reach* quite a number of Southern Senators . . . for instance the two Alabama Senators, the two Louisiana Senators, the two Maryland Senators, the two Virginia Senators, especially Martin. Of course *there ought be no difficulty in reaching* O'Gorman of New York . . ." (1:46)

## CHAPTER X
## WOODROW WILSON'S "DEAL" WITH "FEDERAL" RESERVE CONSPIRATORS FOR PRESIDENCY

At the time that duped and unsuspecting Sen. Aldrich was writing the quoted letter, his Rockefeller in-laws had jettisoned him and his bill and were preparing to oust the Republican Party from the White House. Indifference to political allegiances and control of all political parties is a Rockefeller tradition. Their only loyalty is to themselves, their loot, and their purses.

42

With the purpose of validating their agent's dictum ("the Republican Aldrich bill ceased to be possible legislation") Laughlin was assigned the task of faking a "Midwest grass roots" demand for banking reform, and aligning it behind a bill that he was employed to draw up for completely fulfilling the thievish purposes of his crafty, underhanded employers. For carrying out this slimy scheme, he organized in Chicago, in May 1911, an outfit that he sententiously named the "National Citizens' League For The Promotion Of A Sound Banking System". (1:56) It was falsely represented as "free of any banking influence," "a businessmen's organization bent on 'educating' the public on a 'proper solution' of the banking problem (from the viewpoint of his thievish gangster masters)." Similar subsidiary organizations were set up in forty-five other states.

## WILSON MADE "DEAL" FOR PRESIDENCY IN EXCHANGE FOR "FEDERAL" RESERVE BILL

Woodrow Wilson, corrupt Governor of New Jersey, was chosen by the conspirators to force the passage of the banking bill that they desired. From close observation of Wilson throughout his career, the conspirators knew that he could be depended upon to carry out their orders,—or else—. They knew him as a lecherous, depraved, smooth and sententiously spoken scoundrel and rake who was as devoid of ethics and principle as he was of morality.

At Princeton University, Wilson had been a classmate and boon companion of Cyrus H. McCormick and Cleveland Dodge, kinsmen of the Rockefellers. They knew where all of his skeletons were buried or closeted. This was particularly true of Cleveland Dodge, who had repeatedly rescued Wilson from unsavory, scandalous scrapes. From the beginning, they promoted and subsidized the career of their maverick, woman-chasing classmate. Jointly with Moses Taylor and Percy R. Pyne (scion of the founder of National City Bank of New York) in their capacity of Trustees of Princeton, they had subsidized, or "kept", Wilson in the appointments that they gave him as Professor and President of the University. And they were ever ready to finance his amorous, adulterous escapades and supplement his salary. (5:IV:397)

Dodge is reported to have furnished the $75,000 that was required as a campaign fund by New Jersey Democratic boss, former U.S. Sen. James Smith, Jr., as a condition for giving Wilson the gubernatorial nomination in order to quickly and gracefully get him off the Princeton campus in order to avert a threatening scandal. (6:30) Dodge, likewise is reported to have rushed to Boston to offer payment of $50,000 to a woman, Mrs. Peck, with whom Wilson had had a notorious affair, in order to avert threatened publication of the lascivious letters that, as was his habit, he had written her, after the President had exhausted efforts to recover them by intimidation. (12) It is reported that this matter had eased the way to the Supreme Court bench of her attorney, Louis Brandeis. A distortion of this episode is the basis of a chapter of the ghostwritten book, *Profiles in Courage*, that was published in the name of the late President John F. Kennedy. (83)

Wilson had already amply proved his capacity for doubledealing and treachery. One instance was his "welching" on an agreement that he had authorized George Harvey to make, a deal to back Sen. Smith's reelection as payoff for giving him the Democratic gubernatorial nomi-

43

nation. (:32f) Wilson's contemptible lack of character is aptly described by William F. McCombs, his pre-nomination campaign manager in his book *Making Woodrow Wilson* President as follows:

"I write . . . as an opponent of the subversion of the American constitution and the destruction of our system of Government, through vanity and greed for individual power. . . .He (Wilson) was always actuated by the purpose of the moment. He was an opportunist. Suave of manner, he constantly strove to advance himself. He saw only himself—and only his own personal individual exaltation. He played the game . . . always to win—never to lose. Winning was his passion. . . . He was brutal in victory. He was the first to run when threatened with defeat. . . . Mr. Wilson was insensible of political obligations. He recognized no debt to the giver. . . . His strength lay in his cleverness of expression. . . . One became intoxicated with the veneer of his intellectuality. The Wilson ideal was Alexander Hamilton. . . . Like Hamilton he believed in a limited monarchy—a life tenure for the President. . . . While President he regarded himself not only as President, but Premier. . . . It was during the Paris Peace Conference that he proclaimed himself Premier of the United States. . . ." (6:17f)

Despite his shiftiness, the conspirators were sure of their ground. For them, he was an ideal candidate. He was financially dependent on them. He was sufficiently vulnerable, on the basis of his record known to them, to insure that they would have no difficulty in crushing and disposing of him if he failed to carry out their orders. As Governor of New Jersey, he had proved himself by forcing ratification by the State of their un-Constitutional XVIth Amendment.

At the Westchester estate of their agent, Frank Vanderlip, President of their National City Bank, Gov. Wilson made a deal with the conspirators, represented by their kinsmen, William Rockefeller and James Stillman. In return for their securing his Presidential nomination by the Democrats and effecting his election, Wilson agreed that the first act of his Administration would be to force through Congress the corrupt banking bill they desired. He also agreed that he would express no views on money and banking other than speeches ghostwritten for him by Vanderlip. (4:20) For the purpose of duping the public and hiding the extent of his prostitution and sell-out to them, Wilson required them to communicate with him only through his prospective son-in-law, William G. McAdoo. A contemptible hypocrite, it was his plan to pretend that he was an enemy of the Satanic conspirators to whom he had sold his soul. (4)

### DEMOCRATIC PRESIDENTIAL NOMINATION BOUGHT FOR WILSON

The conspirators had little difficulty in delivering their end of the "deal". The craftiness of the conspirators' maneuvers, at the 1912 Democratic convention in Baltimore, marked them as "masters of deceit"; and clearly indicate that their control of that Party was, and still is, as complete as is their control of the Republican Party. The prime obstacle was the perennial Democratic Presidential candidate, "silver-tongued" William Jennings Bryan. They "leaked" the story, through their propagandist George Harvey, that they would support

Champ Clark for the purpose of directing Bryan's attack at him. The ruse succeeded. Bryan vigorously attacked Clark. With the convention thus brought to an impasse, they had directed Harvey to swing the Alabama delegation to Wilson. At the same time, another agent of theirs, Tammany chief, Charles Murphy, pretended to align the New York delegation against Wilson, and thus duped the "liberal" delegates into giving him the nomination. (8:211f)

The conspirators were then confronted with the problem of winning for their hireling Wilson the support of Bryan to effect unification of the Party. For this purpose, they flattered his vanity by letting Bryan write the Party platform plank on money and banking. Bryan's program was the very opposite of what they were conspiring to adopt. But it served their purpose by the attack that it made on the Aldrich-Warburg bill. It read:

"We oppose the so-called Aldrich bill or the establishment of a central bank, and we believe the people of the country will be largely freed from panics (Ed. sic) and consequent unemployment and business depression by such a systematic revision of our banking laws as will render temporary relief in localities where such relief is needed, with protection from control or domination by what is known as the 'Money Trust'."

Laughlin pointed out:

' The plank was meaningless . . . and left the party practically free to adopt any plan of banking reform which should be brought before them in the future. As it turned out, *what should be proposed really lay in the hands of Mr. Wilson."* (1:98)

And he exulted:

"He (Bryan) gave the coup de grace to any attempt to pass the Aldrich bill." (1:83)

For the purpose of "diverting the peasants" and camouflaging their plot, the conspirators launched, through their agents in the Democratic House Banking Committee, an investigation of what they called the "Money Trust". It served the dual purpose of deflecting attention to themselves as controllers of the nation's fianances, and sidetracking those members of the committee and of the House who might oppose their plans. They were assigned to a subcommittee headed by a retiring chairman, Pujo. Laughlin reported:

"The radicals, led by Robert S. Henry of Texas, wished to play politics with the Trust issue, and leaders, like Underwood, proposed to let them blow off steam before the Presidential election..." (1:100)

The attorney for the Pujo Committee was Samuel Untermyer, a New York lawyer who was identified with the Aldrich-Warburg group whom the Rockefellers wished to sidetrack.

### ROCKFELLER AGENT WROTE BILL FOR GLASS & "PACKED" COMMITTEE

Untermyer and his clique tried to extend the scope of the Pujo Committee to the drafting of the banking bill. The conspirators blocked them by assigning its drafting to another subcommittee headed by a trusted pawn, Carter Glass who they had arranged to succeed Pujo as Banking Committee Chairman. As "adviser" of Glass and his subcommittee, they planted Laughlin's pupil, H. P. Willis (who had served them in writing the report of their Indianapolis Monetary Commission, preparing the way for their "Gold Standard" Act) for the purpose of steering them into adoption of the bill written for them by Laughlin, who wrote:

"Meanwhile the work of the League (Ed. the propaganda agency he had set up for the Rockefeller) intended to secure banking legislation was necessarily connected with . . . the committee serving Mr. Glass . . . aiding in the creation of a bill which should be taken up by the Congressional machinery and end in the Federal Reserve Act. The immediate nexus was through Mr. Glass and his expert, Mr. H. P. Willis. Mr. Glass . . . could not possibly have created a banking measure suitable for a great emergency like that of 1911-13. It required some agency thoroughly familiar with the history and principles of money and banking. This was supplied to Mr. Glass and his subcommittee by Mr. Willis." (1:104)

Willis had served the conspirators as Washington correspondent of the N. Y. Journal of Commerce; and he wrote for them a chapter of a book on "banking reform" that Laughlin was publishing to further the conspiracy. Laughlin acknowledged himself to be the real author of the bill that Willis is supposed to have written for Glass.

"As regards the origin of the Glass bill, after many conferences between Mr. Willis and me, the first tentative draft was made by him on May 2, 1912." (1:107)

Laughlin verifies this by quotation from Willis' letter (1:106f) to him, relating:

". . . I began seriously to put together the provisions for a bill which in an unexpected emergency could be used to assist Mr. Glass' subcommittee in drafting their own bill." (1:111)

Following Wilson's election, Laughlin interviewed Glass personally, and related:

"After my interview with Mr. Glass (November 14, 1912) I had gone to work actively on completing the bill in accordance with the suggestions made by him *and according to what had already been decided upon in my own mind.*

"Mr Glass himself made no suggestions as to the particular provisions of the measure. His main point was to get the measure so drawn that it would not antagonize the Democratic platform or call up objection on the ground of some centralization." (1:111)

Since the conspirators had seen to it that the platform adopted by the Baltimore Convention was virtually meaningless, this presented no problem. Shortly thereafter, Laughlin wrote to A. Barton Hepburn. chairman of the Banking Committee of the American Bankers Association:

"Permit me to ask as a favor that my name be kept out of connection with these plans, and also if parts of the measure are discussed by you with anyone, there shall be no suggestion that it comes from the League. We are working very hard to prevent association of the name of the League with any bills that may come up under the auspices of the Democrats." (1:116)

On November 21, 1912, Glass asked Laughlin to draft a bill for him:

"This was to be known only to him and Mr. Willis . . . in December, 1912, I submitted to Mr.Glass as complete a measure as possible, which would contain a plan for an organization different from that

46

of the Aldrich plan, and yet have the correct banking principle . . .
instead of beginning at the top and working down, my suggestions
were to begin with regional organizations and work upward to a
coordinating body in the form of a Treasury board . . . *we centered
our efforts on getting Mr. Glass to understand our plan* . . . by the
end of November I had made a rough tentative draft of the bill . . .
and later (December 22, 1912) . . . I sent in a final—third—draft
of the bill. . . . The main features of the early plan laid before
Mr. Glass through Mr. Willis, before their first visit to Mr. Wilson,
December 26, 1912, set the outlines of the final enactment." (1:119f)
Laughlin confirms this by a quotation from Willis:

> "As matters later developed, the adoption of the Federal Reserve
> Act was rendered possible only by reason of the fact that it had
> been practically completely shaped, in finished form, before Pres-
> ident Wilson took office, and consequently before many subtle in-
> fluences which are always set at work upon a new Chief Executive
> had had opportunity to accomplish their results." (9:114)

The conspirators' agents did their best to keep their activities in the
dark lest, as Laughlin ironically expressed it:
". . . *it would seem as if the official processes of Congress might be
influenced by forces from without.*" (1:124)
Laughlin reported that he tried to reach Wilson after his election,
through men who had "kept" him, including Rockefeller kinsmen Cyrus
McCormick (a member of the League in Chicago) and Cleveland H.
Dodge. Dodge advised him:

> "Mr. Wilson's belief (was) that it would be undesirable to have it
> understood that he was consulting on this question with anyone
> outside of his coming organization." (1:179).

Arch hypocrite and venal scoundrel Wilson was extremely cautious to
avoid any public suspicion of his sell-out. But it is significant that
Rockefeller agent, Col. House, who was so useful to them in the control
of Texas, and in swaying Wilson in other directions, was not taken into
their confidence in this phase of their conspiracy. House tried to influence Wilson to accept the bill advocated by Sen. Aldrich and his ally
Paul Warburg. But Laughlin reports he was unsuccessful (1:157f).

It was not until December 26, 1912, that Wilson consented to meet
the Congressional agents of the conspirators who controlled the House
Banking Committee, Glass and Willis. Laughlin reported: (1:127f)
"While no formal bill was presented at this meeting, much of the
basic matter inserted into the Federal Reserve Act, matter which
had been threshed out by me with Mr. Willis since May and June,
1912, were laid informally before President Wilson." (9:146)

Willis reported Wilson's scheme to avoid the appearance of a central
bank. Wilson proposed that for this purpose, the regional banks be
labelled "Federal Reserve Banks". He suggested "rigging" the Committee hearings; and he undertook to confer with the witnesses that
were to be called before the Committee in order to influence their
testimony in favor of the bill. (1:128f) Wilson's plans for the "rigging" were elaborate. Laughlin explained:

"The confidential relations existing between myself and Mr. Willis and Mr. Glass were such that it was assumed that I should not speak of them, and when the public hearings were held, it was understood between us that I should not refer to the matters already incorporated into the coming bill. . . . Mr. Willis and Mr. Glass already knew all that I had to propose." (1:130f)

## PRES. WILSON, OBEYING CONSPIRATORS, CALLED SPECIAL SESSION OF CONGRESS

On demand of the conspirators made through Laughlin (1:183f), Pres. Wilson called a special session of the 63rd Congress to pass their "Federal" Reserve Act. To avert suspicion, the session was called for the pretended purpose of tariff legislation which was represented to the public as a device "to improve employment." By this time, Laughlin's underground work for his Rockefeller bosses was completed; and he was returned to his Rockefeller-subsidized professorship at their University of Chicago (1:136). The rest of the job was left to the fellow agents of the conspirators, Pres. Wilson and Congressman Carter Glass. Concerning Wilson's role in the conspiracy, Laughlin stated:

". . . he managed himself in this connection with great skill, and *if he had not taken up the bill finally in an extra session, the bill would probably never have been passed.*" (1:137)

Laughlin reported that the indoctrination of the submissive collaborators of the conspirators on the Committee was left to Glass. (1:139)

The bill was violently opposed by many of the members of Congress, especially the Democrats. Some of the opponents were imbued with the traditional American opposition to central banking. They were aligned with William J. Bryan, in their opposition. Other Congressmen discerned the vicious character of the bill and the conspiracy that lay behind it, led by such men as Congressman Charles A. Lindbergh and Sen. LaFollette.

## PRES. WILSON ORDERED & BROWBEAT CONGRESS TO PASS THE "FEDERAL" RESERVE BILL

Pres. Wilson ordered and browbeat Congress into passing the "F"R Bill. He personally addressed Congress, on June 23, 1913, with a message on the "Federal" Reserve, and openly threatened to keep it in session until they passed the bill.

None of these acts of Pres. Wilson sufficed to beat down the determined opposition to the bill. In their ranks were followers of Secretary William Jennings Bryan. Glass reported on the August 11 Democratic caucus:

"No such scenes were ever witnessed before, nor have any been enacted since." (10:133)

## PRES. WILSON HOODWINKED BRYAN & INCREASED THE LARCENY OF THE "F"R BILL

The opposition had hoped for the support of Bryan in fighting the bill. But, related Laughlin:

"Mr. Wilson's foresight, tact and *management*, both in taking Bryan into his Cabinet, and in adjusting Mr. Bryan's pet currency beliefs to the Glass bill was very effective." (1:139)

The principal of Bryan's "pet currency beliefs" was:

"The issue of notes by the Government has for years been pure Democratic doctrine." (1:156)

The chicanery and larceny by which Pres. Wilson effected this "adjusting" to Bryan's views is reported by Laughlin, as follows:

"Mr. Bryan felt that *his reputation depended* on the insertion of Government issues in the Glass bill. . . . Not only was the passage of the Bill in the House imperilled, but in the Senate. The President, knowing that he must permit some changes sufficient to save the bill, asked Mr. Glass to make the reserve notes 'obligations of the United States'. The astonished chairman of the House Committed emphasized that in the bill the notes were the promises of the Federal Reserve Banks . . . *when Mr. Glass insisted that the Federal Reserve notes could not possibly be regarded as Government notes since they could be put out only by a bank, the President expressed his COMPROMISE as follows:*

" 'Exactly so, Glass. Every word you say is true; THE GOVERNMENT LIABILITY IS MERELY A THOUGHT. AND SO, IF WE CAN HOLD THE SUBSTANCE OF THE THING AND GIVE THE OTHER FELLOW (BRYAN?) THE SHADOW, WHY NOT DO IT IF THEREBY WE MAY SAVE THE BILL?*

"Consequently, Section 16, on note issues, as finally passed, was changed to read:

" 'Federal Reserve notes, to be issued at the discretion of the Federal Reserve Board for the purpose of making advances to the Federal Reserve Banks through the Federal Reserve agents as hereinafter set forth and for no other purpose, are hereby authorized. THE SAID NOTES SHALL BE THE OBLIGATIONS OF THE UNITED STATES and shall be received by all national and member banks and the Federal Reserve banks for all taxes, customs and other public dues. They shall be redeemed in gold on demand at the Treasury Department of the United States. . .!', (1:152f; 25:56)

This fraud of Pres. Wilson was confirmed by Carter Glass who had distaste for its criminality, in his books ADVENTURE IN FINANCE. (10:124f) Pres. Wilson made the debts incurred by the "Federal" Reserve the obligations of the people, deliberately committing a crude fraud on the nation.

### PRES. WILSON REJECTED, FOR THE CONSPIRATORS, "FEDERAL" DEPOSIT INSURANCE

Bryan acquiesced in this fraud. But he demanded that the public be given insurance of its deposits in the "F"R Banks. (1:131) Pres. Wilson and Glass rejected this on behalf of the conspirators. Had Bryan's plan been adopted at the start, it might have saved millions of persons their savings and/or their fortunes twenty years later.

It is an interesting commentary on the hypocrisy of Bryan, some trace of which emerged in his "CROSS OF GOLD" orations, that he accepted this thoroughly dishonest and larcenous proposal of Pres. Wilson. On the day following Pres. Wilson's message to Congress, June 24, 1913, Bryan issued a public letter approving the bill containing the provision, recommending its acceptance by his followers. The letter read:

"When the bill is considered on its merits, *one at once realizes that it is written from the standpoint of the people rather than from the standpoint of the financiers.* The latter are quite unanimous in the belief that the issue of money is a 'function of the banks' and that 'the Government ought not go into the banking business.'

"The Democratic Party, however, has consistently taken the position that the issue of money is 'a function of the Government' and should not be delegated to the banks." (1:153f)

For sheer hypocritic misrepresentation, this statement is a masterpiece.

## BRYAN ABANDONED HIS "PRINCIPLES" & INSURED CONSPIRATORS" SUCCESS

Bryan furnished Glass with a letter, on October 22, 1913, that consummated his "sell out". It read:

"If my opinion has influence with anyone called upon to act on this measure, I am willing to assure full responsibility for what I do when I advise him to stand by the President and assist in securing the passage of the bill at the earliest possible moment." (10:138)

After a month of stormy sessions, on September 11, 1913, Glass read Bryan's letter to a turbulent House Democratic caucus. It sufficed to put an end to all House Democratic opposition to the bill. The "Federal" Reserve Act was passed by the House by a vote of 287-85. Only three Democrats voted against this thoroughly fraudulent measure that surrendered complete control of the Treasury and of banking and credit to the Rockefeller conspirators, and laid the foundation for intensive looting of the nation. The Republicans, on a partisan basis, voted two to one against the bill.

## SEN. OWEN'S HONEST CURRENCY PLAN BLOCKED BY CONSPIRATORS

When the Senate Banking Committee was organized, on March 13, 1913, Sen. Robert L. Owen was appointed its chairman. Of Cherokee Indian origin, he was as sincere and honest an American as the author has ever met. When he visited the author, in 1935, for the relief of painful blindness that he suffered after two operations for glaucoma performed by Professor Alan C. Woods, the head of the Department of Ophthalmology of Johns Hopkins University Medical School, he recounted the true and not widely known story regarding the role in which he had been impressed in the writing of the bill that bore his name, the Owen-Glass "Federal" Reserve Bill, of which he was thoroughly ashamed.

Sen. Owen had sought to secure the passage of a banking bill that would block dishonest manipulation, so-called "management", of the nation's finances and currency. Prof. Irving Fisher, of the Yale Department of Economics, had aided him in drafting a bill that widened the monetary base to include, in addition to gold and silver, all of the staple commodities, designed to eliminate the possibility of either inflation or deflation. It could have been used to create true freedom of employment implied in "freedom of life"; and made certain a job for every man willing to work.

50

But Sen. Owen's bill was exactly what the Rockefeller conspirators did not want. It would have made it virtually impossible for them to "manage", or manipulate dishonestly, the money and economy of the nation to create booms and panics, and chronic unemployment.

The conspirators determined to block the adoption of the Owen bill. They had Prof. Fisher summoned before the Yale officials and confronted with the charge that he was so "foolish" as to advocate money based on commodities other than gold. He was warned related Sen. Owen, that there would be no place at Yale, or in any other university, for anyone so "foolish." Prof. Fisher was keenly aware of the side on which "his bread was buttered"; and was no more principled, unfortunately, than are the multitude of "professors" prostituted to the conspirators and their foundations. He succumbed to the conspirators' blackmail, doublecrossed Sen. Owen and withdrew his professorial support of the honest remedial bill that he had helped draft. In its place, Prof. Fisher announced his advocacy of what he mockingly labelled a "commodity" dollar the value of which was to be determined by a "gold index", that would block stabilization of the economy by making speculative the value of commodities, of gold and of the dollar, and would enhance the power of the conspirators to manipulate, or "manage", the economy to enable them to more readily swindle the nation. The coup de grace was given Sen. Owen's honest, stabilizing currency and banking bill by its flat and categoric rejection by Pres. Wilson. (1:161)

### COL. HOUSE, ROCKEFELLER'S TEXAS AGENT, WAS DOUBLECROSSED

The intrigue that centered on the Senate bill illustrates the Rockefeller practise of leaving in the dark and doublecrossing their own agents and pitting them against one another. The principal opponents of the Rockefeller-dictated "Glass" bill were the advocates of the Aldrich bill drafted by Warburg. Col. House, Rockefeller's Texas agent, spearheaded the effort to induce Wilson to accept the Aldrich bill. He was joined in this effort by Wilson's future son-in-law, Secretary McAdoo, who had drawn up a bill of his own, that had been rejected by the Rockefeller conspirators; and by Samuel Untermyer. (1:157f; 13:162) House's letters reveal how cunningly he was duped by Wilson and his conspirator bosses.

Though Wilson had urged the conspirators to keep the Glass bill secret, he himself had divulged it to Col. House. (1:186f) House had given abstracts of the bill to the McAdoo-Aldrich-Warburg-Untermyer clique. He tried to prevail upon Wilson to let Untermyer present to him the McAdoo scheme in a privately-arranged personal interview. But Wilson turned it down. House then suggested to the clique that Untermyer be slipped into the White House by Secretary McAdoo and Sen. Owen, for the same purpose. (1:159) Warburg managed to sneak into the Senate bill one of his ideas; but it was brusquely thrown out, at the instance of the Rockefeller conspirators, by the Congressional conferees. (1:169; 10:210) Thus it was that both Col. House and Paul Warburg were as completely barred from having any more to do with its authorship than did Sen. Owen whose name it bears. Glass denounced, as false, the rumors that Warburg had anything to do with the writing of his "Federal" Reserve bill. (222:211) Prof. Laughlin stated:

"June 10-14, Mr. Wilson decided against the McAdoo bill in favor of the (conspirators') Glass bill, passing by the Owen bill." (1:161)

## WILSON THREATS FORCED THE SENATE TO PASS THE CONSPIRATORS' "F"R BILL

The Senate passed the emasculated version of the bill by a vote of 54 to 34, on December 19, 1913. Wilson effectively blackmailed the Congress by threatening to keep it in session continually until it had passed the bill, and to deny them their Christmas recess. The bills passed by the House and by the Senate differed widely and materially. Under direction of Pres. Wilson, the two bills were sent to a joint Congressional conference, the stacking of which he had personally supervised, with six Democrats and two Republicans. Their report was, in effect, dictated to them by the conspirators, through Pres. Wilson. It was hastily prepared and immediately accepted and ratified by the House of Representatives, on December 22, 1913 by a vote of 298 to 60. The bill that emerged was that drawn up by Laughlin for the conspirators, practically intact and made even more thievish by the amendment dictated by Pres. Wilson.

In the House, the persistent opposition of Congressman Charles A. Lindbergh (father of the aviator who was to pay dearly for that opposition when it became apparent that he might be sufficiently popular to win the Presidency, through the kidnapping of his son) was of no avail.

"This Act establishes the most gigantic trust on earth," Lindbergh, Sr., with rare insight, truthfully proclaimed on the floor of the House.

The bill, as reported out by a joint conference, was bitterly opposed in the Senate. One of its most vociferous opponents was Sen. La-Follete, who was subsequently replaced by the conspirators with Joseph McCarthy. The bill was finally passed under intense pressure exerted by Pres. Wilson. It passed in the Senate by a vote of 43 to 25, with 27 Senators refusing to vote.

Pres. Wilson signed the fraudulent "Federal" Reserve Bill before its ink was dry. He delivered to the Rockefeller conspirators the bill that they had bribed him to force through Congress.

## "FEDERAL" RESERVE SYSTEM: A MONUMENT TO WILSON'S TREACHERY & DECEIT

The praise heaped on Pres. Wilson by the conspirators and their agents for making possible the "Federal" Reserve swindle was fulsome. Prof. Laughlin wrote:

". . . Mr. Wilson kept his hand on the wheel and influenced the actual character of the Legislation which passed the House. In short, he guided the bill through critical stages and deserved credit for its character and success. . . . In the Senate, Mr. Wilson had a much more personal influence, and there increased his repute as a friend to banking reform. Without him the bill might not have found its way to successful passage. Indeed, in one other respect, in that he himself decided to bring up the reform in an extra session of Congress, he can claim to have saved its existence; as we look back it is unquestionably true that if the bill had not been pushed forward, in spite of a sluggish Senate, just at that juncture, it would never have been passed at all. Hence in summing up the forces that led to its enactment, WE MUST UNHESITATINGLY ASCRIBE THE CHIEF CREDIT FOR ITS PASSAGE TO PRESIDENT WILSON." (1:190)

Rockefeller propagandists are experts in faking public opinion and polls. One of them openly boasts of their success in this direction in the ANNUAL REPORT for 1948 of their "Foreign Office", the Council on Foreign Relations and described their fraudulent tactics in effecting it. (14, p. 36) Immediately after the passage of their "Federal" Reserve Act they filled the press with acclaim of it by "leaders of public opinion." Pres. Wilson professed to see in this propaganda that he collaborated in broadcasting, "public acclaim." Laughlin reports that while signing the bill, Wilson announced:

"I have been surprised at the sudden acceptance of this measure by public opinion everywhere." (1:190)

Laughlin explains, however,

"This was, in fact, an acknowledgement of the campaign of *education* (which is the conspirators euphuism for false propaganda) conducted by the Citizens' League for the period from 1911-1913. This result obviously came from the active and persistent campaign by the League beginning about eighteen months before there was any Glass bill." (1:190)

Wilson's statement about the "acceptance" of the Act is as much in character as his venality and rejection of any sense of gratitude for help given him in obtaining the Presidential nomination by anyone other than the conspirators. It probably is rooted in the fact that Wilson shared with Kaiser Wilhelm the delusion of his "divine right to rule." McCombs reported that Pres. Wilson, in all seriousness stated:

". . . God ordained that I should be the next President of the United States. Neither you nor any other mortal or mortals (Ed.: this includes the entire body of registered voters) could have prevented that." (6:208)

It appears that there was as much delusional as hypocritical in Wilson's attitude. His mental state was aptly described by Col. Henry Watterson in the headline of his special dispatch to the Herald of March 31, 1919:

"PRESIDENT'S 'MEDIOCRE MIND AND COLOSAL VANITY . . .

"MR. WILSON A PUNISHMENT FOR SOME NATIONAL SIN . . ." (6:248)

In view of the record, there can be attributed to nothing other than mendacity and duplicity the statement attributed to Pres. Wilson by his pressagents, and widely quoted:

"I am a most unhappy man. UNWITTINGLY, I have ruined my country."

No one can question that it was ruin and disaster that Pres. Wilson brought to our country by his venal execution of the dictates of his conspirator bosses and employers. His bogus "Federal" Reserve takes its place besides his "14 Points," that he mouthed repeatedly and insistently to serve the purposes of his bosses as the essential bases for their conspiracy to undermine, disrupt, destroy and loot empires and nations, including our own. For his shibboleth, "self determination"

## CERTIFICATE ISSUED TO STOCKHOLDERS OF FEDERAL RESERVE BANK OF NEW YORK

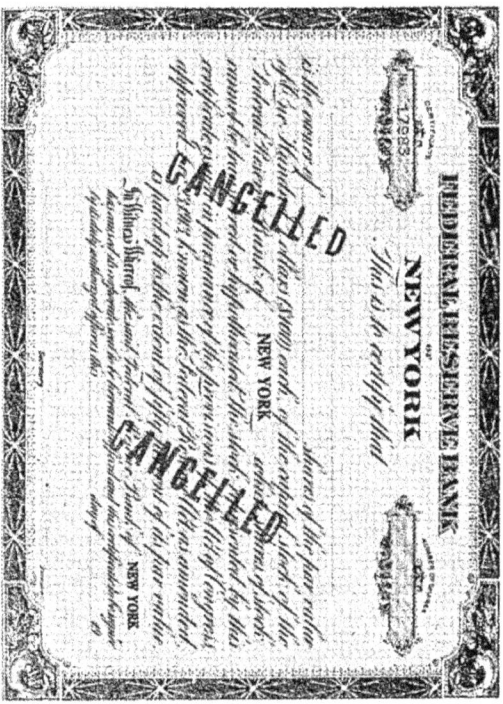

Private banks and persons, the owners of the "Federal" Reserve, receive certificates, as do the owners of other private corporations. The stock has the characteristics of cumulative preferred stock that bears a 6% rate of interest on the paid in capital. Only $50 dollars, half of the $100 par value has been called for and paid in, because the enormous "take," or profits, from the start have made further capital requirements unnecessary. If at any time there develops a need for further capital, the taxpayers are required to furnish it through purchase of stock in the 12 "F"R banks through the Treasury. The Treasury and the taxpayers are responsible for the liabilities of these private "Federal" Reserve banks under the terms fraudulently written into the "F"R Act by Pres. Woodrow Wilson, though they share in none of the profits and are systematically looted to provide them.

may prove to be the device whereby the destruction of our Union, that the Civil War averted, may be brought about through their "Civil Rights", agitation and their "United" Nations.

## CHAPTER XI
### PRES. WILSON'S "PAYOFF" TO CONSPIRATORS: FRAUDULENT "FEDERAL" RESERVE IS THEIR PRIVATE STOCK CORPORATION

The so-called "Federal" Reserve System is a group of private stock corporations. The stock certificate of the Federal Reserve Bank of New York is shown in the photographic illustration, here presented, of certificate 17983, furnished the author by the bank should set at rest any belief that may be held by the unwitting public that the "Federal" Reserve is a public, Government agency.

### "CONTROL" BY GOVERNMENT & PRESIDENT: A SHAM

Numerous devices were written into the law to mask the absolute control of the "F"RS ("Federal" Reserve System) by the conspirators. These included the appointment of the Chairman of the Board of Governors by the President who invariably has served the conspirators loyally and appointed the man dictated by them from among their loyal employees. Other such coverup devices are the classification of banks into various categories, with each group having certain voting powers; appointment of representatives of commerce and industry to three seats on the nine member board of directors; and other provisions of this type.

The bogus "Federal" Reserve System has been owned and controlled from its beginning by the Rockefeller conspirators, indirectly through the ownership and control of member banks. The Act reads:

"Sec. 5. The capital stock of each Federal reserve bank shall be divided in shares of $100 each...A bank applying for stock in a Federal reserve bank after the organization thereof must subscribe for an amount of capital stock of the Federal reserve bank equal to six percent of the paid-up capital stock and surplus of said applicant bank..."

### PUBLIC MAY BE "PERMITTED" & TREASURY REQUIRED TO BUY "F"R STOCK

"Sec. 2:8. Stock offered to the public.

Should the subscription by banks to the stock of said Federal reserve banks or any one or more of them be...insufficient to provide the amount of capital required therefor, then and in that event the said organization committee may, under conditions and regulations to be prescribed by it, offer to *public subscription* at par such amount of stock in said Federal reserve banks, or any one or more of them, as said committee shall determine, subject to the same conditions as to payment and stock liability as provided for member banks." (25:4)

The conspirators provided that, if necessary, the nation would be required, by "allotment," to furnish the capital required by them, in the provision:

"Sec. 2:10. United States stock

"Should the total subscriptions by banks and the public to the stock of said Federal reserve banks, or any one or more of them, be...insufficient to provide the amount of capital required therefor, then and in that event the said organization committee shall allot to the United States such amount of said stock as said committee shall determine. Said United States stock shall be paid for out of any money in the Treasury not otherwise appropriated..." (25:5)

TREASURY & PUBLIC BARRED FROM VOTING THEIR STOCK

But the conspirators very carefully guarded against any interference in their schemes by either private stockholders or the Government in the provision:

"Sec. 2:11. Voting rights

"Stock not held by member banks shall not be entitled to voting power." (25:5)

TREASURY SECRETARY & CURRENCY
CONTROLLER OUSTED

The government has virtually no control over the "F"RS. It was solely for the purpose of duping the public and maintaining a sham pretense of governmental control that a number of provisions were introduced into the original Act. One of them, as mentioned, provided that the Secretary of the Treasury and the Comptroller of Currency should be, ex officio, a small minority of the seven member Board of Governors of the "F"RS. (After the amendment by the Banking Act of 1935, it was designated the "Federal Reserve Board.") By the amended Act, both Government officials were eliminated from the Board in the words:

"...the Secretary of the Treasury and the Comptroller of Currency shall continue to serve as members of the Board until February 1, 1936." (25:28)

This left the conspirators free of any "interference" or "spying" by Government officials into their manipulations. An effort at "face saving," at masking the subordination of the Secretary of the Treasury to the Board, is obvious in the provision:

"Sec. 10:6. Nothing in this Act contained shall be construed as taking away any powers heretofore vested by law in the Secretary of the Treasury which relate to the supervision, management and control of the Treasury Department and bureaus under such department, and wherever any power vested by this Act in the Board of Governors of the Federal Reserve System or the Federal reserve agent appears to conflict with the powers of the Secretary of the Treasury, such powers shall be exercised subject to the supervision and control of the Secretary." (25:31)

COMPTROLLER OF CURRENCY IS SUBORDINATE TO
CONSPIRATORS' "F"R AGENTS

But no such efforts were made to "save face" for the Comptroller of the Currency, as is made clear in

"Sec. 10:8. Issuance of national currency and Federal reserve notes. Section three hundred and twenty-four of the Revised Statutes of the United States shall be amended to read as follows:

Sec. 324. There shall be in the Department of the Treasury a bureau charged with the execution of all laws passed by Congress relating to the issue and regulation of national currency secured by United States bonds and, *under the general supervision of the Board of Governors of the Federal Reserve System*, of all Federal Reserve notes, the chief of which Bureau shall be called the Comptroller of the Currency and shall perform his duties under the general directions of the Secretary of the Treasury." (25:31f)

This makes it clear that the Comptroller, though supposedly representative of the Government and the people on the Board, was and is in effect a subordinate of the Board.

### PRESIDENT HAS ONLY PRETENSE OF POWER OVER "F"R: "APPOINTS" 2 BOARD MEMBERS & CHAIRMAN

Further effort was made to maintain the appearance of Government control of the "F"RS by ostensibly giving the President, during each term, the power of appointment of two Board Governors in the words

"Section 10. Board of Governors of the Federal Reserve System

1. Appointment and qualification of members.

Sec. 10. The Board of Governors of the Federal Reserve System (hereinafter referred to as the 'Board') shall be composed of seven members, to be appointed by the President, by and with the advice of the Senate, after the enactment of the Banking Act of 1935, for terms of fourteen years. . . . In selecting the members of the Board, not more than one of whom shall be selected from any one Federal Reserve district, the President shall have due regard to fair representation of the financial, agricultural, industrial and commercial interests, and geographical divisions of the country.

2. Members ineligible to serve member banks; term of office; chairman and vice chairman

The members of the Board shall be ineligible during the time they are in office and for two years thereafter to hold any office, position or employment in any member bank, except that this restriction shall not apply to a member who has served a full term for which he was appointed. Upon the expiration of the term of any appointive member of the Federal Reserve Board in office on the date of enactment of the Banking Act of 1935, the President shall fix the term of the successor to such member at not to exceed fourteen years, as designated by the President at the time of nomination, but in such manner as to provide for the expiration of the term of not more than one member in any two-year period, and thereafter each member shall hold office for the term of fourteen years from the expiration of the term of his predecessor, unless sooner removed by the President. . ." (25:28f)

To further strengthen the deceptive appearance of Government control of the "F"RS, this section states:

"...Of the persons thus appointed, one shall be designated

by the President as chairman, and one as vice chairman of the Board. The chairman of the Board, subject to its supervision, shall be its active executive officer..."

It requires little thought to realize how specious and false is this pretense of Presidential and Governmental control of the "F"RS. Presidents are, and must be, above all things else, politicians. To be elected, they require money and the support of banks and bankers. Is it reasonable to assume that a President will appoint to the Board any Governor who has not the support and approval of the bankers and of the conspirators who control them? Is it not unreasonable to assume that the conspirators will approve of anyone who is not subject to their discipline and control?

## BOARD OF GOVERNORS NOT GOVERNMENT EMPLOYEES, BUT ARE RULERS OF "F"RS

The Governors of the "F"RS are not employees of the Federal Government. They are the absolute rulers of the nation's monetary and credit system, of all private and national wealth. Over them the nation has absolutely no control. For there is no provision written into the law for their punishment or removal for any malfeasance. On the contrary, their power is virtually unlimited. They are empowered to tax the banking system to provide for their salaries and financing:

"Sec. 10:3. Assessments on Federal reserve banks

The Board of Governors of the Federal Reserve System shall have the power to levy semiannually upon the Federal reserve banks...an assessment sufficient to pay its estimated expenses and the salaries of its members and employees...(25:29)

"Sec. 10:4 Principal offices; expenses...(25:30)

The Board shall determine and prescribe the manner in which its obligations shall be incurred and its disbursements and expenses allowed and paid...and the salaries of its members and employees, whose employment, compensation, leave and expenses shall be governed solely by the provisions of this Act...and regulation of the Board not inconsistent therewith..."

AND DICTATE THE ISSUE OF THEIR NOTES BY TREASURY.

To the rulers of this private corporation, the "F"RS, was surrendered by the Act the absolute and almost exclusive power to issue paper currency.

"Sec. 16. Note issues

1. Issuance of Federal reserve notes; *nature of obligations*: ... Federal reserve notes, to be issued at the discretion of the Board of Governors of the Federal Reserve System for the purpose of making advances to the Federal reserve banks...and for no other purposes, are hereby authorized. *The said notes shall be obligations of the United States and shall be received by all national and member banks and Federal Reserve Banks and for all taxes, customs and other public dues.* They shall be redeemed *in Lawful Money* on demand at the Treasury Department of the United States..." (25:56)

Thus was worded the fraud dictated by Pres. Wilson as a gift, a bonus to his briber bosses. Their privately issued notes were given a status that the Supreme Court, under the direction of Chief Justice Salmon P. Chase, denied to *"greenbacks,"* the currency issued by the Federal Government itself under Lincoln. Curiously, the wording of the last sentence of the section acknowledged that the "F"RS notes were not *"Lawful Money."* However, by a 1933 amendment of the Legal Tender Act, passed by dictate of the conspirators to Pres. Roosevelt, the notes were given the status of "lawful money." (25:200)

## TREASURY PROVIDES NOTES IT MAY NOT ISSUE ITSELF, TO "F"R TO ISSUE

The "F"R notes "issued at the discretion of the Board of Governors," the Act dictates, shall be printed under the direction of the Secretary of the Treasury.

"Sec. 16:9. Engraving of plates; denomination and form of notes.

In order to furnish suitable notes for circulation as Federal reserve notes, the Comptroller of the Currency shall, under the direction of the Secretary of the Treasury, cause plates and dies to be engraved in the best manner to guard against counterfeits and fraudulent alterations, and shall have printed therefrom and numbered such quantities of such notes of the denominations of $1, $5, $10, $20, $50, $100, $500, $1,000, $5,000, $10,000 as may be required to supply the Federal reserve banks...

11. Custody of plates and dies; expenses of issue...

The plates and dies to be procured by the Comptroller of the Currency for the printing of such circulating notes shall remain under his control and direction, and the expenses necessarily incurred in executing the laws relating to the procuring of such notes and all other expenses incidental to their issue and retirement, shall be paid by the Federal reserve banks...

13. Appropriation for engraving etc.

...the Secretary is hereby authorized to use so much of any funds in the Treasury not otherwise appropriated for the purpose of furnishing the notes aforesaid..." (25:60f)

## TREASURY CHARGE FOR NOTES SUPPLIED "F"R IS NOMINAL

The charge made by the Treasury for the money that it supplies the "F"RS is reported to be several dollars per hundred notes of whatever denomination. Thus each $1 note or each $10,000 note may cost the "F"RS the enormous sum of a fraction of a penny, or pennies.

A pretense is maintained, by the Act, of the Treasury maintaining some slight measure of control of the issuance of the "F"RS notes in

"Sec. 16:10. Custody of unissued notes

When such notes have been prepared, they shall be deposited in the Treasury, or in the subtreasury or mint of the United States nearest the place of business of each Federal reserve bank and shall be held for the use of such bank subject to the order of the Comptroller of the Currency for their delivery, as provided by this Act." (25:61)

This pretense was converted to sheer mockery by the subsequently passed Act of May 29, 1920 (41 Stat. 654) that abolished the subtreasuries, and turned over the duties of subtreasuries and their functions to the "F"RS. It reads:

"The Secretary of the Treasury is hereby authorized, in his discretion, to transfer any and all of the duties and functions performed or authorized to be performed by the assistant treasurers above enumerated, or their offices, to the Treasurer of the United States or the mints or assay offices of the United States under such rules and regulations as he may prescribe, *or to Utilize Any of the Federal Reserve Banks Acting as Depositaries or Fiscal Agents of the United States, for the Purpose of Performing Any or All of Such Duties and Functions, Notwithstanding the Limitations of Section 15 of the Federal Reserve Act, as Amended or Any Other Provision of Law...*" (25;113)

## "F"R BANKS PAID FOR STORING OWN NOTES & FOR HOLDING TREASURY FUNDS

This means that the banks of the "F"RS were made the trustees for the funds printed for them by the Treasury, as well as depositaries for all Treasury funds, including income, customs, excise taxes and all other funds. Furthermore it was provided in the various sections of the law involved, that the "F"RS banks be paid by the Treasury for receiving these funds thereby swelling their deposits and the moneys available to them, gratis, for profitable lending at prevailing interest rates in the conduct of their businesses, instead of their paying the Government for the use of the money. For example:

"Sec. 5703 (of the Revised Statutes of the United States)

Expenses incident to the deposit of taxes (Treasury-Post Office Appropriation Act, 1955; 69 Stat. 72)

...That the Federal Reserve banks and branches may be reimbursed for necessary expenses incident to the deposit of taxes in Government repositories." (25:114)

Thus the "F"RS banks are paid for safeguarding from themselves their money printed for them under direction of the Treasury. In this, the fraud of the law in regard to the "F"RS reaches one of its many heights of mockery and absurdity. No doubt investigation would reveal that the banks charge the Treasury for this activity more than they pay the Treasury for the notes.

## POWERS OF "F"RS BOARD OF GOVERNORS VIRTUALLY UNLIMITED

The powers of Board of Governors of the "F"RS over our personal and national wealth are virtually unlimited. Those powers, exactly like those wielded by the British Board of Trade, against which our progenitors rebelled and fought furiously, rest in their treatment of currency as a commodity and medium of control, for the purpose of extracting usurious profit, rather than as a medium of exchange.

The Board is empowered to provide, on a steadily more exclusive scale, currency in the form of their notes issued on the basis of our personal credit or national debt. All of the forms of indebtedness on which it issues its notes that bear no interest, yield the "F"RS interest at rates set by its Board. In this manner, the con-

59

spirators derive one of several forms of profit, that they extort from one and all, through the currency monopoly that they have tricked the nation into giving them. Among the bases for these collections for their "kitty" are: specified:

"Sec. 13. Powers of the Federal Reserve Banks

2. Discount of commercial, agricultural and industrial paper. ...any Federal reserve bank may discount notes, drafts and bills of exchange issued or drawn for agricultural, industrial or commercial purposes, or the proceeds of which have been used, or are to be used, for such purpose, the Board of Governors have the right to determine or define the character of the paper thus eligible for discount, within the meaning of this Act... but such definition shall not include notes, drafts or bills covering merely investments or issued or drawn for the purpose of carrying or trading in stocks, bonds, or other investments, *except bonds and notes of the government of the United States* . . .

3. Discount for individuals, partnerships and corporations. Under unusual and exigent circumstances, the Board of Governors of the Federal Reserve System, by an affirmative vote of not less than five members, may authorize any Federal reserve bank, during such periods as the said board may determine, at rates established in accordance with the provisions of section 14, subdivision (d), of this Act, to discount for any individual, partnership, or corporation, notes, drafts and bills of exchange of the kinds and maturities made eligible for discount for members banks under the provisions of this Act when... endorsed or otherwise secured to the satisfaction of the Federal reserve bank...subject to such limitations, restrictions and regulations as the Board of Governors of the Federal Reserve System may prescribe." (25:43f)

This section of the Act became handily useful to a wealthy and influential friend of the author's and to other henchmen of the conspirators, in tiding over the losses sustained in short-sales in the 1929 market during the period of the violent rally that occurred shortly before the conspirators precipitated the 1929 panic. These loans saved them from taking huge losses during the rally. And it enabled them to make enormous profits in the course of the subsequent market crash that they precipitated.

## "F"R DICTATES AMOUNT OF OUR OWN MONEY & CREDIT WE MAY USE & HOW IT IS USED

An important role is played by the absolute control by the conspirators, through their "F"RS, in manipulating the amount of currency and credit that shall be available for commerce and industry, and for personal and national financing by

"Sec. 14. Open Market Operations.

1. Purchase and sale of cable transfers, banker's acceptances...

Any Federal reserve bank may, under rules and regulations prescribed by the Board of Governors of the Federal Reserve System, purchase and sell in the open market, at home or abroad, either from domestic or foreign banks, firms, corporations, or individuals, cable transfers and bankers' acceptances and bills of exchange of the kinds and maturities by this Act made eligible for rediscount, with or without the endorsement of a member bank." (25:52)

This unrestricted power of the "F"RS, that is international in scope, may determine the nation's balance of payments and may defy the power of the Treasury to effect a favorable balance. This section then proceeds to define other aspects of the "open-market operations."

"2. Dealings in, and loans on, gold

Every Federal reserve bank shall have power:

(a) To deal in gold coin and bullion at home or abroad, to make loans thereon, exchange Federal reserve notes for gold, gold coin or bullion, giving therefor, when necessary, acceptable security, including the hypothecation of United States bonds or other securities which Federal reserve banks are authorized to hold;

3. Purchase and sales of obligations of the United States...

(b) To buy and sell, at home or abroad, bonds and notes of the United States, bonds of the Federal Farm Mortgage Corporation having maturities from date of purchase of not exceeding six months...bills, notes, revenue bonds and warrants...issued in anticipation of collection of taxes or in anticipation of receipt of assured revenues by any State, Country, district, political subdivision, or municipality in the continental United States, including irrigation, drainage and reclamation districts, such purchases to be made *In Accordance With Rules And Regulations Prescribed By The Board Of Governors Of The Federal Reserve System: Provided that...the aggregate amount of such obligations acquired directly from the United States which is held at any one time by the twelve Federal Reserve banks shall not exceed* $5,000,000,000." (25:53)

## "F"R OBLIGATION TO NATION LIMITED TO $5 BILLION
## USE OF NATION'S CREDIT

In return for its unlimited use and control of our personal credit and national wealth and credit, the deposit of virtually all government funds in their banks without payment of interest thereon but with payment by the nation to them therefor, to aid them in amplifying their loot, the conspirators, through their "F"RS, limit the Government's own credit, or currency printed by it for the "F"R, that may be drawn on, even on the security of Government notes and bonds bearing interest, to $5 billion, a small fraction of the credit extended to them by the nation. This is comparable to a person offering to "lend you back" five dollars, requiring payment of interest thereon, of a thousand dollars you had loaned him, charging him no interest. Some exceptions were made by later Acts of Congress to this restriction or use of Treasury credit by the "F"R.

## CONSPIRATORS' PURPOSE: TO STEADILY INCREASE
## NATION'S INTEREST BEARING DEBTS

This absurdly ironic situation—the conspirators' refusal to "lend" the nation its own money is cunningly designed to force the Government to constantly increase the issue of interest-bearing bonds, steadily increasing the national debt that imposes on the nation an ever huger burden of interest payments that accrue to the conspirators. With the rise of national indebtedness, the conspirators further increase their looting of taxpayers through the larger number of Government notes and bonds that they cash at the Treasury, obtaining notes "equal in amount to the par value of the bonds so deposited" (25:8), but continue to draw interest on, thus increasing their usurious returns.

## "F"R POWER TO FIX DISCOUNT RATES, DETERMINANT OF INTEREST RATES, IS ABSOLUTE

"Sec. 14:5. Rates of discount

(d) To establish from time to time, subject to review and determination of the Board of Governors of the Federal Reserve System, rates of discount to be charged by Federal reserve banks for each class of paper, which shall be fixed with a view to accomodating commerce and business; but each bank shall establish such rates every fourteen days, or oftener, if deemed necessary by the Board." (25:53f)

## CONSPIRATORS' FINANCIAL POWER HAS BEEN MADE ABSOLUTE BY THEIR "F"RS PLOT

The provisions of the Act enable one to discern the extent which the conspirators have empowered themselves to rob, swindle and defraud the nation and ourselves. The recent alarming reports in their press about the lower rank racketeers who have infiltrated banking, elicits a smile from the informed. For, long ago, back in 1913, they, the nation's most dangerous and ruthless racketeers, acquired complete monopolistic control of credit, finance and banking through their "F"R Act, "muscling in" with the help of Pres. Wilson. The "enforcers" are their agents, the Board of Governors of their "F"RS. They have arrogated unto themselves absolute domination and dictatorship over the financial, industrial, commercial and credit organization of the nation and of the world. Their power usurped from the Government contrasts with the nation's complete surrender and impotence. The only parties with whom they are now required even to confer only in certain matters, in a capacity other than "advisory," are five bankers appointed from subordinates in "F"R banks who are selected to join them in the "Federal" Open Market Committee. Amendments to the Act, some of which have been mentioned, which will be more fully discussed in later chapters, have steadily increased the power of the conspirators, both nationally and internationally, to such extent that they are now empowered to menace our survival as a nation.

They arbitrarily and capriciously, usually for their own piratical advantages, dictate the volume of money and credit that shall be available, by such devices as: manipulation of bank reserve requirements; manipulation of the stock market by dictating the amount of his own credit an individual may use in purchases; by dictation of the amount of currency and credit that they will make available for stock purchases; by arbitrary juggling of margin requirements; by manipulation of the amount of currency and credit that shall be available for the purchase and sale of property; by manipulation of the amount of money and credit available for industry and commerce. They dictate whether industry can and dare use enough of its own money and credit to provide employment; and by withholding the right of industries to use their credit and restricting the volume of currency, the conspirators can and have forced on the nation and its industries depression, unemployment, panic, and bankruptcy.

They can and do dictate, with an eye to available loot, whether we can use our own credit to purchase the things that we need or want; whether we can buy homes, and on what terms we may buy them; whether we may borrow money on collateral; whether the prices of stocks and commodities shall rise, thus creating a boom, or fall, thereby creating panic, depression and unemployment.

The device that is represented as giving the nation representation on the directorate of the "F"RS and its banks is a transparent fraud. It consists of grouping the member banks into various categories on the basis of their capitalization and permitting each of the categories to appoint directors; of appointing directors from various groups and interests in the community. These devices are meaningless flim-flam. The subordinate directors and officers take their orders from the Board of Governors, vis a vis whom they have little, or no, real power or influence. Equally flim-flam is the pretense of "decentralization" of banking control by dividing the nation into twelve districts and placing a "F"R branch in each of them. Impressive bank edifices built in each of them have served to salve local vanity and to further the deception. But the "F"RS always has been ruled by the Chairman of the Board who, like the present incumbent, William McChesney Martin Jr. (who followed his father's footsteps in the "F"RS) usually is a member of Rockefellers' dangerously subversive agency, the Council on Foreign Relations.

## CONSPIRATORS RESTRICT "F"RS BOARD OF GOVERNORS WITH "GOLD STANDARD"

The conspirators, ever distrustful of their own agents, did put one effective check on the powers of their "F"RS Board of Governors, in order to make sure that they would not be able to give the nation the promised currency that would expand with its needs. For if the Board did so, it would frustrate the conspirators real purpose of despoiling the nation. The conspirators restricted the operations of their "F"RS to operate within the scope of their Gold Standard Act of 1900, that they had imposed to facilitate national looting by their "cornering" of gold:

"Sec. 16:3

Every Federal bank shall maintain reserves in gold certificates of not less than 25 per centum against its deposits and reserves and reserves in gold certificates of not less than 25 per centum against its Federal Reserve notes in actual circulation." (25:57)

But the Board of Governors, nevertheless, sardonically state:

"An important purpose of the Federal Reserve Act was to provide an elastic supply of currency—one that would expand and contract in accordance with the needs of the public." (27:89)

## AND BLOCK SUPPOSED FUNCTION OF EXPANDING CURRENCY TO NATIONAL NEEDS

With complete contempt of public intelligence, however, they acknowledge that the "gold standard" incorporation in the Act bars the way:

"Gold is the basis of Federal Reserve credit because as explained in Chapter III, the power of the Reserve Banks to create money through adding to their deposits or issuing Federal Reserve notes *is limited by the requirement of a 25 per cent reserve in gold certificates* against both kinds of liabilities. That is to say, the total of Federal Reserve notes and deposits must not exceed four times the amount of gold certifiicates held by the Reserve Banks. *Thus the ultimate limit on Federal Reserve credit expansion is set by gold.*" (27:97f)

Consequently the nation is in no better position to obtain adequate currency for its business expansion and growth of wealth than it was before the "F"RS fraud was imposed on it. Whenever they wish, the conspirators are free to manipulate the nation's gold supply, and thereby restrict the nation's economy. Until this provision of the Act and the "gold standard" is abandoned by the conspirators because it is more profitable for them to do so, the nation faces the same situation described by the Board of Governors as prevailing prior to the establishment of their "F"RS, to wit:

"Prior to 1914...forms of currency were so limited in amount that additional paper money could not be supplied when the nation's business needed it. As a result, the currency would become hard to get and at times commanded a premium.

"Currency shortages, together with other related developments, caused financial crises and panics." (27:89)

The conspirators' objective in tying the currency creating power of their "F"RS to gold was identical with their purpose in imposing the "Gold Standard" on the nation. The "Gold Standard" Act is no, less fraudulent in its purpose than is their "Federal" Reserve Act.

In sharp contrast to the gold notes issued to the public prior to the conspirators' theft of our gold, were the gold notes, or certificates, issued under authorization of the "F"R Act by the Treasury to their "F"RS. They tolerate no such fraud as they perpetrated on the public. They provided in their Gold Reserve Act of 1934:

"Sec. 14.-(c)...The amount of gold certificates outstanding shall at no time exceed the value, at legal standard of gold so held against gold certificates." (25:206)

These gold certificates in denominations of ten thousand dollars each, can be held through their "F"RS by the conspirators only Evidently "what is sauce for the goose (the 'sucker public') is *NOT* sauce for the gander," when the conspirators gold loot is at stake. Though the Act has provided only 25% gold coverage for the money and credit issued by the "Federal" Reserve, it provided 100% gold coverage for themselves. They did not permit to be perpetrated by the Treasury on themselves the same fraud that they perpetrated on the nation.

## CONSPIRATORS HAVE BARRED AUDIT OF THEIR "FEDERAL" RESERVE FRAUD

One of the most significant aspects of the "Federal" Reserve Act, is that in spite of control of the nation's money and credit given by it to the conspirators through their "F"RS, no provision is made for public audit of its books. One can readily understand that the conspirators have no desire to let the public know the extent of their looting. This situation was first brought to light by a rider by Chairman of the House Banking Committee, Wright Patman, attached to a 1967 bill extending the conspirators' power to dictate interest rates that may be paid by savings institutions, that provided for an audit by the Government's General Accounting Office of the books of the "Federal" Reserve Board and its twelve subsidiary private corporations, its "Federal" Reserve Banks; and for turning over for audit their examinations of private member banks. If the "F"RS were honestly operated, there is no sound reason why there should not be a public audit of that private agency that has such wide and sweeping powers over the wealth of the nation and of its citizenry. The "Federal" Reserve Board, however, on behalf of the conspirators has vigorously opposed the plan for this public audit. The obvious motive for this opposition is that it seeks to avert exposure of the dishonesty of the "F"RS. It speciously alleged that "the audit could become a wedge for a monetary policy different from the one the Board may wish to follow" (323), which is, in effect, a confession of guilt. The rider was rejected by the House. Patman represented to the author, in a telephone conversation with him at his Texarkana home late in December, 1967, that he still hopes to secure its passage. That his hope is a bit "naive" may be indicated by his impatience with the idea of Rockefeller domination of our country's monetary system.

## "FEDERAL" RESERVE'S TAX EXEMPTION HAS AGGRAVATED THE FRAUD

Climaxing the treasonous delivery of the nation and its wealth into the piratical hands of the conspirators, is the provision that exempted their "Federal" Reserve loot, its profits and dividends, from taxation:

"Sec. 7:3. Exemption from taxation.

Federal reserve banks, including capital stock and surplus therein and income derived therefrom shall be exempt from Federal, State and local taxation except taxes upon real estate." (25:16)
The Act also provided, most generously:

"Sec. 7:1. After all necessary expenses of a Federal reserve bank shall have been paid or provided for, the stockholders shall be entitled to receive an annual dividend of 6 per centum on the paid capital stock, which dividend shall be cumulative. After the aforesaid dividend claims have been fully met, the net earnings shall be paid into the surplus fund of the Federal reserve bank." (25:15)

This, incidentally, is no deviation from the "accepted practise" of the conspirators of exempting from taxation the loot that they derive from their numerous and varied devices that they have conceived for looting the taxpayers through the agency of governments. They have extended it to their numerous plundering agencies such as their New York City Transit Authority, their New York-New Jersey Port Authority, their Tri-Borough Bridge Authority and the numerous "authorities" set up for their turnpikes and their bridge projects throughout the land.

The "F"R Act provided that the System pay a nominal franchise tax in return for its rich, highly lucrative, thievish monopoly, on notes other than those issued on the basis of deposit of Government bonds with the Treasurer. (25:66,102f) Between 1914 and 1932, at which time it was abolished, this tax amounted to a total of a little more than $149,000,000. This was a bit less than the net earnings of the "F"RS for the single year, 1920, that preceded its precipitation of the "Agricultural Panic." The loot derived from its monopoly by the "F"R System, however, is infinitesimal as compared with that derived from it by the member banks. (47:136f)

After the amendment of the Act abolishing the franchise tax, the "F"RS paid the Treasury during the twelve years between 1935 and 1947, the munificent sum total of a bit over two million dollars! There are no records available to show how much more the Treasury paid the "F"R banks for "accepting" Government deposits to increase their earnings.

## PRES. WILSON JOINED RACKETEERS IN WREAKING VENGEANCE ON OPPONENTS

From the very beginning, there was vigorous protest from many public spirited individuals and groups against the dishonesty and the national betrayal involved in the fraudulent "Federal" Reserve Act. Mention has been made of the vehement opposition and castigation on the floors of Congress, especially those of Sen. LaFollette and Congressman Charles Augustus Lindbergh. This invoked the vengeance of the conspirators "on their children's children."

Pres. Wilson exerted every effort to help his Rockefeller bosses defeat the opposition to the "F"RS conspiracy and to help the conspirators complete their monopoly of banking. In a speech that he delivered in October 1917, Wilson proclaimed that "membership in the Federal Reserve System is a distinct evidence of patriotism." The obvious implication of his statement was that all bankers who did not fall in line with the conspirators' "Federal" Reserve swindle were traitors.

Opposition to the "F"RS fraud was particularly spirited and strenuous in the agricultural districts of the Middle West. They saw "the handwriting on the wall," and discerned the hand of the commodity speculator in the conspiracy. Vengeance of vicious character was visited on them for spurning the "F"RS in the so-called "Agricultural Panic" of 1921. The "Federal" Reserve System deliberately raised the discount rates on agricultural loans to the usurious figure of 7%; and ruthlessly bankrupted numerous rural banks and their customers and communities by forcing calling of their loans.

The same pattern was used by the conspirators, subsequently, in the 1930s, to bankrupt banks that they did not control or that would not join the "F"RS. In addition to manipulation of interest and discount rates, they also dragooned the banks to subscribe during the late 1920's to their so-called "foreign loans" which were swindles. The subsequent panic and depression was thus deliberately planned and precipitated by the conspirators to permit them to enjoy the full fruits of their racketeering.

## THE "FEDERAL" RESERVE SYSTEM HAS TAKEN TOP RANK AMONG THE RACKETS.

The "Federal" Reserve System, takes top rank among the rackets that prey upon and loot mankind. The crooked gambling room of Las Vegas assume the aspects of benevolent philanthropies by comparison. Las Vegas can not force anyone to submit to fleecing. But no one can escape fleecing by the "F"RS. All of us "suckers" are forced to play, day in and day out, at its counters, whenever we have occasion to use money.

It is a notorious fact that if one plays long enough at gambling tables, one is wiped out by the percentage that "the house" takes out of each bet for its "kitty." None of us can stop playing at the counters of the conspirators' "Federal" Reserve, so long as we have need for money This makes it obvious that, in the end, all of our personal and national wealth will inevitably end up in the pockets of the "F'RS conspirators. Thus far the "take" of the "F"RS directly, is represented by its profit of more than forty billion dollars rolled up on a capital of approximately six hundred million dollars of *Our Money And Credit.*

## "F'R UNLOADS PRINTING PRESS MONEY ON NATION AT HIGH COST TO TAXPAYERS

The "kitty," or loot, of the "F"RS is built up in a number of manners, of which some of the more interesting are:

1. The interest rates that we, the taxpayers, pay this private corporation on bonds issued by the Treasury. The "F"RS pays virtually no net sum for these bonds. For it deposits them in the Treasury and withdraws the full amount of their face value in "F"R notes which bear no interest, merely for the cost of printing them. The difference between the interest rates paid on the bonds by the taxpayers through the Treasury and the cost of the notes to the "F"R represents, in the aggregate, a handsome fortune. The item of interest charges on Government bonds in the current budgets amounts to more than $13,000,000,000, approximately ten percent of the 1967 national budget.

2. The so-called "discount rate" which is the interest charged by the "F"RS for the money thus obtained that is loaned to its member banks. The latter are assured of a profit on the moneys thus borrowed by the wide difference between the interest, and more importantly, the discount rate that they obtain on loans to their customers, and that which they are charged by the "F"R, less the differential on the reserves that they are required to maintain on deposit with the "F"R.

3. The charges made by the "F"R member banks on the deposits made in them by the Treasury and for "services rendered."

In effect the profits of the "F"R are a tax levied on the taxpayers and the Treasury for the use of the latters' own funds. Instances of such levies that amount to more than 30% of the Governments' own deposits in "F"R banks for the use by the Government of its own money came to this author's attention during World War II with its numerous War Loans.

These and other profits on "F"R notes offer an explanation of the cooperation by the "F"R in effecting the retirement of other forms of currency.

One of the most impressive adventages that the "F"RS offers the conspirators over Las Vegas in looting the nation, is that whereas Las Vegas has to pretend that its games are honest and "on the level," the "F"RS openly and systematically "rigs" national finances, money supply, interest rates, margins and every other device at its command to insure and facilitate the looting of the nation and the world. Entirely within the law, it is the superlative racketeering device. And if it proves defective from their viewpoint, in any respect at any point, new laws or amendments of the old ones can always be put through Congress or imposed by edict of the prostituted Supreme

Court, to remedy the defect to the conspirators' complete satisfaction. For, they allege, only, they and their agents "understand money," *as they want it understood.*

## CONSPIRATORS TERMED ORIGINAL ACT "THE BEST WE COULD GET," BUT IMPROVABLE

The intent of the conspirators to warp the "Federal" Reserve Act to serve their malignant purposes, even better than did the Act as originally passed, was clearly expressed by one of Rockefellers' trusted banker pawns Jacob Schiff, of Kuhn Loeb & Co. In a letter to another Rockefeller agent, Col. Mandel House (who was father-in-law of Jacqueline Kennedy's kinsman, Gordon Auchincloss) on the date of the passage of the "F"R bill, Schiff wrote:

"...We know that an entirely perfect bill satisfactory to everyone, would have been an impossibility and I feel quite certain fair men will admit that unless the President (Wilson) had stood firm as he did, we would likely have had no legislation at all. The bill is a good one in many respects, anyhow a good one to start' with and to let experience teach us in what direction it needs perfection, which in due time we shall then get..." (13:I:179)

## CONSPIRATORS MADE USE OF THE WORD "FEDERAL" BY OTHERS, A FELONY

An amusing aspect of the "Federal" Reserve fraud is the conspirators usurpation of the word "Federal" as their own monopoly under

"U.S.C. Sec. 709. False advertising

Whoever, except as permitted by the laws of the United States, uses the words 'national' 'Federal,' 'United States,' 'reserve'...as part of the business or firm name of a person, corporation...or other business entity engaged in the banking, loan, building and loan, brokerage, factorage, insurance, indemnity, savings or trust business...Shall be punished as follows: a corporation...or other business entity, by a fine of not more than $1000; and officer or member thereof...by a fine of not more than $1,000 or imprisonment for not more than one year, or both." (25:245)

That should suffice to make sure that no one "muscles in" on the racket.

## CHAPTER XII
## XVITH AMENDMENT & "FEDERAL" RESERVE: ESSENTIALS FOR WORLD WAR I PLOT

*"For The Safety Of The Republic We Now Decree That The Dangerous Conspiracy Must Be Ended By November 15 (1911)."* Thus wrote the Supreme Court in its dissolution decree, of May 15, 1911, directed against Rockefellers and their Standard Oil Co. Unfortu-

nately for the world, the conspirators thumbed their nose at the Court and the nation, and proceeded to plot and to perpetrate even vaster, more criminal and villainous conspiracies. The XVIth Amendment, the Federal income and capital tax that they contrived through it, and the "Federal" Reserve Act (which gave the conspirators control of the Treasury and the wealth of the people) were essential features of their plot to loot the nation and force it to defray the cost of world-wide expansion of the Rockefeller Empire. These measures amplified the nation's support of Rockefellers' vicious rackets, of which John D. boasted *'One Of Our Greatest Helpers Has been (and still is more than ever) The State Department In Washington."* (*16:63*)

A patriotic Congress was fully aware of Rockefellers' criminal and villainous intent. It openly predicted their plot to use and destroy our Republic. It attacked them and refused to become their accomplices. It repeatedly rejected in 1909, 1910, 1911 and 1912 bills introduced by their in-law, powerful Republican boss of the Senate, Sen Nelson Aldrich (grandfather and namesake of Gov. Nelson Aldrich Rockefeller) that would have given the Rockefellers a national charter for the Foundation they wished to set up. The projected Rockefeller Foundation was rightly attacked on the floors of Congress as a conspiratorial device for the criminal and treasonous purposes of subverting the nation and betraying it, and of evading the taxation that the conspirators planned to impose on the rest of the nation. No truer words have ever been uttered in Congress—or more patriotic. But the resourceful Rockefeller conspirators planted their agent, Sen. Robert F. Wagner, in the New York State Senate. And he secured for them the passage the bill that chartered their bogus "philanthropy," the Rockefeller Foundation (15:147f)

It is noteworthy that the members of Congress stated that it was no secret that the Rockefeller conspirators planned to undermine the Constitution and destroy our Republic, at the expense of the nation through the use of tax-exempt Foundation funds. The criminal character of Rockefeller activities has never been a secret except to the duped among the public who have been brainwashed by Rockefeller subverters of public opinion parading in an endless array of posts with numerous titles under which they ply their trades in the service of their malign masters: "publicity men"; press agents; "historians," who pervert history; "educators," who blind their students with lies and leave them brainwashed and purged of natural intelligence, in a state of befuddled bigotry that is worse than ignorance; "statesmen" and "public officials," who consistently and persistently betray the nation to serve their masters; and a vast array of others.

Depending on these verminous pawns of theirs, and on their own bogus repute as "philanthropists," the conspirators make little effort to hide their evil purposes. They rely on the moronity to which their agents have been able to reduce their victim public, that takes the place of the natural intelligence and initiative that characterized the pre-Rockefeller Americans, patriots, whom they now denigrate as "extremists" and place in their Museum of Primitives. The present-day "mass men" whom they have created are so devoid of mentality that they distrust their own senses. They are willing to see, hear and believe only what the conspirators dictate. In meaningless blotches of paint, they "see" beautiful women and landscapes. In raucous noise they "hear" harmony and music. In Communist treason they discern "moderation"; and in patriotism they find "extremism."

## CRIMINAL PSYCHOPATHY & INSANE FEAR OF
## POVERTY: DYNASTIC BASES

The desire to camouflage their psychopathic criminality and gangsterism by which they had seized their immense wealth is readily understandable. For the Rockefellers' status was not enviable at the turn of the century. They were justifiably reviled by the nation as ruthless, vicious criminals and racketeers. They were outcasts who were so hated that they feared for their safety when they appeared in public. This fear played a role in the remigration of John D. to New York. He had originally emigrated from New York to Ohio, as a youth, when the family followed their father in his flight. "Doc" William Avery Rockefeller, his father, a quack patent medicine vendor, usurer, swindler, horse thief, bigamist, rapist and all-around scoundrel, had been compelled to flee a half century earlier to avoid apprehension on rape and other indictments, pending and threatened. (79:1f)

John D's fear of public retribution for his exposed crimes led him to connect the homes that he built for his family, on the site of Rockefeller Center, by underground tunnels. The psychopathic fear of poverty that he made the motive force of the Dynasty that he founded, was more powerful even than his fear of physical violence. Coupled with the criminal psychopathy that was familial, it impelled him to scheme vaster and more heinous crimes against civilization, the nation and mankind. Involved therein was the pride which he shared with his father in his criminal craftiness and his exultation therein. Joe Alex Morris, the Rockefeller biographer and pressagent, reported the gleeful memories of the younger Rockefeller generation of the tales of his treachery, deceit and entrapment of both friend and foe, with which John D. would regale them. And he related that Nelson Rockefeller undertook in his college themes, in a spirit of adulation, to justify the piracy of his grandfather, indicating that this perverted pride has become a tradition of the Rockefeller clan. (17:57)

## BOGUS "PHILANTHROPY" MADE MASK FOR
## WORLD CONQUEST & LOOTING

Under cover of the false pretense of "philanthropy," for which purpose, as has been related, he had been advised by his pressagents and propagandists to establish foundations with the objective of appeasing public opinion and hatred of him and camouflaging his racketeering and gangsterism, John D. Rockefeller plotted grabbing the oil and other resources of the nation and of the whole wide world. This plot he made a family and dynastic goal in much the same manner as are feuds in the backwoods. It found expression in the words of his alter ego, his son, John D. Jr., that are quoted by his attorney, agent and biographer Raymond B. Fosdick, as follows:

"So it may come to pass that someday, someday...no one will speak of 'my country,' but all will speak of 'our world.'" (18:390)

The initial impetus to the plot for world control, for "One (Rockefeller) World," was quest for monopolistic control of the world's oilfields. The principal obstacle to this Rockefeller-Standard Oil goal was its most powerful and fiercest competitor in Eurasia, the Royal Dutch Company. Royal Dutch had the support and backing of the Dutch and British Empires. And the Russian Empire had granted them a monopolistic concession for all its oilfields, as had the British and Dutch. The company was controlled by a wealthy group of Jewish bankers, the Rothschild, Sassoon and Isaacs families who later merged with Samuels' Shell interests. The company had a virtual monopoly of oil in the many parts of the world where it operated; and it later invaded the North American markets.

Royal Dutch was able to supply oil to some European markets at prices that defied Rockefeller-Standard Oil competition because of the proximity of some of its fields, such as Baku and Ploesti, and the materially lower shipping costs. It also competed fiercely with the Rockefeller interests in gaining control of oil resources in the Western Hemisphere, especially in the U.S., Mexico and Latin America. (15:183; 46; 65) The Royal Dutch was winning out in the fiercely competitive trade war that Rockefeller's Standard Oil had waged on it since it had begun shipments of kerosene to the European markets during the Civil War.

For John D. Rockefeller this situation implied only one remedy. It meant the extension of the gangsterism and racketeering, in which he had been so successful in the domestic field, to the international field; and ultimately the destruction of the worldwide Empires that stood in the way of an oil empire of his own, the Rockefeller Empire, the masking slogan for which is "One World." This promptly became the fixed mania of the Rockefeller Dynasty, the tradition of which is to tenaciously pursue a set goal, generation after generation, no matter what it may cost the rest of mankind.

John D. and his mad schemers were keenly aware that many other individuals and groups seek to make themselves rulers of the world. First and foremost of these are numerous religions, including the religion of Illuminist Communism. From the start the crafty Rockefeller conspirators set about joining forces with all of them, with the objective of making them serve his purposes. The cost of buying their support and cooperation was shifted to the shoulders of American taxpayers by the device of the Foundation and its tax exemption. Rockefeller, keenly aware of the hatred and fear that he inspired, carefully hid behind the scenes craftily pulling the strings and, like a huge and ugly spider, wove a vast net in which to entrap mankind. From the very start, as has been noted, the U. S. State Department has servilely played the role of his agents and mercenaries, (16:63)

The European key of the conspiracy has been Germany. It had failed to develop, in its extensive Empire, adequate oil production of its own. And it had been shut out from the oil resources and production by the British, French, Dutch and Russian empires, exactly as had the Rockefellers and their Standard Oil. Both coveted the same goal, the oil resources from which they were shut out.

The first efforts of the Rockefeller interests at a solution of the problem was an attempt to make their peace with the Royal Dutch group, in line with the Dynasty's tradition: "If you can't

71

lick 'em, join 'em." But Sir Henry Deterding, the Royal Dutch director, was too well aware that a partnership with the Rockefellers is an invitation to a back-stabbing, when the first opportunity presents; and refused to deal with them. The next Rockefeller-Standard Oil move was an attempt to induce the Czarist regime to cancel the monopolistic concession it had given to Royal Dutch and to give them some concessions for Russian oilfields. This plan the Czarist regime rejected, with words to the effect that they wanted no quarrel with their British cousins.

The situation left only two methods open to the Rockefeller interests to gaining access to the Russian oilfields, other than the prohibitively expensive and futile attempt to purchase control of Royal Dutch in the open stock market. Their first approach was to create a breach between the Czarist regime and the Royal Dutch management. Their second was to oust the Czarist regime by financing, with the funds of American taxpayers derived through their tax-exempt foundations, a revolution in Russia. The conspirators adopted both approaches.

## CONSPIRATORS EFFECTED PUBLICATION OF FORGED "PROTOCOLS OF ZION"

For the purpose of attempting to create a breach between the Czarist regime and the Royal Dutch Co., there was effected the publication in Russian, and widespread distribution, under the name of a Captain Linus, a notorious forged document labelled *Protocols of Zion*. (223:3f) The document was a falsified translation from the German teachings of the Jesuit, Adam Weishaupt, written by him as instructions for the trusted members of his Communist organization, the Order of Illuminati. (29:58;85;86)

Weishaupt's success in forcing the Vatican to reestablish the abolished Jesuit order, through revival of the Church's original Nazarene Communism in the form of present-day Communism, led to the conspiracy's control by the Society of Jesus. This undoubtedly is the significance of the admonition to the Jesuit Order by Pope Paul VI at the time of their assembly, in May, 1965, to elect their new General, Fr. Pedro Arrupe. The situation explains why wherever a totalitarian movement erupts, whether Communist or Nazi, a Jesuit can be found in the role of "adviser," or leader; in Cuba, Castro's Fr. Armando Llorente (167:3) and in Argentina the neo-Nazis are led by Fr. Menvieille.

## CONSPIRATORS INCITED POGROMS

The plot drafted by Jesuit Weishaupt for world dictatorship was translated in Russian in the name of a Capt. Linus, at the instance of the conspirators, under the title of *"The Protocols of Zion,"* and broadcast widely by them as the supposed work of mythical and non-existent "Elders of Zion." The text was faked to create the impression that Jews and Masons were plotting to overthrow the Czarist regime and make themselves absolute, dictatorial rulers of the world. Henry Ford was duped by the conspirators' agent into promulgating this forgery in the U.S. (87:2) The forgery failed to effect the breach between the Czarist regime and the Jewish dominated Royal Dutch. Instead, the conspirators succeeded in inciting massacres of Jews in various sections of Russia, and elsewhere.

72

## CONSPIRATORS FINANCED LENIN & TROTSKY IN FIRST RUSSIAN REVOLUTION

The second approach of the conspirators to gaining control of Russian oil was their financing of Lenin and Trotsky in the Russian Communist revolt of 1905. The conspirators' purpose was to accomplish, themselves, exactly what they falsely represented in their *Protocols of Zion* was being planned by the Jews and Masons. Rockefellers' Jewish banker, Jacob Schiff, of Kuhn Loeb & Co., acknowledged at a Congressional hearing that he turned over the funds to the Communists to finance the revolt. But the questioners carefully avoided asking Schiff who had furnished the funds and for what reason. Nor was he questioned about the well-known plot of the conspirators to steal control of Baku oil from Royal Dutch. This was all the more notable because the committee had already elicited from John D. Rockefeller that he had acquired, thus far, a total of $15,000,000 of the bonds of his competitors, Royal Dutch and Shell, with the obvious objective of trying to take them over and thus gain control of their Russian oilfields, a project in which he eventually succeeded.

With the usual slimy craftiness and ruthlessness, the conspirators had undertaken to reinforce their false propaganda in the *Protocols of Zion* (that the Jews were conspiring to overthrow the Czarist regime and take over control of Russia and the world) by using the prominent but curiously naive, or venal, Jacob Schiff as their agent. It might be seriously questioned whether venality did not play a larger role than naivete in the service that he rendered his Rockefeller masters.

A factor in the failure of both phases of the conspiracy was the close kinship between the Crown heads of Russia and England. Another factor that counted heavily was the Jewish blood strain that runs in the British royal family and nobility, and indirectly in that of Russia, much of which had originally been Jewish by conversion. (322)

Having failed in both of these treacheries, the conspirators planted Lenin and his cohorts in Switzerland, where their foundations maintained them at the expense of American taxpayers, by way of tax exemption, for use at a later date. For, once they have embarked on an enterprise, however mad, they tenaciously persist in it generation after generation, with an intensity that marks their paranoia.

Bronstein, alias Trotsky, was brought by the conspirators to the U.S. where he is reported to have been maintained, without visible means of support, on Standard Oil property at Bayonne, New Jersey. The conspirators' Communist agents were being kept in reserve for future use for overthrowing the Czarist regime when they had created the opportunity.

## FRUSTRATED IN RUSSIA, ROCKEFELLERS TURN TO NEAR EAST FOR OIL

Frustrated in their plots to steal or otherwise secure the readily available Baku oil, the Rockefeller-Standard Oil conspirators turned their attention to undeveloped oilfields in the Near East that were dominated by the British in an uneasy alliance with

73

the French and the Germans. The Germans had been given by Sultan Abdul Hamid a concession, in 1904, for the Anatolian Railway Co. with an option to drill the Bagdad-Mosul oilfields that previously had been promised to an American, Admiral C. M. Chester. Before the Germans had begun the development, the Sultan cancelled the concession and began to negotiate with the British. A revolution financed by the conspirators ousted the Sultan. And Admiral Chester got his concession for his masters, in writing. The British then joined forces with the Germans to pressure the Turkish government to restore the German concession and cancel that which it had given the Americans.

The conspirators then played on the cupidity of the Kaiser and the Germans with plans to finance the building of the Berlin-to-Bagdad Railroad that would give them joint control of the entire concession, eliminating the British and their control of Suez and the Near East, thus severing the lifeline of the British Empire. This move was well planned to precipitate World War I, exactly as every other war of this century has been deliberately planned and precipitated by the Rockefeller-Standard Oil interests for oil and for the expansion of the Rockefeller Empire by destroying every other empire that might contest its world domination. (65:22;15;46;79)

## PAUL WARBURG, CONSPIRATORS' GERMAN AGENT, PROVED HIS WORTH

Paul Warburg, even though he refused to draw up a central banking, or "Federal" Reserve Bill that was sufficiently crooked for his Rockefeller masters, proved his value to them as a German "contact man." His brother was the chief of the German espionage system and afforded the conspirators their contact with the Kaiser and his regime. This was his special value to the conspirators. In addition there was his knowledge of central banking and his value as a Jew that would serve them well in distracting attention from their own malign role and in affording a scapegoat with the inflammatory value of "Shylock" and Jew. All in all, these added up to making tolerance of his Prussian personality well worth the while of the conspirators.

The international oil developments at this juncture indicate the conspirators' urgent need of the "Federal" Reserve and Warburg's role therein, and of the XVIth amendment. Both measures were essential parts of their crafty plot for making American taxpayers bear the burden of precipitating and waging World War I for the expansion of the oily Rockefeller Empire and the destruction of all rivals.

## ROCKEFELLER BANKS USED "F"RS TO FINANCE GERMANY'S START OF WORLD WAR I

Rockefeller banks — Chase National, Equitable Trust, Mechanics & Metals, Bankers Trust and Kuhn Loeb & Co.—financed Germany's launching of World War I on the basis of the deal they had made with Kaiser Wilhelm through their joint agents, the Warburgs. (272:I:138; 20:169) Supplying Germany with the estimated $300 millions involved was facilitated and largely made possible by their "Federal" Reserve System. (21; 23) The "Federal" Reserve Act assured the conspirators that any loss that might have been sustained by their treachery would be the "obligation of the U.S. Treasury" and of the taxpayers, under the terms written into the bill by Pres. Wilson. By the time that they doublecrossed their German partners and assured the British, under the terms of the deal that they made with Winston Churchill through their agent Pres. Wilson, of control of the seas and American support, those debts had been repaid and their German agent, Paul Warburg, had been removed from their "Federal" Reserve.

## "F"RS ENABLED CONSPIRATORS, ALSO, TO FORCE ALLIES INTO SUBMISSION

Through their same "F"RS device, the conspirators brought pressure to bear on the Allies, who had been financed by Rothschild agent, J. P. Morgan, to the extent of $400 million. The Allies realized that they had fallen into a trap laid for them by the conspirators; and that they were doomed to defeat unless they yielded to the oily terms laid down. For this reason, Winston Churchill who had led the British opposition to the Rockefeller-Standard Oil gang (15:189f), yielded to their demand that they be given the rich oilfield prizes including the enormously rich fields of British vassal Saudi Arabia, and other concessions in their sphere of influence in the Near East. In return, the conspirators and their puppet, Pres. Wilson, pledged American wealth and lives to finance and fight the war for the Allies to rescue them. (15:183)

## CONSPIRATORS DOUBLECROSSED GERMAN PARTNERS & EFFECTED RED RUSSIAN REVOLUTION

The Rockefeller deal with the British involved one of their usual treacheries and double-crosses on which they pride themselves. The German sojourn of their reportedly Turkish ancestors and the experience of their ancestor, Johannes Roggenfelder (German for the rye fields, where he had worked), who had been sent to the American colonies as a Hessian mercenary to fight in the Revolutionary War, had bred a mistrust in the conspirators of their German partners. They wisely did not trust them to carry out the deal made for Near East oilfields. As soon as Winston Churchill and the British had awakened, at Verdun, to the realization that they could not win World War I, and had agreed to permit their vassals in the Near East to grant concessions to the Rockefeller Standard Oil interests, the betrayal of Kaiser Wilhelm and the Germans was set.

The conspirators, however, kept their scheme secret until they had used the German General Staff, with the aid of Warburg and his brother, to further the plot on which they had launched with the Communists to overthrow the Czarist regime in Russia. The Germans were induced to transport the conspirators' agents Lenin and Trotsky, with their cohorts, through Germany in a sealed coach to the Russian border. On the coach, according to Col. Nikitine of the Russian intelligence and others, the Bolsheviks were provided by the conspirators with hundreds of millions of counterfeit ten ruble notes. With these notes the Communists purchased the votes that gave them control of Russia without firing a shot. The Communist takeover of Russia by the conspirators through criminal craftiness is a model of their fraudulent transactions that require, on their part, neither courage nor force, but merely ruthlessness and unbounded treachery.

## PRES. WILSON JOINED CONSPIRATORS IN TREACHEROUS WAR DEAL FOR OIL

The most viciously treacherous figure in the perfidious conspiracy to involve the U.S. in World War I, as a payoff for oil concessions, was the conspirators' shameless, ruthless, "bought-and-paid-for" agent, Pres. Woodrow Wilson. The record clearly indicates that Wilson was acutely aware of the nature and purpose of the conspirators whom he served as an eager pawn. When questioned by Sen. McCumber, Wilson freely acknowledged that the War, into which he deliberately plunged us at the very time that he was running for reelection on a platform in which he pledged "to keep us out of the war," was a matter of "economic rivalry," of an oil deal. He was asked:

"Do you think if Germany had committed no act of war... against our citizens that we could have gotten into the war?"

Wilson answered, flatly and unabashedly, that we would have entered the War in any event. The only loyalty that he ever manifested was his absolute dedication to the oily conspiracy of his Rockefeller-Standard Oil masters whom he served with unflinching and unquestioning obedience.

## WILSON'S "14 POINTS" SPELL "DIVIDE & RULE" FOR CONSPIRATORS

Wilson's nauseating hypocrisy in his obedience to his masters emerges especially plainly from his enunciation for them of the "fourteen points" that have been so essential for them in destroying the Empires that blocked their way to absolute world control and looting. His "point" regarding "self-determination" served them well in raising the cry of "colonialism" that they have used so effectively in despoiling European powers of the colonies that they had undertaken to civilize at enormous costs in money and lives; and in stealing, for themselves and their Soviet confederates, the investments in those colonies by the customary thievish device of "expropriation." As the conspirators have planned, the majority of the "liberated" colonies have been plunged into turmoil, savagery and destitution, to facilitate their brigandage, exactly as envisioned by them and their eager agent, Pres. Wilson.

In retrospect, Pres. Wilson stands out as an evil scourge that has aided and abetted plunging mankind into an age of turmoil, violence, misery and savagery, whose acts fully justify his characterization by Italian Prime Minister Pantaleone as a

"*Pecksniff Who Has...Disappeared Amid Universal Execrations.*"

As stated by one of his disillusioned Princeton supporters, Louis Jay Lang,

"Retribution came but a few months before the President-Maker gave up his life." (6)

He probably was referring to the carefully suppressed fact that was well-known in official circles, that his last illness, his stroke, was brought on by a violent blow to his head with a wine bottle by his consort.

## DECEIVING & BETRAYING THE NATION — "DEMOCRATIC PRINCIPLES"

When one considers that the treachery of Pres. Wilson in betraying the U.S. into World War I, in his "keep us out of the war" campaign deceit, was repeated by another agent of the conspirators, Pres. Franklin D. Roosevelt, with his "again and again" speech, one may well wonder whether the contempt that the conspirators have for the moronity of the American public, whom they have so thoroughly brainwashed through their bogus "educational philanthropies," is not entirely justified. Can it be that juggling the truth, trifling with patriotism, treachery and treason are established "principles" of the conspirators, the Party and its leaders? Do they differ in that respect from their Communist collaborators?

## CONSPIRATORS' AGENTS WERE WELL AWARE OF PERFIDIOUS PURPOSE

That Wilson was not alone in his awareness of the conspirators' purposes is attested to by many of their number. Thus one of the more active of their agents, Cordell Hull, discussed the roles of Federal income taxes and the "Federal" Reserve conspiracy in making possible the financing of World War I, and acknowledged:

"The conflict forced the further development of the income tax principle. Aiming, as it did, at the one great untaxed source of revenue, *the income tax had been enacted in the nick of time to meet demands of the War...And the conflict also assisted in putting into effect of the Federal Reserve System, likewise in the nick of time.*" (23)

The excitement of the war served to divert public attention from the intensity of the tax looting. The tax was initially levied at the rate of one-half per cent but was rapidly increased to oppressive dimensions. Secretary of the Treasury McAdoo, Wilson's son-in-law, commented on the effectiveness of the "F"RS in this looting, in his Treasury Report for 1917, as follows:

"The Federal Reserve System has been of incalculable value during this period of war financing on the most extensive scale ever undertaken by any nation in the history of the world. *It would have been impossible to carry through these unprecedented financial operations under our old banking system.*"

The Federal income tax and the "Federal" Reserve, into which the conspirators had betrayed us, were both absolutely essential, the *sine qua non*, of the conspirators' war plans and our involvement in them. And they have been equally essential for other phases of the conspiracy and the other wars in which they involve us. What better reason can be offered for putting an end to both? These views were fully confirmed by Professor Edwin W. Kemmerer, one of the conspirators' trusted authorities on money, who wrote:

"Think of pouring the crisis of 1914-1918 into the bottles that broke in the crisis of 1907." (24:117)

## CONSPIRATORS' OBJECTIVES ARE CLARIFIED BY THEIR TREATMENT OF WARBURG

Confirmatory evidence of the objectives of the conspirators in these phases of the conspiracy is given by their treatment of their agent, Paul Warburg. Warburg, though they detested his "uncouth" personality, his overbearing demeanor, his argumentativeness, his crude vanity and his guttural Prussian accent that grated their ears, had served their purposes well in propaganda for their "Federal" Reserve. He was equally valuable as their German agent and contact with the Kaiser, through his brother who headed the German espionage and intelligence system. Even more important was the service that his father rendered the Kaiser as a banker, as later his firm served Hitler in the same capacity. He consequently was the ideal pawn in their plan to use Germany to precipitate war with their foe, the British Empire, and to effect the undermining of both the British and the Germans. As vice chairman (207:354) of their "Federal" Reserve, he was effectively used to lure the Germans into the war by being in a position to extend to them "authoritatively," on behalf of the conspirators, financing of their entry into the war, that was, as related, one of the prime purposes of the "F"R Act. Furthermore, he served to divert from the conspirators the hatred and approbrium that opponents of the "F"R vented on him, its supposed creator. This was a doubly effectively served role by virtue of the traditional role of the Jew as moneylender and "Shylock," the use of which by "good Christians" was customary.

Nothing more clearly reveals the role in which Warburg was deliberately used by the conspirators than their treatment of him, after he had served his purpose. As soon as they had forced the British into submission and agreed to bring the U.S. into World War I, to finance and fight it for the Allies, Warburg was ousted from their "Federal" Reserve, never to return to it either directly or indirectly. He had served in his role of "fall guy." So soon as the nation's morons had been duped into accepting the "F"RS, and danger of violent reaction against its personnel had passed, he went the way of most agents who serve the Rockefeller interests. Whether he served them in helping plant on Pres. Wilson the German agent and former mistress of the German spy-ambassador, Count von Bernstorff, as wife and executioner, is a matter of conjecture.

CHAPTER XIII
## "FEDERAL" RESERVE REQUIRED "PERFECTION" TO MATCH XVITH AMENDMENT FOR LOOTING

The conspirators recognized from the start that their "Federal" Reserve System lacked the perfection of their XVIth Amendment. The discontent of the conspirators was expressed by their banking agent, Jacob Schiff, in his cited letter to a fellow agent, Col. Mandel House. He pointed out, however, that:

"The bill is a good one in many respects (Ed. from his point of view), anyhow a good one to start with and to let experience teach us in what direction it needs perfection, which in due time, we shall then get..." (13:I:179)

## FEDERAL INCOME TAX MAKES POSSIBLE UNLIMITED LOOTING OF NATION

One readily understand the contentment of the conspirators with the XVIth Amendment and the maze of income tax, capital gains taxes, bureaucratic rules, regulations and edicts woven about it. The brushing aside of the provisions of the Constitution and the elimination by the Amendment of a fundamental and vital principle embodied in it and of any restrictions in draining the wealth of the nation's taxpayers into the coffers of dictatorial conspirators by use of the Federal Government as their thievish agent, was much to their liking. For the un-Constitutional XVIth Amendment has been made by them a device for unlimited looting of each and every one of the nation's taxpayers, that has been given an appearance of legality and Constitutionality thereby. The Federal income tax devices clearly violate the provision of the Bill of Rights that offers security in the private ownership of property, and rob us of that protection. One of the aspects of the Federal income tax setup that makes this un-Constitutionality of the Amendment ultra obvious is that in it there is no limit to the percentage of our vital and basic property, our incomes, that can be taken from us by governmental edict. Congress is free to tax us one hundred percent of our incomes, if it so elects. And Gov. Nelson Rockefeller is demonstrating to New York's citizens that he so elects.

But the taxes levied on our incomes is merely a beginning of the looting that we suffer. Without authorization of Amendment or law, in further violation of the Constitution, the conspirators have, by bureaucratic edicts, converted the income tax to a capital tax. They have done this by decreeing that capital gains are current income in whatever measure they dictate. Short term gains, defined by them in any manner that the conspirators may desire, are all current income. But long-term profits, also defined by them in any manner that the conspirators may desire, are current income to the extent of fifty percent, or to any extent that they dictate. Capital losses, however, they dictate are not income losses for the individual, and can not be treated as such except in a limited extent of one thousand dollars a year. For their corporations, their attitude is the reverse. Capital losses of corporations and their depreciation allowances are decreed to be what they are in reality, loss of wealth, and may be deducted in full from current and past income.

79

## CONSPIRATORS "MUSCLED IN" AS OUR PARTNERS IN PROFITS BUT NOT IN LOSSES

In effect, the conspirators have decreed themselves to be our unlimited paterns in our income and profits, but not our partners in our losses. This is the supreme example of their crooked confidence game: "Heads I win, tails you lose."

With an eye to intensifying their looting, the conspirators have adopted the thievish criminality of the Weishaupt-Marx, Illuminist-Communist scheme in their income tax looting as they have in their "Federal" Reserve. They have made the income tax "progressive." This means that the more one makes, the more they steal and the less one has left, proportionately, unless one can evade taxation entirely, as they have made it possible for themselves to do.

For the purpose of winning popular support for their thievery, and of representing it to the gullible and the moronic as a "soak the rich" scheme, the conspirators wrote into their laws and regulations an exemption of six hundred dollars for each dependent. In 1913, when this measure was adopted, six hundred dollars was an adequate sum to provide a comfortable living for an individual. In the same year the average income tax rate was one-half of one percent; and the nation was falsely assured that the levy would never rise much above one percent. The rank and file were thus induced to accept, delightedly, this "soak the rich" fraud.

It was not long before the nation awoke to some fragmentary awareness of the fact that they had been duped. The tax rate rose steadily, bringing with it steady inflation; and with it rose rapidly the cost of living. But never has the "cost of living" exemption of six hundred dollars been raised by a single penny, except for senior citizens and the blind, although it soon became inadequate for either food or shelter. Ironically, the morons who had been delighted at the prospect of the "soak the rich" program found themselves trapped as its pitiable victims.

## CONSPIRATORS HAVE EXEMPTED THEMSELVES FROM TAXATION

The conspirators, by all odds the wealthiest people in the world, whose incomes have been swelled by these devices to more than a million dollars a minute, have written into the code provisions which virtually completely exempt themselves from taxation except for politically limited taxes on some of their real estate holdings. Thus the Director of Internal Revenue Caplin announced in 1964 that dozens of persons with incomes of a million or more, as well as seventeen persons with the highest incomes in the land, pay no income tax whatsoever.

## ROCKEFELLER CENTER LOW ASSESSMENT VIRTUALLY TAX EXEMPTS IT

The taxation of Rockefeller Center points up the success of the conspirators in averting their fair share even of property taxes, which they dare not completely evade because of fear of public reaction. The assessment of Rockefeller Center, with its eighteen skyscrapers built on more than thirty acres, is less than four times the assessment on the neighboring Tishman Building at 666 Fifth Avenue that is smaller than any of the Center's, and is assessed thirty-five million dollars. Though assessments and taxes have risen more than one hundred percent in New York City during the interval between the nineteen fifties and now, Rockefeller Center buildings assessments are unchanged since the 1930's when both were far lower. Despite further construction and improvements, the current assessment is only three million dollars more than that in the 1930's — a total of one hundred and twenty-eight million dollars. This absurd underassessment of property that has a real valuation of several billion dollars represents a shift of the burden of real estate taxes to the rest of the community. Rockefeller's 4500 acre Pocantico Hill estate with land valued at $180 million is assessed a bit over $5 million. (319)

## TAX EXEMPTION OF "PHILANTHROPIES" & EVASIONS ROB HONEST TAXPAYERS

The evasion of taxes by devices aforementioned and by the bogus pose of "philanthropy" under which the Rockefellers attain their objectives has a built-in source of additional gain for them. Their continued ownership and control of the "philanthropic" funds and the use of them, indirectly or directly, in the conduct of their affairs, enables the piling up of tax-exempt profits. In defiance of the law, the moneys are used also to further their political interests. Whether in spite of the law they derive, personally, millions of income directly or indirectly from the foundations, is rumored but not known.

The significance of this tax evasion and exemption has been aptly stated by Congressman Wright Patman in his Report To The Select Committee On Small Business of the House of Representatives of the 87th Congress, as follows:

"...when an organization is tax exempt, it means that all other taxpayers must pick up the tab. Correspondingly, when any taxpayer reduces his tax by a deduction for contribution to a foundation, it means that all other taxpayers must make up for that tax deduction.

"Tax exemption is a costly thing. *It Explains in Part Why Only One-third of the Income of the Nation Is Actually Taxed.*" (89:133)

"Now, the multimillion-dollar foundations have replaced the trusts which were broken up during the Theodore Roosevelt administration...

"The use of subterfuge — in the form of Rockefeller-controlled foundations — in effect produces the same result as if Standard Oil Co. (New Jersey) owned substantial stock interest in Continental Oil, Ohio Oil, Standard Oil (Indiana), et al." (89:v)

The tax-exemption of the conspirators means, in plain language, looting of the Treasury and of the nation. The cost of government which the Rockefellers evade, through their tax-exemption and other dodges, must be borne by the rest of us. It is we, the victims of their skulduggery, who are the involuntary, drafted and real philanthropists. And they are the self-imposed beneficiaries of the charitable handouts that they exact from us. They compel us to pay the taxes that they evade — with vengeance. For they add insult to injury by using their tax-exempt loot to hold us up con-

81

stantly for more, by an endless array of new imposts for the various schemes that add to our burden and to their incomes, or loot, such as so-called "foreign aid," worthless "bomb shelters," "slum clearance and urban redevelopment" steals and land-grabbing, and absurd and useless "Buck Rogers" projects that yield them and their companies fabulous profits. It is safe to say that the bulk of the taxes, levied on us by them, flows into Rockefellers' tax-exempt purses, to add to their million dollar a minute income.

If the process is permitted to continue, it is inevitable that the ruthlessly dishonest constant increase of the burden of taxes imposed on us by the conspirators, at all levels of government, means a steady and rapidly increased concentration of our wealth in the hands of the "philanthropists." This will serve to dispossess and disinherit the nation, and lead us inevitably to confiscatory inflation and bankruptcy. In the interim, it is reducing most of the nation to a hand-to-mouth, marginal or submarginal existence. This is quite obviously the deliberate purpose of the conspirators.

With the funds looted from us, the conspirators bribe, corrupt and purchase our officials for the purpose of further looting us, of destroying our Republic, of "electing" themselves to public office with the aid of crooked voting machines manufactured by their interests (79:186f; 227; 228), and of usurping rule over the nation and converting our government into a totalitarian dictatorship. In the meanwhile, with supreme insolence, they use the looted funds and usurped power to force us to serve them as self-paid mercenaries in the hot and "cold" wars and revolutions that they engineer for extending their conquest around the world. And they mock us with the phrase "Free World."

## ROCKEFELLERS' "PHILANTHROPIC" FOUNDATION TRUST A MENACE TO NATION

By their control of the Government and of the Treasury, the conspirators have been enabled to create, through tax-exempt organizations, including foundations and various super-governmental "authorities" (both those established by themselves and by others), a vast monopoly of commerce, industry and even of charities (56) that menace the nation and the world with absolute dictatorship. To fatten their loot, they have decreed that the limited individual exemption from taxation for charity is granted only if the donations are given to the "Social Service & Charitable Trust" that they have established. (56) Through this vast concentration of wealth that supplements their own loot, they control and "manage" the economy and politics of the nation and the world to serve them in their gangsterism, and thievish and murderous racketeering. Both in the internal affairs of the nation and in international affairs they have been enabled to supplant Washington as well as State and local governments.

## NELSON ROCKEFELLER VIOLATES INCOME TAX LAW WITH COMPLETE IMMUNITY

The law which bars the use of tax exempt funds for political purposes they disregard and mock. When Nelson Rockefeller sought the Republican Presidential nomination, the entire wealth of their

Foundation Trust was devoted to his campaign through such devices as the Rockefeller Reports propaganda. (79:172) Not content with this enormous subsidy of his campaign, Rockefeller is reported to have diverted more than half a million dollars to payments that were such clear-cut violations of the Internal Revenue Act regarding the use of foundation money that, despite his power, he was cited by the I.R.S. Though the penalty of such violations that are written into the code provide for recovery of all of the capital of the foundation and recovery by the Treasury, retroactively, of all moneys on which taxation has been evaded by the culprit, plus other penalties including prison terms, Rockefeller is reported to have been let off after promise not to repeat the criminal act. (79:231)

Likewise, the Logan Act which bars any party whatsoever, even members of Congress, from meddling in the nation's foreign affairs or influencing international relations, is openly disregarded and flagrantly violated by the conspirators, their foundations and other interests. A large proportion of the funds withheld by the conspirators from the Treasury are diverted, in violation of the law, from the uses for which the diversion was permitted, promoting the welfare of ourselves. (210:8564) Instead the moneys have been expended on enterprises in foreign lands that serve the interests of the conspirators and betray those of our country. As in the instance of the Rockefeller foundations, their moneys are used to finance subversion and all other aspects of the Illuminist-Communist, Fascist and Nazi totalitarian conspiracies of theirs. In this they are aided and abetted by their Central Intelligence Agency (CIA) planted in the government.

## EVASION OF TAX BY OTHER THAN CONSPIRATORS: THE MOST HEINOUS OF CRIMES

The conspirators have made sure that no one other than themselves can escape tax looting at their hands by way of income taxes. They have written into the Internal Revenue Code provisions that make such tax evasion the most heinous of all crimes. Unlike all other crimes of the types in which they and their henchmen engage on a wholesale scale, income tax evasion is a "crime" in which one is required to give self-incriminating evidence and denied the shelter of the Constitution and the Fifth Amendment which they and their henchmen so frequently use; in which their minions of the IRS act as prosecutors, judge and jury, whose every whim is law; in which appeal from bureaucratic decisions of their minions is so costly that their victims have no other recourse, even when innocent, than to accept the verdicts that were arbitrarily arrived at by bureaucrats, long before trial. In no instance, except possibly in court martials, is the Constitution so completely disregarded and a dead letter, as in the "crime" of withholding tax loot from the conspirators and their political henchmen. For this "heinous" crime, they have revived the infamous "debtors' prison."

## FOUNDATION SWINDLE "LEGAL" SOLELY FOR CONSPIRATORS & THEIR CLIQUE

When persons other than the conspirators and their clique follow their example and set up so-called "philanthropic" foundations that operate in exactly the same manner as does Rockefellers' "Philanthropic" Foundation Trust, they are pounced on by the conspirators' agents in the Federal government, as criminal devices. An enterprising group headed by Robert D. Hayes, of Barrington, Ill., established an organization that they named Americans Building Constitutionally, for the purpose of advising and aiding interested persons in following the Rockefellers and their fellow conspirators in dodging taxes through the establishment of foundations for the conduct of their affairs.(324) After it had helped eight hundred persons to follow in the Rockefeller "philanthropic" footsteps, the conspirators and their political henchmen became so alarmed about the cut in their tax loot that criminal investigations were launched by the attorney generals of California, Illinois, New York and other States into the competitor "philanthropies"; the Federal government, through the Internal Revenue Service launched a criminal investigation against the outfit (325); and Wright Patman took advantage of public interest in charges against foundations identical with those he had made selectively against certain larger foundations, and launched an investigation by his House Small Business Subcommittee. (324)

The discriminatory character of these investigations, persecutions and prosecutions of these rivals of Rockefellers' bogus "philanthropic" foundation setup is clearly revealed by the investigations launched by Gov. Nelson Rockefeller's minion, New York Attorney General Louis Lefkowitz, into competitor foundations. (326) His assistant, Julius Greenfield, head of the newly established Charitable Foundation Division, announced for him:

"...some men set up charity foundations and then used the money for their own businesses...to buy expensive paintings and sculpture for their own homes, to pay salaries to relatives, and for other personal uses."

Attorney General Lefkowitz refrained from launching prosecution of Gov. Rockefeller for the acknowledged and publicized use of the funds of the foundations that he controls, in violation of the law, to pay the expenses of his 1960 campaign for the Presidential nomination, brought to light by the IRS (79:231); and though he assured this author that he would do so, he carefully abstained even from an investigation of the proved and acknowledged charge of corrupt payment of his employees engaged in his private quest of the nomination with public tax funds, in flagrant criminal violation of the law. (79:203f;404)

## CONSPIRATORS RULE OUT TAX EXEMPTION
## FOR REAL CHARITY

Further evidence of the corrupt nature of the foundation and charity laws and their administration is offered by the treatment accorded the Happiness Exchange and associated Chai Foundation operated by Joe Rosenfeld over radio station WOR for giving direct charitable aid to the needy public. In 1963, the IRS revoked the exemption from taxation of the charitable funds of the foundation on the ground that, exactly as in the conspirators' foundations, part of the net earnings had benefited individuals associated with it. (327) Direct charity to anyone other than themselves and their agents is abhorrent to the Rockefeller "philanthropists"; and in the effort to eliminate it, they have had the IRS and other laws written to bar it; and long ago have taken over control of all "charitable" organizations, and incorporated them into their bogus "Charity" Trust. (56:17f) As a consequence individuals can not make personal charitable gifts, even to members of their own family, over and above the wholly inadequate dependent tax exemptions, without the additional penalty of denial of deductibility of the money from their incomes for tax purposes; and are penalized by having to pay taxes thereon. The only untaxed "charity" permitted by the law, is to the "philanthropic" conspirators and their organized "charity" rackets. (56) To them, we their American "peasants" are privileged to give 15 percent to 30 percent of our incomes without paying taxes thereon.

## CONSPIRATORS ORGANIZED TO PROTECT RACKETS & PROMOTE SUBVERSION

The conspirators do not rest for a moment on their laurels, with respect to their thievish, bogus "philanthropies"; nor do they let up for a moment in their program of subversion through the agency thereof. They have organized a Council on Foundations, located at 345 E. 46 St., New York, headed by David F. Freeman, that coordinates their activities and "sets up better communications between foundations and government," which is their way of stating they transmit their bosses' dictates to officials as a supposedly independent organization. (328) In a joint statement released on January 30, 1967 (329), two of the conspirators' agents, Dr. George Harrar, president of the Rockefeller Foundation, and McGeorge Bundy, president of the Ford Foundation over which the conspirators have gained absolute control in the manner predicted by this author in 1952 (15:348), announced their intent to devote their efforts to the promotion of the political activities of their Rockefeller bosses by agitation among the Negroes in the field of so-called "Civil Rights." Their "success" in that effort, in which they joined the Jesuits and other churchmen and the Communists, is attested by the Negro riots in which sections of Newark and Detroit that the conspirators seek to grab through their thievish "slum clearance and urban redevelopment" programs were burned down. This arson they "successfully" promoted, under direction of agitators whom they joined in the program for fostering crime among the Negroes that they launched in the government through their agent, Pres. Kennedy, under the prophetic designation of "Poverty Program." It is designed to impoverish the provident elements in the Community while enriching improvident and criminal elements, especially among the Negroes; and to buy their support for the conspirators' political agents.

The tactics whereby they are succeeding in inculcating subversion and treason through so-called "education" was perfectly demonstrated by their appointment of the Red, so-called "Liberal" ousted president of the University of California, Clark Kerr, to the post of chairman of a committee of their Carnegie Foundation for the "Advancement" of Teaching. Kerr was summarily dismissed by California officials for virtually encouraging treasonous rioting by the students on the Berkeley campus, led by a group of Communists, including the daughter of one of the top leaders of the Communists, Aptheker. (330) Nothing could make more clear the subversive, or perfidious, purpose of the conspirators in the operation of their tax-exempted, bogus "educational philanthropies" and their foundations. But so stupidly apathetic and/or paralyzedly helpless are the intelligently patriotic elements in the nation, and so subverted are the majority of their representatives in Congress, that nothing has been done to put an end to the financing of this treason at the expense of the nation that is being betrayed, through tax exemption granted the traitorous "philanthropists" who have the temerity and brashness to call themselves "moderates."

## NOT EVEN IN DEATH DO WE, THEIR "PEASANTS," ESCAPE THEIR TAX LOOTING

For the dual purpose of robbing the dead and of barring the way to the accumulation of wealth and the power therein involved, by others, the conspirators have converted the inheritance taxes, both Federal and State, into devices that serve them well. Whereas it depletes the estates and fortunes of others, often to the point of impoverishment of survivors, it in no wise materially affects adversely the conspirators' hold on their accumulated loot.

The inheritance tax treatments accorded the estates of John D. Rockefeller the First and his son, John D. the Second, his dynastic heir, make clear the extent of their looting of the nation even in death. As early as 1905, the swag of John D. was reliably estimated as more than $5 billion. Confirmation was given this estimate by his assertion that he had sluiced off into his bogus "philanthropies" a tithe, or ten percent of his loot. That "tithe" totalled more than $500 million, indicating that the estimate was low, if it was in error at all. In the years that followed, the depression, wars and revolutions engineered for the purpose of multiplying their looting, the depression of 1907, World War I, the Agricultural Panic, the 1929 Panic and the depression of the 1930's, the fortune multiplied to trillions of dollars, by the time piratic John D. the First died. His heirs are willing to acknowledge that his fortune was billions of dollars. This has been stated by one of their biographer pressagents, Jules Abels, in his book *The Rockefeller Billions*. (90) After his death, his total fortune was reported to the tax authorities to be a mere $25 million. And they never questioned it but were compelled to accept this crumb from their late master's table.

After the death of John D. the Second, several decades later when the 1905 fortune had multiplied many thousandfold, through the conspirators' control of the government, of their "Federal" Reserve racket and national wealth and the wealth of the entire world that was garnered as loot in World War II, his fortune was announced to be a mere $150 million; and at the same time it was announced that neither the Federal Government nor the State would receive a single penny from it in inheritance tax.

Columns, written by this author (354) and others, that ridiculed the alleged "pittance" left behind by a "poor Rockefeller" and berated the authorities for permitting them to evade the heavy inheritance tax levy on the estates of others, brought about a change of heart. In the final report accepted by the authorities, the total estate was reduced to a mere $140 million, and less than $5 million levied in inheritance taxes. In contrast, a short time before a mere millionaire had died and left a fortune acknowledged to be $80 million. More than $70 million inheritance tax was levied on his estate. Such is the power of the Rockefeller Dynasty over our Treasury.

It is estimated that the Rockefeller income at the time of his death was more than one million dollars a minute. This represents a total income of more than a trillion dollars a year. The capital value of such an income can scarcely be less than ten to fifteen trillion dollars. If our Federal and State governments had collected the tax levied by the law on such a fortune, the nation would have been relieved of payment of income taxes during the next half century or more. But the conspirators do not pay taxes. They levy and collect them.

## CONSPIRATORS "PERFECTED" THEIR "FEDERAL" RESERVE FOR MORE LOOT

Although World War I, in the words of Cordell Hull:

"...forced the further development of the income tax...And the conflict also assisted in putting into effect the Federal Reserve System..." (23)

the "Federal" Reserve fraud did not "develop" as smoothly as did the income tax swindle. The conspirators' war propaganda successfully duped the more gullible elements in the nation and silenced the wiser folks who knew better than to oppose the hysteria stirred up thereby. Rising wages in the war industries took some of the sting out of the rapidly mounting tax rate.

Their "F"R operates in the field of banking where many keenly alert opponents and competitors were acutely aware that they were fighting a ruthless band of racketeers bent on establishing an absolute monopoly by bankrupting the rival banks in order to close their doors and wipe out competition. Though the conspirators were intent on destroying their rivals and opponents, they craftily bided their time and waited until they had made them highly vulnerable before giving them the coup de grace.

## CONSPIRATORS FRUSTRATED IN TRAPPING U.S. IN THEIR LEAGUE OF NATIONS

World War I had incredibly enriched the conspirators through looting of the U.S. and of the entire world. As acknowledged by their agents who have been cited above, their "F"R had made possible the financing of the war at the expense of the mercilessly looted American taxpayers. At the same time, it had bankrupted both friends and allies, and foes; and put them at the mercy of the conspirators, who were in a position to dictate, to facilitate or hamper, their financial survival by the terms of repayment, if any, of their wartime debts and loans from the American taxpayers imposed by them through the Treasury.

The conspirators sought to capitalize on their financial power and their political ascendancy to effect the word-wide dictatorship that was envisaged and plotted originally by Jesuit Adam Weishaupt as a part of his Illuminist-Communist plot. Their servile puppet, Pres. Wilson, carried out this phase of their conspiracy by undertaking the organization of the League of Nations at Versailles. But they were blocked in securing the adherence of the U.S. to the League by a group of patriotic members of Congress who were keenly alert to the perfidy that was contemplated. The best that the conspirators could attain, as concerns the U.S., was to secure its representation by an "observer."

## CONSPIRATORS GAINED CONTROL OF WORLD'S BANKS OF ISSUE THROUGH LEAGUE

The conspirators were able, however, to further their purposes by appointing one of their trusted agents, their biographer (224) attorney, Raymond Fosdick, Secretary of the League. (88) One of his secretaries was the "crown prince" John D. Rockefeller the Third.

The arrangement proved quite fruitful for them in the matter of banking and finance. The impoverished lands all sought financial help from the U.S. The Secretariat of the League of Nations, Rockefeller and his agents, laid down the rule that no nation could get a so-called "loan" from the American taxpayers unless control of its bank of issue were turned over to the conspirators. Those lands that lacked banks of issue were required to permit the conspirators to set up for themselves private banks of issue there, patterned after their "Federal" Reserve fraud. This was the first step in the conspirators' plan to extend their looting of nations through control of money, credit and banking around the world. It also enabled them, subsequently through their IMF, to extend their so-called "gold standard" to those lands.

## 1929 PANIC & DEPRESSION OF 1930'S WERE EFFECTED & PROLONGED THRU "F"R

The tremendous financial and political power that the conspirators had usurped through their "F"R and other devices, made it a simple matter for them to create the boom of the 1920's by expansion of currency, credit and the industry, trade and commerce dependent thereon. It was an equally simple matter for them to precipitate panics by deliberate and malevolent manipulations of money and credit by use of the many devices with which they had armed themselves through their "Gold Standard" and "Federal" Reserve conspiracy.

Thus armed, the conspirators readily bring about booms and panics by "Federal" Reserve manipulations. Their arbitrary rulings on issue of currency, availability of credit, interest rates, discount rates, reserves, agreeing or refusing to let the Treasury use its own money and credit, so-called "open market operations" and other shady tricks, make them absolute bosses of our personal and national wealth, freely to manipulate it as their monopolistic racket for piratical looting of the nation whenever it suits their purposes.

Thus they engineered the "Agricultural Panic" of 1921 by raising the discount rate on agricultural loans to an exorbitant seven percent (7%). By this holdup, they forced the calling of agricultural loans, and threw the farmers, agricultural district banks and communities into bankruptcy, in revenge for their resisting domination by the conspirators and their "Federal" Reserve that was so clearly exposed thereby, as bogus. Hundreds of thousands of farmers lost their farms by foreclosure of their mortgages, and found their lifetime work and savings wiped out. Thousands of rural banks that were not controlled by the conspirators were shut down. And whole sections of the country were thrown into a depression by the conspirators through the "Federal" Reserve brigandage. They were thus enabled to steal millions of acres of rich farm land, by the process of foreclosure.

The conspirators then eased up on their gold manipulations, and dictated and directed their "Federal" Reserve policy of "easy money," with low interest and discount rates. They slyly created and stimulated by intensive propaganda an orgy of speculation, a tremendous boom in which their minions in the ranks of labor staged a constant series of strikes for the deliberate purpose of engineering a steadly rising wage spiral that inevitably priced their workers out of the labor market while enriching themselves; and these engendered a parallel boom in real estate, building and the stock market.

### CONSPIRATORS' "FOREIGN LOAN" SWINDLES

For the purpose of "sweetening the pot" for themselves, they intensified their planned looting of the country, by floating numerous bond issues in the names of lands around the world. These issues were forced by the conspirators, on their correspondent banks around the country; and they were palmed off on the sucker public as "high-grade investments." In numerous instances, only a minor fraction of "foreign loans" ever reached the lands in the names of which the bonds were issued, except for payoffs to political bosses of those lands. Most of the money was stolen by the conspirators, drained from the public into their own "tin boxes." Within a short time these bonds defaulted in interest payments and became almost worthless. Many of them were eventually "redeemed" at pennies on the dollar, paid to the public "investors." In the case of some of the German bond issues, the general public were paid off in worthless marks. But the conspirators' kinsman, John Foster Dulles, (15:267f) their agent in the operation of the State Department, is reported to have arranged to have the conspirators paid off in dollars.

The most spectacular of these bond swindles of the conspirators were perpetrated for them by their agent, the Swedish "financier," Ivar Krueger who specialized in match monopolies and in palming off entirely counterfeit bond issues on both bankers and the public. With few exceptions, all of his bonds became absolutely worthless when he disappeared from the public scene, a supposed suicide.

### CONSPIRATORS' GOLD MANIPULATIONS INTENDED
### TO PRECIPITATE DEPRESSION

The U.S. Department of Commerce Reports of 1928-32 (30) clearly depict the conspirators' manipulation of gold on which they based the contraction of currency and credit during the depression. In 1928 $620 million in gold was exported by way of New York, of which more than $500 million is reported to have been shipped out of the country by Rockefeller's Chase National Bank. The excess of gold exports over imports amounted to about $400 million. The resultant contraction of currency and credit effected by the conspirators on that basis was a key factor in precipitating the panic and depression.

Four years later, in 1932, the conspirators again resorted to gold exports for the purpose of deepening and prolonging the depression. It served the conspirators well in shutting down all banks by order of Rockefeller puppet, Pres. Franklin Delano Roosevelt, in order to eliminate their competitors who were not permitted to reopen. It also served as a pretext for robbing the citizenry of all their gold, by way of their "Federal" Reserve, of which more will be related anon.

The profits that accrued to these brigands through their manipulation of the gold shipped overseas, in the interim, was enormously enhanced by the control that they had gained over world finance by the extension of their "Federal" Reserve conspiracy through the League of Nations. The gold was shipped by the conspirators successively to France and England, where they had built up huge debts and obligations, in gaining monopolies of their commerce and industries, and then precipitated violent inflation by the various devices at their command. The conspirators were able to depress the value of the currencies in terms of gold and thereby wipe out their debts and obligations with relatively worthless, inflated pounds sterling and francs purchased with gold withdrawn from the U.S.; and to literally steal, with the aid of the exported gold, large blocks of industries in those lands, as they had previously done post-war, in the 1920's, in Germany, Austria, Italy and other lands.

Rockefeller kinsman, Sen. Joseph Clark, of Pennsylvania, who is acutely aware of the conspirators' "purpose and policy" (22), inadvertently exposed part of the truth in a discussion of the effect of the "Federal" Reserve "tight money" policy on homebuilders and small business men in a taped radio-television program broadcast over Pennsylvania stations on July 31, 1966, released in an AP dispatch.

He stated:

"We have a managed economy run by the Federal Reserve Board, chaired by Bill Martin. They could do away with this (money "shortage") overnight..."It's not a question of supply and demand in the monetary business. *It's A Man-Made Shortage.*" (208)

Sen. Clark resorted to the usual trick of blaming conspirators' agent, "Federal" Reserve Chairman Martin, for the skulduggery they had ordered; but made it clear that their "Federal" Reserve defrauds the nation and rigs its economy.

CHAPTER XIV

ROCKEFELLER USED F.D.R. TO LOOT NATION'S GOLD
THROUGH THE "FEDERAL" RESERVE

"...the wise course for the Administration to have followed was an early return to the gold standard with full convertibility of paper money into gold coin..." (24:186)

"The continuance of the abandonment of the old gold standard

90

*at this time...Was Not A Matter Of Necessity, But A Matter Of Deliberate Choice." Kemmerer: The ABC Of The Federal Reserve System (24:185)*

John D. Rockefeller's piratical descendants have cockily thrown his stealthy caution to the winds; and brazenly carry on, in the open, his malevolent plot. They have the same pathologic, mad fear of poverty and of being stripped of their loot and booty, and of their personal "security," either by more cunning and ruthless criminals than themselves, or by revolt of a nation aroused by their vicious conspiracy. Their fear of reactivation of the hatred bred in an erstwhile more virile American people by the criminal activities on which the wealth and power of their Dynasty rests, that, at the beginning of the century, impelled the Supreme Court to brand them as conspirators that menace the survival of our Republic, lingers. But it has been abated by the success of their bogus "philanthropies" and the poisoning of all media of mass communication with false propaganda regarding their "benevolence," that has robbed many of us, their American "peasants," as they delight in calling us, of our native intelligence. This process has been carried to the point that the nation fawns upon them as "benefactors" and scrambles to elect and appoint them to public office, thereby speeding their dictatorship over the nation and facilitating their looting us.

The average American has been so completely brainwashed and duped, especially if educated, as to make an accomplished fact the objective stated by John D. and his almoner, Gates, in their Occasional Letter No. 1 as the purpose of their "educational" conspiracy, to wit:

"In our dreams, we have limitless resources, and *The People Yield Themselves With Perfect Docility To Our Molding Hands...* and unhampered by tradition, *We Work Our Own Good Will Upon A Grateful And Responsive Rural Folk."* (15:29)

The public has no suspicion of the conspirators' criminal psychopathy (79) and is duped into electing them to public office even though they acknowledge themselves to be "Public Enemy No. 1;" and are prepared to accept them as our dictators and rulers even though they frankly confess betrayal of the nation and the world. (106:132)

The public are completely oblivious of the conspirators' abysmal scorn of them that is clearly expressed in everything they seek to impose on it: "modern art" (209); "purpose and policy" (22); "creative statemanship"; "the future of Federalism" (133); "civil rights" wrongs; drugs and "hippies"; ruinous financial, monetary, economic, political and "international" schemes. The public does not recognize that it has been duped into accepting the patterns of thought, belief, conduct, attire and mode of life that will destroy it as a nation.

The public has been tricked, more particularly the "youth" element, into believing that in these measures, so cunningly directed by the conspirators, it is engaging in a "spontaneous revolution." With ruthless contempt and disregard of human rights, the nation's youth are drafted, exposed to slaughter in pestholes around the world that are not and never will be a part of our Constitutional Republic to which alone they owe loyalty,—for expansion of the "One (Rock-

91

efeller) World" Empire. In this process there is sacrificed their "freedom of life, liberty and pursuit of happiness." The conspirators and their puppets mock their victims with pretenses such as giving the Vietnamese the "freedom of choice" that thereby are denied to their American victims who are further mocked by bearing the burden of taxation that pays for their victimization by the bogus "philanthropist" racketeers.

The pirates have ample reason to exult in having reduced the American victims of their "foundations," by subversion masked as "education," to the level of imbecility and "mass man." This has served to allay the conspirators' cowardly, psychopathic fears; and has served to give them "Dutch courage." Nevertheless they have provided themselves with remote and inaccessible estates in all parts of the world (such as Nelson Rockefeller's widely publicized Venezuelan fortress estate), vehicles ready to take them there at a moment notice, and their own bodyguards that represent a standing army of thugs and gangsters.

Thus shielded, the present generation of Rockefellers, according to their biographers (17), have set themselves the goal of proving themselves "worthy" of their psychopathic criminal paternal ancestry on the one hand, and their slightly less psychopathic Red, abolitionist and so-called "religious" and "liberal" maternal ancestry. (79) They were "educated" in the Red, or "liberal," tradition, in frankly Communist schools, (15:79) institutions that have been richly subsidized by the conspirators through their General Education Board and by other foundations founded or taken over by them and incorporated into their "Philanthropic Foundation Trust." (15:341)

> "They...received their preliminary education at the Lincoln School of Teachers College (Columbia University). The school was guided by the Marxist 'liberalism' of John Dewey and his "progressive education" so dear to the heart of the Communist. The school was heavily supported by the General Education Board and was one of the strongholds of the Rockefeller brand of totalitarian indoctrination of the younger generation, a 'model school' from which the schools of the rest of the country were infected. But thanks to home influence...the boys penetrated the moronic concept of Marxism to the discernment of the device for attainment of power that is the true essence of Marxism; and they have become adept in its use." (15:41)

ROCKEFELLER "CROWN PRINCES," JOHN D. III & IV
SWITCH LOYALTY TO JAPAN & ASIA

Upon completion of their college education and their traditional home training (79:7f), the princes of the Rockefeller Dynasty divided the world into realms among themselves, each choosing his respective principality and domain. John D. III chose Japan & Asia as his domain. He continued his Red indoctrination in the Rockefeller-Soviet Institute of Pacific Relations (IPR) and its ultra-treasonous *AMERASIA* subsidiary (15;103;107:158f)

In this Rockefeller-financed agency, John D. III associated with Alger Hiss, Owen Lattimore; and closely with Frederick Vanderbilt Field, Communist editor of the *New Masses*, whom he served as secretary at its 1929 Kyoto conference where foundation was laid for treasonous engineering of the 1941 Japanese attack on Pearl

Harbor, with the cooperation of Richard Sorge, Soviet spy, operating in the Tokyo German Embassy, as acknowledged in the September 24, 1964 issue of Pravda. Sorge, grandson of F. Adolf Sorge, Secretary of Moses M. M. Levy, alias Karl Marx, and of the "First" International, transferred to U.S. was supplied by the conspirators with spies by Rockefeller-financed IPR to divert the Jap attack from the Soviets to the U.S. to trap us in W. W. II. (15:223f;91) At Kyoto Rockefeller's predatory interest in Japan was kindled, satisfaction of which cost the U.S. and the world untold war suffering.

Correspondence seized by the subcommittee headed by Sen. Joseph McCarthy and in the possession of this author, reveal that Crown Prince John D. III was not a stranger in the mahogany-finished office camouflaged as a dilapidated barn on the Lee, Mass. farm of YMCA and IPR secretary and CFR agent, Edward C. Carter, that McCarthy described as the most dangerous spynest in the country.

John D. III has spent a large part of his time, since the war, in Japan, supervising the low labor cost industries, seized as their war loot, that flood the American and world markets with low-priced exports. These Japanese manufactures have been traced, in wartime, to North Korea, North Vietnam and other of our foes. Among the products thus traced have been materiel of war, including oil, arms, munitions and electronic devices. When not used to mow down our GIs, they serve to wipe out the jobs of the very American workers who are taxed to defray the costs of the Rockefeller "Crusades" and are drafted to fight in them to make possible the conspirators' plunder.

John D. the Third, like his brother Nelson, served in World War II after helping engineer it,—as far away from the front as possible. He held a swivel-chair job in Washington, as executive of the American Red Cross that ever thereafter bore the stamp of his quest for "profits," or loot. With few exceptions, all of the Rockefeller heirs have followed the familial tradition of dodging military service in the wars that they engineer for the expansion of their empire.

After the war, during the period of American occupation of Japan, John D. III with his wife and retinue have spent most of their time in Japan. They learned the Japanese language, customs and other essentials for ingratiating themselves with the Japanese. John D. III personally directed his Japanese agents and employees in the conduct of the Japanese businesses that they have grabbed as the loot of the victory gained for them by GI self-paid mercenaries. With a view to having the Rockefeller "Crown Prince" undergo a seven year period of training to take over their Japanese "duchy," John D. the Fourth was sent to live in Japan on the "maximum allowance the family could afford" twenty seven dollars a month. His reprehensible activities in Japan will be related.

*Amerasia* involved the theft of about 1700 "top secret" documents from various Government agencies, including the Army and the Navy, by an organization that numbered in its ranks known Communist agents. These documents were adequate to enable deciphering of our code in use in the war. The crime involved ranks as treason and in wartime is usually penalized by death.

The key executives and editors of *Amerasia* included:

William W. Lockwood, editor and successor in that capacity of

93

Owen Lattimore, both of whom were members of Rockefellers' top so-called *"Establishment"* agency, their Council on Foreign Relations, and intimate associates of theirs. Subsequently, Lockwood headed the Woodrow Wilson school of diplomacy, Princeton University. Lattimore headed the Johns Hopkins University school of diplomacy.

Philip Jaffe, an acknowledged Communist agent.

By special arrangement made possible by the influence of the traitorous thieves, the case was heard before a judge chosen by them for the purpose, in the early hours of the morning, long before courts usually open, in order to make sure that neither the public or the press would witness the proceedings. Absolutely rigid censorship was maintained regarding the hearing. The only culprit penalized by the court was Philip Jaffe, who was merely fined the sum of five hundred dollars. (15:287;103)

The most ironic phase of the case did not leak out until years later. This may be the first publication of the fact. *Amerasia Was Published Under A Contract With Our "New Deal" Government Which Required Payment Of The Cost Of Publication In Advance! Such Was The Power Of The Conspirators That The Administration Financed Treason Against Itself!*

The treasonous Institute of Pacific Relations served the conspirators faithfully in diverting the Japanese attack from their Soviet partners to the American fleet they ordered bottled in at Pearl Harbor.

## NELSON ALDRICH ROCKEFELLER HAS USURPED RULE OF WESTERN HEMISPHERE

Nelson Aldrich Rockefeller, though unable, according to himself and his pressagents, to spell, or read or write except with difficulty and reluctance, (79:66;66) graduated with high honors and with a Phi Beta key, from that "center of culture and higher education," Dartmouth University. Directly thereafter, he married the extremely plain but inordinately wealthy Mary Todhunter Clark, Philadelphia "mainline" heiress of a former Pennsylvania Railroad president. The newlyweds' honeymoon was a trip around the world that was a continous round of receptions by the royalties of the various lands visited, who bent in obeisance to the Rockefeller Dynasty that had so far outstripped them in their racketeering. For, the crowned heads of the world were acutely aware of the fact, that the United States had become a minor Rockefeller duchy. As early as 1913, this situation had become quite obvious to visitors from abroad although it was not suspected by most of us. Grand Duke Alexander, of Russia visited our shores after an absence of twenty years, and noted, he relates in his autobiography entitled *Once A Grand Duke:* (80:242)

"The rustic republic of Jefferson was rapidly giving way to the *Empire Of The Rockefellers*, but the average mentality of the man-in-the-street had not caught up with this new order of things..."

Nor have the overwhelming majority of the people caught up with it yet, so well have they been brainwashed into regarding the conspirators as "philanthropists" by the pressagents, propagandists and more "erudite" perverters of the truth. On the other hand, the

94

Grand Duke himself was probably unaware that it was the same Rockefellers who had shaken Czarist Russia in the oily revolutionary attempt of 1905 and were preparing to overthrow it.

## NELSON ROCKEFELLER LAUNCHED ON CAREER AS "TEN PERCENTER:" SPECIAL WORK INC.

Immediately after his return from his "grand tour" of the world, the "grandiose ideas," the delusions of grandeur, with which Nelson Rockefeller acknowledges he is afflicted (66:14;79:65f) became dominant. He demanded that he be given the major voice that the "matureness" of his years, (he was then twenty-five years old) and his "vast experience" merited in the Dynasty's affairs, rackets and conspiracies. (66:66) Joe Alex Morris reported, on behalf of his Rockefeller patron, that "he pushed his father to give him greater authority in family affairs." This puts the situation in rather mild terms. The truth of the matter is that Nelson Rockefeller, in effect pushed aside his timid, fearful, "odd' father and took over control as his domain of the Western Hemisphere.

Nelson Rockefeller took over the construction of Rockefeller Center. He handled the job with an eye to personal profit which his biographers make clear is always his first and foremost objective. (17:33) With two friends he organized Turck & Co. for collecting "kickbacks" on supplies and contracts involved in the construction of the Center. Before long, the business was broadened to include "tenpercenting" on all types of contracts that Rockefeller influence could swing, including government contracts with the firms that they control. This deal became so lucrative that Rockefeller eliminated his partners and incorporated it under the name of *"Special Work Inc."* in the Rockefeller Brothers "philanthropy."

## MAFFIA AGENTS INSURE "PERFECT" ROCKEFELLER LABOR RELATIONS

Rockefeller boasts that he had no labor difficulties in the construction of their Center. Under the circumstances, this is readily understandable. For when the construction laborers began to rebel against the munificent depression wage, set by the conspirators through an NRA code, of fifteen dollars per week, they threatened to organize and strike. Joe Adonis, one of the ringleaders of their Maffia and Murder Inc. set-up (94:183,312) was assigned the task of "convincing" the workers that they did not want a wage increase, it is reported. His efforts met with their usual "success." But when Adonis demanded a fee commensurate with his "services" that was regarded "in line of duty and uncalled for" by his employers, it is related, he was rewarded by deportation. Under such circumstances and auspices, "perfect labor relations" are to be expected.

## "NEW DEALER" NELSON ROCKEFELLER HELPED ROOSEVELT PLAN WORLD WAR II.

The most profitable phase of Nelson Rockefeller's assumption of dominion over the Western Hemisphere was his role as "principal adviser" of Pres. Franklin D. Roosevelt. (39) The conspirators' tactics in putting Wilson and Roosevelt in the White House were identical: doublecrossing and ousting the Republicans. Failure of Republican Pres. Hoover, a long-time Rockefeller agent, to abjectly serve

95

them and their Standard Oil interests in China by declaring war on Japan accounted for it. The conspirators had long enjoyed an absolute monopoly of the sale of kerosene for the lamps that they had "philanthropically" given the Chinese peasants. For lighting their "gift" lamps, kerosene yielded the Rockefeller-Standard Oil outfits in China more than a dollar a gallon, as compared with a U.S. domestic price of five to ten cents. This unconscionable gouging of the Chinese was made possible by suppression of oil production from the numerous oilfields in that land, through the Soong agents of the conspirators and their control of the Chinese government. The manner in which the conspirators trained their employees for mulcting of the Chinese was told in the book *Oil For The Lamps Of China*, (353) by an authoress, Vera Teasdale, who was the wife of one of the Standard Oil employees engaged in that task in China.

Revolting warlords of several Chinese provinces granted a concession to the Japanese to drill for oil, in violation of the conspirators prohibition of it. Large oilfields were brought into production in those provinces by the Japanese. Under pressure of the conspirators, the Japanese were driven out by the Chinese government after spending millions on the development of the fields. (15:150) The Japanese vowed to return and seize China, if necessary, to recover their oil investment. Jap attitude toward Rockefeller-Standard Oil interests who they knew had been responsible for their ousting, can be surmised. It found its expression, when Japan invaded China in the 1930's, in their destruction, wherever they conquered in China, of Rockefeller-Standard Oil property to the extent of billions of dollars in value, as their first acts. (15:381)

## QUAKER PRES. HOOVER REFUSED TO DECLARE WAR DEMANDED BY CONSPIRATORS

In this situation, complete subservience of the State Department, of which John D. had openly boasted (16:63), was of no avail unless it could bring about a declaration of war on Japan by the U.S. and send the Armed Forces to the conquered areas of China to recover and protect their loot. Henry L. Stimson, who like all Secretaries of State of the past half century, was a Rockefeller attorney and agent, approached Pres. Hoover on behalf of the conspirators with their proposition that they would terminate the depression and call off the campaign of vilification instituted against him, if he would declare war against Japan, and send American Armed Forces to rescue their properties in China.

## HOOVER STANDS OUT AMONG PRESIDENTS AS GREAT PATRIOT

Though Hoover had loyally served the interests of the conspirators throughout his career (331), he refused to go along with them in precipitating a war because that violated his conscience as a Quaker. In this respect, he stands out creditably among the Presidents of the past half century; for no other of them has refused to accept the dictates of the conspirators to involve us in wars for the expansion of the Rockefeller Empire.

Prof. Harry Elmer Barnes, distinguished historian, author and editor, who had long been "a fair-haired boy" in the camp of the

96

conspirators, but as a loyal American, revolted against their treason, relates this incident in his pamphlet entitled *The Struggle Against the Historical Blackout*, and protests against the deliberate falsification of history financed by the Rockefellers with their tax-exempt loot, in order to suppress the truth of charge of treason hurled against them by kinsman Harry Shippe Truman (15:3f), and avert the wrath of the nation. (32:43)

Hoover had previously made clear, in 1931, to his Cabinet his attitude toward the treasonous proposal made by Stimson on behalf of the conspirators, in patriotic terms that accounted for the continuance by them of the depression and their vilification campaign against the President (that so closely paralleled that which they launched two decades later against another patriot, Sen. Joseph McCarthy) in the following words:

> "These acts (the Japanese invasion of China and their destruction of Rockefeller-Standard Oil property there) do not imperil the freedom of the American people, the economic or moral future of our people. *I do not propose ever to sacrifice American life for anything short of this.*"

It is regrettable that these words have not been engraved on a multitude of memorials to Pres. Hoover. For they rank among the sublimest and most patriotic words uttered by a loyal American President. If our country is to survive the treasonous plots of the conspirators, these words will have to become the sentiment of the nation and its leaders. And the traitorous plot to substitute subversive "internationalism" or religious hypocrisy for the Constitution, must be defeated, and the "international" involvements into which they have entangled us, such as their dis-"United" Nations, must be undone.

## SHOULD NOT PRES. F. D. ROOSEVELT BE RATED AS TRAITOROUS AGENT?

Shortly thereafter, the conspirators' errand-boy, Secretary of State Henry L. Stimson, approached Gov. Franklin D. Roosevelt with their war proposal that had been patriotically rejected by Pres. Hoover. Roosevelt, who had already placed himself under the domination of the conspirators by accepting from them bribes in the form of large contributions to his pseudo-philanthropic business enterprise, Georgia Warm Springs (95:40; 56:82; 7:116) figuratively clapped his hands with glee at having his own war to "immortalize" him in history, and eagerly joined the conspirators.

In so doing, Roosevelt was merely falling in line with the family tradition of leadership of the Illuminist-Communist conspiracy in our country since pre-Revolutionary days, as a consequence of which more than a dozen U.S. Presidents are to be found on their family tree. (29) Under the designation *"America's Royal Family,"* Eleanor Roosevelt, Franklin's "colorful" consort, hung it in the Hyde Park memorial to Roosevelt betrayals of our nation and the world to the "tender mercies" of the Soviets, in which we are still clutched. It remained there until this author spotlighted it in his *Strange Death of Franklin Delano Roosevelt.* (7:10; 332:IV:1)

## ELEANOR ROOSEVELT'S COLOR STRAIN

In this connection, it is interesting to note that Eleanor Roosevelt refrained from hanging in that "chamber of horrors" the family tree of her maternal ancestry. In a letter to the author, she boasted of her maternal tree tracing back to the Livingstons. When that family tree was traced, it was found to lead back to Edwin Livingston, Mayor of the City of New York in the early days of the nineteenth century, who was indicted for the theft of more than forty-five thousand dollars of Federal funds, and fled to New Orleans to escape prosecution. There, as refugee from justice, he undertook to recoup his fortunes by stealing Federal lands along the Mississippi River; and incidentally introduced the colored strain in the bloodline that later mingled with the Marrano, Van Rosenvelt strain.

Sumner Welles was Roosevelt's cousin in the Livingston strain. His appointment as Undersecretary of State was dictated by Eleanor to Cordell Hull who was rewarded by the post of Secretary of State for his services to the conspirators in looting the nation by way of the Federal income tax bill which he had introduced in the House. Welles retained his post for ten years, until his "homophile" vagaries became notorious as a result of a scandal in connection with his representation of our government at the Rio de Janeiro Conference. His article that was subsequently published in Harper's Magazine, entitled *Roosevelt & the Far East* (96), fully confirmed Roosevelt's eagerness to join the conspirators in their war plans that had been presented to him by Stimson prior to his nomination and election.

In 1940, Stimson was rewarded by Pres. Roosevelt with the post of "bipartisan" Secretary of War, from which he could supervise the execution of the plot on behalf of the conspirators. (48) Stimson himself made no effort to mask his role in his biography (128) that was ghosted for him by McGeorge Bundy, Rockefeller agent, member of their Council on Foreign Relations, later planted as chief "adviser" of Presidents Kennedy and Johnson.

## "GRANDIOSE" NELSON ROCKEFELLER WAS ROOSEVELT'S NEW DEAL "ADVISER" & BOSS

Following the purchase of the Presidency by the conspirators for Roosevelt, as it was purchased for numerous other Presidents in the past half century (including McKinley, Wilson, Eisenhower and Kennedy), Nelson Rockefeller assumed the role of chief "New" Deal adviser of the conspirators' Presidential puppet. This role has been acknowledged by the Rockefeller Dynasty in its official publication, the New York Times, on page 88 of its magazine section of May 22, 1960, in an article by Richard and Daz Harkness entitled *"Where Are Those Rampaging New Dealers?"* that was intended to aid "New" Dealer Nelson Rockefeller's attempt to seize the Republican Presidential nomination. The article states, among other facts:

"Rockefeller became a Roosevelt intimate, spending secret holidays with the President at Shangi-la (now Camp David)..." (39:88)

Rockefeller was boss of social service racketeer, Red, corrupt, fortune-hunting philanderer, and intimate of Eleanor Roosevelt, Harry L. Hopkins (15; 79; 95; 210), who was the real leader of the Communist Hal Ware cell in the Department of Agriculture, and initially used him to direct Pres. Roosevelt on the public stage. "New" Dealer Nelson Rockefeller was from the start the unofficial, behind-the-scenes, "closest adviser" of Roosevelt and policy dictator. (39) Rockefeller applied his "mature wisdom" that he had acquired from his Red and Communist teachers and his "wealth of experience" acquired in his life span of twenty-five years, to the nation's problems, most of which had been precipitated by his Dynasty, in advising Roosevelt to adopt policies that would be most profitable to himself and his family interests. In so doing he followed the Rockefeller "instincts."

SON-IN-LAW DALL CONFIRMED CONSPIRATORS' "EXPLOI-TATION" OF PRES. ROOSEVELT

The story released by Rockefeller's pressagents in the New York Times, as part of his buildup for the Republican Presidential nomination (39:88) was backhandedly confirmed by the President's son-in-law, Curtis B. Dall. In his biography entitled *F.D.R. My Exploited Father-In-Law*, he related that the legislation robbing Americans of their gold was "inspired" and dictated "from above." He related that that bill and other legislation had been prepared, in New York, months in advance, and had been rushed through Congress. (376:90f) He identified the plotters and planners of the legislation as members of Rockefeller's Council on Foreign Relations. But either naively, or to serve the purpose of the conspirators, he attributed the control of the CFR to the conspirators' Jewish, "pro-Zionist" agents instead of attributing it to the Rockefeller bosses and financiers of the Council. (15:237) He related that he was convinced that Roosevelt was ordered to raise the price of gold by the "C.F.R. bankers" who had planned it long in advance. (376:93); and that it had been facilitated by their bipartisan control of both the Republican and the Democratic Parties.

Insight into the motivation and veracity of Dall in his attribution of the source of the "Gold Order" can be derived from his personal business interests and connections. At the time of the "New" Deal, before his divorce, Dall was an employee of the Rockefeller dominated Kuhn Loeb & Co. banking firm, and an intimate friend of its Warburg partners. They were, in turn, the dominant Jewish banking firm represented in the membership of Rockefellers' CFR; and it would have been they who would have had sufficient support in dictation of "New" Deal financial policy as agents of the conspirators, in which case Dall would have been "in the know," and would be specific regarding who gave the order for the gold price increase. Since then, however, Dall has left the firm, and become an independent and not too successful operator who has sought the support of Rev. Billy Hargis and his anti-semitic "Christian Crusade," which has served the conspirators, as has Rev. Gerald K. Smith, in collaborating with them and diverting attention from their treason by blaming their Jewish, Zionist agents.

## CONSPIRATORS CLOSED & LOOTED COMPETITOR BANKS & "PERFECTED" "FEDERAL" RESERVE

The conspirators used gold exports to contract currency volume, create runs on competitive banks, and prolong and intensify the depression. With this criminal purpose, President-elect Roosevelt, acting on the "counsel" of the conspirators, was "advised" to refuse to join outgoing Pres. Hoover in measures that would relieve the depression, and thereby reduce their loot. Since the conspirators privately control their "Federal" Reserve System, Pres. Hoover was unable to force it to perform its supposed function, to relieve the monetary stringency, even though the Administration was then represented on its Board by the Secretary of the Treasury and Comptroller of the Currency.

The conspirators' malevolent, thievish purpose more clearly came to light when Roosevelt, on the counsel of his closest "adviser," Rockefeller, ordered a shutdown of all banks from March 4 to March 15, 1933. No banks were permitted to reopen except by consent of the conspirators and their virtually private "Federal" Reserve fraud. This enabled them to bankrupt banking institutions that competed with their own that in many instances were more insolvent than their doomed competitors.

The conspirators' banks, that were often truly hopelessly insolvent, were given unlimited support with taxpayers' funds by way of "loans" from the Treasury, from the Reconstruction Finance Corporation and numerous agencies that were set up for the purpose at the expense of the taxpayers. The Reconstruction Finance Corporation, that was established during the Hoover regime to bail out the conspirators' banks, in 1932 alone, advanced more than $850,000,000 of tax funds derived from depositors who had been looted, to 5,600 conspirators' banks, members of their "Federal" Reserve. In many instances these banks had been plunged into insolvency by looting from within by the conspirators or their agents. In only one instance was a defalcating agent of theirs jailed for his crime.

The treatment accorded by the conspirators to competitor banks, even though they were completely solvent, contrasted sharply with that accorded their own banks, even those that were rendered insolvent by looting. This was especially true of banks controlled by Jews that were not affiliated with them. A clear-cut instance of the deliberate purpose of the conspirators with regard to these competitors is offered by the case of the solvent, Jewish-controlled Manufacturers Trust Co. of New York. It was threatened with permanent closure and bankruptcy by looting through forced liquidation, by agents of the conspirators. Rather than submit their depositors to merciless looting, the honorable principals turned the bank over to them.

## CLOSED BANK OF U.S. PROVED SOLVENT BY THIEVISH "LIQUIDATION"

Another instance of bankrupting of a Jewish bank that proved to be completely solvent even under looting by forced liquidation, was the Bank of the U.S. of New York City. A State bank, it was shut down on behalf of the conspirators by Gov. Franklin D. Roosevelt. Roosevelt's firm, Roosevelt & O'Connor, from which he did not resign even after his inauguration (7), is reported to have participated in the looting, or so-called "liquidation," of the bank's assets through the appointment of an agent, Carl Austrian, to take charge of it. The first fee received by the liquidator, after a few months' work, was reported to have been about one million dollars. In spite of forced liquidation of the assets of the bank in the lowest depths of the depression and the merciless looting involved, the solvency of the Bank of the U.S. was proved by the payment to the depositors of almost one hundred cents on the dollar.

## ABOUT 15,000 BANKS & THEIR DEPOSITORS BANKRUPTED IN HALF DECADE BY "F"R

A tabulation of bank suspensions and failures effected by the conspirators through their fraudulent "Federal" Reserve that was exultantly published by its subsidiary, the Federal Deposit Insurance Corp., in its report for 1934 (31:92) impressively illustrates its effectiveness, as follows:

| YEAR | BANK SUSPENSIONS | LIABILITIES |
|---|---|---|
| 1908* | 178 | $222,316,000 |
| 1921** | 505 | 627,402,000 |
| 1929 | 659 | 230,634,000 |
| 1921-1929 | 5,714 | 1,626,000,000 |
| 1930 | 1,352 | 853,000,000 |
| 1931 | 2,294 | 1,690,699,000 |
| 1932 | 1,456 | 715,626,000 |
| 1933 | 4,004 | 3,598,957,000 |

*Following 1907 panic. **Year of "Agricultural Panic."

"This disgraceful record," wrote Prof. E. Kemmerer, one of the conspirators' monetary experts and agents, "was unequaled in any country" (31:168), a signal tribute to the thoroughness of the conspirators' looting of their rivals.

In passing, it might be noted how clearly is refuted, by the above instances of treatment accorded banks controlled by Jews who were not agents of the conspirators, the myth of Jewish control of our banking system that their pressagents continually turn out as a smokescreen for their thievery. The conspirators went one step further in diverting public hostility from themselves to their Jewish agents by replacing their Secretary of the Treasury, William H. Woodin. He had "reorganized" the Treasury to serve their purposes and placed in its posts their agents, including Nelson Rockefeller's collaborator, Lauchlin Currie, associate of Alger Hiss and other traitorous Communist agents from their Council on Foreign Relations, and his pawn, Harry Dexter White. Their new "fall guy" Secretary of the Treasury was Jewish apple grower Henry Morgenthau Jr. Morgenthau's naive diary is so damaging to them that they have suppressed its publication, except for some carefully edited and expurgated portions of it. (97; 101; 385) Morgenthau, a Hyde Park neighbor of Roosevelt's, is reported to have helped him financially, in some of the scrapes into which the latter's notorious incompetence and lack of honesty and principle had led him; and was acceptable to the conspirators as a foil for their crimes, and as a "red herring" to cover up their thievery.

# CONSPIRATORS LOOTED NATION OF GOLD THROUGH THEIR "FEDERAL" RESERVE

The Executive Order that Roosevelt issued at the instance of his "intimate" adviser, on March 6, 1933, not only provided for the shutting down and looting of the banks, but also prepared the way for the conspirators' theft of the nation's gold through their "Federal" Reserve, by blocking the exchange or transfer of gold, and "taking the nation off the gold standard." The conspirators had transferred their gold holding oversea in the years prior, and were not affected by the order, which enabled them to filch the gold holdings of the private citizenry and the gold remaining in the Treasury.

To give an aspect of legality to this arrant thievery, Roosevelt was advised to simultaneously call a special session of Congress to pass what was labelled "emergency legislation" to ratify the illegitimate bank closing and the crooked gold order. This the "rubber stamp" Congress dutifully did in the Emergency Banking Act of March 9, 1933. And it also empowered Roosevelt, on behalf of the conspirators, to license the reopening of any banks that they chose to reopen, whenever and on whatever terms they chose.

One month later, on April 5, 1933, Roosevelt issued on behalf of the conspirators an Executive Order that required the surrender, by holders, of all gold and gold certificates to their "Federal" Reserve Banks. Two weeks later, Roosevelt issued, on their behalf, another Executive Order that barred all "earmarking" or export of gold. The conspirators thus assured themselves that none of our gold could escape them by the same device whereby they had prepared their piratical coup. Roosevelt followed in the footsteps of his corrupt and thievish cousin, Pres. Ulysses Grant, in rigging a "Gold Corner" for the conspirators. He went one step further. He became the "spotter" and "finger man" for the brigands and converted the Government into an agency for carrying out their looting of the nation's gold.

Nelson Rockefeller, in his omniscence and "supreme wisdom," Roosevelt's "intimate adviser," had overlooked the obvious fact that the nation still accepted the Constitution as its basic law in spite of the emasculation of it that had been effected by the conspirators. The Executive Order on gold was obviously un-Constitutional. In a letter to the New York Times of October 11, 1933 (355) that escaped the then imperfectly developed censorship, this author pointed out that though the Constitution permits the confiscation of property for public interest and benefit, under the eminent domain clause, it does not permit it for the profit of a private corporation, such as the "Federal" Reserve System or its principals. This section of the Constitution, it should be mentioned in passing, has since been completely nullified by the conspirators to ease the way for their gold and numerous other steals, including the land-grabbing so-called "slum clearance and urban redevelopment" racket. (79)

Concern for the surviving public regard for the Constitution impelled Roosevelt, acting on behalf of the conspirators, to silence the controversy thus stirred up, by requiring his "rubber stamp"

Congress to pass the Gold Reserve Act of January 30, 1934. It appeared to provide for vesting the title of the gold, gold notes and bullion looted from the nation in the Treasury. That would be Constitutional, provided that it was requisite to serve public interest. (25:210) But instead it provided for turning over to the conspirators' "Federal" Reserve title to the gold, in the form of gold certificates that constituted certificates of deposit, or warehouse receipts for specific amounts of gold. (25:206: Sec. 14c) In short, the bill was designed to dupe the nation with respect to the theft of its gold and the violation of the Constitution involved.

There are a number of interesting features about these gold certificates. They are issued to the conspirators exclusively, through their "Federal" Reserve, in amount exactly equal to the gold held. The conspirators do not tolerate fraudulent overissue of the notes in the ratio of two and a half dollars for each dollar worth of gold held, as in the issues, under the "Gold Standard," of the Treasury to the public; or a four to one ratio, as in the notes issued to the public by the "Federal" Reserve itself. They tolerated no such fraud on themselves as perpetrated on the public!

The notes are issued only in denominations of ten thousand dollars each, and are redeemable solely by the conspirators through their "Federal" Reserve. Though the "F"R may withdraw the gold from the Treasury solely on demand of foreign central banks, in settlement of unfavorable trade balances, this presents no problem to the conspirators. For, as has been related, they had gained control of foreign central banks through their League of Nations.

The irony of this "trade balance" feature, as will be recounted in a later chapter, rest in the fact that the sums involved in the so-called "foreign claims" that create the unfavorable balances that the conspirators use as a device to divert and "earmark" their gold, is and always has been, during this era, largely looted from the U.S. by a never-ending array of frauds that include: flotation of loans to themselves in the names of foreign lands, few of which were honored even by payment of interest, until the conspirators had bought them up at bankrupt prices from the sucker public and from the victimized and often thereby bankrupted rural and correspondent banks that were duped into purchasing them; UNRRA; Lend Lease; the "Marshall" Plan; the Point IV Program; the AID; the Alliance for Progress, and numerous others that have been promoted for the looting of the nation by the "intimate" adviser of Roosevelt and his successors, Nelson Rockefeller.

## THEFT OF NATION'S GOLD: "NOT A .. NECESSITY, BUT AN ACT OF .. CHOICE"

For a frank and honest evaluation of the conspirators' "New" Deal gold policy, one can do no better than to accept the statement made by one of their accepted authorities on the subject of money, who is cited by them as one of "the seven men in the world who understand money" — as they wish it "understood" — Edwin Walter Kemmerer, Walker Professor of International Finance at Princeton University. In his book, *The ABC of the Federal Reserve Act*, he wrote:

"'...the emergency which justified temporary drastic measures

103

during the banking holiday was passed. The situation was well in hand...the wise course for the Administration to have followed was an early return to the gold standard with full convertibility of paper money into gold coin...(24:186)

"The continuance of the abandonment of the old gold coin standard at this time, in the judgment of the writer, was not a matter of necessity, but a matter of deliberate choice..." (24:185)

In short, it was motivated by the conspirators' chronic "choice" to loot the nation.

## URGENCY IN "CHOICE": PREPARATION FOR PLANNED WORLD WAR II

Actually, however, there was some urgency motivating the conspirators' "choice" that was unknown to Kemmerer. The original "Federal" Reserve Act was planned by the conspirators as an urgent prelude of their deliberate precipitation of World War I for the expansion of their oily Empire, at the expense of the nation. The "New" Deal expansion and intensification, so-called "improvement," of their "Federal" Reserve fraud was planned, at the instance of Roosevelt's "adviser" and boss, Nelson Rockefeller, for further intensification of stripping of the nation by prolongation of the depression as a device for "conditioning" the nation for the acceptance of World War II to break the hold of competitive British and French Empires on their Saudi Arabian and other loot of World War I. (15) By their prolongation of the depression they had been able to propagandize the idea that war was the only way out of the depression; and that an endless series of wars and revolutions are essential for the well-being of the nation. This program of theirs has been published since in the form of *Report From Iron Mountain on the Possibility & Desirability of Peace* that was "leaked" under a pseudonym. (296)

The conspirators' puppet, Pres. Roosevelt, as related, sought to launch the country on war on Japan to save Rockefeller-Standard Oil property in China, as he had pledged in the Stimson deal, to induce them to purchase the Presidency for him. (32) James Farley reported in his *James Farley Story* that at the behest of the conspirators Roosevelt proposed declaration of war on Japan at the first meeting of his Cabinet; and it was only with difficulty that the members of the Cabinet were able to dissuade him from undertaking to make good on his pledge by convincing him that the Constitution was still the basic law of the land, and that it provided that declarations of war could be made only by the Senate, which was then opposed to war ventures. (33:39) Roosevelt was induced, with difficulty, to scheme and plot for the war that he had pledged, at a future date. In the meanwhile Joseph Grew, Rockefeller agent and member of their Foreign Office, the Council on Foreign Relations, was appointed Ambassador to Japan, to devote his efforts to encouraging the Japanese to expand their rearmament while exercising his diplomacy in the effort to shield Rockefeller-Standard Oil property in China. (334)

The Japanese had little difficulty in financing the purchase of raw material for their armaments in the U.S. The steel scrap of the entire Sixth Avenue Elevated Railroad of New York, for example, was shipped to Japan by Sailing Baruch, an agent of the conspirators. The Rockefeller-Soviet Institute of Pacific Relations, as has been related, and its Amerasia subsidiary, became the special project of John D. the Third. It was richly financed by the Rockefellers and their "Philanthropic" Foundation Trust with grants amounting to more than two million dollars from the Rockefeller Foundation alone. Japanese close to the military were subsidized and courted. Communist spies were supplied the Richard Sorge spy ring, with tax-exempt foundation funds of the IPR, for the express purpose of inducing the Japanese to attack the U.S. at Pearl Harbor, instead of attacking the Soviets as they originally planned to do. (15:274f; 91:276)

In Europe, likewise, the Rockefeller-Standard Oil gang was confronted with a problem created by British resentment at the Rockefeller takeover of the Dye Trust, the I. G. Farbenindustrie. As a consequence, they could not secure visas for personnel and clearance for their vessels that would enable them to develop the Saudi Arabian oilfields. The concession had been granted them by the British vassal King Ibn Saud, as a prized bit of loot in return for forcing the U.S. to come to the rescue of the Allies in World War I. The conspirators built up Hitler, through their agents and through their I. G. Farbenindustrie (15:115f) as a menace to England to force her to remove the barrier to their development of that bonanza, Saudi Arabia. (7; 15)

### PROJECTED WAR REQUIRED "F"R "IMPROVEMENT" FOR MAXIMUM U.S. & WORLD LOOTING

By all odds, the most important phase of their "New" Deal to the conspirators, who eternally seek larger profits, was "improving" and "developing" their "Federal" Reserve conspiracy in such manner that would enable them to draw on the wealth of the American taxpayer, as well as on that of the world, to finance their war and insure themselves of bigger and better loot. The depression which they had precipitated and deliberately prolonged provided as perfect an opportunity for this as had their panic and depression of 1907 for the passage of the "F"R Act. It was a "made-to-order" occasion for converting their "Federal" Reserve into a "more perfect" device for plundering the nation and the world, and making of it a thieves' paradise.

### CONSPIRATORS DICTATED "AMENDMENTS" TO THEIR "FEDERAL" RESERVE ACT

A significant step in putting an end to any Government "interference" in their "F"R conspiracy, as has been related, was the elimination of its nominal representation, in the persons of the Secretary of the Treasury and the Comptroller of the Currency, on the Board of Governors of the "F"R after February 1, 1936. (25:28:Sec.10:1) Actually this was a meaningless gesture. For neither of these officials, who were in hopeless minority on the Board, had been able to exercise any significant influence on its actions. The conspirators accomplished this purpose of theirs as one of the features of the final step of their cautiously and slyly attained "improvements" in their "Federal" Reserve Act, the Banking Act of 1935. This "improvement" had been "put over" on the nation for the supposed purpose of relieving the financial stringency and the depression, which the conspirators had deliberately precipitated and were quite as deliberately prolonging while they continued their international manipulations of gold with enormous profits to themselves, in land after land.

The conspirators' first step in the process of inflicting these so-called "improvements" on the nation, as has been related, was the selective bailing out of their own "F"R banks that they had unscrupulously rooked and looted. This they accomplished through the Reconstruction Finance Corporation that was established for the purpose on January 22, 1932, by an act of Congress. Financed by the taxpayers, the RFC was the first fruit of the dishonest act of Pres. Wilson that made the nation responsible for the liabilities of the fraudulent "Federal" Reserve. As pointed out by Hanks & Stucki, in their *Money, Banking & National Income* (44:299) the RFC was nothing more than the intervention of the government to salvage the "Federal" Reserve at taxpayers' expense, thereby strengthening the "F"R's control of money at a time when the fraudulent nature of the representations that had been made in its favor (44:297) had become completely obvious to the nation.

One month after the RFC had been established by Congress to bail out their monopolist "Federal" Reserve banks, on February 27, 1932, Congress passed a bill that the conspirators' agent in securing the passage of the original fraudulent "F"R Act, Carter Glass (who had been advanced for his services to them to the Senate) had introduced to "improve" the "F"R as an agency for looting the nation. The *Glass-Steagall Act* "amended" the "F"R Act to enhance the conspirators' powers in the following manners:

1. It authorized them to advance money to their "F"R member banks on their promissory notes with the questionable security of dubious assets, or of endorsement of the notes jointly by four other borrowing "F"R banks.

2. It allowed the use of government securities, without the limitations required by the original "F"R Act, as collateral for the issue of "F"R notes.

In effect, the Act made the "F"R sole arbiter of the nature of the collateral given by its members for the issuing of notes and incurring of liabilities for which Wilson's dishonest clause makes the taxpayers responsible.

The next step in the process of "improvement" of the "F"R Act was masked as "extension of monetary power" to the newly inaugurated Pres. Roosevelt under the emergency provisions of the Constitution. The *Emergency Banking Act* of 1933, passed by a special session of Congress called by the President, on March 9, 1933, five days after his inauguration and three days after he had been ordered to close all banks in the so-called "bank holiday." The speed with which this Act was put on the statute books suffices to make it obvious that it was written, as reported by Dall (376:93) in advance by agents of the conspirators and at their behest. It provided, among other things, the following:

1. The President was given dictatorial authority over money and finance including control of foreign exchange, gold and cur-

rency movements, and banking.

2. The purchase of the conspirators' national bank stocks, when it suited their purposes, by the RFC.

3. Regulated the abuse of bank credit that had been prevalent, by: a. Barring loans by banks to their administrative officers. b. Regulating the investment policies of the banks. c. Restricted the use of bank credit for speculation.

4. Dictated larger profits for the conspirators' banks by: a. Barring interest payments on deposits. b. Eliminating competition with "F"R member banks by giving the "F"R Board the power to dictate rates of interest paid by banks to their depositors.

5. Undertook to reestablish some measure of confidence in the shaky, crooked banking system by establishing a limited amount of insurance of deposits through a Federal Deposit Insurance Corporation that, in effect, required the taxpayers to insure their own deposits.

6. Tightened the conspirators' monopoly of banking by: a. Increasing the capital requirements for newly organized national bank. b. Granting national banks the right to establish branches.

7. Authorized frank and open centralization of banking by the establishment of the so-called "Federal" Open Market Committee that is given monopolistic control of the "F"R banks' trading in securities, including specifically, government securities.

The next step in the conspirators' process of "improving" their "Federal" Reserve was accomplished by them under the pretense of "relieving the depression by creating inflation," and by the un-Constitutional delegation of power by Congress to the conspirators, through their puppet, Pres. Roosevelt. For the purpose of deluding the nation, the measures were incorporated in an amendment, sponsored by their agent, Thomas, to their Agricultural Adjustment Act of May 12, 1933.

## CONSPIRATORS RIGGED AGRICULTURAL ALLOTMENT ADMINISTRATION SWINDLE

The Agricultural Adjustment Act (AAA) was a measure that had been drawn up, at the instance of the conspirators by a Hindu by the name of Svirinas Wagel who was economist for Bernard Baruch's firm, Hentz & Co., many months before Roosevelt's election. Its pretended purpose was to help the farmers whose incomes had been wiped out by the drop of agricultural product prices that had been engineered by the conspirators in spite of the development of extreme shortages in grain and other food commodities. The real purpose of the AAA was to enrich the conspirators by speculation in those commodities, raw materials of the necessities of life, with absolute safety and insured profits.

The plan, its originator agreed with this author, assured a relatively high fixed price to the marketer of a product, by government subsidy of the difference between the speculative market price and an abitrarily fixed "fair price." However, by failing to provide loans for the bankrupt farmers to finance the purchase of seed and the cost of cultivating and harvesting the crops, it compelled them to turn to the conspirators for this financing. In this manner, the conspirators became owners of the crops through liens on them,

107

and were "long" of the commodities. By control of the speculative market that was made possible by their control of money through the "F"R, the conspirators were able to force up the prices of the commodities in advance of their growth; and were thus able to set the "fair price" that would determine the size of the subsidy which they would be paid by the Government. They then "sold short" the commodities for future deliveries with the protection of the "long" position that they obtained through financing the farmers. They thereby made huge speculative profits; and eventually depressed the prices of the commodities to levels far below the "fair price" that they had had their agents in the Government set; and insured themselves of enormous subsidy payments at the expense of the taxpayers. It was a crude and ruthless swindle of the farmers and of the nation that did much injury to both.

## THOMAS AAA AMENDMENT: BASIS OF CONSPIRATORS' GOLD PRICE SWINDLE

The Thomas Amendment to the AAA swindle granted the power to the conspirators' agent, Pres. Roosevelt, to insure them further loot by the issuance of three billion dollars of interest-bearing Treasury securities and of money; by manipulation of the gold content of the dollar, and consequently of the price of gold, up to a limit of 50%; and by the issuance of two hundred million dollars of silver certificates. This was coupled by Presidential authorization of manipulation by the "Federal" Reserve Board of the reserve balances required of banks against their deposits, that implied extending to it even more absolute monopolistic powers for juggling of the nation's wealth.

This swindle was rapidly followed, on June 5, 1933, by abrogation, or nullifying, of the gold clause in all contracts by a joint resolution of Congress. This act constituted the wiping out of the most fundamental civil right assured by the Constitution and the Bill of Rights. It laid the basis, with the other gold measures, for the "Gold Corner" being developed by the conspirators.

## ROOSEVELT "GREENBACKS" PROVIDE INDIRECT INTEREST PAYMENT TO CONSPIRATORS

On August 29, 1933, Pres. Roosevelt, issued an order that did much to clarify the real objectives of the Thomas Amendment. The conspirators had blocked a provision, that had been introduced as a sop to the traditional pose of the Democratic Party, for the issue of three billion dollars in non-interest-bearing greenbacks. Instead, the Treasury was directed to issue $3 billion of interest-bearing bonds which the "F"R banks "purchased" with non-interest-bearing currency issued on collateral of the bonds. The cost to the taxpayers of the interest on those bonds amounted to sixty million dollars a year, an additional tax levied by the conspirators through their "F"RS.

## SPECULATIVE MANIPULATION OF GOLD BY CONSPIRATORS AUTHORIZED

Roosevelt's Executive Order directed the Secretary of the Treasury to *sell* domestically mined gold on the world market at the best price available, then set at twenty dollars an ounce. This served the dual purpose of depressing the price of gold; and of enabling the conspirators to purchase, through their foreign agents, the large amount of gold that had been mined in this country since the holding and purchase of gold had been prohibited to other of our nationals by Roosevelt's Executive Order of March 6, 1933.

Adequate time was given the conspirators to corner this gold. On October 22, 1933, Roosevelt announced in one of his mendacious and cynically false "fireside chats" that revealed his aptitude as a confidence man, (7:95) that trading in gold would bring about recovery in commodity prices. Reversing his previous Order of August 29, 1933, (two months earlier) he required the conspirator-directed RFC to purchase domestically mined gold at prices dictated by themselves, to buy and sell gold, and support their market in gold by trading in it, *At The Taxpayers' Expense.*

Three days later, their RFC began to buy from them, at $31.36 an ounce the gold, that they had bought up cheaply under the earlier Order, which represented a profit of more than 50%. One week later they had their RFC make their "Federal" Reserve its agent in this gold trade. Finally, several months later, on January 16, 1934, they had manipulated the price of gold to $34.45 an ounce, netting themselves additional profit at the expense of the taxpayers looted and improverished by the depression that they had engineered and maintained, and by their "New" Deal.

## CONSPIRATORS LURED "PEASANTS" BACK TO THEIR BANKS WITH DEPOSIT INSURANCE

For financing of the "Federal" Depositors Insurance Corp. established for the purpose of creating confidence in their banks, the taxpayers were required to furnish through the Treasury one hundred and fifty million dollars of the private corporation's capital, in order to "ease the burden" on the "Federal" Reserve swindlers. No interest was paid by it to the Treasury for the use of the money.

At the end of fourteen years the FDIC profits had become so large that the initial financing was repaid to the Treasury. But Public Law 363, Sec. 4, was passed by Congress, requiring the Treasury to supply the conspirators' FDIC, whenever it may need it, with the sum of $3 billion. In short, the depositors insure their own deposits; and the conspirators' banks enjoy its business-getting benefits with no diminution of their loot.

Insurance of depositors' funds had been proposed by honest members of Congress, in 1913, at the time of the passage of the original "F"R Act. But it had been fought bitterly by the conspirators, and especially by their Congressional agent, Carter Glass, who now advanced to the Senate for his services, introduced the deposit insurance measure.

## PRES. ROOSEVELT FOLLOWED COUSIN, PRES. GRANT, IN "GOLD CORNER" RIGGING

For the purpose of giving some semblance of legality to the theft of the nation's gold, as has been related, Pres. Roosevelt was required to demand the passage by Congress of the *Gold Reserve Act* of 1934. The Act was hurriedly passed by the "rubber stamp" Congress on January 30, 1934; and it was equally hurriedly signed by Roosevelt, on the same day. It nominally transferred to the Treasury title to the gold loot that had been fenced for the conspirators by their "Federal" Reserve. Actually, the control of the gold was left in the conspirators' hands by a simple device. The Act required the public and the "Federal" Reserve to turn in their gold to the

Treasury. The public was paid in paper dollars; but the "F"R was given "gold certificates" for the gold turned in. The special character of the gold certificates is described in Sec.14 of the Act, as follows:

"(c) The Secretary of the Treasury is authorized to issue gold certificates in such form and in such denominations as he may determine, against any gold held by the Treasurer of the United States, except the gold fund held as a reserve for any United States notes and Treasury notes of 1890. *The Amount Of Gold Certificates Issued And Outstanding Shall At No Time Exceed The Value, At Legal Standard, Of Gold So Held Against Gold Certificates.*" (27:206)

These gold certificates, warehouse receipts for the gold which vested ownership of it in the conspirators through their "Federal" Reserve, to which they were issued as receipts for looted gold turned in by it. Gold can be withdrawn only by the conspirators on the basis of real or fictitious "foreign" accounts which they control. Contrasting sharply with the pretense of the "gold standard" and the fraudulent "gold reserve" that had been provided for the nation at large, the conspirators' gold certificates are one hundred percent backed by their gold, part of which is held for them by the Treasury. Ironically, the Act provides for the guarding of the gold looted from the nation, at Fort Knox, for the thievish conspirators at the expense of the robbed taxpayers.

The Act provides, also, that no gold shall be coined; that neither U.S. currency or "Federal" Reserve notes will be redeemed in gold; that the gold shall be kept in the form of bullion, or bars. It limits the amount of gold that can be withdrawn from the Treasury for industrial and other technological private uses to the amount approved by the Treasurer. It authorized the Secretary of the Treasury to deal in gold and to sell even the gold required as a reserve for currency

"...Provided, however, That the Secretary of the Treasury may sell gold which is required to be maintained as a reserve or as a security for currency issued by the United States, only to the extent necessary to maintain such currency at a parity with the gold dollar." (27:204)

It also authorized the Secretary of the Treasury, with the authorization of the President, to change the gold content of the dollar and to reduce it by not more than sixty percent. Roosevelt promptly reduced the gold content of the dollar to fifteen and five twenty first grains of gold ninety percent fine, thereby increased the value of the conspirators gold from twenty dollars an ounce to thirty-five dollars per ounce. The Act permitted the revaluation of the silver content of the dollar proportionately. Roosevelt thus followed the familial tradition established by his cousin, Pres. Grant, in rigging a "gold corner" for the conspirators.

Within the following year, according to the "Federal" Reserve report, more than a billion ounces of gold, much of which had been exported by the conspirators when it was valued at $20 an ounce, was reimported by them for redemption at $35 an ounce. This netted them a "trifling" profit of more than seven hundred millions dollars at the expense of the taxpayers. By 1940, their gold imports had risen to more than five billion dollars for the year. Their total gold

110

imports in the period of 1934-40 amounted to more than sixteen billion dollars, and involved for them a profit of more than seven billion dollars.

## CONSPIRATORS' "NEW" DEAL SILVER STEAL

In the course of manipulation of the nation's wealth and economy facilitated by their "Gold Standard," the conspirators had stolen control of the principal mining interests. As a result they had gained control of the production of silver. Consequently, their attitude toward its monetization became more favorable, especially inasmuch as it gained for them the adherence and support of the Western States. And, as might be expected, silver became in their hands a device for further plundering the nation.

Extension of the conspirators' brigandage, on the basis of silver, to the world at large was effected by them in the World Economic Conference that was held shortly after the passage of the Thomas Amendment. At the Conference, they entered into an international agreement on silver, that became the foundation for a number of "angles" of the conspiracy other than profitable silver speculation. For example, it prepared the way for the further looting and impoverishment of Asia (320) and for the Communization thereby of China. Also, it provided, by way of silver options, a device for bribing and silencing enemies. An option on one hundred thousand ounces of silver accounted for a discontinuance of attacks made upon them by Fr. Coughlin (97:185) in his Social Justice campaign, and false and corruptly motivated diversion of his attacks to the "Jewish international bankers."

On December 31,1933, Roosevelt launched a silver purchasing program that was subsequently ratified by a "rubber stamp" Congress in the Silver Purchase Act of 1934. It established a ratio of one silver dollar for every three gold dollars in U.S. monetary stock; and authorized Treasury trading in silver within the price range of 50¢ and $1.293 per ounce. At the time, silver was selling in the world market at 25¢ to 35¢. The conspirators played their usual hypocritic and crafty game of pretending to be "opposed" to this deal of theirs. But when a list of speculators in silver was published, it listed their agents and nominees, including Frank Vanderlip, and Fr. Coughlin's employee. (97:185f) Their pretended opposition insured the adoption of the program. The delay of Roosevelt in issuing the order had given them ample time to "corner" silver in the world market and import it, for sale to the Treasury for looting of the taxpayers.

Morgenthau related in his diaries (97:183f) how he naively played the dupe for the conspirators and their pawn, Roosevelt, in their pretended opposition to the silver coinage bill introduced by Martin Dies; and insured their speculative profits in silver by juggling the silver market to suit their purposes. This made a success of their scheme for impoverishment of Latin America and China where the inflation that they created by their silver speculation insured the takeover by their Communist partners.

Before forcing up the price of silver, the conspirators barred the export by others of American silver, by an embargo. This enabled them to make sure that others would not follow their example and ship abroad American silver for the purpose of reimporting it when they had "rigged the price of silver and effected a "corner." When aggressive buying by the Treasury, dictated by the conspirators, had raised silver to 49¢, on August 9, 1944, Roosevelt issued an Executive Order that dictated that all silver in the country must be delivered to the Mints within 90 days against payment of 50.01¢ an ounce.

Rockefellers' Chase National Bank was the agency through which Morgenthau was required to make silver purchases, thus assuring that at all times the conspirators sat at the helm in this silver manipulation around the world. (97:197) They juggled the price of silver from 64.64¢ in late 1934, to 77.57¢ when election approached in 1936, after hitting a high of 81¢ in April 1935. The conspirators unloaded their silver holdings on the Treasury and taxpayers, and won the election with the help of their duped confederates, the silver producers and champions. They then smashed the world silver market by dumping huge blocks of Treasury silver on the world market in order to add to the pressure on the market by Chinese offers of 200,000,000 ounces and British Hong Kong offers of an additional 100,000,000 ounces. They thus manipulated silver to a low of 45¢ on January 20, 1936. On December 8, 1937, they set the price of silver at 64.5¢ an ounce, after the London Silver Agreement, in which Roosevelt had entered our country, at their behest, with resulting extension of their thievery on an international scale.

The potential for brigandage and looting of taxpayer "peasants" offered by the silver corner becomes obvious from the figures on silver certificate issue by the Treasury. From a total of $40,000,000 in 1934, it rose to $1,230,000,000 in 1938. It would not be wide of the mark to estimate that the profits from this "deal" of theirs amounted to half the latter sum. With the help of their agents in the White House, they tremendously increased their profits from the silver after mid-1967.

## CONSPIRATORS RETIRED CURRENCY AND "STERILIZED" GOLD: FOR MONEY STRINGENCY

Clear-cut proof is available that both the gold and the silver "corners" by the conspirators in their "New" Deal were nothing more than "confidence" games perpetrated on the nation for the dual purpose of looting it and prolonging the depression. They were in no wise intended or designed to relieve the monetary stringency and the world-wide debacle that they had precipitated with their 1929 "Gold Corner" engineered through their "Federal" Reserve. In the instance of the silver certificate issue, the conspirators deliberately arranged the retiring of an almost equal amount of their "Federal" Reserve and National Bank notes and thereby "minimized the inflationary dangers" of the silver program." (97:188; 24:225-7) Likewise, the gold purchases were engineered by the conspirators in such manner as to carefully avoid relieving the monetary stringency and the consequent depression and, instead, to prolong and intensify them.

Proof of this is clearly apparent in the treatment accorded their gold when it was purchased by the Treasury, and the reason offered therefor. The threat to the conspirators' schemes for prolonging their depression thievery, offered by expansion of the nation's currency to a point adequate for the needs of a prospering commerce and industry by the use of the purchased gold as a basis for the issue of currency, was carefully avoided. The depression was deliberately prolonged, by a process that was labelled "sterilization" of the gold. Under orders of their puppet, Pres. Roosevelt, the Secretary of the Treasury announced on December 1, 1936, that the gold would be paid for with interest-bearing Government bonds instead of with currency issued on the basis of the gold. This meant the gold was converted into an even more costly liability, instead of being treated as an asset. It meant that the conspirators burdened the taxpayers with interest on the bonds in addition to the increase in national debt involved in the issue of the bonds for the purchase of gold for them. (24:217)

## SEC CREATED TO INTENSIFY CONSPIRATORS' POWER THRU STOCK MARKET LOOTING

By the passage of the *Security & Exchange Act* of June 6, 1934, the piratic power of the conspirators "Federal" Reserve was extended to the absolute domination and control over the finances and securities of all corporations and over the stock exchanges on which they are marketed and traded. Their "Federal" Reserve is empowered by it to dictate whether money can be borrowed, by whom, how much, and on what conditions, from their member banks or from the public directly. It is also empowered to dictate whether and to what extent a person or corporation can use its own credit in the purchase or sale of securities and other items, and on what terms. It empowers the conspirators to capriciously and arbitrarily juggle those terms in a manner that facilitates their looting of the nation by manipulation of markets in securities, commodities and money. This power has been used by the conspirators to systematically and periodically swindle the public to the tune of billions of dollars of investments and savings.

The swindling of the public by collaboration of their "Federal" Reserve conspiracy and of the SEC as then directed by their agent, Joseph Kennedy, in railroad and public utility holding company (under the "death sentence" rigged by them) has cost the public hundreds of billion dollars in investments and savings that were wiped out and/or stolen by the conspirators, and infinitely intensified the depression. (7:178f) Under its present management, the SEC has been largely, though by no means entirely, converted to public service, though often too belatedly to offer protection to the public. Excepted from SEC protection are issues involving the Rockefellers and their agents, as in the case of their Horizon Titanium Co. fraud. As for the "Federal" Reserve, its Board and chairman serve their bosses, the conspirators, loyally in "rigging" the market for them to facilitate looting the public. Its "Open Market Operations" that are apparently dictated by the conspirators, are kept secret from the public; and pronouncements by "F"RB chairman and members, regularly serve to boom the market when the conspirators are "long" and to break it when they are "short" of it.

## BANKING ACT OF 1935: CONSPIRATORS' "NEW" DEAL "PERFECTING" OF "FEDERAL" RESERVE

The Banking Act of 1935 gives insight into the conspirators' concept of "perfecting" of their "Federal" Reserve fraud. It is viewed by them as "superb" in that it served

"...to a greater degree than any previous law *To Concentrate Responsibility For National Credit Policies In The Hands Of The Federal Reserve System's Principal Administrative Agency.*" (44:306)

Thus reads Professors Hank and Stucki estimate of the conspirators' success in establishing an entirely illegitimate monopoly of finance and control of personal and national wealth.

Among the provisions of the Act were the following:

1. The "Federal" Reserve Board was reconstituted into the Board of Governors of the "Federal" Reserve System, who are wholly beyond the reach of Congress and the nation during their fourteen year tenures, and are absolute dictators of the nation's and the people's wealth, finances, credit and even survival. Loyalty of these agents is assured by the fact that they can expect to find employment, after their terms, principally, if not solely, in the employ of the conspirators or their agencies. Their specified powers are:

A. Absolute authority over both reserve and margin requirements.

B. Final determination of discount rates set by the reserve banks.

C. Dictation jointly with the Comptroller of the Currency and the conspirators' FDIC: (a) whether there is need in a community for a bank that will be permitted to join the "F"R and FDIC; whether the bank proposed for the community is financially adequate; both of which judgements determine whether the conspirators shall have local competition to impair their banking monopoly.

D. As a sop to the "peasants," individual accounts were given double the FDIC insurance that they had previously, or $5,000.

An additional protection of the conspirators' banking monopoly incorporated in the Act, gave the FDIC power to control the rate of interest on time deposits, and to prohibit interest on demand deposits of all insured banking institutions connected with their "F"R.

Professors Hanks and Stucki proclaim exultantly that the Act provided both more centralized and greater control over money and banking. This is correct. But they erred when they stated that the control is "national." That it definitely is not. It is strictly private racketeering control by the conspirators that is nationwide and world-wide in scope. (44:307)

## MORGENTHAU WAS DUPED, BUT HONEST & HONORABLE

Secretary Morgenthau stands out in this "New Deal" mess of perfidy and corruption as duped, but honest and honorable. He regarded the orders of the conspirators transmitted to him by their pawn, Pres. Roosevelt, as stupid. (97:196) He boldly stated his suspicions, to the press in the words:

"...we are not going to let fifteen or twenty people clean up twenty-five or fifty million dollars through a monetary program of the Government." (97:187)

His estimate of the number of people who did "clean up" is high. His estimate of how much they "cleaned up" is absurdly low.

114

A more accurate estimate of the loot immediately and directly derived from these aspects of their "New" Deal, is $5 to $10 billion. Their indirect profits from it by way of the brigandage facilitated by their deliberate prolongation of the depression and theft of the major part of the industry of the nation and the world, by way of their fostering of violence, crime and lawlessness and profiting therefrom, by way of World War II for which the "improvements" were part of the preparations, this loot of theirs might well amount to many trillions of dollars.

Though he clearly discerned their thievery and was incensed by it, Morgenthau was forced by the conspirators' order transmitted to him through their agent, his boss, Pres. Roosevelt, to accede to it.

## TREASURY'S DAILY BALANCE SHEET CLEARLY REVEALS THEFT OF NATION'S GOLD

The theft of the nation's gold is clearly discernible from the daily balance sheet published by the Treasury. The real ownership of the stolen gold is revealed by the simultaneous balance sheets of the "Federal" Reserve, which are published each Friday in the New York Times.

The Daily Statement of the United States Treasury lists under its assets in the first week of August, 1962, a total of 461,601-974.9 ounces of gold valued at $16,148,054,120.11. By way of comparison, it states that the gold held by the Treasury one year prior, was valued at $17,601,421,523.11.

Directly opposite the listing of the Treasury "Assets," one finds "Liabilities." The first heading is "Gold Certificates (Series 1934) etc.," totalling $16,029,992,466.31. Those gold certificates are, as has been related, certificates of deposit, or warehouse receipts, for specified amounts of gold which is the property of certificate holders. The only gold momentarily owned by the Treasury, was valued at $118,-061,653.80, or less than one percent of the gold held in storage by the Treasury.

The true owner of the supposed gold "Assets" of the Treasury and the nation, the holders of the gold certificates, is revealed in the report of the "Federal" Reserve of the same date, in the item labelled "Twelve Federal Reserve Banks Combined." Under the heading "Assets" is the entry, "Gold Certificate Account, $14,673,000,-000.00." Directly beneath it appears another gold item labelled "Redemption Fund For Federal Reserve Notes," $1,201,000,000.00. The total of these two items that are listed as "Total Gold Certificate Reserves" is $15,874,000,000. The conspirators, through their private enterprise the fraudulent "Federal" Reserve, own all the gold that was stolen from the nation through the agency of their "New" Deal plus all that was purchased subsequently in the world market with interest-bearing Government bonds, liabilities of the Treasury and the taxpayers.

## ON BALANCE, NO GOLD HAS LEFT COUNTRY IN PAST DECADE

This situation raises the question: What has happened to the gold that has been "withdrawn"? It would be nothing short of incredible that such consummate thieves and confidence men had permitted any part of their fabulous loot to be taken away from them.

One is assured by inquiries at their "Federal" Reserve that none of it has slipped out of their claws. This author was informed, on inquiry made, in 1965, of the New York Federal Reserve Bank, that on balance, none of the "withdrawn" gold has left the country for "foreign central banks." The bulk of this gold that has been supposedly "withdrawn" for "foreign" accounts has merely been "earmarked" which means that it has been transferred from one room of the bank to another room in the same bank. Inquiry at the time of the above detailed Treasury and "Federal" Reserve reports elicited the amount of the "earmarked" gold to be more than ten billion dollars in value. (38) Adding this sum to that falsely listed by the Treasury among its "assets," reveals that thanks to the enforced, but real "philanthropy" of the American public, the conspirators now own approximately two billion dollars more of gold than the maximum previously held! But the Treasury and the nation own no gold.

By 1966, the "earmarked" gold held by the Federal Reserve Bank of New York was stated by its officials to be $13.032 billion.

CHAPTER XV

NELSON ROCKEFELLER ADDED "FOREIGN AID" TO "NEW" DEAL "F"R, GOLD & SILVER THIEVERY

"Perfecting" the thievish mechanics of the conspirators' "Federel" Reserve, in his capacity of "New Deal" wheeler-dealer and "adviser," merely whetted the appetite of Nelson Aldrich Rockefeller. The ambitious youth repeatedly expressed his boundless admiration for the master-criminal precepts and examples of his ruthless ancestors, that made them the "most successful" gangsters of their times. His is a driving lust and "ambition" in the same direction. He has a peculiarly malevolent genius and inventiveness. He has dedicated himself to attaining the Rockefeller dynastic goal of assuring themselves "security" by making themselves world dictators and thereby destroying the security of the rest of the world. (17; 66; 79)

The regal tone of the Rockefeller Dynasty, as has been pointed out, is reflected in the naming of the heads of the clan in successive generations, John D. the First, John D. (Jr.) the Second, John D. the Third, John D. the Fourth, etc. Possibly some day there will also be added the title of Emperor, as well there might be today. Then it may be merely a matter of time before the idea intimated by John D. the Second, in his 1945 speech to the Protestant Council, of the acceptance, in the Roman tradition, of their status as *"Rex, Imperator et Deus"* (King, Emperor & God) comes to be established.(84)

116

## NICKERSON'S BLUEPRINT OF "ONE (ROCKEFELLER) WORLD"

The pattern of the program was clearly and contemptuously published by the Rockefeller associate, intimate friend and spokesman on matters of social organization, fellow member of their Union Club, Hoffman Nickerson in his book entitled *The American Rich.* (100) Published by Doubleday Doran in 1930, it has been the pattern of the conspirators' "New" Deal and all subsequent developments. The plot that is outlined in considerable detail in the book, is the destruction of our Republic and of the Constitution on which it is based, by the establishment of a class who are "perpetually rich" because they have usurped the power to loot the rest of the nation by picking its pockets through such devices as taxation and their "Federal" Reserve, which were already accomplished facts. He expressed the conspirators' contempt for the democratic concept of equality before the law as a basis for human organization; and their rejection of the concept of representative government, a republic, as "absurd." The only "perfect" form of government from their viewpoint, he relates, is a hereditary monarchy with absolute dictatorial power. He then proceeded to outline the conspirators' program for converting our Republic into an elective, absolute monarchy until such time as the nation could be brainwashed, or otherwise induced, into accepting a hereditary, absolute monarch. In effect, he blueprinted the process of imposing on our country a government "of, by and for the Rockefellers."

The initial step in the plot was the creation by the conspirators of the myth of the "indispensable man" by propaganda and by the simple device of stirring up, behind the scenes, antagonism between various minority groups. The master conspirator, the "indispensable man" would be built up as the "one and only man who can compose the differences." This phase of the conspiracy is a modification of the Machiavellian scheme, "divide and rule." By setting Protestant against Catholic, black against white, Christian against Jew, workers against employers, etc., they create their "elective monarch" and repeatedly reelect him, until the nation will have accepted him as its ruler. The ultimate aim would be to finally dispense with elections as "unnecessary," and to make the monarchy hereditary as well as absolute, *by letting the monarch pick his successor.* In this manner, the conspirators plan, they would establish "perfect" government in our land and eventually in the world. (100:274)

The extent of the conspirators' success in brainwashing the nation, through their "Philanthropic" Foundation Trust and at the expense of the nation, into acceptance of this subversion and treason is made obvious by the words of their agent, Nickerson, regarding the attitude that prevailed in the nation in 1930 with regard to hereditary political power.

"...since no trace of hereditary political power exists in the Republic, it is much better not to innovate unless compelled. *Nor is it easy to imagine circumstances capable of soon compelling us.*" (100:302)

In the three decades that have elapsed, it has come to be accepted by the bulk of the nation that public office is the property of the officeholder, that it is his "right" to transmit to his heirs. Thus following the death of Sen. Carraway, his wife inherited his seat, without a public voice of dissent. Likewise, following the death of Sen. Neuberger, his wife was appointed to his seat. When Sen. Robert F. Wagner became so obviously non compos mentis that it could no longer be hidden, his family refused to withdraw him from the Senate (to which the majority of his duped electorate would have been delighted to reelect him in reward for the corrupt service he had rendered) until an agreement was made with the conspirators to advance his son as his political heir. Following the death of Pres. Roosevelt, his consort, Eleanor, and other members of his family were regarded as entitled to public office in continuance of the role of the Roosevelt-Delano Dynasty (self-titled *America's Royal Family* in a family tree hung by Eleanor, at Hyde Park) in giving the U.S. more than a third of its Presidents because of its leadership of the "liberal," or Communist, movement in the land since the Revolution. (7:10) Nelson Rockefeller, as will be related, has dictated the incorporation of personal handdown of the rule of the nation in the XXVth Amendment to the Constitution.

For the purpose of insuring the usurping monarch absolute rule, a number of devices already had been put in operation under the direction of agencies controlled by the conspirators, that include among numerous others: their *Public Administration Clearing House* and its hundred of subsidiary organizations such as the Governors' Conferences, Committee for Economic Development, American Bar Association, and numerous other subverted or subversive organizations listed in their publication *Public Administration Organizations, a Directory* (102; 15:162f); and their propaganda agencies, such as *Interpublic Inc., Infoplan* and numerous others. (79:186f)

The most effective of their subversive devices was created by the elimination of the Constitutional provision for a check and balance on the power of the President. They have nullified that clause in the Constitution that gives the power to initiate budgetary legislation, the power of the purse, to the House of Representatives. Elimination of this check on the absolute monarchic power of the President is essential for the conspirators, wrote Nickerson; and progress he pointed out had already been extensive in this direction in the form of the "executive budget plan." This plan consisted of having the executive, the President in this instance, draw up a budget asserting the financial needs and taxes requisite to meet them, for presentation, originally in advisory capacity, to Congress. The "executive budget" should be so large, he advised, that no Congressman would dare add to it; so complex, detailed and voluminous that Congress would not have time to examine it; and so full of "pork barrel" and graft for each and every member of Congress as to content them and their constituents and make them fearful of disturbing it. Such a budget assures acceptance by the majority of the Congressmen interested solely in "what is in it for them." They willingly abdicate the power and right given them by the Constitution. When, as in the case of their "New" Deal, this process is repeated year after year,

118

and becomes the "accepted practise," the monarchic executive has usurped the power of the budget and eliminated that check on his power. And, wrote Nickerson:

"The first step toward complete monarchial initiative is the executive budget plan *now prevailing in the Federal Government and in thirty-four of the forty-eight States. Even the logical step of limiting the Constitutional powers of the legislative bodies has been taken in seven of the thirty-four, Maryland, West Virginia, New York, Massachusetts, California, Nebraska and Wisconsin. The rich might do well to help forward such a development."* (100:261)

It is well to bear in mind that there is no material difference between the totalitarian objective of the conspirators and of their spokesman, Nickerson. He takes pride in his Nazarene Catholicism, and is fully in accord with the Nazarenism of the frank and open Communist who places his faith in the Weishaupt-Marx pseudo-philosophic justification of the avowed thievery contemplated. This identity of their true objective better enables one to understand the Rockefeller-Soviet Axis collaboration. (15:204)

For the purpose of eliminating any check on the power of the President, become monarch, by any initiative exercised by Congress, the remedy, Nickerson points out, is quite simple. The Constitution provides that the President shall inform Congress on the state of the nation by means of messages. By the use of "emergencies," deliberately created by the President and his fellow conspirators, Congress can be badgered with numerous messages that demand the passage of "must" legislation for which public support has been engineered by propagandists. The Congressmen can be so completely entangled in legislative processes thus demanded by the President that they would have no time to consider or introduce any measures initiated by themselves. And they are thus converted to mere puppets, or "rubber stamps," of the "President-become—monarch." Nickerson states on behalf of the conspirators:

"While increasing disrepute of legislatures will doubtless in the long run prevent their continuance as the chief organ of government, still it would be unwise to abolish them...(100:260)

"...if legislatures continue to wallow in their present disrepute, it will be easy to prune their sovereignty. There will be no need for the rich to hasten such development..." (100:273)

The other check placed by the Constitution on the absolute power of the President, as well as on the power of Congress, is the Supreme Court. This block in the way of the conspirators would have been eliminated when in the course of his repeated terms in office, the President would have appointed the majority, or all, of the Justices, and would have "packed" the court. This part of the conspiracy temporarily miscarried, when Roosevelt followed the counsel of his impatient "intimate adviser," Nelson Rockefeller, and undertook to denounce the Supreme Court for its "sick chicken" decision that declared un-Constitutional the NRA, key measure of the "New" Deal plot for monopoly of all industry. Eventually, the conspirators have succeeded, however, in slyly packing the Supreme Court with their own breed, converting it into one of the principal agencies in carrying out their plot to destroy our Republic.

The plot, as outlined by Nickerson in his *American Rich,* was to make intensive use of minorities such as Negroes, Jews, foreign elements and "liberals" of breeds differing from their own, in subverting our Government and institutions. It provides, however, that as soon as the Constitution had been destroyed or made a dead letter, the "problems" posed by these minorities would be solved by eliminating those "vermin."

## JOHN D. THE SECOND HAILED THE "ONE (ROCKEFELLER) WORLD"

Some of the objectives of this conspiracy had been attained, as has been related, by the year 1933 when Franklin D. Roosevelt and his brash "adviser," or boss, Nelson Rockefeller, had loomed on the national scene. Usurpation of the nation's finances, money and credit by way of the "Federal" Reserve had already vested the conspirators with the power of the purse that extended more deeply and widely than the power that had ever been vested in Congress; and had forced abdication by Congress of whatever power might have been vested in it.

John D. the Second had openly expressed his wish, or command, that there be surrendered to the conspirators our national sovereignty by way of "internationalism." That is as requisite for the expansion of the Rockefeller Empire as it is for that of their partners, Communist Soviets. As early as 1924, he had announced his "internationalist" objective in a talk to a group of students, that is quoted by his "mouthpiece," agent and biographer, Raymond Fosdick, as follows:

"We are standing tonight on the mountain top, with the world spread out at our feet — your country, your country, my country — all about us... So it may come to pass that some day, some day, the people of all nations will stand on the mountain top together, and no one will speak of 'my country' but we will speak of 'our world,.'" (49:390)

The editorial "our" indicates that the Weishaupt-Marx concept of rulership of the world through a "United Nations" had given way to that of "One Rockefeller World."

## ROCKEFELLER'S INSTITUTE OF PACIFIC RELATIONS & AMERASIA

Nelson Rockefeller's role in the advance of the "New Deal" phases of the conspiracy, as has been stated, has been acknowledged. (39) The personal role of the Rockefellers in the activities of their Institute of Pacific Relations and its Amerasia subsidiary, that a Congressional investigation pronounced to be a treasonous agency serving the Communist cause, has been related. (103:104;105) To what extent the failure of prosecution of the *Amerasia* crew was due to personal involvement of the "sacrosanct" Rockefellers in the IPR can only be a matter of conjecture. It constitutes, however, one of the most extraordinary cases in American law.

## "NEW" DEAL WAS "PACKED" WITH ROCKEFELLER-SOVIET AGENTS

One of the conspirators' first "New" Deal moves had been the ouster by Pres. Roosevelt of more than 600,000 loyal Government employees in a pretended "economy" campaign. Directly thereafter, more than 2,000,000 Reds and other brands of subversive agents of the conspirators were packed into the Government departments. Among them were such frank Communists as Rockefeller associate and fellow member of their CFR, Alger Hiss, who served them with such complete satisfaction that he won rapid promotion to the highest ranks of their Government agents. He was promoted more rapidly when it became widely known that he was a Communist agent. Nelson Rockefeller confided to a New Hampshire contractor's association, in the course of his 1964 primary campaign for the Republican Presidential nomination, that he had aided and abetted Alger Hiss in his perfidy, when serving the conspirators as the Secretary of United Nations Organization Conference in San Francisco, by shielding him from exposure by the FBI as a Communist agent. (106; 79)

## CONSPIRATORS' AGENT, HARRY L. HOPKINS, WAS RINGLEADER OF "HAL WARE CELL"

Alger Hiss was one of many Rockefeller Red agents who were planted in the Department of Agriculture under Henry Wallace in what came to be known as the "Hal Ware Cell." Hal Ware was a kinsman of the Civil War Communist leader and pro-Negro agitator, Thaddeus Stevens, and son of "Mother" Bloor, the Communist agitator among the Pennsylvania coal miners. He was not, however, the real ringleader of the conspirators in that cell.

According to Murray Garsson, who acknowledged having unwittingly played host to the cell members in an apartment that he maintained at the Wardman Park Hotel in Washington, the real leader of the cell was Eleanor Roosevelt's "heartthrob" at the time, Harry L. Hopkins. (7; 84) Garsson stated that he had been helped by Hopkins in securing Government contracts; and in return, he subsidized Hopkins and paid his gambling debts and racetrack losses. Hopkins requested the loan of the apartment that Garsson maintained in Washington, during the weekends when he returned to his family home in New York, for entertaining his friends. Later Garsson discovered that the charges to his account made by Hopkins' friends were in the name of the members of the "Hal Ware Cell" who were later exposed.

Rockefellers, through their Council on Foreign Relations, planted numerous of their agents who freely associated with Alger Hiss, Owen Lattimore and the other Reds in its roster, in the Roosevelt Cabinets and more particularly in the higher ranks of "New" Deal executives. These included: Henry L. Stimson, Secretary of War; Harold Ickes, Rockefeller and Standard Oil attorney and Secretary of the Interior; John Foster Dulles, Rockefeller kinsman, attorney for their German interests, who during three decades was their agent in directing the State Department, joined them in sponsoring his intimate associate, Alger Hiss, and fronted for them in the subversive Federal (alias National) Council of Churches of Christ, and with Alger Hiss, in the World Council of Churches; Edward Stettinius Jr., Secretary of State and Yalta participant; Gen. George C. Marshall, head of the Joint Chiefs of Staff, Secretary of State, and the conspirators' agent in forcing China into the camp of their Soviet confederates; Dean

121

Acheson, Rockefeller-Standard Oil attorney, attorney for Soviet Poland in the U.S., and Secretary of State who would not "turn his back on" Alger Hiss.

## LAUCHLIN CURRIE, CANADIAN RED & ROCKEFELLER TOP AGENT IN "F"R

By far the most important agent of Rockefellers in their "Federal" Reserve and the Treasury was the Canadian Red, Lauchlin Currie. Currie was born in Nova Scotia, in 1902, the son of Lauchlin Currie and Alice Eisenhauer. After training at the Rockefeller subsidized London School of Economics where he secured a B.S. degree, he became instructor and tutor at Harvard University, where he obtained his Ph.D., in 1931, and became associated with another student, Harry Dexter White. A professorship in international economics at the Fletcher School of Law & Diplomacy was followed by his appointment as senior analyst of the U.S. Treasury, in 1934. There he was instrumental in planting his fellow alumnus, Harry Dexter White, in the position of assistant director of research in the Treasury, late in 1934. Then he had been transferred by the conspirators to their "Federal" Reserve, as assistant director of research and statistics of its Board until 1939, when he was planted in the post of Administrative Assistant to the President. There he remained until Pres. Roosevelt's death. His importance to the conspirators was so high and the trust that they placed in him so complete, that he was sent by them, in 1941, as the head of an economic mission to China; and subsequently, in 1942, as the "President's personal representative" on a "diplomatic" mission to China. In 1945, he was sent to Switzerland at the head of an economic and financial mission.

The dominant role played by Lauchlin Currie in the conspirators' monetary manipulations as well as in their "Federal" Reserve swindle and the Communist takeover of China, is richly documented. The *Harry Dexter White Papers* (59) clearly reveal that the line of command was from Rockefeller to Lauchlin Currie, to recalcitrant Harry Dexter White. The same picture emerges from the slanted portions of the Morgenthau diaries that have been released. (97:394;101) Currie's book entitled *The Supply & Control of Money in the U.S.* (61) reveals the extent of his domination of the operations of both the "F"R and the Treasury on behalf of the conspirators.

## RED, LAUCHLIN CURRIE RAN "F"R FOR CONSPIRATORS

The clearest picture of the power exercised in the Government by the Rockefeller agent, Lauchlin Currie, is given by Congressman Jerry Voorhis in his autobiography, *Confessions of a Congressman*. (34:176) Voorhis was assigned by his House Committee to ask Pres. Roosevelt to put an end to the "Federal" Reserve fraud, by having the Government purchase its stock and take it over. Roosevelt, with his usual deceit, "agreed" that it would be good for the nation to do so. But, Roosevelt said, he would like to have Voorhis discuss the matter with the Chairman of the Federal Reserve Board, Marriner Eccles. When Voorhis took the matter up with him, Eccles stated he was powerless to act in the absence of Lauchlin Currie, who was then in China (busy arranging its delivery to the Communists). Roosevelt thus craftily frustrated, on behalf of his bosses, the plan of the House Committee. Obviously Lauchlin Currie's role in the "F"RS overshadowed that of the Secretary of the Treasury and his subordinates in the same measure as the "F"R dominated the Treasury.

## CURRIE JOINED MARSHALL IN DELIVERY OF CHINA TO COMMUNISTS

Lauchlin Currie served his Rockefeller-Soviet Axis masters loyally and well. As a representative of their treasonous Institute of Pacific Relations, he went to China in 1941 as Roosevelt's personal emissary. (108; 109:4462; 15:822) He was named by Elizabeth Bentley, the confessed Communist courier, as one of her sources of important espionage data. (38) This leaves no question as to where his interests lay.

When Gen. Wedemeyer recommended that light arms and munitions seized from the Germans be shipped to the Chinese Nationalists, with the approval of the Joint Chiefs of Staff, Lauchlin Currie, as Presidential Assistant ordered the first shipment of 20,000 rifles stopped en route. The Lauchlin order, on White House stationery, forbade any such assistance to Nationalist China. (107:36) He ordered Army supplies, urgently needed by the Chinese Nationalist forces, dumped in the Indian Ocean. (15:287) There seems to be little question that Lauchlin Currie played as important a role in delivery of China to the Communists as did another of the Rockefellers' Red agents, Gen. George Catlett Marshall. (15:294f)

Lauchlin Currie was able to serve the conspirators especially effectively because he exercised supervision over the Foreign Economic Administration and was able to by-pass the Office of Far Eastern Affairs and the State Department and to transmit to superiors false reports favorable to the Communists. (107:117)

## ROCKEFELLER AGENT CURRIE MASTERMINDED IMF ORGANIZATION

Currie was revealed by Congressional investigations into internal subversion to have been particularly active in the Treasury in formulating the plans for the Bretton Woods Conference and the resultant International Monetary Fund, and placing his pawn, Harry Dexter White, at its head. (59)

For the purpose of averting complete exposure of his activities in connection with the Alger Hiss case, and of evading service and subpoenas and escaping indictments, Lauchlin Currie was shipped to Colombia (the South American hotbed of Communism that harbored such characters as Fidel Castro) after he had served them in Switzerland as chief of an economic and financial mission in connection with his brainchild, the International Monetary Fund and its subsidiaries. (321) In Colombia, he served the conspirators, in 1949, first as chief of the economic mission of the International Bank for Reconstruction and Redevelopment. In the following year, he was appointed chief of the conspirators' monetary mission to Colombia. In 1952, he was promoted to the post of adviser to their National Planning Council of the Colombian government. (60:613) The "success" of his mission and the effectiveness of his services to the conspirators is clearly indicated by the complete financial debacle of Colombia, the total breakdown of law and order there, with concomitant stimulus to the Communist cause, and the eventual takeover by the Communists of the Colombian government.

## CONSPIRATORS GIVE CURRIE REFUGE IN BRITISH COLUMBIA

Currie's departure to Colombia to take up permanent residence there is reported to have been timed, in 1950, to avert questioning by a Senate committee regarding his Communist activities. (321) When questioned in 1948, at the same time as was White, he had shown the aplomb of an experienced agent, in contrast with White's shocked collapse, and had employed the conspirators' influential "mouthpiece," former Secretary of State Dean Acheson, to defend him. He then had brazenly held his ground and denied amply verified charges, depending upon the friendliness of the committee that held a number of collaborators.

When, in 1953, Attorney General Herbert Brownell made public the report of Bentley to the FBI made in 1945, and ample corroborative evidence, Currie was safe from indictment, in exile and become a citizen of Colombia, with a contract for reorganizing its administrative setup for the conspirators, for a fee of $150,000. In 1967, when his former associates and confederates had risen to posts as high as Supreme Court Justice, his Rockefeller bosses had emerged as open rulers of the U.S. and the world, and his crimes all but forgotten if not barred from prosecution by the Statute of Limitations, the conspirators promoted his rehabilitation as they did that of another of their agents who had been convicted of perjury in connection with treason, Alger Hiss, through the influence of their "educational" philanthropies. Lauchlin Currie was appointed visiting professor at the Simon Fraser University, Burnaby, British Columbia. Whether his salary there will be paid by Rockefellers' Foundation, as was their agent's, William McKenzie King, at McGill University, or whether their immense influence in the educational world was involved, has not come to light. He will join the ranks of Rockefeller agents, including Alger Hiss, in subverting another generation, through "education."

## NELSON ROCKEFELLER PROMOTED "FOREIGN AID" TAX-PAYER LOOTING TO EVADE JOHNSON ACT

While Rockefeller agents were busily engaged in carrying out phases of the conspiracy, Nelson Rockefeller turned his acquisitive "genius" to other of its aspects for personal and familial profits. The "foreign" bond racket had been thoroughly exposed and scotched by the Johnson Act of 1934, which barred the sale in the U.S. of bonds issued in the post-World War I era, in the names of other countries through which the conspirators had been enormously enriched, and purchasers swindled by default by the foreign countries that had received only small fractions of the money raised in their names. These bonds had enabled the conspirators to swindle both the public and their correspondent banks throughout the country out of billions of dollars. And they had helped the conspirators to bankrupt thousands of banks. What better field was there for the operations of the Rockefellers and their "Philanthropic" Foundation Trust than to find some method of perpetuating such fabulous brigandage?

Accordingly, it is hardly to be wondered that the Rockefeller

124

Foundation and its subsidiaries and affiliates began to issue bleating, plaintive reports on the subject of the "necessity" for rendering "Christian charity" and "aid" to all "needy" lands where they discerned ample plunder. They propagandized the treasonous concept that we are a "Christian nation," and must substitute Christian, Nazarene doctrine, which is "internationalist" Communism, for our Constitution as the law of the land. By this means they have deluded the nation into hastening the doom of our Republic.

## THE FUNDAMENTAL ANTITHESIS BETWEEN RELIGION & GOVERNMENT

If it were more widely realized how basically the function of government is the very antithesis of that of religion, especially of Jewish, Nazarene Communism that now parades under the name of Christianity (58), there might be more hope of salvaging our Republic and our Constitution from the destruction that has been wrought by the conspirators. The function of our Government, as defined by the Constitution, is to serve us *in our present existence*, to safeguard our sovereignty and to protect our country and ourselves against the rest of the world in order to insure our "life, liberty and pursuit of happiness."

The prime purpose of religions, including the Judeo-Christian faiths, is to induce people and nations to surrender their sovereignty to the power-mad and loot-hungry peddlers of deities who are represented as *"internationalist"* rulers of the world acting through their intensely *nationalist* vicars on earth; and to surrender our personal liberty, our wealth upon which it rests, and if required, even our lives, in this present existence, in return for their assurance of *"salvation" in an alleged future existence*. Until this antithesis is universally recognized, the existence of nations and of peace among them is all but impossible. For the strife between religions and sects has accounted for more brutality, bloodshed, massacres and wars than any other criminal pretext.

## RELIGION VS. "PHILANTHROPY"

Briefly stated, both lay and religious politicians seek power and control of wealth. Government, through which the lay politician operates, rightly should undertake to provide security in the present existence. The religions, through which priesthoods operate, require varying measures of sacrifice of security in the present existence in return for a promise of security in an alleged future existence.

The conspirators, posing as "philanthropists," with their so-called social service agents, require sacrifice of other persons which they allege will bring security and rewards in the present existence. They craftily evade informing us, their victims, that the security and rewards in the present existence will be for themselves only.

## MAGNA CARTA HISTORY REVEALS THE FUNDAMENTAL CLASH OF RELIGION & FREEDOM

The little known history of the basic charter of human freedom in modern times, the Magna Carta, reveals clearly the fundamental and basic clash between religion, as exemplified by Christianity, and the concept of human liberty and freedom. The story is succinctly related in a publication of the British Museum, in connection with its exhibit of the original documents, written by

G. R. C. Davis, entitled *Magna Carta*. (211).

King John had refused to accept Stephen Langton who had been designated Archbishop of Canterbury by Pope Innocent III. As a consequence, England had been placed under Papal interdict in the following year, 1208; and in the next year, King John himself had been excommunicated. The barons had taken advantage of the Pope's withdrawal of support from King John to rebel against him and threaten his overthrow unless he would grant them the basic human rights that they incorporated in a draft of the Magna Carta. At the same time he was threatened by invasion by the French king, His Catholic Majesty Philip Augustus, that had been instigated by the Pope.

Faced with defeat by these forces aligned against him by the Vatican, King John ran for cover, and sought to regain the support of the Pope. He returned the title to his kingdoms of England and Ireland to the Pope, as vassals, swore submission and loyalty to him, accepted Langton as Archbishop of Canterbury, and offered the Pope a vassal's bond of fealty and homage, an annual tribute of 1,000 marks (equivalent to a bit more than 666 pounds sterling) and the return of the Church property he had seized when he had rebelled against it. Two months later, in July 1213, King John was absolved of excommunication, at Winchester, by the returned Archbishop of Canterbury Langton. Three months later, on October 3, 1213, King John ratified his surrender of his kingdoms to the Pope, who by virtue of his position as vicar of Christ claims ownership of everything and everyone on earth in the tradition of the Nazarene-Communist supercapitalist superdictatorship that is true fundamentalist Christianity. (356)

On April 21, 1214, the Pope, in Rome, formally accepted King John's surrender of his kingdoms and his pledge of vassal (together with the moneys paid in tribute); and three months later, in July 1214, Pope Innocent III raised the interdict against the English. Thus the Pope assured the English of "access to Heaven," from which they had been "barred" by their king's opposition to the Church's Nazarene, or Communist, totalitarianism and denial of civil rights to mankind.

In the meanwhile, on August 25, 1213, at St. Paul's Cathedral, Archbishop Langton asserted his role as ringleader of the rebellious barons and swung those who were not satisfied by King John's surrender to the Pope into line, by supporting their demand that the king sign a draft of an agreement assuring their rights as humans, to appease them and put an end to the rebellion that he and the Holy See had been instrumental in inciting. For, without subduing the insurrection, the Vatican would lose the advantages gained in the deal with King John. The signing of the document was deferred pending a campaign by King John in France to counter the threat of invasion.

On return from his defeat in France, King John was confronted, in January 1215, at the Temple in London, by an armed and. insistent band of barons requiring that he sign the documents incorporating their demands for human rights.

As vassal of the Pope, King John dispatched envoys to Rome to receive instructions from him, after securing a delay from the barons until the Sunday after Easter on the pretext that their demands were too complex for immediate decision. The Pope's reply to the king's message was a suggestion of delay by the device of "arbitration." On May 9, 1215, the king proposed to the barons "arbitration" before a court consisting of representatives of himself, of the barons and of the Pope, after the barons had besieged the royal castle at Northampton. This proposal was rejected by the barons. And they answered on May 17, 1215, by capturing London. The king's negotiators, who included Archbishop Langton, finally effected an agreement with the barons, about June 10, 1215, at a conference at Runnymede, that was signed and sealed by King John on or about the date that the Magna Carta bears, June 15, 1215.

After he had been forced to sign the Magna Carta by threat of defeat by the barons, King John sent word of it, by envoy, to the Pope. The envoys returned several months later, bearing Papal bulls, dated August 24 and 25. Pope Innocent III declared the Magna Carta to be:

*"...unlawful and unjust as it is base and shameful...whereby the Apostolic See is brought into contempt, the Royal Prerogative diminished, the English outraged, and the whole Enterprise of the Crusade greatly imperiled."* (211:14)

On these grounds and on the ground that "the king had been compelled to enter upon it by force and fear" (211:14), and on the implied ground that it violated the basic tenets of Christianity in its denial of dictatorial rights to him and his henchmen, *Pope Innocent III denied on behalf of the Church the Declaration of Human Rights as embodied in the Magna Carta, because possession of rights by anyone violates the tenets of the Church.*

The Papal bulls were greeted by the barons with a resumption of the civil war in England. The Pope was so enraged at the failure of Archbishop of Canterbury Langton to destroy the rebellious barons and carry out the orders incorporated in his bull, that he suspended him from his office when he visited Rome at the end of September 1215, to attend the Fourth Lateran Council. Undoubtedly with the consent, and probably at the direction of the Vatican, the French invaded England under Prince Louis and joined forces in a treacherous alliance with the barons, as pretender to the throne of King John.

The sudden death of King John, in October 1216, brought to the throne his nine-year-old son, as King Henry III. His supporters revived the Magna Carta to appease the barons and gain their support against the pretender who was badly routed. These circumstances barred any further effective opposition to the Magna Carta by the Pope, without risking loss of the 666 pounds tribute.

## PAPACY'S INCITEMENT TO STRIFE OBEYED CHRIST'S VERIFIED TEACHING

Pope Innocent's rejection of the Magna Carta and the bill of human rights that it embodied, did more than uphold the totalitarianism of the Church. In inciting to strife he followed implicitly one of the few teachings of Jesus Christ, "The Prince of Peace," that is verified in the Gospels by two of His Apostles. Thus St. Levy (Mark 2:14; Luke 5:27), alias Matthew, cites Jesus as follows:

127

*"34 Think not that I am come to send peace on earth: I came not to send peace, but a sword.*

*"35. For I am come to set a man at variance against his father, and the daughter against her mother, and the daughter-in-law against her mother-in-law.*

*"36 And a man's foes shall be they of his own household.* (Matthew 10:34-36)

Repeated by St. Luke, this one of the few teachings of Jesus found in the Gospels that is verified by two witnesses, reads:

*"49. I am come to send fire on earth; and what if it be already kindled?*

*"51 Suppose ye that I am come to give peace on earth? I tell you nay; but rather division.*

*"52. For from henceforth there shall be five in one house divided, three against two and two against three.*

*"53 The father shall be divided against the son, and the son against the father; the mother against the daughter, and the daughter against the mother; the mother-in-law against the daughter-in-law, and the daughter-in-law against the mother-in-law."* (Luke 12:49, 51-3)

Nothing more clearly reveals the antithesis of government and religion than these facts. It is the function of government to maintain law and order to further peace in our present existence, if it be good government; and not to promote strife in the present existence for the purpose of insuring "salvation" in an alleged future existence. And it is the function of good government to assure those true civil rights that imply equality before the law; and not do deny them, as do religions, for the purpose of giving wealth and power to its priests or a class designated by them, for one purpose or another, as "privileged." An understanding of these facts enables one to better understand and evaluate the attitude of religious leaders in the matter of the so-called "Civil Rights" of Negroes, that are in reality gross civil wrongs in that they deny to whites the freedom of choice of associates and promote strife. (273) It better enables one to understand the role of the clergy in inciting strife by this subversive activity of theirs.

## NELSON ROCKEFELLER "GETS RELIGION," & PROFITS FROM "FOREIGN AID"

Nelson Rockefeller, "New Dealer" and Roosevelt "intimate adviser," supported by the Rockefeller and allied foundations, dedicated himself to solving the problem of circumventing the Johnson Act and continuing the looting of American taxpayers through the agency of foreign lands. His "solution" of the problem was substituting duped, voluntary participation in what was represented to the nation as profitable "investment" in bonds for the supposed "aid" to foreign lands, with compulsory, nationwide looting of taxpayers in the name of other lands. The Constitution bars the taxation of the nation for the support of any other land than our own. But the conspirators enlisted the support of the clergy in this looting of theirs with the lie that the U.S. "is a Christian nation";

and "it must show Christian Nazarene charity" to all other lands, including especially their Soviet partners. This new confidence game the conspirators accordingly gave the name "foreign aid."

Nelson Rockefeller displayed inordinate zeal in the use of this "religious" swindling device that has become a tradition in the Rockefeller Dynasty. (79) He dedicated himself, during decades, almost exclusively, to imposing on the American taxpayers so-called "foreign aid" schemes that convert the Government into a device for their merciless looting. He and his fellow conspirators made a dead letter of the Constitution and of the law, and mocked the nation while looting it through an endless array of "foreign aid" tricks and swindles that, charitably speaking, are little short of treason. (79)

## ROCKEFELLER CONSPIRATORS AND FOUNDATIONS FLAUNT CONSTITUTION & LAW

Rockefeller's "foreign aid" schemes, in addition to violating the provisions of the Constitution, also violate the Logan Act which bars any individual or group from meddling in the foreign affairs of the nation. This Act is never mentioned or applied nowadays, except to those who oppose the conspirators. Even perfidious interference in the nation's international relations, and meddling in the pattern followed by the son of the Rockefellers' Baptist minister, their agent, Cyrus Eaton and his Pugwash cells, are completely immune from interference or prosecution.

The Rockefellers and the foundations that they control, including the Carnegie and the Ford foundations, openly boast of their complete disregard of Constitution and law. Thus the Rockefellers boasted in the 1935 report of their Rockefeller Foundation:

## "THE FOUNDATIONS HAS LONG BEEN CONCERNED WITH INTERNATIONAL RELATIONS"

"Through the promotion of . . . two types of enterprise, i.e., the stimulating of more intelligent (sic) public opinion by a variety of activities and the furnishing of experts for specific planning...the Foundation has achieved some results, and it is hoped will accomplish more in the future." (110:216)

This is a frank and open statement of violation of the laws under which the foundations are chartered. Inasmuch as their capital funds are moneys withheld from the Treasury by tax-exemption, they are public funds that rightly can only be used in and for our country. The laws also provide that none of their moneys may be used for political purposes, either at home or abroad, under penalty of abrogation of their charter, confiscation of their capital funds by the Treasury and imposition of taxes on their incomes, with additional penalties for tax evasion.

Nothing would better serve the interests of our country and of the world than the wiping out of the bogus "philanthropic" foundations and of their "philanthropic" sponsors for their flagrant contempt of the law. But the Rockefeller dominated "Philanthropic" Foundation Trust is a super-governmental agency that figuratively "thumb their noses" at governments and enable the Rockefellers to adopt the attitude: *"La lois c'est moi."*

Little need it be wondered that the Rockefellers have sent

their obedient puppet John J. McCloy (15) to Salzburg, Austria, to "advise," or dictate, in an address before the conspirators' international seminar for diplomats at Klessheim Palace, the extension to other lands of their super-governmental agencies, their foundations. Agent McCloy is quoted as pleading:

"I wish that there could be erected in Europe a complex of foundations whose representatives could exchange thoughts with those of American foundations and thus form a sort of informal approach to some of the great problems of the day." (112)

The dispatch made it clear that McCloy was speaking in the role of Trustee of the Rockefeller Foundation.

The value that the conspirators place on their foundations and their super- and supra-governmental powers, it has long been recognized, far exceeds their value as tax-exempt dodges. The Jesuit master conspirator, Adam Weishaupt, had conceived of the use of pseudo-philanthropic foundations as a device for gaining worldwide dominion through a "United Nations" more than a century earlier. The conspirators are merely following the same pattern of their use for the brainwashing of nations by control of education and all forms of mass communications, including the subsidy of authors, columnists and reporters, for which efforts Weishaupt had set the pattern when he enlisted the aid of Rousseau, Voltaire, Goethe, Payne and Thomas Jefferson.

## CONSPIRATORS BAR CONGRESS FROM EXPOSURE OF THEIR FOUNDATION CRIMES

The conspirators brook no interference with the power that they wield through their foundations, or exposure of them. This was made clear by their actions when Congressman Carroll Reece was appointed by the House to investigate their foundations. Reece invited this author, as an authority on the subject, to come to Washington for the purpose of serving as the Committee's chief investigator into the foundations. It can hardly be regarded as more of an "accident" that Carroll Reece became deathly ill, shortly after the interview, than were the deaths of Senators Robert A. Taft and Joseph McCarthy when they voted against "foreign aid," of Larry Duggan who "squealed," or of James Forrestal who carried his investigations into their treason too far. (15; 79)

During Reece's "ailment," the conspirators rigged the committee with scantily informed personnel, including some of their agents. One of the personnel of the Committee, Red Wayne L. Hays, Congressman from Ohio, blocked the investigation by abusing, attacking and outshouting informed witnesses, and forcing a discontinuance of the investigation. As a consequence, that great menace to our Republic and to human freedom, the bogus Rockefeller "Philanthropic" Foundation Trust, continues to flourish.

## KINSMAN, COL. McCORMICK, EXPOSED ROCKEFELLER "FOREIGN AID" PROFITS

Rockefeller "foreign aid" thievery was exposed by a kinsman of theirs, Col. Robert McCormick, in an editorial in his Chicago Tribune of December 13, 1948, as follows:

"ROCKEFELLER PROFITS FROM THE MARSHALL PLAN

"THE TRIBUNE has examined official records of Marshal. business for the 45 day period ended September 15 — one-eighth of the first year of the plan. It appears, for example, that the Anglo-American Oil Company, Ltd., obtained permission from the British government to go shopping for petroleum products in America. The record shows that it was able to buy $7,258,332 worth of products from the Esso Export corporation and the Standard Oil Export corporation, both of New York. Thus the British concern got the oil it was after, and was doubtless able to make a good profit selling it to its customers. The two American companies were paid in dollars in New York for the oil supplied to the British companies, likewise on a remunerative basis.

"What makes the transactions notable is that the British buyer, Anglo-American, is owned 100 per cent by the Standard Oil Company of New Jersey. The American sellers, Esso Export and Standard Oil Export, are also owned 100 per cent by Standard of New Jersey. Thus what the Marshall Plan actually did was to enable the biggest American oil company to shift some merchandise from one department to another, collecting two profits on the operation, at the expense of the American taxpayer.

"Esso Export corporation also sold $4,020,210 worth of its products to a certain French concern, called Standard Francaise des Petroles, with ECA footing the bill. This French concern is 83.63 per cent owned by Standard of New Jersey. Other subsidiaries of the leading Rockefeller concern, operating in Norway and other countries, also made deals with sister companies. If Standard Oil of New Jersey continues such transactions all year at the rate attained in the 45 days covered by our study, it will buy and sell itself $ 120,000,000 worth of oil in the period, at the expense of the American taxpayer.

"Meanwhile, another French concern, Les Raffineries de la Vacuum Oil, got permission to go shopping for some crude oil, too, and wound up making a deal with its parent company, Socony-Vacuum Oil Company, formerly the Standard Oil Company of New York. The transactions amounted to $2,249,877 in a 45 day period. If this rate is continued for a full year under the Marshall Plan, another huge Rockefeller concern will buy and sell itself $18,000,000 worth of oil at the expense of the American taxpayer.

"This lucrative oil business, with the Rockefeller companies collecting double profits, is the real Marshall Plan in operation. It is undoubtedly true that if the plan to aid Europe never had been conceived, the Rockefeller interests would have found means to carry on their export business in petroleum, though not as profitably, of course.

"It should not escape notice that members of the Rockefeller family played an important part in getting the Marshall Plan through Congress. They worked through an organization called the Committee for the Marshall Plan to Aid European Recovery. *John D. Rockefeller Jr., the demonstrated boss of all Standard*

*Oil companies, was on the inner executive council of the committee. Nelson A. Rockefeller, the son of John D. Jr., was on the main body of the committee.*

"Here is more evidence that the people who put the Marshall Plan over on the American people are cashing in on it. It already has been revealed that Anderson, Clayton & Co. has received more money from the Marshall Plan in operation than any other concern. The head of that company is William Clayton, who, while a top figure in the government, did more to shape the foreign aid program than any other individual.

"The big New York banks, whose directors also played an important role in promoting European aid in Congress, have been repaid with a nearly exclusive franchise on the letter of credit business resulting from the program. Banks in the interior of the country were formerly very active in financing exports. The interior banks had no part in promoting the Marshall Plan and they have been cut out of this highly profitable, risk-free business.

"A leading member of Congress, Chairman Walter Ploeser of the House Small Business Committee, issued a statement Wednesday calling upon Congress for an investigation of the circumstances under which Clayton has been able to monopolize the ECA cotton business. Reports are current that the Senate will be asked to look into the monopoly of the Wall Street banks in ECA transactions. The investigation also should cover multiple commissions and profits under the Marshall Plan, such as those enjoyed by the Rockefeller oil companies."*

## NELSON ROCKEFELLER "DEDICATED" TO "FOREIGN (ROCKEFELLER) AID"

The extremely lucrative character of Rockefeller's bogus "foreign aid" plan explains his extreme dedication to it. He devoted himself tirelessly to lobbying it through Congress and to propagandizing it personally throughout the nation. He placed himself on call twenty-four hours a day for this task. And let it be known that he would appear anywhere in the nation, at any time of the day, to sing its praise and urge its adoption. It was for him, obviously a work of love and rare devotion — to the looted dollars. "Foreign (Rockefeller) aid" has proved to be far more profitable to the conspirators than either their "foreign" bond or Dawes Plan frauds, and has proved to be a way of life for them that has cost the nation the burdens and grief of endless wars and give-away programs. They have cost the American taxpayers between fifty and one hundred billion dollars a year in current taxation, a total of more than one hundred billion dollars in "loans," and a national debt that is variously estimated to be between three hundred billion and a trillion dollars.

## ROCKEFELLER'S ENDLESS STREAM OF "FOREIGN (ROCKEFELLER) AID" SCHEMES

Nelson Rockefeller's return from his honeymoon trip around the world marked the beginning of his interest in foreign affairs.

---

* © 1948. Reprinted by permission of Chicago Tribune.

Significantly, it also marked the beginning of the rise of Hitler and the Nazis as a power that would menace the conspirators' British enemies, the Royal Dutch & Shell interests and their Jewish principals. This was materially facilitated by their League of Nations, which Rockefeller controlled, as has been related, through their appointment of their attorney, Raymond Fosdick, whose efforts were seconded by John D. the Third, in person, as its "Under" Secretary General. (224:188) They were completely successful in blocking any power, in or out of the League, from interfering with the "coups" that the conspirators "inspired" Hitler to undertake, in the course of the buildup of Nazi Germany. They provided Hitler and the Nazis with both oil and refineries essential for his "conquests" that they dictated. From their "philanthropy," the Rockefeller Institute, they sent their agent, Alexis Carrel, author of *Man the Unknown*, to inspire and advise Hitler on "the extermination of the unfit." This was a project that profitted them hugely by the income derived by their I. G. Farbenindustrie from the rendering of the fat of concentration camp victims. (79:101f)

In order to mask the endless flow of the "foreign aid" looting, they gave it an assortment of names in various stages of decades of its continuance. Each of them was planned and plotted in advance by Rockefellers' Foundation and their Council on Foreign Relations. After the Dawes and Young Plans that were designed to help the resurgence of Germany and incidentally of Hitler and the Nazis, there came the "Lend-Lease" Plan that the conspirators arranged for the material and financial aid to Great Britain and its allies whom their agents, Hitler and the Nazis, had driven to war and were defeating. This help, they granted, after Winston Churchill, on behalf of the British, had agreed to permit the Rockefeller-Standard Oil interests to develop the Saudi Arabian concession for which they had engineered World War I. (15:375) They contented themselves with this measure of entry into World War II, until they arranged, as has been related, to effect, through their treasonous Institute of Pacific Relations and spies that they furnished the Richard Sorge spyring, the Japanese attack on the U.S. at Pearl Harbor.

In the meantime, Nelson Rockefeller played a stellar role, as "New" Dealer, in lobbying through Congress the Universal Military Training Act which provided for the drafting of Americans to serve as self-paid mercenaries of the Dynasty in the expansion of its Empire. At about the time of our entry into the war, Nelson Rockefeller evaded the draft by emerging into the open as the Poo Bah of "foreign aid" swindles, in which role he has since continued in various capacities, up to the present. He dictated to his puppet, Pres. Roosevelt, his appointment as "Co-Ordinator of Inter-American Affairs." This self-dictated appointment served him in a number of manners. It enabled him, most importantly, to evade military service in the draft that he had helped impose on others of the same age. Incidentally, it enabled him to carve out for himself a Latin American duchy at little or no cost to himself; to further his clan's oily interests; and to pave the way for the eventual takeover of the Continent by planting the seeds of Communist revolutions that are planned to serve to make him its effective dictator. He is keenly aware of the "profits" that can accrue from such predatory seizure and the consequent totalitarianism. This clearly emerges from the ghostwritten "encyclical" that appeared in his name in *Foreign Affairs*, the official publication of the conspirators' Council on Foreign Relations, entitled *Purpose & Policy*. (22)

Meanwhile, Nelson Rockefeller managed to make his job adequately profitable, for the nonce, by demanding of Congress a granted appropriation that was reported to add to a total of six billion dollars, to use for his purposes, with no accounts rendered. The Latin American press reported that Rockefeller informed South American lands that they could not expect any of the funds appropriated by Congress for their so-called "defense," unless a deal of interest to himself and his associates was forthcoming from them. Included among those deals was return of expropriated properties of the Standard Oil companies. Latin politicians feathered their nests with such deals.

## "CO-ORDINATOR" ROCKEFELLER USED POST TO BUILD HIMSELF S. AMERICAN EMPIRES

Nelson Rockefeller, personally, acquired vast empires in South America at the expense of U.S. taxpayers. His widely publicized holdings in Venezuela are minor in comparison with those he acquired in a deal with Brazilian President, G. Vargas that later cost the latter his life, in the Province of Minas Gerais that is enormously rich in natural resources. It is thought that this deal had some bearing on the plan to move the capital of Brazil to the wilderness adjoining Minas Gerais, at Brasilia, expenditures for which have strained Brazilian solvency.

## NELSON ROCKEFELLER'S COFFEE CORNER

An incidental profit was derived from the conspirators cartelization of coffee around the world for the purpose of steeply raising the market price of their Brazilian production. Rockefeller had become a major producer of the coffee as a result of this deal. This world-wide monopoly of coffee was financed by the conspirators at the expense of American taxpayers, through the Export Import Bank. And as a result of the setting up of this Coffee Trust, that has been made a subsidiary of their U.N., the conspirators raised the cost of coffee to us, their American "peasants," from twenty-five cents to a high of one dollar and fifty cents a pound. (79:111; 386)

"Co-Ordinator" Rockefeller chose as his employees and collaborators a host of his Council on Foreign Relations agents and numerous Communists and Nazis of varying degree of notoriety. He chose as his fiscal agent, Paul Nitze, nephew of North German Lloyd agent Paul Hilke who was a close collaborator of German Ambassador-spy Count von Bernstorff. Bernstorff was ousted because of his involvement in the Black Tom explosion. Paul Nitze subsequently was made by the conspirators Secretary for the Navy in the conspirators' munitions and arms sales agency that they named "Defense" Department. Communist and Nazi agents were planted throughout South America to serve the conspirators. Some dedicated their efforts to protecting the interests of the conspirators in I. G. Farbenindustrie. (79:107)

## "UNITED" NATIONS — A ROCKEFELLER
## CREATION & CREATURE

Through the "Rockefeller Committee" Nelson Rockefeller managed to transplant himself and his subversive crew into the State Department, entering it "through the back door." Subsequently he personally directed the surrender of our national sovereignty to the Rockefeller-Soviet Axis through their dis-"United" Nations agency. This he accomplished with the treasonous collaboration of his intimate associate and agent, Alger Hiss, and other Council on Foreign Relations agents. Later Rockefeller boasted that he had abetted Hiss's treasonous role. (387) The "United" Nations aspect of the conspiracy originally conceived and launched by Jesuit Adam Weishaupt, father of modernday Communism, in 1776, prior to the American Revolution, was only slightly revamped by the conspirators and their foundations in the years prior to their consummating it at San Francisco in 1945. Evidence on this subject is offered by the organization by the CFR agents of the conspirators of the *United Nations Relief & Rehabilitation Administration*, popularly known as the UNRRA more than a year before they launched their "United" Nations conspiracy.

As soon as the thievery and treason of the UNRRA became notorious (113:297), the conspirators were at hand, once again under the leadership of lobbyist Nelson Rockefeller, with another name for it with which to dupe the nation, the so-called "Marshall" Plan, that was operated by another dummy front of theirs, the "Economic Cooperation Administration."

## EARL BROWDER & COMMUNIST PARTY JOIN ROCKEFELLER
## IN "POINT 4"

When Congress rebelled against the conspirators' "foreign aid" looting, "Marshall" Plan, Nelson Rockefeller was ready at hand with another camouflage for its thievery and its treasonous role in the Korean War in providing Saudi Arabian oil to the North Koreans and Chinese Communists with which to slaughter our GI's at the expense of American taxpayers. (15:417-23; 79:141) "Point 4" is so characteristic of the machinations of the conspirators that it deserves detailed study. It was originally launched in the Rockefeller Foundation as a device for the development of industries in foreign lands that had been grabbed by the conspirators for cutthroat competition with American industries that they plan to ruin with an eye to stealing them; and for the purpose of breaking the back of Organized Labor in those industries by creating vast unemployment in them with imports from such cheap labor markets that they control, as Japan.

For the purpose of intensification of the situation, the conspirators have effected virtual elimination of tariff protection for those industries by such of their devices as GATT. For the purpose of avoiding expense to themselves of transferring American knowhow to their cheap labor markets overseas and for training the cheap labor in the requisite skills, they impose the cost of the "Point 4" scheme on the very American workers whom they plot to impoverish and the industries that they plan to bankrupt, or embarass financially.

135

Intensive propaganda was arranged for this program by the conspirators by having their card-holding Communist agents, who constitute the backbone of the "Party" in the U.S., make it an integral part of their "Party-Line." This was done by Earl Browder in his book, *The Road to Teheran*, that was published by the Communist *International Press*, in 1943. Browder dilated on the conspirators' plans as follows:

"Our government can create a series of giant industrial development corporations, each in partnership with some other government or group of governments, and set them to work upon large scale plans of railroad and highway building, agricultural and industrial development...in all the devastated and undeveloped areas of the world. America has the skilled technicians capable of producing the plans for such projects..." (50:79)

Browder also divulged the programs that the conspirators had drawn up for Africa after they had taken it over by an "anti-Colonialism" campaign that was designed to mask their looting, now being carried out, as follows:

"America can underwrite a gigantic program of industrialization of Africa..." (50:53)

This plot was next transferred from the Communist "Party-Line" to the January 20, 1949, Inaugural Address of the conspirator's kinsman, Pres. Harry Shippe Truman, in which it is cited as "Point 4," whence it derives its title. Cousin Truman dutifully and promptly appointed Nelson Rockefeller chairman of a "committee" to bring in a "report" on his scheme. The so-called "committee" consisted of a group of Rockefeller agents, employees and sycophants who could be depended upon to comply with his every raving. They included:

Robert P. Daniel, Baptist minister, v.p. of Conference of Presidents of Negro Colleges that are liberally subsidized by the Rockefellers.

Harvey S. Firestone Jr., member of Rockefellers' CFR, who has extensive interests in Liberia and might expect to benefit from "foreign aid."

James W. Gerard, former U.S. Ambassador to Germany who served the conspirators well in that role.

Thomas Parran, former Surgeon General of the U.S. Public Health Service, who served the conspirators loyally in their "health" and drug rackets.

Jacob Potofsky, member of Rockefellers' CFR, president of Amalgamated Clothing Workers (Union) of America, CIO.

After a lapse of two years, Nelson Rockefeller submitted his scheme as a "Committee Report." In the interim, bills providing for appropriations for the so-called "Marshall Plan" narrowly averted defeat in Congress, in spite of Rockefeller's insistent and persistent personal lobbying for it. The usual Rockefeller tactics were employed, of bringing to bear on the Congressman every available measure of pressure and coercion, as was his practise throughout the forties and fifties whenever any of his "foreign (Rockefeller) aid" measures were under consideration.

Senators Joseph McCarthy and Robert Taft earned Nelson Rockefeller's undying hatred, which they did not long survive, because of their opposition to his "foreign aid" steal measures in the 1949 and 1950 sessions of Congress. Neither of them lived long thereafter.

Rockefeller's "Committee" report was published in his name under the amusing title of *Partners in Progress* (84). As might be surmised, the "Report" urged immediate adoption of his scheme in as glowing terms as his ghost writers could find. "Point 4" looting, it represented, would prove the salvation of the world and provide eternal peace, so long as the conspirators collected their plunder. With the support of Pres. Truman, Nelson Rockefeller lobbied his "Point 4" plot through Congress, personally. As was his unvarying practise where "foreign (Rockefeller) aid" was concerned, he dedicated all his time, day and night, to pressuring Congress for passage of the bill. Where billions of loot are concerned, Rockefellers are always most dedicated.

Long before the "Point 4" program was exposed, the conspirators had ready at hand numerous "new" camouflages for their "foreign aid" brigandage. They included their so-called "Administration for International Development" and their "Alliance for Progress" that is dedicated to intensify their looting of South America. Nelson Rockefeller's "foreign aid" plots have cost the American taxpayers more than a hundred billion dollars in monetary outlay. It has seriously impaired the solvency of the Treasury and deliberately created for the nation an unfavorable balance of payment. Its use for undermining our continued existence as a nation is the problem that now confronts us.

The Rockefeller profits from their "foreign aid" plots have been huge. The hundreds of million dollars of multiple profits of their Standard Oil companies that kinsman Col. McCormick exposed in his above-cited editorial, are minute fraction of their loot. "Foreign aid" has been proved "Rockefeller aid" in thousands of their enterprises around the world. Their refineries and other facilities in numerous lands were rebuilt, and many an old one enlarged and new ones built, with "foreign aid" funds. A gas recycling plant in Saudi Arabia was built with "foreign aid" moneys, at the expense of American taxpayers, for Rockefellers' Arabian American (Oil) Co. Aramco's oil was treasonously supplied to the North Koreans and Chinese Communists during the Korean War, at the expense of American taxpayers for use in slaughtering our GI's. (15:79)

The list of this treasonous "foreign aid" looting could be extended into volumes. Since our topic is the "Federal" Reserve and the influence of "foreign aid" on our finance and monetary system, the author refers the reader to other works, including his own, for more detailed discussion of the thievery and corruption involved. (15; 79; 114) It is a safe guess that a minimum of 70% of all so-called "foreign aid" went into the coffers of the conspirators, in one way or another. And much of the balance of it went into bribery at home and in the lands in the names of which the funds were granted to themselves by the conspirators.

## MOFFETT SWINDLED TAXPAYERS FOR ROCKEFELLER-S.O.
## & WAS SWINDLED BY THEM

One instance of bribery at home that illustrates the "philanthropy" of the conspirators deserves mention at this point. It came to light through a lawsuit brought against the Rockefeller-Standard Oil group by a kinsman of the conspirators, James Moffett. Moffett was a Standard Oil executive who had been "loaned" by the company to the Government during World War I "to supervise the purchase of oil during the war" in the manner desired by the conspirators. This "loan" proved immensely profitable to him and to his bosses. And at the end of the war he returned to his Standard Oil job.

Once again, during the "New" Deal Moffett was "loaned" to the Administration for nominal purpose of serving as Housing Administrator. The real and ulterior purpose behind this move of the conspirators was to "induce" Pres. Roosevelt to give them $160,000,000 of the two billion dollars appropriated by Congress to spend as he saw fit and without rendering any account, for development of the Saudi Arabian oilfield. For "inducing" Roosevelt to divert this money from the war effort into their purse, the conspirators contracted to pay Moffett a commission of 5% of the sum, or eight million dollars.

Moffett's efforts were crowned with complete success. He had no difficulty in convincing Roosevelt that he should be "liberal" to his patron bosses. What role Roosevelt's "intimate" adviser, Nelson Rockefeller played in plying the President was not revealed.

With characteristic chicanery, the conspirators refused to pay Moffett the contracted commission when the deal was consummated. They also refused to give him back his job from which he had been "loaned," when he left the government service; and left him stranded. Moffett brought suit against Standard Oil Co. to recover his eight million dollars commission, won the suit and was awarded a verdict of $1,800,000.00. But the conspirators appealed the case and arranged to have it heard before one of their legal pawns, a retired judge, in the role of "referee."

The judge handed down a most curious verdict, denying Moffett the commission required by his contract. He ruled that the deal was "against public interest"; and that, therefore, the beneficiaries were entitled to keep the entire proceeds of the conspiracy and did not have to pay the commission and share the loot with Moffett. This situation truly depicts the "honor among the thieves." The shady nature of the "deal" is apparent from the ultra-rapid withdrawal of a bill introduced by a Senatorial agent of the conspirators, prior to the Moffett contract, that provided for an appropriation of the $160,000,000 for the same purpose, as soon as it was exposed by some editors and columnists, including this author. (79)

## CONGRESSMEN DISREGARD WARNING, VOTE FOR
## "MARSHALL" PLAN & ARE DEFEATED

The extent of the malign power of Rockefeller over our Government is further illustrated by the action of the Republican majority of the 78th Congress in following his dictation and voting in favor of his "Marshall" Plan, in spite of the fact that they had been warned against it by this author in a talk at the dinner of the "78th Club." They were warned that they would face defeat in 1948 if they would vote for the plan, because the funds that Rockefeller importuned them to appropriate for it would be used for the same subversive purposes as the conspirators' OPA. Unfortunately, Rockefeller's lobbying prevailed. And the prediction proved too accurate. Most of the Congressmen who voted for the "Marshall" Plan were defeated in a campaign in which "New" Dealer Rockefeller played a large role—behind the scenes. As a consequence, control of Congress returned to the hands of the "New" and "Fair" Dealers.

An interesting sidelight on the continuity of the Rockefeller Dynasty's plottings from generation to generation and the wholehearted collaboration of its members is presented by little brother David Rockefeller's "improvement" on the "Point 4" plot. As launched by Nelson Rockefeller, the program had a serious defect. Though it provided technologists to train their cheap foreign labor, it failed to provide the executive ability without which these foreign enterprises of the conspirators would be certain to fail.

Brother David devised a way to provide the needed executive ability at no cost to the conspirators. He organized the executives, that their enterprises slough off and "retire," into a group who were induced to volunteer their services at no cost, to the overseas enterprises in order to insure their success. This is acknowledged to have been a huge success in making "foreign (Rockefeller) aid" more effective in their ruinous competition with American industry and labor.

## ROCKEFELLER'S IBEC OPERATES MOST PROFITABLY ON "FOREIGN AID" MONEYS

Rockefellers organized the International Basic Economy Corporation for the pretended purpose of "service" around the world. It profitably operates a wide variety of enterprises around the world with the funds levied on American taxpayers for the bogus "foreign (Rockefeller) aid." This involuntary charity of the taxpayers was arranged by the conspirators in the terms of the "aid" agreements which insured that the major part of the so-called loans would never be repaid to the Treasury and us looted "peasants." These arrangements provided that the "loans" shall be repaid by the foreign lands in their currency, at a highly depreciated rate, into special accounts maintained for use in those lands. The conspirators craftily arranged, subsequently, the passage by Congress of bills that provided that a certain percentage of those funds, termed "counterpart funds," shall be used by "unspecified" persons to establish and finance industries in the respective lands.

Under the terms of these Acts of Congress, Rockefellers' IBEC has established a chain of supermarkets in Italy that offers ruinous competition to the native grocers and greatly intensifies the hatred of Americans, with the financing of 600,000,000 lira of "counterpart funds." The company's President assured this author, at a meeting of IBEC, that the money was obtained "on the most favorable terms," intimating that may never have to be repaid, or if repaid, it would be in lira become almost worthless.

139

## "ROCKEFELLER'S CHICKEN WAR"

Another "extraordinarily successful" Rockefeller IBEC enterprise is a chain of chicken farms throughout Europe and around the world initiated in collaboration with Arbor Acre Farms, which was "absorbed" into the Rockefeller enterprise in the usual manner. In a single farm in Aprilia, Italy, the conspirators produce millions of chickens and innumerable eggs. The success of the enterprise financially is assured by the use of "counterpart funds;" and by the virtually free provision of feed for the chickens by American farmer and taxpayer funds by way of "foreign (Rockefeller) aid." The American farmers and poultrymen who supply the feed for the conspirators' chickens, as taxpayers, are rewarded by the conspirators by exclusion from the foreign markets, including the EEC, of American poultry which had previously been exported in a volume totalling more than $50,000,000 a year. Naturally, this has the further implication that our balance of trade and payments is rendered more unfavorable by the $50,000,000 loss of exports. But for Rockefellers' IBEC, this is a "most highly profitable enterprise." The enterprise has come to be known popularly as *"Rockefeller's Chicken War."* (115; 79:236).

"Foreign (Rockefeller) aid" has proved so valuable a device in the conspirators' brigandage that the Rockefellers have voiced their intent to have it continued during the balance of this century, if not forever. (155)

The vast expansion of these IBEC enterprises fraudulently financed by American taxpayers' moneys diverted into "foreign (Rockefeller) aid" is proudly illustrated by the conspirators in the *Annual 1965 Report* of their International Basic Economy Corporation in a map on its pages 16 and 17, on which are graphically portrayed the various enterprises it has undertaken around the world. The chicken farms, portrayed by the figure of a chicken in a square, have spread around the world to sixty countries, many of which had imported American poultry, including Canada, Venezuela, Colombia, Peru, Argentina, Brazil, United Kingdom, Netherlands, France, Spain, Germany, Switzerland, Lebanon, Pakistan, Zambia, Rhodesia, India, Japan and the Philippines. (416)

As Rockefeller "Chicken War" profits rose, U.S. poultry trade dropped and payment balance suffered. By 1968, the exports of American poultrymen who financed Rockefellers' chicken farms and provided them with free feed by way of "foreign aid" with their taxes, dropped from $76 million in 1962 to $46 million in 1967. On February 15, 1968, the council considering the General Agreement On Tariffs & Trade in the "Kennedy round" appointed a panel of eleven members, at the mocking instance of the conspirators, to consider the American industry's complaint that subsidized exports and protective domestic policies had severely hurt their business. (377) It is almost incredible that the conspirators' censorship of the news regarding their "Chicken War" had been so effective that the industry failed to recognize that Rockefellers and their IBEC are ruining their businesses.

## ROCKEFELLER'S "FOREIGN AID" IMPOSED SOCIALISM & INJURED RECIPIENT NATIONS

Dr. Kurt Block, Associate Editor of *Barron's*, revealed that

Rockefeller's "foreign aid" conspiracy also has undermined the lands that were supposed to be its beneficiaries, insofar as they have received any of it. He stated that Rockefeller's "Marshall" Plan undertook, like their CIA, to impose Marxism on the world; and that it enabled the conspirators, for example, to force devaluation of the British pound sterling. (378) The injury it is inflicting on the U.S. is gravest and most aggravated. It has materially aided them inflate and devalue the dollar and to bring the U.S. to the verge of fraudulent bankruptcy.

CHAPTER XVI
"HARRY DEXTER WHITE": ROCKEFELLER "FALL GUY"
IN GOLD & MONEY CONSPIRACY

The deliberate purposefulness of the brigandage of the Rockefeller "foreign aid" plot and the importance of its role in carrying out their "Gold Standard" and "Federal" Reserve conspiracy to its ultimate goal of thoroughgoing looting of the U.S. and of the world was most completely exposed by the character whom they used as a dummy front and "fall guy" in the scheme—"Harry Dexter White." His role and the services that he was called on to render the conspirators clearly emerge from the data which they have treacherously and repeatedly published through government agency, that has been obviously deliberately slanted to cast him in the role of "the villain" and "master spy." These publications that were issued by their agents on the Senate Committee on the Judiciary in the form of so-called hearings on Interlocking Subversion In Government Departments, include: *The Harry Dexter White Papers* (59) and the even more obviously slanted excerpts from his boss, Morgenthau's diaries that were "edited" by an agent of theirs, Prof. Kubek, and published by the Committee under the title *Morgenthau Diary (China) & (Germany)*. (101; 385)

The persistent effort of the conspirators to divert public suspicion from themselves by portraying White, an obvious pawn of theirs, as the ringleader of the monetary conspiracy that they had launched when he was not yet born, is made more ludicrous by each successive attempt. It is also made transparently clear and obvious by their studied efforts to cover up the obvious ties between White and Nelson Rockefeller and his top agents.

Harry Weiss, alias "Harry Dexter White," Harvard PhD, was beyond any question a "liberal," or Red. For had he not been a Red, he would never have been able to graduate from that traditional hotbed of Communism, even as an undergraduate student. His biography that is quoted in *The Harry Dexter White Papers* recounts

141

## ROCKEFELLER'S "CHICKEN WAR" FINANCED LARGELY BY "FOREIGN AID."

This illustration from the centerfold of the 1965 annual report of International Basic Economy Corp. (IBEC), the business established by Nelson Rockefeller for diverting "foreign (Rockefeller) aid" into the conspirators' purses by such of his devices as "counterpart funds." It is through this outfit that Rockefeller is waging his "Chicken War" on American farmers and poultrymen, who as taxpayers supply part of the funds and free feed for

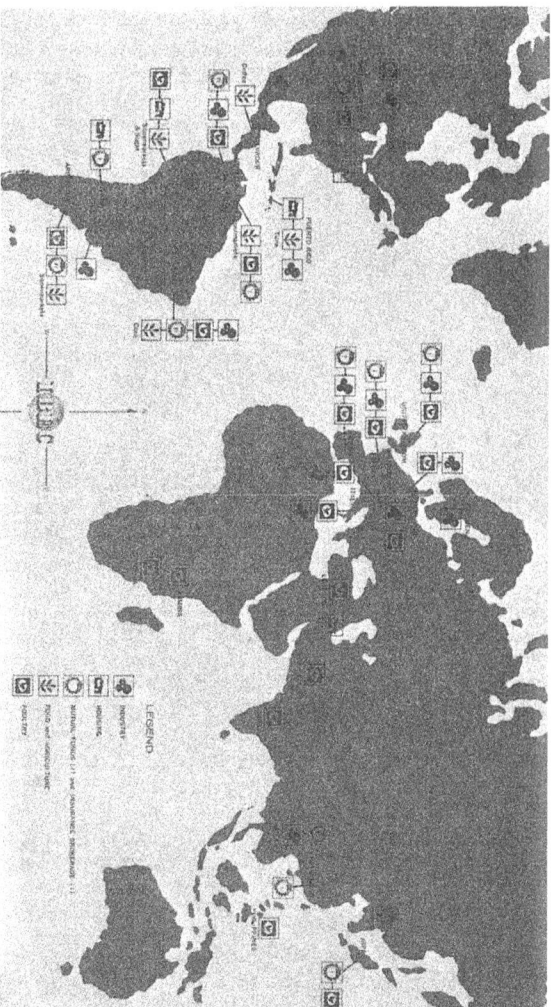

## WORLDWIDE IBEC BUSINESSES

his chickens. As a reward for helping, American producers are increasingly shut out of an ever larger number of countries, further impairing our payment balance. Through their domestic corporation, Arbor Acres, which has been incorporated in the "philanthropists'" Rockefeller Bros., they are competing ruinously with American producers at home, probably with an eye to setting up a Chicken & Egg Trust to parallel their Milk Trust.

"Born in Boston, Massachusetts, October 29, 1892, Harry Dexter White did not decide upon an academic career until he had reached his late twenties. Early years in business were interrupted by the First World War, in which he served overseas as a lieutenant in the infantry. On his return to the United States, White directed an A.E.F. orphan asylum for two years. Then resuming his education at Stanford University, he earned his B.A. in 1924, and a year later an M.A. (In 1929 he became instructor at Harvard in economics; and then had gone to Lawrence College in Appleton Wisconsin, as professor.) In 1935 White received a Ph. D. from Harvard.

"In June 1934 Professor Jacob Viner of the University of Chicago brought White to the Treasury Department to make a special study. White has since stayed there, having become Director of Monetary Research, a title created for him. In 1935 he was dispatched to England to study economic and monetary questions, the first of his official posts as Treasury spokesman there and in other countries. White took over the managing of the Treasury's two billion dollar stabilization fund in 1941, and he has represented the Treasury at the committee meetings of the Economic Defense Board. He also sits on the board of trustees of the Export-Import Bank of Washington, and is a member of the Committee on Reciprocity Information." (59:2601-2)

## ROCKEFELLER CFR, IPR & "F"R AGENT & WHITE BOSS PROVED A SOVIET AGENT

A most significant sidelight on White's career, to which no reference is made in the above biography, was the fact that he was shadowed in his early career and dominated in his later career by Rockefellers' top Communist (35; 107:117) Council on Foreign Relations monetary agent, Lauchlin B. Currie. As stated by Currie in a letter of condolence to Mrs. White on August 17, 1948:

"I met Harry at the first meeting of Ec 11 (presumably Economics 11 at Stanford University) in 1925. Thereafter our paths crossed and recrossed and our careers were roughly parallel, even to our appearing together last Friday (before the House Committee on Un-American Activities) to answer the same charges, almost exactly 23 years after our first meeting." (59:xxvi)

Currie was, as has been related, beyond any doubt a top Rockefeller-Soviet agent in the monetary field, who rated intimate association with his Rockefeller masters in their subversive agencies, that they prefer to have dubbed *The Establishment*. They include both their Foreign Office, the Council on Foreign Relations, and their treasonous, Soviet espionage agency, the Institute of Pacific Relations. In both of them Currie was associated with Prof. Jacob Viner, another Rockefeller Red from their University of Chicago, who joined him in sponsoring White.

## WHITE PAPERS PROVE THAT HE HAD NO AFFILIATION WITH COMMUNIST PARTY

By way of contrast, in all the venomously slanted propaganda directed against White by the Senate Committee on the Judiciary and other agencies of the conspirators, released as a smoke screen to shield themselves, the real traitors, there never has been adduced any proof that White was ever a member of the Communist Party or that he ever committed a provably treasonous act. Likewise the House Un-American Committee never found any record of affiliation of White with any of the numerous Communist fronts which the conspirators' agents infested. The cited Committee publication merely lists the contacts and meetings that White had noted in his carefully kept diary that was turned over to the Government after his death, with the Rockefeller-Soviet top agents that had been planted in swarms in all branches of the Roosevelt Administration, with whom he was required to meet and confer by his official position. The foreword of the *Harry Dexter White Papers* presents, ironically, this particularly pertinent advice for evaluation of its content:

"It should be understood, however, that the mere appearance of a reference to or correspondence with Harry Dexter White by any individual does not necessarily have any subversive connotation and that such references and correspondence were in many instances *inherently relevant to his official duties* and those of his associates." (59:v-vi)

Unfortunately there is no such excuse for the members of the Senate Judiciary Committee and of their staff participating in such gross distortion of the truth contained in the foreword of the *HDW Papers;* nor can they offer valid excuse for their collusion with the treasonous conspirators in shielding their treachery from exposure by besmirching the name of a dead man who can not rise to his own defense with the convincing proof offered by his carefully kept and preserved records of all his activities presented in the text of the volume. Where is the Committee's presentation of the records of the known traitors, of Lauchlin Currie agent of Rockefeller and his notorious "Establishment," or of his agent Alger Hiss, convicted of perjury in connection with treason, whom Nelson Rockefeller acknowledged shielding? (106; 132)

The close tab that Currie kept on White's activities, especially those involving China, is evident in the listing of their conferences on that subject in the Foreword of the *Papers.* (59:xxvl-vii) Seven of the thirty-one are specifically noted as dealing with China. Can it be questioned that Currie's position, as Assistant to President Roosevelt and the President's personal representative in China, was such as to make his advices, directions and orders the decisive factors in White's actions in the matter, or that his status of "aid to Soviet Military Intelligence" (103:418) determined any treason involved therein?

## HARRY DEXTER WHITE TOOK ORDERS FROM ROCKEFELLER MONETARY CONSPIRATORS

The publications of the Senate Committee on the Judiciary are virtually complete proof of the falsity of the allegations that the activities in which Harry Dexter White engaged were motivated by either his disloyalty or by treason, conscious or deliberate, on his part. On the contrary they offer complete proof that his activities were dictated by the conspirators through their agents, government employees whose collective voicing of the orders of their perfidious ringleader constituted the consensus of the ma-

143

jority of conferring officials that effectively dictated his acts. In the words of the committee itself, his activities were

"...*inherently relevant to his official duties...*" (59:v)

No evidence has been adduced by the Committees or their investigators to indicate even that White was aware that his acts conflicted with the interests of the nation, or were treasonous.

On the contrary, the evidence contained in the published portions of the *Morgenthau Diaries* (97; 101) and *The Harry Dexter White Papers* (59) quite clearly reveal that both of them went out of the way to protect our national interests from the conspirators, and to expose the conspiracy to the nation by way of their diaries. This is apparent from the entries by Morgenthau, to which reference has been made, that he was required to permit Rockefeller's Chase National Bank to juggle the gold and silver markets with public funds and that he knew that they were looting the taxpayers of millions of dollars but could do nothing about it. (97:174, 187) White undertook, as will be related, to expose the conspirators' plans for gold manipulation but was blocked from so doing by suppression of his article on the subject that would never have come to light if the Committee had not published it.

The motivation of both the appointments, of Morgenthau and White, and of the false charges of disloyalty levelled against them is revealed by the response of Pres. F. D. Roosevelt to a remark made to him by a friend of the author's, who pointed out that Morgenthau's father had expressed to him the opinion that his son knew little or nothing about finance. Roosevelt replied that Morgenthau's knowledge of finance was of no consequence but implied that his appointment would prove of advantage in shifting responsibility for the depression on the Jews. The appointments served the conspirators well in diverting attention from them and their notorious Nazarene Communist (Christian) agents and in relieving them of the responsibility for their acts of treason.

## OCCUPATION CURRENCY TREASON NOT WHITE'S OR MORGENTHAU'S

An instance in point is the widely circulated and false story regarding the delivery of matrices and plates for the printing of occupation money to Communist Russia, by Morgenthau and White. The truth of the matter was clearly revealed in the Hearings Before the Committee on Appropriations of the Senate Subcommittee on Armed Services, Banking & Currency, on Occupation Currency Transactions. (117) The record indicates that both the Army and the State Department had agreed with the Allies that there be adopted a uniform occupation currency in Germany. Early in 1944, Ambassador to Russia Harriman had reported to the State Department that the British Government urged the inclusion of Russia in the currency arrangement (117:147), in which Secretary of State Cordell Hull concurred; and offered to print the currency for Russia.

Russians demanded, however, that they be given plates and paper for printing their own occupation currency to insure "a constant supply." In response to Ambassador Harriman's request for instructions in the matter, Sec. Hull stated that the Combined Chiefs of Staff would not favor delivery of plates. And the Treasury Department, at the same time (March, 1944) concurred in this refusal. (117:150, 178) Russia thereupon threatened to issue her own occupation currency. (117:151) The State Department, fearful of the "effect on the relations in many other aspects of Soviet, British and United States Governments" recommended giving the Soviets duplicate plates for printing the currency. (117:152) Thereupon Morgenthau was required to furnish the Soviets with the plates and materiel for printing the currency. (117:186) One month later, Major Jordan reported, the first of three shipments, five plane loads, were dispatched to Russia. (118:227)

## OCCUPATION CURRENCY TREASON PERPETRATED BY THE CONSPIRATORS

White pointed out, correctly, at the hearings, that the money that the Soviets printed was not American money, but was Allied occupation currency. *Whatever treason there may have been involved in the situation was in the lobbying through Congress, by the conspirators, of appropriations for redemption by the Treasury, at the expense of American taxpayers, of all the occupation currency.* There has been no investigation even suggested to determine which of the conspirators, and their banks, lobbied these appropriations through Congress, which Congressmen were "induced" to vote for it, and who were the traitors who profited most from this brigandage. Their identity can be surmised from past records: the conspirators and their Chase National Bank.

## SPIES DO NOT KEEP RECORDS FOR INSPECTION BY COUNTRY BETRAYED, A LA WHITE

For obvious reasons, spies, foreign agents and traitors do not make a practise of keeping records of their every activity, associate and meeting, unless they are very stupid. No one has ever charged that White was lacking in intellect. Nevertheless, like his superior, Secretary Morgenthau, he kept complete and detailed records of his every activity in a form that was readily available to the Senate investigators and has been reproduced, in part, in *The Harry Dexter White Papers.* One is compelled, for this reason, if for no other, to accept the judgement of Sen. Eastland that was concurred in by Senators Welker and Jenner, in commenting on the diary of Morgenthau, as applying with equal validity to those of Harry Dexter White. They acknowledged that:

"The very existence of these diaries is the strongest possible assertion of your good faith in connection with your every official act..." (101:1697)

Equally notable are several other features of White's actions. When questioned regarding his relationships with known Communists, he never resorted to the Fifth Amendment, as is their custom. (59:-2651) A veteran of World War I who had risen from the ranks, he took so keenly to heart the questioning of his loyalty that it precipitated his death. Such sense of honor and patriotism has not characterized the avowed Communists in our midst: Hiss, Currie, Chambers, Bentley, Budenz, Matthews, their bosses, the conspirators, and the rest of the breed. These facts fully confirm the open acknowledgment of Whittaker Chambers in his *Witness* that White was not a Communist. (59:xxxviii) Though a "liberal," or Red, as are all "social(ist) scientists" as a product of their indoctrination, and in that sense a "fellow traveler." Chambers acknowledged that

145

White was not a subject of "Party discipline." He was as loyal an American as a "social scientist" can be. And as will be related, he was blocked by the conspirators and unsuccessful in his attempt to forewarn the nation on the gold and monetary aspects of the conspiracy.

## NELSON ROCKEFELLER COVERTLY
## USED WHITE AS PAWN

White's *Papers* clearly reveal in how minor a role he was cast by the conspirators. Omitted from the index, as is usual where His Dynastic Majesty is concerned, are records of his being "honored," by two personal conferences, by the "top boss," Nelson Rockefeller. The first was on October 15,1941, at 4:10 to 4:25 p.m. (59:2732) The second was in "Co-Ordinator" Rockefeller's office, on Feb. 18, 1942, at 2:30 to 3:55 p.m. (59:2757) for "discussion on financial implication in balance-of-payments study on Latin America." Inasmuch as this matter vitally concerned the purse and interests of Rockefeller and the Dynasty, it serves to explain the approach in person rather than through trusted, CFR Rockefeller-Soviet agents. It does indicate, however, that direct personal "guidance" was exercised by the conspirators when the occasion was deemed "urgent" and "vital." What is impressive about this record of White's is that it presents an exception to the almost awesome deletion of the Rockefeller name from most reports of the Governmental agencies.

Both the White *Papers* and the *Morgenthau Diary* disclose that although Nelson Rockefeller did not deem it necessary to personally direct and supervise these lowly pawns of his in the Treasury, his authority was exercised on behalf of the conspirators by numerous of the "liberal," Red and frankly Communist top level associates and agents of his "Establishment, including those of his CFR and "Philanthropic" Foundation Trust."

They literally infested and swarmed in all the "New Deal" Government agencies and even those few loyal and patriotic officials who would have shunned them if they were free to do so, were required by their posts and duties to associate with them and take orders from them as superiors or as representatives of overwhelming majorities in Government councils. In short, it was "...inherently relevant to his official duties..." (59:v)

Lauchlin Currie, the "Soviet Army Intelligence agent," and Rockefeller-subsidized University of Chicago Professor, Jacob Viner, to whom White owed his appointment, both of them CFR members and close associates of Rockefeller, virtually directed and dictated White's every act. Twenty-seven conferences with Currie and twenty-one with Viner were listed by White in his *Papers*. These conferences took place with greatest frequency at times when decisions were to be made on matters of such importance as supplying the Soviets with plates for printing of occupation currency, the support of China or the organization of the International Monetary Fund. Great as was the influence on White exercised by those two Rockefeller agents who were his mentors, it was tremendously amplified by the host of agents of the conspirators who regularly constituted majorities of the conferees whose majority rulings White was compelled to accept. Among them were the following figures from Rockefellers' "Foreign Office," the Council On Foreign Relations:

146

Owen Lattimore who was characterized by Congressional investigators as a "Communist agent." (119:15)

Edward C. Carter, Secretary of the Institute of Pacific Relations, Rockefeller financed and dominated; and characterized by Congress as an agency serving the Soviets. (119;15)

Herbert Lehman, (15) "liberal," or Red, CFR member who served the conspirators in many capacities, including direction of their UNRRA, "foreign aid" program.

John J. McCloy, CFR member related by marriage to the Zinssers and Adenauer, who was given charge of the American occupation of Germany to protect the interests of the conspirators, after serving them in capacity of attorney in connection with those interests; subsequently, he was made by his Rockefeller masters, president of their Chase National Bank that they required, of Secretary of the Treasury Morgenthau, be made the sole and exclusive agency of the Treasury in the world market manipulations of gold and silver despite his protest against their looting of the Treasury in the process. (15;97)

Gen. Lucius Clay, CRF member, who has loyally served the conspirators in many capacities. (15)

Beardsley Ruml, CFR member who spent his life in the service of the Rockefellers and first openly diverted funds from their foundations to the support of Communist agitation around the world; and wrote the tax measures with which the conspirators misappropriated ever large amounts of our national wealth to the expansion of the Rockefeller-Soviet Axis and Rockefeller Empire. (15)

This partial list of agents who served to swing the consensus of conferences and committees which controlled, supervised and directed the actions of White and other Government officials in the directions ordered by their Rockefeller masters, could be extended through many pages. But the above suffices to indicate the manner in which Rockefeller operates to insure that conferences and "committees" of his creatures operate to enforce the conspirators' will. Action was taken only after numerous such rigged "conferences" and "committees" had "yessed" the dictates of the conspirators handed down to the President who echoed his "intimate adviser." Consequently, attribution of those decisions and acts to anyone other than the "top man on the totem pole" is absurdly false.

Pres. Roosevelt was notorious for pretending to acquiesce with any adviser. But he acted only at the dictation of the Dynasty that put him in the White House. (7:134f) Initially the dictates and orders were percolated down to the President through Harry L. Hopkins, a trusted agent of the conspirators, until the way had been paved for "adviser" Nelson Rockefeller by adequate intimacy and "greasing of the palm." Policy was dictated by no one else, in order to make sure that the conspirators' objectives were attained.

In matters of finance, White was "advised" concerning Rockefeller's Latin American "co-ordination" by the Dynasty's Chase National Bank officer, Rovensky (79;66:113) who had first introduced Nelson to the potentialities of brigandage in South America; and by other of their bank employees. (59:2732) On one occasion, Rovensky's mission was reinforced by Ruml. (59:2735) Agent Currie's efforts in securing the adoption of monetary plots sought by the Dynasty and the "Federal" Reserve "reforms" were ably seconded by a crew of

147

his subordinates in that organization. (59:2750; 2751; 2752; 2753; 2755; 2756; 2764; 2766-9; 2777-8) Lord Keynes from the Rockefeller-subsidized and dominated London School of Economics & Political Science was cunningly pitted against White for the purpose of organizing their International Monetary Fund conspiracy in the exact manner they desired. But it was trusted CFR agent, assistant to the President and Communist tool, Lauchlin Currie who was sent to Switzerland, in 1945, as "chief of economic and financial mission" that effected the organization of the IMF, (60:569) and who dictated the appointment of Harry Dexter White as his pawn in running it.

Lauchlin Currie's efforts were ably seconded by Rockefeller CFR agent, Gen. George Catlett Marshall who, under the instructions of the conspirators, had forced Chiang Kai-shek to turn over to the Communists half a million Nationalist troops (who were later shot from behind their lines), under threat to withhold American aid. The conspirators had prepared the way for the Communist takeover by precipitating the financial debacle of China with the silver manipulations effected by their Chase National Bank. Both Currie and Viner were on hand to represent the conspirators at the earlier conferences on China, on February 2, and March 5, 1942. (59:2734-5). Freda Utley reported that Currie had no first-hand knowledge of China, but was invited in as "Chinese expert" on the basis of his monetary views that had helped inspire the monetary and silver manipulations that had precipitated the violent Chinese inflation that played so large a role in its Communist takeover. (107:117f) He blocked the shipment of arms and munitions, seized from the Germans, to the Chinese Nationalist that had been ordered by Gen. Wedemeyer and the Joint Chiefs of Staff. (107:36) Instead these arms were treacherously turned over to the East Germany Communists.

Elizabeth Bentley testified that, as a Communist courier, she derived vital information from Lauchlin Currie, both directly and through Michael Greenberg, a British Communist whom Currie had appointed as his assistant. (59:2537; 919:414) She stated:

"...the secrets had been stolen by Lauchlin Currie... a full-fledged member of the Silvermaster (Communist espionage) group." (59:119:243)

She stated that White had been instrumental in her obtaining information regarding our breaking of the Soviet code; but she did not indicate that it was intentional on his part.

CONSPIRATORS' COMMUNIST AGENTS MADE
EXTRAORDINARY EFFORTS TO FRAME JEW WHITE

Communist agent, Prof. Bystrov, (59:2537), did his best to cast suspicion on White, including openly sending him rich gifts, thus clearly proving that White was not a Soviet agent. Whittaker Chambers reported that Col. Bykov was incensed because White refused to give the spies vital information; and that he had suggested that White "be controlled," or "framed," coerced and blackmailed. Chambers reported that he remonstrated to Bykov that *White was not a member of the Communist Party and not subject to its discipline.* (59:2497). This makes clear the motive of the Rockefeller-Soviet conspirators in singling out White for "framing" as the "villain" on whom to shift the odium of their own perfidy. White's death,

148

that was precipitated (so uncharacteristically for a spy) by the shock of the accusation, made simpler and safer their carrying out the age-old practise of using a Jew as scapegoat to cover up their own crimes, and avert exposure.

The Rockefeller-Standard Oil conspirators made good use of the services that they exacted of White in connection with their brigandage that launched us into the war. White's *Papers* list the following conferences with them:

July 21, 1941. Messrs. Walden and Singer, of Standard-Vacuum Oil Co. of New Jersey, (with Mr. Ullman) re oil from Dutch East Indies. (59:2731)

December 17, 1941. The same Ullman brought another Standard Oil official E. J Sadler to confer with White. (59:2733). Ullman who served the Rockefeller-Standard Oil interests so well, was an associate of Rockefellers' CFR agent, Lauchlin Currie, in the Silvermaster spyring. (59:lii)

August 11,1943. Meeting with Messrs. McGuire and Livesy of State Department, Garry Owen, of California Saudi Arabian Co.; Mr. Bernstein. (59:2750)

January 19, 1944. Meeting on Saudi Arabia with Messrs. James Landis, Bernstein, Glendenning, Friedman: Parker, McGuire and Livesey from State Department. (59:2755) Constantine E. McGuire and Philo W. Parker were Rockefeller CFR agents.)

Feb. 17, 1944. Meeting on Saudi Arabia. Present: Grant and Barrett of British Treasury; McGuire and Parker of State; Bernstein, Friedman and Glendenning. (59:2756)

They were followed shortly by another Rockefeller CFR agent and employee:

Feb. 24, 1944. Mr. Shepard Morgan, vice president of Chase National Bank.

## POSTWAR PLAN PROPOSED FOR DEFEATED GERMANY BY EISENHOWER & ROOSEVELT

The item that contributed most to intensify the venom directed against Morgenthau and his Assistant Secretary White was the so-called *Morgenthau Plan* for postwar Germany. Ironically, it was the White *Papers* that  first disclosed that the plan was actually conceived by Gen. Dwight D. Eisenhower in his mess tent in Southern England in a discussion with Morgenthau and White, at lunch on August 7, 1944. (59:2637) On August 26,1944, Pres. F. D. Roosevelt sent a memorandum to the Secretary of War commenting on the Army's "Handbook" on postwar Germany,  that reveals that he was unjustly robbed of his share of the credit for it. It read:

"MEMORANDUM FOR THE SECRETARY OF WAR

"This so-called 'Handbook' is pretty bad. I should like to know how it came to be written and who approved it down the line...

"It gives me the impression that Germany is to be restored just as much as The Netherlands and Belgium, and the people of Germany brought back as quickly as possible to their prewar state.

"It is of the utmost importance that every person in Germany should realize that this time Germany is a defeated nation. I do not want them to starve to death but, as an example, if they need food to keep body and soul together beyond what they have, they should be fed three times a day from Army soup kitchens. That will keep them perfectly healthy and they will remember that experience all their lives...

"Too many people here and in England hold to the view that the German people as a whole were not responsible for what has taken place—that only a few Nazi leaders are responsible. That, unfortunately, is not based on fact. The German people must have it driven home to them that the whole nation has been engaged in a lawless conspiracy against the decencies of modern civilization...          F.D.R. "          (59:2580-2)

## WHITE VAINLY UNDERTOOK TO EXPOSE MONETARY CONSPIRACY IN "FUTURE OF GOLD"

If the keeping of their detailed diaries regarding the every activity, contact and associations, their frank and open admission of dealings with exposed Communists and traitors into which they were forced by their official positions, without recourse to the Fifth Amendment, and. in the case of White, his record as a war veteran, were not adequate proof that they were naive victims of the conspirators, White's draft of a complete exposure of the conspirators' monetary plot that was drafted by him in his role of Assistant to the Secretary of the Treasury should make that fact transparently clear. It was suppressed and never published until the Senate Committee dug it up and published it without realizing that it offers additional proof of the self-serving treachery of their plot to depict him as a traitorous mastermind. Can anything be more absurd than expecting a supposed foreign agent and spy, in which roles the conspirators and their Senatorial agents seek to cast White, to keep such records and perpetrate such follies?

The extent to which White went in seconding the effort of his chief, Morgenthau, in exposing the conspirators' thievish monetary plans and plots is clearly revealed in the draft of his article entitled *The Future of Gold*, that was unwittingly published by the Subcommittee on Internal Subversion of the Senate Judiciary Committee of the 84th Congress, in its effort to "frame" White. (59:2664-92)

White's expose of the conspirators' monetary and gold manipulations was cunningly written as a pretended defense of their "Gold Standard," which they had imposed on the nation and planned to impose on the world for their thievish purposes. This is made clear by the first paragraph of his article. It relates:

"The outbreak of the war has intensified the already chronic discussion concerning the future status of gold. There is concern in particular about the large quantities of gold flowing into this country. One frequently hears that we are getting the large volume of gold because we pay the highest price in the world for it, that owning about 65 percent of the world's monetary gold already, we shall accumulate almost all of it before the war is over, and that there will then be no way we can use our gold. Other nations it is said, will ultimately refuse to accept or hold gold as money. We

150

will be left with over $30 billions of gold, acquired mostly at $35 an ounce, for which there will only be a trifling demand—to fill teeth and fashion wedding rings. (59:2665)

"What role will gold play after the war? Will it cease to be used as a monetary metal? Will it lose its monetary value and have use only in industry and the arts?

"*It must be made clear at the outset that Gold is not an indispensable element in a monetary system.* The evolution of monetary systems has long since reached a stage where the business of a country can be transacted without the aid of gold..." (59:2670)

This statement of White's clearly contradicts the falsity of the representations of the conspirators when they effected the imposition on our nation of their "Gold Standard" Act of 1900; and it represents so dangerous a contradiction and exposure as to constitute what they regarded as ample justification for suppressing the publication of his views and for "disposing" of him as soon as they had made planned use of him. White continued:

"The significant question, therefore, is not whether the business of the world can or cannot be transacted without gold, but rather whether it can be transacted as well without gold as with it, and *whether the difference is worth the cost. Gold is an expensive metal...When gold ceases to perform all important monetary functions better than can be done in some other way, then, gold as money will be doomed.* The crucial question therefore, is: 'Is gold as a monetary instrument superior enough to any other device to justify its continued use?" (59:2671)

From the viewpoint of the conspirators who have long used gold as a medium of national looting and control, no ranker heresy could be uttered and no more complete betrayal be effected. White explained:

"For some domestic purposes gold is no longer used at all, for others it plays a lesser role than formerly, while its hitherto most important function within a country—that of constituting a specie base for note issue and deposits—is being regarded as an unnecessary anachronism...now (1940) *There is no country left in the world where a holder of paper currency can actually convert that currency at will into gold at a price fixed by law and hold that gold wherever he pleases.* Today the United States is almost the only country left where gold can be purchased at a fixed price, and *even here it can be so purchased only when it is to be used for export under specified conditions.*" (59:2671-2)

There is an element of amusement in the fact that White, the "textbook banker" who constantly quoted doctrinaire "monetary authorities" and the differences in their theories, naively failed to discern in the above situation that he cited, the process of development by the conspirators of the tightest "Gold Corner" in world history. It was this naive impracticality and willingness to accept the instructions of his mentors and teachers that made him a tool who was so useful to the conspirators that they forgave, but suppressed his "heresies." And it later led to his being used by them to tighten and "perfect" their gold conspiracy as the "author" of their International Monetary Fund. White dismissed the supposed function of gold in the domestic economy with the words:

151

"The chief purpose which the requirement (that there be some gold reserve against notes and deposits) *is supposed to serve* is to prevent an undue expansion of money supply by limiting, to some previously determined ratio to gold, the maximum amount of currency notes that may be issued, and in some cases by limiting the amount of demand liabilities... that may be created... The system so described *is supposed to be 'automatic' in contrast to 'managed' currency*

"Whether fractional gold reserve requirements do in fact act as a restraint against inflation... is a much debated question among monetary theorists... an issue on which there is no unanimity... (59:2672-3)

"Taking all these considerations together, it appears that notwithstanding the widespread support of the view that gold plays a useful and important role in the domestic monetary system and can perform a more helpful role if the gold standard were adhered to, *there are arguments upholding the contrary view weighty enough to arouse fears for the future of gold were its usefulness as a monetary metal wholly or chiefly dependent upon its continued use for coins, to provide metallic convertibility for currency, or a basis for note issues or credit expansion...*" (59:2674-5)

Though the conspirators did not approve of White's plan to popularize his views regarding the value of gold in the domestic economy, and suppressed their publication, they did welcome his acceptance of their gold and monetary schemes in the international sphere. It would have required little intelligent insight on the part of White, and of other "learned" economists, to realize that if gold was inadequate for monetary needs on the domestic scene, it would be infinitely more inadequate on the far vaster worldwide financial scene. Had White been a mental heavyweight, a profound thinker, he would have anticipated the present monetary and financial collapse engineered by the conspirators on the basis of the world-wide acceptance of gold as the only legitimate medium for settlement of unfavorable balances of payment.

White did anticipate moderate unfavorable payment balances, which he regarded, in accord with what he had been taught, as most desirable. He did not anticipate the ruthless, treasonous devices, such as looting in the guise of "foreign aid" that was used by the conspirators to attain those imbalances. He wrote:

"Whether the replacement of an unfavorable balance of payments for our present favorable balance be rapid or long delayed is impossible to forecast. But rapid or slow, its development after the war is as well-based as is the hope for world economic recovery." (59:2670)

"In years to come a combination of circumstances may emerge which would cause for many years a large sustained outflow of gold from the United States. We cannot forecast what the relative degree of prosperity, of investment opportunities and of security, will be among the nations of the world 5, 10, or 15 years from now... The United States may be just in the right position of being willing gradually to develop an unfavorable balance of payments and thus steadily export gold, while numerous other countries, after regaining their essential level of imports—following their period of immediate postwar reconstruction—may be just in the position to build up their gold reserves.

"He would be bold man indeed who would say that it is improbable that we should have an unfavorable balance of payments as large as $1 billion a year for many years..." (59:2688)

"...the only gold that is of potential use to the United States is that amount which may be used some time in the future to liquidate adverse balances of payments." (59:2687)

"...gold really derives its importance as a monetary metal not from its use within a country but because of its utility as a medium of international exchange. *In the performance of that function gold is as yet without a peer.*" (59:2674)

White then proceeded to explain that there were other means available for settling imbalances of payment, that led some persons to believe that gold can be dispensed with in international exchange by use of an international, universally accepted paper currency or by exchange stabilization. He decried such views (that are currently being advanced by the conspirators for their nefarious purposes) as fallacious, He explained:

"...though credits and foreign exchange earning assets can be used in part, or for a short time, to avoid equating inpayments and outpayments,... in the main inpayments and outpayments must be kept equal so long as countries engage in international transactions.

"There are only four possible ways in which a country can keep its international accounts in balance without resort to foreign borrowing or foreign lending. (A deposit in a foreign country is in this connection equivalent to a loan to a foreign country...) These four ways...are:

(1) By adopting strict foreign exchange and/or import controls...

(2) By permitting fluctuation in exchange rates to take place freely so as to balance the demand for any supply of foreign exchange.

(3) ...conduct international trade exclusively on a barter basis.

(4) ...permit trade to operate without any restrictions...and depend entirely upon gold as a means of settling any difference in balance of payments." (59:2676-7)

White, however, related that though gold has no utilitarian value, it had been the most efficient device for settling balance of payments, in spite of a vital handicap that bars its use to many nations that can not afford it:

"Gold is for many countries an expensive tool and despite the fact that it has great usefulness as a stabilizing element and that it yields large dividends because of its convenience as an international medium of exchange, a poor country can ill afford to have much of it." (59:2679)

153

## WHITE AVERRED THAT POWER PLAY MAINTAINS
## STATUS OF GOLD DESPITE COST

White made perfectly clear the basis on which the "efficiency" of gold in international exchange rests in spite of its uselessness, cost and unavailability to many nations; and explained why there need be no fear for the future of gold and its acceptance by all nations. He detailed as insuring the continued monetary use of gold, other than its physical stability, a number of predatory powers and influences.

"Monetary authorities here (as elsewhere) are fully cognizant of the need to leave inviolate the unquestioned acceptability of gold as a means of international payment; there is no danger that they will do anything to diminish in the slightest . . . its general acceptability . . .

"Another important consideration overlooked by those who fear that gold will cease to be acceptable as money is that numerous countries have a large and continuing stake in maintaining the value of gold and will do nothing to jeopardize the use of gold as a medium of international payments. The British Empire, for example, produces half the world's gold supply. It is a source of vital revenue to one of the Dominions and of considerable to several other parts of the Empire and the shares of the British gold-mining companies constitute an important block on the London Stock Exchange. Therefore she would never refuse to accept gold in settlement of debts or in payment for her goods or services. And there are other countries that produce gold. Mexico, Peru, Colombia, Venezuela, Japan and Russia likewise produce gold in large enough quantities to prevent those countries from doing anything to interfere with the efficacy of gold as a means of international payment.

"In addition to the gold-producing countries, there are the gold-holding countries...Countries holding gold will be as little desirous of jeopardizing its value as countries producing gold. Sweden with its stock of $300 million of gold, or Argentina with its $400 million, will be no less reluctant to have gold lose any of its purchasing power than would be Netherlands with her $700 million, or South Africa with its $100 million of holdings and ½ billion of annual output. (59:2680)

"The value of gold as a means of international payments rests on much firmer ground than its value as part of any country's monetary system. Its use as required reserves against note issues or deposits rests largely on psychological grounds, upon historic precedent, upon traditional faith in gold, and upon prejudice buttressed by foggy understanding of principles underlying the role of metallic reserves in modern monetary systems. In its role as a medium of international payments, however, the prestige of gold rests on something far more substantial..." (59:2681)

That "something far more substantial" is the use of a "gold standard" and gold as a means of control of national and world economy. White thus clearly exposed the purposefulness and the objectives of the conspirators in their current monopoly of gold:

worldwide looting and totalitarian rule. But he failed to discern the conspiracy which he unwittingly abetted.

## WHITE WISELY DISCOUNTED INTERNATIONAL MONETARY AGREEMENTS

It well may be that White's vision was deflected from the developing "Gold Corner" by the very device he was chosen by the conspirators to spearhead for them, the International Monetary Fund that they used so effectively in their conspiracy. Despite the role that he played in the IMF, White realistically doubted the possibilities of internationalism in finance. He wrote:

"There may possibly come a time when gold will no longer retain its superiority over other devices, but that can be only when national monetary systems and national monetary policies cease to exist and are replaced by an intergovernmental authority which will decide the monetary credit, and trade policy that each national is to pursue, a sort of monetary League of Nations which would control world economic policy. *If and when that time arrives* gold possibly will be no more needed to settle international balances than gold is now needed to settle balances among the States within the country. But *until that millenium arrives* gold will continue to be sought by various governments as a combination war chest and protective cushion against shocks of international change, as well as an efficient and smooth instrument for balancing international payments, and a reserve stock of international purchasing power.

"There are some who believe that a universally accepted currency not redeemable in gold (or in some other specified universally accepted commodity) is compatible with the facts of national sovereignties, but a little thought reveals the impracticability of any such notion..."

"...*There is nothing in past history and certainly nothing in current events which gives assurance that a group of major countries will agree to resign their sovereignty on so fundamental matter as the value of their currency in terms of other currencies.*" (59:2682)

*This statement clearly reveals the truth of Whittaker Chambers report that White was not a member of the Communist Party.* For "internationalism" and an economy "managed" through an international monetary system are basic tenets of Communism. White's view of the role that could be played by such international organization as the IMF was merely to "make a redistribution of gold easier and enhance the effectiveness of gold shipments as an aid to autonomous monetary policy." (59:2684).

For insight into the meaning of the current "Gold Corner" of the conspirators, it is well to bear in mind White's pithy and accurate statement:

155

"Were gold to cease to be used as a medium of international exchange, the only salvage value it would have would be its industrial use. *Separate gold as a metal from gold as money and you would find that its industrial value is small indeed."* (59:2684)

## WHITE'S USEFULNESS TO THE CONSPIRATORS RESTED IN HIS ECONOMIC BRAINWASHING

White was a completely inexperienced money and banking theorist whose capacity for thought went little beyond what his teachers and professors, including Rockefeller-Soviet agent, Lauchlin Currie, had taught him. His views largely parroted those of the Rockefeller-Soviet agents that surrounded him in the "New" Deal. Those views did involve sufficient independent thought to lead him to expose incompletely the nature of their "Gold Standard" conspiracy; but were not supported by adequate knowledge of monetary history or a keen insight into the nature of money. He, like others who must earn their living as economists, ignored the questions: "What value has money if it will not purchase for us the necessities of life?" "Are not the real bases of wealth and the ultimate media of exchange, or security behind money, the raw materials of the necessities of life?"

White, like other economists, completely ignored the economic wisdom of the ages embodied in the Biblical story of Joseph's stewardship of Pharaoh's gold, and in the myth of Midas and his "golden touch." He, like other economists, was blind to the lessons of rationing in World War I, and of the drought freshly experienced by the nation in the 1930's.

White viewed money in the same light as the moneylending bankers self-interestedly wish to have it viewed: as the only stable and "essential" commodity, which they alone shall be empowered to create and manipulate at their own will for unlimited profit or loot. The concept that money should be a mere medium of exchange, like a hat check, for the true essentials of life and luxuries, and that its volume should expand automatically with the expansion of national wealth, is abhorrent to them because it would spell an end to their control and periodic systematic looting of the nation and the world by manipulation or "management" of money and finance. In this respect, the capitalist bankers and the super-capitalist Communists are in full agreement. They both ardently advocate a "managed" economy. Their only disagreement is on the question of who shall "manage" the economy and for whose benefit.

White made it quite clear that gold, though it is the most useless of the commodities, is valued by the conspirators as the most desirable form of concentrated storage of wealth, so long as they can dupe nations in their belief in its value at the rate arbitrarily set by themselves.

The extraordinary efforts of the conspirators and their agents in the Senate to depict White as the mastermind of a conspiracy that had been hatched by them before he was born and has continued long after his death, are obviously as absurd as the portrait is false. Spies and traitors do not keep records of their treacheries available to the nations that they betray, as did White in his

156

*Papers.* (59) Nations that benefit from their treason do not expose their agents by ostentatiously sending them gifts, as in the instance of Prof. Bystrov; nor do spies and foreign agents keep such evidence around as did White. (59:2537) Spies do not openly acknowledge association with known agents of powers for whom they work, as did White in more than one instance. (59:2651) Instead they plead the Fifth Amendment, which White did not do.

## CHAMBERS AFFIRMED THAT WHITE WAS NOT A COMMUNIST AGENT

Whittaker Chambers, as has been related, clearly stated that White was not a member of the Communist Party or subject to its discipline. (59:2497;119:429-30) He reported that Bystrov who had undertaken to cast suspicion on White, fumed because he could not be "controlled" by Soviet agents. The statement by Elizabeth Bentley that White had made it possible for the spies to obtain certain information, viewed in the light of these facts, impel the conclusion that whatever aid White may have given the spies was unwitting, involuntary and unintentional, and "inherently relevant to his official duties." (59:vi) It indicates that White was used by the host of Rockefeller-Soviet agents that infest the Government and completely surrounded him, and more particularly by Lauchlin Currie, the most powerful Rockefeller-Soviet intelligence agent in the "New" Deal, and by his boss Nelson Rockefeller. This domination adequately explains White's innocent involvement. It should be borne in mind that White alone in the entire crew was a loyal World War I veteran who rose from the ranks to lieutenant. And he did attempt, insofar as he was capable of so doing, to expose the nature of the "Gold Standard" conspiracy; but was thwarted in it.

## HISTORY PROFESSOR, SERVING CONSPIRATORS, FALSIFIES HISTORY

Prof. Kubek, head of the Department of History of the University of Dallas, who was employed by the Senate Committee on the Judiciary to help in the "framing" of White in his "editing" for the Committee of the *Morgenthau Diary (China)* (101; 385) falsely wrote in the foreword:

"Ultimately, White was revealed as a Communist agent." (101:4)

This author phoned Prof. Kubek in August 1965 to ask him what proof he had for this false statement. The Professor hemmed and hawed. When pressed for a reply, he said that he thought that Whittaker Chambers had denounced White as a Communist. When Chambers' denial of White's membership in the Communist Party was quoted to him, Prof. Kubek was nonplussed. This author asked him to check his records and mail on any proof that he might have for his misrepresentation. No such references have been forthcoming, despite the professor's promise to inform this author of the source of his misstatement. Nevertheless, in the preface of additional abstracts from the Morgenthau diaries published by the Committee and edited by the same "scholar," Prof. Kubek, he asserted that the FBI had reported that White was a Communist. (385) In reply to a question posed to J. Edgar Hoover, Director of the FBI, inquiring for a copy of the cited report on White, this author received a denial of such publication.

## PROF. KUBEK ACKNOWLEDGED FALSITY OF HIS LIBEL OF HARRY DEXTER WHITE

Prof. Kubek, in a rare moment of truth, questioned the truth of the "safe" libel of dead Harry Dexter White that he uttered on behalf of the conspirators and real, traitorous culprits, to shield them. In the introduction to his slanted abstracts, *Morgenthau Diary (Germany)* prepared for the Committee on The Judiciary Of The United States Senate, at the end of eighty pages of inuendo and quotation based on statements of acknowledged criminals, spies and traitors, he states:

> "*If In Fact Harry Dexter White Was Himself An Active Agent Of Soviet Espionage, As J. Edgar Hoover Of The FBI Has Charged (Ed. On The Basis Of "Testimony" Of Confessed Traitors, But Questioned By Him) The Implications Are Indeed Profound.*" (385:80)

The implications are profound indeed. They are that Prof. Kubek and his employers have undertaken to shield traitorous conspirators by throwing up a smoke screen and charging a dead Jewish, "Liberal" economist, patriotic war veteran and unsuspecting tool of theirs, with treacheries and crimes that anteceded his birth and continue decades after his death. There can not be any question that this does make them ex post facto as well as ante facto accomplices of this continous perfidy and treason that accounts for the slaughtering the cream of our youth in Vietnam, Korea and around the world, has undermined the stability of our government and may well threaten our survival as a nation.

## CHAPTER XVII
## "INTERNATIONAL" MONETARY FUND ORGANIZED BY ROCKEFELLER-SOVIET CONSPIRATORS

Their League of Nations had been most useful to the conspirators, in forcing nations seeking loans from the U.S. dominated by their "Federal" Reserve, to turn over to them and their agency control of their finances and monetary systems. This control was centralized by them in their Bank for International Settlement that they established in 1930 as an agency of their League. But their BIS fell short of giving the conspirators absolute, complete control of the finances and economies of the nations, that would facilitate their totalitariah control, because it did not establish a stranglehold on them by forcing their adoption of their "Gold Standard." This defect was described in their BIS Report of 1944, as follows:

"In order to make a real contribution to increased exchange stability, the Fund must gain an influence over those essential factors which determine the currency developments in the different countries, and these are largely of a domestic character." (52:114)

## CONSPIRATORS' IMF EXTENDED THEIR "GOLD STANDARD" & "F"R PLOT AROUND WORLD

The devices which the Rockefeller-Soviet conspirators had found most effective in their plot to "gain influence over those essential factors which determine currency developments...of a domestic character" were their "Gold Standard" coupled with their "Federal" Reserve fraud. The huge indebtedness into which the nations around the world had been plunged by the war, engineered by the conspirators, and reconstruction needs, constituted an ideal opportunity for throttling and straightjacketing the economies of all lands so as to make them as ready prey for looting as the U.S. This was the purpose and objective of their "International" Monetary Fund (IMF).

The Rockefeller conspirators craftily camouflaged as a "philanthropic" scheme their plot to force the nations of the world to surrender to them their sovereignty, in the same manner as they had forced the U.S. to do so, through surrender of their financial independence. Their various foundations and organizations, as well as their "Foreign Office," the Council on Foreign Relations (15) all served in planning it as an ulterior phase of their Rockefeller-Soviet "internationalist" schema that was designed to facilitate the organization of their "United" Nations.

In June, 1943, they arranged the meeting at Hot Springs, Virginia, of the United Nations Conference on Food and Agriculture as an expression of their pretended concern for the starvation that they had inflicted on many parts of the world (from which the U.S., by good chance, narrowly escaped) by the war that they had planned and precipitated. In November, 1943, they had arranged the meeting of the United Nations Relief & Rehabilitation Administration Council. These were all represented as fulfilling the proposals of the conspirators mythical "Atlantic Charter," that was conceived to give official sanction to their plot. This followed on the *Joint Declaration of the United Nations*, of January 1, 1942, that was signed by twenty-six nations. (15:398) The purposes which the conspirators envisaged for their "United" Nations was related by their CFR agents Grayson L. Kirk, then Acting President of Columbia University, and Walter R. Sharp in a pamphlet that was published in October, 1942, in Rockefellers' *Foreign Policy Association Headline Books* series, entitled *Uniting Today For Tomorrow, The United Nations In War & Peace.* (120)

On the basis of a Tripartite Agreement between the U.S., Great

Britain and France, Harry Dexter White was assigned the task of drafting the working plan on behalf of the U.S.; and John Maynard Keynes on behalf of England. White acted in his capacity of Assistant Secretary of the Treasury and chairman of committees assigned to the task, who arrived at their decisions on the basis of a majority vote. At four of the key meetings regarding the plot, Rockefeller-Soviet top agent Lauchlin Currie was present to voice his bosses' requirements. (59:xxvi) And at few of the meetings on the matter were the Rockefellers represented by less than half of the conferees all of whom were fellow members of Currie in Rockefeller's Council on Foreign Relations. Keynes represented the Rockefeller subsidized British Fabians (2) and had been called in by the conspirators to "advise" Pres. Roosevelt to tax and spend, and to buy back prosperity by rolling up deficits and mounting debts. Keynes expounded this specious theory that hugely delighted the conspirators, in his book *Treatise On Money*, and amplified it in *The General Theory Of Employment, Interest And Money*. (121) In all of his work, in spite of his "liberalism, Keynes was a special pleader for the British. But because of the usefulness of his subversive doctrine in looting the U.S. he was nevertheless favored by the conspirators.

The conspirators craftily pitted White against Keynes. White's plan was dictated by them through their agents on the committee, who constituted a majority. It was labelled the "International Stabilization Fund of the United and Associated Nations." It provided for a capitalization of $5 billion, $2 billion of which was to be supplied by the U. S.; and half of the capital was to be paid in gold. The feature of the plan that clearly reveals that it was not drawn up by White, in view of his expressed disbelief that any country would surrender its sovereignty by yielding control of its money (59:2683), that he expressly stated in his *Future Of Gold*, was its provision for the creation of a new international currency named "unitas".

Keynes' plan was approved by the Rockefeller-Soviet conspirators, because he advocated an "international" currency. But it did not suit their thievish purposes because though the currency's value was expressed in terms of gold subject to changes in valuation, it was to be merely a bookkeeping device labelled "bancor", and no actual gold would be turned over to the conspirators for looting. The bookkeeping credit on the books of what Keynes labelled the International Clearance Union, was to be based on each nation's pre-war trade volume.

On October 8, 1943, White announced on behalf of the conspirators the "bait" that they offered to secure acceptance of their scheme, the United Nations Bank for Reconstruction & Development, that would supplement the IMF in providing them with billions more loot largely at the expense of American taxpayers. This "bait" clinched the deal. On May 26, 1944, Pres. Roosevelt extended invitations for a United Nations Monetary & Financial Conference to be held on July 1 of that year at Bretton Woods. Roosevelt at the same time dictated that the conference must accept the plan dictated by his bosses, the conspirators.

Even the noisome Russian delegation, who submitted every proposal for approval to Stalin (54), in their satisfaction with the

160

acceptance of the basic tenet of Weishaupt, Marx and Lenin on the "internationalist" currency as the monetary base of a world-wide "managed" economy, accepted the conspirators' scheme as dictated by "adviser", Nelson Rockefeller through his pawn, Roosevelt. They expressed their delight with it by subscribing more than their quota to the Fund thereby assuring themselves of larger borrowing power under its rules. American taxpayers were nicked more than $3 billion dollars to provide more than 30% of the capital, for which we received a "generous" 27% of the total votes in IMF and World Bank councils. As usual, the conspirators undertook to divert suspicion from themselves by pretending to "oppose" the scheme exactly as they had pretended to "oppose" their "Federal" Reserve conspiracy. (59:2601-5)

## IMF TIES GOLDEN NOOSE TIGHTLY ABOUT WORLD ECONOMIES AND FINANCES

There is no room for questioning that the conspirators designed the IMF as a subsidiary of their "Federal" Reserve fraud. This is borne out by the publication of the monetary rules of the IMF as an appendix to the official "F"R publication of laws affecting its activities. (25)

The rules supposedly carry out the provisions of the Lend-Lease Agreement required of the nations receiving that "aid": to stimulate "production, employment, and exchange and production of goods... elimination of discriminatory treatment in international commerce and reduction of tariffs and other barriers."

This pretended goal, it provided, was to be attained by requiring each land to fix and maintain, within a variance of only 10%, the exchange value of its money relative to the dollar and the currency of other signatory nations; and to maintain free convertibility of the money into Dollars and other units, *And/Or Gold." Each And Every Country Is Barred From Purchasing Or Selling Gold At Any Price Other Than That Dictated By The IMF*. Change in the par value of the currency of any nation requires the consent of the IMF. However, a uniform change in the value of gold by all nations simultaneously may be proposed by any member, or by the IMF itself, and submitted to a vote. (25;53) This provision clearly indicates that the conspirators plan to compensate themselves for their loss of interest on the stolen gold by world-wide increases in the price of gold to any figure that they might desire. (44:417-25) No serious obstacle would be presented to this plot by the provision that they had written into the Bretton Woods Agreement Act, Sec. 5, in order to allay the suspicions of Congress. It reads:

"Unless Congress by law authorizes such action, neither the President nor any person or agency shall on behalf of the United States...

(b) propose or agree to any change in the par value of the United States currency under article IV, Section 5, or article XX, section 4 of the Articles of Agreement of the Fund, or any general change in par values under article IV, section 7..." (27:252-3)

Congress was always pliable at the hands of the conspirators, and as workable as fresh putty. They have many kinfolks and paid agents in its ranks. They need merely fake one of their periodic "crises," or precipitate, if necessary, one of their panics, to herd the nation into submission with the aid of their prostituted media of "mass communication," or indoctrination.

In this manner, the conspirators have set the stage for use of their "Federal" Reserve gold loot and the powers with which they have endowed themselves through the dis-"United" Nations and their IMF, to plunder any and every part of their "One (Rockefeller) World," unmercifully and on an unprecedentedly vast scale, by dictating that their gold hoard shall be revalued and inflated to any price they may choose, whether it be seventy or seven hundred dollars an ounce, when they so decide. This will instantly devalue, or even wipe out the savings, insurance, pensions, investments and wealth of all mere mortals, overnight.

## PLIANT AND RUTHLESS ROCKEFELLER AGENTS RUN THEIR IMF FOR THEM

Although Harry Dexter White was used as a pawn by the Rockefeller-Soviet conspirators in the drafting of the Bretton Woods scheme, under the direct control of their top echelon of agents, he was not trusted by them sufficiently to be given free rein in putting it over because he was not, as Whittaker Chambers stated and Col. Bykov complained, subject to Party discipline. (59:2497) One of the conspirators' most trusted Red agents who has long been personally associated with the Rockefellers, as Chairman of their treasonous Institute of Pacific Relations, in their subversive Council on Foreign Relations, in the State Department and numerous other capacities, Prof. Philip C. Jessup (15) was appointed by them Assistant Secretary General of the Bretton Woods Conference to ride herd on its puppet President, White's superior, Secretary of the Treasury Henry Morgenthau. Jessup's record of affiliations with Red and Communist front organizations was so notorious (116:1093, 1097, 1206, 1210) that Senate refused to confirm his 1951 appointment by Pres. Truman as U.S. Delegate to the UN.

## PER JACOBSSON, "ADVISER" OF INTERNATIONAL SWINDLER, HEADED CONSPIRATORS' IMF

In the post of Director of the IMF, the conspirators placed a man who had served them with highest distinction, a Swede named Per Jacobsson. It is a curious fact that Swedish Reds however subversive or criminal, such as Jacobsson, Gunnar Myrdal, Dag Hammarskjold (79), and numerous others, are regarded by the conspirators as "in better odor" and less suspect, and therefore more useful on the world scene. Per Jacobsson had served, as adviser," with the "highest distinction," a fellow conspirator, Ivar Kruger, in the perpetration of one of the hugest international swindles in history, the International Match Co. fraud. This brigandage had proved especially helpful and profitable to the conspirators because it helped prepare the way, on an international scale, for the market crash of 1929, and the panic and depression of the 1930's. This left no doubt in the minds of the conspirators that Jacobsson was a "genius." For, the International Match affair ranks as one of the major frauds of history, though it does fade into insignificance beside the "F"R, IMF and "Gold Corner" which the conspirators are presently perpetrating. Jacobsson continued to serve

162

the conspirators loyally, in their IMF, until he died in the 1960's. His name was always reverently whispered in the conspirators' prostituted media of mass communication as "that outstanding authority on finance, Per Jacobsson." Rockefeller's high admiration of Jacobsson's "talents" was effusively expressed in by David in his memorial eulogy at the 1967 Rio de Janeiro IMF conference. (301)

## CONSPIRATORS DUPE, DISCARD & DESTROY
## HARRY DEXTER WHITE

Harry Dexter White, the unwitting pawn of the conspirators, was "induced" to resign from his IMF post on March 31, 1947, (59:2631) before his honest convictions on gold and monetary policy could hamper the conspirators' plot. Correspondence of his with Mayor William O'Dwyer, of New York City, indicates that he expected to be employed in New York. (59:2533-4) It is difficult to believe that he had ever been entirely comfortable in his post. Even in his role of U.S. Delegate to the Bretton Woods Conference, he had never been a free agent, but was bound by instructions of committees packed with agents of the conspirators. This is clearly evinced by the instructions given him by Secretary of State Cordell Hull at the time of his appointment, on June 23, 1944, which read as follows:

"...you and the other delegates will be expected to adhere to the joint statement of principles of an International Monetary Fund announced April 21, 1944.

"You will apply the same principles in your discussions and negotiations with respect to the proposed Bank for Reconstruction and Development, except that you will be governed by the principles agreed upon by the American Technical Committee." (59:2617)

His fellow delegates numbered an ample quota of dedicated Rockefeller agents, including their attorney and CFR associate, Secretary of State Dean Acheson, and their pawn, Sen. Robert F. Wagner, who had secured for them a New York State charter for their Rockefeller Foundation when Congress repeatedly refused to grant them a charter because of their avowed subversive purposes. (15:75)

Shortly after White resigned his post, the conspirators began their usual process of destroying their distrusted and discarded agents. Subjected to attacks in Congress and in the media of mass communication controlled by the conspirators, and to continuous harassment, and Congressional investigations in which he frankly told the truth that is borne out by the records, never adopting the Communist tactic of resorting to the Fifth Amendment, he took the treachery to heart as does no conspirator. He quickly succumbed and is reported to have died of a heart ailment in August 1948. Rumors were circulated that White had committed suicide. They were subsequently stamped as false. White was recovering from a heart attack at the time he was subpoenaed for questioning by the Congressional committee. He arose from his sickbed to appear, in sharp contrast with what might have been expected of a Communist agent, who would have delayed his appearance on the well-founded ground of illness. White, in his

163

indignation at the falsity of the charges against him, did not hesitate or stall, even though ill. Disregarding the risk of death, he promptly made his appearance before the committee to deny and disprove the charges. That was not the act of a spy or traitor, but was what might be expected of an indignant patriot.

The treatment accorded White by the conspirators contrasts sharply with the VIP treatment accorded the conspirators' notorious Communist agent, Lauchlin Currie. Like all of the Rockefeller-Soviet agents, he lived a sheltered life until the schism in the faith of the Soviet and Chinese Communists in Colombia endangered it. Then he was promptly provided with shelter by the conspirators, by transfer to British Columbia.

CHAPTER XVIII
DAVID ROCKEFELLER TAKES OVER AS DYNASTY'S
WORLD MONETARY BOSS

David Rockefeller, the youngest of the Rockefeller "princes," chose as his duchy the continent of Africa the wealth of which had recently begun to intrigue the Dynasty. As a more immediate source of prodigious pelf and loot, he took over the ultra-profitable world-wide financial and monetary racketeering that the Rockefeller imperialists had developed about the nucleus of their "Gold Standard" and "Federal" Reserve frauds. In this activity he is supported by the continued activity of his brother, Nelson, with whom he avidly collaborates. In the meanwhile, Nelson had gone on to cultivate a field that offered more promise of "profits" to the Dynasty: the Governorship of New York that he has hope will serve as a stepping stone to the White House, and national and "One (Rockefeller) World" dictatorship.

As New York Governor, Nelson Rockefeller scorns any reference to "conflict of interest," and instituted a frank and open spoils system for the benefit of the Dynasty. He headed the list of bills that he demanded that the State Legislature pass with measures that were frankly designed to increase their power and loot in the State. These included: bills that were designed to enable the Rockefellers to extend their New York City Bank Trust throughout the State without resort to subterfuge; a bill that would make it possible for their Milk Trust (so labelled by Henry Wallace in his Wallace Farmer) to enhance their profits from the sale of spoiled milk by eliminating the New York requirement that milk containers bear the date on which they had been filled (56:101; 57; 79:201-2); a bill that he succeeded in forcing through Legislature that increased the State income tax to the point where he, personally, would have been required to pay a combined Federal and State income tax total of 101% of his income *if he were not able to entirely avoid the payment of any income tax by hiding behind the tax exemption dodges which the conspirators have written for themselves into the tax laws.* In the message he read to New York State Legislature on January 3, 1968, Gov. Rockefeller acknowledged that his most costly and corrupt Administration in the State's history has reduced it to insolvency and no more taxes can be levied short of confiscation. As usual he pretended that his tax looting was due to citizens' demand for "services." However, the only service he has rendered is that a bull gives a cow. (335)

## DAVID ROCKEFELLER, AN INTENSIVELY TRAINED & DEDICATED RED

David Rockefeller, the youngest of the brood, who was born on June 12, 1915, is the Rockefeller most thoroughly groomed in Communism and its uses. At the Columbia University "experimental" and so-called "Progressive" Lincoln School, he received a "permissive," "liberal" or Red indoctrination in the pattern advocated by Professors John Dewey, Count and others, for the purpose of creating a "new (Communist) social order." Studious and intensive by nature, his bent took him initially into the field of science, the study of entomology, beetles and other bugs. He freely acknowledges the shortcomings of the so-called "education" he there received: that it failed to teach him to spell correctly or to read well, at both of which accomplishments he acknowledged himself still to be deficient (as is his brother Nelson). (125:68)

It is significant of the state of degeneration at which "education" has arrived as a result of Rockefeller "philanthropic" control of it, that these basic deficiencies did not preclude his receiving degrees from both Harvard University and the University of Chicago. It appears probable that if he had adhered to entomology and the world of bugs, the world of humans would have fared better. His pressagents note that at Mt. Desert, Maine, where the Rockefellers have a summer home, David joined a neighbor, Henry Ford II (whose interests have since fallen under Rockefeller domination) in nature studies. (15:347) The Rockefeller psychopathic greed and Weishaupt-Marxist economics were merged by his scholarship and, unfortunately for mankind, directed into other channels that now menace the world.

Undergraduate training at Harvard University intensified David's "Liberal" bent. And his interests were still further turned in that direction by a friend and agent of his father, by the "Liberal" Canadian Premier, William McKenzie King, who had served the Dynasty in laying the foundation for its takeover of American labor unionism as well as in robbing Canadians of their subsurface property rights and of their natural resources. King's services were so profitable to them that the Rockefellers provided for him in his old age, at the expense of American taxpayers by way of their Foundation and its tax exemption, by a grant to McGill University for the supposed purpose of defraying his expenses in writing his autobiography. (122:54; 15)

King advised David Rockefeller to follow, in reverse, the trail that he himself had followed in his education as a Red. King had started his training at Rockefeller's University of Chicago, pro-

165

ceeded to the London School of Economics and finished at the Harvard hotbed of Communism. He counselled David, a Harvard graduate, to reverse the process in seeking indoctrination that was regarded as vital for a Red, totalitarian takeover of the world through the channels of business, finance and government.

Following King's advice, after a year of graduate work at Harvard, David turned for indoctrination to the violent Red, Harold Laski, at the London School of Economics, and John Maynard Keynes, the crafty Fabian proponent of the scheme of "restoring" American prosperity with deficit financing leading to national bankruptcy that was plotted by Lenin as the device for Communizing the U.S., and was adopted by the conspirators as the financial basis for their "New" Deal. David might well have expected to be welcomed with open arms at that center of British, Fabian Communism. For it had been heavily financed, at the expense of American taxpayers by way of tax exemption, by his grandfather and father, John D. I and John D. II, personally and through their "Philanthropic" Foundation Trust (2:199, 204) and had furthered their efforts to destroy the British Empire from within.

For the purpose of completing his "Liberal," Red and subversive indoctrination, semi-literate David sought and obtained his Ph.D. at the Rockefeller-subsidized, radical, Baptist University of Chicago. The Communist character of his economic instruction at that institute is clearly indicated by the records of those characters whom he thanked, in the preface, for guidance and advice in the writing of his Ph.D. thesis, Professors Jacob Viner and Oskar Lange. (128:vi)

Both of these characters are notorious Reds. Prof. Jacob Viner's collaboration with Soviet Intelligence agent Lauchlin Currie as mentors and monitors of Harry Dexter White, has been related. Even more significant is the career of Oskar Lange. Lange was a Polish Communist who came to the U.S. in 1934 as a missionary for the Polish Marxists. Four years later, he was placed on the faculty of the Rockefeller-dominated University of Chicago, as economist and "social(ist) scientist." There David went to sit at his feet and drink in the "wisdom" of Lange and his ilk.

Several years thereafter, in 1945, Lange resigned from the university to assume the post of Soviet Polish Ambassador to the U.S. and U.N. These posts gave Lange ample opportunity to publicly express what he had previously reserved for the privacy of academic halls, shielded by "academic freedom": his bitter hatred of the U.S. and contempt for its institutions. (59:2650) In the conspirators' "United" Nations, he invariably voted with the Soviet block. (129) Recalled to Warsaw in 1949, he became the conspirators' top agent in Poland, "their man behind the scenes," and Premier Gomulka's boss. When Vice-President Nixon visited Poland, it was the conspirators' agent Lange who entertained him and acted as his guide in Warsaw.

## RED MAYOR LAGUARDIA BOSSED BY DAVID FOR THIEVISH CONSPIRATORS

After he received his Ph.D., David Rockefeller married Margaret McGrath, and then assumed the task of controlling, or "guiding," the conspirators' "liberal," or Red, agent, New York City's

Mayor Fiorello LaGuardia, and his frankly Communist "soul-mate," Congressman Vito Marcantonio. This chore he described in his correspondence as "a hectic time with my new job with Mayor LaGuardia and finishing my thesis." In the guise of political intern, he served as sentinel who sat guard over the Dynasty's local interests, sitting in the front office and controlling access to the Mayor. The situation explains LaGuardia's false reputation of "honesty" in spite of the fact that his was one of the most corrupt administrations up to that time (prior to Mayor Lindsay) as well as most costly, in the history of New York City. It was marked by no petty graft for wardheelers. The graft was on a grandiose scale that redounded almost exclusively to the profit of the conspirators.

LaGuardia had been put in office by the Rockefellers by their usual device of a so-called "Reform" movement that is a clearcut expression of their absolute control of all political parties. The conspirators effected his election, by the fair and foul means that they can always bring into play, for the specific purpose of finally accomplishing a huge steal that they had vainly tried to put over during several decades. This "piece de resistance" of corruption of the LaGuardia regime centered about the unification of the city's transit system. The conspirators had controlled, mismanaged and mercilessly looted the system and brought it to the verge of bankruptcy. Their objective was to unload on the taxpayers at one hundred cents on the dollar the transit bonds that they had bought, during depressions and market breaks, at the price of pennies on the dollar; to merge and unify the several companies involved under their own indirect management through a "transit authority"; to force the taxpayers to shoulder the cost of rebuilding, improving and expanding it; and to sharply increase the fares while continuing to milk and loot it. Many hundreds of million dollars of loot have been involved in this scheme, the foundation for which was solidly laid by LaGuardia "managed" by David Rockefeller.

"Honest" agent LaGuardia is reputed to have received no payoff for setting the scene for this steal. But his kin are said to have profited to the tune of $1.5 million. New York's subways have been greatly extended at the expense of the taxpayers, but are in a constantly more neglected and deteriorated condition. Fares have been steadily increased as fast as public opinion and political expediency permitted, to its present level of quadruple the original fare, or twenty cents; and further increases are in prospect. With the help of the Rockefeller controlled transit labor unions, the public have been milked to the tune of many hundreds of million dollars. (7:132, 214)

## CONSPIRATORS CREATE SLUMS FOR THIEVISH "CLEARANCE"

While bossing their agent LaGuardia, David Rockefeller promoted a number of other thievish interests of the Dynasty. One of the most menacing of these was land grabbing racketeering under the guise of pretended "slum clearance and urban redevelopment." For the purpose of depressing some of the nation's most valuable real estate, New York City properties, to an even lower level than they had succeeded in doing with the depression-constructed Rockefeller Center and their unethical and dishonest prac-

167

tises in operating it, they converted much of the city to slums. (15:173f; 79:74f; 130)

## DAVID ROCKEFELLER: STAR "BLOCKBUSTER"

The creation of slums for depressing real estate values was effected by the conspirators by the process of "blockbusting" which they reduced to a fine art. Negroes from the South and Puerto Ricans were lured to New York and other cities around the country by the conspirators, and ruthlessly, but profitably crowded into all properties that were available. They were uprooted from their environments, in which they had managed to make a living, by various crafty devices. David Rockefeller, as Mayor LaGuardia's "aide," or boss, is reported to have been responsible for posting of advertisements in buses and other public vehicles in Birmingham, Atlanta and other southern towns, inviting them to migrate to New York, promising them immediate support by metropolitan taxpayers through "Relief" if they did not find employment that they fancied.

Spanish-speaking Porto Ricans were the special protegees of Nelson Rockefeller, who had studied Spanish with gusto when he set out to loot Latin America as "Co-Ordinator." (79:105f) They were lured to New York with an eye to providing tens of thousands of votes for the conspirators' agent, Mayor LaGuardia, and with an eye to Nelson Rockefeller's political designs for which purpose they have been assiduously and successfully wooed and duped by him. They also have been profitably plied with the conspirators' dope.

Numerous of the most undesirable elements, especially the Southern blacks with long and dangerous criminal records and outcasts in their home communities, gladly accepted the conspirators' enticing invitation to prey upon New York and its taxpayers. Maintained in relative luxury and idleness on Relief, they have been free to indulge their fancies in breeding illegitimate offspring and to ply their criminal trades. It is a matter of debate whether this undesirable and/or criminal element lured into the city by the conspirators do not exceed the better elements seeking honest employment. At any rate these activities of the conspirators have created a steadily increasing wave of crime in New York and other cities of the North.

## NEGROES & PORTO RICANS PROFITABLY USED, ABUSED AND ABANDONED BY CONSPIRATORS

The lured immigrants have been craftily colonized by the conspirators' agents, with the help of their "open housing" and "desegregation" frauds, in the desirable sections of cities that they want to steal. There they are crowded into apartments, rooms and cellars in numbers far exceeding their capacity and mercilessly fleeced. Cunning and unscrupulous persons among blacks serve the interest of the conspirators in preying on their fellows and plying them with drugs.

All laws of housing, sanitation and health are waived for the conspirators and their agents. Their Relief Administration often packs several families into single apartments, rooms or cellars, paying the owners exorbitant rents at the expense of the taxpayers, helping raise the budget for these activities to figures that now exceed the entire tax roll of New York two decades earlier. Tenants have been encouraged to destroy the properties in which they reside, though some of the riff-raff among them, who are

168

accustomed to fouling their own nests, require no encouragement. It is quite usual for some of them to rip out the plumbing in their own toilets and sell the stolen parts for enough money to buy a dose of dope.

By the administration of the law, these tenants have been exempted from prosecution for their crimes; and the landlords, who have fewer votes than the tenants, are held liable for the destruction wrought. Rigid rent controls imposed by the conspirators deny the landlords sufficient rental income to meet the barest expenses of maintenance and taxes that are constantly increased to meet the cost of "Relief"; and leave nothing for repairs of the damages, in a scheme of progressive confiscation of property.

When the conditions thus created become intolerably vile and menacing, and the neighborhoods converted into vicious slums, the conspirators launch their "Slum Clearance & Urban Redevelopment" scheme to use the government to steal the property and finance its profitable exploitation. The power of eminent domain of the government for confiscation of property with fair and adequate compensation for public, non-profit benefit, has been converted into a device for looting the property owners and the rank and file of taxpayers for the personal direct and indirect profit of the "philanthropists."

Properties designedly converted into slums are seized and virtually stolen from their owners by condemnation at confiscatory prices that represent a small fraction of their worth, at the expense of the taxpayers. They are then sold to the conspirators or their agents, at a small fraction of the price paid by the taxpayers. In many instances, the properties continue to be rented by the purchasers until they are ready to begin redevelopment. The buildings are then demolished, at the expense of the taxpayers.

With loans provided them by the Housing Administration, at the expense of the taxpayers, that often far exceed the cost of the proposed developments and yield the conspirators windfall profits, they proceed to erect high rental and other profitable structures. To further enhance their thievish profits, the conspirators have dictated that their development be exempted from taxation for periods as long as thirty years, as in the case of Rockefeller Center. Thus the conspirators have arranged to be rewarded handsomely and to be further greatly enriched for their brigandage. This thievery has been nation-wide in scope. And it has netted the conspirators ownership of much valuable property in town and country, throughout the land.

## ROCKEFELLER RAPE OF NEW YORK CITY & STATE IS THOROUGH

Rockefellers property steals in New York have been especially intensive and give color to the report that they plan to take Manhattan out of the United States and put it all under the sovereignty of their dis-"United" Nations, making their holdings forever tax exempt, as soon as they have stolen all of it. They have succeeded in grabbing the homes of countless thousands of New Yorkers, and after dispossessing them, forcing them, if they wish to remain in the city, to become their tenants at exorbitantly high rents. Thus far they have grabbed, directly or indirectly, the entire waterfront of Manhattan and much of the most valuable property in the city. The property which they supposedly have "given" their dis-"United" Nations racket will, under the terms of their contract with it, revert to themselves with all its buildings, free of all charge, if and when it suits their interests to move it elsewhere. Several of their realty operations in New York give insight into their modus operandi in these steals.

## ROCKEFELLERS' LINCOLN CENTER: DEDICATED TO THE "ARTS" — OF LANDGRABBING

When the Rockefellers set up their Rockefeller Center deal to intensify the real estate crash that accompanied their "Federal" Reserve precipitated 1929 panic, they adopted their favorite pose of "philanthropic patrons of the arts;" and they cadged public support and contributions on the pretense that they planned to supply a new home for the Metropolitan Opera. When it suited their purposes, their control of the Opera enabled them to secure abandonment of that pretense in favor of a highly profitable commercial enterprise that was materially helped by the passage by the 72nd Congress, in 1932, of Public Bill 296, introduced by their pawn, Sen. Robert F. Wagner, that made Rockefeller Center the only freeport in the U.S. (15:173f) Nelson Rockefeller made considerable money on "kickbacks" obtained by him through his 10% agency Special Work Inc. which became an integral part of the Rockefeller Brothers "philanthropy." (79:73; 31:58; 43:93; 44:7)

The Rockefellers worked the same scheme to supplement their Slum Clearance & Urban Redevelopment taxpayer-subsidized steal. Once again, posing as "patrons of the arts," the Metropolitan Opera and other "art" projects most of which are as ardently maintained and supported by "Liberals" as is their Communist rooted Museum of Modern Art (209), they cadged money from the public once again "to provide a new home for the Metropolitan Opera." In the prosperous period of the 1960's the square block Manhattan site of the old Metropolitan Opera House had become immensely more valuable than it had been in the 1930 depression; and more valuable than the property of the slum-surrounded Lincoln Center that the conspirators had obtained for virtually nothing. The old Metropolitan Opera site is leased for a period of ninety nine years for the sum of half a million dollars a year, for the construction of a skyscraper that will be enormously profitable. The principals in this deal are hidden by the same devious devices of nominees, agents and corporations as the conspirators have adopted in their "Federal" Reserve setup.

The buildings of Lincoln Center were planned by the conspirators' architectural firm, Harrison & Abramovitz, and was built under their supervision at a fantastically high cost. What role the Rockefeller Brothers firm, Special Work Inc., that specializes in "tenpercenting" and "kickbacks" (79:74; 17:58; 66:93f), may have played in siphoning off the funds contributed naively by the sucker public, is not revealed.

As is the conspirators' practise in "slum clearance" and kindred enterprises, the construction work was so shamefully gerrymandered that the structures began disintegrating before they were completed. Defects in the acoustic properties of the new Metropolitan

Opera House, the theatres and the concert halls were so glaring as to require repeated demolition and reconstruction. The entrance stairs of the buildings were "ideally" designed to subject to injury those who sought to enter, and led to numerous negligence suits by injured persons. The decorative fountain on the grounds was so faultily constructed that its water leaked continually into the offices and cafeteria beneath it, and precluded their use; and for years the leak has defied the efforts of the architects to repair the defect. Three rooms were completely sealed off, with windows but no entrance doorways. Audition rooms were built so small that they scarcely offer sufficient space for artist, piano and accompanyist.

## CHASE MANHATTAN BANK & CENTER
## ARCHITECTURAL "PERFECTIONS"

Illustrative of even craftier real estate operations are the structures that they built for their Chase Manhattan Bank and Chemical Bank New York Trust companies on several acres of land in the Wall Street section at Pine and Nassau Streets, directly opposite their New York Federal Reserve Bank. The structures are stark, ugly steel and glass towers. They are devoid of windows that can be opened to admit air and natural ventilation; and are dependent on central airconditioning systems that regularly break down. Like most structures of this type they can not be weatherproofed. Only intermittently can they be kept comfortable, cool in the summer and warm in the winter; and rarely can snow and rain be kept out. Not infrequently, the secretaries can keep comfortable in the summer time only in their negligees, and in the winter, in their fur coats. Their pressagents admit that windstorms regularly levy a toll of blown out windows. (121:78) that endanger the lives of the inmates and of passersby; and they are enormously costly to replace.

Other landgrabbing "slum clearance" enterprises of the conspirators in New York are their Port Authority "Trade Center" and New York State office buildings about which will be related in a later chapter. They are all of the same pattern. And all of them have the same architects.

Harrison & Abramovitz, the architects have been especially closely identified with Nelson Rockefeller who in younger years toyed with the idea of becoming an architect. (66:74) One of the delusions to which he acknowledges himself to be prone, (79:66) is that he is possessed of architectural "genius." Harrison is a kinsman, a remote in-law, (17:174) whom Nelson regards as trusted adviser. It is rumored that Nelson Rockefeller is a "moving spirit" in the Harrison & Abramovitz firm, a sort of silent partner. This would be fully in character. The Rockefellers spurn the idea of "conflict of interest" and make no secret of the fact that they seek extraordinary profits from their every involvement.

It is interesting to note that none of the buildings which the Rockefellers themselves own, in which they have no partners and have their own money invested, are of the same steel and glass architecture as those built for others. This raises the suspicion that there may be a deliberate purpose to this defective architecture. The excessively high cost of maintenance of these structures insures their foreclosure, at an early date.

171

## CHURCHES "SANCTIFY" CONSPIRATORS' "SLUM CLEARANCE" STEALS & JOIN IN

One of the ugliest aspects of the "slum clearance and urban redevelopment" thievery is the unprincipled participation in it of religious leaders and their institutions. For the purpose of deluding the public with regard to the crude brigandage involved in their landgrabbing activities, the conspirators make it a practise to share a part of the loot that may range to 25% of the stolen land, with religious institutions. Religious leaders make it clear by their participation in looting the public, often their own followers, how little morality, ethics and principle are basic ingredients of their religions. And the situation reveals how flagrantly is being violated the Constitution's provisions on separation of church and state.

## JESUITS' FORDHAM UNIVERSITY SHARES CONSPIRATORS' LINCOLN CENTER STEAL

The lion share of that part of the stolen land that the conspirators share with the religious confederates, through the country, is "fenced" by the Catholic Church. It has been estimated that about 20% of all property stolen by this device is split by the conspirators with the Holy Roman Empire, with the Catholics. The remaining 5% is the swag pounced on by all other religious outfits.

This situation is well illustrated by the Lincoln Center land steal. For the purpose of "deodorizing" that steal and of "sanctifying" it and making appear to be a "holy" cause, the conspirators gave a sizable portion of the confiscated property involved to the Society of Jesus as a site for a branch of their Fordham University, which even its alumni pronounce to be an inferior and foundering institution. (336:32) To its everlasting discredit, the Church eagerly participated in the property theft that despoiled many of their parishioners, dispossessing them from their homes and destroying their businesses and livelihoods from the proceeds of which they had paid their tithes and other offerings. Jesuit Br. James M. Kenny, Fordham University's vice-president gloated over the situation in a story published in the New York Times of December 4, 1967, in an article entitled:

*"College Town" Is Rising On Fringes Of Lincoln Center*

In the article is one line that unintentionally stresses the inhumane and mercenary aspect of the thievery involved. It reads:

"The...projects are the latest in an area that has been transformed from a drab slum to a shimmering center of culture, education and *High-Rise Apartment Living." (306:49)*

The article made no mention of the fact that the "drab slum" had housed the homes and businesses, and provided the livelihoods of many of the poor parishioners of the Church of the Blessed Sacrament and of the Church of St. Paul the Apostle, who can not afford the rents of the "high-rise apartments" for which they had been ousted. Possibly a motivation for collaboration in the theft of the property might be found in the higher income to the Church from the wealthier parishioners that would replace those looted and displaced.

The situation is reminiscent of that presented a decade ago by an Italian Capuchin monastery that sought to expand its land holdings. Small neighboring landowners were readily convinced

172

that yielding their land to the Order would pave their way to heaven. But a more intelligent, large property owner refused to turn over his property. The monks, with Maffista collaboration, murdered the property owner and stole his property. When caught, their sentence was a few years in jail. (310)

### JEWISH YESHIVA UNIVERSITY "WANTED IN": REJECTED AS "UNDESIRABLE."

That lack of principle and inhumanity are traits shared by too many faiths is apparent from the efforts of the Jewish, Yeshiva University crowd to share in the Lincoln Center land steal. They sought a site for the expansion of their university. The conspirators turned down the yarmulke-topped Jews as "undesirable neighbors." But the Rockefeller attitude is quite different when they seek the votes of the Jews.

### ROCKEFELLER CAMOUFLAGE, A POSE OF "PHILANTHROPY" ADOPTED BY DAVID

In accord with the conspirators' traditional pose of "philanthropy" originally advocated by Jesuit Adam Weishaupt as mask for predatory activities, David Rockefeller played a role in the organization of a Public Health Research Institute in New York City's Health Department, at the expense of the taxpayers. It was designed, as are all Rockefeller "philanthropies," to mask one of their endless patterns of thievery. Its real purpose is to direct the enormous drug and medical supply purchases of the City to the firms that are controlled by the conspirators and affiliated with their Drug Trust, licensees of their I. G. Farbenindustrie cartel. The "Institute" supplanted the famed Health Department Laboratory that had conducted brilliant researches under its illustrious director, Dr. Park, and done a magnificent public health job in eliminating infectious and contagious diseases. Rockefeller "modestly" assumed the role of Director of the "Institute."

### AGENT ANNA ROSENBERG'S SKIRTS SHIELDED DAVID ROCKEFELLER

When the conspirators were bringing to a head their plot to precipitate World War II and drag the U.S. into it, David Rockefeller transferred himself to the shelter afforded by a longtime Red agent and employee of theirs, Anna Rosenberg, (since married to another of their Red agents, Paul Hoffman) as her assistant regional director in the U.S. Office of Defense, Health and Welfare Service (122:62), which his brother, Nelson, later dictated be reorganized under his direction into the Department of Health, Education and Welfare boodle. (79:155)

### DAVID ROCKEFELLER'S "ARDUOUS" MILITARY SERVICE SERVED DYNASTY

In May, 1942, when faced with the draft that the conspirators had engineered for securing manpower for the expansion of their Empire, David Rockefeller went into the service. He was assigned to a "front line" berth, close to home at New York City's Governors Island Army post. When winter came on, his transfer was arranged to the more clement climes at the "front" in Miami Beach, Florida, where he is reported to have been given the assignment of groom of a colonel's horse. (122:62) Tiring of this chore, he transferred to the Engineer Officer Training School, at the "front" at Belvoir, Virginia, whence he emerged, in March 1943 with the rank of second lieutenant. (17:130; 124:787) With the effect of delaying his transfer to active service, he then went to the Engineering School, at Camp Ritchie, Maryland, until June 1943. After this prolonged course of training as an engineer, he obtained an assignment "mostly in intelligence work," in Algiers, Africa, (17:130)

Africa had become what was for him a safe hotbed of intrigue of Rockefeller German and French financial agents, that proved most highly profitable to the conspirators. (123) At the end of the war, promoted to the rank of captain for his "heroic," distinguished and arduous service, to horses and purse, he went to Paris as Assistant Military Attache. There he luxuriated until December, 1945. For his "signal service" he was awarded by the French minions, the Legion of Honor, and Legion of Merit. Through this record of "heroism," David joined his odd brother, Winthrop, (131:230; 260) in departing from the Rockefeller tradition to which brother Nelson adhered, of scorning and evading a show of patriotism by joining the Armed Forces drafted for the purpose of serving their interests.

CHASE NATIONAL BANK TAKEN OVER BY ROCKEFELLERS
The Chase National Bank was organized by a Wall Streeter named John Thompson, in 1877, as a "wholesale," banker's bank. He named it, as an expression of his admiration, after Lincoln's Secretary of the Treasury, Salmon P. Chase. Chase had induced Congress, as has been related, to make greenbacks legal tender; had then been appointed Chief Justice of the U.S. Supreme Court; and had taken advantage of the assassination of Lincoln to seek the Presidency by courting the votes of the newly liberated Southern Negroes (as did his successor in the post, Earl Warren, almost a century later); and had ingratiated himself with President U.S. Grant, by declaring un-Constitutional the measure that he had induced Congress to pass, making greenbacks legal tender. Thus he made possible the killing made by the Grant crowd in the Gould-Grant "Gold Corner" that Gould and Fisk had engineered with the bribed collaboration of corrupt and venal President Grant, the closest kinsman to Pres. F. D. Roosevelt of the twelve Presidents on the Roosevelt-Delano family tree. (7:10,24)

The Chase bank was taken over by the Rockefeller in a merger deal with their Equitable Trust Co. The two banks collaborated in financing Germany's entry into World War I through the newly organized "Federal" Reserve. (20:159; 21) Rockefeller's uncle, Winthrop Aldrich whose father had initiated for the conspirators the "F"R, was president of their Equitable Trust. When it was merged with Chase National Bank, he became the chairman of its board of directors.

DAVID ROCKEFELLER "STRUGGLED" TO TOP, & CONTROL
OF CHASE NATIONAL BANK
On leaving his "arduous" duties in the Armed Forces, David Rockefeller assumed the post of assistant manager of the foreign department of the Chase Bank. In the following decade he "struggled" his way to the Presidency of the bank, that has been merged with the Bank of Manhattan Company one of the oldest banking

174

institutions in the country. The objectives of the merger included entry of the institution into what might be called "retail banking," the acceptance of accounts from the general public and dealings with them. The Manhattan Company had sixty-seven branches throughout New York. The merged bank ranks next in size to the Bank of America, which is the largest in the country. In the process of the merger, the Chase Manhattan Bank was converted to a bank operating under a charter from the State of New York. The merger enabled the bank to enjoy the special advantages which the State charter offered, until such time as those and still greater advantages could be derived from resuming a national charter. More recently the Chase bank has once again applied for a national charter for the purpose of enjoying the benefits with which the conspirators have endowed it.

Rockefeller pressagents stress the "close ties" of the Rockefeller brothers to the Chase Manhattan Bank, that they cite to justify its designation as the "Rockefeller bank." Actually, it is one of numerous "Rockefeller banks" around the country and the world. The First National City Bank, which is the second largest in New York City, is headed by Rockefellers' cousin, James Stillman Rockefeller. The Chemical Bank New York Trust, which represents a merger of several of the larger banks in the city, has its share of Rockefeller nominees and directors. Congressional investigations reveal the extent of the use of nominees and dummies by the conspirators in their nation-wide interlocking control of banks throughout the country. (213)

Rockefeller stock in the Chase Manhattan Bank that is registered in their own names, rather than in the names of nominees, has a total value (as of January, 1965) of $70 million. (121:61) This represents only 5% of the outstanding stock. At the same time David Rockefeller's personal holdings were reported to be valued at $15 million. (121:62) This makes him the largest stockholder. Additional holdings are in the names of members of his immediate family.

## "LOAN SHARKING" AND USURY ARE
## ROCKEFELLER TRADITIONS

"Loan sharking" and usury are Rockefeller traditions that trace back to the origin of the Dynasty with their great-grandfather, "Doc" William Avery Rockefeller. (79:1)

"Doc" Bill Rockefeller, operating under the alias of "Doc" Levingston, under which he contracted another of his bigamous marriages (in this instance to Miss Allen) attempted to steal control of one of the first oil companies in the U.S., Bissell's Pennsylvania Rock Oil Co. by the device of usury. He loaned the company and its principals a sum of money, on notes secured by ample collateral, at exorbitantly usurious rates of interest. He desired the oil for his quack patent medicine "cancer cure" that he labelled "Seneca Indian Oil." For advertising purposes, he required the company to change its name to Seneca Oil Co.

When the oil company was forced to suspend operations because of the drain on its resources by "Doc" Levingston's usury, the principals brought suit in the local court to break the usurious

175

contract. Fortunately for them, it was brought to light in the course of the proceedings that "Doc" Levingston was none other than "Doc" Bill Rockefeller, a criminal fugitive from justice in New York State. This fact plus the flagrant nature of the usury led the court to order the culprit to cancel the loan and return the collateral. Later, Bissell and "Col." Drake managed to raise enough money to complete the first drilled oil well, at Oil City, that launched the oil industry in the U.S. (43;89;380)

This oily swindle was the experience that led "Doc" Rockefeller to finance and direct the entry of his oldest son, John D., in his stead, in racketeering in the oil industry. His interest charges to his son were more modest than those levied on Seneca Oil Co. principals. Unaffected by his unhappy experience in the Seneca Oil swindle, "Doc" Bill Rockefeller persisted in making his basic business "principle": "Dishonesty is the best policy." (43:44)

### MODERN-DAY ROCKEFELLER STOCK SWINDLES

How well the Rockefeller Dynasty has learned the tradition of "Doc" and his usury, is indicated by various episodes of swindling of stockholders by floating worthless stock, or stock priced far beyond its real value, that is periodically resorted to by them in spite of their enormous wealth, income and loot.

Several such instances, recently perpetrated, are at hand. Illustrative of the first type of swindle, the sale of worthless stock, is the sale by Rockefellers, through their brother, stockmarket operator, Laurance, to the public of the stock of the Horizon Titanium Co., a subsidiary of their Horizon Co. of Cleveland. That Company had no assets other than license of some patents for the production of titanium by a process that is materially more expensive than those which they held in another of their companies. They were consequently worthless. Through their fiscal agents. Lehman Brothers and Lazard Freres, Rockefellers sold to the public one million shares of Horizon Titanium Co. stock at sixteen dollars a share. The stock was sold on the basis of a prospectus filed with the Securities and Exchange Commission that failed to reveal many material facts. It was jiggled up to twenty dollars a share and "roped in" the public. A couple of years later, the stock was selling for pennies and acknowledged by the principals to be worthless Their political and financial power made them immune to prosecution. The SEC refused to investigate the matter.

An example of the second type of swindle is the Itek Corp. According to the stories released by Rockefeller agents, the corporation was financed by them, through Laurance, in a deal in which they took for themselves more than two hundred thousand shares at forty cents a share. It was then loaded, under their potent influence, with enormous Defense Department contracts. Less than two years later, stock was disposed of to the public at $375.00, and up, a share. The shares were split and unloaded on the sucker public. Within one year, the stock had sold down to as low as $9.00. Defense Department contracts had been withdrawn and the research workers and projects had been dispersed to other of their organizations. This was a truly "philanthropic" jiggle. The SEC agency has very studiously looked the other way and carefully refrained from investigating. After the sucker public had been robbed of their stock, the company was revived with more Defense Department and other contracts, regained its earnings and market value, and in 1967 sold as high as $172 a share after most of the public had been squeezed out.

## DAVID ROCKEFELLER CONVERTED CHASE BANK TO USURY & "LOAN SHARKING"

David Rockefeller, in his capacity of officer of Chase Manhattan Bank, has dedicated it to the traditional family pattern: usury and loan sharking.

A "tight money" policy was dictated by David Rockefeller at the meeting of the American Bankers Association. CFR agents, including Chairman of their "F"R Board, William McChesney Martin, have intermittently, but progressively, imposed it on the nation. The "tight money" policy means that enterprises that are not controlled by the conspirators and their henchmen, are either denied legitimate loans at fair and legal rates of interest that make it possible for them to operate at a profit; or they are denied any loans for the conduct of their business and payment of their employees, on the pretext that, there is no money available." Their "Federal" Reserve fraud implements this scheme for throttling the commerce and industry of the nation by periodically creating shortage of money thereby increasing interest and rediscount rates and by "open market operations." The so-called "principle" underlying these financial manipulations, is that money is a commodity rather than a medium of exchange; and that it must be made scarce in order to yield their banking fraternity the highest profits by means of their manipulations which they mockingly name "the operation of the law of supply and demand."

## "PERSONAL LOANS": "YOU HAVE A FRIEND AT CHASE MANHATTAN BANK" LURE

As a rule, the conspirators and their upper echelon agents operate within the letter of the laws that they have written and had passed to shield their activities. Such violations of the law as they perpetrate are blinked at and ignored by their agents that they have placed in public office. Under the law they are free to charge corporations as much as they choose for the money that they lend them. Only in larger corporate loans are they restricted by the limited measure of competition that they allow.

It is in the field of so-called "personal loans" that the bank's "loan sharking" confronts the individual. Some judgement of profitability of this "personal loan" racket can be discerned from the intensity of the bank's quest for borrowers. Every medium of mass communication is brought into play: the press, signs and placards, and radio and television broadcasts importune prospective borrowers with the slogan:

*"YOU HAVE A FRIEND AT CHASE MANHATTAN BANK."*

The full extent of this "friendship" can be judged from an examination of the usury and "loan sharking" involved in "personal loans."

Before the takeover of banking by the conspirators, loans were made to borrowers either at the legal rate of interest, or at a lesser rate, paid solely on the amount of the loan outstanding at

177

the expiration of the period during which it had been earned.

Their "friendly" personal loans, however, are discounted. This means that the interest is deducted in full from the amount of money that is borrowed, in advance, before it is earned. Thus, if one borrows $100 at the "legal" rate of interest, which is 6%, one receives only $94. The six dollars deducted in advance represents a true interest rate, on a one year loan, of more than 13% paid in advance. But out of that $94, the borrower is often required to pay a number of additional charges such as legal and investigating fees and insurance on his life to insure repayment of the loan if he should die. It is not unusual for the fees to amount to an additional $10. This raises the cost to a bit over 18% of the $84 net received by the borrower.

The borrower, however, is required to repay the "personal loan" in weekly or monthly installments. This implies that the borrower only enjoys the use of an average of half the sum borrowed, for which double the amount of interest and charges has been levied in advance. The actual charge to him for the use of this fractional sum is 36% or more, materially exceeding the rate allowed pawnbrokers in New York City and smacks of the "vigorish" of gangster loan sharks, some of whom are agents of the conspirators and financed by their banks.

## RELIGIOSITY IS NO BARRIER TO USURY & "LOAN SHARKING"

Control of the laws of the land by the conspirators, and its enforcement, is manifest in the immunity from prosecution of themselves and their banks for misrepresentation and fraud in connection with these loans. Public indifference to this usury and fraud, except when personally involved, can hardly be viewed with surprise in view of indifference of religious leaders to this problem. This indifference is especially pronounced in the instance of the Canon Law. Originally, under the Canon, charging of any interest on a loan, or even making a profit on a business transaction, was a cardinal sin and a capital offense. This was completely reversed in the first, 1918, codification of the Canon as published by Jesuit Frs. Bouscaren & Ellis, which states:

"The present canon states implicity that in modern times there is always present in a loan some just reason for demanding the legal rate of interest and *Explicitly Allows An Even Greater Rate Of Interest* provided there be just and proportionate reason for demanding it. The canon however, studiously avoids determining what these just reasons are, leaving that to Catholic morality and economists to determine.

"...it is not per se unlawful to make an agreement for the legal rate of interest...or even for a higher rate, provided that there be a just and proportionate reason." (127:825)

One is forced to ask oneself, wherein lay the fault of Shylock. He had what he regarded a "just" reason.

## BANKS' PROFITS ENHANCED BY MAFFIA "LOAN SHARKS" & "ENFORCERS"

In the quest for greater loot than that yielded by their own "loan sharking," the "bankers" have enlisted the cooperation of their Maffia "sharks" and their "enforcers." This was brought to light by an investigation of extortion practised by the underworld that was instituted by New York State Attorney General Louis Lefkowitz, in connection with numerous incidents of violence and murder perpetrated in these operations. "Vigorish," which is the underworld term for the extortionate interest rates that they extract from their victims, rises as high as can be extorted. If the borrower fails to pay the weekly installment, he is subjected to physical violence, or even murdered. In a few instances, the victims have squared up their accounts by murdering the lender. Businesses unfortunate enough to borrow from these racketeers are frequently bled into bankruptcy, or taken over, by them.

The "arrangements" that these cruder "banking" racketeers and "loan sharks" have with their more powerful and legitimatized colleagues of the member banks of the "Federal" Reserve racket, was uncovered by the investigators. It was found that the Maffia racketeers were financed in their "loan sharking" operations by the banks... "for a consideration." Shortly thereafter, Attorney General Lefkowitz who is a loyal puppet of Governor Rockefeller and of the same stripe, lost interest in the investigation, and nothing further was heard of it.

Their pressagents acknowledge that Gov. Nelson Rockefeller has closely collaborated with his brother, David, in promoting and protecting their Dynastic interests, especially in the field of banking. A New York State legislator is quoted as asking:

"Is this state being run by the Governor or by the Chase Bank?" (121:38)

In the meantime, considerable alarm was raised among the conspirators by their criminal subordinates "kicking over the traces" and taking over banks in various parts of the country for quick looting. Smaller banks in the West and mid-West were rapidly bankrupted and shut down by these impatient "bankers." The sums stolen by means of faked loans were, from the viewpoint of the conspirators, mere "chicken feed." But the incidents were menacing to their own rackets of slowly and patiently bleeding the nation of its wealth and destroying its solvency by their "Federal" Reserve and banking frauds year after year. And since the looted banks were members of the Federal Deposit Insurance Co., the looting did cost them relatively minor sums. Their agents in Washington promptly initiated moves to block entry into the banking field by minor racketeers, in order to preserve the loot in the field for the "top drawer" racketeers, the conspirators and their henchmen.

## CHASE MANHATTAN BANK COLLABORATION
## WITH NEGRO "BANKERS" EXPOSED

The role of Rockefeller's Chase Manhattan Bank in collaborating with "loan sharks" and banking racketeers was exposed, however, in the case of the Crown Savings Bank of Newport News, Virginia, by a report that was published in the New York Herald Tribune of July 23, 1965 under the headline *Chase Buying of Defaulted Notes Told*. The dispatch related that Wright Patman, chairman of the House Banking Committee had revealed that Rockefeller's Chase Manhattan Bank had bought, on July 3, 1964, from the Crown Savings Bank, represented by its Negro President LeRoy F. Ridley, $500,000 in notes. Of the total, notes valued at $108,000 were

179

for loans extended largely to Peter D'Agostino of New York and Alvin D. Townsend of Atlanta, and were more than six months in default, at the time of purchase by Chase Manhattan Bank. Subsequent testimony by "Dukie" Goldberg, of Norfolk, Va., who introduced D'Agostino to Ridley, however succulent, was not revealed. The Rockefeller predilection for Negroes emerged once again in this incident. Ridley was asked by Rep. Wright Patman why "...toughminded officers of the Chase Manhattan Bank...bought the notes..." He replied: "I think they did it to help us."

## RACKETEERING CONSPIRATORS ARE ALARMED
## AT COMPETITION BY MINOR RACKETEERS

Newspapers bearing the alarm headlines: *Racketeers Are Taking Over Banks* are particularly amusing in view af the fact that the conspirators, the top rank racketeers, took over our entire financial and banking system more than half a century ago through their "Federal" Reserve fraud. Operating within the laws that they dictate, or in contempt of the law, through their agents, they steadily victimize the nation through brigandage and racketeering.

## CHASE BANK COMPLETES CONSPIRATORS' ESPIONAGE
## VIA THEIR INCOME TAX DEVICE

Some measure of how completely the devices and orders of the conspirators nullify and supersede the laws of the land, can be gained from the action of the New York City Council on September 20, 1966, reported in the N. Y. Times of the following date. (212) One of the strenuous objections raised to the un-Constitutional Federal income tax when it was first proposed by the conspirators, was that it would constitute a dangerous device for industrial espionage and for illegal search in violation of the Bill of Rights. To allay that fear, it was represented that the detailed reports of income that it required, would be confidential and would not be accessible to anyone but authorized officials of the Internal Revenue Service. Access to income tax reports has been barred to the members of Congress and even to other Government officials, except under extraordinary circumstances involving crime. The same provision was made in the New York law when the conspirators imposed a State income tax. Later, by an amendment that greatly increased the New York tax demanded by Gov. Nelson Rockefeller, the State income tax report was made identical with the Federal report in most basic respects.

When a few years later, the conspirators imposed a third income tax on the citizens of New York City, they arranged to provide for themselves maximum facilities for espionage into the affairs of individuals and industries, that completely nullifies the code of secrecy enjoined by the first Federal income tax measure that they imposed on the nation. This has been accomplished by putting into their hands, through their Chase Manhattan Bank, the processing of all the confidential financial dealings of the citizenry, that are embodied in the Federal income tax reports, including those of their competitors, the private property of the conspirators. And for this privileged nullification of the law and potential of criminal espionage, the conspirators' Chase Manhattan Bank is rewarded by payment of $1,775,000 by the city's taxpayers.

According to the Times report, Chase Manhattan Bank came by

this windfall as a result of Gov. Nelson Rockefeller's designing refusal to permit the State to process the municipal income tax reports, knowing well that New York City had no facilities for doing it and that it would have to be turned over to a private concern that had the facilities. Then, "by odd chance" the conspirators' Chase Manhattan Bank entered "the lower of...two bids" by banks that alone were permitted to bid for this golden opportunity. The true motive underlying Gov. Rockefeller's opposition to the State processing the City's income tax reports, is more clearly revealed by the fact that he was quite willing to have the State process the City's sales tax receipts that are of far lesser significance, espionagewise.

## CONSPIRATORS WANTED N. Y. LOTTERY TO BE OPERATED BY CHASE MANHATTAN BANK

As soon as the conspirators had engineered the establishment of a lottery, in New York State, for further fleecing of the citizenry, while protesting their opposition to its "immorality," they announced that they wanted their Chase Manhattan Bank to be given the sale of tickets. The racketeers are most anxious to preserve for themselves the loot hitherto derived through their Maffia agents in the operation of the lesser gambling rackets, such as the numbers racket. (15) If the loot is great enough, the "immorality" of the racket becomes converted into one of the "trusts" that they hypocritically allege was imposed on them by God! (225)

The N. Y. Times of January 6, 1967, (225) reported:

### "CHASE BANK SEEKS LOTTERY AGENCIES

"In a recent letter to legislative officials, a Chase Manhattan representative said the bank would be willing to sell the tickets (of the lottery) in all of its 140 branches and would like to control and supervise the ticket sales in all other banks in the state.

"Having the state lottery tickets sold by banks is already being considered by the leaders of Legislature, *The Governor's Office* and the Departments of Taxation and Banks, who are working together to draft a plan to put before the Legislature.

"Chase suggested that it be compensated for its administrative expenses. Under its plan, the bank would also have the use of all lottery funds, which come from bets on horse races in the state, deposited with it and be able to earn interest on these funds before it turned them over to the state.

"It is a good thing for the banks, one official said. It could mean a lot of dough for them.'

"In its letter, Chase said it did not foresee any technical problems, since the bank already handles several fiscal operations for the state...for years been an authorized state fiscal agent. This means that it is depository for collateral (government bonds) that other banks must put up when they receive deposits of state funds.

"Also Chase is one of eight banks that collect and process the money from the state sales tax, and it has a similar role with New York City income tax, which went into effect last year.

"In handling the sales tax, Chase gets no compensation from the state for its administrative services, *Such As It Requested In Its Lottery Proposal, But Only The Temporary Use Of The Money For Investment Purposes.*"*

As soon as the "principle" of sale of lottery tickets by banks controlled by the conspirators had been established, they demanded, in addition to the profits that they would derive from lending out the money at their usual usurious rates, a charge of ten cents, or ten percent, on each ticket sold by them. To allay the sharp public protest against this gouging, the conspirators compromised and dictated that they be given "merely" five percent for the sale of lottery tickets. A few banks, not controlled by the conspirators but by bankers more honest and principled, such as the Franklin National Bank, refused to sell the tickets because they regard the function of banks as the encouragement of thrift and not of gambling.

## PROFITS SALVE THE ROCKEFELLER
## RELIGIOSITY & "CONSCIENCE"

It evidently in no wise violates the Baptist religiosity and conscience of David Rockefeller to have converted the operation of the Chase Manhattan Bank to usurious "loan sharking." His Time Inc. pressagent reflected his exaltation at having raised the bank's profits by greatly increasing its volume of "personal loans," (125:69) from a "paltry $9.8 million in 1947" to $166 million in 1961; and thereby increased net earnings to $70.5 million in spite of an increase of savings accounts on which interest must be paid, from $22 million to $1 billion in the same period. As of 1964, the savings accounts had risen to $1,248 million, the profits to $84 million, and the installment loans proportionately. Evidently many more persons have been duped into believing: *You Have A Friend At The Chase Manhattan Bank*, and have tasted Rockefeller "philanthropy."

## DAVID ROCKEFELLER, "WORLD'S MOST
## IMPORTANT BANKER."

David Rockefeller immodesty but truthfully announced through his *Time* pressagent that he is *"The Most Important Banker In The World."* (125:67) He would not be stretching the truth if he also announced that as the financial head of the Rockefeller Empire and of the Rockefeller-Soviet Axis, he dominates world finance and monetary systems, and is in effect the *Sole Remaining International Banker* of any account.

His pressagents acknowledge, however, that his prominence as a banker does not arise from his ability, or knowledge of banking, but is primarily an outgrowth of the volume of loot accumulated by Rockefeller criminality, and pathologic greed, and the enormous, overshadowing power that he exercises as a consequence; and of his own cupidity by which he has come naturally, as a matter of heredity and training. A colleague is quoted as correctly evaluating his banking ability in the words:

"It's a good thing for David to have somebody around who can

---

* (c) 1967 by the New York Times Company Reprinted by permission.

tell him that some visionary idea he has won't stand up bankingwise."
(121:61)

An added factor in Rockefeller's success as a banker, is the familial power that makes their slightest wish the law of the land and enables them to contemptuously disregard all existing statutes. As a consequence, financial racketeering, diversion of public funds into their own purses and "loan sharking" have been made by them "accepted practise" in banking.

### DAVID ROCKEFELLER'S COMMANDMENT: BANKS MUST EARN 9% NET, MINIMUM.

David Rockefeller has replaced the Ten Commandments with his *One Rockefeller Commandment*, enunciated to the American Bankers Association, to wit: banks must earn a minimum return of 9% net. It matters not that a gross rate of more than 6% charged individuals constitutes a violation of the laws on usury in many States of the Union. Rockefellers' Commandment supersedes all laws in a world that has become *"One Rockefeller World."* Their dictates are promulgated in our institutions of learning, all of which are controlled by them through their bogus "philanthropies," by their prostituted "economists;" by the media of mass communication, most of which they control; by religious institutions, most of which are subservient to them; and by governments, the majority of which are their vassals. And their financial dictates are carried out by their fraudulent agency, the "Federal" Reserve System and its subsidiaries around the world, including the International Monetary Fund. The people of the world indeed *Have A "Friend"* At The Chase Manhattan. Having such a "friend," they need no enemies.

### CHASE MANHATTAN IS FRIENDLIEST TO SOVIET RUSSIA AND COMMUNISM

Long before the Rockefellers joined their agent, Cyrus Eaton, in openly financing our Communist enemies in the midst of the Vietnam War and serving the Soviet Russian Amtorg as espionage agents, (270) with American taxpayers' funds, their Chase Bank loyally served their Bolshevik confederates. After they financed Lenin and Trotzky in the first and second Russian Revolutions, Rockefellers' bank became the depositary and agents of the Soviets. The lengthy array of Rockefeller-Soviet Chase Manhattan accounts in addition to the Soviet Treasury, have included its agencies such as the espionage service, *Amtorg*, the propaganda unit, the *Four Continent Book Corp*, and their *"United"* Nations, as well as the "mysteriously" vanished deposits of the Czar and Russia. For their domination of the UN finances they have not relied solely on their control of it to assure their Chase Manhattan of its accounts. They maintain as their "envoy" for the bank at the UN, the former representative from the U.S. to its Economics and Social Council, their agent, Christopher W. Phillips. (121:56)

### CHASE BANK HAS UNLIMITED FUNDS FOR SOVIETS; NONE, AT LEGAL RATES, FOR AMERICANS

Though the conspirators and their Chase Manhattan Bank have unlimited funds for their Soviet partners, and for other foreign lands and enterprises where usurious interest rates prevail, they

183

often represent that they have no funds for Americans and their enterprises, at the legal rate of interest. But for usurious "personal loans," for which they advertise in all media and clamor continuously over radio and television, for the "loan sharking" by themselves and their Mafia agents, they also have unlimited funds.

There is abundant evidence that the periodic tightening of the supply of money and credit dictated to the banks by the conspirators "Federal" Reserve, that creates a shortage of funds available for domestic industries and their payrolls, are deliberate "squeeze plays" and frauds. Most obvious is their failure to lure deposits as intensively as they do "personal loans," and their failure to actively compete for funds other than long-term bonds, notes and savings deposits and certificates of deposit that they plan to pay back with depreciated or worthless dollars.

## CONSPIRATORS RESTRICT, OR BAR, BANKING COMPETITION THRU "F"R MONOPOLY

Through their "Federal" Reserve banking monopoly, the conspirators are able to severely restrict or to absolutely bar the methods of competing for business that prevailed prior to its establishment. What measure of competition their "F"R permits in seeking deposit of funds, is largely limited, as has been indicated, to savings accounts, especially long term deposits and certificates of deposit. These forms of deposit involve a large measure of fraud that is inherent in the conspirators' plan and plot to wipe out the dollar through their current "Gold Corner."

The fixing of the maximum rate of interest on long-term savings deposits by the conspirators through their "Federal" Reserve, enables them to loot the public of the differences between that rate and the rate of their devaluation of the dollar, which they constantly accelerate. Thus thru difference between the allowed 5% maximum rate on savings deposits dictated by their "Federal" Reserve and the current rate of their annual devaluation of the dollar, about 15%, the conspirators' brigandage nets them loot of 10% in addition to the profits of their "loan sharking" with the money. They dupe the public into depositing money of relatively high purchasing power that they plan to pay back with money of lower purchasing power, and eventually with practically worthless money.

The same is true of all the institutions that lure money for longtime holding, such as life insurance companies, pension funds, ordinary bonds, social security and government bonds. The plan on which the conspirators operate is: the more money they owe the greater will be their profit when the dollar is eventually devalued to the point where they will be able to repay their debts with worthless dollars. By the same process the conspirators make the wage increases, with which their "Labor Baron" agents dupe their vassal workers, a snare and delusion, and a device for speeding the devaluation of the dollar.

The conspirators have managed with their usual impunity, to give their Chase Manhattan Bank a competitive advantage in luring saving accounts by giving their depositors a slightly higher interest rate than they allow their less directly controlled banks, that in reality constitutes a violation of the rule issued by their "Federal" Reserve on saving interest rates allowable. They do this by the

184

device of compounding the interest on their savings deposits daily; and by paying interest on their savings accounts up to the day of withdrawal, instead of only on set quarterly dates.

Profiting from their devaluation of the dollar, lies behind the issue of notes in the amount of $250 million at an interest rate of 4% by Chase Manhattan Bank. The public will be paid back in 1990 with devalued or worthless dollars; and the swindle will repay the conspirators handsomely. It is noteworthy that the rate of interest paid by the conspirators on these notes of theirs, indicates that they do plan to maintain interest rates, through their "Federal" Reserve, at or above that level during the term of the notes.

## CONSPIRATORS' BANKING MONOPOLY DISCOURAGES ORDINARY CHECKING ACCOUNTS

In sharp contrast with the wooing of trusting savings depositors for covert swindling and looting concerning which law enforcement officers maintain a discreet silence, the conspirators' "F"R banking monopoly deliberately discourages checking accounts and makes them ever more costly. In the past, banks competed for checking accounts by payment of interest on balances maintained in the accounts, as well as by rendering services of various characters at no cost. Now however, the conspirators have dictated through their "Federal" Reserve that banks may not pay interest on balances on checking accounts though it would as readily be possible, with the help of modern computers, for the banks to pay interest on daily balances in checking accounts exactly in the same manner as the Chase Manhattan Bank pays daily compounded interest on its savings accounts. Charges are made for checks blanks, "special accounts" and other previously free services.

Instead of paying interest on those balances and thus encouraging deposits in checking accounts, the conspirators have made it the practise to charge 10¢ for each deposit made, and three cents for each check deposited. Instead of the interest on balances that they have ordered themselves not to pay, the conspirators' banks allow depositors an absurdly low allowance, that they avoid calling "interest" but label "credits" on end-of-month balances. The uniformity of those charges in various communities attests to the extent of monopoly in restraint of trade established by the conspirators in banking.

## CONGRESS HAS PROVED THAT CONSPIRATORS INTERLOCK CONTROL OF NATION'S BANKS.

Congressional investigation has proved conclusively that Rockefellers have seized nationwide control of banking by the devices of direct and indirect stockholdings, interlocking directors, bank holding companies and other devices. The report issued by the House And Senate Joint Economic Committee, under the chairmanship of Wright Patman, listed a few of the numerous devices other than control of their "Federal" Reserve, by which this monopoly of banking has been established by the conspirators. The report names numerous of their nominees, agents, "dummy" stockholders, and interlocking directors. But it omits mention of their agents on the Federal government, their Federal Reserve Board and the Treasury; and it makes no mention of the role in their money and banking monopoly of their foundations, their trust companies, including

185

their U.S. Trust Co. of New York, and their foreign agencies. (412) Though Congress has conclusively proved their effective monopoly of banking, it has done nothing more than rainforce that monopoly by its acts. (89)

## ROBERT KENNEDY'S FAKE ANTI-BANKING MONOPOLY SUIT SHIELDS CONSPIRATORS

Under the pretense of "protecting the public," the conspirators' agent, Attorney General Robert Kennedy, in 1962, brought a "test case" against two minute New Jersey country banks, correctly charging conspiracy and monopoly in restraint of trade, because they resorted to the usual practise of making identical charges on ordinary and special checking accounts. The size and insignificant character of the banks made the suit absurdly comical if its nefarious purpose had not been to shield the conspirators by quashing the indictment, thus legitimatizing the monopolistic practises.

This phase of the banking monopoly was overlooked in the December 1962 Report of the Select Committee To Conduct A Study & Investigation Of The Problems Of Small Business, in which its Chairman, Wright Patman, affirmed that the conspirators had fortified the banking monopoly that they had established through their "Federal" Reserve by nation and world-wide interlocking of directorates of banking institutions, generally by the use of numerous "dummies" and nominees, some of whom were listed in the report. (213)

## CONSPIRATORS' POWER RENDERS THEM IMMUNE FROM PROSECUTION FOR FRAUD

It is a tribute to the power of the conspirators that no law enforcement officer dares expose and prosecute them for the fraudulent misrepresentation involved in their "loan sharking" in the various aspects of their banking business, including their "personal loans." Less powerful shylocks in the installment loan business have been attacked by the authorities. Bills have been introduced to compel them to tell the truth in their advertising and contracts about their usurious interest rates and other charges. Gov. Rockefeller's minion and sidekick, Attorney General Louis Lefkowitz, made a noisy issue of the matter, for a time, to dupe the public. At no time, however, was any reference made to the equally usurious charges of the banks for their "personal loans." This matter was covered up with a silence as dead as that accorded the involvement of the Chase Manhattan Bank in financing of the Maffia agents. Thus protected, Rockefeller's Chase Manhattan Bank is beginning to compete so vigorously with the pawnbrokers that it appears to be merely a matter of time when one will witness the raising of the three-gold-ball symbol over its door of the patron saint of the pawnbrokers, St. Nicholas, or Santa Claus.

## SHYLOCK DAVID DETERRED NEITHER BY PAYMENT BALANCE OR "EQUALIZATION"

David Rockefeller demands that others be required to act to improve the nation's payment balance or be penalized by an "equalization tax." But his own outlook is "global" and his investments scattered around the world without regard to payment balance or "equalization tax." His pressagents report that his investments are scattered around the world usually where interest rates are most

186

usuriously high and enormous profits unscrupulously gained. His personal holdings specifically mentioned include: a cattle ranch in Brazil; part of a sheep ranch in Australia; a motion picture theatre in Nigeria; "a joint enterprise" with a "foreign (Rockefeller) aid" Agency for International Development, in a combined agricultural and industrial community in the Philippines; a textile plant in the Congo. (112:73) The investments, in foreign lands that offer the best monetary return and opportunity for "loan sharking," are many of them financed, as in the case of IBEC, with American taxpayers "foreign aid" and "counterpart" funds that are exempted by them from the "equalization," income and all other taxes that apply only to their American peasants.

ROCKEFELLER TAX EXEMPT "INVESTMENTS"

These enterprises have one thing in common. They are all in lands that rate as "underdeveloped." Under the laws which the conspirators have placed on the statute books, their loot is protected, both as to capital and profit, by the selfsame American taxpayers who have provided the loot. And the State Department that John D. I boasted serves them so well (16:63) is ever ready to protect their loot with the lives and fortunes of the same boob "peasants," the American taxpayers, as in the case of Japan, Korea and Vietnam, down to the last draftee. We boobs, their American "peasants" pay for these ventures with both our money and our lives.

The conspirators have exempted themselves from the tax that they levy on other investors in foreign securities and investments, the so-called "equalization tax" imposed, for the supposed purpose of reducing the imbalance of payments, even on investments of foreign currencies that constitute no drain on the dollar. The total value of such investments by others is infinitesimally small as compared with the enormous volume of dollars drained off in foreign investments and "foreign (Rockefeller) aid" by the conspirators, without payment of either "equalization" capital tax or income tax on the profits. In these overseas "investments," Rockefeller deliberately accentuates the monetary crisis that he pretends to decry.

"INTERNATIONAL EXECUTIVE SERVICE CORPS"
YIELDS ROCKEFELLER HIGHER PROFITS

David Rockefeller has shown a high measure of ingenuity in enhancing the conspirator's "foreign (Rockefeller) aid" profits. He is credited with conceiving of and organizing the so-called "International Executive Service Corps" that craftily serves the purpose of providing high calibre executive skill and know-how for the operation of the conspirators' foreign enterprises. Mature executives are "induced" to volunteer to serve *At Their Own Expense And For No Salary* to insure successful operation of overseas enterprises in "underdeveloped" lands. These executives are selected for their experience, in this country, in succssfully operating enterprises of the character projected. Some of the volunteers may have been forced into retirement in the conspirators' domestic enterprises for the specific purpose of serving in some needed capacity, at no cost. Such wage-saving serves to enhance the "philanthropists," profit, or loot, from their highly rewarding foreign enterprises.

187

## INCOME & "EQUALIZATION" TAXES ENHANCE LOOT
## AND INCREASE PAYMENT IMBALANCE.

"Foreign (Rockefeller) aid" and "counterpart funds" loot of the conspirators are in no wise diminished by any of the numerous taxes that they have imposed on us to provide the funds therefor. Their foreign earnings would not be subject to income tax even if the conspirators had not exempted themselves from domestic taxation and from the absurd and wholly un-Constitutional so-called "equalization" tax that they have imposed on us "peasants" for the pretended purpose of remedying our imbalance of payments. Its actual purpose is to prevent us from escaping looting by the devaluation of the dollar that they have planned and are bringing about with ever increasing speed. This is made clear by the provision of the so-called "equalization tax" that bar us "peasants" from investing money derived by us from foreign holdings that constitute no drain on the dollar whatsoever, unless we pay the tax.

It is difficult to discern what the tax on us for such investments does "equalize" in view of the fact that virtually all the "foreign (Rockefeller) aid" funds of ours that they steal and "invest" constitutes a drain of dollars from our economy that is acknowledged to equal the entire volume of our imbalance of payments; and under the provision of the law, they are free to invest unlimited hundred millions of dollars in foreign plants without payment of the tax that we are required to pay for our minor investments of foreign funds. The use of the term "equalization" is another of those semantic perversions for deceptive propaganda that characterize all the activities of the Rockefeller-Soviet Axis. Thus do they mock and "thumb their noses" at us "peasants."

## CONSPIRATORS HAVE WIDELY EXTENDED THEIR
## LOOTING THRU AGENCY OF GOVERNMENTS

Their "slum clearance and urban redevelopment" thievery represents only one of the numerous devices whereby the conspirators have extended their looting of taxpayers through the agency of governments. Scarcely a year goes by without their introduction of a new one through the "1313," Public Administration Clearing House, through which they make their governmental rackets widespread and universal "accepted practise." They have an advantage over the forms of racketeering practised by their gangster and Maffia henchmen because laws that they have passed, "legalize" them.

## "IN REM" FORECLOSURE ACTIONS ENABLE
## THEFT OF PRIVATE PROPERTY

One of the most thievish "legalized" devices for property theft is their "in rem" foreclosing of tax liens on property that enables them to sell at auction, without notifying the owner and without redress, parcels on which there has been as little as one cent in arrears for a period of years. The entire salesprice over and above the taxes due is then stolen by the government. If this were done by a private individual, he would be prosecuted as a felon. Perpetrated by the conspirators through the agency of governments, it becomes "legalized felony."

Similar "legalized felony" is the law of escheat, whereby savings left in bank accounts that are inactive for a number of years, or money due one from any source such as insurance, not claimed within a specified period, are irrevocably confiscated, or stolen, by the State. Other forms of "legalized" thievery promoted by the conspirators are considered in other chapters.

## CONSPIRATORS' ABUSE OF GOVERNMENTAL POWERS DESTROYS RESPECT FOR LAW, & ORDER

Dishonest and criminal use of government accounts for youthful and less disciplined persons scorning ethical principles and the law, and resorting to crimes of violence as a way of life. When a Gov. Rockefeller hypocritically and mockingly "justifies" his merciless tax looting and fiscal brigandage with the bald lie that the impotent public "demand more service and must expect to pay for it" his dishonesty fools no one. Folks recognize that they are being looted, and that the service he renders differs only in variety from that which the bull renders the cow. They are sick unto death of his stud service.

## "AMERICANS, DAVID & NELSON ROCKEFELLER: AS UGLY AS THEY COME," WROTE NKRUMAH.

Rockefeller pressagent Kahn quoted a feature article in the *Ghanian Times* published in the spring of 1963, that shows exceptionally keen insight into the characters of David and Nelson, and their brothers, that was gained by the Africans after suffering for five years from Rockefeller bogus "philanthropy" extended to their country by the Rockefeller Brothers Fund. It read:

"Whilst the Governor of New York concentrates on changing the political climate in Washington to open up the trade in nuclear arms, the President of Chase Manhattan is most concerned with commodities like copper and bananas."

The Ghanian article then proceeded to detail some of David's malign activities, which his pressagent falsely declares were "imaginary." These included:

1. Preventing the Organization of American States and the Alliance for Progress from interfering with the conspirators' Latin American business interests (which are being promoted by those programs at the expense of U.S. taxpayers)

2. Plotting the overthrow of the governments of Bolivia and Peru( to further their interests)

3. Sustaining the governments of Portugal and the Union of South Africa and furnishing them with arms, (so long as they served the conspirators' interests)

4. *Dominating the Government of the United States through Congressional stooges and a kept press.* (In this the primitive Ghanians show keener innate intelligence than do most of our "civilized" Americans, unfortunately)

5. Using the Central Intelligence Agency and the Department of State to watch over his bank's foreign investments. This John D. openly acknowledged with greater candor and honestly than has been manifested by his heirs. (16:63)

The Ghanian article continued:

"His contempt for the liberty and happiness of other people doesn't embrace the whole of humanity, but only the sections falling under the scope of his bank's business, which dominates all other investors in Latin America, and is coming into South Africa, the Congo, Angola and South-West Africa in a big way." (121:39)

## CHAPTER XIX
## DAVID ROCKEFELLER'S GOAL: WORLD-WIDE "GOLD CORNER" & NATIONAL BANKRUPTCY

Our most vital concern, and that of the peoples of the world should rightly be: *What Does David Rockefeller, World Financial Dictator And Ranking Usurer, Plan As Our Fate?* His dictates pronounced by him before meetings of the American Bankers Association, were that interest rates must be raised to yield the conspirators' bank a return commensurate with that which they obtain with "foreign (Rockefeller) aid" in "underdeveloped lands," a minimum of 9% net, by the adoption of a "tight money" policy. By the time that the 1966 elections had rolled around, the conspirators' scheme had attained the desired political effects. They had brought on a violent stock market crash, a slowdown of commerce and industry, and the threat of widespread unemployment that became a reality in many countries of the world, including England, Germany and Japan. This effect had been further intensified by the conspirators' deliberate unfavorable rigging of the U. S. balance of payments; and by the pretended "withdrawal," by "earmarking," of gold that the conspirators falsely represent is owned by the U.S. Treasury.

As has been related, Brother Nelson's "New" Deal had looted American citizens of their gold through their "Federal" Reserve conspiracy. As undercover boss and "fixer" in the Eisenhower regime (79:155), he had made it a felony for an American to own or hold more than a few hundred dollars worth of gold anywhere in the world; and the conspirators had made it a criminal offense for anyone, other than their agencies, to import or export gold in virtually every country in the world. Capping the climax, in 1966, their pawn, British Prime Minister Wilson had required Parliament to pass legislation making it a felony for anyone to own more gold than two gold coins both of which must have been issued prior to 1838, in the very land that launched the "Gold Standard." What better foundation could be laid by the conspirators, for a world-wide "Gold Corner" far vaster than any attempted in world history?

### IS 1969 THE TARGET OF THE CONSPIRATORS?

*The Rockefellers are traditionalists. Can it be that they plan to celebrate the centennial of the Gould-Grant "Gold Corner" with one far vaster, in 1969?*

190

## IMPEDIMENTS THAT CONSPIRATORS MUST SURMOUNT
## FOR SUCCESS OF "CORNER"

There remained a single group of technical barriers to the complete control and disposition by the conspirators of the gold that they had stolen. This technicality was set up by the conspirators themselves when they established their "Gold Standard" and their "Federal" Reserve in order to support the myth that our currency rests on a valid gold base, and to mask the fraud involved. Under the conspirators' "New" Deal Gold Reserve Act of 1934, Sec. 6, it is provided

"...That the reserve for United States notes and for Treasury notes of 1890, and the security for gold certificates...shall be maintained in gold bullion equal to the dollar amounts required by law..." (25:203)

The Federal Reserve Act has required in Sec. 16:3

"Every Federal Reserve bank shall maintain reserves in gold certificates of not less than 25% against its Federal Reserve notes in actual circulation..." (25:57)

The reserve for the U.S. and Treasury notes is nominal, involving on October 29, 1955, little more than $156 million. (137:1) This sum has remained constant during the years that supervened since passage of the G.R. Act. The reserves of gold that were tied up by the "F"R Act were considerably greater, amounting in early 1964 to about $14 billion. (138:1) This amount of gold constitutes more than 25% of the world's supply. It is an impediment to a successful "Gold Corner" that would be virtually unsurmountable. And failure of the conspirators to include it in their "Corner" would not only jeopardize its "success" but would also reduce their loot therefrom enormously. That, for them, who are trained to squeeze the last drop of blood out of their very deal, is an intolerable situation.

"New" Dealer Nelson Rockefeller arranged to transfer by his "aid" and other schemes the bulk of the conspirators' golden loot from their domestic account, through their "Federal" Reserve, to their "foreign" accounts. On balance, none of this golden loot had been permitted to leave the U.S. For they trust neither their partners and allies nor their foreign depositaries. The conspirators who have so cunningly looted the nation and the world of their gold, do not risk its being stolen from themselves. They prefer to keep it here, in the U.S., under the guardianship of the U.S. Army in Fort Knox vaults, at the expense of American taxpayers; and gold they have "earmarked" for supposed transfer to "foreign agencies," which they control, in the vaults of their N.Y. Federal Reserve Bank. There they are able to watch it from their Chase Manhattan Bank. In 1964, officials of the N.Y. Federal Reserve Bank informed this author that they held "earmarked" for the "foreign accounts," more than $10 billion in gold. By 1966, their "earmarked" gold there held was more than $13 billion.

## IMMENSE UNDERGROUND VAULT AT POCANTICO
## HILL REPORTED

In this connection, it is interesting to note the existence of an immense underground vault at the Pocantico Hill, New York, estate of the Rockefellers supposedly intended for removal of "trash and

191

garbage." The report states that it is so large that huge trucks can enter it and maneuver within it. It is reported that trucks bearing heavy loads from the Federal Reserve Bank have been observed to enter it and to depart unloaded. One might well speculate on what are the contents of these "heavy loads," in view of the fact that the law constitutes no impediment or barrier to the conspirators, who "are the law."(243:123)

## CONDITIONS THAT WILL ASSURE SUCCESS OF WORLD-WIDE "GOLD CORNER".

The success of the conspirators' world-wide "Gold Corner" hinged on their succeeding in transferring to their "foreign accounts" more than $13 billion of gold, filched from the nation, that their "Federal" Reserve Act required must be held in their domestic accounts as reserves. Approximately $5 billion of the gold was required as a reserve against member bank deposits with the "Federal" Reserve. An additional $9 billion has been required by the law to be held in their domestic accounts, as a reserve against their "F"R bank note issue.

Mention has been made of the manner in which wheeler-dealer, Nelson A. Rockefeller, succeeded, (in his various roles as "New" Deal adviser, or boss, of Pres. Franklin D. Roosevelt, as "Fair Deal" dictator of kinsman Pres. Harry Shippe Truman, and as "mastermind" of Pres. Dwight D. Eisenhower's "Ike Deal") in establishing foreign credits for the conspirators against the gold in their American account that far exceeds its total. Among these thievish devices were:

1. His endless series of "foreign (Rockefeller) aid" that had drained off the money of American taxpayers into Rockefeller coffers in foreign lands.

2. His "Point 4" export of American skills and know-how to foreign lands to insure the successful competitive operation of their "foreign aid" financed operations exemplified by IBEC chicken farms.

3. Foreign, more or less localized wars and dis-"United" Nations "police actions" that the U.S. was tricked and trapped into fighting and financing for the expansion of their Empire and the pretended "cause," of "fighting Communism." These wars are used by the conspirators as a "show case" for the sale of the arms and munitions that they manufacture, to allies and foes alike. (275-280) Their "demonstrators" of their murderous wares are drafted GI's who are rewarded for their efforts with the shells, shrapnel and bullets for the manufacture of which their taxes have paid. The Daily News, of New York, while refraining from crying treason, commented editorially, on January 17, 1967, sardonically, under the headline *On Trade With The Enemy* in connection with the Rockefeller-Eaton belated announcement of their longtime financing of the Soviets:

"...it would be sad to see some Rockefeller or some Eaton marched off to the jug for having... sold strategic goods to an enemy nation."

All of which makes the pretense of the conspirators involving us in wars around the world for the "containment of Communism" patently absurd. This is especially true in view of their role in financing the Soviets who have been their agents and partners from the start, while fostering Communism at home, especially in Washington; and their real and actual purpose of weakening and exhausting the U.S. by spreadeagling our Armed Forces around the world, more especially in Korea and Vietnam, to serve in protecting their Japanese, and other Far Eastern interests and holdings, from their Soviet partners.

4. Flooding the U.S. with the products of their "foreign aid" financed, tax-exempt, low-wage, competitive industries the products of which are admitted to the country under special, "most favored" nation clauses that they have written into their GATT. This tremendously increases their overseas dollar holdings and the claim that they make on their filched domestic gold holdings. They have recently extended it through another "Kennedy round."

Only Congress could have authorized, by legislation, the release of the gold loot from the conspirators' domestic account to their foreign account, to permit consummation of their "Gold Corner" and the consequent debacle of the dollar to virtual worthlessness. To this task, David Rockefeller dedicated himself.

## CONSPIRATORS PREPARED WAY WITH RIGGED "COMMISSION ON MONEY & CREDIT" REPORT

For the purpose of duping the nation, the conspirators resorted to their usual tactics of rigging a so-called "Commission on Money and Credit," composed of their puppets, agents and pawns, to proclaim as their alleged "expert opinion" the malign wishes of the conspirators. More than half of the membership of the committee were Rockefeller Council Foreign Relations agents, many of them old "war-horses" who had served their masters entirely to their satisfaction on earlier committees. The membership was as follows (42:vi-vii):

* David Rockefeller, President, Chase Manhattan Bank, whose role can not be assumed to have been passive in view of previous and subsequent developments.

* Frazer B. Wilde, Chairman, Connecticut General Life Insurance Co., Chairman of the CMC, member of the CFR.

* H. Christian Sonne, Vice Chairman of the CMC, member of the CFR.

* Adolf A. Berle Jr., "New" Deal security officer for the State Department at the time it harbored a Communist cell that included Alger Hiss as well as Nelson Rockefeller's Communist holdovers from his "Co-Ordinator's" office. CFR member.

James B. Black, Chairman, Pacific Gas & Electric Co.

* Joseph M. Dodge, Chairman, Detroit Bank & Trust Co., CFR member and interlocking member of its subsidiary Detroit Committee on Foreign Relations.

Marriner S. Eccles, former Chairman of the Federal Reserve Board, Chairman of the First Security Corp.

* Lamar Fleming Jr., Chairman Anderson Clayton Co., member of CFR and interlocking member of Houston CFR.

* Henry H. Fowler, attorney, Fowler, Leva, Hawes & Symington, who resigned to assume post of Under-Secretary of the

193

Treasury, later appointed its Secretary, placing him in a position to carry out the conspirators' plot; and CFR member.

Gaylord A. Freeman Jr., Pres., First National Bank of Chicago.

Fred T. Greene, Pres., Federal Home Loan Bank of Indianapolis.

Philip M. Klutznick, who resigned to become U.S. Representative to the Economic & Social Council of the U.N.

Fred Lazarus Jr., Chairman, Federated Department Stores, Inc.

* Isador Lubin, Prof. of Public Affairs, Rutgers University, CFR member.

* J. Irwin Miller, Chairman, Cummins Engine Co., CFR member.

* Robert R. Nathan, Robert R. Nathan Associates, Inc., CFR member.

Emil Rieve, Pres. Emeritus, Textile Workers of America, AFL-CIO

* Beardsley Ruml, former Director of Laura Spelman Rockefeller Memorial, Trustee of Rockefellers' Museum of Modern Art and general, all-around pawn of the Rockefellers, Chairman of the N. Y. Federal Reserve Bank, and CFR member, (deceased).

Stanley H. Ruttenberg, Director, Department of Research, AFL-CIO

Charles Sawyer, member of Rockefeller law firm, Taft, Stettinius & Hollister.

William F. Schnitzler, Secretary Treasurer, AFL-CIO.

Earl B. Schwulst, Pres. & Chairman, Bowery Savings Bank

Charles B. Shuman, Pres. American Farm Bureau Federation

* Jesse W. Tapp, Chairman, Bank of America, CFR member

J. Cameron Thomson, Chairman (retired), Northwest Bancorporation

* Willard L. Thorp, Director, Merrill Center for Economics, Amherst College, CFR member.

* Theodore O. Yntema, Chairman Finance Committee, Ford Motor Co., CFR member, interlocking member of Detroit CFR.

* Marks the member of Rockefellers' Council on Foreign Relations.

As might be expected under the circumstances, Rockefeller's "commission" parroted his wishes and recommended that the country accept all the financial and monetary measures he required for the furtherance of the conspiracy. Though various members noted minor dissents, which were included in the published report, none of them dissented with that section which was most vital for consummation of the conspirators' "Gold Corner." They unanimously agreed that:

"The Commission believes that the threat of a confidence crisis would be greatly reduced if it were generally recognized, both here and abroad, that all of the U.S. gold is available to meet our international obligations. Any doubts about the U.S. policy should be removed *by elimination of the gold reserve requirement* at the earliest convenient moment so that all of the U.S. gold stock is available for international settlements." (42:234)

This section of the report raises a question as to either the honesty or the intelligence of the members of the Commission. Assuming that each and every one of them is able to read a financial statement, and is able to understand it, they could not fail to be aware that the U.S. Treasury has not owned a single ounce of gold (with the exception of that in transit) since "New" Dealer Nelson Rockefeller directed Pres. Roosevelt to order the nation to submit to looting of its gold through the conspirators' "Federal" Reserve. Consequently, there is no U.S. gold available "to meet our international obligations." Under the circumstance, they could not help but be aware that they were recommending that the gold hijackers, their masters, be authorized to withdraw the imaginary gold support behind the dollar by transferring it to their foreign accounts, thus consummating their obvious "Gold Corner" plot.

The unreliability as well as the falsity of their report is made clear by the failure to mention the information that is readily admitted by the "Federal" Reserve officers, that on balance, no gold has left the U.S. in the past decade, and that more gold is held in this country by the conspirators today than ever before in our history. Beyond any question Marriner S. Eccles and Beardsley Ruml, both of whom have served as "Federal" Reserve Chairmen, must have been as well aware of these facts as their boss, David Rockefeller.

## DISLOYALTY OF "COMMISSION" CONTRASTS WITH WHITE'S HONESTY IN RE GOLD

One might well contrast the disloyalty and lack of candor of the members of the Commission with the loyalty and honesty of that reputed "traitor," Harry Dexter White, who honestly acknowledged in his suppressed article, *The Future Of Gold* (59), that gold is a costly burden on the economy of nations, and by implication, of the world; that the total world supply of gold is inadequate for the conduct of the business of the nation, even more inadequate for the settlement of international payments, though he favored it for the latter; that the conspirators were fearful that gold would be abandoned as a medium of exchange and monetary metal and that this contingency was only avertible by their plotting and planning, of which he approved and in which he participated as their agent. Furthermore, they failed to point out, in all honesty, that at this time, the total gold holdings filched by the conspirators would be woefully inadequate to satisfy our rigged unfavorable payment balance that they had created by their nefarious activities. This fact, the excessively candid (from the viewpoint of the conspirators) White would have readily admitted had the same circumstances existed at the time that he wrote his report. If Harry Dexter White was a traitor, as the conspirators would have one believe, what can one say of the members of the Commission and their boss?

By contrast with the forthrightness of White, the members of the Commission undertook to dupe the nation with regard to the true purpose behind their heeding "their master's voice" in recommending the release of the domestic gold holdings: bankrupting the Treasury and the nation that had been tied by them, for that

195

deliberate purpose, to their mythical "Gold Standard," placing the nation and the world at their mercy.

## ROCKEFELLER'S "COMMISSION" RECOMENDED MEASURES FOR GREATER BANK PROFITS

The chief concern of the David Rockefeller dominated CMC, as might be expected in view of the character of its sponsorship, was directed to methods of increasing the profits of the conspirators' banks and the power of their "Federal" Reserve conspiracy. They expressed satisfaction with the advance of the conspiracy to date in the words:

"The recommendations do not call for any wholesale overhaul of our financial structure. They consist of many small changes..." (42:6)

They treated the matter of the life of the nation, its production, employment and other aspects, as secondary to money control and a managed economy. It is a interesting comment on the fundamental identity of what is regarded as "capitalism" and Communism, that there was no basic disagreement between the representatives on the "Commission" of banking, commerce and the Marxist Labor delegates. They all averred that:

"In the United States, monetary policy is essentially Federal Reserve..." (42:46)

Even though the conspirators' direct return on their investment in their "F"RS is now limited to a mere 6% net on the par value of their stock of which half is paid in, above any and all expenses that they wish to incur, it is obvious that the indirect returns from control of our personal and national money and credit is so incredibly enormous that it contents even their Shylock spirit. But in character, is the recommendation that extension of their banking monopoly be facilitated, and their loot increased, viz:

"The Commission recommends that all insured commercial banks should be required to become members of the Federal Reserve System."

The Commission was fully in accord with the views that had been expressed earlier by David Rockefeller, with "their master's voice." Most of these recommendations were desired by the conspirators to tighten their grip on money and credit, though a few of them were meaningless concessions to political pressures.

## CONGRESSMAN WRIGHT PATMAN ACCEPTS ROCKEFELLER DICTATES VIA THE COMMISSION

The wishes of David Rockefeller expressed as "recommendations" of his Commission on Money & Credit, assume especial significance in view of their acceptance by Wright Patman. He, member of the House of Representatives Banking and Currency Committee of long tenure, and more significantly, is chairman of the House and Senate Joint Economic Committee, who was long a ringleader of the Congressional group who fought the "F"R fraud. The extent of Patman's bowing to the dictates and peculiar "charm" of Rockefeller can be discerned by comparison of his Bill H. R. 11, introduced on January 4, 1965, and referred to his Committee on Banking and Currency, with the recommendations of David Rockefeller's "Commission."

"The Commission recommends that the present form of capital stock of the Federal Reserve banks should be retired. Instead, membership in the System should be evidenced by nonearning certificate of, say $500, the same for each member bank."(42:91) Patman's bill parrots and provides:

"(a) Retiring Federal Reserve bank stock;... (381:1)

"Not later than thirty one days after the date of enactment of this Act, each holder of stock in any Federal bank shall surrender such stock to such bank which shall, as of the thirty-first day after the date of enactment of this Act, cancel and retire the same and pay or credit to such former holder the par value thereof, plus interest at the rate of one-half of one percentum per month from the date of the last dividend, less a membership fee of $10, which shall not be refundable. (381:1)

Rockefeller dictated through his "Commission:"

"The need for coordination, however, is very important. Isolation may mean weakness, and presidential support can be very helpful at times. The real ability of the system to influence national economic policy might well be increased rather than diminished if its ties to the President were closer. The *Commission Believes That Somewhat Closer Ties are Advisable*.

"Of the means to this end, one has already been tried and discarded: ex officio memberships of the Secretary of the Treasury and the Comptroller of the Currency on the Board..." (42:86) Patman's bill parrots, as follows:

"(b) Coordinating Federal Reserve bank policies and programs with those of the President of the United States in keeping with the provisions of the Employment Act of 1946." (381:1) The "master's voice" of Rockefeller speaks through his Commission:

"The FRB should consist of five members, with overlapping ten year terms, one expiring each odd-numbered year; members should be eligible for reappointment.

"The FRB chairman and Vice-Chairman should be designated by the President from among the Board's membership, to serve for four year terms coterminous with the president's." (42:87)

Patman echoes Rockefeller's wishes as follows:

"(c) Reducing the number and term of office of members of the Federal Reserve Board.

(d) Making the term of Chairman of the Board coterminous with that of the President of the United States." (381:1)

H. R. 11 fully bears out the charges of Patman's former associates in the battle they waged since the introduction of "Federal" Reserve bill that the Congressman has betrayed their cause with his bill. They ridicule false title of his bill:

"A Bill to make the Federal Reserve System responsive to the best interests of the people of the United States and to improve the coordination of monetary, fiscal, and economic policies." (381:1)

Instead, they aver, Patman's bill confirms the betrayal of the

197

nation into the hands of the conspirators, in obedience to the dictates of the "Commission" rigged by ringleader, David Rockefeller. They regard this betrayal by Patman as particularly vicious, because it comes at a time when the conspirators are bringing to a culmination their plot to undermine, and possibly to topple, our Republic in the manner sought by Lenin and his Communist followers, the destruction of the value of the dollar and national bankruptcy. It comes at a time when only an amendment to our Constitution that will place in the hands of the people and Congress the power to issue an honestly based and unmanipulable currency, to take its place beside the power now granted by it to coin money and to charter and control banks, can save our Republic and ourselves.

## AVERTING LOSSES TO THEMSELVES AND INCREASING LOOT IS ROCKEFELLER PURPOSE

Only an imbecile can fail to realize that the real purpose of the "recommendations" of Rockefeller's "Commission" is to avert losses to the conspirators and to increase the loot of their brigandage and that their purpose is served admirably by the Patman bill. Leaving the conspirators in control of their "Federal" Reserve as its "members" while permitting them to reclaim the 3% of the capital which they had been previously required to invest in its stock, would enable them to avert the loss that they would sustain on that investment when they had made the dollar worthless. The loss to all the member banks would be the entire sum, more than $600 million, that they now have invested. For Rockefeller's Chase Manhattan Bank, the loss would amount to more than $5 million; but the Rockefeller "philanthropists" do not take kindly to such losses, even though the consequent profits of the destruction of the value of the dollar will net them an untold fortune. Undoubtedly they appreciate Patman's offer to spare them this loss by arranging timely return to their banks of the investment required by the original "F"R Act.

The promotion of their profits by Rockefeller's "Commission" is the obvious purpose of numerous others of their "recommendations." These include:

"Because capital is a scarce resource, the economic system must provide a system for allocating it efficiently among competing uses. In a perfectly working market, the allocation would be done by interest rates, used in its broad sense to mean price paid for funds...Intermediaries would allocate their funds among all potential borrowers willing to pay *Rates Of Interest At Or Above the Going Rate...*" (42:154)

This is a clear-cut plea for further official sanction of their usury.

"1. The provision of the National Banking Act should be revised so as to enable national banks to establish branches within trading areas' irrespective of state laws, and state laws should be revised to provide corresponding privileges to state-chartered banks." (42:166)

"The Commission recommends continuation of the present prohibition of interest payments on demand deposits." (42: 167) These provisions are obviously designed to amplify the power

198

and profits of the conspirators' banking monopoly.

## GOV. NELSON ROCKEFELLER NEPOTISTICALLY PROMOTES DYNASTY'S BANKING INTERESTS

Rockefellers' pressagents freely acknowledge that Gov. Rockefeller has used his office to lobby for legislation that will permit unlimited expansion of his family's banking interests and control. Their *Time* magazine related that Gov. Rockefeller prodded New York State Legislature to pass a bill, in 1960, that would permit their New York City banks to extend into Westchester and Nassau counties. (125:69) Their pressagent Morris made it unmistakably clear that the prime motive in everything that they do, is to make the money that they so direly need; and that they permit nothing to stand in their way in so doing. (17:33,171) Gov. Rockefeller made this ultraclear when he pointedly refused to press for the adoption of a "conflict of interest code" for New York. Traditionally the Rockefeller code bars no vice or crime in their "making money ." And their "educational philanthropies" have succeeded in making that the code of the younger generations that have come under their subversive influence, with a consequent rise of delinquency and crime.

## DAVID ROCKEFELLER "ADVISED" CONSPIRATORS' PAWN, PRES. J. F. KENNEDY

Pres. Eisenhower, whose nomination had been purchased for him by the conspirators through Rockefeller kinsman, Winthrop Aldrich, (79:154) had served them well and to the limit of his capacity. He had delegated the appointment of his Cabinet and the "reorganization" of the Government, the virtual control of his Administration, to Nelson Rockefeller. (79:155) Rockefeller had promptly turned over the burden of carrying the bulk of Dynasty's bogus "philanthropy" propaganda machine directly to the taxpayers by establishment of the Department of Health, Education and Welfare; and had "reorganized" the Defense Department to acquire even more absolute control of the tens of billions expended by it, for the purpose of draining an even larger share of those funds into their coffers and making it an exclusive sales agency of their munitions. (275:80) By those means and by the support of "foreign aid" frauds, he had materially aided in bringing the Treasury to the verge of bankruptcy through unfavorable balances of payment and in facilitating the development of their projected "Gold Corner." (79:138)

The ideal execution of the conspirators' schemes required the subsequent (1960) election of Nelson Rockefeller as President. At Chicago, however, because of some undercover, patriotic activities, he failed to secure the Republican nomination. Reliable reports prior to the election, that were fully confirmed by post-election developments, related that the conspirators were able by virtue of the control of the "F"R and the banking system of the country, to effect a deal whereby the election of John F. Kennedy was "fixed" by the conspirators, in return for advance assurance that, when elected, he would serve them and permit them to name the key policy-making figures and Cabinet members of his Administration. Pres. Kennedy appointed key Rockefeller agents from their Council on Foreign Relations (which Kennedy is reported to have joined, undercover). To the key post of Secretary of State, Pres. Kennedy appointed Dean Rusk, President of the Rockefeller Foundation, whom he is reported never to have met prior, and who was "loaned" to the Administration by the Rockefeller Foundation, (79:217) to boost their arms and munition business in Vietnam in cooperation with their agent, Secretary of "Defense," McNamara.

Their pressagents report that David Rockefeller had personal contact with Kennedy when both were being indoctrinated with Communist "philosophy" at the ultra-Red Rockefeller-subsidized London School of Economics. In the mid-1950's they had been rival candidates for the Board of Overseers Red Harvard University, of which both were alumni. Pres. Kennedy showed his appreciation for Rockefeller efforts on his behalf, by making him his "adviser" in matters of finance, and inviting him to White House dinners.

The conspirators' use of their foreign dollar holdings built up in the illicit manner that has been related, and the use of them to drain off the gold from their domestic to their foreign accounts, served as a pretext for the fellow conspirators to alarmingly brainwash the nation with regard to the "crisis" that had been created by their "withdrawals."

This "alarm" is cited as the pretext for an invitation extended by Pres. Kennedy to David Rockefeller to personally sponsor the thievish scheme and dupe the nation to acceptance of it from a "philanthropist," from "the horse's mouth," by writing him an open letter for publication. Prior to election Joseph P. Kennedy had tipped off some of his cronies that if his son were elected, the price of gold would be raised. As a consequence, there was wild speculation in the British and world gold markets that led to a transient increase in the price of gold. (121:68)

### ROCKEFELLER LETTER, REQUESTED BY KENNEDY, PROMOTED RELEASE OF GOLD

There is confirmation of the reported Rockefeller-Kennedy corrupt pre-election deal and the inclusion in it of a gold "fix" in David Rockefeller's "open letter" sent to Pres. Kennedy at his request. It was identical in its tenor with the "report" of his "Commission" on Money & Credit. David Rockefeller undertook, in effect to dictate acceptance of looting to Kennedy and the nation. The circumstance of its publication makes even more ugly the picture of Pres. Kennedy's abject submission to the conspirators. Kahn reported that Pres. Kennedy personally authorized his friend and Rockefeller CFR agent, Henry Luce, of *Time Inc.* to publish this humiliating directive of David Rockefeller, ordering the nation's monetary and fiscal policy. (121:68) Luce, a longtime friend of Kennedy, had written the preface to his ghosted book entitled *Why England Slept.* (140)

The letter was published in the July 6, 1962 issue of *Life* as a widely publicized lead article. (41:30) To further bolster public acceptance of Rockefeller's dictates to Kennedy, there was subsequently published as a lead article in the September 7, 1962 issue of *Time*, a panegyric by Luce on David's financial piracies and usury, lauding his greedy acquisitiveness and ruthless craftiness. Luce was keenly aware that he was writing about his boss.

200

The letter that was obviously intended as a sounding board for David Rockefeller and the conspirators' gold plot, is reported by Kahn to have been "compiled" by his Chase Manhattan Bank employees. (121:58) It lauded Pres. Kennedy for his adherence to such phases of the conspiracy as "managed economy," "foreign (Rockefeller) aid," "defense" and space looting, and others that have redounded so richly to profits of the conspirators. But it waxed eloquent on the topics dearest to the Rockefeller heart: usury. Rockefeller demanded the maintenance of "tight money" and high interest rates. He demanded release of "F"R Act required gold reserves held by the conspirators in their domestic account. (41:33)

With a view to spotlighting the conspirators' gold "withdrawals" Pres. Kennedy appointed a "Balance of Payments" Committee. Kahn reported that Pres. Kennedy had refrained from accentuating the picture of the conspirators' dictation of his policies by not appointing David Rockefeller to the chairmanship of the "Committee." He directed the chairman he did appoint, however, to include in its membership "a nigger in the woodpile," David Rockefeller, in full realization that he would dominate the "Committee" and dictate its "report." (121:68) Pres. Kennedy subsequently joined his adviser, Rockefellers' CFR agent whom they have since then made president of their Ford Foundation, McGeorge Bundy, in sponsoring the establishment of the Business Group For Latin America, by David Rockefeller to serve their Latin American thievery. (121:68)

Pres. Kennedy further promoted the conspirators' plot for inflation and destruction of the value of the dollar. A UPI dispatch, published in the N.Y. Times of January 23, 1962, announced: "U.S. Would Drop Silver Standard. Kennedy Asks Congress End Currency Relationship." President Kennedy thereby insured the conspirators an ultraprofitable culmination of the silver conspiracy that they had launched during their "New" Deal, under the direction of "New" Dealer Nelson Rockefeller, through their Chase National Bank (97) that had enabled them to turn China over to their Communist partners, with the help of their CFR and Institute of Pacific Relations agents and spies.

## CONGRESS OBEYED CONSPIRATORS' DICTATES TO ELIMINATE SILVER FROM CURRENCY

Congress obediently passed the bill for abandonment of silver coinage demanded by Pres. Kennedy on behalf of the conspirators. Their "Federal" Reserve, in the meantime hastened to empty the Treasury of its silver, with the help of intensive publicity that stimulated speculation in silver. Until mid-June, 1967, one needed merely to call up the N.Y. Federal Reserve Bank and order thousand ounce of silver bars, to secure their full cooperation in withdrawing silver from the Treasury by way of the Assay Office. Silver dollars and half dollars were withdrawn from the banks and the Treasury in sacks containing $1,000.00 each.

The Treasury withheld until the last, three thousand bags, of a thousand dollars each, of the relatively rare Carson City minted dollars that command prices as high as several hundred dollars each among coin collectors. Employees of the N.Y. Assay Office informed this author, that these bags of silver dollars were turned over to the Chase Manhattan Bank. This has not been publicized. Instead

201

the Treasury announced that these Carson City silver dollars were being held back for sale to collectors at auction to raise money for charitable cause. "Charity begins at home" is a motto to which the Rockefellers eagerly subscribe.

## CONGRESS VIOLATED NATION'S CIVIL RIGHT BY RENEGGING ON TREASURY CONTRACT

By June 1967, the Treasury was faced with depletion of its reserve of silver to a point below the requirements for redeeming the outstanding silver certificates that the Government contracted with the nation to redeem with silver; and for minting the only coin that now contains silver, the half dollar, the silver content of which has been reduced from 90% to 40%. The conspirators had no more qualms about having Congress order violation of the contract to redeem the silver certificates in silver, than they had previously manifested in ordering violation of the contract of the "Gold Standard Act" to redeem currency in gold. Congress passed bills, at their behest, limiting the redemption of silver certificates to those presented prior to June 24, 1968; and totally cancelling more than a hundred million silver certificates that were arbitrarily deemed to be "lost."

## CONSPIRATORS' IMF GAVE STAUNCH "INTERNATIONALIST" SUPPORT TO THEIR PLOT

The fears that White expressed on behalf of the conspirators:

"We will be left with over $30 billion of gold...for which there will be only a trifling demand—to fill teeth and fashion wedding rings." (59:2664)have been rendered vain by the organization that he naively served them to establish, the "International" Monetary Fund. As might be expected, their IMF supports Rockefeller's dictates to Pres. Kennedy. Its Director was then the previously mentioned character who had played an unsavory role as aide to the conspirators' agent, the arch-swindler, Ivar Krueger in his gigantic International Match swindle, Per Jacobsson. Jacobsson faithfully seconded "his master's voice" and "valiantly" rushed in to support "banker" David Rockefeller's orders at the September, 1962 meeting of the Fund. The spirit in which Jacobsson undertook to "assure" the nation and the world on the monetary situation brings to mind the similar job done by another of the conspirators' "distinguished economists" and agents, Professor Irving Fisher, in 1929, when he falsely assured the nation that "all is well" at the very time when they were getting the crash and panic under way.

The IMF meeting ended on the note that there must continue the juggling of their "commodity," money, by the conspirators and their agents (to insure them profits to their liking); that money must be maintained in the proper degree of scarcity, "tight," to assure their malign purpose of manipulating all commodities that are truly essential for existence. There was also intimation that the "withdrawal" of gold from the U.S. Treasury would be terminated temporarily by juggling and "kiting" of "international" loans.

## CONSPIRATORS' SET STAGE FOR GOLD WITHDRAWAL & SCARE

While reassuring the nation through their IMF' and other agencies in regard to the unfavorable balance of payments that they had engineered they set the stage for continuance at an even more rapid pace of their gold "withdrawals." They pressured Congress into reducing the duties on their cheap foreign merchandise by the so-called "Kennedy rounds." They blocked import controls for all of their overseas imports with the exception of oil, but imposed quotas on oil in order to enable them to squeeze the domestic oil independents who needed oil.

## JEAN PAUL GETTY FORCED TO WALL BY ROCKEFELLER CONSPIRATORS.

Shortly after the conspirators' *Fortune* had mockingly labelled Jean Paul Getty, whose total wealth is less than Rockefellers' daily income, the "richest man in the world," they proceeded to pluck him of a major part of his assets, by their oil quota device. Getty had undertaken to escape from a squeeze, into which they had trapped him, by building, on the Delaware River, the most modern refinery for processing the oil from the discovered Libya oilfield. The conspirators were able to prevent Getty from securing enough oil to operate the refinery which they coveted; and threatened him with bankruptcy, until he turned over a large part of his holdings to them.

## VIETNAM WAR FURTHERS CONSPIRACY

The Rockefeller-Soviet Axis, jointly with the Jesuits, further their American conspiracy by plunging the nation in turmoil, currently the Vietnam War and the "Black Power" guerrilla Civil War. This is the meaning of Nelson Rockefeller's ghosted "encyclicals" *Purpose And Policy* (22) and *Policy & The People* (392) written for him by Red Harvard policy adviser of the Rockefeller Brothers Fund Inc. and CFR member, Prof. H. A. Kissinger. (393) In the first he hails this as an era of war and revolution, that he has so effectively promoted, and so richly profited the conspirators. The N.Y. Post pointed out (393) that Rockefeller adopted a "harder line" of foreign policy, "defense" and military policy than either Pres. Eisenhower or the Democratic Presidents who succeed him. (393) In view of his draft evasion and munition and arms profits, Rockefeller's approval of the Vietnam and all other wars is understandable.

The Vietnam "policy action" has an especially high value for the conspirators. The cream of American youth are there completely surrounded, infiltrated and entrapped by Communists who slaughter them almost at will. Those GIs who escape slaughter fall victim to a host of loathsome and debilitating, incurable tropical diseases such as malignant forms of malaria, virus hepatitis, amebic dysentery, melioidosis, leprosy, exotic venereal diseases and others. As a consequence many of them will not procreate viable offspring, much to the satisfaction of the conspirators who dread the babies other than their own breed, as a "population explosion" that frustrates the population control that they regard as so essential for their planned dictatorship. Another advantage of Vietnam and the spreadeagling of our Armed Forces around the world, to be entrapped and either decimated or held as hostages, is that it leaves us virtually defenseless at home against invasion from without, against guerrilla Civil War waged by the conspirators' savage Negro and other Communist agents at home, and takeover by them.

## CONSPIRATORS REGIMENT & TRAIN SUBVERSIVE FORCES AT TAXPAYERS' EXPENSE

The conspirators have been subsidizing the subversive elements in our country, with special stress on the Negro and Comunist, indirectly at the expense of the taxpayers with the tax exempt funds of their foundations; and more recently they have succeeded in placing the costs directly on the shoulders of the taxpayers through their "Civil Rights," "Poverty" and OEO programs. They and their Jesuit and other religious, professorial, social(ist) service, Negro and political pawns have cunningly suggested, invited and incited rioting and crime under the pretense of "predicting" its occurrence, unless the taxpayers submit to further looting by them to "prevent" it. With the moneys thus looted from the taxpayers, they reward the agitators and rioters, subsidize and incite them to further lawbreaking and rioting with the promise of further rewards—at the expense of the taxpayers. Consequently the greater the Relief, "Civil Rights" and "Poverty Program" appropriations become, the closer the nation approaches bankruptcy, anarchy and takeover by themselves as dictators. That is the true meaning of Nelson Rockefeller's "encyclicals" and David Rockefeller's financial "advices."

## PRESIDENT'S COMMITTEE ON CIVIL DISORDERS URGE MORE REWARDS TO HASTEN ANARCHY

The "Report" of the conspirators' hack Negro and political agents appointed by the President as a Committee On Civil Disorders is a perfidious enunciation of their plot to stimulate rioting, and hasten national bankruptcy, anarchy and dictatorial takeover. It embodies incredible and suicidal pandering to the Negro and other subversive elements that emerges, clearly, from consideration of its contents and accredited authors.

The members of the Committee consist of a pair of "professional Negroes and several white hack politicians, including the conspirators' kinsman and agent, New York's scourge, unprincipled "Liberal," Mayor Lindsay. It is incredible that they are not well enough informed to be aware of the falsity of the premises and the damaging, self-defeating character of the recommendations of their "Report."

1. Do they not know the falsity of the myth that "wrong" was done the Negroes' ancestors by slave owners who purchased them at high cost, from their fellow Negroes who sold them into slavery, and thereby saved them from sacrifical slaughter and cannibalism? If they are so ignorant of the subject that they do not know this fact, they should educate themselves in the matter by reading the authentic report of Negro Communist, Richard Wright, in his book "Black Power," in which he described the human sacrifice and cannibalism that still prevails in Africa in what is now the Negro "republic" of Ghana. (347:291)

2. Do they not know that slaves cost their owners an average of $5,000, were valuable property and were solicitously cared for, fed, sheltered, educated, civilized, and often literally loved too well by their masters?

3. Do they not know that the more civilized Negroes did not desire to be "liberated" and denied the shelter they had been given by their masters; whereas the more savage and uncivilized Negroes, were incited by white carpetbaggers, to brutally and shamefully abuse their former white masters, exactly as today they are being incited by the conspirators and their agents on the Committee; and the consequence was hatred and degradation?

204

4. Do they know that there exists in this country, today, a shortage of labor so serious that the only excuse for unemployment is refusal to work?

5. Do they not know that the great majority of the rioters are "Reliefers" who are being maintained by provident, taxpaying citizens in comparatively luxurious (lace curtains and salad forks) idleness and vice, that gives them the leisure to procreate profitably and engage in riots to demand larger bribes for their political support that are breaking the backs of provident good, citizens and bankrupting our governments?

6. Do they not know that if the rioters were given jobs, other than "Liberal" "Civil Rights" and pro-Communist agitation, they would refuse to work and allege that they were being "denied their 'rights,' abused and discriminated against;" that if they were given mansions, they would be privileged, under present housing laws, to quickly tear them apart (either because of primitive mentality that leads them to foul their own nests, sheer savage destructiveness, or for the purpose of selling the stolen material for the purchase of dope) and convert them to slums in which alone they feel comfortable; and if they were given richer bribes, as the Committee demands, in its Report, that would merely encourage and incite them to make greater and more insolent demands supported by more heinous violence and crimes?

7. Do they not know that the students who swell the mob of rioters in Summer are being incited by their Red and too often frankly Communist teachers and professors who should be ousted as the first step in improving the situation?

8. Do they not know that their pretense of "predicting" further violence and riotings is a thinly veiled invitation and incitement thereto?

If the members of the Committee do not know these well-known facts, they are incompetent to hold public office. On the other hand, if they made their false "Report" with full knowledge of these truths, they have exposed themselves as dishonest hack politicians who betray their trust, their oaths of office and the nation; as crooked and perfidious officials seeking princely handouts and graft for themselves and their henchmen for building for themselves political machines at the expense of the taxpayers. One begins to wonder how much of the tens of billions of dollars that the Committee members demand for the pretended "solution" of the problem, will flow in the usual direction, into the pockets of the conspirators.

## WHITE & BLACK PUBLIC OFFICIALS OPENLY SUPPORT CONSPIRATORS ON NEGRO RIOTS

A wide array of the conspirators' agents in public office as openly support, encourage and are involved in the conspirators' program for precipitating riots and anarchy as the members of the COCD have shown themselves to be. Virtually all elected and appointed Negro officeholders have openly acknowledged themselves to be involved in or sympathetic to, this phase of the conspiracy, thereby betraying public trust and violating their oaths of office. The more civil among them do so under intimidation by their more savage brethren; and in fear of being characterized as "Black Toms." They thereby lend their support to the conspirators in inciting guerrilla warfare on communities with ill-disguised or openly expressed intent of genocide, "to wipe out the 'whiteys,' 'white devils'." Avowal of complicity in this conspiracy has been made by many of them before Congressional Committees, in meetings in public schools and other buildings to which they have free access, in public and in private, over radio, television and all media of mass communication which the conspirators dominate and have placed at their disposal. In all of these felonies they are actually supported and encouraged by their Communist, "religious" and "philanthropic" confederates and accomplices, thus far with absolute impunity. Politicians do not dare enforce against them the laws that they flagrantly violate because of fear of losing their votes, from which conviction for felony would bar them.

### N.Y. OFFICIAL ANNOUNCES PLOT TO USE VIETNAM-TRAINED BLACKS TO EXTERMINATE WHITES

Percy E. Sutton, Negro Borough President of Manhattan, New York, announced in a "keynote address" before the National Conference of Antipoverty Agencies (for the subsidy and bribery of Negro savages) held at Red, Rockefeller subsidized Columbia University's Teachers College on February 22, 1968, the intent to use thousands of returning Vietnam Negro veterans to apply their wartime skills in bloody guerrilla war against American white folk throughout the country. He proclaimed:

"I am afraid that the greatest battle of the era—of the Vietnam war—will not be fought in the demilitarized zone north of Da Nang, but will be fought in the streets of America." (382)

Sutton's open announcement of this plan of Negro blackmailing of the nation, brought down on him neither protest and demand for his removal from office, nor arrest under the law that makes criminal conspiracy a felony, so customary has become the use of public facilities by Negroes for plotting anarchy and inciting their race to criminality.

There may well be approaching the day when the cream of our youth, including our professional men, scientists and scholars, drafted in the service of the conspirators and scattered around the world, may serve the conspirators as hostages used to force acceptance of their dictatorship after they have effected our actual, or virtual, defeat abroad by monstrous betrayals of our country. The complete breakdown of law and order that they have plotted and a disastrous inflation that they will have effected through their "Federal" Reserve fraud will have brought it about.

### CONSPIRATORS PROFIT FROM SACRIFICE OF GI "DEMONSTRATORS" OF WEAPONS

In the meanwhile, these foreign and domestic wars are yielding huge profits to the conspirators. Congressional investigations have brought to light their treacherous use of wholly un-Constitutional war involvements at endless cost to the nation in money, materiel and lives, but without even the dubious reward of clear-cut victory, to garner for themselves fabulous profits from the sale of arms and munitions of which they are the chief manufacturers around the world. Pres. Eisenhower rewarded the conspirators for purchasing his nomination and "arranging" his election by turning over the "reorganization" of the government to Nelson Rockefeller. His interest was the War Department, which with characteristic chicanery, he renamed the "Defense" Department and converted into a sales agency for the conspirators' arms and munitions business.

When the charge was made on the floor of the Senate that the "Defense" Department, as reorganized by Nelson Rockefeller is an arms sales agency, the N.Y. Times launched an investigation into it, omitting the Rockefeller involvement. The findings of the investigation were published in the Times in a series of articles entitled as follows:

*"Armament Sales: U.S. Is Principal Supplier to the World"* (275)
*"U.S. Arms Sales Spurred by Large Field Force & Complex Credit System"* (276)
*"American Does Brisk Business in Surplus Weapons"* (277)
*"16 Concerns Get Major Share of U.S. Arms Profit"* (278)
*"U.S. Arms Salesman, Henry John Kuss Jr."* (279)
*"Private Arms Dealer, Samuel Cummings"* (280)

### PENTAGON: ROCKEFELLERS' MUNITION & ARMS SALES DEPARTMENT

The gist of the report is "Defense" Department, as "reorganized" by Nelson Rockefeller, has become a gigantic munition business conducted at the expense of the taxpayers and yielding profits of fabulous billions to the conspirators, through companies controlled by them. On the basis of demonstrations of the vaunted superiority of their munitions and arms by GI's at the risk of their lives in the endless series of wars which conspirators have engineered for us, they use the so-called "Defense" Department to cajole and cudgel nations around the world to purchase their deadly wares.

The report relates that they maintain in the "Defense" Department, at the Pentagon, an official salesman named Henry John Kuss Jr., with the title of Deputy Assistant Secretary of Defense for International Logistics Negotiations, who has made for them sales and profits so huge that their dummy, Secretary of Defense Robert S. McNamara, was directed to award him the Meritorious Civilian Service Medal for his "unparalleled ability as a negotiator." That means that he has been unusually successful in engineering, for the conspirators, arms races between nations that scare them into purchasing their death-dealing devices, and into putting them into use and consumption. Rockefeller's "Defense" Department would have been named Rockefeller Munitions Sales Department & Merchants of Death, if there were even a trace of honesty in him.

Resistance to sales to both friendly and enemy nations is minimal. For the conspirators have arranged to saddle the cost of the weapons for friend and foe, alike, squarely on the shoulders of American taxpayers while sluicing off the enormous profits into their own purses in the same manner as in their other "foreign (Rockefeller) aid" deals. The taxpayers pay part of the cost of this trade in the form of an arms-sales credit fund of $383 million to provide down payments to the conspirators' companies on more than $1.5 billion in sales; and in addition credit is extended by the U.S. Government in unlimited amounts. Still another source of taxpayers' money for payment of arms for foreign lands is provided by the conspirators through their Import-Export Bank. (276) On the basis of past experience in "foreign, (Rockefeller) aid" loan repayments, the conspirators will steal such repayments of the arms loans as will be made, through such devices as "counterpart funds" and thereby further enhance their profits from this trade in death; and all the costs of rearming lands around the world will be borne by American taxpayers, in contemptuous disregard of the Constitution.

## "PHILANTHROPISTS" EMERGE AS MERCHANTS OF DEATH

The report relates:

"The business is so complex and the relationship between the Government and industry so interlocking that it is virtually impossible to determine where Government begins and industry action ends." (278)

This is in no wise surprising in view of the fact that the conspirators have made the U.S. Government a minor bureau of their Rockefeller Empire, and American taxpayers involuntary financiers of their thievish "philanthropic" war mongering.

The "Defense" Department announced on behalf of the conspirators that it planned to serve the "philanthropic" merchants of death uninterruptedly, and expected to earn for them $4.5 billion by 1972, to "settle trade balance." (345)

### CONGRESS APPROVED TAXPAYER FINANCING OF "PHILANTHROPIST" MERCHANTS OF DEATH

The full extent of the conspirators' control of Congress was illustrated by the action of the Senate on the bill to extend the life and lending authority of the Export-Import bank subsidiary of their "Federal" Reserve. Efforts of the minority to amend the bill were defeated, to the extent of blocking provision

"...that would prohibit the bank from making any loans for the purchase of any United States products by a Communist country, or by any other country if the products were destined to end up in a Communist nation." (281)

This amendment that might have restricted the extent of the criminal aid to Communist lands by the Rockefeller-Eaton (270) deal to facilitate the provision of arms and munitions for the slaughter of our GI's in Vietnam, was defeated by a vote of 51-35. (283) With few exceptions the members of the Senate staunchly supported the use by the conspirators of the "Defense" Department as an agency for the sale of arms and munitions, and for their war-mongering. (282)

### GI DEMONSTRATORS OF THEIR MUNITIONS IN VIETNAM ARE BETRAYED

An even uglier and more vicious picture of betrayal of our GI's in Vietnam by the conspirators was revealed in investigation, by a House Armed Services subcommittee, of the jamming of their M-16 guns by defective powder supplied the Armed Forces by the conspirators through their Olin Mathieson Chemical Company to which their agent, Secretary of Defense McNamara gave an exclusive contract for its production from "reprocessed" defective waste. (301) This treachery, which cost the lives of numerous GI's, did not preclude the conspirators from having their "Defense" Department

208

agents give their oil companies, including their Humble Oil subsidiary of their Standard Oil of New Jersey, their Standard Oil Co. of California and their Mobiloil Co., the major portion of $305 million contracts for oil for the Armed Forces, and the granting of further contracts for powder, to their Olin Mathieson Chemical Company. (302)

## ROCKEFELLER'S "PHILANTHROPIC" WARMONGERING AIDED BY "DEFENSE" DEPARTMENT

The report makes it clear that it is one of the prime functions of the "Defense" Department, as reorganized by Nelson Rockefeller, to promote the conspirators' warmongering. In some instances, it is done under the pretext of "improving the balance of payments." This was the case when Kuss dumped on Germany discarded F-104 Starfighters, sixty-one of which crashed, killing their crews. As a consequence, the last half billion of the more than $4 billion arms purchase commitment of West Germany was replaced by a German pledge to purchase half a billion dollars of Treasury bonds that will further unfavorably affect, ultimately, our balance of payments. Such devices as NATO and SEATO, the report acknowledges, are used by the "Defense" Department and its military salesmen, to exert pressure on the nations involved to buy and put to destructive martial use the conspirators' arms and munitions. One of their most important sales devices is to point to the performance of their wares in the "demonstration wars" staged in Korea and Vietnam. (276)

## WARMONGERING PLAYS A ROLE IN TIMING GOLD WITHDRAWALS FOR MAXIMUM SCARE EFFECT

Warmongering helps the conspirators transfer gold from their domestic to their "foreign" accounts. (141) During 1962, the conspirators' gold "withdrawals" totaled about $1 billion. This accentuated the "advice," or order, of David Rockefeller to Pres. Kennedy to release all their domestic gold for transfer to their foreign accounts, for the pretended purpose of settling our imbalance of payments that had been created by them deliberately. Under-Secretary for Monetary Affairs of the Treasury, Robert V. Roosa, their Council of Foreign Relations agent, like his chief, Secretary Dillon, added fuel to the scare propaganda by announcing on behalf of the conspirators that they planned to "withdraw" even larger volumes of gold, facilitated by the enormous costs of the Korean, Vietnam and "Cold" war "demonstrations" of their "philanthropic" death-dealing merchandise and the foreign loans to finance their use and consumption.

## PRES. KENNEDY FAILED TO GET SUPPORT OF CONGRESS FOR CONSPIRATORS' GOLD RELEASE

Pres. Kennedy failed, much to the conspirators' annoyance, to secure the support of Congress to carry out their dictates on the release of gold tied up in their domestic accounts by the "F"R Act. He had "shot his bolt" in carrying out the conspirators' dictates on making the Western Hemisphere safe for their Communist partners, in a deal involving the pretended removal of Soviet missiles and bases from Cuba (where they continue to be) and the betrayal of Cuban Freedom Fighters at the Bay of Pigs. The sham "resistance" of Kennedy and his "New Frontier" to the military takeover of Cuba by the Soviets covered up the deal made by the Washington Rockefeller-Soviet agents to deliver the island to Russian Communist occupation, the permanence of which appears secure. It fooled no one except imbeciles and idiots who were propagandized into acclaiming it as a "magnificent victory" for Kennedy's "diplomacy," instead of a deliberate perfidious delivery to the Soviets of a military and missile base at our very threshold.

Cuba presented to a scoffing, derisive and contemptuous world the absurd spectacle of a trapped, vanquished but blustering U.S., that either could not, or would not, or both, protect itself from Communist encroachment at home, while pretending to "stop" it on the other side of the globe, in Europe, Africa and Asia. The obvious implication of the situation, a deal to serve the Rockefeller-Soviet Axis, was not lost to the world. And it is bearing fruit in world-wide contempt for our country, as expressed in current events. In particular, it has aided the conspirators in undermining any remaining trust in our country and its finances.

## KENNEDY'S ASSASSINATION PAVED WAY FOR EXECUTION OF ROCKEFELLER'S ORDER

Pres. Kennedy's timely assassination was quite fortunate for the conspirators' program, not because he was not willing to carry out their dictates, but because he had not sufficient control over Congress to secure passage of the required law. The assassination projected into the White House a man who by various devices had attained an almost absolute control of Congress, Lyndon B. Johnson. Pres. Johnson "cracked the whip" over Congress; and without delay it passed that part of the gold legislation dictated by David Rockefeller that the White House wanted passed.

Johnson was too wily a politician to give the conspirators the whole loaf that they demanded. They were forced to be content with part of the golden loaf. Pres. Johnson directed Congress to eliminate the gold reserve that the conspirators' "Federal" Reserve Act required them to maintain against the deposits of member banks with the "F"R. This released about $5 billion in gold for transfer from their domestic to their "foreign" account. The law still tied up in their domestic account the $9 billion of gold that was then required as a reserve against "Federal" Reserve notes in circulation.

As soon as the bill had passed, the conspirators began their moves to "withdraw" all of the freed gold as rapidly and discreetly as the spotlight of publicity on gold permitted. The withdrawals by their French and other foreign collaborators were intensively publicized. Little mention was made, however, of the gold from Russia and other lands that was purchased for them by the Treasury at the expense of the taxpayers, and imported. Between June 30, 1964 and July 30, 1965, the gold falsely and deceptively listed among the assets of the U.S. Treasury dropped from $15.46 billion to $13.85 billion, "withdrawals" totalling more than $1.6 billion, fulfilling Rockefeller CFR pawn, Roosa's, "prediction." (137)

Several measures speeded the gold withdrawals. The Treasury was required to subscribe an additional $800 million to their International Monetary Fund. Of this sum, it was required that $200 million be paid out in gold. Subsequently, the Treasury was required to subscribe $200 million for a bank that will finance the conspirators' Asiatic ventures. There seems to be no end of such ventures dictated by the conspirators as a pretext for the gold "withdrawals." By these devices, the conspirators confront us, their American "peasants," with a constant array of scare gold headlines such as those carried by the N.Y. Times of July 2, 1965, reading:

*"Gold Stock Falls by $359 Million*
*"Holdings of U.S. Decline to $13.9 Billion, the Lowest Level since 1938*
*"65 Loss at $1.4 Billion"*

## CONSPIRATORS PROFIT FROM "WITHDRAWALS" ADVANCING THEIR "GOLD CORNER"

The most obvious consequence of the "withdrawals" was contraction of the nation's and the world's currency effected by reduction of gold available for the maintenance of their "Gold Standard." The restriction of the supply of currency on this basis, by the "Federal" Reserve, without regard to the needs of the nation and of its business and industry, served as justification for its raising the rediscount rate. The rediscount rate determines the profits made by the member banks by raising the legal rate of interest and discount which they charge their depositors and customers. And it increases the loot which they receive from the taxpayers by way of increased interest rates on Government bonds and notes. As the "withdrawals" increased, the "Federal" Reserve successively raised the rediscount rate in July, 1963, from 3% to 3½%; in November, 1964, from 3½% to 4%; and on December 6, 1965, from 4% to4½%, and in 1966, to more than 6%, the legal rate of interest in most States.

The increase of the rate of interest that had been insistently dictated by David Rockefeller to the banking fraternity, and to Pres. Kennedy in his letter, was obediently imposed by his minions on the "Federal" Reserve Board, headed by its Chairman, his CFR pawn, William McChesney Martin. To be sure, Martin and the Board dared not immediately raise the rate to the usurious level demanded by Rockefeller, who laid down the rule that a bank's minimal earnings on its capital must be 9% net, or 3% higher than the legal rate of interest in New York. Such a jump in interest rates would be politically dangerous to the conspirators. But the gradual raising of the rates has been tolerated by the nation duped by propaganda into the belief that it is "a necessity."

## STOCK MARKET "SHAKEOUT" IS SOURCE OF ADDED LOOT FOR CONSPIRATORS

Each rise in the "F"R rediscount rate is a signal for a crack in the stock market that yields the conspirators fast and fabulous profits from "short sales" in the stock market safely made on the basis of advance information. To facilitate the dumping of their stock, the conspirators make it a practise to make money "easy," or plentiful, and to encourage stock speculation, for a period of months prior to the date when they plan to simultaneously tighten the supply of money and to increase the rediscount rates. In this manner, they stimulate the wild speculation and inflation when they are disposing of the stock and "going short of stock," unloading it on the sucker public; and then bring about the crash which enables them to loot the "peasants" of both their stock and their money, if they are operating on margin, find themselves short of cash, or scare easily.

An insight into the modus operandi of this phase of the swindle can be gleaned from the operations of the conspirators during 1965. The "Federal" Reserve Board reported that it had reduced the nation's monetary supply prior to June, 1965. (145) On June 1, 1965, "F"R Board chairman, William McChesney Martin, took advantage of the deliberately created monetary shortage to bring about a major crash in the stock market by announcing that a situation comparable to that preceding the 1929 crash and the depression had been brought about by his fellow-conspirators' "management" of the economy. This market break permitted the insiders to cover their "short sales" and loot the scared public of billions of dollars.

## STOCK MARKET RIGGING BY CONSPIRATORS' "FEDERAL" RESERVE

Directly after this engineered break in the market, later in the same month, June 1965, the "Federal" Reserve agents of the conspirators reversed their action and rapidly flooded the market with money, making it "easy," after giving the conspirators a perfect opportunity to pick up cheap stock. By June 25, 1965, the "F"R announced that as a result of its action in making money "easy," the nation's money supply had increased more than $1 billion; and the market boom resumed with the blessing of the "F"R. Five months later, on December 6, 1965, Martin announced the increase of the "F"R rediscount rate from 4% to 4½%, precipitating another break in the stock market of sharp but transient character. Since this move meant that the Government and industry would have to pay higher rates on their loans than prevailed prior, this initiated a more gradual but steady drop in the bond market. In 1966, the conspirators repeated this swindle.

In the meantime, while the supply of money that the conspirators made available in the U.S. rose, their International Monetary Fund announced that they had diminished the world supply of money, (as was reported by Edwin L. Dale Jr. in the New York Times on August, 1965). (146) An earlier article in the same publication, by Robert Frost, on July 2, 1965, revealed and exposed the manipulations of the conspirators in the international field and threw light on the situation and on their purpose. It announced that $258 million in gold had been "withdrawal" from the Treasury and transferred to their International Monetary Fund. And it pointed out that the U.S. (i.e. the conspirators') domestic gold holdings had been reduced to the lowest level since 1938. In addition to the sum transferred to the conspirators' IMF, $100 million of gold had been transferred to their "Exchange Stabilization Fund;" and that total represented the largest weekly "withdrawal" since June 24, 1959, when the bulk of $364 million "withdrawal" had likewise been effected by transfer to their International Monetary Fund. (147)

The world-wide manipulation of money and the stock markets constitute an extra source of loot for the conspirators. Frost made it clear in his dispatch that these huge "withdrawals" of gold to the conspirators' IMF had been specifically authorized by Congress in obedient response to the dictates of Pres. Johnson a few days prior; and that the President had hastened to promptly sign the bill immediately after passage by Congress.

## "PREVENTION OF INFLATION" IS THE FALSE
## EXCUSE GIVEN FOR MANIPULATION

Most transparently false are the excuses given by all the parties involved in these monetary manipulations, to wit: the *"prevention"* *of inflation.* It has been obvious for decades that it has been the *deliberate objective* of both our national and local governments *to* *cause inflation.* Every service provided or controlled by the governments has been priced steadily higher. Postage has been increased from 2¢ to 6¢ for letters; from 1¢ to 5¢ for postcards; from 20¢ to 75¢ for registered mail; postal services have been steadily reduced and the public has been virtually sabotaged. Local, State and Federal taxes have mounted by leaps and bounds. Fares of municipal transportation services have mounted from 5¢ to as high as 30¢; and transfers have been eliminated, requiring the payment of an additional fare. Support is being gained by the conspirators for this vicious inflation from labor elements that have been organized by their agents, so-called "labor leaders," or Labor Barons. This steady inflation is directed by the Rockefellers on a nation-wide basis, through their Public Administration Clearing House of 1313 East 60th Street, Chicago, that is known popularly as "1313." (15:162;7)

## CONSPIRATORS' WAGNER LABOR ACT: GOONS'
## "MAGNA CARTA," PROMOTES INFLATION

Organized labor is doing a yoeman's job in helping the conspirators engineer the steady spiral of inflation that consumes the "wage increases" that they extort from industries that are not completely controlled by themselves. This is accomplished by a process of collective blackmail that by semantic perversion has been named "collective bargaining." A "Magna Carta" was given to the Labor Barons to regiment workers by a process that is often open coercion of criminally violent character, and to levy a special tax on them for the privilege of working. This is an obvious and flagrant violation of the basic freedom that is supposed to be assured under the Constitution. This was done by the "New" Deal law drawn up by a subservient agent of the conspirators and named after him the Wagner Labor Relations Act. By the Act both employer and employee are denied their basic Constitutional rights. (7:210) Under various pretexts, extortion is practised on both, with the full support of the Government, under the direction of the conspirators.

As a consequence of these dangerously subversive activities, the nation, the public and the workers are being constantly more intensively driven by the conspirators to an ever more marginal existence, no matter how high their wages are raised. And an ever larger proportion of the populace are being forced on the Relief roles, where their support is further increasing the taxation on the rest of the nation.

The phase of the deliberately engineered inflation that is hitting the people ever harder is the rising cost of food and the bare necessities of life. Thus in the early 1950's, green vegetables and fruit could be purchased in most sections of the country for and average of 9¢ a pound. By 1961, under the Labor-sponsored Kennedy "New Frontier" for select Labor Barons, the price had risen to 19¢ a pound. In the following five years, the price had risen further to 29¢ to 39¢ a pound, and the supply of both vegetables and fruit on the

213

markets dropped steadily. An important factor in the situation was cutting off from the farmers and ranchers the supply of labor for harvesting the crops and preparing them for the market, by the Secretary of Labor, Wirtz. Maintenance of shortages and of high prices was insured by the operations of the conspirators through their controlled truck and transport workers unions.

## ROCKEFELLERS' LOOT FROM LABOR UNION RACKETS THEY SPONSOR & SUPPORT

Victor Riesel, the Hearst labor columnist, under the caption *New Type of Partnership*, reported on the curious, long-time partnership that exists between Rockefellers and their Labor Barons who regiment for them "working stiffs" and "peasants." The bulk of the money extorted from union members and employers under the guise of "pension funds" and other "fringe benefits," Riesel related, have been put at the disposal of the Rockefellers and their Chase Manhattan Bank. (148) George Meany, Walter Reuther and other AFL-CIO "leaders" have turned over much of their treasuries to a Mortgage Investment Trust operated by the conspirators and their bank. The money, that is expected to amount to $50 million, is certain to be partly or completely wiped out by their "Gold Corner" inflation, and the long term mortgages paid off in depreciated or worthless dollars, enabling the conspirators to steal part or all of the funds. The same plan, as has been related, underlies the long term $250 million note issue of Chase Manhattan and similar issues of companies controlled by the conspirators. These acts of betrayal of trust and thievery follow the tradition Rockefeller pattern and the precept of "Doc" Bill Rockefeller, the founder of the Dynasty: "Never give a sucker a break. Betray all who trust you. Partners deserve to be rooked."

## ROCKEFELLER'S LABOR BARONS LEND THEIR SUPPORT TO MONETARY FRAUD

Rockefeller's Labor Baron partners reciprocate for favors received by giving full and unconditional support to the "F"R and monetary frauds, even though it is certain to eventually wipe out the funds that they have entrusted to his care and leave their deluded followers destitute of the "benefits" that they have hoped for and often sacrificed employment and wages to obtain by way of strikes. The measure of their support of the planned "Gold Corner" is reflected in their assignment of their agents and personnel to give their stamp of approval to Rockefeller's Report of the Commission on Money and Credit (42:vii) including:

Emil Rieve, President Emeritus, Textile Workers of America, AFL-CIO

Stanley H. Ruttenberg, Director, Department of Research, AFL-CIO

William F. Schnitzler, Secretary-Treasurer, AFL-CIO

These tools of the conspirators were belatedly "drafted" by Rockefeller to rubber stamp his thievish scheme, in April and May 1960, after it had been drafted according to his dictates. Though these characters raised minor remonstrances to the conspirators' scheme, they gave it their complete approval.

## DAVID ROCKEFELLER CONTEMPTUOUSLY BROADCAST
## HIS BRIGANDAGE AS "CURE"

The canvas of treachery incarnate presented would not be complete without depiction of David Rockefeller contemptuously broadcasting to the nation, while chuckling quite obviously, the brigandage and looting that he has dictated through the "Federal" Reserve-IMF setup and puppets in the government. The conspirators' control of NBC made it no problem for "liberal" usurer David to obtain, at no cost, one choice Sunday noon hour of television broadcast time to sneeringly dictate, once again, to the nation submission to looting by their monetary and gold manipulations and increased taxation. The broadcast, filmed in advance, on November 30, 1967, was one of the WNBC Television "Speaking Freely" series that contrary to the implication of the title, was well edited in advance of going on the air. (363)

The broadcast was in the nature of an "alibi" in which the perpetrator of the evils was cast in the role of "benevolent adviser" to the nation. It partook of the odor of a production of Faust in which Mephistopheles masqueraded as a saint. In response to carefully slanted questions by host, Edwin Newman, David Rockefeller as President of the Chase Manhattan Bank reiterated the policy he had dictated in the form of "advice" to the nation to accept the conspiracy already carried out.

He "advised" governmental economy, in the same breath as he urged increased spending in all directions that would swell the coffer of the conspirators: "foreign aid" that must not be cut back, but avoid making loans that would not be paid back (Ed. to the conspirators as usual?); "slum clearance and urban redevelopment" on an ever larger scale and subsequent private sales of the properties built at public expense (Ed. to the conspirators, as usual?); higher taxes (Ed. with continued exemption of the conspirators?); birth control (Ed. for other than the conspirators); the gold "outflow" must be stopped (Ed. though it has never occurred except in the transfers of stolen gold from the conspirators domestic to their "foreign" accounts); and he found it "no hardship" to be a Rockefeller. The deceit of the presentation was palpable to the informed, replete with dishonesty and treachery, however plausible the propaganda may have been to the uninformed. Implied in the "advice" was false counsel on how our country could avert the devaluation of the dollar, as the pound had been freshly devalued. Given by the very character who has been the master plotter in the "Gold Corner" which will force devaluation of the dollar, it was craftily designed to shift the blame for future events on scapegoats. The intensive campaign that has been long subsidized by the conspirators has made certain that they will be the traditional scapegoats: the Jewish "international bankers."

CHAPTER XX
PLUTOCRATIC DYNASTIES MATCH "FEDERAL"
RESERVE IN THREAT TO REPUBLIC

Media of mass communication are brainwashing the American public into acceptance of the hereditary monarchic rule of either the Rockefeller or the Kennedy Dynasties, or both. The public, especially the younger generation and the self-styled "intelectuals" and students, have been completely "molded" into the pattern of "mass man" by pressagentry parading as "education" launched by Rockefeller in his bogus "philanthropy," the General Education Board as exemplified in his *Occasional Letter No. 1*. They accept subversion with enthusiasm. It matters not to the average, unthinking and brainwashed American that acceptance of the rule of either Dynasty means nullification of our Constitution and the end of our Republic and the freedom that it assures. This is the planned and expected result of the "philanthropy"-inculcated inability to think beyond immediate gratification of desire and the quest for so-called "security;" and of deliberate suppression of information that might enable one to evaluate the consequences of rule by those Dynasties.

The so-called "principles" that guide those Dynasties, that they seek to mask with their bogus "philanthropies," are most incisively illustrated by their attitude toward the Negro problem. Both Dynasties have actively and intensively financed and promoted the agitation among the Negroes that was originally launched in the early 19th century by the Jesuits for the purpose, pledged in the secret Treaty of Verona (1822), of destroying our Republic, as the "work of Satan" that violates the Church's "principle" of "divine rule" dictated by it. (72:71f) The evidence is conclusive that the attitude of the Dynasties toward slavery in general and slavery of Negroes in particular is no different from that of the Jesuits and their Church, that is cited by Gury in his *Doctrine of the Jesuits*. It reads:

"Slavery does not constitute a crime before any law, divine or human...When one thinks of the state of degradation in which hordes of Africans live, *the slave trade may be regarded as a providential Act...*"

The Church and its Orders reduced to serfdom and enslaved their parishioners as the price of their "salvation." The basis and justification therefor is the claim that the Pope, as the vicar of Jesus on earth, is the rightful owner of the earth and of everything and everyone on it. Throughout the Middle Ages the rank and file of Christians continued as serfs until the monarchs and the nobility had successfully staged their revolt against the Vatican and asserted some measure of personal freedom and title to their domains. (364) The Canon Law of the Church has never relinquished its claim to all human rights as its exclusive prerogative; but it respects the rights of slave owners in sections:

"987, 4. Slaves in the strict sense of the word are impeded (from ordination,) until they obtain their liberty. This case is still a possibility in certain missionary countries, though it rarely occurs." (127:430)

"Canon 1083...Second, marriage is invalid if a person who is free marries one whom he believes to be free but who is a slave

216

in the real sense..." (127:548)

Though it has practised slavery, finds no fault with it and countenances it in many lands, the Church supported the Jesuit scheme for overthrowing our American Republic, in accord with the Order's agreement at Vienna that was the condition exacted by the Vatican for its reestablishment, by waging its first war on slavery, in the U.S. Ruining the American economy and bringing about the secession of the Confederacy by agitating revolt among the Negroes, and by craftily enlisting duped "Radicals," Protestants and Jews as Abolitionist pawns, was the Jesuit plot launched, in 1822, through the missionary St. Leopold Society. (72) The Civil War was brought about with the intent of setting up, with the collaboration of the agent Maximilian who was crowned by the Pope as Emperor of Mexico, a Papal State extending from Mexico to Quebec. Current events in Quebec indicate that the plan has never been abandoned by either the Jesuits or the Church.

Inasmuch as Jesuit Adam Weishaupt launched the Illuminist-Communist conspiracy, it is not surprising that the Communist in the U.S., who were then known as Illuminists and later as Radicals, have been the faithful collaborators of the Church in the subversive plot to overthrow our Republic by persistent subversive and treasonous agitation among the Negroes. Under the direction of Jesuit Communist leaders (they have a blanket dispensation to join in "heresies" to serve the interests of the Church) (72:16) a steadily larger proportion of the Negroes have been seduced into the Communist ranks. The majority of present day Negro agitators and so-called "leaders," of the NAACP, SNCC, "American" Mau Maus, Black Muslims and other criminal elements, have come from the ranks of the Communists.

## ROCKEFELLERS COOPERATE WITH JESUITS: FINANCE & FOSTER NEGRO AGITATION & CRIME

Rockefellers have been the most liberal financiers and sponsors of subversive "education" and agitation among the Negroes, through the agency of their own foundations and other that they control, including the Carnegie and the Ford Foundations. Though the Rockefeller motivation is partly perverted attachment to the Negroes, and partly a family tradition of Abolitionism, it is in the main part identical with that originally conceived by the Jesuits: the use of the Negro to destroy our Republic by inciting them to savagery to effect a complete breakdown of law and order that will serve as a perfect pretext, in combination with a crashing economy that will be brought on by their "Gold Corner," for establishing a dictatorship under themselves that will be welcomed by a terrified nation. Negro "education" or agitation was the prime purpose of John D. Rockefeller the First, and the Second, in setting up their "educational philanthropy," the General Education Board. It was only with difficulty that they were dissuaded, by their Baptist collaborators, from devoting it exclusively to the "education" of Negroes. (77:II:483)

The Rockefeller conspirators have made excellent use of the ground-work of the Jesuits, their Communist agents, their duped Protestant and Abolitionist pawns and subversive agencies in the Negro agitation. They are honorary officers of many of the subversive Negro organizations that they have endowed and supported with their tax exempt funds, in effect using taxpayers money for subversion. They have used their vast influence to secure for their key agitators prize awards, including a Nobel prize, that is now awarded almost solely for services to the Soviets and Communism, for their associate and oft-honored guest, the Red irreverent Negro agitator Rev. Martin Luther King.

## POPE PIUS XII IN "SERTUM LAETITIAE" EXPOSED VATICAN USE OF AMERICAN NEGROES

Whatever may have been his qualities as a family man and master of foreign exchange, Pope Pius XII can hardly be regarded as being diplomatic in his exposure of the Vatican's design to use for its purpose the American Negroes. Though there is no record of his having any interest in Negroes enslaved in Africa, Asia, and elsewhere, with full approval of the Church and support of its Canon Law, Pope Pius XII, in his first encyclical expressed "concern" for the American Negroes. In his *"Sertum Laetitiae"* issued in 1939, first year of his reign, as an encyclical commemorating the first hundred and fiftieth year of the Church in the United States, he announced:

*"9. We confess We feel a special paternal affection...for the Negro people dwelling among you..." (375)*

He directed that they enjoy the special "solicitude" of the clergy "in the field of religion and education." He also intimated that the U.S. should be led to adopt a syndicalist form of government akin to that of the Nazis and Fascists, whom he favored, in which industry would be cartelized and all labor organized. Obviously his interest in the U.S. was as much political as religious; and it fully coincided with the program for the nation to which the Society of Jesus had pledged itself at the Congress of Vienna. And equally obviously, that accounted for his special "solicitude" for the Negro in America specifically. It paralleled the hyperintensive activities of Jesuit Fr. John Lafarge, editor of the Order's weekly, ironically named *America*, of agitation for "Civil Rights" among the Negroes which has been memorialized in the Fr. John Lafarge Institute.

## ROCKEFELLER LIAISON WITH JESUITS IN CONSPIRACY: FRS. HESBURG & AVERY DULLES

The presence of Jesuit Theodore M. Hesburg, of Notre Dame, on the Board of Trustees of Rockefellers' Foundation, side by side with its chairman, John D. Rockefeller the Third, indicates the complicity and accord in their activities, including agitation and incitement of the Negroes. An additional link with the Society of Jesus is their kinsman Fr. Avery Dulles, apostate son of their agent, former Secretary of State, the late John Foster Dulles.

## JESUIT GENERAL PEDRO ARRUPE ORDERED HIS VASSALS TO INTENSIFY NEGRO AGITATION

Fr. Pedro Arrupe, General of the Society of Jesus, had the temerity and hypocrisy to openly incite American Negroes with a command to his followers issued on November 5, 1967, at the time when their rioting, arson and murder was beginning to subside. (340) In it he made reference to the Jesuit program of agitation and subversion among the American Negroes launched in connection with their pledge embodied in the Treaty of Verona to undermine our Republic and upbraided them for their failure to make good their pledge. He fulminated:

218

"...our record of service to the American Negro has fallen far short of what it should have been."
The implication of his order was that he was dissatisfied with

what they had accomplished by merely inciting the Negroes to riot, burn and murder in Watts, Cleveland, Detroit, Newark and dozens of other towns and cities.

Fr. Pedro Arrupe ordered his Jesuits to intensify further and more fruitfully their efforts among the Negroes, and, in effect, to complete their chore of destroying the country from within. He ordered Jesuit purchasing agents to discriminate against whites by joining in boycotts of businesses that "discriminate against Negroes," or in other words that do not oust white employees and replace as many of them with Negroes, whether qualified or not. He ordered the faithful to fight for more "equality" for the Negroes than for the whites.

## ROCKEFELLERS' FEDERAL ALIAS "NATIONAL" COUNCIL OF CHURCHES & ADL: ECHOES

Rockefeller domination assured the full collaboration of many other religious denominations in the Jesuit led and Rockefeller financed subversive agitation among the Negroes. The Federal Council of Churches of Christ in America, that Rockefellers directed through their kinsman, John Foster Dulles, was pronounced by the U.S. Navy to be one of the most subversive organizations in the nation. (365) The dozens of Christian denominations that adhere to it accept the teachings of its leaders that Soviet Communism is Christianity. (365)

A strange adherent, or fellow-traveller and collaborator, of the Council and equally under the conspirators' domination, is the Anti-Defamation League. The ADL is a Communist organization that controls the Jewish Bnai Brith society that is supposed to control it; and pretends to present the view of the American Jews most of whom repudiate it and its subversiveness, which fully matches that of its sister organization the FCCCA. The latter organization's treasonous attitudes became so notorious that during World War II it adopted the alias "National" Council of Churches of Christ in the U.S. These subversive organizations, as might be expected, have joined their Rockefeller sponsors in the agitation among the Negroes.

## MYRDAL'S, ROCKEFELLER-FINANCED, PRO-NEGRO COMMUNIST PROPAGANDA: AMERICAN DILEMMA

The basis for the current wave of Negro rioting and savagery was laid by Rockefellers with foundation tax exempt funds. In 1929, they imported and awarded Rockefeller Foundation Fellowships to two avowed Swedish Reds, Gunnar Myrdal and his wife Alva. (284: 155) Myrdal is Professor of "international economics," which in simple language means he is Professor of Communism at Stockholm University.

The award was made for the specific purpose of laying an Illuminist-Communist, or Marxist, pseudo-scientific foundation for more intensive agitation among the Negroes. Though a dedicated Marxist, Myrdal undertook to belie the teachings of his better-informed master, Karl Marx, that

"...niggers are an inferior breed of animals."

Marx held, however, that Negroes could be used by Communists to destroy the United States, in which he was fully in accord with his Jesuit mentors, especially Weishaupt whose Illuminist organization he joined as a student. Myrdal's propaganda was published by the conspirators under the title of "An American Dilemma." (285)

## NEGRO SLAVE TRADE WIDESPREAD. ROCKEFELLERS' ARAMCO SHIELDS IT IN SAUDI ARABIA

The are many section of the world where the Negro slave trade flourishes and the status of blacks can not compare with their advanced economic status and freedom in America. Viscount Maugham reported to the British Parliament, on July 14, 1960, as follows:

"...Saudi Arabia is the greatest slave-buying area in the world; and there are over half a million slaves there today. The main oil company operating in Saudi Arabia is the Arabian-American Oil Co. (the headquarters of which are located at 505 Park Avenue, New York City), Aramco...Aramco wields considerable influence in Washington; and the Foreign Office do not want to embarrass the Government of Britain's largest ally." (348)

Aramco is a Rockefeller-Standard Oil subsidiary that developed the rich Saudi Arabian oilfields that the conspirators acquired from the British as the price for forcing the U.S. into World War I, to finance it at the expense of the American taxpayers with the help of their "Federal" Reserve conspiracy, and to draft our Doughboys to fight it for them and purchase the oil with their blood.

## ROCKEFELLERS FINANCE MOSLEMS IN "HOLY WAR" ON CHRISTIANITY & NEGRO SLAVE TRADE

With the money paid out to the King of Saudi Arabia as royalties, the Rockefellers have financed the revival of Mohammedanism and its invariable corollary, a "Holy War" on Christianity, in which Christians and their ministers, priests and converts are frequently crucified by the "gentle, kindly Arabs." Rockefellers, who pose as "God-fearing" Christians, when they do not pose as "gods" (99), are well aware of their role in financing this war on Christianity. It was first reported publicly at a meeting of the Silver Bay Conference on Christian Missions, on July 16, 1956, sponsored by them through their "National" Council on Churches of Christ in the U.S., in a dispatch to the New York Times that was carefully hidden in its shipping news section at the back of the paper. (366:51;139:1)

The Rockefellers also sponsor and finance, through those royalties, and possibly more directly, the brutal and horribly gruesome Negro and white slave trade that has been so graphically described by Sean O'Callaghan, in his book *The Slave Trade Today. (287)* The "excuse" given for complicity in these vicious crimes by the conspirators, is that they "fear reprisals." (366) The only "reprisals" that seem to stir the Rockefeller conspirators to action are those that threaten their purses. Lives of others, humanity and principles appear to be "of no account" and "meaningless" to those sham "philanthropists."

## CHAMPIONS & AGITATORS OF NEGRO "CIVIL RIGHTS" SPURN CHALLENGE TO EMANCIPATE NEGRO SLAVES

None of the champions of so-called "Civil Rights" for Negroes, that are in reality uncivil wrongs, has raised a voice in protest against the Negro slave trade sponsored by their Rockefeller confederates. Gen Pedro Arrupe and his Jesuit priests have failed to demand deletion from the Canon law of the Church the sections that give approval and support to slavery. (127:430;548) This is understandable in view of the fact that the Order itself has enjoyed the benefits of Negro slavery in the Congo, practised by their business agency, the Societe Generale Belgique and the Union Miniere du Haut Katanga, as well as in other regions.

Neither the Rockefeller subsidized "National" Council of Churches of Christ nor its Anti-Defamation League affiliate have raised a whisper of protest against the Negro slave trade sponsored and financed by their "moneybag" bosses. No priest, minister or rabbi has made himself heard in denunciation of the Aramco slave trade or even in protest against it. There haš been no word uttered against it by either the Pope, the Archbishop of Canterbury or any Chief Rabbi that has reached the public ear with any of the intensity of all their drivel and humbug.

More strikingly still, not a single Negro "leader," or agitator, has raised a murmur in protest against the Negro slave trade, even though publicly challenged to do so by this author under circumstances that could be expected to assure a measure of success. One might well wonder if Rockefeller subsidy had some bearing on the failure of Roy Wilkins and his Urban League, the NAACP, Stokely Carmichael and his SNCC, Rap Brown, the "religious" demagogues, the irreverent Revs. Adam Clayton Powell, the defalcating Congressman, and the frankly hypocritic, Red Nobel prize winner, Martin Luther King and his Southern Christian Conference, the Black Muslims who accept as their deity Mohammed who put this stamp of approval on Negro slavery and eunuchs, (287:79;57f) its most crudely boastfully vociferous muscleman spokesman, Cassius Clay alias Muhammed Ali, the Black Power and American Mau Mau savages, and the host of elected and appointed Negro officials, including the Negro Supreme Court Justice, who might well have undertaken to act as spokesman for his race—none of them uttered a murmur on behalf of their fellow Negroes sold into slavery. It might be that they agree with the Jesuit attitude expressed by Gury, that "their enslavement is a providential act."

### AUTHOR CHALLENGED NEGROES TO REQUIRE ROCKEFELLER TO STOP S.A. NEGRO SLAVE TRADE

The arrant hypocrity of champions of so-called "Civil Rights" for Negroes was strikingly highlighted by this author in advertisements placed in several newspapers, including the Negro gazette, the New York Amsterdam News, in connection with the 1966 gubernatorial reelection campaign of Nelson Rockefeller, that challenged them to put an end to the denial of the basic civil right, that is freedom, for the Negroes sold into slavery, one of them read:

### "NEGRO SLAVES FOR SALE
in Saudi Arabia

in slave makets financed by Rockefeller-Standard Oil royalties
Read About It In

221

THE TRUTH ABOUT ROCKEFELLER,
by Emanuel M. Josephson
and
THE SLAVE TRADE TODAY,
by Sean O'Callaghan
Learn about the half million slaves in Saudi Arabia. The enslavement of Negro Moslem religious pilgrims to Mecca. The brutal
castration of Negro boys to serve as eunuchs in Moslem harems.
Action by the U.S.A. and the U.N. to stop it blocked by the Rockefeller-Standard Oil Aramco influence and pressure. Hypocritic
financing of desegregation here and of Negro slave trade in Saudi
Arabia." (256;287)

One might reasonably have expected the Negroes and the pro-
Negro agitators of all categories, Communists who have taken up the
Negro cause, to use for their subversive purposes, to challenge the
Rockefeller candidates running in elections in New York, Arkansas
and West Virginia, to put a stop to this horrible trade. One might
have expected Gunnar Myrdal and his Red pal, Chief Justice of the
Supreme Court, Earl Warren who precipitated more than a decade
of Negro savagery, Communist and criminal sabotage on the nation
by his desegregation decision that denies basic civil rights to the
nation's white folks, the right to choose their associates and environment, on the basis of Myrdal's false and subversive propaganda that
he treated as "law" as "legal precedent," to have raised, in concert,
a storm of protest and organize action to stop the slave trade. It
would have been a manifestation of their humanity and intelligence
to challenge the qualification of the Rockefeller candidates on the
basis of their support of the trade, demand that they withdraw
their support and use their immense power to put a stop to it. One
might have expected the clergy who have so violently agitated for
"Civil Rights" for Negroes only, to fulminate against the inhumanity
and "ungodliness" of the slave trade and traders. Certainly one
might have expected that the professional "bleeding hearts" and
social(ist) service parasites would have discovered a "cause" that
offered them potential of profit, in a campaign for liberating the
slaves and ending the slave trade.
NONE OF THE PROFESSIONAL PRO-NEGRO & NEGRO
AGITATORS INTERESTED IN NEGRO SLAVES.
None of the professional pro-Negro and Negro agitators and
"champions," showed the slightest interest in the Negro slaves or in
bringing pressure to bear on the Rockefeller fiendish culprits to
liberate the slaves and stop the slave trade. Instead, most ironically,
the editors of the New York Amsterdam News, on the editorial page
of the same issue in which they carried the advertisement on page
8, two pages later, on page 10, *advised their readers to give their vote
to the culprit, Rockefeller.*
CONCLUSIVE PROOF: CONSPIRATORS MOTIVE IS
SUBVERSION & ANARCHY, NOT NEGRO WELFARE
In view of these facts, can there be any question that the motive
of the conspirators and their motley agents is subversion by fostering
rampant crime and anarchy as an pretext for destroying our Republic
and establishing themselves as totalitarian dictators? Obviously, they
222

have no use for Negroes other than to further the conspiracy to take over the rule of the land as its dictators, or commissars, as their agents have in Russia, China and numerous other lands, to reduce both whites and blacks to the same level of serfdom.

This is clearly evinced by the concentrated restriction of their agitation to the U.S. where hundreds of Negro millionaires, numerous Negroes in all ranks of public office and all walks of life, attest to the fact that the American Negro is free to improve himself and rise in the world, if he desires to do so and is willing to work and apply himself; and where the Negro has attained the highest standard of living. These Negroes offer ample proof of how little truth there is in the allegations that Negroes are discriminated against unjustifiably merely because they are Negroes, are confined to ghettos, and are denied adequate education, as misrepresented by the conspirators, and their Illuminist-Communists, Gunnar Myrdals, Martin Luther Kings, National Council of Churches, priests, ministers and rabbis.

## MYRDAL GAVE "CIVIL RIGHTS" CONSPIRATORS PSEUDO-SCIENTIFIC, FALSE BASIS

The conspirators' agent, Gunnar Myrdal, like all Communist and other totalitarian propagandists, including the Jesuits and the clergy, had little regard for the truth. In his so-called "research" involved in his propaganda on the Negro, that he named *An American Dilemma*, he presented only the traditional lies that have been the stock in trade of Negro agitation since it was first launched by the Jesuits and their Communist and Abolitionist dupes. It can be summed up in the absurdly false fiction that "the Negroes have been wronged, but can do no wrong."

## THE TRUTH REGARDING THE HISTORY OF THE NEGRO IN AMERICA

The vital truth regarding the history of the Negro in America is generally the reverse of the misrepresentation by the subversive propagandists, that are useful to them because they are more palatable to the average Negro.

Few Negroes are more than five generations removed from African savagery and the cannibalism still rampant among black natives in many lands. This is illustrated by the recent reports from the Congo and other black African "republics" that have been "liberated" from colonial civilizing influences, by the conspirators with the aid of their "United" Nations and Communist aids. It is gruesomely depicted in the Reuter dispatch of August 13, 1967 (286) from Dar-es-Salaan, capital of a "liberated republic" in E. Africa. It related that native Mahola Petikite, one of the prototypes of Negroes whom unsocial "social(ist) workers" and their Gunnar Myrdals, Red propagandists who parade as "professors" of "social sciences," characterise as "gentle underprivileged victims of psychologic trauma" inflicted on them by unsympathizing civilizing discipline. The headline read:

## "KILLS AND EATS FAMILY" (286)

The report related that Petikite had naively confessed that he had developed an atavistic "irresistible desire for human flesh." That desire is so characteristic of primitive, uncivilized mankind that it has found its way, in real or symbolic form, in many religions. It is

223

the basis of "the eating of the flesh and drinking of the blood of Jesus" symbolized in Mass.

Petikite was baffled by being held prisioner for satisfying such a "natural" desire in a manner traditional among his people. He remonstrated:

"I killed and ate only members of my own family. So whom was I offending?"

## ENSLAVED NEGROES WERE SAVED FROM THE STEW KETTLES OF THEIR OWN PEOPLE

The Negroes were enslaved and sold to American and other slave traders, as they are today, by members of their own families and tribes, or by other black captors, as "weaklings." Had the traders not come to their rescue by purchasing them, they would have been slaughtered, carved and stewed or eaten in the raw, exactly as Petikite ate his own family.

Nkrumah's powerful Ashanti tribesmen who rule the first of the new "liberated" African "republics," Ghana, (that was previously known as the Gold Coast) were the most active and successful of the Negro enslavers and traders. Richard Wright, the Communist Negro author, luridly describes in his book, *Black Power*, (347) relating his experiences on his 1954 visit, the ritual currently used by the Ashantis in their sacrifice of the blood of humans to their ancestors bones that precedes their "Masses," filling their bellies with the flesh of the victims. He related:

"You see, they have a way of seizing you quickly, running your cheeks and tongue through with a long knife so that you cannot speak. They cut off your head and take your blood in a brass pan and bathe the bones of their ancestors with that blood, mumbling and praying the while..." (347:291f)

This is one of the charming Mass rituals that the ancestors of the American Negroes escaped when they were providentially and mercifully sold into slavery. In passing it is noteworthy that this slave trade continues today, most actively engaged in by the followers of the same Mohammed whom presentday Black Muslims worship as their deity, though his teachings justify and enjoin Negro enslavement. (287;79:57f)

## NEGROES SOLD INTO AMERICAN SLAVERY HAD REASON TO REGARD SELVES AS FORTUNATE

Negroes sold into slavery in America commanded an average price of $5 thousand each, in the slave markets. They were valued possessions of their purchasers. They were trained in the ways of civilization, "converted" to the acceptance of Christian mythology, cared for, pampered and not infrequently loved and bred by their masters. Only madmen and criminal kidnappers were so stupid as to abuse such valuable property as slaves. These were the instances seized upon by the Jesuits and other religious agents provocateurs and their pawns, the Abolitionist.

### JESUITS, EARLIEST NEGRO AGITATORS, CONTINUE: FR. JOHN LAFARGE INSTITUTE

The prime elements in stirring up the savagery of the Negroes in the early 19th century, as is the case today, were the Jesuits, and allied religious characters. The motive of the Jesuits, obviously, was not the desire to develop a source of income by "saving the souls" of the penniless blacks. Their objective was stirring up riots, rebellion and civil war that would enable their Society of Jesus to destroy our Republic as it had pledged to do at the Congress of Vienna, (72) as the price for reestablishment of their Order that had been abolished four decades earlier by the Pope Clement XIV, in his breve *Dominus AC Redemptor,* as immoral and a menace to the faith and the Church.

This purpose was made doubly clear by the treacherous practise of the Jesuits of establishing schools for the education of the children of the plantation owners, teaching them to hold the Negroes in subjection and slavery, while agitating revolt and freedom among the slaves. One of the earliest Negro slave revolts instigated by the Jesuits, was that in Charleston, S.C., led by a revolting Negro named Denmark Vesey, in 1822, shortly after the missionary funds of the St. Leopold Society were made available for their subversive purposes. (72)

The continuing, presentday dedication of the Jesuits to subversive agitation among the Negroes, paralleling that of their Communist pawns, as enjoined on them by the present Black Pope, their General Pedro Arrupe, is attested to by their establishing the *Fr. John Lafarge Institute,* with headquarters in the office building of their publication, at 106 W. 56 St. New York City, ironically named *America,* after the Republic they aim to destroy. The Institute is a memorial to the agitation among the Negroes by its editor during the first half of the century, Fr. John Lafarge. (273;367) Fr. Ryan, editor of America, informed this author that the Institute holds forums attended by Jesuit, Communist and Negro "Civil Rights" agitators in true "ecumenical" dialogue. (368)

## TRUE SIGNIFICANCE OF NEGRO "CIVIL RIGHTS" & DESEGREGATION RIOTING

Unfortunately, for themselves, far too large a proportion of the Negroes have not undertake to improve and advance themselves much beyond an attentuated form of their African mental and physical lethargy and savagery. This is clearly evident in their current riots, slaughter and arson, most of the victims of which are their fellow Negroes. One can sense that if they were hungry, they also would not hesitate to carve and eat their fellow man.

The ascendency of the primitive instincts of the savage in them is manifest at every turn. The instinct to seize by force what they desire, that characterizes savages, and in lesser degree infants and immature persons, is obvious in the brazen looting that is the practise of every Negro mob. This is the inner significance for the Negroes of the so-called "Civil Rights" and "Black Power" agitation and rioting: it is for them an open sesame for attaining by whatever crime they choose the things that they want but do not want to work or lack the mental capacity to attain. The practise of Negro "leaders" and public officials and of too many white officials of justifying and thereby encouraging criminal acts on the basis of alleged "deprivation" makes it clear that they are of the same mind.

## TRUE SIGNIFICANCE OF "DESEGREGATION" AGITATION

Since the large semi-savage element among the Negroes are indiscriminate in choice of victims, it is understandable that the better elements among them do not want to associate with Negroes. They seek however, to deny white folks the choice of associates that they demand for themselves; and to force them to associate with the very Negroes whom they themselves scorn and spurn. Recently some of the better elements among the Negroes, either as a matter of choice and benefits or of coercion and intimidation, have given their support to the *Black Power* rabble. Those among them occupying public office are clearly betraying public trust when they do so.

## LARGE ELEMENTS AMONG NEGROES DELIBERATELY CONVERT THEIR ENVIRONS INTO SLUMS

The African psychology of many Negroes accounts for their conversion of their environments into slums and consequent segregation. It makes them prone to the full range of vices, including drug addiction and preying on one another. Superstition makes them ready victims of religious racketeers, and peddlers of gods and voodooism. And that accounts, in part, for the support that their agitation has had from other religious leaders than the Jesuits. "Thar is money in them thar blacks" opine the vendors of any and all gods. It appears to be a matter of indifference to which "Heaven" they buy tickets. Judging by the number of Negroes who have abandoned Christianity for Mohammedanism, in the Black Muslim movement, the choice of a deity of many of them is determined largely by what they think they can get out of it.

Sloth makes many of them untidy and filthy in their personal and environmental hygiene. Many of them seem to lack the animal instinct of avoiding fouling their own nests; and they scatter filth about them, destroy their own homes as effectively as do the arsonists among them with their Molotov cocktails. This is further aggavated by the practises of dope addicts among them of ripping out plumbing and fixtures from their homes to sell them to junkmen to obtain money for the purchase of dope. In short, they deliberately convert any environment in which they are placed into slums. As a consequence, landlords are compelled to raise their rent to the point that equals 100% of the value of the building in a year. Landlords, in some instances, consider themselves lucky if their buildings survive more than a year of this class of Negro tenancy.

The inferior housing conditions of Negroes of which the conspirators and their agents and agitators make a "desegregation" issue, is created in most instances, by themselves. No landlord is so shortsighted as to hasten the destruction of his own building and the wiping out of his own investment, under ordinary circumstances. It is the practise of politicians, under direction of the conspirators, to blame landlords for slum conditions over which they have no control, because they are a small minority as compared with tenants who have more votes; and make them whipping boys while exonerating destruction by tenants. Rent control, which is progressive confiscation of property and tenant subsidy, aggravates matters. Public housing projects supposed to eliminate slums, in spite of vigilant policing, often have been converted instantly into vile slums when occupied by the same element of the Negroes.

## MYRDAL SUPPRESSED FACTS REGARDING NEGRO "RECONSTRUCTION ERA" ABUSE OF WHITES

Entirely omitted in Myrdal's Red propaganda is the brutal abuse of Southern whites by some Negroes incited by insane Congressman Thaddeus Stevens, his Negress wife and carpetbaggers, in the era following the Civil War that is ironically called the "Reconstruction Era." In some sections of the South the whites were denied franchise, and only Negroes and carpetbaggers were allowed to hold public office. White folks, other than carpetbaggers and Union soldiers assigned to protect them, were mistreated and brutally assaulted. White women were raped by Negroes with complete impunity, until the Klu Klux Klan was organized as a necessity, to terrorize the savage Negroes with their own brand of terrorism. That is the only language that many savage Negroes did and do understand.

The era proved, as does the current "Civil Rights" anarchy, how thin is the veneer of civilization of too many Negroes, what a profit-seeking sham is their religiousity, and how readily even the better elements among them are cowed into following the leadership of the more violent, vicious and criminal among them. When given the opportunity, a majority of Negroes prove themselves as incapable of ruling themselves and others as are their African kinsmen. These facts are dishonestly omitted from Myrdal's propaganda, exactly as they are omitted from the textbooks of their history that Negroes now demand be used in our classrooms.

## TRUE AMERICAN NEGRO BELIES ALLEGED "ABUSE" OF NEGROES.

An outstanding Negro and American of the type that the black rabble never accept as their leader, Rev. E. F. Yearling, has truthfully attacked the "Civil Rights" agitation as a Communist-directed plot. He evidently is unaware of the Jesuit origin of both. He has patriotically undertaken a campaign to awaken the Negroes to the use being made of them by the conspirators. It is certainly predictable that he will never receive a Nobel prize for his efforts. (291)

## COMMUNISTS CLAIM CIVIL WAR & "RECONSTRUCTION ERA" AS THEIR "VICTORY"

The Communist fully confirm Rev. Yearling's charges. They vociferously campaigned for the celebration of the Civil War Centennial; and claimed it and the "Reconstruction Era" that followed as their "victories." To signalize those "victories" the Party's International Publishers put out a series of biographies of their members involved in precipitating and waging the Civil War and in directing the "Reconstruction."

One of the most interesting of the biographies is that of *Joseph Weydemeyer*, reputed ancestor of Gen. Wedemeyer, who was a German Communist military officer and journalist associate of Karl Marx. After the failure of the 1848 revolution in Germany, he went underground for a time and then migrated to the U.S. at the instance of Karl Marx, to carry on Communist propaganda with the cooperation of Charles A. Dana, New York publisher of the Tribune. (369:28) He played an active role in the agitation that precipitated the Civil War and rose to the rank of general in the Union Army. In 1944, a Liberty ship was named in his honer.

## SUBVERSIVE WHITE CLERGY, & BLACK & WHITE
## OFFICIALS INCITE NEGROES.

A group of subversive organizations of white clergymen, including The Protestant Council of New York, the U.S. Catholic Conference and the Synagogue Council of America, issued a 1967 Labor Day release alleging that there have been "wrongs done the Negroes," that they implied justified the savagery of their rioting. The unprincipled clergy appear to be more interested in lining their purses with the coins of the gullible and superstitious Negroes, the Sammy Davises and others, than they are in the truth and the preservation of law and order, and our Republic. (292) Their statements were as openly incitations and invitations to the Negroes to continue their rioting, as have been the statements of white and black public officials, including New York's Mayor Lindsay at the time of his appointment to "investigate" the riots, and later in the report of the Committee.

## VENGEFUL, CONCEITED JEWISH RABBIS ARE NOW
## CONSPIRATORS' STUPIDEST AGENTS

Probably the most stupid pawns of the conspirators in the "Civil Rights" and "desegregation" agitation that besets the nation, are the Jewish rabbis, their misled, sheep-like followers, and the violently Red Anti-Defamation League, that is controlled by the conspirators and in turn controls for them its supposed mother organization, Bnai Brith. The ADL is, in effect, an affiliate of Rockefellers' Council of Churches, and like it, a subsidiary of the Communist Party, that has treacherously usurped the role of spokesmen of the Jews to serve the interests of the conspirators.

A large proportion of American Jews, as a consequence, have been duped into supporting the "Black Power" agitators, in retaliation for the discrimination practised against themselves, under the misrepresentation that the elimination of the supposedly unjustifiable discrimination against certain classes of Negroes will, in turn, break down the barriers against themselves. This basely motivated revenge, fortunately, has backfired in the "Black Power" situation exactly as the support of Communism by the same stupid Jewish element has backfired in the Soviet. The savage element among the Negroes has turned on its Jewish supporters with hate and fury. Mayhap this paranoid element, who fancy themselves "chosen people" and inordinately smart, will learn their lesson.

## JESUITS ARE STILL RINGLEADERS IN THE CONSTANT
## AGITATION AMONG NEGROES.

Burke McCarty points out in her *Suppressed Truth About The Assassination Of Abraham Lincoln:*

> "Disruption has always been the first motive of the Jesuits and black slavery was the rock upon which they planned to rend this government. There was no other principle or ethics involved, never is, so far as Jesuitism goes, except the fundamental principle of the divine right to rule of the popes of Rome." (72:71)

That this is still true, is demonstrated by the current role of the Church in the so-called "Negro Revolution" that they continue to promote and agitate with the collaboration of the Communist clergy of

228

other denominations. This is manifest in the participation of priests and nuns in the bacchanalian Selma march; in the activities of such priests as Fr. Groppi inciting Negroes to riot; in the excommunication of such powerful politician as Louisiana's Leander Perez because of his justified opposition to the horrors of school desegregation. How little "principle" is involved in these stands of the Church, other than the determined purpose to undermine and take over our Republic, is revealed with startling clarity by the failure of either Jesuits or Church to withdraw its Canon-dictated support of slavery. Equally telling is the revival of the criminal agitation of the "Reconstruction Era" and the "religious" brand of totalitarianism by the first President of the faith, by Pres. John F. Kennedy and his clan.

"BLACK POWER": ITS TRUE MEANING & SIGNIFICANCE

There is a measure of irony in the adoption of the title *Black Power*, as the name for their political organization. Richard Wright used it as the title for a book that relates his findings that the only basis he could find in the Gold Coast(Ghana) for self government was the savagery of Negro tribes. (347) He depicted the lust for human blood and flesh of the natives; and clearly indicated how fortunate were the American Negroes to escape the stew kettles of their black brethren by being sold into slavery. The "Black Power" and American Mau Mau groups seek to bring about an atavistic reversion to savagery among the American Negroes, primarily directed against white folks, to avenge the mythical "wrongs" done their ancestors.

This planned atavism of Negroes, and the use made of them by the conspirators, has highly dangerous consequences for both whites and blacks, and for the nation. It means the conversion of a large proportion of the Negroes into a privileged criminal class, for whom a black skin means a perfect defense for any crime, however heinous. It endangers both national and personal security for both whites and black.

It also threatens to require eliminating Negroes from an ever widening field for employment in hospitals and nursing homes. The employment of such Negroes in the care of helpless persons, especially white, in positions that enable them to vent their savagely sadistic and venomous, though falsely rooted, hatred whipped up by the conspirators and the clergy, is at times, dreadful to behold. How many of the innocent victims lose their lives, as a consequence, can only be surmised; and evaluated as the "blessings" of the rabbis, ministers and priests involved. They have created on the basis of deliberately false representations bolstered by "religious" nonsense and abacadabra and their support of the more noisome, unscrupulous and criminal elements among the Negroes, an intense hatred directed against dissenting blacks and all white folk. So intense is their animosity and hatred that the only possible solution may be their elimination from communities, and as Abraham Lincoln foresaw, from the country.

PRES. KENNEDY MADE JESUIT CONSPIRACY THE
"POLICY" OF HIS ADMINISTRATION

Pres. Kennedy unified the groups adhering to the Jesuit 1822 plot to use the Negroes to destroy our Republic. (72) He supplemented the "Civil Rights" program that has been launched by the conspirators during the Administration of their pawn, Pres. Eisenhower, with his OEO "Poverty Program," at the head of which he placed his kinsman Shriver. It was designed to bribe the worst and most numerous Negroes to vote for him, and as its name indicates, to impoverish provident, honest taxpaying elements in the community, in the effort to reduce them to levels of existence below that of the largely Negro beneficiaries of the program.

## CONGRESS PROVED: "POVERTY PROGRAM" FINANCES RIOTS & CIVIL & CRIMINAL DISORDERS

Hearings held by Senate Committee On Government Operations subcommittee disclosed in 1967 (346) that tax funds appropriated for the Kennedy-Shriver "Poverty Program" pour very largely, and sometimes almost exclusively, into the pockets of Negro criminals and their organizations. This is part of the conspirators' program to gain Negro votes to keep themselves in power, and to assure black co-operation in a breakdown of law and order, anarchy and overturning of our government to facilitate their takeover as our dictators. The report is full of evidence of instigation and financing of nationwide riots and civil and criminal disorders by leaders and employees of the program, at the expense of the taxpayers. A Chicago project of the program was found to employ, at salaries ranging from five to six thousand dollars, exclusively Negro felons under indictment or parole for crimes ranging from arson and murder to rape. (346) One of the ugliest aspects of the conspiracy is the use of subversives including Rev. Martin Luther King, Rev. Adam C. Powell, Rap Brown, Stokely Carmichael, Alger Hiss and Lauchlin Currie, and others of the breed, in all media of mass communications, including schools and colleges, to serve as "models" and to "inspire" youngsters.

A thorough investigation reveals that the Kennedys, and more particularly Bobby Kennedy, have merged the ugliest aspects of the conspirators' use of the Negroes with those of the Church, the Jesuits and their Communist puppets, in their "New Frontier" Poverty Program. They have rapidly developed it into a holocaust of violent rioting, arson and murder that undermines our Republic and threatens its survival. Supposedly informed commentators such as CFR member David Lawrence, has cautiously advanced the idea that there is a planned conspiracy behind the outbreak of riots in 110 cities across the country. The Federal authorities involved falsely deny this obvious fact, in an effort to cover up their complicity. Lawrence intimates, however, that there is reason to believe that:

> "...agents of subversion have been busily engaged in supplying guns and giving instruction on how to make 'Motolov cocktails'." (414)

He suggested that the Negro "revolution" is part of a guerrilla war being waged by the conspirators on the nation, using the Negroes as their pawns.

A visit to Pres. Kennedy's Poverty Program project, *Mobilization For Youth* in New York City, disclosed that the conspirators brazenly have given it a name that accurately describes its function and activities. It is an agency for military mobilization and training of Negro youths, most of them on Relief, for waging guerilla warfare on the nation, and for breeding hatred of white folks. The youngsters are taught to support Rev. King's "non-violent Negro revolution" while being trained by Red Negro instructors to stage riots, to make "Molotov cocktails" and use them for arson, divert and attack the police, and when caught to allege "police brutality," support their "social(ist) service" accomplices with pleas of mercy on the allegations of "underprivilege," and avow their support of "nonviolence." They are also instructed to join agitation for support of local control of education for the purpose of converting the schools to the same uses. While they are undergoing training, and for complicity in rioting, they are paid wages out of the Poverty Program funds provided by the taxpayers.

## BOOBY KENNEDY & REV. KING JOINED TO CARRY OUT
## PLAN OF COMMUNISTS

Sen. Robert F. Kennedy's plan for Negro agitation aimed to carry out strategy that was published in the February 1968 special issue of *Political Affairs*, the theoretic strategy journal of the U.S. Communist Party. In the article *"The Battle For Black Liberation"* there is laid down the Party's program for creation of a new "front" in American politics, the "Peoples' Party." It proclaimed, one month in advance, the false allegation of the President's Advisory Commission On Civil Disorders, headed by New York's Red Mayor Lindsay among others, that "white racism" is responssible for the riots which they precipitate.

The Party's journal disclosed that the Communist-planned new "Peoples' Party" is identical with that which was being negotiated by Sen. Kennedy with "Rev." Martin Luther King before his assassination, that may have played a role in it. The scheme, in which Kennedy and King followed the Communist Party line. is to build the new "Peoples' Party" front by a coalition of anti-war, Negro, student, "Civil Rights" and "Poverty Program' agents of the conspirators. (15)

## WATERBURY'S FEAR OF DESTRUCTION BY
## NEGRO-SET CONFLAGRATION

Following an alerting editorial by William Loeb in the *Connecticut Sunday Herald* of February 4, 1968 and inspired "predictions" of the burning down of Detroit and Waterbury in the course of the year, the citizens of the latter town have become highly alarmed over a number of local incidents about April 12, 1968. The first was the purchase by Negroes from a local bottling plant of numerous Coca Cola bottles of the type recommended for use by the conspirators in the manufacture of "Molotov cocktails." The second was the clamping down by the local police on the purchase of guns and ammunition by white folks while Negroes were being supplied with them from outside the town. They fear that the Negroes will execute literally the teaching of Jesus:

"I come to send fire on earth..." (Luke: 12:49)

## "REV." KING'S ASSASSINATION IS WARNING TO
## BLACK & WHITE AGITATORS

"Rev." Martin Luther King was a Negro, rabble rousing agent of the conspirators. His "mission" was to blackmail and loot the responsible elements of the nation, in collaboration with the conspirators, under the customary cover of "religion" and champion-

231

ing the mythical cause of the supposedly "wronged" and "abused" improvident elements among the Negroes. On behalf of the conspirators he set the goal of his blackmail and looting of the nation at a "modest" $100 billion a year. Dissembling his racketeering as "non-violence," he stirred up among his black rabble followers rioting, looting, arson, rape and murder wherever he went. He was closely identified and collaborated with the Communist and other subversive agents of the conspirators; and the effectiveness of his efforts on their behalf were materially enhanced by their arrangement to have him granted a Nobel Prize with unlimited access to all their media of mass communication to further their subversive goals.

Subversive agitator King's assassination may prove a blessing in disguise for the conspirators, his followers and the nation, if it alerts them to certain facts, and drives them home. There must be an end to the un-Constitutional denial of human rights to white folks and the better elements among the Negroes, and the discrimination against them in favor of the improvident, incompetent, scantily civilized and semi-savage elements among the blacks. There must be an end to maintaining them on Relief, in idleness and relative luxury at the expense of the more provident elements, white and black, to engage in vice, unlimited procreation and "population" explosion, thievery, arson, rape, murder, genocide, treason and other crimes. There must be an end to the coddling of Negro incompetents and misfits by the conspirators and their "social(ist) service" parasites who pamper their inferiority complex about being black by making the color of their skins a perfect defense for any crime, however heinous. There must be an end to the imposition on the nation of so-called "Civil Rights" that are un-Constitutional un-civil wrongs, and constitute the denial of basic human rights such as choice of associates and neighbors, to the white folk. There must be an end to ousting of white employees who have proved their competence, in response to blackmailing by Negroes supported by the discriminatory and wholly un-Constitutional laws placed on our statute books by the unscrupulous, vote-seeking politicians often at the instance of the conspirators.

Rabble rouser King is a victim of the violence tinted with hate that he and his ilk have stirred up in the nation by their Red, subversive activities, and unbridled crime colored by treason. His death should serve as a warning that there are still at hand red-blooded Americans who will take the law into their own hands if the government and the courts prove to be too cowardly and dishonest to uphold the rights of everyone without regard to politically motivated distortion and violations of justice and the law. King would still be alive, but behind bars, together with numerous clerical and lay treasonous collaborators and venal vote-seeking politicians, if our government officials were not derelict in enforcement of the law which clearly defines conspiracy, incitement to blackmail, theft, burglary, arson, rape, murder, genocide and treason as felonies, and dictates penalties of incarceration and/or execution. The officials who fail to enforce the laws are accomplices in these crimes. They must be inpeached, removed from office and meted out the punishment for them dictated by the law. This penalty has been stiffened by the Civil Rights Bill signed on April 12, 1968 by Pres. Johnson.

Intelligent elements in the nation are shocked, disgusted and incensed by the insincere sham of mourning for the death of this rabble rouser who used religion as a cloak for his subversive and criminal activities. Those public officials who have ordered flying of flags at half mast and manifestations other than celebration of riddance of the nation of him, clearly reveal themselves as his sympathizers and collaborators. For the preservation of our Republic and to avert its overthrow by the conspirators and its replacement by them with a totalitarian dictatorship, we must eliminate them and all other public officials who put maintaining themselves in public office above maintaining law order. Mayors like Lindsay who proclaim over all media of mass communication their "fear," or wish, that some incident such as this may stir mobs to violence and crime are deliberately inciting them. Their subsequent failure to provide adequate police protection, as in the case of the Harlem riots celebrating King's assassination, proves malevolent intent. Their obvious collaboration with the conspirators should forever eliminate them from public office, no matter how high and exalted their positions. Only by such rigid enforcement of the law and order can there be any hope of avoiding a totalitarian takeover of our Republic.

Viewing the honoring in death and memorializing of this Red rabble rouser, one begins to wonder if our political and religious leaders have gone so far down the path to Communism that we may expect to witness the spectacle of our flags at half mast in mourning for a Khrushchev or Kosygin. And in view of the absurd comparison by Pope Paul VI of the justified assassination of King with the crucifixion of Jesus, one begins to recognize that his campaign of "non violent" incitement to rioting, arson, rape and murder served the interests of more than one group of conspirators.

## KENNEDY REPUDIATED DECLARATION OF INDEPENDENCE: ADVOCATED "INTERPENDENCE"

The intent to betray our Republic to an overriding loyalty to his faith emerged in Pres. Kennedy's July 4, 1962 address in Independence Hall that he specifically directed to Archbishop John Krol. (179) He scoffed at the Declaration of Independence and alleged that the Constitution "stressed *not Independence but Interdependence.*" He proclaimed his Jesuit inspired, treasonous "internationalist" *Declaration of Interdependence* on Vatican and Europe:

"... I will say here and now, on this Day of Independence, that the United States will be ready for a *Declaration of Interdependence*, that we will be ready to discuss with a United Europe...

"And for the support of this declaration, with a firm reliance on the protection of Divine Providence, we mutually pledge to each other our Lives, our Fortunes and our sacred Honor."

Pres. Kennedy therein set the clock back to the time when Pope Innocent III ordered nullification of the Magna Carta because, as the stated it, (211) it violates the prerogatives of the Church to

233

grant rights to anyone. Kennedy's *Declaration* obviously implied rejection of both the Constitution and the Bill of Rights.

Kennedy's religiously motivated subversive, reactionary attitude gives added significance to the relegation of the Magna Carta Memorial to an almost unreachable spot at Runnymede; whereas Queen Elizabeth violated the British Constitution by granting the larger and more prominent portion of the Runnymede field to the United States for a grandiose memorial to the conspirators' pawn, Pres. John F. Kennedy and his *Declaration* that nullifies the Magna Carta, the Constitution and the Bill of Rights, and proclaims the ascendency of the Nazarene totalitarianism of the Church.

## KENNEDY MYTH IS PROPAGATED TO MASK TREACHERY
### WITH PRETENDED "GREATNESS"

For the purpose of perpetuating the Kennedy Dynasty and the grip of the Jesuits on the White House, an army of pressagents employed by the Kennedys themselves, as well as those of the Democratic Party and of the Church, have undertaken to "immortalize" him and his betrayals as "great." Some have even suggested that Pres. Kennedy be elevated to sainthood.

Stewart Alsop, in an article in the Saturday Evening Post entitled *"Was John F. Kennedy A Great Man?"* mockingly cites as his claims to "greatness" the treacheries and betrayals above-cited, his fortunate inability to induce Congress to pass any part of his program, and his setting of male hair styles by the manner in which he combed his hair. (218:16)

In the same mocking spirit and in the same issue of the Saturday Evening Post, Tom Wolfe, in an article entitled *the courts must curb culture*, stresses another disservice rendered our land in copying the other autocrats of history (his master, Nelson Rockefeller, Hitler and the Nazis, Stalin and the Communists, the Medicis, and numerous others) in beating the drums for "culture." He cites the "explosion of culture" at the Kennedy inauguration at which Cardinal Cushing, a Protestant minister and a rabbi were followed by senile poetaster Robert Frost pathetically lamely reading one of his effusions representative of the "Religion of Culture" that the Kennedys have inflicted on the nation. It was characterized by the courting of such characters as Carl Sandburg, of Pablo Casals and other Communists and so-called "Liberals," invited as honored guests at the White House, to use it for the dissemination of their subversions; by the government subsidy throughout the nation of centers for the dissemination, at public expense, of these subversions, that was culminated by the appointment Mayor Lindsay, of a Commissioner of Culture; by the fostering of a "national" theatre for dissemination of subversion by such crimson propaganda plays as *"Goodbye My Fancy"* and the vile, pathologic filth of Tennessee Williams; by the fostering of juvenile delinquency and criminality by personal example on an even more intensive scale than have the Rockefeller bogus "philanthropies;" by fostering the "sloppy slut" attire modelled after that which the Soviets wear as a matter of necessity, African coiffures, African savage dances and pool dunkings in full attire.

Summed up briefly, shanty Irish graduated to "lace curtain" Irish, has supplemented the Rockefeller "educational" subversion, by converting "culture" to rhyme with "manure." And our two aspiring dynasty, Kennedys and Rockefellers, have combined to rob Americans of their native intelligence and loyalty, and to make us a nation of queers, phonies, "beatniks," hippies, and poseurs. They seek not to raise the level of the Africans, but to reduce us all to the same level of drug intoxication, imbecility and savagery. Rightly, Tom Wolfe recommends that our Supreme Court, if it ever departs from its subversiveness, should declare the expenditure of public funds on this bogus "culture," un-Constitutional, and undo these and the other evils done by the dynasties.

Then there may be ended the nauseating campaign of the Kennedy clan and their pressagents, allies and affiliates to glorify their "martyr" by naming everything except lavatories after him, and setting up "shrines" to him to promote the public careers of their clan and dynasty. And there will be a stop to the portrayal of the most treacherous acts of their "hero" by hired, licensed, censored and taxed pressagent biographers, as "noble acts" that should serve as "inspirations" and models in future betrayals of the nation.

## DYNASTIC DISSENSION: ASSASSINATION A LA BORGIAS

It is not merely the ostentatious fostering of "culture," reminiscent of the earlier totalitarian dynasties of the Borgias and the Medicis, that is observable in the current scene. The Kennedy assassination and its utilization by his would-be heirs and successors partakes of some of the same odor.

Two weeks prior to Pres. Kennedy's assassination, the Secret Service, the FBI, the New York City Police Commissioner and other Federal and local agencies had been alerted to a threat to the life of the President. This is made clear by the extreme security vigilance surrounding the President when he visited New York on the 9th of November, 1963. This was the day following the announcement by Gov. Nelson Rockefeller that he was going to seek the Republican nomination for President.

The announced purpose of President Kennedy's visit to New York was to give a talk before the Protestant Council of New York, a Rockefeller subsidized organization, at the Hilton (Rockefeller) Hotel. Following his usual practise, Pres. Kennedy came to New York to spend the night at his suite at the Carlyle Hotel, at Madison Avenue and 76th Street, in the type of orgiastic "partying" to which he was addicted. The liquor concession at the hotel is still owned by the Kennedys; and it is operated by them in the bartending tradition of that clan, as are the other activities.

The extremely peculiar circumstances surrounding this New York visit of Pres. Kennedy were mentioned by only one newspaper, the Sunday News of November 10, 1963. Under the headline *JFK So Closely Guarded Only A "Why" Gets Through*, Joseph Cassidy and Lester Abelman announced that the President was cloaked "in the tightest security vigilance to enfold a President on a New York visit in recent years..." They related that he was "rigidly shielded from public approach during all his appearances." Even the reporters were barred from approaching him. And they were denied any explanation for the "beefed-up Secret Service vigilance." Deputy Police Commissioner Arm acknowledged, according to the report:

"It was added vigilance, but I don't think it should have included the press." The report noted that the President's motorcade to the airfield on his departure on Saturday, November 9th, "was led by a 35-man police motorcycle escort." (216)

Attorney General Robert F. Kennedy, boss of the FBI, and through his brother, of the Secret Service, could not help but be aware of the fears of his subordinates in those agencies for the life of his brother that had led to the adoption of those extreme precautions including a bullet-proof, bubble-topped car. This throws a sinister light on his subsequent actions.

There can be no question that Robert was aware of the notice given by Pres. Kennedy to Vice President Johnson that because of the notorious activities of his associates, Jenkins, Estes and Baker, he would be dropped in 1964, as Vice-Presidential candidate from the Democratic ticket. Former Vice President Nixon had promptly made the story public, when he visited Dallas, Texas, on the following day.

The wave of hatred of the New Frontier and of President Kennedy in Vice-President Johnson's bailiwick, Texas, ran high and was notorious. The Vice-President undertook to induce Pres. Kennedy to visit Texas in the third week of November, and begin his Presidential reelection campaign in an effort to charm and win over the natives. His effort was without success the press reported until he enlisted the help of brother, Robert Kennedy, in inducing the President to make an immediate visit to Texas.

Robert must have overcome his brother's objection that it is one of the worst mistakes, in politics, for an office-seeker, especially an incumbent, to begin to campaign far ahead of the election. He probably overcame the President's fear of violence of the natives that had been visited on another standard-bearer of the "New Frontier," Adlai Stevenson, in Dallas the very morning of the projected visit. It was brother, Bobby, according to the press, who supported the Vice-President's efforts and finally prevailed upon his brother to invade the intensely hostile Texas scene.

The violent attitude of Texans toward President Kennedy and his Administration were common knowledge and amply proved. Equally common was the knowledge of the especially violent character of the Vice-President's Texas henchmen and the trail of crimes with which they had marked his career. (217) Obviously the rigid and extreme security precautions adopted on the President's New York visit, less than two weeks earlier, were in order. In view of the assault on Adlai Stevenson, on the same morning, the minimal precaution that was justified was the normal security measure when the President slowly parades through a town: placing him in a bullet-proof, bubble-top car. (It is most curious that Johnson, who always sought to ride in the same vehicle as Kennedy, chose on that day to ride in the sixth car behind him.) (338) Had this been done, President Kennedy would have escaped death during the parade.

*No valid explanation has ever been sought, or offered, for the discarding by Bobby's FBI or the Secret Service, of this ordinary, routine precaution for the security of the President. Bobby's widely advertised concern for his brother's widow, contrasted sharply with his lack of concern for the security of his brother.*

One finds oneself wondering if the spirit of rivalry between the

Kennedy brothers may have been factor in Bobby inducing the President to visit Texas at the time. It has been widely reported that there was intense rivalry between the Kennedy boys, in spite of their uniting in a common cause. There can be no question that President Kennedy owed his election to the shrewd and unscrupulous politicking of his brother Bobby. It is reported that Bobby demanded and fought to be given the post of Attorney General, for which he was completely unqualified because of lack of experience. The appointment and other appointments of members of the family and their entourage present the ugly picture of nepotism that characterizes the Kennedy Dynasty as it does the Rockefeller Dynasty. It presents the picture of the planned establishment of an absolute American monarchy a la Nickerson, detailed in his book *The American Rich.* (100)

## MORE "MODEST" THAT ROCKEFELLERS, KENNEDYS AIM TO BE SAINTS, NOT GODS

In one respect, the Kennedy Dynasty aspiration is more "modest" than that expressed by John D. Rockefeller the Second. The Kennedys merely aspire to sainthood, as is indicated by an "inspired" article in the World Telegram & Sun of December 24, 1964, reading as follows:

"UNION LEADER URGES KENNEDY SAINTHOOD,,

"A union leader suggests that President Kennedy be elevated to sainthood. The idea was put forth in an editorial in a union publication by Patrick E. Gorman, secretary-treasurer of the Amalgamated Meat Cutters & Butcher Workmen. 'President Kennedy, in our opinion, was a martyr to the same extent as St Peter who died for his faith,' Gorman wrote. He said Kennedy 'performed miracle after miracle...He washed from the face of the land...the ugly image of religious intolerance. *God walked with Him...*" (341)

There can be no question that Pres. Kennedy performed "miracles," if bowing to Khrushchev at Vienna, delivery of Cuba to the Soviets as a missile base, trapping our GIs in Vietnam, duping the public, and spurning the Declaration of Independence in Independence Hall and getting away with it, are "miracles." And since he did "walk with Rockefeller," it might be alleged that "God walked with Him."

## ARE KENNEDYS CATHOLIC, NAZARENE, ROCKEFELLER OR MARXIST REDS?

Pres. Kennedy's record presents a puzzling picture to the searcher for his mental attitude. Though Catholic by birth, he was by education and training, less inclined to the Church and its Nazarenism than he was to the Rockefeller brand of Marxism, and to Sovietism. He obtained his education at two Rockefeller subsidized, violently Red institutions, after a three months stay at Princeton University in 1937, Harvard University and the London School of Economics and Political Science. At the latter, he sat at the feet of the more or less frankly Communist, so-called "Fabian," propagandists, Harold Laski and John Maynard Keynes.

As Senator, he emulated his father in his service to the Rockefeller interests. Joseph Kennedy served, in the capacity of head of the SEC, as agent of the conspirators in swindling the public out of tens of billions of dollars investments in utilities and railroads (7:180f); and as Ambassador to St. James, their liquor interests.

The Kennedys, father and sons, joined Cardinal Spellman, as will be related, in putting pressure on the Eisenhower regime to protect the Vietnamese Catholics who had been made refugees from persecution by irate Bhuddists as a result of the driving out of the French from Indo-China by the conspirators bent on seizing for themselves its huge oil reserves. The Church, and in particular the Jesuit Order, sustained heavy losses as a result of the conspirators' success in driving the French (and incidentally the Church) out of Algeria, assisted by Sen. Kennedy's demand made, on their behalf on the floor of the Senate, that the French forthwith withdraw from that country after the discovery of oil there. As a result, the Catholic and other French have been subjected to persecution and confiscation of their wealth there.

Following his inauguration as President, Kennedy's first act was to appoint to his Cabinet a clutch of Rockefeller "Liberals" or Reds. And his next move was to hustle to Vienna for the purpose of rendering homage to the conspirator's Soviet agent, Khrushchev. This he followed up by delivering Cuba to the Soviets as a missile base, while belatedly pretending to block its takeover. Thanks to the treachery involved in blocking Castro's overthrow attempt in the Bay of Pigs incident, Cuba remains a Soviet missile base at our very shore, while lying pressagents and propagandists of the conspirators heaped praise and laurels on the President for his supposed "defeat" of the Soviets.

In Vietnam he made the U.S. the laughing stock of Asia and the world by sending our GIs into a trap in which they are completely surrounded by the Communist population of that pestilential land, to fall victims of diseases (that they will bring back to plague our land) and to die at the hands of our treacherous native "allies." This treason was compounded by the felony of the assassination of the selfsame Diem whom they had placed in power and discarded when he no longer served the conspirators' purposes. Our betrayal was effected under the pretense of "blocking" the spread of Communism in Asia, while here in the U.S., the conspirators foster Communism and make the White House the haven of every Communist agitator.

Pause for thought as to the religious aspect of the Vietnam situation, and the Communist, is given by the contradictory attitude taken by Pope Paul VI and his insistent peace propaganda and calls for Xmas truces on the one hand, and on the other hand, the insistence on victory by Cardinal Spellman and by Saigon Catholics. (231) The Xmas and other truces have always been used by the Communists for shipments of arms and munitions as well as reinforcements of their armed forces in South Vietnam; and in the slaughter of our troops. Tompkins has reported in his *Italy Betrayed*, that the Vatican was antagonistic to ourselves and our allies in World War II. (232) That attitude is fully compatible with the pledge exacted of the Jesuits. (72) But it is incredible that any one of the faith would favor the slaughter of the Catholic refugees in Vietnam that would certainly follow the withdrawal of our troops there, as demanded by Pope Paul. The courting of the conspirators' Communist partners

238

by the Pope and by "beatnik" Bobby Kennedy who was largely responsible for our involment in Vietnam, presents a picture of almost incredible treachery.

## BOBBY KENNEDY DUPES HIS BOBBY-SOX, BEATNIK & RED FOLLOWERS ON VIETNAM WAR

Whtever may have been Bobby's role, he made good political use of the sympathy aroused by his brother's assassination. Rejected as running-mate by Pres. Johnson in the 1964 campaign, Bobby scorned and flaunted the spirit of the Constitution regarding popular representation. He advanced the "rotten borough" system which has been discarted even in England, the land of its origin, by joining the rank of "carpetbaggers" as candidate for the post of U.S. Senator from New York, where he was not a resident, in a campaign in which he posed as "loving brother" of the assassinated President.

His platform aimed to win for him the support of all the subversive and Red elements in the electorate in addition to those bound to him by his faith, and of the Negroes whom he had used in the furtherance of his plans. One of the major planks in his platform, and in that of his cheat brother, Edward, is a pretended repudiation of the Vietnam war and of our involvement in it.

The sheer hypocrisy of this Kennedy platform is incredible. For it is a matter of record that the Kennedys betrayed the U.S. into military involvement in Vietnam after the conspirators had instigated the ouster of the French from Indochina in order to get sole control of the oilfields that underlie it and the China coastal shelf. The ouster of the French left the Vietnamese minority who had been converted to Catholicism, refugees in danger of extermination by Bhuddists and/or Communists.

The Kennedys joined Cardinal Spellman in bringing pressure to bear on President Eisenhower to sponsor their coreligionist Ngo Dinh Diem, as Vietnamese ruler, and to send American GI's to Vietnam to support him. (215) Sen. John F. Kennedy, after introduction to Diem by rosy Red Supreme Court Justice Douglas devoted several of his rare appearances on the floor of the Senate, in 1954, to speeches demanding American intervention in Vietnam on behalf of Diem. (220:2904, 4672-82,5120,10003-6;App.727) Eisenhower rejected the demand for shipment of GI's to Vietnam, but sought to placate the religious element for which Kennedys fronted, by sending only military advisers. It was not until Kennedy was placed in the White House that GI's were sent by him to wage the avowedly religious war there, in which we have been hopelessly entrapped by him. This Kennedy "Crusade" has, and will continue to, cost the lives of thousands of our GIs and endless billions of our taxpayers' money. Robert Kennedy fully supported our national betrayal by his brother, a flagrant violation of our Constitution that permits the drafting and taxing of ourselves only for the support and defense of our country. However, neither he or any member of his clan volunteered in the U.S. Armed Forces for service in Vietnam in the religious war to protect their coreligionists.

## CAMPAIGNING BOBBY KENNEDY FALSIFIES HIS VIETNAM RECORD & BETRAYS U.S.

In spite of his treacherous role, with his father and brother, in entrapping us into inextricable involvement in Vietnam and neighboring lands, Sen. Robert Kennedy hypocritically represents to his bobby-sox, "hippie," "beatnik," "Liberal" and Communist devotees that he is "dedicated' to getting our boys out of Vietnam and to putting a stop to drafting them for service there. He makes these misrepresentations for the dual purpose of advancing himself to the White House and embarrassing the Administration that is forced to carry out the Vietnam policy that he was instrumental in disloyally launching, and that can not be reversed without sacrificing hordes of his native coreligionists, numerous GIs and our national "face" and honor.

Treacherous betrayal of our country with the objective of advancing his career and fortunes, has become a set habit of Sen. Robert Kennedy. As in the instance of Benedict Arnold, he has deliberately undertaken to embarrass our country in its international relations and in the conduct of the very war into which he was instrumental in plunging us. With the advice and coaching of a clutch of "Redvisers," who can not be regarded as anything short of treasonous, he has sought to make himself President of the U.S. by wandering around the world currying the favor of other lands by attacking the policies of our Government which he was instrumental in launching. In flagrant violation of the Logan Act, he has undertaken to obstruct the foreign relations of our country and to supersede the President and his official agency, the State Department, in the conduct of our foreign affairs. Since, under the Logan Act, this is a felony, if not treason, one can only wonder at the benign tolerance of the Administration in failing to prosecute and jail him for it, except as another device for wooing the Catholic vote. This is all the more to be wondered at in view of the fact' that his treachery is certain to prolong the conflict and to cost the lives of numerous of the GIs whom he pretends to desire to rescue.

## SEN. ROBERT KENNEDY & HIS AGENCIES
## ENDANGERED NATIONAL SECURITY

Sen. Robert Kennedy, on his visit to France, in February, 1967, for the avowed purpose of undermining our Government and its policies in negotiations with De Gaulle's hostile regime, deliberately broadcast, or had broadcasted by agencies controlled by him, the rumor that he had been approached with fresh North Vietnamese overtures for peace. These rumors were published, with an eye to promoting his political stock, in *Newsweek* magazine, that is controlled by him and his family. He announced that the offers would be made by the North Vietnamese and the matter would come to a head in the following "critical two weeks." Two weeks later, the complete falsity of the Bobby's release was proved by the slaughter of ever greater numbers of GIs, the innocent victims of the treachery. The false rumor had stimulated intensification of the war.

As in the case of all madmen who seek to make themselves rulers and to dominate the world, the lives of others are of little concern to this scamp who seeks to make himself our President. One wonders about his relations to Lee Oswald who conspired against his brother's life, but probably was not his sole assassin. Attorney General Robert Kennedy had placed Lee Oswald under obligations to himself by blocking presecution of him for the attempted assassination of Gen. Walker. One wonders about reports of his involvement in the death of Marilyn Monroe reported by Jesuit trained Frank Capell (233); without naming openly, by Walter Winchell; and intimated by electronic sleuth Bernard Spindel when his Putman County home and workshop was raided in December, 1966, his wiretapped recordings of phone conversations of those involved in Marilyn Monroe's death seized; and he was indicted by Democratic Manhattan District Attorney Hogan. (234)

At interesting angle is presented by the Lee Oswald involvement. His cousin is reported to be a Jesuit priest. And it is a matter of record that Lee Oswald was invited to address the Jesuit college in Springhill, Alabama, on the subject of his activities, two weeks before the Kennedy assassination. The Jesuit involvement closely parallels that in the Lincoln assassination. (72;199) New Orleans suspect Ferrie was said to be an ex-priest.

## "BOBBY" KENNEDY USES CHURCH, BUT SCORNS
## ITS PRIESTS & FOLLOWS JESUITS

Bobby Kennedy defies his Church and disregards its discipline in his courtship of the Marxist Communist vote. This once again became strikingly obvious when he went out of his way to challenge the opposition of eight American bishops to any amendment of the New York State law barring abortions. A week after the reading of a pastoral letter of eight Roman Catholic bishops in all New York diocese churches, Kennedy addressed a "standing-room only" audience of woman students of Skidmore College at Saratoga, N.Y., on February 22, 1967, and told them that he favored amendment of the law to permit abortions. When challenged by Fr. Joseph F. DiMaggio with the statement that the views expressed by Bobby are "definitely not the teachings of the Church," Bobby shut him off with the comment: "I don't think that there is much to be gained by continuing this discussion." (235) In this address he reiterated his earlier statement defying the teachings of his Church in a lecture to the students of the Syosset (L.I) High School. (236)

The attitude of Sen. Kennedy obviously parallels that of the founders and real leaders of modernday Communism, the Jesuits. The views of the Jesuits and their activities were startlingly challenged by Pope Paul VI in a warning that he gave their delegates to a convocation in Rome on November 16, 1966, in which he expressed his "surprise and...grief" caused by their activities. (237) Even more stringent were the words of Cardinal Cushing, who on January 22, 1967, addressing a Church conference in Boston, charged the Jesuit Order with "lying." (238)

## KENNEDYS EMULATE THE JESUITS & ROCKEFELLERS
## IN USE OF THE "BIG LIE"

As has been related, the Jesuits are not alone in the use of the "Big Lie" technique which is the common practise of all faiths. Hyperintensively exploited by Jesuit Illuminist, Adam Weishaupt, as the basis for his revival of Nazarenism of the Church in the form of modern-day Communism and of the bogus "philanthropy" that is used as a mask, it is the very essence of the pretended "benevolence" of the Rockefellers and their fellow conspirators. The "Big Lie" has been intensively and shamelessly used in the promotion of the

Presidential aspirations of Sen. Robert Kennedy, by him and his confederates.

## SORDID EXPLOITATION OF PRES. KENNEDY's ASSASSINATION IS "BIG LIE" AT WORST

Seldom in history has there been an uglier exploitation of the "Big Lie" than in the commercial and political uses of Pres. Kennedy's assassination by his family and entourage. Their rush to convert his death into a source of income and of political advantage is utterly devoid of sincere and dignified grief. As stated by a personal friend of his widow, Jacqueline's conduct "is marked by her habitual exhibitionism." Her mother and the Auchincloss clan into which she married are reported by the Ladies Home Journal to find disgusting and intolerable the cheap publicity that she attracts in her extraction of every conceivable advantage and gain from the death of her husband from whom she was oft estranged and of whose absence she was so fond that she left him for a prolonged stay in Europe, leaving him to his own devices and fancies, (239) and her "secretary." Her exhibition of grief was too calculating and dramatic to be convincing to the discerning. This is especially true since it is common knowledge that only the monetary blandishments of Joseph Kennedy accounted for the survival of the marriage.

The "Big Lie" technique as it is practised by the Kennedy Dynasty, was most clearly exposed for all to see in the affair of "The Book." Manchester was appointed by the Kennedys to write a slanted account of the *Death of a President*. The deal made with the author, Manchester, and his publisher by the Kennedys provided for a huge payments, from the expected profits from this business venture, exploiting the assassination, into organizations controlled by the Kennedys and operated to serve directly and indirectly their interests. Jacky and Bobby then proceeded to censor and suppress the truth, the facts that they themselves had given Manchester, and to twist the record to suit their purposes. This was done by them on the hypocritic pretense that while obviously seeking publicity and profit, they were in quest of "privacy." The "quest for privacy" was handled for them by their pressagents in such manner that they obtained world-wide, first page publicity that might be expected to increase the sale of the book and their "kickback" from it enormously; and won a settlement, that contented them, from its serialization. It is reported that the total amount of the "kickback" will amount to millions of dollars that will come under their control, in addition to the millions contributed for the ostensible purpose of setting up memorials, and incidentally of aggrandizing themselves and promoting their conspiracy to take over control of the government, and of further exploiting the nation.

## KENNEDYS EFFECT PROSTITUTION OF HARVARD U. & THE PRESS, TO THEIR CONSPIRACY

The Kennedy "Big Lie" technique follows the Adam Weishaupt pattern that is used by their Rockefeller bosses, in their effort to establish theirs as a rival, but cooperative, dynasty. They subsidize prostituted professors of institutions that are bribed by endowments to serve them and their conspiracy in subverting the nation. The Kennedys, however, are even rawer in their technique of making the public finance their vicious activities. They use the funds that the public has been induced to contribute to the aforementioned "memor-

242

ial" for the subversion of "education" that is, in substance, false propaganda in their interest, and for the seduction of the personnel of all media of mass communication that are susceptible thereto.

The covert and thorougly dishonest use of the moneys cadged from the gullible public around the world for the personal aggrandizement and political advancement of the Kennedys and particularly of Robert Kennedy, and their exploitation of the contributors, was courageously exposed after thorough and fearless investigation by a British journalist, Henry Fairlee. (240) It is highly significant that this matter that so vitally concerns us all, was not brought to public attention by American newspapermen. This makes it clear to what extent they and their organization, the Newspaper Guild, have been seduced, intimidated and bribed by the conspirators to serve them as their pressagents and false propagandists. As a consequence the nation's press is far more rigidly censored than even the Soviet press; and the nation is fed only such information, and more often misinformation on vital matters, that the conspirators wish it to know.

Fairlee's investigation revealed once again, that the professors and so-called "authorities" that the conspirators use in their subversion and looting of the nation, are merely venal "intellectual" prostitutes who serve them and their interests abjectly and ruthlessly; that these professional harlots are mouthpieces for the super-Mafia that the conspirators have induced the public to identify as "the Establishment." Throughout American history the most subversive and most subservient of these prostitute professors have been identified with Harvard University.

It is a matter of record that only one president of Harvard has ever been known to attack the Weishaupt-Marx Illuminist-Communist conspiracy: David Tappan, in 1798, when the drive against Communism in this country, reached the highest intensity that it has ever attined. (29:25;241) Before and since, Harvard has been the outstanding tool, among American universities of other faiths, of Weishaupt and his Jesuit colleagues in furthering their conspiracy. Throughout American history it has been a haven for the subversive agents of the country's first ruling dynasty, the Roosevelt-Delano Dynasty(7); and has well served its successor, the Rockefeller Dynasty.

Fairlee revealed that the money that has been cadged by the Kennedys from the public for the ostensible purpose of "immortalizing" Pres. Kennedy and his kith and kin, and of aggrandizing and promoting themselves as an American ruling dynasty in the spirit of the Irish kings, falls into their hands through their Kennedy Library Corporation. This corporation consists of the Kennedy family and some friends and members of the Kennedy administration, including Eugene Black (who was the former head of the World Bank and is now connected with the Chase Manhattan Bank) its chairman, George Meany and Arthur Schlesinger. Its business is run by Sen. Robert Kennedy, who brooks no interference from any other member of the family. Fairlee reports that when Sen. Edward Kennedy undertook to advise in the management of the KLC, Bobby rebuked him with the admonition:

"Now, Teddy, remember that father said (after the assassination) that I am the head of the family."

243

Joseph Kennedy adheres to the Biblical rule and Irish tradition of primogeniture, hereditary transmission of power, and succession in the order of birth, the rule for the dynasty that he has aimed to establish as rulers of an American monarchy.

Bobby Kennedy dictated to the Harvard Corp. that operates the University, according to Fairlee's investigation that in return for a $3.5 million of Kennedy Library Corp. funds ($1 million of it cadged from the public and $2.5 million diverted to it from Ford Foundation funds by Pres. Kennedy's "special assistant," McGeorge Bundy who is now the Foundation's president) the name of the University's Graduate School of Administration be changed to the John F. Kennedy School of Government. He also dictated that there be established in the School an Institute of Politics that he required was to be endowed by others in the amount of $10 million and to be supervised by an "advisory committee" of which one must be a member of the Kennedy family. (The Kennedys are now represented by that paragon of "beauty, wisdom, virtue, modesty shyness, shrinking self-effacement and fidelity," Jacqueline Kennedy.) Its organization makes it quite clear that this Institute of Politics of Harvard U., that poses as an "educational" institute, is nothing more than magnified ward-heeling establishment for promoting the "Big Lie" in the interest of duping the public into betraying the nation by advancing the political careers of the Kennedys and their henchmen.

The array of characters whom the Kennedys have chosen as their agents in advancing their "Big Lie" propaganda, in the role of Harvard "professors" is most illuminating. They include the following:

Adam Yarmolinsky, formerly Deputy Assistant Secretary of Defense, (whose long familiar "Liberal," or Red, tradition has been commented on by a number of patriotic organization) in the Kennedy Administration; and now professor of law at Harvard.

Daniel P. Moynihan, also a member of the Kennedy Administration whose prime role was agitation among the Negroes designed to gain their political support at the cost of betrayal of the nation; and now Harvard professor.

Richard Neustadt, "Liberal" adviser to Presidents Truman, Kennedy and Johnson; Harvard professor and director of the Institute.

For the purpose of indoctrination of its students with the "Big Lie" propaganda technique, a wide array of lower rank bureaucrats from Washington and pressagents are being drawn into the Institute for the obvious purpose of building up a Kennedy political machine, Fairlee reported. It is noteworthy that no educator from the Jesuits or other priests are included in the ranks of the Institute. Fairlie explains that all of them are "potential members of any future Kennedy administration."

Harvard University has a long and thoroughly dishonorable record of prostituting education to political services. With the one exception that has been mentioned, President Tappan's attack on Illuminist Communism in 1798, that "education" has been slanted in the direction of one or another type of Communism, especially Nazarene and Weishaupt-Marxist. It especially distinguished itself in the support of the witchcraft agitation of one of its more "distinguished" faculty members, Rev. Cotton Mather. (58:65) Harvard has eagerly offered "educational" berths for indoctrination of its students by political hacks who had been ousted from office and power, until such time as they could delude the public into voting them back in office. But never before has Harvard demeaned itself to so low a level as to serve as a precinct clubhouse for political hacks and wardheelers. (7:51;15) In this subversion of education, the Kennedys' activities are far more brazen and in keeping with their shanty Irish, bartending, wardheeling tradition, than those of their mentors and fellow conspirators, the Rockefellers and their bogus "foundations."

## KENNEDYS PLAN TO MAKE SELVES NATION'S RULERS AND/OR DESTROY IT

The intensity of the drive of Robert Kennedy for the Presidency and the money spent on it is illustrated by the fact that early in 1967 it was announced that twelve of his pressagents were preparing books of propanganda for him that would be published within a year. It is to be expected that their nauseating drivel will depict him as the nation's "saviour" whose services outstrip those of George Washington. The truth regarding him was diplomatically stated by a good American of Kennedy's own Party and faith, former Postmaster General James A. Farley, at the Jefferson-Jackson Day Dinner of 1967, at Hartford, Connecticut. He benevolently portrayed the treacherous activities of Sen. Robert Kennedy as follows:

"One can forgive his lack of experience — but not if he proposes to continue gaining it by imperiling the safety of the nation. This he does when he explores diplomatic channels which can only lawfully be done by the President."

On Kennedy's return from the treacherous visit to France to which Farley referred, it was reported that he was roundly trounced by the President and threatened with an early end to his career. But the reports did not make mention of the fact that, under the Logan Act, Sen. Robert Kennedy's imprisonment for a crime that ranks with treason, was mandatory.

## KENNEDY DYNASTY IS MINOR, BUT CURIOUS, SATELLITE OF ROCKEFELLER DYNASTY

Though the Kennedy Dynasty is "one up" on the Rockefeller Dynasty, in that one of its members has seized the Presidency and White House, it must be borne in mind that John F. Kennedy succeeded in so doing only with Rockefeller help. It is a matter of record that Joseph Kennedy, seeking bank financing for his son's nomination and campaign, was shunted to Nelson Rockefeller and made a deal with him.

Under the "leaked" terms of the deal that were amply verified by subsequent developments, Rockefeller offered to support Kennedy's campaign, in event that he himself could not get the Republican nomination — on the condition that John F. would serve the conspirators as loyally and ruthlessly as had Joseph Kennedy himself; and, also, would agree to appoint on his Cabinet and to key policy-making jobs, the trusted agents of the conspirators.

Pres. Kennedy lived up to this deal, as is evidenced by his giving the key appointment, Secretary of State, to Rockefeller's employee,

President of Rockefeller Foundation, Dean Rusk, even though it was reported that the two had never met. And Kennedy's entire Cabinet, with the exception of his brother, Bobby, were trusted Rockefeller agents largely picked from the ranks of their "Foreign Office," the Council on Foreign Relations. (79:217) Sen. Robert F. Kennedy has served his Rockefeller masters and their most notorious Red agents and confederates, as abjectly as did his father and brother.

The mode of takeover of our government by the Rockefeller and Kennedy Dynasties has differed. The Kennedys brazenly infested our government with their breed as soon as they had bought the Presidency for John F. Every available male member of the clan — Bobby, Eddie, Shriver — and all their wardheeler henchmen no matter how shameful their records, were saddled on the taxpayers, on the public payroll, in an unabashed display of nepotism and the spoils system.

## BOBBY KENNEDY HAS MENACED NATION & FORCED OUT PRES. JOHNSON

Threats, corruption, violence and gang tactics, that featured the entry of the Irish in ward politics, has been extended to the national scene by Bobby Kennedy and his Dynasty. It has been crudely intensified by the Dynasty's Prohibition era experience, when Joseph Kennedy became an important factor in the flow of liquor into the nation through various channels. Political bosses and leaders have been bribed and intimidated, or otherwise forced by them, to support the Presidential aspirations of the Kennedy mob. Refusal means subjection to ruthless force, pressure, violence and "heat." Opponents were vilified by circulation of false rumors, viciously attacked and, in some instances the object of physical violence and mob threat, as well as numerous other mean and ugly devices at the disposal of the Dynasty.

It is a matter of record that no American President has ever been demeaned and subjected to such vitriolic abuse, by mail and on the public platform, and threats of mob violence as has Lyndon B. Johnson. Vicious attacks have been made on him personally, on his Administration and on our national policy by viciously treacherous Robert Kennedy. His attacks on the nation's efforts in the Vietnam war into which Kennedy and his Dynasty deliberately plunged us, escalated and forced on the successor Johnson Administration, have been little short of treasonous, as has his joining the Communists in inciting the nation's Negroes, youth, bobbysoxers, beatniks, hippies and subversives of all stripes, in his "Children's Crusade." It has cost the lives of numerous GIs and undermined our war effort and attempts to extricate ourselves from the Vietnamese Crusade in which he and his Dynasty have entrapped us.

The threats on the President's life have become so vicious and numerous and incited mobs and demonstrations so violent as to force the Secret Service to resort to such extraordinary measures as keeping his travel plans and movements secret and, in Los Angeles, barring his stay in hotels, confining him to his plane during his overnight stay. By these tactics, the Dynasty, the so-called "Irish Mafia" succeeded in forcing Pres. Johnson to announce his withdrawal from the 1968 nomination campaign.

## JOHN D. THE SECOND'S MEMORABLE SHERIFFS' BALL ORGY

The Rockefeller Dynasty, on the other hand, were mindful of the adverse public reaction to their criminal record; and their personal infiltration of the government was most cautious and stealthy, and was extended over generations.

The first entry of the Rockefellers into governmental role was the appointment of John D. the Second (Jr.) by Tammany boss Charley Murphy, as chairman of a committee to investigate prostitution and the White Slave trade in New York City. It is reliably reported that Murphy made this appointment "with tongue in cheek" because he had learned that Junior was himself maintaining a mistress and keeping her undercover in a brothel; and that he had quarreled furiously with a minister who had taken fancy to her and sought her favors at the brothel. Junior showed his appreciation for the appointment, as was the custom, by giving New York's sheriffs a lavish ball. This ball was long remembered by those who attended it. Junior is reported to have demonstrated his "high religious and moral principles" by making his Sheriffs' Ball one of the most outrageous sex orgies in New York's history. (242)

## OPEN TAKEOVER OF GOVERNMENTS BY ROCKEFELLER DYNASTY IS RAPIDLY PROGRESSIVE

The story of the progressive undercover takeover of our government by the Rockefeller conspirators, and the rapidly galloping open seizure by Nelson Rockefeller and the current "generation of vipers" has been related. (15;79;243) It first forcibly struck public attention in the 1966 elections when Nelson Rockefeller was reelected New York Governor, Winthrop Rockefeller elected Governor of Arkansas, John D. the Fourth elected to the West Virginia House of Delegates, and his father-in-law, Charles Percy, elected U. S. Senator from Illinois. In the meantime, Laurance Rockefeller was appointed by his brother, Nelson, to the post of Park Commissioner of New York State; his son, Laurance Jr., found shelter from military service in VISTA; the Aldrich cousins placed in minor New York State posts by their uncle, Gov. Rockefeller; and numerous more remote kinsmen occupy, with the help of the conspirators, other government offices. Among the latter are Red Sen. Joseph Clark, of Pennsylvania, cousin of ex-Mrs. Nelson Rockefeller; Sen. William O. Proxmire, who was married to Ellen Rockefeller, and has represented Wisconsin in the U.S. Senate since the conspirators disposed of Sen. Joseph McCarthy; Congresswoman Frances Bolton, senior member of the minority of the House Foreign Affairs Committee who celebrated the Japanese attack on Pearl Harbor (244), and her Congressman son, both from Ohio; and many other close and remote kinsmen, including Mayor John V. Lindsay, of New York City, who is ably abetting them in looting the City more ruthlessly than it ever has been looted before, even by the notorious Tweed Ring and by the conspirators' Red agent, Fiorello LaGuardia, who was bossed by David Rockefeller personally.

The conspirators' pressagents allege that the flocking of the Rockefellers and their agents into public office is motivated by the desire to "serve" the public, in order to mask their true, and openly acknowledged, motive of profiting from public office and looting the public. They adopt the pretense of Nelson Rockefeller that he aims to give the public the services that they demand, and to make them pay for it by steadily increased taxes or other devices. But the steadily increased looting by taxation that quite regularly flows into the conspirators' purses, the public can discern only one service, that which the bull gives the cow. And the public most definitely does not ask for that service.

## CONSPIRATORS' "FEDERAL" RESERVE IS MOST EFFECTIVE DEVICE IN STEALING ELECTIONS

Of all the corrupt devices for usurping the power to rule the nation that have been recounted — their crooked voting machines, their bogus "philanthropies," their Federal income tax, their power of unlimited looting of the nation by taxation, their virtually complete tax exemption, their universal military training and draft laws which exempt themselves, their "internationalist" self aid through so-called "foreign aid" and wars of expansion and conquest, and their dis-"United" Nations conspiracy — none has been as effective as their bogus "Federal" Reserve conspiracy. This is perfectly illustrated by their engineering of their 1966 election victories.

The plot began about a year before the election. They suddenly brought to an end the wave of employment and prosperity around the world that they had rigged with "foreign aid" thievery, wars "to contain Communism," nuclear energy and astronautic promotions and a "soft money" policy dictated through their "F"RS allowing the U.S. and the world to make use of their own wealth without restrictions. The conspirators suddenly and deliberately restricted the money and credit available for the conduct of American business by raising their "Federal" Reserve rediscount rate and interest rates, and by contracting the amount of the nation's money and credit that they permitted to be used for the conduct of business. The obviously false excuses that the conspirators gave the world through their "Federal" Reserve, banking and government propagandists, included the unfavorable U.S. balance of trade that they were deliberately creating with their "foreign aid" thievery, their "gold withdrawals" in the names of their foreign agencies and banks of issue which resulted in no loss in their gold holdings in their domestic depositories, the shortage of money and credit which they deliberately created, and the rising interest and discount rates that they dictated to the foreign banks of issue that they own and those that they control indirectly through their International Monetary Fund and other agencies.

## ROCKEFELLER CONSPIRATORS REVEAL OWNERSHIP OF FOREIGN BANKS OF ISSUE

The above statement that foreign central banks are owned by the Rockefeller conspirators is made on the best conceivable authority: on the basis of their own published statement. With their usual supreme contempt for the moronity into which they have "educated" the nation through their bogus "educational philanthropies," the Rockefellers openly boasted in the *New York Times*,

248

on March 13, 1967, in a special dispatch by Paul L. Montgomery, under the headline *Chase Convening Big Parley in Rio*, that their Chase Manhattan Bank owns controlling interest in foreign, Latin American central banks, in the words:

> *"Chase Has Controlling Interests in National Banks in Honduras, Peru, Brazil and Venezuela..."* (245)

## CONSPIRATORS RIGGED RECESSIONS & PANIC TO WIN ELECTION

This control, whether direct or indirect, enables the conspirators to rig interest and rediscount rates in any land to suit their purposes. The conspirators rigged a shortage of money through their IMF and other agencies, around the world. Industries that were not controlled or favored by the conspirators were denied funds or credit to meet their payrolls and other costs. Trade slumped, stock markets crashed, mortgages were foreclosed, droves of workers were thrown into the ranks of the unemployed and panic prevailed in the U. S. and around the world. The conspirators' financial sabotage was as effective in creating what their agents called "a recession" in England, Germany, Canada and Japan as in the U. S.

Recessions and depressions thus rigged are the favorite devices of the conspirators for effecting defeat in elections of the agents whom they have placed in governmental power who no longer serve their immediate interests. The rigged "recession" insured the defeat of most of the candidates of the Party that they had placed in power, the Democrats, and assured the victory of two Republican Rockefeller Governors and of many of their Republican henchmen in the 1966 election. Once again the conspirators proved that their *control of the "Federal" Reserve is their most potent political weapon.*

## AFTER WINNING ELECTION, CONSPIRATORS ENDED MONETARY STRINGENCY

Proof that the "recession" with its usurious rises in rediscount rates was rigged became completely evident within several months after the conspirators' election victories. The conspirators' "Federal" Reserve lowered rediscount rates and reserve requirements, banks lowered their interest rates under the competitive pressure of Rockefellers' Chase Manhattan Bank, money became plentiful and stock markets began to boom. In March 1967, the N. Y. Times headlines read *Banking Reserves Reach 4-Year High.* And on April 6, 1967, the conspirators' "Federal" Reserve announced a reduction of its discount rate to 4% "to loosen credit." (266) At the same time it was announced that for the conspirators' Chase Manhattan (and others of their Banking Trust)

> "...the last three months have been the most prosperous in the bank's history with earnings running about 7 per cent ahead of the same period last year."

David Rockefeller, chairman of the board, announced that his Chase Manhattan Bank had seized control of the London Standard Bank Ltd. and of banks in South Africa through which it was planned to extend the conspirators' subversive Negro "civil rights" agitation in that land, to serve their malign purposes there. He

Illustration.
BANKER DAVID ROCKEFELLER DANCES A PERUVIAN WALTZ WITH
EMPLOYEE OF BANCO CONTINENTAL OF PERU, TAKEN OVER
BY HIS CHASE MANHATTAN BANK

This is one of the numerous banks around the world that the conspirators have taken over through the agency of their "Federal" Reserve, their League of Nations and dis-"United" Nations, their International Monetary Fund and other agencies of theirs, as part of their worldwide banking monopoly and "Gold Corner" plotted for looting the U.S. and the world.
UPI Photo.

expressed it in the words:

"We are convinced that over a period of time the Standard Bank can exert a *constructive* influence on racial conditions in South Africa." (267)

At the same time Rockefeller announced that the reports that had been disseminated by his pressagents that he would openly take over the operation of the U. S. Treasury as its Secretary instead of controlling it through his CFR agent, the incumbent, Fowler, was "strictly rumors...with no foundation whatever."

## CONSPIRATORS USE NATION'S WEALTH TO MAKE CAMPAIGNING COSTLY TO OTHERS

The conspirators' use of their "Federal" Reserve, and through it, of our personal and national wealth, to support their own political campaigning while making it prohibitively costly to their opponents is not their only advantage and profit therefrom. Through their monopolist ownership of the most effective media of mass communication, the air channels, radio and television, that they have usurped by fair means and foul, they make their opponents campaigning, as well as their own, a source of enrichment and profit for themselves. (79:182f) They have so completely usurped the nation's airways, that are the property of the people, denying its use to the nation for even so vital a matter as election of their representatives, and made its use so costly, that only they and their agents can afford to seek public office in its higher echelons. Elections are now openly acknowledged to be attainable solely by purchase. The Kennedys are reported by their kinsman, Gore Vidal, to spend freely for election and promotion of their Dynasty, including "an estimated million dollars a year" to purchase the Presidency for Bobby. (246)

Nelson Rockefeller's 1966 gubernatorial campaign was acknowledged to have cost more than 5 million, but is reported to have cost more than $20 million. The difference, according to the reports, was accounted for by various dodges used to evade "honest election" laws. Rockefeller's stepmother is reported to have contributed $600,000; and the rest of the family $145,000 of the acknowledged expenditures. The advertising firm, Jack Tinker & Partners, was paid $144,588 for its handling of the "Big Lie" propaganda. The Chemical Bank New York Trust Co. is reported to have "loaned" $200,000, and the Bankers Trust Co., $150,000, to the campaign in its last days. (247) A dummy organization, Friends of the Rockefeller Team Committee, was reported to have "borrowed" $2.5 milion from a group of banks, including $700,000 from the Manufacturers Hanover Trust Co., $500,000 from Bankers Trust Co., $545,000 from Empire Trust Co., and $800,000 from the Chemical Bank New Vork Trust Co.

These latter "loan" reports were charged by Sen. Manfred Ohrenstein to constitute a violation of the election laws inasmuch as no interest was reported to have been paid on them to the banks. Sen. Jack Bronston stated:

"From this we conclude that either the interest has been forgiven or that the loans have been paid. If the interest has been forgiven, this raises grave public questions with regard to the banks involved and their relationship with the Governor." (248)

The banks' "relationship to the Governor" are quite obvious. They are members of the conspirators' "Federal" Reserve and directly or indirectly controlled by them; and they have profited hugely from various measures forced through the New York State Legislature for them, including the law that permits them to acquire or establish branches outside of New York City, where they had been previously barred. It is interesting to note that the bank most closely identified with the Rockefellers, their Chase Manhattan Bank, was not "touched" by the conspirators. It is also noteworthy that reelected Gov. Rockefeller has already provided some measure of reward for the banks that were so generous in support of his campaign, through some of the many ways available to the ruler of the State, including permitting them to share, with the Chase Manhattan Bank, in the loot from the proposed lotteries, by holding funds collected for long periods of time without payment of interest, by paying to them commission on the sale of lottery tickets, billions of dollars of bond issues, and other devices.

FIXING VOTING MACHINES & STEALING ELECTIONS

Almost the sole value of support of various groups, such as labor unions, churches, public contributions and bank loans, to the conspirators' candidates for public office, is in securing nominations. For the conspirators have perfected the mechanics of stealing elections and made it automatic by use of automatic voting machines marketed and "serviced" by companies that they control. Their control of voting machine companies makes the stealing of elections by fixing voting machines 100% "safe" and irreversible. This so completely nullifies franchise that it has become immaterial to the conspirators who is permitted to vote. That is what accounts for their willingness to extend the franchise to everyone, no matter how unqualified. With their voting machines it is as easy to steal the vote of minors, Negroes and illiterates as it is to steal those of qualified voters.

PURCHASE OF AUTOMATIC VOTING MACHINE CO. INSURED ROCKEFELLERS' ELECTIONS

Voting machines were originated and marketed by a group of our "most honorable" citizens. They included Al Capone, Frank Costello, Jimmy Roosevelt and other equally distinguished citizens of the type identified with the Mills Manufacturing Co. and "slot machine," "one arm bandits" and other gambling devices. The first voting machine used publicly was marketed by the Automatic Voting Machine Co.

As might be expected, in view of the character of the sponsorship, the voting machines can be "fixed" readily to insure stealing of elections. The "fixing" of the machines for election stealing is effected by servicing employees of the company prior to, or even during, the election. The voter knows, from the lever which he moves, only how he intends to vote. But he has no knowledge of how his vote is recorded, at the back of the machine. (79:186f)

A voting machine is merely a bank of counters, and it would

be readily possible to enable the voter to see the actual recording of his vote on the counter of his candidate. From the viewpoint of the conspirators, however, that is absolutely undesirable. For it would make impossible stealing of elections by such devices as affixing decalcomanias over the numbers on the counter wheels, reversing connections of the levers with the counters, relays that apportion votes among the candidates in the manner requisite for stealing the election for a particular candidate.

The function desired by the conspirators for their voting machines is stealing of elections, for which they are ideally adapted. For once an election is stolen by "fixing" of vote machines, there is no possibility of a recount and reversal of the results. Automatic Voting Machine Co. machines were rented or purchased for use in the elections of New York and other States as soon as they had been "perfected."

About half a year before Nelson Rockefeller sought the gubernatorial nomination in New York, control of the Automatic Voting Machine Co. was purchased and merged into Rockwell Manufacturing Co. Their performance was so excellent in giving Rockefeller a resounding victory in his election as Governor, in spite of public distrust and dislike of him, that the decision to oust all minority stockholders from the A.V.M.Co. was made. The minority stockholders, including this author, were compelled to accept the generous offer of twenty dollars a share for their stock that had never sold above four dollars, and relinquish any right to "snoop" in that company's affairs.

### LOUISIANA INVESTIGATION PROVED SHOUP MACHINE IS MORE EASILY "FIXED"

Complaints about much to obvious stealing of elections by use of voting machines in Louisiana resulted in precipitating there, in 1960, an investigation of voting machine frauds on the basis of the House Concurrent Resolution No. 33 of the 23rd Regular Session of the Louisiana State Legislature. At the hearings of the Investigating Committee, voting machine experts, who had defected, demonstrated some of the various methods of "fixing" the machines that had been used in stealing elections. The demonstrations revealed that the voting machine marketed by the Shoup Voting Machine Co. could be "fixed" more readily, and in more manners, for stealing elections, than could the Automatic Voting Machine Co. device. (227; 228)

### CONSPIRATORS DISCARD NEW YORK'S AUTOMATIC MACHINES FOR MORE "FIXABLE" SHOUPS

The inferiority of the Automatic Voting Machines, that had been installed throughout New York State, for stealing elections aroused the conspirators to prompt action. The Automatic Voting Machines were promptly disposed of, at what is reported to be a considerable loss; and promptly replaced with the more readily "fixable" Shoup Voting Machines. Rockwell Manufacturing Company discarded its Automatic Voting Machine Co. by "spinoff" of its stock that dropped back to four dollars a share. And Shoup Voting Machine Co. was purchased and merged into General Battery & Ceramics Co.

## SHOUP COMPANIES TAKEN OVER BY MYSTERIOUS
## ASSOCIATES OF CONSPIRATORS

On October 25, 1965, there was freshly incorporated in New York by the firm with which Gov. Nelson Rockefeller's campaign manager, Sen. Jacob Javits, has been identified, the Automatic Tolls Systems Inc. that took over from General Battery & Ceramics Co. one of the divisions of the Shoup company that had previously been merged into it. At about the same time, there was taken over by a mysterious company, Merion Industries Inc. located at 555 E. City Line Ave., Bala Cynwyd, Pa., that is not far removed from the conspirators' Humble Oil Co. office, the Shoup Voting Machine Co.

Merion Industries Inc. is quite secretive and refuses to give much information to credit agencies. It banks with Chase Manhattan and Mellon National banks. It has diversified holdings into which a voting machine company would not appear to fit. But it has an acknowledged holding of about a third of the Shoup Voting Maching Co. stock.

The Shoup machines have a surprising breadth of market wherever the conspirators are most active. They are reported to have been used in the 1967 Vietnam election under supervision of a Presidentially appointed committee of "observers" that included a Catholic priest, "to insure an honest election." The Shoup machines ran true to form. Despite the Catholic minority in South Vietnam, the Catholics won an "overwhelming victory," *Electing All The Senators.*

## SHOUP VOTING MACHINE USE MAKES POSSIBLE
## "AMAZINGLY ACCURATE" POLL

The takeover of the Shoup Voting Machine Co. by the conspirators may explain how it was that a Rockefeller biographer and pressagent on the staff of the New York Daily News, James Desmond, was able to predict the exact outcome of an election held one week later. (149) The election was the Mayoralty race in which the Democratic Party had little desire to win because of various adverse developments in prospect, including a planned subway strike and fare increase. The Democrats, with the object of "throwing" the election picked as their candidate a relatively unknown Jewish politician, Beame, who was in disfavor with the organization because of his honesty and straightforwardness.

The Republican candidate was a distant kinsman of Rockefellers, from the city's social fringe, member of their Council on Foreign Relations and Congressman from the "silk stocking" district of New York City, song and dance man and clown, John V. Lindsay. His election was assured by the use of the Shoup voting machines, though he was the only Republican winner in the election. The vote was most complexly split, between the two Parties. Nevertheless Desmond, in the know, was able to predict it with incredible but *Absolute Accuracy.* That can be explained only by "inside information" on the "fixing" of the voting machines.

It is noteworthy that a post-election check on the figures tabulated from the voting machines revealed in two of the election districts checked, "padding" of the reported vote for Lindsay by the conspirators' "Liberal" Party, of ten thousand votes in each district. It is an interesting commentary on the lack of desire of the Democrats to win the Mayoralty that they demanded no recount in the obviously corrupt situation. It was quite evident that they did not want to win the Mayoralty for their candidate. Lindsay runs New York as "Fun City" for local talent and imported "gay" lads, "AC-DCs," and "Commissioners,, at an unprecedented high cost, to the taxpayers of $35,000 each and as much additional as they can make "on the side."

## GOV. ROCKEFELLER PUT MAFIA IN CHARGE
## OF LOTTERY & LIQUOR AUTHORITY

A cursory examination of the record rolled up by Gov. Rockefeller reveals that the present generation of the "philanthropist" Dynasty, the so-called "Establishment," is as closely identified with subsidiary criminal elements as were their ancestors. Walter M. Conlon was given by Gov. Rockefeller "a political plum," with a salary of $26,980 a year, as the third ranking official in the State Tax Commission. He "assisted in some State lottery drawings." Conlon's qualification was his role as "front man" and partner of a Long Island gangster with the "highly creditable" record of convictions for "burglary, armed robbery, counterfeiting, assault and robbery, homicide and, forgery." (307) While in office, he was indicted for an illegal land deal, and ousted from his post, like so many of Rockefeller's criminal appointees and associates. (308)

Judson Morhouse, Gov. Rockefeller's political sponsor, campaign manager and pal, was convicted of a felony, extortion in obtaining a liquor license from the State Liquor Authority for the New York City Playboy Club, an outfit that operates in an atmosphere patterned after the old-fashioned brothels. Subsequently the Playboy Club was exposed by a complaint to the SLA of "aggravated assault" on a member by "musclemen" operating it, as harboring a criminal element. The Club retains its license, fortified in it by the exposure that appears to have convinced the SLA that its mob is in control. Gov. Nelson Rockefeller has valiantly risen to the defense of his convicted pal and agent, Morhouse, and boasted, in a TV broadcast, that, despite conviction, he has not served his jail sentence, and implied that he never will do so. (79:206)

Rockefeller appointed SLA Chairman Martin Epstein, who fronted for the Governor's Administration in the liquor license payoff racket that mulcted millions of dollars from liquor licencees, refused to waive immunity when summoned before a Grand Jury. He escaped prosecution on the plea that he was dying of cancer. Epstein had been recommended for his post by Brooklyn Republican boss John Crews who had "delivered the vote" for Rockefeller's election. (79:205)

This pattern of corruption pervades the entire Administration of Gov. Rockefeller as an aspect of "making his every endeavor richly repay him." Exposures and convictions have made no change in the situation. Former FBI agent William D. Kane identified SLA agent John J. Aliegro who attempted to extort $25,000 from Daniel Segal, a licensee, as a Mafia associate. (309) This feature appears to be characteristic of the efforts of "philanthropist" Nelson Rockefeller to make a living, that he so direly needs, and "to make his every effort pay handsomely." He scorns the concept of "conflict of interest.' (79)

## IS ROCKEFELLER DYNASTY, THE "ESTABLISHMENT," THE SUPER-MAFIA?

The long term associations of the Rockefeller dynasty with the Mafia are numerous. John D. the First, in the 1880's, is reported to have put the Mafia in control of the Brooklyn waterfront to prevent competitors shipping kerosene abroad. John D. the Second was involved in the employment of the Mafia to break the 1913 Colorado Fuel & Iron Co. strike at Ludlow Colorado. (94:181) The New York headquarters of the Mafia have been located at 24 W. 55 Street, New York City, in Rockefeller property, (94:312) directly next door to Gov. Nelson Rockefeller's other properties, including his "unofficial State Capitol" at 22 and 20 W. 55 Street; and behind his supersecret offices in 13 W. 54 Street and his adjacent property at 15 W. 54 Street, part of which he has converted (for the purpose of securing tax exemption) into the so-called Museum of Primitive Art. Undercover visits and communications are facilitated by underground tunnels between the buildings, that the New York Times of November 25, 1967 reported his "aides call 'the secret passageway'... that the Governor and other officials use...to leave their offices when pickets or reporters are pacing on 55th Street." (311:41) Mention has been made of the employment of Maffista Joe Adonis, head of Murder Inc., to assure Nelson Rockefeller, in his construction of Rockefeller Center, "perfect labor relations." (79:77)

Gov. Rockefeller's program for institutionalizing drug addicts helps the Mafia drug pushers as does also the suppression of essential research into the chemical and biologic causes of addiction that might lead to its cure. This is especially significant in view of the Rockefeller ownership and control of the world-wide Drug Cartel. The results of Rockefeller's program on which he based his campaign for reelection attest to its efficacy from the viewpoint of the conspirators' purses. His appointee, Dr. Efren Ramirez, head of N.Y. Addiction Service Agency, testified before the N.Y. Joint Legislative Committee On Penal Institutions, on December 13, 1967, one year after Rockefeller's program had been launched, that the army of New York City's drug addicts had increased to 100,000 and that they steal $10 million a day to purchase drugs. (312) Simultaneously, the Federal Trade Commission reported that the drug trade had outstripped the auto industry, and had become the nation's most profitable industry. (313:65) Rockefeller control of the indoctrination, or "education," system facilitates regimenting the nation, from youth, in any vogue, madness or suicidal fad that augments their loot, or "profits." Control of mass communication media and the Crime Syndicate, simplifies promotion of the addictive drugs spewed into the market by the conspirators' Drug Trust. The N.Y. Times, in series exposing drug usage, lauded addiction as a new "American way of life." (337) The rations of our GIs in Vietnam contain their addictive drugs. (383)

As soon as the formerly ethical drug firm E. R. Squibb & Sons had been taken over by the conspirators' Olin Mathieson Chemical Corp., it began patent medicine promotion, in the most vicious quack tradition of "Doc" Bill, over radio and television, of dangerous addictive drugs for self administration. The conspirators' U.S. Food & Drug Administration closes its eyes to the dangerously false advertising that atavistically reverts to the ugliest phase of the Dynasty's tradition.

255

## "EDUCATION" USED TO PROMOTE DRUG ADDICTION
## & CREATE "HIPPIE" MODE & PROFITS

The vilest and most successful of the conspirators' drug promotions is their use of control of the educational system, through such "professors" as Leary and the hokum of religion, to regiment youthful students into the ranks of drug addicts and ready victims for their Mafia drug "pushers." The aforementioned Times article exults: "Usage by youth grows most." (337:22) That "profits" can be derived by the "philanthropic" conspirators from their joint control, of the Drug Cartel, the Mafia and education was again brought to light by a raid by 200 narcotics agents, in the early morning hours of January 17, 1968, on the Stony Brook campus of New York State University. Sixteen students, ranging in age from 16 to 23 years, and an additional seventeen persons on the campus were arrested for narcotics violations, after undercover agents had purchased drugs there with ease. (357)

The New York State University, a State Department, is under direct control of Gov. Rockefeller. The character of "educator" appointed by his Administration is indicated by the statement of local Police Commissioner John Barry that he had found the administration of the college "uncooperative and not to be trusted." This is fully confirmed by the statement of Dean David Tilley that he found it "impossible to be an educator and cooperate with the police in serving students in the searching stage." (358) Police Commissioner Barry accused Dean Tilley of "warning students, at a 'pot' party, of an impending raid." He also charged that members of the faculty were suspected drug users under investigation by the Suffolk County grand jury. The suicide, in 1965, of a young student "educated" in the use of marijuana, at the college, was belatedly brought to light. John Toll, President of the institution stated in his testimony before the Joint Legislative Committee On Crime that the "success" of the conspirators' "philanthropic educational" program was such that one out of every five students of the State University have become narcotic addicts. (360) The situation leads one to wonder if drug addiction has not become a prerequisite for graduation.

The use of narcotic addiction for domination of nations is one of the oldest tricks of Oriental conquerors. Cannabis indica, or hashish, a drug similar in its action to marijuana (cannabis sativa) has been widely used, to bolster the murderous lust and "courage" of men, by conspirators to profit triply: from the sale of the drug, 'from the hold over men and their crimes attainable by supplying and withholding the drug, and from the breakdown of law and order paving way for dictatorship.

## "SUCCESS" ATTAINED BY CONSPIRATORS THROUGH
## THEIR GENERAL EDUCATION BOARD

Within half a century, the Rockefeller conspirators attained complete success in John D. I's subversive objectives of his General Education Board, as stated in his Occasional Letter No. 1. They fully confirmed the predictions made by a number of wise and patriotic members of Congress, including Sen. Chamberlain, of Oregon, who said, on March 26, 1917:

"The Carnegie-Rockefeller influence is bad. In two generations they can change the minds of the people to conform to the cult of Rockefeller...rather than the fundamental principles of American democracy." (15:3)

A large segment of the nation and the world have been duped by the "philanthropists'" Madison Avenue propaganda into believing that they are "free" and exercise "self determination" only when they surrender themselves to duping and doping by the conspirators. Their subversive propaganda has been enhanced by their success in transplanting the agencies and activities launched by them through their tax exempt foundations into the Federal and local governments for operation at the expense of the taxpayers. Thus their subversive General Education Board's activities were transferred and incorporated with the *departments of health and welfare by its original Assistant Secretary, Nelson A. Rockefeller. At the same time, the conspirators arranged to have their own foundations and agencies engaged in subversion and support of their political advancement financed by the taxpayers through their so-called Central Intelligence Agency (CIA).* (395:400;401)
Products of the "success" of the conspirators' GEB of which we are now suffering include: juvenile delinquents, gang warfare, "beatniks," "hippies" who emulate the lowest strata of Negro riff-raff and have sunk to subhuman levels, "sloppy sluts," dope addicts galore and a progressive deterioration of the level of civilization we had attained prior to their "philanthropies." They have been "taught to do in a perfect way" muggings as well as slaughter on a grand scale, as exemplified in the Near East, Korean and Vietnam holocausts engineered for the expansion of the oily "One(Rockefeller)World" Empire. These dupes of the conspirators are eloquently portrayed by press photographs of their bodies and those of their victims strewn over battlefields, that should bear the legend: "*...they yield themselves with perfect docility to our molding hands."*
Other products of the success of the conspirators' GEB are the "Civil Rights" rioters, murderers and arsonists in Watts, Detroit and Cleveland; and the draft card burners, Vietnam sit-ins and school and college picketers and rioters. Their function is the breakdown of law and order at home to serve the conspirators' dictatorship aims.

"A ROCKEFELLER FUND SUCCESS: IT GOES BROKE"
The above was the headline of the deceptively false story in the *N. Y. World Telegram & Sun* of November 18, 1965, on the shutdown of the General Education Board after its function had all been transplanted into the government. The story represented that the GEB, established by John D. the First, had shut down after sixty-two years of *"giving aid"* to U.S. education, *"particularly for Southern Negroes."* It related that "almost all major colleges and universities" had received grants from it. But it made no mention of the real purpose of those grants: seduction and bribery of teachers and professors to "yield with perfect docility" and serve the conspirators in subversion of the nation and the world. It made no mention of the enormous increase in the costs of the "education" purveyed, and the fabulous profits that it has yielded the conspirators through their control of the industries involved and through, subversion.

257

## ROT & CORRUPTION ARE EARMARKS OF ROCKEFELLER POLITICS & ADMINISTRATION

Rot and corruption pervade every aspect of public life of Nelson Rockefeller and his cohorts. It is marked by atavistic reversion to "Doc" William Rockefeller's, his great grandfather's, swindling carnival and medicine show tactics: the use of felons, confidence men and "shills" to lure gullible suckers. The deterioration that he has produced in law enforcement has become manifest in the multiplying instances of officers of the law resorting to crime and its promotion. One of the most recent instances was the arrest, on December 12, 1967, of five New York and one Federal narcotic agents for the sale of dope to "pushers." (314;315)

New wrinkles in crime developed by themselves and their agents, manifestations of their "genius," constantly come to light. The latest was disclosed in testimony before the N.Y. State Investigation Commission on December 13, 1967, was the advance of waterfront thievery practised by the Mafia gangsters of the Vito Genovese "family" during past decades, that has been extended to the airports operated by the conspirators' Port Authority. The racketeers have taken over the airlift industry by a criminally led union, stealing many millions of cargo every year, with violence and sabotage. (316;317)

## ROCKEFELLER SEEKS PRESIDENTIAL NOMINATION WITH AID OF "SHILLS"

Nelson Rockefeller's most amusing use of the carnival-type "shills" that proves him to be "a chip off the old block" of his felonious ancestor, swindling quack "Doc" Bill, has been his tactics in drumming up for himself a "draft" for the 1968 Republican Presidential nomination. He is employing all available Madison Avenue advertising and huckster "talent" drafted to fake "public opinion" and "demand" for his candidacy in so clumsy and obvious a manner that it is highly probable that the "Doc" would have rejected them as too crude to sell his oily "cancer cure," even though financed entirely at the expense of the taxpayers. Fulton Lewis III reported that Rockefeller offered campaign managers who managed to swing Texas into the Goldwater column in 1964, $30,000 to work for him until the 1968 nomination, whether he won or lost; and an additional $30,000 a year for nine years if he would win the nomination, at the very time he was publicly lying that he did not want the nomination and was pretending to support his dupe and catspaw, Romney. The treachery that he showed in doublecrossing Romney is a device that he has used in the past several decades to destroy all Republican leaders who were potential Presidential candidates, (79:147) and to throw the election to fellow, "New" Deal, Red, and what he calls "moderates" or Democrats. (396)

While Rockefeller still posed as a non-candidate, a Madison Avenue "shill" placed a two page advertisement in the N.Y. Times, on March 3, 1968, congratulating Romney for his "quitting" and accepting his doublecross, inviting himself to seek the nomination and asking the sucker public to contribute to his campaign. (397) On the following Sunday Rockefeller showed his treacherous hand by summoning stooge employees and Republican Governors, who had enjoyed the hospitality and rich gifts and "samples" when guests of the conspirator-financed-and-controlled Governors Conferences, to his New York home for the purpose of "drafting" him. The "enthusiastic" response was cited by the N.Y. Times as consisting of seven Governors, including his "odd" brother, Winthrop, Governor of Arkansas; three Senators, including his doublecrossed pawn Javits whom he had promised to back as a "favorite son" candidate from New York in repayment for managing his reelection campaign; two New York and three out-of-State Representatives; and seventeen of his subordinates. Their "command performance" clearly indicated no great enthusiasm for him. Rockefeller's customary release to the press stated that he had been "drafted," but like Julius Caesar, he rejected the crown. It was not reported who would play the role of a much needed Brutus. (397;398) The Republicans have little stomach for Red, "New" Dealer Nelson Rockefeller who has refused to campaign as a Republican and has regularly betrayed the Party.

In his desperate determination to seize the Presidency Nelson Rockefeller has publicized the conspirators' ability to steal elections through control of voting machine companies. He announced on April 11, 1968, that if he could get the nomination, he could guarantee his election. (413)

The manner in which Rockefeller has attained his "acclaim" has been experienced by this author. On Sunday April 22, 1968, one week before he announced his candidacy, this author was approached by a person who asserted he represented Rockefeller, and offered payment of $150,000 in cash for suppression of this book and *The Truth About Rockefeller*. The publisher of columns by this author was offered an equal sum to refrain from further exposures of Rockefeller malfeasance and skulduggery.

## EXTENSION OF TAX EXEMPTION TO LABOR
## HENCHMEN ENRICHES CONSPIRATORS

The menace of illicitly usurped power coupled with tax exemption that is extended by conspirators to their pawns, partners and co-conspirators in regimenting American "peasants," the Labor Barons, gangsters and goons, was dramatically illustrated by the January, 1966 New York City transit strike that paralyzed the City for a period of twelve days. Rockefeller's stooge Mayor Fiorello LaGuardia, under the personal direction of his "secretary," David Rockefeller, had served them in the rigging of an enormously profitable deal, or steal, for "unification" of New York's transit system. It bailed them out, at par value, of the securities of the various companies involved, that they had acquired for a small fraction thereof. As this author has recounted in *Strange Death of F. D. Roosevelt*, (7:132) it was reported that the conspirators had looted $150,000,000 from New York's taxpayers in this "deal." Rumor has it that Mayor LaGuardia received no direct "payoff" in this steal; but that it was paid to his kin. The Rockefeller interests retained control of the transit system through their extra- and supra-legal Transit Authority, for the purpose of continuing to mulct and loot it, and of deliberately mismanaging it to the point where public outcry would force extension, improvement and increased fares. (7:214)

## TRANSIT WORKERS UNION AID CONSPIRATORS
## IN LOOTING NEW YORKERS.

Since the 1940's the conspirators assigned the role of dramatizing

259

the process of looting New York through the transit system to the TWU's crude, semi-literate, uncouth goon Labor Baron, Michael Quill, an Irish Red who has been identified before the Dies Committee as a former member of_the Communist Party (with fifty-two Communist "front" citations in Appendix IX) who was ousted from it when he breached its discipline. He was not otherwise disposed of by it in the customary manner, murder, probably because of his proved usefulness. At the time, Quill identified his lieutenant and understudy in the TWU, as a card-holding member of the Communist Party, which the latter proudly acknowledged. Red Mike Quill was lent added prestige in his role of President of the International TWU, in the 1940's, by his post of New York City Councilman. (7:215) Every two years, with the regularity of clockwork, Quill, joyful, blustering and arrogant, threatened to paralyze the City with a transit strike. In the early 1950's he played up to the public by demanding wage increases *with no rise in the fare.* This suited the purpose of the Democratic Party at the time and of its Mayor Robert F. Wagner Jr. with whom Quill was closely allied.

Mayor Wagner was a Rockefeller agent of the second generation. His father, Sen. Robert F. Wagner, whose religious apostasy from Judaism, to Protestantism and then to Catholicism, was a standing joke among the clergy, was notoriously a mere Rockefeller puppet and a mental case who often did not know the contents of the bills that he was given by the conspirators to introduce. He earned his first Rockefeller laurels when he was sent to the New York State Legislature to secure the passage of a bill granting a State charter for the Rockefeller Foundation, after Congress had repeatedly refused to grant it a charter because of the subversive purposes for which it was planned. (15) No heavyweight mentally, in the last decades of his public life he was an advanced case of senile dementia who had to be accompanied by a guardian to find his way home. All bills Wagner introduced at the behest of the conspirators advanced the Rockefeller-Soviet conspiracy; he served them with loyal servility. The most acclaimed of those bills is the Wagner Labor Relations Act, the Magna Carta of the conspirators Labor Barons, Mafia gangsters and goons who regiment American working "peasants" for them. (7)

CONSPIRATORS' DEMOCRAT MAYOR WAGNER<br>RIGGED THEIR TRANSIT LOOTING

As might be expected in view of his ancestry, Mayor Wagner served the conspirators with absolute fidelity in their looting of New York. They, in turn, maneuvered the rewriting of the charter which they had imposed on the City, several decades prior, to conform with the latest plan for looting municipalities that their agents had promulgated through their "1313," Municipal Clearing House agencies and their Institute of Public Administration. (15:162f) They have transformed New York's Mayor, following their scheme for Sovietizing the U.S., to absolute ruler of the City under their direction.

As a reward for the financial support that the unions, the TWU in particular, had given his three election campaigns from the tax-exempt loot extracted from their member serfs for the privilege of working, he arranged, under the cover of the process of collective blackmail mockingly named "collective bargaining," to repeatedly increase the wage of the unionized transit workers. By 1965, Mayor Wagner and the conspirators had so well succeeded in bringing New York City to the verge of bankruptcy, that it was deemed wiser for him to refuse reelection.

The wage of unskilled transit laborers had been raised to a minimum of $140 per week. This is higher than the pay of many professional, highly skilled workers, and was among the highest wages in the country, at that time. Exercising the absolute power over the wealth of the city which the conspirators had endowed him under their "revision" of the city charter that made him "Commissar," the Mayor generously doubled his own salary to $50,000 a year with proportionate pension and "fringe benefits." In addition he maintained the residence (provided for New York's Mayor since the days when "Liberal" LaGuardia had bridled at having his Negro constituents move into the same apartment house on Fifth Avenue, and usurped the use of one of the city's historic landmarks, Gracie Mansion), in regal style, at the expense of the taxpayers. A retinue of household employees and retainers, with their upkeep, cost the taxpayers a million dollars a year in wages, upkeep and pensions.

## CONSPIRATORS' RED "REPUBLICAN" MAYOR LINDSAY PICKED TO SPARK STEAL

Public outrage at this unabashed looting made it "time for a change." The conspirators engineered the election of another of their stooges, a kinsman of theirs, a Liberal," or Red, of their own stripe, (who prefer to dupe the "peasants" by calling themselves "moderates") and alleged "Republican." Congressman John V. Lindsay's election was effected by the usual devices of the conspirators, control and rigging of voting machines, stealing elections and nullifying the franchise of the citizenry whom they mockingly implore to cast their ballots.

Directly after they had elected their "song and dance man," Lindsay, Mayor, the conspirators set about intensifying their looting of the City. They rigged another transit strike that served as a justification for an increased transit fare and additional subsidy of their Transit Authority by the taxpayers. Before the election, in November, the conspirators' Chase Manhattan Bank arranged for the rental of buses to convey their workers to and from work during a transit strike that was to be called in the following January

Several weeks later, their stooge Mike Quill announced a preposterous set of terms for the new labor contract for his union. These included a four day week at a salary increase of 30%, six weeks vacations and numerous other absurd demands, the cost of which would require tripling the fares and increasing the deficit-ridden city's budget. In his loutish manner and affected Irish brogue, he made it clear, in all media of mass communications, freely put at his disposal to heroize him as a "champine of the workers," that he planned to use the irresponsible power with which the conspirators had endowed him to vent his spleen and deliberately endanger the welfare, security, health and lives of the people and inflict huge losses on commerce and industry. His elegant expression of this intent was: "Let the people waddle to work;" and "I'm gon-oo reduce the City to

261

a shambles." His mentally aberrant state was obvious, in the act which he staged with excessive reality, and crude, vulgar abuse of the public officials involved.

As part of the act, the Transit Authority obtained a last minute injunction against the strike. Tragedian Quill replied: "Let the judge drop dead in his black robes!"; and "I'll rot in jail before I call off the strike." He melodramatically defied the injunction that made the strike illegal, and before television cameras and microphones, he insisted on going to jail to play the martyr. But no sooner did he get to jail than he staged a "heart attack." The conspirators arranged to make him an honored and pampered guest of the City in a private room at Bellevue Hospital with a retinue of nurses, doctors and guards that cost the taxpayers a small fortune, instead of confining him to the jail ward. He rested in luxury rejoicing in the "shambles" to which he did reduce the City, in defiance of the Court's injunction.

## CONSPIRATORS DELIVERED NEW YORK
## INTO HANDS OF THEIR LABOR GOONS

Gov. Nelson Rockefeller celebrated the calling of the transit strike by entertaining a galaxy of Labor Barons (the favored leader of whom had been convicted of murder, forty years prior, but released on a technical appeal), goons and racketeers, in his private apartment at Rockefeller Center. The "distinguished affair" constituted derision of the Court ruling that declared the strike illegal and a conspiracy against the public. It forcibly underscores the failure of Gov. Rockefeller to make any move by the State of New York to enforce the laws barring a strike of public employees and a conspiracy against the government and the public. Rockefeller's only public utterances during the strike dealt with such shams as his fake "drive against narcotic addiction." In support of his minions, Rockefeller flagrantly violated his oath of office.

## MAYOR LINDSAY ALSO GAVE THE CONSPIRATORS
## HIS FULL COOPERATION

Song and dance man, Mayor Lindsay, gave his full cooperation to the conspirators, with the smirking air and ham acting that is his forte. The conspirator-controlled press, radio, television and other media of mass communication played him in the role of "the hero" who aimed to foil the villain, Mike Quill. But his only action was collusion with the lawless goons to help make their sabotage of the public more effective and crushing. Instead of heeding the Court order and requiring the strikers to return to work or be subject to penalties, Mayor Lindsay condoned their illegal acts and contempt for the law and the Court. He commiserated with them and told them that they had grievances that he falsely implied *justified their violations of the law*, that they were "underpaid" and that he was anxious to make amends to the extent that he could find more money extractable from the taxpayers, the State and the Federal governments.

The stranded and grievously injured public, Mayor Lindsay ordered, in full accord with Labor Baron Quill, to "waddle," to either stay home and forego their earnings, walk endless miles to their places of employment, or if it was absolutely necessary for them to do so, to get to their destinations in the severely restricted private vehicles he allowed to travel in the city. Lindsay had been vociferous in his support of the "Civil Rights," which are civil wrongs, accorded to the conspirators' Negro confederates for political purposes. However, he collaborated in denying to the entire community their real and vital right of adequate transportation, and the civil right to be protected from a conspiracy that injured public and private welfare by public officials sworn to uphold the law.

## MAYOR LINDSAY JOINED LABOR GOONS IN SABOTAGING THE CITIZENS

Instead of complying with the Court order, Mayor Lindsay made himself an accomplice of the lawbreakers and courted them by engaging with their representatives in the process of collective blackmail. He disregarded numerous demands of press and public to provide emergency transportation with public and private vehicles that were available and could have been operated by other public employees.

On the twelfth day of the strike, the New York Times espoused public interest, in a change of policy undoubtedly dictated by its costly experience with its unions. It accepted an advertisement from this author, at his personal expense, outlining the facts above stated, pointing out that the City and the public officials involved, including the Mayor, were legally liable for their illegal acts and negligences, as were also the union and its members and officers personally. (174) Within twenty-four hours after the appearance of the author's advertisement with its exposure of the true nature of the conspiracy, a prompt reaction took the form of a full page advertisement in the New York Herald Tribune of January 13, 1966, headlined *Time Is Running Out*. It was signed by John D. Rockefeller the Third, Winthrop W. Aldrich, his uncle, and one hundred and four of their associates, agents and stooges, a cross section of their Council on Foreign Relations pawns. (176) The conspirators called a halt to the strike and the sabotage that it involved. They acknowledged that:

"New Yorkers...should not be called upon to endure longer the sacrifice imposed on them by the wilful conduct of a few. To a large extent, those least able to afford it have suffered the most. Thousands of men and women cannot get to work; many others cannot put in a full day's work. Thousands are not being paid; small business firms are threatened with collapse, and essential health, educational and other services of the City are seriously threatened."

They sought to absolve their agent, Mayor Lindsay, of the charge made by this author, collusion with the lawbreakers, but admonished him to do his legal duty of protecting the community instead of collaborating with union agents.

"...we now urge Mayor Lindsay, *who has acted thus far with infinite patience*, to employ the full services and capacities of the City and State in the restoration of the transportation facilities of the City."

They also sought to absolve their confederate, Gov. Nelson Rockefeller, for his nonfeasance and malfeasance, as follows:

"Specifically, we urge the Mayor, if the strike is not ended promptly to request the Governor of the State and any other appropriate authorities to join him in making use of all the available manpower resources of the community, including, if necessary, and as a last resource, the National Guard, to man and operate buses within the City for as long a time as may be necessary."

## CONSPIRATORS, SCARED, CALLED A HALT TO THEIR STRIKE

The influence of this cabal and the role that they played in this conspiracy against the public is manifest from the termination of the strike at the very moment the newspaper containing their advertisement appeared on the street. The same recommendations had been made by numerous groups, daily, from the very start of the strike. But it was only when the clique, that tagged itself *Citizens' Committee For Public Safety*, responded to exposure of the collusion of their agents in the conspiracy against the public, and advice that lawsuits for recovery of damages due to their malfeasance and negligence be brought against them personally, that they acted to terminate the conspiracy.

## "I AM THE MAYOR" LINDSAY MADE DETERMINED EFFORT TO RAISE FARES

New York State made available to the City the sum of $84 million to turn over to the conspirators' Transit Authority, to make up its "deficit," and make an increased fare unnecessary. Mayor Lindsay had full authority to do so, under the new City Charter, which gave him virtually absolute power to rule New York as a "commissar," including its finances. But he refused to turn the money over to the Transit Authority, presumably on the basis of a secret agreement with his confederate, Rockefeller, to dupe the public. As a consequence, fares on all public conveyances were increased from 15¢ to 20¢; and the way was prepared to further intensify transit looting of the citizenry by the proposal advanced by Gov. Rockefeller to "unify" the transit looting by the establishment of another of the conspirators' supra-governmental "authorities," the Metropolitan Transit Authority. Through that device, the conspirators have enabled themselves to raise New York's transit fares whenever they please and as much as they wish, with no redress possible on the part of the public, by the simple device of forcing each transit system to pay for itself while they continue and intensify their unlimited looting on an ever more grandiose and ruthless scale. To facilitate this arrangement, Gov. Rockefeller duped the public into voting, in the 1967 election, for a $2.5 billion bond issue for the pretended "transit improvements." Previously, a $500 million appropriation for the purpose of building a new Second Avenue subway had "vanished" (into the pockets of the conspirators?). There is little reason to believe that the $2.5 billion, or most of it, will not suffer the same fate.

## RACKETEERING EXPOSURE COMPELLED LINDSAY TO "SAVE FACE" IN GARBAGE STRIKE

Exposure of the collaboration of his Water Commissioner Marcus with the Mafia in looting the City by "kickbacks" on contracts, forced Mayor Lindsay to "save face" by pretending to oppose the Sanitation Union's demand, in January 1968, for pay and other increases exceeding those that he had agreed upon with union

264

"leader" DeLurey that had been rejected by its members. Posing as a "champion" of public interests, Lindsay asked Gov. Rockefeller to call out the National Guard to move the week-long garbage accumulation that filled the streets, though it would have cost the taxpayers many times the demanded wage increase. Rockefeller helped Lindsay "save face" by refusing to call out the troops. Instead, he courted the unionists by offering to violate the Taylor Act that had been passed on his own demand, by offering to have the State take over the City's Sanitation Department and put his stamp of approval on their violation of the law by granting them $250,000 demanded wage increase.

Lindsay played his role with a pose of righteous indignation at Gov. Rockefeller's collusion in violating his own Taylor Law, and his violation of "Home Rule" by intervening, as requested, in the City's affairs. He made an issue of the $250,000 that amounted to less than the salary of eight carpetbagger and "gay boy" Commissioners that he has dragged in from all parts of the country. For Health Commissioner, Lindsay imported from Canada, by way of Seattle, a character whose sole acquaintance with New York and its problems was a few days' vacation spent there, years earlier. In these appointments, Lindsay adhered to the pattern decreed by the conspirators and promulgated through the "1313" Public Administration Clearing House, as an essential device for denial of home and self rule and supplanting our Republic with their totalitarian regime by imposing "carpetbagging" officials, "managers," whose sole allegiance is to the Dynasty and its looting. (102)

### LINDSAY SHOWED LOYALTY TO CONSPIRATORS: IMPOSED CITY INCOME TAX

Mayor Lindsay demonstrated further his loyalty to the conspirators and their subversive conspiracy by betraying his campaign pledge of economy and promptly collaborating in their tax looting by imposing on the taxpayers, a third, New York City income tax superimposed on the Federal and State taxes. Patterned after the Federal income tax they imposed on the nation, it virtually completely exempts them from taxation, while permitting them to loot the citizenry and spy on their affairs. Mayor Lindsay followed their program further by mercilessly looting property owners, other than the conspirators, by tremendously increasing both their assessments and taxes, to provide for the swollen salaries and other graft of his Commissioners and "gay boys" and their absurdly fantastic "ins." He has been highly successful in driving industry and commerce out of New York City by confiscatory taxation and harassment by favored union gangsters and racketeers.

### LINDSAY ADMINISTRATION FOLLOWS PATTERN OF ROCKEFELLER CORRUPTION

The Lindsay administration has adhered to the Rockefeller pattern and has been characterized by rampant corruption and crime. It is difficult to believe that his Commissioners have been appointed for any other reason than to serve their conflicts of interest. His Commissioner of Housing was closely identified with owners of slum tenements full of violations of all varieties.

His Commissioner of Police was imported from Philadelphia, where he was a favorite of the "Liberals," labor union racketeers, blacks and assorted criminal elements favored by the Reds. His chief other qualification was that he was completely ignorant of conditions existing in New York. He has been extremely successful, with the help of the conspirators, in fostering crimes of all categories in the city. Obstruction of streets by queues of theatregoers for whom theatres no longer find it necessary to provide shelter while waiting for the show to start, block passage and endanger pedestrians. "Hippies" addicted to drugs marketed by the conspirators and their agents assemble in filthy quarters or in public parks, luring youngsters with seductive publicity carried in all media of mass communication controlled by the conspirators, from their homes to lives of vice. Though the Commissioner can find unlimited police for protecting labor union racketeers with their picket lines, Black Power and Mau Mau criminals, ragged, bearded draft protesters and Communist demonstrators, he can find none to protect the law-abiding citizens from crimes by daylight, in the center of the City, ranging from mugging, battery and assault, murder, burglary and arson. As a consequence, there has been a staggering rise in major crime in New York City during the Red Lindsay administration. The ultimate in the "perfections" of Lindsay's Police Department was the complicity of its narcotics squad in the supply and sale of narcotics to "pushers," or vendors. One wonders if they gained their promotions as rewards for boosting the conspirators' highly profitable drug and fencing businesses. (379;399)

## LINDSAY'S COMMISSIONER MARCUS COLLABORATED WITH MAFFIA IN LOOTING CITY

The most "perfect" of Mayor Lindsay's appointments was that of his pal Marcus as Commissioner of Water Supply, Gas & Electricity. Marcus, son-in-law of the conspirators' Brahmin socialite CFR agent, former Governor of Connecticut Lodge, has a shady record that is readily discoverable. His first public act as Commissioner was to double the City's water rates; and to propose the health-endangering measure of metering the water supplied homes and apartments, that would penalize healthful cleanliness. It was later discovered that his plan was motivated by expected "kickbacks" on the hundreds millions of dollars involved in the purchase and installation of the meters which he represented would be a boon to the citizens.

The only attention Commissioner Marcus paid to the shortage of water threatened by the then current drought was to declare the cleaning of minor reservoirs to be "emergency" measures that required contracting without bids. He gave those contracts to Maffia-affiliated firms and shared a kickback with a notorious Maffista, possessed of a long criminal record, Tony "Ducks" Corallo. The pattern of the conspirators' association with the Maffia is strikingly followed in this instance. The Maffia tie-in arose when they seized control of bars that cater to the "gay" lads, until scandal forced the State Liquor Authority, most tolerant of Maffia penetration and corruption under the Rockefeller administration, to cancel their liquor licenses. Whereupon, the Maffia opened clubs for the "gay" lads, for which no liquor licenses were required.

## LINDSAY, VICE CHAIRMAN OF NACCD BEGINS TASK BY INCITING BLACKS TO RIOT

An amusing aspect of the rapidly increasing New York crime under the Lindsay administration is his appointment by the President, as an "expert" on riot and crime prevention, in the role of vice chairman of the National Advisory Commission on Civil Disorders. No doubt what recommended him for the post is his Red "Liberalism" that belies his designation as a Republican, as well as his courting of the criminal black and subversive elements of the nation. As soon as his appointment was announced in Washington, he proceeded to demonstrate his lack of qualification for the job by deliberately inciting Negroes to rioting, violence and crime by the usual formula of the Communist agitators. He predicted that the riots of next year would be more violent and criminal, offering the usual Communist apologetics for the felons— unless they were paid off at the expense of the taxpayers with more handouts to maintain them in luxurious idleness and were offered jobs that they neither desire nor are competent to fill.

## "LIBERALS" COURT CRIMINAL ELEMENTS AS KINDRED SPIRITS & NATURAL ALLIES

Mayor Lindsay has followed, faithfully, the conspirators' "Liberalism" in protecting their Labor Barons in their violations of true civil rights of the community. Numerous police are diverted to protect picketers and strikers whose object it is to prevent proprietors' use of their property. In effect this means that police are used to violate basic rights of the party picketed, to commit crimes. So many police are diverted to protection of inciters of violence and other criminal activities that New York City has become a hotbed of crime, with innumerable, often unrecorded, murders, muggings, rapes, burglaries and other crimes. Even in the center of town it is not safe to walk the streets in daylight. Furthermore, if by good and rare chance the felon is apprehended, as often as not the influence of the conspirators effects his release to further prey on us "peasants."

The failure of the "Liberal" Mayor Lindsay, Gov. Rockefeller and their appointees to do their sworn duty and uphold the law, in order to gain favor with their subversive, Negro and criminal agents who are given the use of all media of mass communication to exultingly announce their intent to violate the law and to incite others to do so, has made the City and State unsafe for law-abiding citizens. Police are enjoined by those "Liberals" from enforcing the law, and with law-abiding citizenry, are barred from the use of arms that are freely available to the criminal elements. This demonstrates the effectiveness of Rockefellers' "philanthropic" activities in "education": "teaching our children to do in a perfect way, what their fathers and mothers do in an imperfect way": fostering dope addicts, juvenile delinquents and adult criminals, instead of good citizens. As a consequence, the average victim of a crime, if he survives it, is harassed by mobs of police who flock to the scene in cars (in which they travel in pairs to protect themselves from the criminals). But rarely do the victims recover any stolen property, or can they expect the criminal to be apprehended. Indeed, ever more frequently, police themselves are discovered to be ringleaders of criminal bands.

## THE CONSPIRATORS HAVE ARRANGED TO MAKE LIFE SAFER FOR THEIR CRIMINALS

The conspirators have expressed their concern for their criminal agents by making life safer for them. Thus Gov. Nelson Rockefeller conducted a successful campaign to eliminate the death sentence in New York State. A direct sequel was a startling rise in the number of reported rape cases in the State, many of them culminated by murder. The felons in the lower grades including the conspirators' dope smugglers and pushers and their Maffia padrones have been blanketed by the conspirators' agents, sitting on the Supreme Court bench, with an almost complete shield of immunity that includes prohibition of use of wire-tapping evidence and of confessions in their prosecution.

The Maffia or "Cosa Nostra," as the local members prefer to be named, and their dope rings will be materially aided by Gov. Rockefeller's proposed program of enforced isolation and "treatment" of addicts in State institutions. The dope pushers will have made available to them a complete roster of all addicts in the State; and they will be materially helped in their "pushing" by being able to threaten addicts with compulsory incarceration if they do not purchase the dope from the conspirators. It is noteworthy that Rockefeller is no more in favor of using the funds of New York's taxpayers for a study of the underlying mechanism of drug addiction that he is to have the money of his tax-exempt foundations used for that purpose. A discovery of the cause of addiction, the modifications of body chemistry that create the craving for narcotics, would probably lead to the immediate discovery of the remedy. That would hit the pocketbooks of the conspirators a mighty blow!

## SUPREME COURT INCLINED TO SHIELD NEGRO RAPISTS AT INSTANCE OF CONSPIRATORS

Capping the climax of the conspirators' efforts to foster crime is the move of their Supreme Court agents in the case of the Arkansan Negro, William L. Maxwell, convicted in Hot Springs, in 1961, of raping a white woman. On January 23, 1967, the Supreme Court ordered the U.S. Court of Appeals to hear another of his numerous appeals from his conviction and death sentence, on the ground that more Negroes than whites had been convicted of raping white women. (230) The only consequence that can be expected, on the basis of past performance, is that raping of white women by Negroes will be made as safe an occupation for them as are numerous other heinous crimes, including looting of public funds by Negro "leaders," rioting, arson, treason and murder.

The conspirators' tax exempt funds richly finance this fostering of Negro, as well as white, crime. They do not come to the front, however, in these nefarious activities. They operate through their Red agencies and agents. The appeal in question was made by their Red NAACP agency through its director, Jack Greenberg. No doubt their even more violently Red agencies, such as

CORE, SNCC and the Communist Party itself, will rush in to join in this "worthy cause." The appeal was initiated by the sardonically named Legal Defense and Educational Fund Inc. One wonders if the Fund will undertake to "educate" its beneficiaries in the performance of rape on white women.

## ROCKEFELLER QUOTED AS SAYING HE WILL REFUSE TO BUY MORE ELECTIONS

Rockefeller is quoted by several columnists as joining the complaint of many candidates for public office that the cost of "buying elections" has become too costly; and alleging that he will buy no more of them. No effort is made to hide the fact that candidacies and elections are being bought. News media openly relate that the various political parties seek candidates who can supply the funds for campaigns or who command tax exempt funds through such means as control of foundations or unions.

## BUT MAKES DEALS WITH LABOR TO BUY PRESIDENCY FOR HIM AT PUBLIC EXPENSE

Victor Riesel, the reliable "Labor" columnist, repeatedly reported corrupt deals that Gov. Nelson Rockefeller is offering his Labor Barons for their support in his 1968 quest for the Presidency. Under the headline "Rocky's Dinner Party: Groundwork For '68?" Riesel reported that Gov. Rockefeller held "a princely council" at his home at 812 Fifth Avenue, at which his honored guests were practitioners of "street cleaning, janitoring, table waiting, building servicing, carpentering, derricking and administering." All were union leaders who had been invited, or summoned, by telegram to "dine with the Rockefellers," on December 14, 1966, with their wives. Among the guests were the Howard Coughlins of the Office and Professional Employees Union, John DeLury, of the Uniformed Sanitationmen of America, Dick Nolan of the Operating Engineers' Union and "old radicals" such as Jay Rubin of the Hotel and Motel Trades Council and Leon Davis of the Hospital Workers Union. Most prominent among them was Harry Van Arsdale, closest Rockefeller associate among them and notorious as "Mr. Four Hour Day," because of his demand for a four hour day for his Electrical Construction Workers Union. He headed Rockefeller's labor campaign organization and was in turn rewarded by Rockefeller's complete cooperation in the Transit Workers Union that paralyzed New York City during several weeks in January, 1966. At the very time of the dinner, unions headed by some of the guests, including the plumbers' union, were striking and paralyzing enterprises involving hundreds of millions of dollars and throwing tens of thousands of workers out of work. But no mention was made of these "trivial matters" by their Rockefeller host. The guests knew right well that they had been summoned for more important matters, which Riesel summed up with the statement that they were quite certain that Rockefeller had not spent an acknowledged $5 million merely to buy the Governorship, but planned to make a determined effort to buy the Presidency in 1968, or at least the Secretary of State post, and was wooing them for their support with a deal that would be at least as satisfactory a sell-out to them of the public and taxpayers as that which he had given them in the past, for their financial support and the betrayal of their vassal members. (249)

269

Gov. Rockefeller planned his customary attempt to evade his campaign promise that he would not increase taxes, without forfeiting any of the so-called "profit" or loot that he seeks from his office, by proposing two projects that will be enormously costly to the taxpayers, and profitable to himself, the conspirators and their banking confederates through financing by more than $10 billion in tax exempt bonds. One of these steals which is the building of a series of atomic energy power plants by New York State at the expense of the taxpayers for seven private utility companies controlled by the Rockefellers. These plants would profitably supplement the steal by the conspirators' United Nuclear Corp. of atomic energy plants built at a cost to taxpayers of billions of dollars, including that at Hanford. This planned steal was not reported to have been brought to their attention probably because it was too raw, and might have irritated his "close friends and political allies," and impelled them to make higher demands for "payoff."

## ROCKEFELLER ENLISTED LABOR SUPPORT FOR TRANSIT STEAL & HIGHER FARES

Gov. Rockefeller did, however, ask his Labor Barons for support of another outrageous steal in return for a payoff. For the purpose of more intensively looting the public through their transportation needs, covertly and without immediately raising fares and taxes, Rockefeller proposed to create another of the conspirators' "authorities" to merge all New York transit agencies through which New Yorkers have been looted. For this purpose he proposed that his Metropolitan Transit Authority demand authorization by Legislature of an extra-budgetary $2 billion bond issue. The bonds will require increased taxes for interest payments and amortization during the life of the issue, amounting to a minimum of $150 millions a year; and it also means a removal from the tax rolls of property that implies added burden on the taxpayers of at least $100 million a year. Thus the public would be duped with the representation that taxes would not be increased by him.

Gov. Rockefeller falsely represented that subway fare increase would be averted by this steal. Dr. Ronan, Rockefeller's chosen agent for operating the MTA, more honestly stated in a press conference on Station WABC, that it might be possible to avert an increased subway fare for a "considerable time." (268) How "considerable" is that time is indicated by a columnist who reported that while the bill for creating the MTA was pending, the conspirators' Transit Authority was having the coin slots on the subway turnstiles enlarged so that they could take 25 cent pieces instead of the small 20¢ tokens. In February 1968, an increased fare was demanded by the Long Island Railroad, a division of the MTA, and was granted.

Gov. Rockefeller offered the invited Labor Barons a handsome bribe for their support of the bill authorizing this gigantic steal that will amount to billions each year: a guarantee that no man would be permitted to work on any part of the program who does not pay them tribute as members of their unions. But he included a "catch" that would deprive the Labor Barons of one of the most important sources of their illegitimate income: that they agree

270

to forego strikes. Riesel stated that one of the implied and understood terms of Rockefeller's deal was that the Labor Barons have their unions support his Presidential aspirations in 1968 (or earlier) and that they withdraw their support from Pres. Johnson. Riesel said:

"Few insiders here doubt that he (Rockefeller) is making a massive drive for the GOP Presidential nomination." (250)

## ROCKEFELLER GRABS THROUGH HIS OFFICE ALL FALL IN THE SAME PATTERN

Rockefeller's grab of taxpayer funds and property in his capacity as New York's Governor, fall into the same pattern as the conspirators' wartime, "foreign aid" and "coordination" steals. They are brazenly open and predicated on his attitude that public office, like all his other efforts, must pay handsomely without regard to such "nonsense" as "conflict of interest." This is as strikingly apparent in his Albany South Mall building boondoggle and his Hudson River grabs as it is in his "slum clerance and urban redevelopment" and New York Trade Center steals. His attitude is that he is above all law and tenets of honesty and decency. Dictatorially he proclaims in effect: "The Law? I am the Law."

The ownership of any valuable tract of property by others than themselves is "an affront" to the thievish conspirators, and is an invitation to steal it by one of the devices that they have originated for the purpose. Fronting the State Capitol at Albany, on a hill overlooking the Hudson, Rockefeller found twenty blocks, ninety eight acres, of choice property occupied by 3,500 families of the taxpayers, "peasants," with their businesses, livelihoods and homes, that could handily be tagged as slums for the purpose of looting. Loot in addition to the value of the grabbed land was derivable through the costs of its "redevelopment" by Rockefeller's kinsman, architect Harrison of the firm of Harrison & Abramovitz, in which he is rumored to be interested. (293)

This "redevelopment" project was conceived by Rockefeller on his usual grandiose scale, to cost the taxpayers a billion dollars. State laws require that such capital expenditures must be submitted to the taxpayers for approval. Rockefeller's merciless tax looting, during his governorship, made it a certainty that such needless expenditure, and taxes to cover it, would be rejected by the voters. The new "Rockefeller Center," which it was promptly labelled, was opposed by Democratic Mayor Corning of Albany. But this constituted no obstacle to Gov. Rockefeller and his "grandiose ideas." With complete contempt for the "peasant" taxpayers, Rockefeller disregarded and flaunted the law. He made a deal with Mayor Corning in consideration of which the latter dropped his opposition to the steal. It will cost New York's taxpayers a half a million dollars a year, in addition to interest and all other costs, for issue of bonds for State purposes, in violation of both the letter and spirit of the law, in the name of the County and City of Albany.

From past records of Rockefeller deals, such as those of Rockefeller Center and the "United" Nations, some undisclosed part of the deal probably provides that the land and the gerrymandered buildings will revert to the conspirators when the buildings have rapidly deteriorated and become too costly to maintain.

*Fortune* magazine, in an article entitled *New York Rebuilds Its Capital*, reported that in Harrison's (Rockefeller's?) architectural plans:

"... he has come up... with flashy shapes and crammed functions into them...one office building is roughly the shape of an old-fashioned keyhole—an arbitrary shape in which to try to arrange efficient offices." (293)

It quotes *Progressive Architecture* as describing this as "an exercise in architectural pop art."

The thievish potential involved in this Albany "Rockefeller Center" South Mall project and its possible yield to such organization as the ten-percenting Special Work Inc. of Rockefellers' "philanthropic" setup, was revealed by New York State Controller Levitt in a letter, at the end of January, 1968, to the State Legislature asking for an inquiry into its rising cost. He called attention to the steady rise in the cost estimate from $350 million to $610 million and indicated that the eventual cost will be "at least a billion dollars." Sidney H. Schanberg, in a special dispatch to the N.Y. Times published on January 3, 1968 (361:29), reported that Gov. Rockefeller had hurried to send a special message to the Legislature pleading that it disregard the Controller's requested investigation. Schanberg's description of Governor Rockefeller's concern was quite apt: that the Governor's reply was interpreted as meaning that the project was *extremely important to him personally.* In view of the fact that nothing is more important to him than making money, as avowed by him to his biographers (66:44), the inference to be drawn therefrom is much too obvious: corrupt practises.

Rockefeller has undertaken to use his public office to perpetuate another shameful steal in connection with the family's Pocantico Hills estate. To supplement the Dynasty's "meagre income" they plan an industrial development, now barred by zoning, on part of the estate. For that purpose, Gov. Rockefeller has undertaken to have the State put through their estate a new highway from the main highway, miles away. As part of the scheme, it is planned to run a highway along the east bank of the Hudson River that will deprive access to residents of the towns along the river. For the consummation of this and other designs on the taxpayers, Gov. Rockefeller has appointed his brother, Laurance, New York State Park Commissioner. The reader is referred for details of this steal to William Rodgers' *Rockefeller Follies.* (243)

## "BIG LIE" CAMPAIGNS OF OPPONENTS & HIMSELF ARE PROFITABLE FOR ROCKEFELLERS

Rockefeller's concern over cost of campaigning for office is a pretense. For as a result of the conspirators' monopoly of the networks, the moneys spent by his opponents and contributed to his own campaign are a source of immense profits to them. The principal items of cost in modern campaigns are radio and television broadcasts. The more intensive the campaigns, the greater are their profits therefrom. (79:82) In some instances their ownership of the networks is masked to evade the law and protect their FCC agents. Jack O'Brian revealed in his March 15, 1967, column in the World Journal Tribune:

"Belatedly revealed new owners of the Mutual Network includes *Rockefeller heirs* M. P. and B. D. Gilbert..."

Television and radio are ideal media for the dissemination of the "Big Lie," the technique of which depends on psychologic factors: the "conditioning" of the "mass men" created by the "educational philanthropists," that makes them responsive only to stimuli selected by the conspirators, following the technique of Pavlov in the manner indicated by Ortega y Gasset (251), and stimulation of the "mass men" constantly and repeatedly with the "Big Lie," or a series of them, regarding the candidate. By monopolizing prime broadcasting time for short advertisements constantly repeated through days, weeks and months, the conspirators avail themselves of the psychologic fact that lies repeated often enough through media to which "mass man" has been conditioned by them to be responsive, come to be regarded as the truth. In this manner, the conspirators can make heroes of loathsome crooks and vicious traitors. Exposure of their skulduggery is blocked by their control of all media of mass communication. The so-called "debates" that they stage in order to maintain the illusion of freedom of speech and fairplay are so crookedly rigged and limited, in time and scope, that they accentuate the "Big Lie."

ROCKEFELLER PLATFORM: DOPE ADDICT "SOLUTION" DESIGNED TO AUGMENT DOPE PROFITS

The "Big Lie" technique and its effectiveness was beautifully illustrated in Nelson Rockefeller's third gubernatorial campaign. His false past promises that he would not increase taxes had so completely destroyed his credibility on that count that it was little stressed. Greatest stress was laid in his "Big Lie" campaign on the pretense that he would solve the very real problem of dope addiction and crime resulting from it that the conspirators had so deliberately brought about. The solution that Gov. Rockefeller made the basis of this aspect of his campaign was one that had repeatedly been proved to be the very method that would increase addiction and the profits from it to the conspirators and their "lesser Mafia" henchmen: the isolation of addicts for years in institutions. Past experience has amply proved that such a program is mortally feared and shunned by addicts; and that it serves to put the addicts completely at the mercy of the dope "pushers" and their criminal associates, and greatly increases the profits that the "lesser Mafia" make for the conspirators.

There was withheld from the public, during the campaign, the fact that the only possible solution of the problem is research to discover the changes in body chemistry (probably the inactivation of some trace element by the drugs, that creates a deficiency thereof) that is responsible for addiction, and its correction. This truth was disclosed in the second of a series of articles boosting the use of drugs as "the modern way of life," published two years later in the New York Times. (342) The article by Richard D. Lyons, in the January 9, 1968, issue, succinctly reveals the truth in its headline, reading:

273

"SCIENCE'S KNOWLEDGE ON THE MISUSE OF DRUGS &
HOW THEY ACT IS FOUND TO LAG
MORE STUDY IS URGED ON THEIR EFFECTS
Centuries-Old Problem Of Addiction Poses Question
Thus Far Unanswered"
The article does not reveal that the conspirators have studiously avoided sponsoring those needed researches. None of tax funds
diverted into the "Philanthropic" Foundation Trust by the conspirators has ever been used for this vital basic research, though much
of it has been misused, directly and indirectly, to stimulate the production and consumption of drugs. The probable explanation of this
sordid situation is offered in another article in the quoted series.
It relates that drugs have been used since time immemorial by
ruthless enslavers of men to weaken and/or destroy any resistance
to their domination. The reader can judge for himself, bearing
in mind the drugged "hippie" pattern of our society, if that is
the true purpose of our ruler, Gov. Nelson Rockefeller, and of his
Dynasty and collaborators. Biographers report that he offers samples of drugs of controlled firms to his friends. *He never takes any
himself.* (79:70:343)

FAKED "OPPOSITION" SUPPLEMENTED BY "DEAL" TO
LEAVE CONSPIRATORS ON TOP

The rigged character of Gov. Rockefeller's reelection was obvious. His Democratic opponent, O'Connor, did not give up his office
so as to permit election of a successor, and he made no effort to
take real issues to the voters and to expose the obvious absurd
insincerity and falsity of the "issues" on which Rockefeller campaigned. He gave the impression that he was actually fearful that
he might win. Subsequently, a columnist revealed that an "arrangement" had been made by him to appoint one of Rockefeller's Aldrich
cousins to a key post if elected.

KENNEDY DYNASTY SERVES ROCKEFELLER DYNASTY
AS MINOR SATELLITE

The conspirators and their "super-Mafia" invariably "work both
sides of the fence." This was demonstrated with startling clarity
when Sen. Robert F. Kennedy was induced to launch a well-founded
attack on the conflict of interest involved in Rockefeller's planned
atomic energy plant steal. Kennedy initially charged, truthfully, that
Rockefeller's bill would give the Dynasty's private utilities absolute
and uncontrollable monopoly of New York power; and would raise
further the high cost of electric power in the State. (252) Rockefeller promptly slapped Kennedy down with the grossly false and
insulting retort: "Senator Kennedy's statement is phony and a
hoax." (253) "Bobby" Kennedy, obviously terrified at the boss Rockefeller's venomously caustic attack, ran for cover. He hastily rendered abject obesiance to his Rockefeller master. On the following
day, under the headline *RFK, Rocky Seek Pact On Power,* he announced through his spokesman, Leo Goodman, through whom rosy
Red Walter Reuther directs his activities, his willingness to aid and
abet Rockefeller in this steal, and betray, "compromise" was the
euphemistic term used in the report, public interest. (254) Nothing more clearly demonstrates the humble satellite position of the

Kennedys to the Rockefeller Dynasty. In May 1968, Rockefeller pressured passage by N.Y. Legislature authorizing this steal in slightly modified form, with the full collaboration of pawn Booby Kennedy.

## ALL-POWERFUL ROCKEFELLERS HOLD NATION IN CONTEMPT

The utter contempt with which the Rockefeller conspirators regard the nation from their position of absolute monopoly and power emerged even more clearly in the elections of two other members of the Dynasty: Winthrop Rockefeller, elected Governor of Arkansas, and John D. Rockefeller the Fourth, delegate from Kanawah County to the West Virginia House of Delegates as an avowed step in the purchase for him of the carpetbagging governorship of that State.

## ARKANSAS OPPOSITION NEWSPAPERS & RADIO REFUSE ADS ON "WINNIE'S" RECORD

Winthrop Rockefeller's purchase of the Governorship of Arkansas falls into the conspirators' new tactics of carpetbagging in poverty-stricken sections of the country where support and control can be cheaply bought, and where the glamour of Rockefeller wealth and false "philanthropic" repute raises high hopes among the poor. Control of media of mass communication, especially of the "opposition" newspapers and radios in Arkansas was obtainable for a trifling sum. This precluded informing the citizenry by men courageous enough to face ruin, or the conspirators' "enforcers," of the shameful truth regarding the candidate. Such intensive, Mafia-like forces were brought to bear that even confirmed Democrats among the citizenry feared to support openly their Party's candidate. The conspirators had built up a sense of indebtedness by planting some minor branches of industries controlled by them in the State, thereby providing employment to some of the local folk.

An effort was made, with undercover support of local businessmen, to apprize the citizenry of the menace of the takeover by the conspirators and the shameful record of the candidate. They included the better element of Rockefeller's own Party, organized in a committee named *Republicans For Good Government*, who distributed a well documented and illustrated pamphlet that truthfully portrayed the various unsavory characteristics, acts and associations of the candidate. (255) The truth was a futile weapon against a corrupt campaign that is reported to have cost the conspirators more than $4 million. It was reported that Negro voters were assiduously courted and paid for at the rate of ten dollars each; and Negro political leaders around the State were given a total of seventy new automobiles. This makes understandable the rejection by the local radio station catering to the Negroes, as did the local Democratic "opposition" newspapers, of a fully documented advertisement on the financing of the Negro slave trade in Saudi Arabia by the Rockefeller interests.

## JOHN D. THE FOURTH BOASTS OF PERFIDY & EVADES SERVICE IN VIETNAM

An uglier picture is presented by the treacherous career of Rockefeller "Crown Prince," John D. the Fourth, and his projected rise to hereditary ruler of our land. He had been sent to Japan to learn the language and customs, and to train to take over from his father control of the industry and commerce of Japan, now the Dynasty's interests, won for them, as their war loot, in World War II by GI mercenaries. Toward his expenses, he was given "the maximum allowance that the family could afford," announced to be the "generous" sum of twenty-seven dollars a month. In Japan, he proved himself "a chip off the old block," by treacherously betraying our national interests in an act that was characterized as little or nothing short of traitorous. He incited Japanese students and Communists to stage riots and demonstrations against our country, specifically directed against Pres. Eisenhower with the purpose of blocking his projected visit to Japan.

Subsequently the treacherous scamp wrote a letter to a Kyoto newspaper in which he praised the rioters for offering the affront to our country and President who had been "bought and paid for" by his kinsmen and was dominated by them in every move. Then, in cowardly fear of the anti-American hatred that he had stirred up, he cut short his projected seven year stay in Japan, and fled home to the U.S. for refuge. Directly after his return, he authorized the publication in his name, in *Life*, one of the media controlled by the conspirators, of an article in which he boasted of his disloyalty and treachery. (93) As a reward for this treachery, he was given a series of jobs in the conspirators' Democratic Administration, by Pres. Kennedy. None of them took him to the front in Vietnam where drafted GIs were shedding their blood for further expansion and profits of his Dynasty.

## JOHN D IV TOOK PUBLIC OFFICE & ANNOUNCED INTENT TO RULE W. VIRGINIA, AS "START"

John D the Fourth followed the family tradition of evading active military service in their own "Crusades" for the expansion of their Empire and loot. Following the example of his uncle, Gov. Nelson Rockefeller, he obtained, through familial power, an administrative, swivel-chair job in Washington, in the missionary agency set up by Kennedy, the "Peace Corps." Then, moving away still further from the Vietnam front, he had himself transferred to the subversive "Poverty Corps" in the Appalachia region, in West Virginia, that had been effectively impoverished by his Dynasty.

With a view to advancing his status to one befitting a Rockefeller "Crown Prince," the conspirators followed their usual pattern in the takeover of sections of the country. All their press-agents, propagandists and media of mass communications gave him a fake buildup as a "philanthropist." They carefully avoided revealing that their Rockefeller-Standard Oil outfit with the help of their agent, president of coal miners union, John L. Lewis, had driven its coal industry to the wall and thereby made West Virginia the "poverty pocket" that it has been since it felt the curse of Rockefeller "benevolence."

"Crown Prince" John D the Fourth, riding on the fake "build-up" of "philanthropist," to which color was lent by his job in the bogus "Poverty Corps," announced that he would "turn coat," as did his uncle Nelson, and condescend to adopt local citizenship, and rule West Virginia's impoverished "peasants" as a Democrat. The conspirators' agents resorted to their usual, familiar practise of engineering his "drafting" as candidate for the State legislature from Kanawah County. At the same time, they filled the press and all other media of mass communication with stories that their usual fake polls to create public opinion indicated that his "philanthropy" destined his election, in the near future, as Governor of the State and ruler of its duped "peasants." He himself modestly announced that he planned to take over the post of Governor and ruler of the State, at the same time as his notoriously queer uncle, Winthrop, announced his intent to take over the rule of equally backward, impoverished and duped Arkansas. (79;131:230;255)

An advertisement offered to all the local press, detailing these shameful facts and advising the voters not to aid and abet able bodied young men evading their duty to serve the country in Vietnam by voting them into public office, was rejected, so complete and absolute is the conspirators' control of the local media. Instead, the craven specimen has been built up to the point of the citizenry accepting him as their prospective ruler, as their Governor-to-be. How much money the conspirators spent to buy the election for him has not been revealed.

The candidate's contempt for those who voted him into office was openly stated by him to be abysmal. He boasted that he won the election without announcing any platform or condescending to discuss any of the issues vital to the citizenry. He implied that they were too stupid to be concerned with them. And he intimated that he would follow the same tactics when he proceeded to purchase the Governorship of the State. One week after his election he did announce his plan to marry Sen. Percy's daughter, Sharon, to rule at his side. On February 1, 1968, he announced that he would assume the post of State Secretary before taking on the governorship. (362)

## "STATE MARRIAGE," POLITICALLY DICTATED, PLAYS ROLE IN DYNASTY BUILD-UP

An interesting sidelight on the conspirators' dynasty-building is cast by "Crown Prince" John's wedding, it was revealed by the Daily News. Under the headline *Lynda At Wedding, But She Missed The Star Role*, Judith Axler reported:

"Lynda thought an awful lot of Jay (John D. IV's nickname) at one point. She invited the young Democrat...to the LBJ Ranch several times last year to keep her company...She wrote Jay...asking him to come to Washington to see her...she was lonely in the 132-room White House...wouldn't he come and visit? Jay wrote back kindly and gently explaining that he and Sharon were now engaged." (257:3:1)

Ironically, Ladybird Johnson had introduced the bride and groom.


## USE OF "FEDERAL" RESERVE TO PRECIPITATE PRE-ELECTION PANIC PROVED BY RECOVERY

Complete proof of the use by the conspirators of their "Federal" Reserve as a political tool was evident in the rapid reduction of interest rates in the U.S. and around the world within several months after they had used usury-precipitated panic to secure their election victories. The drive for reduction of prime interest rates was led by the conspirators' Chase Manhattan Bank at the direction of the self-same David Rockefeller who had ordered higher interest rates in the year prior to the election. And the rapid lowering of their "Federal" Reserve rediscount rates was directed by them through their CFR agent, Chairman of the Federal Reserve Board William McChesney Martin, who had raised the rediscount rate to an exorbitant level a short time prior to the election, precipitating the panic.

It is noteworthy that Pres. Johnson, who had made a display of his "disapproval" and "opposition" to the rise in the rediscount rate, but invited Martin to socialize with him at his Texas ranch, reappointed him Chairman of the Federal Reserve Board several months after the Democratic defeat in the election. At the same time, it was reported that Ladybird Johnson was a guest of the Rockefellers at their Caneel Bay, Virgin Islands, resort and that her matchmaking had resulted in the marriage of "Crown Prince" John D. the Fourth. (257)

## CONSPIRATORS HAVE AMENDED THE CONSTITUTION: TO USURP THE PRESIDENCY?

Following their custom of leaving no stone unturned in their subversive activities, the conspirators have adopted alternative devices for seizing the Presidency and open rule of the nation, with an eye to Nelson Rockefeller's failure, in repeated attempts, to seize the Republican Presidential nomination. These are even more menacing to the nation than the tactics and successes of the Kennedys. Nelson Rockefeller's attitude toward the Presidency is: "While there is life, there is hope."

The first step in the process was taken more than a decade ago. The conspirators forced the retirement of the patriotic veteran, Sen. Jenner, of Indiana, by a threat of bringing unfounded charges of corruption against him. Suffering from a war injury which is reported to be progressively disabling in character, the Senator withdrew from the race for reelection. The conspirators then sponsored and supported the campaign of Democrat Birch Baye for the Senate seat; and succeeded, by their usual methods, in making him Senator.

Directly after the assassination of Pres. Kennedy, the conspirators launched a campaign of alarm, through all the media of mass communication, about the failure of the Constitution to make provision for succession in case of the death of the Vice-President. The conspirators do value the Constitution when it can be made to serve their own purposes. The appointment of a Congressional committee to sponsor their Constitutional amendment was arranged by them; as was the appointment of their man Sen. Birch Baye as its chairman. Gov. Nelson Rockefeller brazenly addressed an open letter to Sen. Baye, when the subcommittee began its hearings, in which he virtually ordered the Senator to bring in a report recommending the adoption of a Constitutional Amendment providing for the selection of a successor to the Vice-President, in case of death of either President or Vice-President, by the Presidential incumbent. This will give the voters no voice in the matter.

278

## THE ROCKEFELLER CONSTITUTION AMENDMENT

Sen. Birch Baye heeded "his master's voice" and followed his dictates in the report brought in for the subcommittee. The bill that would make Rockefeller's dictate a Constitutional Amendment was promptly passed by the Senate. Obviously, Rockefeller expects to dictate his appointment as Vice-President, under the circumstances in question, without being elected, thus bringing himself "within a heartbeat" of his determined goal.

The Rockefeller-dictated XXVth Amendment became a part of the Constitution within record time. For adoption, it required the ratification of thirty-eight State legislatures. All of the corrupt political power of the conspirators was brought into play to rush the ratification. Considerable payoffs appear to have been involved. Three State legislatures vied with one another to win the "reward" as the last of the thirty-eight States to ratify. That paragon of unselfish, uncorruptible and dedicated "public servant," the Nevada State Legislature, won the prize, and came in, under the line, as the last to give its needed vote to ratify the Amendment. On February 10, 1967, Rockefeller's XXVth Amendment became a part of our Constitution. This adds another star to Rockefeller's record in changing constitutions as often as it suits his purposes. (79:181) It reveals the extent that our Constitution has been replaced by Rockefeller wishes and dictates.

In the conspirators' rush to put over their plot, it was entirely overlooked that the amendment does not provide for Presidential succession in event that both President and Vice-President are incapacitated or die. Obviously, Rockefeller's only object was to get himself into the White House. Thereafter, the conspirators have no concern about establishing their Dynasty as hereditary rulers of our land.

## PLOT TO ASSASSINATE VICE-PRESIDENT HUMPHREY EXPOSED IN GERMANY

It is a curious "coincidence" that less than three months after ratification of Nelson Rockefeller's XXVth Amendment, Vice-President Humphrey, though nominally a U. S. official, was sent to Europe to court the favor of that electorate. The situation brings to mind the tour of Nelson Rockefeller's bailiwick, Latin America, by Vice-President Nixon, for the purpose of wooing that alien electorate, on which occasion he was assaulted and narrowly avoided assassination; and his errand to Ghana, to render homage on behalf of the U. S. to that, since deposed Red savage, Nkrumah, where he narrowly avoided death by crash of the defective military plane on which he travelled. (79:209f)

Vice President Humphrey was greeted on his European pilgrimage with abuse and riots. In Germany, the West Berlin police made a timely discovery of a "mysterious" plot to assassinate Humphrey. The press announced that eleven of the plotters had been seized with an arsenal of bombs and chemicals, shortly before the Vice-President's arrival there. (402) The situation arouses wonder whether Rockefeller's XXVth Amendment will serve to give the U. S. the Latin American and Soviet type of "government by assassination," with Constitutional sanction.

## BOBO ROCKEFELLER EXPOSED PLAN TO USURP PRESIDENCY WITHOUT ELECTION.

The conspirators' purpose in imposing the XXVth Amendment on the nation was disclosed by divorce-bent Bobo Rockefeller, wife of "homophile" Winthrop, who reported that she had overheard discussion by the brothers, at one of their Sunday weekly conferences, of a plan to seize the Presidency for Nelson without an election, presumably by the devices with which he had become familiar in the process of exploiting South American lands as "Coordinator." The exposure so thoroughly alarmed the Rockefellers that their attorneys, who had previously fought bitterly Bobo's divorce action with every device at their command, and were prepared to threaten to take action against her that would deny her the custody of her child, Winthrop Rockefeller Jr., hastened to offer her all her demands—on one condition, directly after her interview appeared in the magazine section of a New York newspaper. The condition is reported to have been a pledge that she would never again expose any of Rockefellers' schemes, plans, plots or private business that she might have overhead. The divorce agreement is also reported to provide that if Bobo ever again opens her mouth with regard to Rockefeller affairs, the few millions, that for them is an insignificant sum, that she was given, would revert to them.

## ARE PIONEERING AMERICANS DUPED TO POINT OF SURRENDER OF FREEDOM TO DYNASTIES?

The rise of the ruling dynasties obviously implies an end to "government of, by and for the people," and an end to freedom in the land. It seems hardly credible that the descendants of bold, pioneering Americans who braved the dangers and hardships of migration to a new land, tamed a wilderness and its savage natives and preserved their freedom, in hard-fought wars, from the oppressive rule of monarchic dynasties, have been duped into surrender of that hard-won freedom. They certainly would not be mindful of the admonition of Ben Franklin's Poor Richard:

"They who give up essential liberty to obtain a little temporary safety deserve neither liberty nor safety."

Nevertheless, too many people have been duped and led to follow their contemptuous leadership as faithfully as the Pied Piper of Hamlin was followed by the rats of yore. So successful have been the subversive plots and plans of the conspirators, that the rank and file of Americans are taxed, regimented and submissively drafted as self-paid mercenaries in the wars for world conquest and the creation of "One (Rockefeller) World," in complete disregard of the Constitution and the basic law of the land.

## THE NATION'S PROSTITUTED PRESS OPENLY HAIL THE RIVAL DYNASTIES AS RULERS

Publications that have the widest distribution and appeal debate which of the two dynasties that seek to usurp the rule of the land, the Rockefellers and the Kennedys, is ahead in its takeover of the government. And they champion the cause of one or the other dynasty. Thus the *Sunday News* of December 18, 1966 (265) published a feature article by Christina Kirk entitled.

## "BILLION DOLLAR DYNASTY

"With two governors and a legislator, the Rockefellers are out-distancing the Kennedys politically...and in giving away money they're in a class by themselves." (265)

The article is entirely characteristic of Rockefeller pressagentry; and it might well have been one of their handouts. It represents the Rockefeller practise of disposing of other peoples' money that they have looted, as "philanthropy," and their draft-dodging, as "noble conduct." The most significant aspect of this handout is the acknowledgement on the part of the conspirators that they are setting up a dynasty in competition with the Kennedys. Even more significant is the recognition that a large section of the American people have accepted the idea of surrender of their freedom to the dynasts as their rulers. The cautious propagandists, pressagents and publicists of the conspirators, who spend unlimited funds on "creating" public acceptance of their subversion (they call it "engineering of consent") have determined by their endless polls that the bulk of the nation is ready to accept domination of the super-Mafia, the conspirators' so-called "Establishment," as their absolute rulers; and that the nation has been induced to accept their complete subversion and destruction of our Republic, and of the Constitution on which it rested, in exchange for a delusion of "security."

There is a material error in the title of the article. The Rockefellers were billionaires more than half a century ago. They are today multi-multi-trillionaires, and mayhap even quadrillionaires; and fully as malevolent as they are rich. Even more openly than their dynastic rivals, their avowed objectives are to loot, despoil and betray our country and the world. They can both truthfully repeat the teaching of Jesus, as reported by both St. Matthew and St. Luke, as their motto and goal:

"Think not I am come to send peace on earth. I come not to send peace but a sword." (Matthew 10:34)

It is difficult to conceive of a more horrible fate for the nation and the world than to be betrayed into the hands of either, of any loot—and/or power-hungry Mephistophelian Dynasty; or of a more dreadful scourge than Rockefeller "philanthrophy."

CHAPTER XXI
## "INTERNATIONALISM" & TOTALITARIANISM OF DYNASTIES: IS IT TREASON?

Patriotism means loyalty to one's country. "Internationalism" means loyalty to no country, that too often implies betrayal of all lands with the motive of totalitarian domination, acquired by

281

intrigue or conquest for the purpose of looting and brigandage. Such "internationalism" means treason, in the strictest sense of the word.

The Rockefeller Dynasty and its subsidiary Kennedy Dynasty are both avowedly and notoriously "internationalist," in their attitudes, policies and activities. The nation must consider for its security the question:

"Wherein are their past performances and projects treasonous betrayals of our Republic that endanger us personally and as a nation?"

The record of our national betrayals by the Rockefeller Dynasty thus far recounted is long and shameful. In this century it involves, among others: the imposition of the "Gold Standard"; the takeover of education and its conversion to subversion through their General Education Board; the 1907 panic; usurpation of control of our national and personal finances through their "Federal" Reserve and Federal Income Tax conspiracies; our involvement in World War I for the expansion of their oily Empire at the cost of a quarter of a million lives of our doughboys and tens of billions of dollars; our betrayal into the hands of their Soviet partners in a 1926 deal with Stalin that was followed by financing and sponsorship of Communism and Communists, through all the foundations over which they gained control, and collaboration with the Soviets implied in the recognition of Russia as a part of their deal for control of Soviet oil; the 1929 panic and the depression that followed and was deliberately prolonged for more than a decade; the emasculation of our Constitution and the subversion of our Republic deliberately effected by them for the purpose of making themselves our undercover rulers, following the pattern described by Hoffman Nickerson; the wholesale looting of our country and ourselves through their control of our finances, taxation, bank closures and foreclosures of our holdings engineered through their "Federal" Reserve conspiracy, further intensified by the fraudulent wiping out of tens of billions of dollars of investments in utilities which they dictated through their utility "death sentence" measures and their corrupt dictation of railroad bankruptcies and reorganizations carried out with crooked control of the Securities and Exchange Commission headed by their agent, Joseph Kennedy; directing the precipitation of World War II and of our involvement in it for expansion of their oil production in Saudi Arabía and the Asiatic sector of their Empire, impressing into the defense of their Soviet partners our national and personal wealth in the amount of hundreds of billions of dollars and our youth, whom they drafted into their service, at the expense of the lives of hundreds of thousands of our GIs, after providing spies and support to the Communist Richard Sorge spy ring in his successful effort to induce the Japanese to refrain from attacking the Soviets and, instead, attack Pearl Harbor and destroy our Pacific fleet there bottled for the purpose; betrayal of the sovereignty of our Republic into the hands of themselves and their Soviet partners through their culmination of the dis-"United" Nations conspiracy; betrayal of drafted GIs impressed into the service of their oily Empire and the Soviets by their Status of Forces agreement and by arranging their encirclement by their Soviet partners in the Berlin enclave; ceding to the Soviets a long handicap in the missile race by turning over to them missile laboratories and researchers seized by GIs; engineering the expansion of their totalitarian Empire by yielding to the Soviets large sectors of Eurasia; plunging China into Communism under their aegis, converting an ally of ours into one of our most menacing foes; involving us in a war in Korea to protect their interests there, in the guise of a so-called "police action to contain Communism" of their Rockefeller-Soviet agency, the dis-"United" Nations, that still continues, and has cost tens of billions of dollars and tens of thousands of our GIs their lives; involving us in Vietnam, with the cooperation of the Kennedy Dynasty, for the dual purpose of protecting their interests and shielding Kennedy's coreligionists, the Catholic refugees in South Vietnam, from slaughter, at a cost in money and lives of our GIs that are less valued than those of the Vietnam refugees, that threatens to be overwhelming, especially in view of the undeclared war, (like that in Korea) that is being waged as a "friendly rivalry" between the Rockefeller-Soviet Axis partners) on a "no-win" basis; persistent looting through "foreign (Rockefeller) aid" programs that has enabled the conspirators, with the help of their "Federal" Reserve and its IMF subsidiary, to hasten the culmination of their "Gold Corner" with devaluation of the dollar. Some measure of the continuous injury inflicted by the conspirators on us and our country by their betrayals, in times of peace and war, can be discerned in the recent developments in Vietnam. (15;79)

## ROCKEFELLERS JOIN AGENT EATON TO FINANCE SOVIET SUPPORT OF VIET CONG ENEMY

Those who doubted or ignored the Rockefeller covert financing of Lenin and Trotsky through their banker, Jacob Schiff, in the first and second Russian revolutions (15:204), and their support and domination of the Communist movement on a world-wide scope, were rudely shocked, and (unless too grossly bigoted to accept the truth) awakened by the announcement on January 15, 1967, jointly issued by Rockefellers and their agent, Cyrus Eaton, that they had entered into agreement with Soviet Russia to finance and develop her industry, commerce and tourism, openly and on a grander scale than hitherto. Even more notable and significant was the deal because it relieved the strain on the Soviet's economy involved in their support of the war that the Communists are waging on us in Vietnam. (270)

The announcement published in the conspirators' official gazette, the N. Y. Times, left no room for doubt of Rockefellers' control, domination and support of Communist Russia and its agencies from the start. It related that in connection with the deal, the conspirators would openly carry out the activities of the various Soviet agencies that they had operated secretly for them through their Chase National Bank. They announced publicly, for example, that the Communist trading and espionage agency AMTORG, that from the beginning had been operated by them through their bank, would be openly taken over and operated by themselves personally. This obviously meant that Soviet industrial and political espionage would be greatly facilitated, extended and amplified by them.

## CONSPIRATORS FURTHER AID SOVIET ESPIONAGE WITH THEIR CONSULAR TREATY

To further aid their Soviet partners in their espionage and trade, thereby ingratiating themselves, the conspirators hyperintensively lobbied through the Senate, and had passed on March 16, 1967, the Soviet-American Consular Treaty that is ideally designed to facilitate wartime agitation and spying at home, behind our lines for our Communist Vietnamese enemies. Liberty Lobby, in its *Liberty Lowdown* of April 1967, reported that Senate Republican "leader" Sen. Everett Dirksen, the "wizard of ooze," was "induced" to withdraw his original opposition to this treasonous measure, joined forces with the subversives and pressured Republican Senators to vote in favor of it. It related:

> "The combination, organized *under the prime direction of Nelson A. Rockefeller, will take over the licensing operations of AMTORG, the official Soviet trading agency in America.*
>
> "*The money-mad businessmen who insist in trading in the blood of American soldiers are saved from the firing squad only by the technicality that the war in Vietnam is not a declared war under the Constitution.*
>
> "*The Consular Treaty's ratification is just a part of the Establishment's (Rockefellers') quid pro the Red oil agreement quo.*"

It is open to question whether the acts are not treason, in spite of the absence of a declaration of war. The Constitution definition in Article III, Section 3 is:

> "Treason against the United States, shall consist only in levying War against them, *or in adhering to their enemies, giving them aid and comfort.*"

Soviet Russia avows itself to be our enemy bent on "burying" us. Satellite North Vietnam and the Viet Cong wage active war on us with her aid. Any land that gives aid to either of them is our enemy. And any person who gives aid and comfort, as do the conspirators, to our enemy is declared guilty of treason by the Constitution.

## HEINOUS PERFIDY OF CONSPIRATORS AGGRAVATED BY "FOREIGN AID" FINANCING

Their perfidious betrayal of our country, which has been entrapped by the conspirators in internecine warfare with their Communist partners, for their oily interests, is all the more heinous because we, their American "peasants," have been given no "freedom of choice" that they profess to wish to have us assure the Vietnamese, in serving them with our lives and financing them with our fortunes. The financing given the Communists by the Rockefeller-Eaton deal is largely, if not entirely, through moneys extracted from taxpayers for "foreign (Rockefeller) aid." The Eaton side of the partnership operates under the name of Tower International Inc. which is operated by Cyrus Eaton and his brother-in-law, Fay A. LeFevre, in open support of Communist industry, commerce and subversion.

284

## EATONS, ROCKEFELLER PARTNERS, HAVE BEEN ROCKEFELLER AGENTS

Rev. Charles Eaton was Rockefellers' Cleveland Baptist minister. The Rockefellers regard shrewd clergymen as the craftiest "con" men, possibly because of their proficiency in extracting money by selling "protection" against the gods that they peddle. Rockefeller was enabled to perpetrate some of his crudest swindles through Baptist ministers, as in swindling the Merritt brothers out of their Mesabi Range, with the collusion of Rev. Fred L. Gates whom they rewarded with the post of their almoner. The Eatons have served their Rockefeller masters, who control the Eastern sector of their Steel Trust acquired with their Mesabi loot, in operating the Western sector of the Trust and in maintaining close relations with their Soviet partners, as in the perfidious Pugwash Conferences.

The Eatons have been trusted agents of the Rockefellers. Cyrus Stephen Eaton was given his first job by John D. the First. Cyrus S. Eaton Jr. acknowledged in an interview with Robert E. Beddingfield, of the N.Y. Times, his intimate acquaintance with the present Soviet pawns of the conspirators, Brezhnev and Kosygin. (226) Once again there was acknowledged the Rockefeller direct control of AMTORG, and the open takeover of its trading and espionage functions.

## IBEC, ROCKEFELLER "FOREIGN AID" LOOTING AGENCY, PERFIDIOUSLY FINANCES SOVIETS

The Rockefeller partnership in the deal with Eaton is through their International Basic Economy Corp. better known as IBEC. Nelson Rockefeller, as has been related, organized it in conjunction with his "foreign aid" activities, for the purpose of filching moneys looted from American taxpayers, by way of "counterpart funds." Those "funds" are moneys "legally" converted from "aid" by legislation that the conspirators put through Congress that provides that a portion be diverted to "private enterprise by Americans," meaning to his uses. This bill Rockefeller lobbied through Congress personally. This means that we have been perfidiously betrayed by him, and his fellow conspirators, once again, into financing our mortal enemies the Soviets and their Vietnamese satellites in the interminable war that they are thereby enabled to wage on us.

Neither Rockefeller nor his fellow betrayers could have had any doubt that financing that they volunteered to Soviet Russia would be used to slaughter our GIs in Vietnam and to exhaust us in that Asiatic quagmire. For, directly after the Rockefeller-Eaton conspirators announced their deal, Soviet Premier Brezhnev exultantly announced that Soviet Russia would be enabled thereby to increase her support of her satellites, the Vietnamese, in the war without quarter that they are waging on us. At the same time, he showed his appreciation of the Rockefeller support and aid, at our expense, by ordering us to withdraw our GIs from Vietnam or have them face extermination. Immediately thereafter the casualty and death tolls of our GIs in Vietnam rose steeply. *If Rockefeller aiding and abetting the slaughter of our GIs in Vietnam in the "opportunity" offered by their agents, the Kennedys who solidly entrapped us there, is not treason, under its definition in the Constitution I know not what is.*

285

## NELSON A. ROCKEFELLER SALUTES THE "AGE OF REVOLUTION" HE CREATES

The Rockefellers craftily seek to mask the interminable anarchy and continual crises into which they deliberately plunge the nation and the world to serve their nefarious purposes, by portraying this as an *"Age of Revolution,"* and a highly desirable state of affairs from their viewpoint. This Nelson A. Rockefeller clearly stated in the ghostwritten article, that bears his name published, in the official publication of the Dynasty's "Foreign Office," the Council of Foreign Relations, *Foreign Affairs*, entitled in the fashion of encyclicals, *Purpose & Policy*. (22:370-90) The satisfaction with which he views the turmoil and bloodshed, is undoubtedly related to the fact that each of the "crises" that has precipitated them has been dictated or engineered by the conspirators themselves to yield them fantastic profits.

The so-called "foreign policy" of the U.S. during the past half century that has been followed by the State Department that John D. the First boasted in his *Random Reminiscences* (16:93) loyally served him, has steadfastly and undeviatingly carried out the "purpose and policy" of the conspirators. This explains fully the consistent betrayal and doublecrossing of all nations allied or friends of the U.S., such as England, Cuba, Santo Domingo, Katanga, Republic of South Africa, Rhodesia and France; and the support by the Rockefellers, personally and through their U.S. "duchy," of all satellite lands of the Rockefeller-Soviet Axis, such as Poland, Jugoslavia, Ghana, Indonesia and India, that at the best pretend to be "neutral." This accentuates the absurdity of the pretense that our national purpose is the support of the "Free World" and "democracies." They use the words "Free World" to designate the lands they are free to loot, and "democracy" in the sense of "proletariat" or mob rule, that is the pretended form of the Weishaupt-Marx-Lenin totalitarianism, that in effect means the absolute dictatorship that Nelson Rockefeller avowed is the objective of himself and his fellow conspirators for the U.S. and the world, in the ghostwritten book that bears his name, entitled *The Future of Federalism*. (133;79:250)

So long as a government stands in the way of the conspirators, and is not absolutely dominated by them, no matter what may be its form, it is subverted or destroyed by them. How much people may suffer, or how many may be slaughtered in the course of these "revolutions" is a matter of supreme indifference to them and actually gratifies the malign conspirators. Especially is this true of Nelson Rockefeller, who aspires to U.S. and world dictatorship, and is paranoid, as are his brothers, on the subject of what he calls the "population explosion," the idea that there are too many of us "peasants" in the world for him to rule conveniently. As a consequence, foundations controlled by them have launched movements for birth control that have made his mania immensely profitable to the conspirators, at the expense of American taxpayers.

## CONSPIRATORS PROFITABLY CHECK POPULATION BY FLUORIDES, PILLS, OVENS & WARS

Thus the American Agricultural Chemical Co., a subsidiary of their Continental Oil Co., markets its waste product fluorides to New

York City and numerous cities around the country, for the wholesale pollution of their water with the pretended purpose of saving infants from that "dread and mortal disease, dental caries." The actual purpose is birth control by fluoride sterilization, and evasion of the Catholic Church's prohibition of birth control. This fluoride sterilization has the "advantage" of causing in later life that "godsend" in shortening lives and reducing population, cancer. (79:196f;417) Their sales of their waste fluorosilicic acid to New York City alone, nets them more than a million dollars a year. The success of water fluoridation in birth control is attested by the report of the U.S. Public Health Service that as a result of the fluoridation of water of several thousand cities, the U.S. birth rate dropped, in 1964, to the lowest figure in the twelve years of their "glorious experiment." Deformities of newborn caused by water fluoridation, still further reduces population.

Even more highly profitable has been the sale and distribution around the world, at the expense of American taxpayers, of steroid contraceptive pills that have netted Syntex and their Drug Cartel many hundreds of million dollars. And incidentally, these "pills" have the "advantage" of reducing population by causing thromboses, strokes, blindness and cancer. Another of their profitable enterprises is provision of condoms to India and other lands. (317)

These "slow" methods of exterminating "surplus" humans who "overpopulate the world," are not the most favored by the impatient, loot-hungry conspirators. Concentration camps and ovens that permit of genocidal and rapid extermination of droves of humans at a time, are less of a trial on the patience of the "philanthropists." And they have an economic advantage of averting the intolerable situation of "unused resources and economic waste" that is so abhorent to the conspirators. For the fat of the victims can be rendered, as it was by their I. G. Farbenindustrie, and prove a source of more loot, or profit. The more rapid methods of human extermination and genocide such as slaughter in Vietnam of both native and Americans victims, are undoubtedly regarded as abhorently wasteful. A bit more economic is the process of civil war in savage lands such as the Congo, where cannibalism yields some use for the corpses, in the process of self-extermination of the natives. (318)

## IMPACT OF KENNEDY DYNASTY'S "INTERNATIONALISM" ON U. S.

The vicious impact of the "internationalism" of the Kennedy Dynasty on the domestic scene has been of more recent origin and largely in the capacity of satellite of the Rockefeller Dynasty, but with its own peculiar subversive overtones. Those nuances are lent it by higher allegiance to the Holy Roman Empire, the Vatican, than that of the Rockefeller Dynasty to its professed Baptist faith, though both are overshadowed by their adherence to its Nazarene Communism as a path to richess. Pres. Kennedy's "Declaration of Interdependence" (on Europe and the Vatican) addressed to Archbishop John Krol, and its spurning of the Declaration of Independence (405) might well be classed as the most perfidious betrayal of his oath of office by any President. His adherence to the Rockefeller-Soviet Axis is attested to by his visit to Vienna, shortly after his inauguration, to render homage to the conspirators' pawn Khrushchev. On the advice of his brother, Robert, and others, he initiated our active involvement in the Vietnam War for the protection of his coreligionist refugees by sending 16,500 drafted GIs on that Crusade shortly after assuming office. On the same advice, he engineered the Bay of Pigs invasion of Communist Cuba and betrayed the invaders, thus effectively yielding to Soviet Russia Castro's domain as a permanent missile base at our very border. He involved our country in missionary work supplementing that of his Church, in the form of the Peace Corps, at the expense of American taxpayers and in violation of the Constitution. He flaunted the Constitution in supporting, with our Armed Forces, the Communist and Church sponsored "Civil Rights" that are the uncivil wrongs, on behalf of Negroes, and denied the basic civil right of freedom of choice in associations, to the whites, thereby constituting the blacks as a privileged criminal group who have effectively destroyed law and order in many sections of the country. (406)

## TRULY "INTERNATIONALIST," DYNASTIES BETRAY OTHER LANDS TO THEIR INTERESTS

In a true spirit of indiscriminate "internationalism," both dynasties as readily betray other lands as they do our own. In these betrayals, the Kennedy Dynasty have been true and trusted satellites of the Rockefeller, to the point of even betraying the Church and its Orders. Rockefellers and their Standard Oil have "muscled in" and undermined the British Empire, their most formidable rival, in Saudi Arabia, Persia, India, Suez, Africa and other of its dominions and spheres of influence, materially aided by Nazi and Irish favoring, Ambassador Joseph Kennedy; on the French Empire in Indo-China, including Vietnam, and Algeria, (and the Church and Jesuit interests there) with the active collaboration of the Kennedys; and on Belgium and the Jesuit-dominated Haut Katanga, with the intensive active collaboration of Kennedys; and wherever it suits their purpose, through their dis-"United" Nations. (79)

The role played by their "United" Nations cabal in the Congo affair has been courageously exposed on the floor of Congress by Rep. Donald C. Bruce, of Indiana. (62) He placed on record the plot of the conspirators that was carried out by their Swedish interests headed by their Bilderberg agents. They included Bo Gustav Hammarskjold, brother of Dag Hammarskjold whom they placed at the head of the "U"N as secretary, for that purpose. He served them so ably in that racketeering, at the cost of his life, that they have undertaken to "immortalize" him as an "international hero." Their "United" Nations forces, led by a Bilderberger, served as their gunmen and "enforcers" who personally participated in the pillage and looting. (61:18137f;-63;79:241f) it is noteworthy that the signal for the outbreak in the Congo was the very moment of the departure from that land of David Rockefeller, accompanied by their "U"N and CFR agent Rockefeller Foundation trustee, Ralph J. Bunche, on an inspection tour of its lootable "unused resources." (79:242)

## "U"N & WILSON'S "SELF-DETERMINATION" ABETS "ANTI-COLONIALISM" BRIGANDAGE

The "choice" victims of the conspirators' "internationalist" brigandage are the savage and backward lands colonized by more civilized powers that undertake the dangerous and oft thankless task of civilization and development. The piratic conspirators systematically vilify other colonialists than themselves, as "exploiters of the natives," using the word in the Weishaupt-Marxian sense. They agitate and stir up the natives to oust the relatively beneficent powers, in order to make it possible for themselves to hijack the resources that have been developed, by "expropriation." The deluded natives are often tricked into destroying each other, thus solving the problem for the conspirators, of disposing of any claimants to the stolen property, and of the effort and expense of completing the civilization of savage and backward peoples. Encouraging the revival of cannibalism and headhunting among them, as was brought to light by the death of Michael Rockefeller, avoids "unused resources and economic waste."

In this brigandage the conspirators have been materially aided by the *"14 Points"* enunciated for them by their pawn, Pres. Woodrow Wilson. They mockingly label their process of brigandage and genocide *"the principle of self determination."* They impress into partnership with themselves, in the requisite violence for securing their loot and in paralyzing their intended victims, their dis-"United" Nations tool, the U.S. Armed Forces and those of any other nation they can dupe or impress. And they proclaim themselves "champions of the Free World," bent on promotion of "Democracy" and on giving their victims freedom of choice that they deny their American and other draftees. Their activities make it transparently clear that what they mean by the "Free World," is a world that they are free to loot and decimate.

## "PRINCE" DAVID IS "PRIME MOVER" IN CONSPIRATORS' "INTERNATIONALISM"

Rockefeller pressagents make it clear that David is not motivated by such "chauvinistic" principle as patriotism. Deviating from the past practises of the Rockefeller Dynasty of trying to hide their wealth by labeling mockingly the next intended victim of their looting, as in the case of Jean Paul Getty, as the "richest man in the world," they now characterize David as "one of the richest men in the world." They describe his face as "round as a moon...smooth... with a needle-like nose that projects sharply" (121:50); his voice high pitched and singing (121:78) and characterized by their CFR agent, Pres. Pusey of Harvard in the words:

"I sometimes think he's got electricity in his head." (121:68)

Through his pressagent, he acknowledges himself to be "enormously and all but incalculably rich;" rated by such Asiatic monarchs as Japan's Emperor and the Prince of Thailand as "outranking royalty," and "Prince of the...American tribe" (121:46). They report that in South Africa he arranged for clandestine meetings with underground black leaders; is active in government affairs, especially in the international field; and is *the prime mover "in banking that controls the course of world economic affairs and history"* and the "most important...banker...in the world." (125:67) It can not be questioned that he ably seconded the efforts of Nelson and the Dynasty in bringing the Treasury to the verge of bankruptcy and in destroying the value of the dollar. It is a tribute to the success of the conspirators' propagandists in convincing a brainwashed, duped and moronized nation that the moral lepers have lost their spots, that the Rockefeller racketeers masquerading as "philanthropists" can do no wrong, to the point that David and his kinsmen boast of their brigandage and treachery and no longer bother to hide behind the shadow of their agents and "fall guys," the reputed "Jewish international bankers."

## "PRINCE"DAVID CREATED NEW, "TOP DRAWER" AGENCY FOR "INTERNATIONAL" BRIGANDAGE THE BILDERBERGERS

"Prince" David's knavish "genius and originality" accounted for his creation of a new, "top drawer" agency for abetting him in his favorite pastimes, usury and brigandage, the *"Bilderbergers."* (79-171f,244f;126;407) The Bilderberg group is the top level super-Mafia, or "Establishment," that operates directly under the supervision of the conspirators in putting in operation throughout the world Marxist "internationalism" in looting nations. Originally "top secret," it was acknowledged by "Prince" David's pressagent to be one of the conspirators' key "internationalist" agencies. (121:68f) It was organized for them in May 1954 to allay the intense hatred of Americans stirred up throughout Europe, by the intensive looting that they engineered with the aid of the "Marshal" (Rockefeller) Plan and other "foreign (Rockefeller) aid" plans, that threatened their hold on their plunder. (126:237) Their agent in organizing it was Polish Red, economist and multiple agent, Dr. Joseph H. Retinger. The German "consort" of the Queen Juliana of the Netherlands, Prince Bernhard, was chosen to serve them as a "front," to divert suspicion from their highly secret "conferences." In this capacity he was later joined by another Royal "Consort," Prince Philip of Edinburgh.

Pressagent E. J. Kahn Jr. has undertaken to "take some of the curse off" the secret Bilderberger Conferences, usually held in isolated spots around the world under strictest "security precautions," most ironically, by revealing that David Rockefeller is its head; and has missed only two conferences of this cabal that far outranks in both secrecy and criminal import the conferences held by the conspirators' Mafia henchmen, such as that held at Appalachin. (121:68f)

The majority of the known members of this cabal are, like their patron Rockefeller, notorious "Liberals," or Reds. They have included British Laborites Hugh Gaitskell and Premier Harold Wilson; Italian Premier Alcides de Gasperi; and Socialist French Premier Guy Mollet. Like the American members, they are all tied in with Rockefeller interests through the organization.

Highly significant was the attendance at the 1957 Bilderberger Conference on St. Simons Island, Georgia, of the darling of Germany's Neo-Nazi movement, Kurt-Georg Kiesinger. The list of invited guests was carefully chosen to avoid offending the anti-Semitic sensibilities of this "former" Nazi. Such specimens as Jacob Javits were conspicuously absent. (408) On the other hand when bootlicking Javits was invited to the conference at Williamsburg in March 1964, the election year, Rockefeller agent, chairman of the foreign policy committee of the Bundestag and darling of the Neo Nazis, Kiesinger was equally conspicuously absent; and Javits could preen himself on his exalted associates and their tolerance of him by spreading the guest list over the Congressional Record. (408)

On December 1, 1966 the conspirators promoted their pro-Nazi agent Kiesinger to the post of West Germany's Chancellor. One may wonder whether Javits mourns having missed meetings so distinguished an "internationalist."

From the U.S., Rockefeller brought to the various Bilderberger "conferences" a vast array of their oft subversive agents and most trusted CFR and governmental pawns. Among them are the following: (408;409)

Secretaries of State, present and former:

Dean Rusk (15:16); John Foster Dulles (15:267); Christian Herter; Dean Acheson (15:264)

Central Intelligence Agency heads:

Gen Walter Bedell Smith ; Allen Dulles (15) ; John A. McCone.

State Department subordinates:

Joseph E. Johnson, former State Department assistant to and successor of Alger Hiss. He was permitted to resign while under fire, during World War II, when a leak of top secret information to the enemy was traced to his office. Thereafter he was appointed by David Rockefeller and his kinsmen, John Foster Dulles, as had been Alger Hiss before him, to posts vacated by Alger Hiss after his indictment, including President of their Carnegie Institute for (Preventing) International Peace. (15;107:121)

Paul Nitze, nephew of World War I German agent, Paul Hilke, who was involved with German Ambassador-spy, Count von Bernstorff, in the Black Tom explosion of munitions. He has been a close associate of Nelson Rockefeller in his various subversive capacities. His appointment was dictated to the sensitive post of Secretary for the Navy by the conspirators to Pres. Kennedy; and when Rockefeller's salesman pawn, McNamara, was expected to resign, in 1966, he was aligned by the conspirators for the even more "sensitive" post of Secretary of "Defense." (79:107f)

President Eisenhower's personal representative and assistant:

C. D. Jackson, who as spokesman for the American delegation led by David Rockefeller at the first Bilderberger "Conference," in May 1954, promised the assembled Reds:

"Whether (Sen. Joseph) McCarthy dies by way of an assassin's bullet or is eliminated in the normal American way of getting rid of boils on the body politic, I prophesy that by the time we hold our next meeting, he will be gone from the American scene." (79:159f;126:242)

Members of Congress:

Jacob Javits, "Liberal," Red Rockefeller CFR agent, foisted jointly by the conspirators and their Communist henchmen, on New York as Senator; campaign manager of Gov. Rockefeller in his reelection campaign, who though doublecrossed by Rockefeller who promised to make him "favorite son" in the 1968 Republican Presidential nomination campaign, grovels before the "golden calf."

J. W. Fulbright, violently "Liberal," or Red, Oxford University Rhodes Scholar, and former President of University of Arkansas, and Arkansas Senator who never misses an opportunity to loyally serve the conspirators and give comfort to our Communist enemies

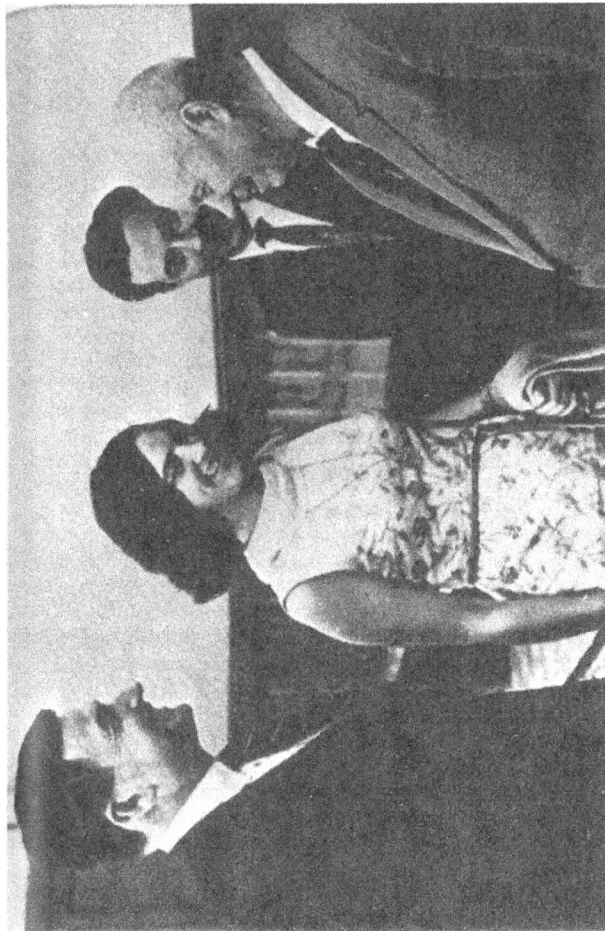

## DAVID ROCKEFELLER, HIS BOSS, ACCEPTS KHRUSHCHEV'S URGENT
## INVITATION TO VISIT HIM AT THE KREMLIN

David Rockefeller held a conference in Leningrad of his Bilderberger "Dartmout group" to discuss politics and stimulate Communist Russo-Chinese business for the branch of his Chase Manhattan Bank he had opened six months earlier, in Hong Kong, for the specific purpose of trading with the Communists. At the end of the two weeks conference, in mid August 1964, Khrushchev phoned Rockefeller and urgently requested him to come to Moscow and discuss his decisions at the Kremlin. Rockefeller agreed to do so. He was entertained, with his daughter, Neva, at the Kremlin. But, shortly thereafter, Khrushchev was "fired" because his controversy with Mao Tse Tung interfered with the Soviet-Communist China trade from which Rockefellers sought to profit. Wide World Photos.

in war and peace.

Gerald R. Ford, Republican minority leader of House of Representatives.

"Adviser" to Presidents:

McGeorge Bundy, Rockefeller CFR agent, "adviser" to Presidents Kennedy and Johnson, biographer of Roosevelt's Secretary of War Stimson, kinsman of his Secretary of State Dean Acheson, brother of one of the contributions to the defense of Alger Hiss, and President of the conspirators' Ford Foundation.

Pres. Kennedy's Cabinet, dictated to him by the conspirators' including:

Sect. of State Dean Rusk, Under Secretaries George W. Ball, George McGhee, Walt W. Rostow; McGeorge Bundy, Paul Nitze and Arthur Dean of the "Defense" Department; and others called by C. D. Jackson, "Bilderberger alumni." (126:148)

## "PRINCE" DAVID SPURNED KHRUSHCHEV'S PLEAS AFTER REVEALING LENINGRAD CONFERENCE

The most amazing conference held by David Rockefeller and his associates, that clearly reveals the Rockefeller control of Soviet Russia, was held, in the first half of August 1964, in that land which notoriously offers its subjects no political freedom, Soviet Russia, at Leningrad. It occurred a bit over half a year after David Rockefeller announced in the press the opening by himself, personally, of a Hong Kong branch of his Chase Manhattan Bank for the expressly announced violation of our law and national interests, trade with the Chinese Communists. In violation of the Logan Act, he undertook to meddle in our foreign affairs, announcing in Hong Kong that the U.S. should trade with Communist China, with recognition implied. (121:42)

It was common knowledge, repeatedly commented on in the press, that Soviet Russian trade with Communist China had broken down almost completely because of the feud between the conspirators' agents, Khrushchev and Mao Tse Tung. Since that was China's major trade, it is understandable that David Rockefeller's personally opened Hong Kong branch of his Chase Manhattan Bank got no business or profits from that trade. The press openly discussed the advantage, for restoring that trade, of deposing both Khrushchev and Mao Tse Tung, the two stumbling blocks.

Since the prime purpose of Rockefeller's Leningrad Conference was profits for his branch bank in Hong Kong, it is understandable that Khrushchev's dismissal would be the major item on the agenda. When the conference was almost over, Khrushchev phoned David Rockefeller and implored him to come to Moscow and discuss the matter at the Kremlin.

David Rockefeller yielded to Khrushchev's pleadings and, with his daughter Neva, visited at the Kremlin. The press around the world carried the picture of the meeting of the two dictators in the Kremlin; and it was reported that David's daughter, Neva, had taken notes of the meeting of the Rockefeller boss with his Communist agent. Khrushchev's pleadings were obviously of no avail; and he was not able to talk his way out. Shortly thereafter, he was ousted. (79;121:37,68) Could there be better proof of Rockefeller control of world Communism?

292

## ROCKEFELLER-EATON DEAL A PAYOFF TO SOVIETS
## FOR DESTROYING NASSER

The urgent motive behind the Rockefeller-Eaton-Soviet deal did not become fully apparent until, after a lapse of almost six months, the Arab-Israeli war broke out and Nasser and his Arab allies were defeated in a fulminating six day campaign. The Arabs had been armed by the Soviets, and in their defeat were solaced by the sympathies and moral, or immoral, support of the Communists.

Nasser's real name is Nasserbaum. His grandfather, lt was revealed in the French press, is buried in the Orthodox Jewish cemetery in Cairo, under their original family name, Nasserbaum. Like Hitler, another apostate of Jewish origin, Nasser was built up by the conspirators as their Red agent in Egypt to serve them in furthering the destruction of the French and British empires, in which the seizure by him of the Suez Canal played a significant role. The conspirators, through their kinsman agent, Secretary of State John Foster Dulles, (15:267f) in 1956, blocked the Israelis when they were joined by the British and French and were at the point of seizing the Suez Canal from the defeated Egyptians. The conspirators came to the rescue of Nasser and saved him from defeat and debacle of his regime.

Contemptible agent Nasser, whose military "prowess" had been bolstered by refugee Nazi military officers who adopted aliases and pose as Moslems, (303) was too stupid to recognize that he was an impotent pawn of the conspirators, and that the rulers of the Soviets were in the same position. His greed impelled him to doublecross the conspirators by making a deal with their Soviet agents in return for aid, financial, military and engineering in the building of the Aswan Dam. With the support of the Soviets, Nasser then undertook to take over the Near East Moslem Arab states, including the conspirators' oily empire centering in Saudi Arabia, and loot them of their wealth.

For the purpose of enhancing his loot, Nasser aligned the oil-producing states and those through which the trans-Arabian pipeline runs, to violate their oil contract with the conspirators and demand the lion share of their profits from oil. The contract of Rockefellers' Caltex and Aramco with Saudi Arabia gave the ruler of that land half of the profits from the production of oil. Nasser, in the characteristic role of Arab beggar and thief, put pressure on Saudi Arabia and other Arabian states producing oil, to demand 75% of the profits of production, refining and distribution of the oil. In so doing he touched the most sensitive Rockefeller nerve, the money nerve. The conspirators, however, could not take any direct action against Nasser without antagonizing the entire Moslem world and the Arabs, and jeopardizing their Near East oily empire to gain which they had precipitated two World Wars. But it was essential for their interests that Nasser, "grown too big for his breeches," be reduced to size and destroyed.

The Rockefeller-Eaton *(Ibec-Tower)* deal was timed to set the trap for Nasser and his "Arab beggars and thieves." The Soviets served the conspirators effectively by supplying defective arms and equipment in a volume apparently adequate for the purpose of "destroying Israel," and by duping Nasser into launching his Tirana embargo as the first move in that war. Neither Nasser or his Nazi army officers had any suspicion that, even if the ignorant Arab soldiers could muster sufficient intelligence to handle the equipment, it would prove a boomerang. The tanks were designed to lose their treads after traveling a few miles; and the missiles were set to travel in circles. The conspirators made doubly sure that the well trained and equipped, highly intelligent Israeli army would make short work of the Arabs.

The conspirators had no fear of Arab reprisals or of closure of the Suez Canal that was expected as repetition of the Egyptians' stupid tactics in the 1956 war. The Arabs could find alternative markets for their oil only among the conspirators' Soviet and other agents. Ironically, the oil that they did deliver to the Soviets was turned over by them to their exclusive sales agent, Standard Oil. And the conspirators have supplied the Israelis with Arabian oil. Nasser stupidly fell into the trap set for him, from which it is reasonable to assume he will never be able to extricate himself. No matter what measures he adopts to prevent a revolt against his rule, he is doomed. And the conspirators are well rid of him. Near East Christians, against whom Nasser's Moslems have been waging a Holy War and crucifying, sub rosa, have been rescued by the more civilized Israelis. (304;305)

## VIETNAM GIS MOWED DOWN WITH ROCKEFELLER-EATON FUNDS PROVIDED BY U.S. TAXPAYERS

One year after "philanthropic" Rockefellers and their agent, Eaton, brazenly announced their perfidious deal to finance Soviet industry with funds derived largely from U.S. taxpayers through "foreign (Rockefeller) aid" and other tax exempt funds, Soviet Russia furnished our Vietnamese enemies, for the first time, with huge tanks and the latest model planes in sufficient volume to enable them to seize towns throughout South Vietnam during the 1968 Tet New Year celebration, and slaughter thousands of our GIs. This situation falls into the same pattern as the treachery of the conspirators throughout the Vietnam war. The conspirators, through their control of their "Defense" Department sales agency, had blocked effective raids by our Air Force on North Vietnamese until they had supplied our enemies with missile bases to destroy hundreds of multi-million dollar planes that they had supplied our Air Force. And even then, they barred our Air Force from destroying many vital targets, presumably because they owned the plants. Through their Standard Oil companies, they supplied our enemies with fuel and with money, alleged to be tribute to avoid destruction of their tanks, plants, installations and other properties by their Red partners. They intensified the slaughter of our GIs by supplying them with defective powder, through their Olin Mathieson Chemical Co., that jams their guns. Also by financing Soviet Russian industry, they worsened our payment balance and deliberately precipitated a financial crisis that undermines our national solvency and ability to carry on, while treacherously barring victorious conclusion of the war. In addition they foster dissension, disloyalty, and breakdown of law and order at home by financing "Civil Rights" agitation, rioting, arson, murder and complete breakdown of law and order.

*Does it make any difference to the slain GI's and their families that, in disregard of the Constitution, the conspirators activities can not be prosecuted and stopped as treason, because to serve their malign purposes, war has not been officially declared? Are they any less treasonous therefore?* Does not service to our dead and wounded GIs justify the demand of Nelson Rockefeller that he be made our ruler? What higher service can people seek than their looting and betrayal? And that, Rockefeller has proved himself ever willing to render us American "peasants."

Should we not be grateful to the Kennedy Dynasty for giving us the opportunity to dissipate our wealth, shed our blood and lay down our lives in their "internationalist" venture in the pesthole that is Vietnam, to protect their coreligionists there, (411;412) even though it may mean undermining of our Republic and the surrender of our freedom, our fortunes and ourselves to the utter ruthlessness of their tribe and Dynasty? Should we not appreciate the blessings they have bestowed on us by slyly supplying our Communist foes a military base in Cuba under the aegis of Jesuit-led Castro (410:3), laying us wide open to attack at home while they scattered our Armed Forces around the world and rendered us almost defenseless? Would it be wrong to label such "internationalism" treason?

Who can question our good fortune in having two such Dynasties offer to assume monarchic power over us? Could we be afflicted with a worse scourge?

## CHAPTER XXII
## WHAT MUST WE DO IN ORDER TO DEFEAT
## THE CONSPIRACY?

The Supreme Court, in its decision directed against the Rockefellers and their Standard Oil, wisely decreed:

"FOR THE SAFETY OF THE REPUBLIC WE NOW DECREE THAT THE DANGEROUS CONSPIRACY MUST BE ENDED..."

Unfortunately, the conspirators thumbed their noses, at the Court and the nation. They vastly expanded their conspiracy against the nation and the world to the point where the menace foreseen by the Court has become a fearsome reality. Our Republic rapidly is being destroyed, is being replaced by a plutocracy dominated by themselves and is in the process of conversion to an absolute, totalitarian monarchy, and a vanquished kingdom of the "One (Rockefeller) World" Empire. They have effectively made themselves the monstrously malevolent masters of the nation and world.

Our only chance of survival as a nation, rests in stripping the conspirators of all the powers that they have arrogated to themselves and usurped, recovering the loot they have stolen, and undoing their emasculation of our Constitution and Republic.

## TAX EXEMPTION: THE DANGEROUS SUBVERSIVE DEVICE OF THE CONSPIRATORS.

Among the most dangerous and subversive usurpations of the conspirators, other than the "Federal" Reserve and the control of money, is the tax exemption of themselves and their conspiratorial agencies and agents. The power to tax is the power to rule or destroy. Tax exemption is intensification of the power to tax. For it implies delegation to its beneficiaries of the power to foist on the rest of the community the burden of the taxes evaded. It infinitely intensifies the power of the purse of the exempted and their consequent political power, in exact proportion as they impoverish the rest of the community by promoting crushing, confiscatory taxation. In time, only the exempt can afford funds for political activities. Tax exemption is allowed only for contributions to "charitable" rackets and bogus "philanthropies" of the conspirators. (56) Corrupting shamelessly and with impunity the body politic by exercise of the power which they thus have usurped, they concentrate the wealth of the nation into their purses and loot one and all mercilessly, using the government as their private agency for that purpose.

The "philanthropist" Nelson Rockefeller, Governor of the State of New York, has given the State the most venal, corrupt and costliest administration in its history. (79:179f) Each increase in the rate of his tax looting attests to the fact that he evades the payment of those taxes. This was made crystal clear when he raised the rate of the State income tax on the highest bracket to 10%. For this would have meant that he had undertaken to raise his own combined Federal and State income tax from 100% to 101% of his income. Former Director of Internal Revenue Caplin confirmed the fact that the seventeen wealthiest persons in the nation, with multi-million incomes reported, pay no Federal income tax whatsoever. There is not much room for doubt that the Rockefellers are to be found in that category. It is understandable that he "felt no pain" in his most sensitive money nerve his purse when he tripled the New York State budget during his term of office, to the 1968 figure of $5 billion plus. How much of this tax loot has flowed into the purses of the Rockefellers and their fellow conspirators we may never know. But it may be surmised from what has been related about diversion of tax funds into the various enterprises in which he has engaged.

The most recent exposure of the diversion of "foreign (Rockefeller) aid" funds to the conspirators' enterprises was reported by Russ Braley, in the New York Daily News in a special report dated Raunheim, West Germany, January 18, 1966, entitled *blast hits new U.S. refinery in Bonn; 1 dies*. The report recounts that the huge new oil refinery of Rockefellers' Caltex Co. that was destroyed by an explosion and fire.

"...*was built by the U.S. in 1964 at a cost of $80 million.*" (173)

This confirmation was really unneeded in view of the special effort Rockefellers' pressagents have directed to impressing on the public that their masters are "keenly interested in making money" (17:33) in whatever they do.

## FOUNDATIONS MENACE NATION & MUST BE ELIMINATED
## FOR SURVIVAL OF REPUBLIC

Though their sham "philanthropic" foundations are by no means the sole device for usurpation of power through tax exemption and national brainwashing, they are important sources of power that is highly intensified by control of foundations set up by others, grabbed by the conspirators through their control of the Treasury Department. Their control of the most richly endowed foundations, including their own, the Carnegie and the Ford Foundations, is absolute; and constitutes the nucleus of what has been termed their "Philanthropic" Foundation Trust. But no significantly endowed foundation has escaped their indirect control.

## U.S. TRUST CO. OF N.Y., FOUNDATIONS' "TRUSTEE":
## ANTI-TRUST LAW EVASION AID?

An overlooked and uninvestigated device of the conspirators for converting the hundreds of millions of numerous less wealthy foundations to the subversive and oft treasonous uses is the U.S. Trust Co. of New York at 45 Wall St. Among the dozens of foundations which it serves them in dominating are the $51 million New York Community Trust, the $21 million Milbank Memorial Fund, the $20 million Sprague Educational & Charitable Foundation and the $1 million Metropolitan Opera Endowment Fund. The concentration of tax exempt billions of the foundations invested in securities is a sacrosanct and unmolested device for maintaining monopolies in restraint of trade.

How well these foundations have served the malignant purpose of the conspirators and how dangerous they are for our national survival, can be discerned from a thoughtful examination of the avowed purpose John D. I stated in his "encyclical" issued as "Occasional Letter No. 1" for his General Education Board that during more than half a century controlled American "education" and brought it to its present abysmally low status:

"In our dreams, we have limitless resources and the people yield themselves with perfect docility to our molding hands."

Those "limitless resources" are our property of which they steadily loot us by the combined devices of taxing us and rifling our purses while exempting themselves and devising numerous new devices for looting us by taxation through the government and other agencies. It is we who have been real, though inwitting and unwilling, "philanthropic" financiers of our own destruction at the hands of the conspirators.

The success of the conspirators in using the funds looted from us to "mold" or brainwash us, is amply demonstrated by the fact that without a whimper, the people have served the conspirators with their fortunes and their lives, in war and in peace, through the agency of our Government. This illustrates how true was the prediction of Sen. Chamberlain, when he said, on March 26, 1917:

"The Carnegie-Rockefeller influence is bad. In two generations they can change the minds of the people to make them conform to the cult of Rockefeller, or the cult of Carnegie, rather than the fundamental principles of American democracy." (15:3)

297

The full significance of the above cited Rockefeller "encyclical" is better appreciated when one considers the purpose of the "molding," or brainwashing, as stated therein:

"So we will organize our children into a little community and teach them to do in a perfect way (Ed. from the Rockefeller conspiratorial viewpoint) the things their fathers and mother are doing in an imperfect way..." (15:3)

We well know now that this has meant the destruction of parental influence, the organization of juvenile delinquent gangs that are fertile ground for the development of the criminal talents and for the "teaching" of Communist subversion and treason, as well as the cultivation of sex degeneracies and perversions involved in financing of the Kinsey Reports for self-justification, that the conspirators require for their malign purposes. (15:79;103)

## "PHILANTHROPISTS" RUN RACKETS FLEECING PUBLIC, WITH TAX EXEMPT FUNDS

The bogus "philanthropic" foundations are especially inimical to public interest, aside from their tax exemption and preying on the nation, in that they serve to camouflage the conspirators' ugliest anti-social activities. They dominate politics and use it to betray the nation. Their medical foundations have served them in gaining control of the medical, drug and hospital industries, which they have converted to enormously profitable rackets that have incredibly increased the cost of illness and medical care, and often made it mortally dangerous by their marketing of virulent poisons as drugs. The conspirators themselves, however, carefully avoid medical care at the hands of the doctors whom they have indoctrinated, and seek medical care largely at the hands of osteopaths, and of chiropractors, who are barred by law from prescribing or administering the poisons that their drug concerns market. Though they distribute samples of the drugs, that they market, to their friends, they carefully avoid taking them themselves. (79:70;229)

## CONSPIRATORS PRICE MEDICAL & NURSING CARE OUT OF RANGE OF PUBLIC MEANS

Their "educational" foundations have not merely subverted education, but have made it enormously more costly. A medical education that prior to their takeover through their "philanthropies" cost a mere $3 thousand, now costs more than $50 thousand. They have brought this about by their seizure, with the help of their "philanthropies," of a wide range of industries that supply and cater to schools and colleges. These they have converted into enormously profitable enterprises, "high fliers" on stock exchanges. One of the "modest" examples is Cenco Instruments, a marketer of classroom scientific devices, the stock of which has risen from an adjusted value of $1 to $48 a share. Medical publications have been made so costly by the commercial exploitation that it is prohibitively expensive for the average physician to keep abreast of medical advances except through free medical magazines and newspapers the distribution of which is financed by drug concerns for advertisement to the profession of the conspirators' drugs.

Dana Hudson, directress of an Atlanta school of nursing pointed out in an address before a national nurse's association entitled *Fac-*

*tors Influencing The Nursing Shortage*, that educational rackets launched in 1918 by the Rockefeller Foundation are responsible for the shortage of nurses that has hugely increased the cost and lowered the quality of nursing care. It joined forces with Rockefellers' "philanthropic" Sealantic Fund in reducing sharply the opportunities for girls to obtain nursing training by restricting accreditation of nursing schools to those institutions controlled by them, and by making the training so costly that only a severely limited number could afford the training. This the conspirators accomplished by requiring expensive tribute to their "education" racket, in the form of a college degree prerequisite for nursing. Then, she reports, they were instrumental in creating further costly barriers to nursing education.

"The National League for Nursing accreditation has set up requirements for accreditation which make it prohibitively costly for diploma schools to continue to exist. In order for diploma schools to be accredited, the student nurses may no longer give nursing care to patients to help defray their expenses. Schools have had to increase their tuition to meet the cost, and this has placed the program beyond the means of many young women. Also this lack of clinical training has impaired the proficiency of the young graduate to the extent that many doctors request older graduates to care for their patients." (344)

Unjustifiable restrictions in licensing nurses has aggravated the situation. Every Rockefeller "philanthropy" has proved enormously costly to the nation.

## LAWS RESTRICTING USE OF TAX EXEMPT FUNDS FLOUTED BY GOV. NELSON ROCKEFELLER

The conspirators persistently violate, with absolute impunity, the laws regulating the use of tax exempt foundation funds, which provide the penalty for use of foundation funds for political activities, of confiscation of their tax exempted capital plus fines and imprisonment, Gov. Rockefeller was caught by the IRS, and confessed, deliberately violating the law by diverting more than half a million dollars of foundation funds to his 1960 political campaign for the Presidential nomination. The drastic, "compulsory" penalties provided in the law were completely disregarded by the authorities. He was reported to have been let off with "a slap on the wrist," with the admonition not to do it again. This breach of the law was perpetrated by the authorities involved, in spite of the fact that the bulk of the funds of the foundations are channelled into subversive political activities, and has given the conspirators complete control of all political parties. (79:231) Rockefeller, despite his plea, has continued to use tax exempt foundation funds for political, purposes by the "committee" device and "reports."

## CONSPIRATORS, UNDER ATTACK, SAY THE FOUNDATIONS CONTROLLED BY OTHERS ERR

Repeated Congressional investigations have fully exposed the subversive activities of the Rockefeller and other foundations controlled by them. This author was requested to serve on the staff of the Committee appointed by the 83rd Congress to investigate the tax exempt foundations, by its chairman, Carroll Reece. This request was made on the basis of published work of this author on the subject. (15) Directly thereafter, Reece developed his strange and almost fatal illness. In spite of the conspirators' efforts to suppress the investigation by incessant interruptions by their agent, Red Congressmen Wayne L. Hays, of Ohio, the Committee did bring to light once again the exclusive support by the foundations of Communist and other subversive political activities. (164) The same fact was revealed by the Congressional investigations of Rockefellers' Institute of Pacific Relations. (15:103;104) Once again violations of the law and the support of subversive and Communist political activities by the Rockefeller dominated foundations, and the use of their funds to finance the conspirators' commercial and industrial activities, was exposed by the Congressional Subcommittee of the Select Committee on Small Business, headed by Congressman Wright Patman, to which reference has been made. The Committee reported that the Rockefellers are evading the law with their foundations. (89:v) Despite these repeated exposures, the law has never been enforced.

The climax was capped when the conspirators themselves acknowledged the abuse of foundations, in a report which one of their agents was delegated to prepare on the subject, published in December, 1965, by the Russell Sage Foundation, entitled *Foundations and Government.* The authoress is Mrs. Marion R. Fremont-Smith, a former state director of public charities and assistant attorney general of the State of Massachusetts. She is reported to have taught political science at Wellesley College. She wrote her book as project director of the Russell Sage Foundation. (165)

The history of the Russell Sage Foundation casts some light on the nature of the report. Founded in 1907 by Mrs. Russell Sage in honor of her husband, an associate of the swindler, Jason Gold, alias Jay Gould. Its $15 million outright gift was supposedly directed to "improvement of social and living conditions in the United States of America." It became one of the cornerstones of the Social Service Racket that did little other than publish statistical studies, improve the living conditions of its executives and workers, memorialize its userer namesake by recommending passage of laws authorizing the usurious interest rates of 36% to 42% on small loans to the poor, and promote Communism. Mary Van Kleeck, director of the Foundation's Industrial Division, has been one of the outstanding promoters of Communism in the U.S. one of the founders of the local Communist Party; and repeatedly one of its candidates for public office. (56:59;7:54)

Writing under these auspices, Mrs. Fremont-Smith lauded American foundations for their "unique contributions to society." The only abuse that she regarded as worthy of any serious consideration was the "glaring abuse" exposed by Wright Patman, of the misuse of his foundation by David G. Blair, of New York, for supplying money for stock market operation to Serge Semenenko, a Boston banker, and other stockmarket operators. In view of her background, it is understandable that she discerned no "abuse" in the subversive and Communist support by the foundations, or the political and treasonous uses of their funds that have been repeatedly exposed. She termed the foundations "charitable institutions," and stated that the threatened revocation of their tax exempt status would hurt the public because the foundations would have less money to give away. How much more the public can be hurt than now by the tax looting to which they are subjected as a result of the foundations' tax exemption and by their forced status of involuntary but true philanthropists, she failed to explain. There is an intimation in her book that the foundations are powerful enough to continue to violate the law with impunity. She suggested that the Federal Government abdicate its control of the foundations and turn it over to the State governments. This presents the totalitarian bent conspirators who persistently press for centralization of government in Washington, in the anomalous role of advocating State's Rights on their own behalf. (166)

The New York Times explained the timing of the publication of the book and its propaganda on behalf of the foundation frauds, as preparation for the hearing to be held by Rockefeller agent, N.Y. Attorney Gen. Louis J. Lefkowitz, whose "dedication" to service to his boss rather than to the public has been noted, (70:203) a week later to "consider" takeover of the control from the Federal Government by New York State of its foundations, the capitalization of which it reports to be 56% of the assets of all major foundations. (165) The situation is tantamount to Rockefeller investigating criminal activities of himself and his kin.

## SAUCE FOR THE GEESE, CONSPIRATORS, *IS NOT* SAUCE FOR THE GANDERS, PUBLIC.

The alarm of the conspirators and their political pawns at the "crime" of the average citizen following their lead in setting up foundations and using their tax exempt funds for personal advantage, has been related. (324:325;326;327) Their daring to follow the example set by the conspirators may lead to their criminal prosecution. But the conspirators are immune from prosecution of their identical frauds that are far more flagrant and injurious nationally.

## LABOR BARONS & THEIR CRIMINAL ASSOCIATES HOLD GOVERNMENT IN CONTEMPT

As a direct consequence of the power with which the conspirators have endowed their Labor Barons and their fellow criminals, especially by extension to them of tax exemption, they hold our government and its laws in absolute contempt. This was most obvious in the acts of their TWU agent, Michael Quill. It found its final expression in his exit from the American scene. His coffin was covered with an Irish flag. There is little room for doubt, however, that if he could have presided at his own funeral, his choice would have been the hammer and sickle.

## ULTIMATE RESULT OF TAX EXEMPTION OF UNIONS: ONLY WORKERS WILL BE TAXED

The ultimate result of the conspirators' extension of tax exemption to their unions and their Labor Barons plus the power of collective blackmail under the guise of "collective bargaining," will be a complete takeover of all industry and commerce by them. That will mean that all industry and commerce will be exempted from taxation. Only the worker will then bear the burden of taxes, as in Russia and other Communist lands. And the conspirators will have attained another of their totalitarian goals.

## TAX EXEMPTION OF CHURCHES IS A SURVIVAL OF ECCLESIASTICAL TOTALITARIANISM

The tax exemption of church property is a residue of the totalitarianism that characterized most religions. Constituting a subsidy of religion, it is an ignored Constitution violation. It is a phase of the picture presented in Israel, for example, by the orthodox rabbinate undertaking to dictate the law of that land and its administration, as supposed spokesmen for the God whom they peddle. In the Christian world, tax exemption of churches is a phase of the claim of the Pope and the Vatican to ownership of the entire world and everything and everyone in it, body and soul, as the vicars on earth of the God whom they merchandise, Jesus Christ. It extends the claims of the Roman Empire, to which it succeeded, as the Holy Roman Empire. This ultra-totalitarian dictatorship is represented by the Church as motivated by its desire to save the souls of mankind. And in the fervor that they bring to bear on this task, they have never hesitated, in the past, to cut a man's throat or to burn him at the stake, "to save his soul;" and rob him of everything that he had, in the process. It is the ecclesiastical version of the Mafia's "protection" racket: they sell "protection" against the wrath of the God whom they vend. In the "auto de fe" there is keenly brought home to the victim the teaching of Jesus in Luke 12:49; "I come to send fire on the earth"!

All religious leaders and institutions, with few and rare exceptions, seek to amass wordly wealth, allegedly "for service of the Lord," and incidentally to provide a living for themselves, their ministers, rabbis, muezzins and priests. Irrespective of their denominations, they extend their palms and ask one to "share with God." It is with mixed feelings that the donors watch them pocket the funds. More than one guileless child has asked: "Is he God?," when viewing this spectacle.

## CHURCHES OFTEN HAVE MONOPOLIZED WEALTH & IMPOVERISHED LANDS.

In virtually every theocratic state in history, the religious hierarchy has eventually gained control of the bulk of the wealth and property. The rank and file of the people are invariably left in poverty with barely enough for a marginal existence, stupidly offering blind devotion to their looters, so forcibly is instilled in them the promise of plenty in a "heavenly," problematic, future existence in return for supinely submitting to mulcting and plucking in their present existence. Those who refused to be duped and plucked found that their religious "benefactors" were so bent on "saving their souls" that they were brutally tormented and assailed by sword and fire, and their worldly wealth stolen as ruthlessly as by the most secular gangsters. More than fifteen centuries of history attest to this. The poverty of the people of numerous lands, including Spain, Italy, Portugal, South America, Tibet and many other Asiatic lands, that were the birthplace of our religions, attest to the consequences of the concentration of wealth of those lands in the clutches of avaricious religious hierarchies.

## TAX EXEMPTION OF CHURCHES MEANS THEIR SUPPORT INCREASES TAXPAYERS, BURDENS'

Religious institutions account for tax exemption of an enormous amount of wealth. It amounts to more than a quarter of the U.S. total.

302

That implies that the taxpayers who contributes to a religious organization thereby increases, in the same proportion, the burden of his own taxation, and that of the rest of the taxpaying community. This means, also, that all taxpayers are forced to contribute, willy nilly, to the churches, synagogues and temples. That is a clear-cut violation of the Constitution that decrees separation of Church and State. It means that the government is taxing the people for the support of religions and that it endows them with the power to increase the taxes levied on the rest of the nation, in direct proportion to the steady and rapid increase of the wealth of the churches.

This concentration of wealth in the hands of the churches and religious institutions and their tax exemption cast a sharp and discreditable light on the pretenses of religious leaders that their goal is to serve the community and eliminate poverty. Churches would materially improve the financial status of the community and of their parishioners by honestly assuming their fair and full share of the tax burden, instead of evading it by tax exemption and other devices. One of the major defects of the so-called "Poverty Program," drafted under the influence of the President's Baptist minister aid and alter ego, Rev. Moyer who wrote for him the sermons he delivered, is that it is a mere political device that pretends to find a solution of the poverty of some sections of the Negro community by impoverishing other sections of the community by taxation that too often spells the transition from a marginal existence to actual want. It involves the same fallacious cunning that underlies all Communism, whether Nazarene of the Gospel, or Illuminist based on revival of Nazarene by Adam Weishaupt and his disciple Moses Mordecai Marx Levy alias Karl Marx: "solving" the problem of poverty by "distribution of wealth" and making everyone poor. In practise, however, the "Poverty Program" is not designed to do anything more than provide the politicians with more graft for themselves and for the purchase of votes among the Negroes; and to maintain themselves corruptly in power.

## A RARE, HONEST RELIGIOUS LEADER ACKNOWLEDGED THE MENACE OF CHURCH EXEMPTION

One religious leader has had the honesty, intelligence and self-interest to acknowledge the menace of tax exemption of religious institutions and their wealth and holdings, to both themselves and the community. Rev. Eugene Blake, the Presbyterian Church leader, has clearly discerned the dangers of the concentration of wealth in churches through their tax exemption, and the creation thereby of supercapitalistic totalitarian theocracies dominated by themselves. In an article which he published in the August 1959 issue of *Christianity Today*, he pointed out the historic fact that wealth and property acquired by the churches and held under the protection of tax exemption, have been responsible for the concentration of the wealth of many lands in the hands of avaricious ecclesiastics with consequent impoverishment of the people. This, he correctly stated, has led, in numerous instances, to denunciation and renunciation of churches and religions, revolt against their tyranny, and expropriations of church properties accompanied not infrequently with exile of the clergy.

Rev. Blake might have detailed numerous instances when the avarice and cupidity of ecclesiastics have so impoverished peoples

303

that they were forced to drive them out and recover the property and wealth that tax exemption had made it possible to amass. He might have pointed to the ruthless impoverishment by the Jesuits of Portugal that led to their being expelled in the mid-eighteenth century by the order of the Marquess de Pombal; subsequently from many other lands; and their eventual dissolution by the breve of Pope Clement XIV. He might have pointed to the ousting of the Church from France in the Revolution, and the eventual imprisonment of Pope Pius VII by Napoleon at the instance of his Jesuit advisers. He might have pointed to the revolt against the Church in Mexico, in the early XIXth century, by the impoverished peasants, led by Father Hidalgo. He might have pointed out the incident mentioned by Bishop Fulton Sheen when acting as radio and television commentator on the visit to the U.S. of Pope Paul VI.

Bishop Sheen mentioned that at the time of the Italian uprising, in the 1860's, the Church had been impelled, by fear of expropriation by the revolutionists of its enormous wealth, to consider moving the Vatican to the U.S. He did not mention the fact that consideration of this move was dropped because of American reaction to the involvement of John Surratt and Papal Secretary of State, Cardinal Antonelli, in the assassination of Lincoln. (72:167;168)

Rev. Blake might have brought the situation up to date by pointing out that one of the motives for the peregrinations of Pope Paul VI, himself, is the threat of the present Italian government to tax the fabulous income and the fantastic wealth of the Vatican. This significance of the Pope's visits to distant lands, establishing a precedent, has not been ignored by the Italian government To avert the exposure of the avarice and cupidity of ecclesiastics, Rev. Blake wisely has suggested that churches forego their total tax exemption and accept voluntarily their burden of taxes. He suggested it not on the basis of justice and ethics. He advised that churches may thereby avoid the danger of public revulsion and desertion, and the menace of expropriation of their property by an aroused citizenry, looted and impoverished thereby. (58:30)

Dr. Blake was later joined by a number of other Protestant prelates and by the National Conference of Christian and Jews in urging fair sharing of the communities' tax burdens by the churches and synagogues. Honest, though spookily senescent, Episcopal Bishop James A. Pike, who courageously and intelligently rejects many phases of Judeo-Christian mythology, stated in an article in the April, 1967, issue of *Playboy* magazine, that citizens would enjoy a material reduction in their tax burden if the wealth and income of church property were fairly taxed; and that the enormous wealth that organized religion makes it a practise to acquire, makes taxation of its property mandatory if our Constitutional government is to survive. He pointed out that the "visible" real estate wealth of organized religion in the U.S.A. alone, amounted to $79.5 billion at its nominal rate of assessment; that more than half of it, $44.5 billion was owned by the Catholic Church, the real property holdings of which alone, were assessed at more than the total value of five of our leading corporations, including the Standard Oil of N.J., General Motors, Ford Motors, General Electric and Chrysler. He related that the Knights of Columbus's $200 million assets include a steel tube mill and several department stores; that the Jesuits derive a yearly income of $250 million from large investments in steel and aircraft companies, and from controlling interests in Phillips Petroleum Co., Creole Petroleum Co. and the Bank of America.

In sharp contrast with the public spirited attitude of the above-mentioned religious organizations is the reported adherence to its traditional attitude by the Catholic Church and its leaders, that despite its enormous extraneous holdings and wealth, including the above corporations, its exorbitantly priced Washington Highgate apartments, business office and commercial property, its New York Hutchinson Sperry office building, and its half billion dollar Montreal Victoria City financial district development,—it "had no income from 'unrelated businesses' and would not be affected by the proposed changes (of taxation) on such income." (284:20) The attitude of the Church persists in the dogma that it is the rightful owner of the earth, its inhabitants and all wealth is rightfully its property; and the communities must carry its tax burden, in addition to the tithes it levies.

## CHURCHES ACCOMPLICES OF CONSPIRATORS IN "SLUM CLEARANCE" BRIGANDAGE

Religious institutions have given unstinting support to the conspirators' "slum clearance and urban redevelopment" confiscation of private property, homes and businesses, land grabbing, piracy and thievery. Indeed, they have eagerly joined the conspirators in this outrageous crime as accomplices and eagerly shared in the loot. It has been estimated that religious institutions and churches, share in the property stolen in this un-Constitutional abuse of the right of eminent domain by confiscation of property in the name of the State, amounts to approximately 20% of the total seized from the unfortunate private owners. Instead of the churches protesting against the heinous piracy, they have joined in it and given it a "holy" aura. Not satisfied with what they cadge from the public and with forcing the community to carry the burden of their taxes, they shamefully join in the plot to rob the community and often their own communicants of their homes and their livelihoods. Catholic institutions are reported to grab more than 70% of the conspirators' 20% payoff to religious institutions; and the balance is shared by the other denominations. The same pattern of cold, calculating, unprincipled exploitation of their communicants is practised by all the "peddlers of gods" across the land. Not content with what they can wheedle and extort from their parishioners with threats of damnation and Hell, or by offers of "protection" against their gods, they practise crimes which would be a credit to their Mafia accomplices.

## ELIMINATION OF TAX EXEMPTION: AN ESSENTIAL FOR SURVIVAL OF REPUBLIC & FREEDOM

The elimination of tax exemption is an absolute essential for survival of our Republic and freedom. There is no provision in the Constitution that empowers the Federal government to exempt anyone from taxation. Such exemptions violate the basic provisions in the Bill of Rights assuring equality of all before the law and barring special privileges for anyone. Tax exemption implies more than mere privilege. It implies granting to the exempt the power to shift their burden of taxes to others; and the authority to place others at a disadvantage by burdensome taxation that is readily converted to unfair competition and domination of the nation. For preservation of our Republic and freedom, the provisions barring tax exemption must be enforced and funds looted from the Treasury by tax exemption must be recovered.

Any resistance to surrender of the tax exempt loot will demonstrate fully the hypocrisy and sham of pretended religious and temporal "do-gooders," and "philanthropists." If they were sincere in furthering the welfare of the nation, their first act would be to honestly share the burden of taxation instead of evading and thrusting that burden on the rest of the nation to handicap it. Furthermore, the tax exemptees would not pursue their present tactics of deliberately increasing taxation of the nation for their own advantage. The only "philanthropy" the nation desires of these bogus "benefactors" is that they carry their full share of the tax burden and not seek and accept the illegal privilege of exemption.

### MONEYS WITHHELD FROM THE TREASURY BY EXEMPTEES MUST BE RECOVERED

Mere elimination of tax exemption, however, is not an adequate remedy in the current state of our affairs. The nation must recover the funds that have been diverted or stolen from the Treasury. In the instance of foundations this means, usually, seizure by the Treasury of the bulk, or all their capital as well as the taxes due on their incomes. Most of them have been capitalized with money withheld from the Treasury for supposedly legitimate uses. But most of them, including Rockefellers' bogus "Philanthropic" Foundation Trust, have been used in flagrant violation of the law for political, financial, industrial, subversive and other illegitimate uses. The penalties provided in law for its violations will more than consume their entire capital. The complete takeover of the foundations by the Federal government will make possible the elimination of all their numerous subversive activities and of the diversion of tax funds to the support of their foreign interests to the detriment of our payment balance, and the unconscionable tax burden that they have saddled on us. And it will place in the hands of the Government the few worthwhile activities which they may have supported. (15) Subsidy of foundations, religious institutions and unions through the CIA and other agencies must be stopped. (400; 401)

Elimination of tax exemption of labor unions will work no hardship on workers. On the contrary, by forcing honest accounting on union officials, it might serve to put an end to the looting of the workers by the Labor Barons, goons and gangsters, and put an end to triple taxation of the workers that exists under the tax exemption of the unions. For workers now pay their withholding income tax; their private tax levy by the Labor Barons in the form of union dues and levies; and they are also called upon to bear, with the rest of the taxpayers, the burden of the taxation that the unions evade on their multi-billion-dollar annual "take." If there can be arranged, by any chance, the elimination of the Labor Barons and the takeover of the unions by the government, that would even further serve the interests of the workers. They rightly should be given full protection of the law, as citizens and taxpayers, including any special protection which their status as workers may require, without the payment of additional taxation or dues levied by private organizations. The takeover of the functions of the unions by the government need not involve the banal consequences of such action by totalitarian governments—if the conspirators are barred from converting our Republic to a totalitarian state—by reestablishing our Constitution as our basic law.

The elimination of tax exemption of churches and religious institutions, as has been pointed out by Rev. Blake, will serve the interests of both the nation and of the churches themselves. It will put an end to the flagrant abuse of the Constitution that is involved in the covert subsidy of religion involved in their exemption. Recovery of taxes evaded in the past that has served to concentrate the wealth of any community in the hands of churchmen could be effected by stripping them of property that is not directly used for the conduct of their religious services. By sharing the tax burden of the community the churches will cease to levy taxes for their support on non-believers and non-adherents, which has been their thoroly dishonest practise in the past through tax exemption. Honest and sincere ecclesiastics will welcome this change that will convert churches to such social uses as they conceive to be their functions rather than to antisocial stripping the community of its wealth, that has been their dominant characteristic in the past.

Even if there were no reason for putting an end to tax exemption of churches, synagogues and other religious institutions and their holdings, it is required by strict compliance with the section written into the Constitution by a Unitarian minister, James Madison, that requires separation of Church and State. Compliance with this Constitutional provision has been persistently ignored and violated, though it would prevent the overthrow of our Republic and its subversion and takeover by any religious conspiracy, of which there have been many. Not the least of them has been the St. Leopold Society, that under Jesuit domination was set up to destroy our Republic in accord with the pledge made to the Holy Alliance, in the Treaty of Verona of 1822 (72:8) and numbers among its subsidiaries the Holy Name Society and the Knights of Columbus, whose unwitting members serve its purpose. (72:28f) In this connection, the rifling of the Treasury of the latter organization by its sponsors, which was recently reported, is of interest.

Inasmuch as the property held by the various religious denominations has been estimated as almost 25% of the developed property in the land, their sharing the tax burden would materially reduce its onus on the rest of us; and it would bring their pressure to bear in the demand that our tax looting cease and our taxes be reduced. There would be demand for an end to the missionary work which the taxpayers are now required to support in such absurd and un-Constitutional ventures as the so-called "Peace Corps," "Alliance for Progress" and others, if the churches and the commercially motivated foundations were required to bear their full share of the cost. In this connection, it is well to bear in mind that religious, or theocratic, totalitarianism (and all religious are by

307

their very character totalitarian) in no wise differ from any other form of that disease of society, including Nazi and Soviet forms.

## "LIBERTY AMENDMENT," REPEALING UN-CONSTITUTIONAL XVITH, IS VITAL

The proposed "Liberty Amendment" to the Constitution that has been promoted by a dedicated group of citizens headed by Willis E. Stone (163), and ratified, thus far, by six State legislatures, is a vital move in the direction of revoking the power usurped over the nation by the conspirators. It is a wise and imperative move to repeal the Rockefeller-Aldrich plotted XVIth wholly un-Constitutional Amendment that violates the deliberate purpose of the writers of the Constitution to abridge the power of purse of the Federal government. The objective of the authors of the Constitution was to avert its becoming an autocratic dictatorship through the power to loot by taxation without limit. They undertook to accomplish this by limiting the Federal government's power to taxation of the States by apportionment. This device took cognizance of the fact that the people can more readily hold to account their local governments, and thus retain some measure of the ultimate power of the purse.

The conspirators attained, through the XVIth Amendment, coupled with their "Federal" Reserve fraud, virtually unlimited power of the purse and unlimited power of search and attainder. Through it they have usurped the power to spy on every enterprise in the land and to force disclosure of the innermost secrets of the dealings of individuals and businesses. In the past there was maintained the pretense that these disclosures were kept well-guarded secrets by the Internal Revenue Service. But the fraud of this pretense has been carelessly brought to light by the acts of Gov. Nelson Rockefeller during his regime to make this confidential data more readily available to the conspirators through their Chase Manhattan Bank.

Repeal of their XVIth Amendment with the endless array of rules and regulations that their agents have issued on its basis for harassment of the nation's taxpayers, would materially help to curtail the power usurped by the conspirators. It would help to restore the freedom that the Constitution was intended to give us, by eliminating the criminal, illegitimate use to which they have put the income tax for looting and oppressing the nation and using its wealth to enrich themselves and enhance their power by numerous criminal devices. It would put an end to their persistent effort to reduce many taxpayers to a marginal existence, and in some instances, to actual poverty, by ruthless taxation; and to their filching the bulk of the taxes extracted from us. It will reduce and minimize the incentive of the conspirators to involve us in their "internationalist" brigandage, "police actions" and wars, by cutting off the flow of "other people's money" into their hands, by way of the Treasury, to finance them. There will be an end to the sluicing off the wealth of the nation by their bureaucratic agents in Washington, and their dictatorship of local affairs attained by the bribery involved in condescending to contribute small fractions of their tax loot to local groups and parties, for political uses for maintaining themselves in power.

Federal taxes will once again be levied by the States by apportionment. Federal expenditures will, once again, be more closely scrutinized by fifty-interested State governments which will be confronted with the task of extracting the money from their local taxpayers and electorates. There will be a return of more responsible government that will spell an end to this phase of the conspirators' racket.

## LIMITATION OF POWER OF TAXATION BY CONSTITUTIONAL AMENDMENT ESSENTIAL

If we are to have the liberty that the Constitution was intended to provide for us, there must be introduced into it, by amendment, a provision, the necessity of which was not foreseen by its authors, to limit the total percentage of our incomes that all levels of government can levy for taxes. We have had ample evidence of the effectiveness of unlimited taxation and capital levies, by so-called "capital gains taxes," in limiting our freedom and in enabling usurpation of power by the conspirators and their political agents. The wisdom of the totalitarian religious leaders of past ages, in limiting their tax, or tithe, to ten percent of net income might well be followed in an amendment to the Constitution limiting taxes that may be exacted of the citizenry by all levels of government, to that figure. It is a fraction of income that few will miss or attempt to evade. And in spite of adherence to the Bill of Rights in elimination of capital levies, such as the so-called "capital gains tax," elimination of all tax exemptions will insure adequate funds for essential services of a government honestly administered and free of corruption and "handout" bribery of voters. Such tax limitation would put an end to the practise of continuous looting of the citizenry by taxation and inflation of currency caused by steadily higher taxation. If such a limit of taxation is not imposed by Constitution, destruction of our Republic and its replacement by a totalitarian State is inevitable, in the course of time, through confiscation of property by taxation.

## CONSPIRATORS' MEANEST THIEVERY: INHERITANCE TAX, SUPPLEMENTED BY PROBATE CRIME

The conspirators' meanest form of thievery is robbing the dead and their widows and orphans. It is complemented by the looting of estates by probation. In addition to quest for loot, the inheritance tax and its administration are operated by them with full legal sanction, by the government, to prevent others from building up fortunes that might rival theirs. There are instances in which inheritance taxes and probation and legal fees have devoured 100% of estates. The survivors find their bereavement intensified by brigandage; and they are hopelessly handicapped in the battle to protect enough of the estate from looting by the conspirators operating through the government to preserve their standard of living without a wage earner.

The notion widely disseminated by the conspirators and their Red associates and dupes is that inheritance taxes prevent dangerous accumulations of wealth in the hands of the idle rich. Its falsity is completely proved by the virtually complete exemption from inheritance taxes of the conspirators' estates as a consequence of loopholes they have written into the law and its administration for their own benefit. The estate of John D. First, who on the basis of his statements that he diverted a tithe of his income, $500 million, to his foundations, left a fortune of at least $5 billion, was taxed on a valuation of $25 million; and the hugely richer estate of John D. the Second, on a valuation of $150 million, that was taxed less than $5 million. Nothing more clearly proves that the inheritance tax is a vicious capital tax for selectively looting the dead and bereaved. This governmental looting must be eliminated, or restricted solely to huge fortunes.

## AMEND CONSTITUTION: U. S. ISSUE OF CURRENCY AND CONTROL OF BANKING IS ESSENTIAL

Equally imperative as a Constitutional amendment for the limitation of taxation by government is the termination of the conspirators' "Federal" Reserve conspiracy and of their control of banking and of credit and currency, the life blood of the commerce and industry of the nation. For this purpose, an amendment to the Constitution is imperative to grant to Congress and to the Federal government the unequivocal power to establish and charter banks and to issue currency other than gold and silver coins. As has been related, the Constitution, for reasons which its framers regarded as valid in view of their experience with the British Board of Trade, denied those powers to Congress and the Federal government. At present the only basis for the Federal exercise of those powers under the Constitution are the emergency power granted the President, and dubious decisions by the Supreme Court regarding what it calls "derivative powers" assumed to be vaguely implied in those specifically granted Congress. It is highly questionable that in a test case before an honest Supreme Court panel that is unbiased by political considerations, these "derivative" powers would be sustained in view of the provision of the Constitution which reserved for the States any powers not specifically granted to the Federal government.

Still another amendment to the Constitution would be advisable if we are to attain the position of abiding strictly by it as the basic law of the land. There should be specifically granted to Congress the right to do what it has long been doing: the right to authorize the coining of money in metals other than gold and silver. This restriction is clearly implied in the provision of Section 10 of the Constitution reading:

"No state shall...make any thing but gold and silver coin a tender in payment of debts..."

The adoption of these amendments would legally empower Congress and the Federal government to perform legitimately the desirable functions that are illegitimately and un-Constitutionally performed by the so-called "Federal" Reserve. It would eliminate the conspirators' perpetual brigandage and systematic looting of the nation and the world by "management," for their own interests, that in reality is deliberate mismanagement. It would mean an end to their use of national and personal prosperity as an "opportunity" and occasion for looting us by precipitating panic, depression and unemployment at home and abroad, by deliberately and suddenly restricting the volume of money and credit available for the conduct of business, using as a transparent excuse the arbitrary ratio of both to the supposed, but looted and non-existent, gold holdings of the nation that they rig and manipulate for their thievish purposes.

The government would be free to issue non-interest-bearing notes on the basis of reserves of staple products, of the real wealth and commerce of the nation, and in anticipation of receipt of taxes, that would be wholly adequate for its needs, instead of issuing interest bearing bonds and notes that are equally the obligations of the taxpayers in spite of the fact that they redound to the private profits of the conspirators and their confederates, who thereby increase the burden of the taxpayers by way of a rapidly and steadily mounting ever huger national debt. The interest on that debt, in 1968, already exceeds $14 billion payable by the taxpayers. That burden is further increased by the conspirators by upward manipulation of interest and discount rates that they "justify" on the ground of the "monetary shortage" that they deliberately create by their manipulations. An honest and unmanipulable monetary and banking system established by the government would eliminate these abuses.

## ENDING "FEDERAL" RESERVE FRAUD & RECOVERY OF CONSPIRATORS' LOOT IMPERATIVE

Pending the adoption of the outlined amendments to the Constitution, the emergency power it grants the President must be rightly used for the takeover by the Federal Government of the banking and monetary powers usurped by the conspirators through their "Federal" Reserve fraud, and to recover the loot they have stolen from the nation through it, by their various forms of thievery and piracy. These moneys recovered by the Treasury must be applied to reduction of those parts of the national debt that have been legitimately incurred. There should be recaptured the enterprises that the conspirators have financed with funds diverted from the Treasury by various means, their "foreign aid" loot, the domains and industries that have been seized by them as war loot at the expense of American lives and fortunes, enterprises financed by "counterpart funds" or by governmental subsidy. There should be promptly seized the gold stolen from the nation through their "Federal" Reserve fraud, including that gold which the Treasury has purchased with taxpayer funds and turned over to them, as well as that gold that they hold in their vaults "earmarked" in the "foreign accounts" of their agents and dummies. "Foreign aid" and "counterpart funds" that the conspirators have diverted into their enterprises, and the profits earned thereon, must be recovered on the basis of the original dollars represented by them.

## INTEREST BEARING BONDS FRAUDULENTLY HELD BY "F"R MUST BE CANCELLED

Approximately $30 billion of interest-bearing Federal obligations are held by the "Federal" Reserve under circumstances that can not be viewed as anything but fraudulent. They are the obligations which have been redeemed by the Treasury, when presented by the "Federal" Reserve, by the issue of currency notes representing their full face value. And although they have been fully redeemed with non-interest-bearing currency notes, they still remain the property of the "Federal" Reserve and yield it their full interest rates. Honesty demands that this fraud be stopped by their surrender to the Treasury by the "Federal" Reserve for cancellation. This is the purpose of the excellent bill, H.R. 7601, that was introduced in the House during the first session of the 86th Congress by Wright Patman.

Patman's bill would be a step in the right direction. It stands in sharp contrast with another bill that he introduced, H.R. 11, which would fortify the conspirators in their control of their "Federal" Reserve.

## CONSTANT DEVALUATION OF MONEY, INFLATION: CONSPIRATORS' LOOTING DEVICE

Constant devaluation of money and steady inflation are the conspirators' most effective devices for looting nations. In addition, the conspirators employ many devices for indirect looting of nations. They have the advantage of duping the public into believing that they are earning more and becoming enriched instead of being looted. A prime example is the steadily rising wage scale. Equally effective and deceptive are the minimum wage acts that the conspirators sponsor to gain the support of the duped public. The raised wages too often serve to reduce employment, increase the ranks of the unemployed, and swell the relief rolls. When the cost of labor outstrips its productivity, the workers are priced out of the market, unless rising cost, or inflation, of the value of the product serves to outbalance and insure a profit.

Artificial shortages of labor and products are effectively used to promote and support inflation. The underlying purpose of labor unionism is to create a shortage of human labor and skills. Unorganized labor is easily manipulated to create shortages by such device as has been used by Secretary of Labor Wirtz in agriculture: barring the entry of Mexican workers has created a shortage of agricultural products that has tremendously increased their cost and threatens to cause malnutrition in a large group that can not afford them.

## ANTI-"SOCIAL" WORKERS' RELIEF, "CIVIL RIGHTS" & "POVERTY" PROGRAMS INFLATIONARY

Among the craftiest and most vicious schemes for the promotion of inflation and looting the nation are those represented as "benevolence" and "social service." The horde of "social service workers," who graduate from "snap" and "bull" courses that pass for "education," can make a living only by joining the conspirators in their subversive activities, exactly as do the "economics" graduates. As this author has related in his earlier works (56; 29; 7) the majority of them depend for a living on becoming parasites on our economy, and undermining and destroying our Republic and social order. They express their intent "to create a new social order," expressed under the pyramid of the Illuminist emblem on the reverse of the U. S. seal as "Novus Ordo Seclorum" (29), by which they mean

312

that they seek to become cogs in a totalitarian machine in which they will "manage," a euphemism for "mismanage," our lives to serve their purposes and provide themselves with a livelihood, as "benevolent" agents of a dictatorship. The prediction made by this author, in the books above cited, that these mobs of social parasites will serve the conspirators in more intensively looting the nation, has been amply verified by subsequent developments.

## "NEW" DEALER NELSON ROCKEFELLER SADDLED NATION WITH H.E.W.

"Social service" racketeers gained their first death grip on the nation in the "New" Deal fronted by the conspirators' stooge, Pres. Roosevelt, but dominated by Nelson Rockefeller, "his closest adviser." (39) The so-called "Relief" program was headed by that utterly unprincipled Red scoundrel, the conspirators' agent, Harry L. Hopkins (7; 56; 79), the ringleader of the so-called "Hal Ware Cell" of Communists. He was as dedicated as is Gov. Nelson Rockefeller himself to the conspirators' policy: *"Tax! Tax! Tax! Spend! Spend! Spend! Elect! Elect! Elect!"* He uttered it frequently and applied it as intensively as does Gov. Rockefeller himself. In both instances there is left unuttered the true intent: *"Steal! Steal! Steal!"* (7; 22; 56) The program was designed to "pacify" the nation while the conspirators deliberately prolonged the depression that they had precipitated through their "Federal" Reserve fraud; and to continue their looting on a minor scale, until they had precipitated World War II that facilitated looting the nation on an ever grander scale. In the meanwhile, the "social service" parasites, most of whom are frankly Communist, built up in the Government a bureaucracy that has been firmly saddled on the nation, in the form of the Department of Health, Education & Welfare, by "New" Dealer Nelson Rockefeller. (79:155)

The currency inflation has been accentuated in both its cause and effects, by the "Relief" and sister programs, "Civil Rights" and "Poverty." Both have been designed to seduce agricultural and Negro workers to migrate to cities and industrial centers, thus reducing available farm help; and at the same time uprooting them from the environments in which they have thrived during many generations producing for themselves and for the nation the necessities of life. Immigrated, they have been duped into maintaining their betrayers, the conspirators, in power, to serve them in creating slums that rig "slum clearance" steals; and, in turn, are maintained in idleness and vice, as a "privileged," oft criminal element, by these "social service" programs—the conspirators' "New Social Order"—to more intensively loot the taxpayers and bankrupt the communities.

## DELIBERATE DISSIPATION OF OUR REAL WEALTH AND RESOURCES MUST BE STOPPED

Next to its pool of usefully and productively employed citizenry, a nation's most valuable asset is its supply of raw materials of the necessities of life. Without them, no nation can survive. Of these assets, we produce enough to furnish abundant reserves. Those commodities are the only real security for money. For if there is none at hand, in reserves, and we can not buy them to stay alive,

313

money has no value for us. This is the truth that the conspirators, bankers and their economist pawns do not want us to realize. They want to keep us deluded in the belief that only money and credit that they create on the basis of our own wealth, is riches. This enables them to manipulate the real wealth produced by the nation and steal it.

The conspirators have made it their practise, for this purpose, to dissipate our essential resources in any manner they can manage. During their "New" Deal, they plowed under crops, slaughtered pigs and doused potatoes with kerosene for the purpose of speculating in commodities that were already in scarce supply because of the drought, and for which the nation hungered because it had been deprived, by the conspirators, of the money or credit with which to purchase them. As a result, the nation lacked reserves in the war that followed; and there were breadless, meatless and sugarless days, and rationing. The nation yearned and hungered for the necessities of life that might have tided us over our days of need, if they had not been destroyed.

The armistice brought about reduction of "New" Deal restrictions and an increase in production. The conspirators hastened to try to eliminate our surpluses and reserves by their "foreign (Rockefeller) aid" and "give aways." This enhanced their speculative profits insured by the AAA programs. Systematically, agricultural commodities "surpluses" that could constitute reserves against times of drought, crop failures and other emergencies, have been dissipated by the "aid" programs or sold by the Government to foreign lands, at a loss. The dissipation of the nation's real wealth is "justified" by talk of the "Christian duty" to feed the "hungry"— abroad only. The conspirators dissemble their malign purpose by eschewing government in favor of religion, the Constitution in favor of the Gospels. But conspirators' misuse of the "aid" furnished at the expense of the taxpayer has made Americans hated around the world.

In Italy, the Rockefellers have used "foreign (Rockefeller) aid" counterpart funds diverted from the Treasury and the taxpayers into their purses to establish supermarkets that compete ruinously with local grocers. Rockefellers' International Basic Economy Corp. (IBEC) reported in its 1964 Annual Report that their Arbor Acres chicken and egg business, around the world, operated entirely at the expense of American taxpayers, has been as highly profitable to them as it has been ruinous to both the native producers and to American exporters who sold more than $50 million of poultry a year in the European market until the Rockefellers shut them out and impaired our payment balance in that amount. (79:237; 142; 143; 144)

### CONSPIRATORS MENACE U.S. SURVIVAL BY CREATING FOOD SHORTAGE BY GIVE-AWAYS

The conspirators' "foreign (Rockefeller) aid" give-away at the expense of American taxpayers has done more than destroy markets, create payment imbalances, and increase taxes. It has threatened the nation with food shortages by reducing reserves below the danger point, resulting in risking actual shortages, rationing and hunger and consequently endangering national security.

The carry-over of wheat, it was reported by Herschel D. New-com, Master of the Grange, on November 8, 1965, was reduced in the summer of 1964, to 819 million bushels, as compared with a 1958-62 average of 1.24 billion bushels; and he predicted that by the summer of 1966, it might be down to 750 million bushels. The reserve of corn, he reported, was even more critical, with a reduction of 35% in the carry-over, to 1.125 billion bushels, the smallest since 1955. The reduced reserves, he stressed, would bring about increases in prices of the commodities, and threatened a shortage that might well leave the nation with an insufficient supply for its needs that could threaten it with hunger if the prolonged drought, of years' duration, the "lean years," in growing sections of the country should continue. In 1966, as a consequence, of the corn shortage, there developed a shortage of hogs and skyrocketing prices for pork bellies, bacon and pork that profited the speculators, but brought about belt-tightening in some quarters. (152)

## DESPITE SHORTAGE, CONSPIRATORS EXPORT GRAINS TO COMMUNIST & HOSTILE LANDS

In spite of the shortage of grain that threatened, the conspirators deliberately gambled with our survival by shipping those commodities to other lands, in enormous volume and largely at the expense of our taxpayers. Much of it was virtually given away by them, directly or indirectly, at the expense of American taxpayers with profit for themselves, to their partners, our enemies in the Cold War, Communist Russia and China, and to hostile, so-called "neutralist," lands such as India. Other lands, including Canada and Australia, with large surpluses, sold grain to them at profits that materially improved their balances of payment. The conspirators treacherously further impaired our payment balance and increased our national debt, while themselves profiting therefrom. Ironically, one of the ultimate sources of profit of the conspirators from their treachery was the purchase of gold to pay for the Canadian and Australian grain, by the Treasury to be delivered to them at $35 an ounce.

While the conspirators were depleting our reserves and threatening our national survival, the virtual gifts, that we were induced to make to enemy and "neutralist" lands, were used, in the case of Soviet Russia, to increase reserves and to supply our enemies in the "Cold War" and in North Vietnam. In the case of "neutralist" India, that has been consistently hostile and opposed to us in world affairs, it has been estimated that almost half the millions of tons of grain that has been shipped by the U.S., largely, if not entirely at the expense of the taxpayers, has gone to feed the rats and other vermin that the Hindus are barred from destroying by their religion. (153) The reason why the conspirators are more "philanthropically" inclined to Indian rats and vermin than to American humans is the virtual monopoly of the Indian oil market that they and their interests have been given, and the site for three oil refineries with adequate capacity to supply all our Oriental enemies with the fuel and oil that they require for tanks and planes to mow down our GIs in Korea and Vietnam. The crude oil has been supplied, for our enemies, out of the Saudi Arabian oilfields developed at the cost of American taxpayers by Aramco, subsidiary of Caltex that in turn is subsidiary of Standard Oil. Indian Pres. Zakir Husian stated in his opening address to its Parliament that in 1968 India anticipated a bumper crop, but would use the American imports to bolster its reserves. (370) The grain given India by the U.S. taxpayers to maintain the conspirators in its good graces, is valued at about $2.5 billion. (154)

American food shipments to Egypt since 1952 have a total value of $1 billion. Like India, Egypt has been consistently hostile to the U.S., thereby showing her "appreciation" for the gifts of the American taxpayers given on behalf of the oily conspirators. It has used the American and other aid to launch attacks on its neighbors, and later to doublecross the conspirators themselves. Pres. Nasser (baum) deliberately incited attacks on American libraries and consulates. Nevertheless, our State Department has undertaken to appease him, on behalf of the conspirators, and to encourage further attacks on us by both Egypt and its Soviet allies by continuing shipments of grain and other foods for which some of our own people may hunger, on a basis that virtually constitutes a gift and reward for violating our national interests.

*What is the explanation for this apparently absurd "foreign policy" of our Government, that has been aptly described as "rewarding our enemies and betraying our allies?"*

It would be absurd error to believe that this "foreign policy" is based on stupidity. Edward S. Mason, Lamont Professor at Harvard University and Rockefeller agent who has served the conspirators on various of their resonator "committees" made quite clear, on their behalf, in his Elihu Root Lectures before their Council on Foreign Relations, of which he is a member, on *Foreign Aid & Foreign Policy,* that:

> "...foreign aid as an instrument of foreign policy implies that foreign aid programs are shaped *with the interests of the aid-giving countries primarily in mind.*" *(155:3)*

Since the "foreign aid" extended by the U.S. so clearly violates its interests, one questions: What interests does the State Department serve in the "foreign policy" that it shapes with the "foreign aid" programs? The answer appears in the volume *Random Reminiscences* that appeared in the name of John D. Rockefeller the First, that has been cited:

> "One of our greatest helpers has been the State Department in Washington. Our ambassadors and ministers and consuls have aided to push our way into new markets. " (16:63)

This makes it reasonably certain that "New" Dealer Nelson Rockefeller's insatiable greed impelled him to make sure that the endless arrays of "foreign aid" programs that he personally promoted and lobbied, served completely and solely the interests of the Rockefellers and the expansionist interest of their world-wide Empire, and of their Rockefeller-Soviet Axis partners. They were obviously "in the mainstream" of the policies he dictated as a member of the State Department. It can not be denied that every phase of the "foreign aid" schemes that he conceived and directed has served the Rockefeller-Soviet interests, to the utter exclusion of our national interests. This was shrewdly discerned by one of their defected African Communist agents, Nkrumah, the Negro dictator of Ghana. (135:162)

The results produced by the policy he has dictated match Nelson Rockefeller's statement in the "encyclical," "ghosted" in his name, in his CFR publication, *Foreign Affairs*, entitled *Purpose & Policy*. (22:370) His "purpose," he stated, is creation of the current "revolutionary period" in which he revels. As a consequence, all that slimy collaborators need to do serve as an excuse for looting American taxpayers by the "foreign (Rockefeller) aid" route and sharing the spoils, is to stage a riot directed against our country and its officials, preferrably massacring a few, burn down an American consulate, trample an American flag, stage a revolution, engage in an invasion or a war, or any other pretext that they can contrive, for a share of the loot.

## GAMBLING WITH RESERVES OF COMMODITIES ESSENTIAL FOR SURVIVAL MUST STOP.

Despite the warning, in the Fall of 1965, that our reserves of wheat were only 150 million bushels above our needs for a year, 600 million bushels minimum, and a continuation of the drought during the next year would leave us with not enough to feed ourselves, the conspirators dictated "foreign aid" shipments. The conspirators announced through the Administration that they were prepared to gamble with the nation's food supply on the odds that the drought would terminate in 1966. If we had lost, the nation would have had to tighten its belt. But that did not concern them. Fortunately adequate rainfall produced a bumper crop in the following year.

Gambling with national survival, however, is not good government. It must be stopped, and the stable commodities that are the raw materials of the necessities of life must be dealt with by those whom we select to represent us as the real wealth that they are. We must not permit the conspirators to force us into acceptance of their dictatorship by threatening us with want and hunger by any of the numerous devices that they have brought into play for that purpose.

## CONSPIRATORS' ATTITUDE: "AMERICA & AMERICANS BE DAMNED"

We have arrived at the point where it is accepted public policy that less and less tax funds shall be appropriated for services to our citizens and taxpayers; and the only funds that are unstintingly granted, as in Relief, "Civil Rights" and "Poverty" programs, are in the nature of bribes to noisome traitors, defiers of the law, law breakers, subversives and felons. We have arrived at the almost incredible situation in which our laws are warped by our highest courts to protect only criminals and leave law-abiding citizens to their mercy. Public officials, following the leadership of the sympathetic conspirators, as in Gov. Nelson Rockefeller's campaign to end capital punishment, seek to make crimes of the most heinous character, safer vocations. Bar Associations advocate change of the law and their administration to reduce the penalties of all crimes and sentences of criminals to minimal terms so that they can be freed rapidly to resume their criminal vocations and prey on the law-abiding. In line with this attitude, the conspirators bend their every effort to harass, handicap and discredit police and other law enforcement officers, to compel them to protect and collaborate with lawbreakers and criminals, espec-

317

ially if they be rioting blacks, violators of other peoples' rights to the use of their own property by labor strikes, or subversives bent on creating anarchy and overthrowing our Republic.

The law abiding citizens and the taxpayers are now habitually sabotaged by our government. The property owner, under rent control laws, is required to subsidize his tenants, permit them to demolish his building with impunity, and accept progressive confiscation of his property. Adequate rent increases are denied him, but freely imposed in public housing. Not only is the administration of the law corrupt, but corruption has taken over the law and nullified both Constitution and Bill of Rights.

## GOVERNMENT PRETENDS TO FIGHT INFLATION, BUT INFLATES POSTAL & ALL OTHER COSTS

Though our Government, under the direction of the conspirators, uses unlimited amounts of taxpayers' moneys to provide "aid" and services to lands around the world, it frequently rejects the provision of adequate, essential services to citizens, except at steadily mounting and comparatively exorbitant cost. That belies its pretense that it is opposed to inflation and seeks to control it. A flagrant example is postal service. Despite enormous expenditures for maintenance and defence of the conspirators' interests in other lands, the Government alleges that it can not afford to supply us reasonable, efficient, subsidized and stably priced postal services. Postal rates are being steadily increased and services reduced. Whenever Congress does not furnish the Postmaster General with all the funds that he demands for the conduct of his Department, a thoroughly inefficient and antiquated patronage machine and political "gravy train," he autocratically further cuts down the services essential for the nation's business. Closing of postoffices in the early evening was followed by their complete shutdown over weekends.

Constantly changes in regulations are issued to harass the public and deliberately aggravate the situation. An instance is a change in label for book mail by Postmaster General Gronouski, that required their reprinting to bear the words "Fourth Class, Special Rate" in addition to that previously required to indicate the contents: "Educational Material & Books." The special rate on book mailing was one of the few benefits of the "New" Deal, that was represented to be intended as an aid to education though it was actually motivated by the self interest of "New" Dealers, all of whom made their positions more lucrative by publication of their drivel. Gronouski evidently put the booksellers to the expense of printing the new labels, as a preliminary to eliminating the special book rate. Never, at any time, did he consider eliminating the special postal rate for the tons of Communist propaganda that the Post Office delivers for Russia, China and their satellites; or the vast scale thievery in the Post Office that makes it possible to purchase U.S. postage stamps, wholesale or retail, at discounts of 5% to 20%. Fortunately, Gronouski was sent off as Ambassador to his Red Poland before he accomplished more domestic injury.

## DAMS FOR AFRICAN SAVAGES & "UNALIGNED" ENEMIES BUT DAMNS FOR AMERICANS

At the behest of the conspirators and in violation of the Constitution that bars taxation of Americans for the support of any land other than the U.S., our Government is building dams for friends and foes alike. For African savages, it is building the Volta dam, at the expense of American taxpayers. But toward our American taxpayers, our Government adopts the attitude that it can spare no funds to build dams to protect them from destructive floods that occur almost annually on the Susquehanna, the Mississippi, the Delaware, the Missouri and others rivers. In this, as in other matters, the attitude of the conspirators that is reflected by their Government agents, is: "Americans be damned."

## "RELIEF" & "POVERTY" PROGRAMS PROMOTE
## CONSPIRATORS' CAUSES & INFLATION

The "Relief" and "Poverty" programs promote the conspirators' interests in several manners other than purchasing Negro votes with the bribery involved. Since the bribery is effected with tax funds, the programs tremendously increase the burden of the taxpayers and inflationary pressure, driving many communities to the verge of bankruptcy. Thus New York City's taxes for those programs today, alone exceeds the entire prior budget of the City. By maintaining an army of able-bodied, shiftless Negroes in luxurious id'əness and vice and subsidizing the breeding of illegitimate children it increases the black population and the voters, rioters, pillagers, rapists and murderers available to serve the conspirators; and at the same time it creates an inflationary shortage of labor.

## CENTER FOR THE STUDY OF DEMOCRATIC
## INSTITUTIONS CORRELATES PLOTTERS

The conspirators have very cunningly shifted suspicion from themselves by using an agency subsidized by the Ford Foundation which they completely control (15:347), the Center For The Study Of Democratic Institutions. Manned by Rockefellers' Reddest and most radical agents, it more rightly deserves the name Center For The Promotion Of American Communism. There the conspirators assemble the most vicious of their pro-Negro and other subversive agents to encourage, inspire and justify sabotage of the nation. These traitorous activities the conspirators proudly publicize through the Center under the title of *A Center Occasional Paper.* (305) The use of the word "occasional" fully betrays it as Rockefeller inspired publication: for the word has been a favorite of theirs since its use by John D. the First in *Occasional Paper No. 1* that outlined the purposes of his bogus "philanthropy."

## WARS & "POLICE ACTIONS": CONSPIRATORS' MOST
## VALUED INFLATIONARY FORCE

Wars for the expansion of "One (Rockefeller) World," and "police actions" under the auspices of their Rockefeller-Soviet dis-"United" Nations, have been the strategic and inflationary devices that are by far the most profitable for the conspirators. Wars provide them with endless varieties of loot in fantastic amounts. The sales of munitions, arms and all varieties of military equipment in which, as related, the "Defense" Department has served them as "demonstrators" and sales force in supplying both friend and foe often at the expense of American taxpayers, have yielded them fantastic profits, while enormously increasing the nation's tax burden, debt and adverse payment balance.

In the past half century, the conspirators have provided the nation and the world with a plenitude of wars that have incredibly increased their loot of all varieties and made them the virtual masters of the world. Our country is involved by them currently in two "hot" wars, World War II and Korean, three "cold" wars, with Communist Russia, Cuba and China, two "police actions," in Congo and Viet Nam. The Viet Nam "police action" bids fair to serve the conspirators in the role of "the straw that broke the camel's back." Like the others, it is a "friendly action" between the two partners of the Rockefeller-Soviet Axis. More than 15,000 of the over one hundred thousand casualties among the cream of American youth have lost their lives, butchered in a trap in that wholly Communist swamp land, protecting Rockefeller-Standard Oil petroleum reserves that underlie the entire Indo-Chinese delta country and the Chinese coastal shelf and protecting 2½ million Catholic refugees resulting therefrom. It is questionable that any of our half million GIs will return free of the loathsome, incurable chronic tropical diseases that infest that hell hole.

The conspirators have no more intention of permitting our country to win in Vietnam than they have had in permitting them to win in Korea. Either victory would breach their deal, now out in the open in the Rockefeller-Eaton-Soviet partnership. It would also put an end to the huge profits that they are making in supplying the Viet Cong and North Vietnamese with oil products, arms and munitions with which to shoot down GIs, exactly as they have been supplying our North Korean enemies, at the expense of American taxpayers. The conspirators make no secret of their plan to prolong the Vietnam hostilities for years. The heads of Rockefeller controlled enterprises were notified in mid January, 1968, that war would continue in Vietnam through most of 1971, and to plan accordingly. The discovery of a large oilfield, at Taching, in north China, and the determination to preserve their oil monopoly there, are added incentives. (181)

### WARS' COSTS WILL ENABLE CONSPIRATORS TO COMPLETE "GOLD CORNER" & TAKEOVER

Prolongation of the wars will not only increase tremendously their wartime profits, but also materially further the conspirators' "Gold Corner" by aggravating our payment imbalance and by impairing our national solvency. It served as a perfect excuse for demanding release of the $11 billions of gold that they were forced by the "Federal" Reserve Act to keep in their domestic account. The cost in American and other lives is regarded as furthering their population control program and is of no concern to them. They have never denied that their slogan is:

*"Oil is thicker than blood, provided it is the other fellow's blood." (15)*

### IMF, UN & STATE DEPARTMENT SUPPORT ROCKFELLER WORLD-WIDE BRIGANDAGE

The story of all the domestic and most foreign national and international "crises" of the past half century has been that of Rockefeller gangsters "muscling in" on the commerce and industry of nation after nation, with the full collaboration of their UN, their Soviet partners and the U.S. State Department. This offers the real explanation of the apparently vacillating U.S. so-called "foreign policy," that has been aptly described by Field, in the words:

320

*"American policy to date has consisted in talking against Communism and acting in favor of it; in weakening and whittling down the power of the Anti-Communist nations and creating vacuums into which Communism can spread. Bretton Woods did the job on the financial end."* (64:47)

Millions of American Armed Forces and peoples around the world have been forced to shed their blood and give their lives to serve the interests of the ruthless, brutal, villainous gangsters of the Rockefeller-Soviet Axis. (15) Our men must be extricated from the trap into which they have been sent in Vietnam, Korea and other lands. And there must be barred, forever, use of our forces for any purpose other than defense of our country and its security.

## "SOLUTIONS" OFFERED BY CONSPIRATORS ARE DESIGNED TO INTENSIFY INFLATION.

With few exceptions, the "economists," "planners" and politicians are directly or indirectly on the payroll of the conspirators. Consequently it should surprise no one that all of their schemes for the pretended "solution" of monetary and economic problems are designed to intensify the evils, for the purpose of increasing their employers' loot. This is quite apparent in the constant accentuation of inflation by the very "remedies" and "solutions" that they join in extolling.

The conspirators' key agency in this national and international looting, is their "Federal" Reserve and its subsidiaries. Alfred Hayes, president of their "F"RB of New York, stated in an interview with H. Erich Heineman that the basic function of the "Federal" Reserve is:

"...to control the size of the nation's money stock." (184)

The volume of money determines the extent of the conspirators' loot derived from their favorite and traditional device, usury. They call it "interest" and "discount," both more "respectable" than their Mafia agents' term "vigorish." Obviously, the scarcer they make money, the more the "philanthropists" can extort for its use. Since the cost of borrowing money is a basic item in production costs, its rise is a determination of rising prices and dropping purchasing power of money. That is inflation, a significant factor in the conspirators' looting of the nation through their "F"R.

## INCREASED TAXATION INEVITABLY INCREASES INFLATION

By far the most important device for reducing the purchasing power of money by inflation through the agency of the government, is mounting taxation. For taxes are an inescapable factor in all costs. Increases in taxes are intensified and multiplied through their addition at each stage in the processes of production and trade. This makes it quite clear how absurdly false is the representation by the conspirators, their pet "economists" and politicians, that the remedy for inflation is increased taxation.

## TAX INCREASES: FAKE "CURE" OF CONSPIRATORS' POLITICAL PAWNS FOR INFLATION

The favorite remedy offered by the conspirators and their polical henchmen for inflation is intensified looting of the public by increased taxation. Since they are tax exempt but derive a large part of

321

their loot from the taxes paid by the public, one can understand their dedication to tax brigandage. The absurd speciousness of the "reasoning" that they offer in favor of increased taxation, is manifest in the questioning of the conspirators' "Federal" Reserve agent, the FRB Chairman William McChesney Martin who has insistently demanded, in his official capacity, increased taxes to "prevent inflation." House Ways and Means Committee Chairman Wilbur D. Mills, one of the rare specimens of honest politicians, who has an honorable and proud record of consistently fighting the conspirators' tax looting bluntly asked Martin:

"Mr. Mills: If I know anything about business, those (increased taxes) are costs, are they not?
"Mr. Martin: They are.
"Mr. Mills: Do they not then make a contribution to the cost-plus inflation that we are fearful of?
"Mr. Martin: . . . yes." (298)

Martin left his bosses' and fellow conspirators' cat out of the bag. They brazenly admit, when cornered, that their real objective is to increase inflation and thereby reduce the purchasing power of the public and further increase their loot.

## TAX INCREASES INVARIABLY INTENSIFY INFLATION & CONSPIRATORS' LOOTING

Increased taxes add fuel to the fire of inflation, and largely account for the conspirators' phenomenal "success" in looting nations, for whom the consequences have been proportionately pathetic. Franz Pick has pointed out that the destruction of the value of currencies of the world is steadily rising to new peaks; and currency values have dropped, by 1966, 60% to 98% below their pre-World War II values. He rightly characterized the process by which the conspirators have brought this about as *"monetary confiscation"* resulting in *"fraudulent bankruptcies" that are represented to the public as "stabilization of price levels and monetary reforms."* (214)

The conspirators are keenly aware that increasing taxes will inevitably intensify inflation and increase their loot by the process of repaying loans and deposits, of paying wages and obligations, with inflated and depreciated currency of lower purchasing power. The insistence voiced by all of their agents that remedy for inflation is higher taxes, that the supposed gold reserve behind their "Federal" Reserve currency be abandoned and the gold released to "foreign" accounts, and a new "international" exchange medium established by them through agencies subsidiary to their "Federal" Reserve fraud, is quite obviously motivated by the conspirators' self interest, their desire to more freely loot the U.S. and the world.

## CONSPIRATORS' IMF VOICES THEIR DEMAND FOR HIGHER TAXES & NEW MONEY BASE

The International Monetary Fund subsidiary of their "Federal" Reserve has joined in the chorus of their agencies demanding more tax loot for the pretended purpose of "fighting inflation," and has added another note: a demand for a new medium of exchange created and controlled by them. For this latter purpose, the conspirators' CFR agent, Secretary of the Treasury Fowler issued a call, in 1966, to the

Group of Ten nations that dominate the IMF, for a monetary conference to devise a new "international" currency of the type advocated by Marx and Lenin, as a means of world control, that will be "managed" by the conspirators in much the same fashion as they "manage" the dollar through their "Federal" Reserve. This meeting paved the way for their IMF conference, in the following year, in Rio de Janeiro.

## CONSPIRATORS' SCHEME IS THAT WHICH HAS BEEN ATTRIBUTED TO "TRAITOR" WHITE

The monetary scheme that is now advanced by the conspirators in no wise differs from that proposed by their supposedly "traitorous" agent, Harry Dexter White and by their British, Fabian pawn, John Maynard Keynes, on their behalf at the Bretton Woods conference, at which their IMF was organized as a subsidiary of their "Federal" Reserve conspiracy. The persistent pushing of this plot long after the death of those pawns, proves conclusively that the conspirators were the authors of whatever treason they seek to attribute to White. Significantly, other of their agents in the original plot, notably White's associate E. M. Bernstein, are acting for them at this stage of their conspiracy.

Their scheme is nothing more than the issue by themselves, through their IMF agency, of a fiat, unsecured currency. It would be a revival of the "wildcat" bank scheme on an even more irresponsible basis than those which defrauded the nation during the 19th century. The unit, instead of being called, as in the scheme that White presented for them, "unitas," and Keynes, "bancor," they now propose to call "cru," an abbreviation of "Collective Reserve Unit." It has been aptly described by an honest and courageous member of their CFR, their *Fortune* editor, John Davenport, as a proposal:

"...to create a new medium of international exchange, so to speak, out of thin air."

He commented:

"To be blunt: can liquidity be managed *from the top down,* short of some kind of super-sovereign international government which, when proposed openly and politically, has again been rejected? *Or are we attempting in the matter of money to create such sovereignty through the back door, or through a trap door?"* (180:214)

## ROCKEFELLER "ONE WORLD" SOVEREIGNTY CAN NOT ENDOW FIAT MONEY WITH VALUE

Davenport hit the nail on the head. The Rockefellers are engaged in world conquest through war and finance on both the domestic and the international scenes, "through the back door" of worldwide Communism that they sponsor and promote, and "through a trap door," as exemplified by the trap in Vietnam in which our GIs are being butchered in a swampland that is completely controlled by their Communist partners.

There is ample proof that even a "super-sovereign" international government, that the conspirators are plotting, can not give "liquidity," in the sense of stable purchasing power, to the fiat, printing-press money that they issue through their "Federal" Reserve on the mythical gold base; and even more certainly it will not be accomplished with the "cru" that they plan to issue on the basis of "thin air."

Necessities of life that determine the value of money do not grow from money. This has been proved repeatedly, in our own history and in the history of the world. The scheme is certain to prove to be a snare and delusion for the lands on which it is imposed; and a device to further facilitate looting and impoverishment of the world by the conspirators This is amply evident from their "Federal" Reserve fraud and its various extensions and subsidiaries, notably their League of Nations and its banking devices, their dis-"United" Nations, IMF and other agencies, and the various political pacts such as NATO, SEATO and the international monetary and finance agreements that they have rigged to blind the world to their looting.

## DAVID ROCKEFELLER USES ALL THE MEANS AT HIS COMMAND TO "PUT OVER" THE FRAUD

David Rockefeller, in the self-proclaimed (through his publicity men) role of "the most important banker in the world," unstintingly dedicates himself to imposing the international printing press currency fraud on the nation and the world. Every medium of mass communication controlled by the conspirators, is used by him to dupe the nation to enter the trap, in which he plays the role of the spider inviting us flies into his web to have our substance devoured by him. Thus on December 17, 1967, he commandeered one hour of prime television broadcasting time, the Sunday noon hour, on their NBC national network, to promote the conspiracy and gloat with scantily dissembled glee and satisfaction at its success in forcing devaluation of the British pound. Billed as "financier David Rockefeller" (351) his propaganda was a rigged "interview" by one of the conspirators' "trained seal" correspondents in whose script were listed "correct" questions calculated to suppress the truth.

## PRES. JOHNSON HEEDS "HIS MASTER'S VOICE" & SOUNDS DEATH KNELL OF DOLLAR

David Rockefeller, as related, had publicly ordered Pres. Kennedy to eliminate both the silver and gold backing of the dollar and "Federal" Reserve currency. Kennedy was unable to carry out the order because of his inability to control Congress and dictate legislation. Shortly after Kennedy's assassination, his successor readily forced Congress, by his "arm twisting" tactics, to pass legislation carrying out part of David Rockefeller's order. On his demand, Congress passed a law releasing that part of the conspirators' gold loot that their "Federal" Reserve had been required to hold against the deposits of its member banks, a reserve of 25% in gold. The conspirators' gold loot thus immobilized in their domestic "Federal" Reserve account, amounted to a third of the gold held, or $5 billion. The excuse offered that element in the public that might be interested in such an "insignificant" action, is that it would "free the gold for settlement of our unfavorable trade balance."

Directly after the passage of the gold bill demanded of Congress by Pres. Johnson, on order from Rockefeller, approximately $3 billion were withdrawn, transferred, cautiously and intermittently, from their domestic hoard to their "foreign" bank of issue accounts. On balance, not a single ounce of gold left the country. It was transferred from one room or account of their "Federal" Reserve or the Treasury, to another. On April 11, 1967, the *Wall Street Journal* announced

324

that $13.1 billion in gold was then held by the U.S. at Fort Knox and in the Assay Offices of the Treasury Department, represented in the article as owned by the country. And it continued: (261)

"But the biggest single store of gold in the world, just under $13 billion worth, reposes five stories below ground level at the New York Fedĕral Reserve Bank in downtown Manhattan, and the U.S. doesn't own a penny of it."

Another article in the same issue of the *Wall Street Journal (262)* entitled *"Gold Drain Plug. Pressure Is Intensifying For A Warning By U.S. It May End Gold Selling,"* related that a Rockefeller employee of their Chase Manhattan Bank, its Vice President John Deaver, had echoed his master's propaganda on gold, in an article published earlier in the month in the Chase Manhattan publication *Business in Brief.* (263) He advocated that the U.S. violate, on the conspirators' behalf, the International Monetary Fund Agreement to buy and sell gold to foreign central banks and international agencies at $35 an ounce, and refuse to sell gold at any price when it suited their purpose. Several days prior, another of the conspirators' pawns, Rudolph A. Peterson, president of the Bank of America which the conspirators are gradually taking over, had added his bit to this propaganda in a speech which he had delivered under the watchful eye of boss David Rockefeller before the New York Chamber of Commerce. The article made it clear that Pres. Johnson and Secretary of the Treasury Henry Fowler, Rockefeller CFR agent, had received their instructions in the matter. But, it intimated that no official announcement had been made by either of them because the conspirators preferred to have the scheme represented abroad as "unofficial," on account of the alarm thereby created.

Less than a week later, Pres. Johnson demanded of Congress that it pass a bill eliminating the 25% gold reserve that the conspirators' "Federal" Reserve has been required to hold against the currency issued by it. (264) The represented purpose of releasing $12 billion of the conspirators' gold held in their domestic account, was to make it available for transfer to "foreign" lands for settlement of accounts. The sheer hypocrisy and mendacity of this misrepresentation is apparent from the conspirators' avowed and broadcast scheme to violate their agreement and sell no gold to foreign lands. The obvious purpose is to enable the conspirators to transfer their gold from their domestic to their foreign accounts so that can violently inflate and destroy the dollar and profit from an eventual revaluation of their hoarded gold loot. In short, the bill demanded of Congress spells the death knell of the dollar, and possibly oᴵ every world currency; and the consummation by the conspirators of the greatest "Gold Corner" in world history. It is designed to saddle the Rockefeller Dynasty openly on the U.S. and the world, and reduce the bulk mankind to poverty and serfdom in a "One (Rockefeller) World" absolute dictatorship and Empire.

The legislation entitled: "To eliminate the requirement that the Federal Reserve banks maintain certain reserves in gold certificates against Federal Reserve notes," had previously been introduced in the 1st Session of the 90th Congress as H.R. 6428 by Congressman Reuss, and had been referred to the Committee on Banking and Currency on March 1, 1967.

In the meanwhile, for the avowed purpose of confusing the foreign banking fraternity who are concerned with the planned unilateral violation of the agreement entered into by the U.S., at the instance of the conspirators, with the IMF, a barrage of contradictory reports and speeches were issued by agents of the conspirators and published in the media that they control. Robert V. Roosa, former Under Secretary of the Treasury, made a widely published speech opposing the refusal to sell gold abroad. The press release did not make it clear that he is a Council on Foreign Relations agent of the Rockefellers, and had on that very day been appointed a Trustee of the Rockefeller Foundation. (269)

## BETRAYAL OF OUR SOVEREIGNTY FOR THE EXPANSION OF THE ROCKEFELLER EMPIRE MUST BE ENDED.

Our Constitution is the blueprint of a nation, our Republic. So long as it remains our basic law theoretically, the betraying of our sovereignty and "internationalism" are violations of it and are treason. Taxation of Americans and drafting of GI's for the defense and support of any other land than our own is a flagrant violation of the Constitution and arrant treason. Likewise, the subordination of our national soveregnty to the so-called "United" Nations, the culmination of Adam Weishaupt's Illuminist-Communist conspiracy, can only be regarded as the act of traitors until such time as the Constitution is revoked and abandoned. And that, we ardently hope, never will be done.

All of the "internationalist" and traitorous activities in which our Republic has been betrayed, including agreements, alliances, "police actions," wars, and "diplomatic" activities of our Federal government, are acknowledged by the Rockefellers (16:93) and their fellow conspirators, to have served their interests at enormous cost to us in money, resources and lives. The conspirators have become so bold, arrogant and contemptuous of us that, as has been related, they have personally emerged in open direction of these perfidious activities. In many instances, including the "Status of Forces" agreements, any pretense of extending the protection of our Constitution and law to us individually, even when drafted in our Armed Forces, has been abandoned. Our GIs are scattered around the world and our Armed Forces "spreadeagled" to serve as virtual hostages for the conspirators and their confederates. Our wealth is being poured out into their coffers by an endless series of treacherous devices.

A halt must be called to the conspirators' treasonous betrayal of our Republic and ourselves, and their contemptuous flaunting of our Constitution as obsolete. And at home, there must be halted their deliberate undermining of our institutions, customs and pattern of life. Unless this is done promptly, we will be, and we deserve to be, reduced to the status of serfs of the conspirators, devoid of all human rights assured by the Constitution.

## "LIBERTY AMENDMENT" PROVIDES A SOLUTION OF HUGE NATIONAL DEBT

The patent national debt that the conspirators have busily rolled up for the nation by their "management" now amounts to more than $330 billion; and the interest thereon constitutes a burden on the taxpayers of approximately $14 billion. In addition to this bond-ed indebtedness, the taxpayer carries the even larger burden of losses incurred by the so-called "authorities" and Government subsidized corporations established by the conspirators to operate in cut-throat competition with unsubsidized private industries controlled by others, at profits to themselves but at huge losses to the nation and its taxpayers. These losses engineered by the conspirators consume virtually the entire sum derived by the Government from income taxes. Their elimination would make the Federal income tax needless as a source of revenue. The true total potential debt probably exceeds several trillion dollars.

The most profitable and least suspect of the so-called "Governmental corporations" established by the conspirators at all levels of government, are their "authorities." They are laws unto themselves and supra-governmental, above regulation and control by any governmental agencies. They are free to loot the nation as mercilessly as they wish. The sole restrictive provision put in their charters is the sardonic rule that they must be "self-supporting," with the help of whatever subsidy they receive from the governments involved. They are invariably operated in such manner as to require maximum and ever increasing subsidies from the governments, at the expense of the taxpayers. They are exemplified by such tax exempt agencies as the Tennessee Valley Authority, at the Federal level; the New York-New Jersey Port Authority that at 1967 yearend announced the value of its holdings as $2 billion, at the interstate level; and the New York City Transit Authority at the local level. They are all tax exempt. And they are all above and outside the control by the law though they are entitled to full protection of the law.

The Liberty Amendment that aims to eliminate the Federal income tax also aims to relieve the taxpayers of the burden constituted by these agencies of the conspirators. It provides for the elimination of those pseudo-public corporations that serve to devour the income tax loot that pours into the conspirators' pockets. The elimination of the huge "losses" which the conspirators arrange in the "management" of these corporations will fully balance the entire yield of the Federal income tax and make it needless. The sale of these corporations to private enterprise will go far in wiping out the national debt.

Cessation of the huge drain on our wealth by the conspirators' "foreign aid" frauds, and the drain of the malevolent foreign involvements into which they have trapped the U.S. for their own advantage (including "police action," wars, dis-"United" Nations, the "International" Monetary Fund and other subsidiaries of their "Federal" Reserve fraud) plus belated forcing of debtor nations to repay their debts to the Treasury and not to the conspirators who have diverted the moneys to their foreign accounts and their agencies in foreign lands, will reverse our unfavorable payment balance and establish a national surplus, will go far to restore the value of the dollar.

## PSYCHOLOGIC VALUE OF RECOVERY BY TREASURY OF GOLD LOOTED BY THE CONSPIRATORS

*The gold looted from the nation by the conspirators through their "Federal" Reserve fraud must be seized and recovered for the nation.* For, though gold, as pointed out by Harry Dexter White, is a relatively worthless commodity, and constitutes a burden on the economy and a real liability, it has a potent psychologic value that necessitates its recovery. The grip of gold as a symbol of wealth on popular imagination throughout the ages makes it readily possible for the conspirators to create fear for the solvency of the nation if it does not hold gold. And that is the device that the conspirators appear to plan to use to thrust our enormously rich country into fraudulent bankruptcy, and to loot us as they have looted other nations around the world with the same device. Since the total value of all the gold in the world represents a minute fraction of the nation's income and wealth, it is wise that we bow to popular psychology and accept the relatively small burden that it places on our economy for the purpose of coping with that factor.

## CONSPIRATORS' GOLD TRAP A BOOMERANG & FACILITATES NATION'S RECOVERY OF LOOT

Repossession of the $25 billion in gold looted from the nation by the conspirators presents no legal problem. For the trap that they have set for us "peasants" also stands ready to entrap them. They represent that their gold hoard is the property of banks of issue of foreign lands. Those lands owe the U.S. considerably greater sums than the value of their supposed "earmarked" gold held in the vaults of the "Federal" Reserve. Seizure of the gold by the Treasury as partial recovery of the debts on which they have defaulted would be quite legitimate.

If, however, the conspirators assert their claim to the gold, they confess violation of the law that they have placed in the statutes of the U.S. and other lands around the world, that make it a felony for any private citizen to own gold, in refined and other forms, beyond the value of a few hundred dollars. If the vital interest of a couple hundred million Americans can be made to prevail over that of a couple dozen conspirators, a few thousands of their henchmen and a million of their agents, pawns and employees, the recovery of the stolen gold will present no problem. Nor will the payment balance or the stability of the dollar give any cause for concern, if this and other phases of the conspiracy are dealt with in equally legal fashion.

Congress, however, must be compelled to safeguard these vital interests of the nation. Thus far, only one Representative has had the courage to defy the conspirators and demand, on the floor of the House, that France and other defaulting debtors of our country be required to pay their debts, long overdue, on which they have shamefully and fraudulently defaulted with the full collaboration of the conspirators who are their confederates in the fraud, and the beneficiaries thereof. Their rigged claims against us represent a small fraction of the principal of the debts they owe us and of fair interest charges due on them.

Prompt action by our Government in this matter would blast the "Federal" Reserve and "Gold Corner" conspiracy and its perpetrators sky high. The conspirators would not merely lose their golden loot, but also would be faced with the penalties for their crime, which they have written into the law. This would be "poetic justice."

# CHAPTER XXIII
## SOLUTION OF MONETARY PROBLEM: THE PRINCIPLES THAT MUST GUIDE IT

There is pathetic irony in the restoring of the words, *"In God We Trust"* on our currency by the conspirators, at the very moment that they busily plot to destroy the value of the dollar and replace it with a worthless fiat currency. Throughout the ages, the most ruthless and unscrupulous criminals have operated behind religious masks and shams. But none have made more crafty and shameful use of pretended "benevolence," bogus "philanthropy" and the cloak of sham "religiosity" than have the Rockefellers. For the latter, full explanation can be found in their madness that has led them to pronounce themselves to be special agents of the Lord, who appointed them "to hold in trust for Him" the loot that they have extorted from us, and to aspire to the status of "gods."

## MAD ROCKEFELLER OFFERS SELF AS "GOD" IN ROLE OF "REX, IMPERATOR ET DEUS"

John D. the Second (Jr.) twice delivered a speech before the New York Protestant Council (first in World War I, and again in World War II) entitled *The Christian Church — What Of Its Future?* in which he madly dictated that the Christian Church, like Lamaism of Tibet, must become the Church of the Living God. (371:5) His numerous utterances respecting his delusion or pretense that the Lord had made him His "trustee" of the loot which he had garnered makes quite apparent that he was intimating that he would make a mighty good "god." It is hardly surprising that his heirs are equally mad and of similar mind; and that they would not take it amiss if we were to accept them as were the Caesars and as are their successors who rule the Holy Roman Empire, as *Rex, Imperator et Deus*.

Like so many tyrants in the past, they are well on the road to being accepted as "gods" by the multitude who have complied with the conspirators' scheme and dictate that they

"...yield with perfect docility to our molding hands." (15:3)

Unlike the mythical deities of yore, they who are our modern bogus "gods" are not content with a mere tithe, with a tenth of our wealth, but demand it all. (84; 15:300; 79:37) They are "superior" racketeers! They are the Western version of Kali, the Hindu deity of thieves and murderers, who far exceed her in sacrificial requirements. They require the slaughter of millions in endless wars to expand their domains, and genocide to enhance their loot.

329

## OUR SURVIVAL REQUIRES ELIMINATION OF PLOTS & DEVICES OF "PHILANTHROPISTS"

We are now at the crossroads. We are confronted with a hyper-acute problem: What can we do to prevent revival of the conspiracy after we recapture from these false "gods" and bogus "philanthropist" thieves and felons our freedom and our looted wealth? How can we restore our Constitution, that the conspirators decree is "obsolete" and in need of alteration to suit their designs, and amend it to serve adequately as our basic law and the bulwark of our freedom? How can we stop the conspirators who are little short of their goal of making themselves our gangster, tyrannical dictators, and firmly establish the Republic designed by the Constitution?

Now, or never, we must eliminate the conspirator "philanthropists" and the aforementioned devices that assure success of their plot. The most important of those devices are those that give the conspirators control of our wealth and our monetary system, notably their "Federal" Reserve conspiracy, and direct and indirect domination of our persons. The answer is most readily arrived at by considering the axiomatically basic functions of government.

## BASIC FUNCTIONS OF GOVERNMENT REQUISITE FOR OUR SURVIVAL

Axiomatically, the basic function of government is to enable its citizenry to live and survive. It is for that purpose peoples organize governments and delegate powers, in a republic, to chosen persons in their midst. For this purpose, governments must serve certain functions.

1. Government must insure the availability of necessities of life. For without those necessities, life is not possible, and without life, government is not possible. Since food and other raw materials of the necessities of life can not be produced instantly:

    a. *Government must provide for availability of the raw materials of the necessities of life, by storing them.*

2. Government must make it possible for the citizenry to obtain the wherewithal to purchase the necessities of life.

    a. To make this possible, government must insure to its citizenry *freedom of employment* that is adequately profitable.

Unfortunately the economic basis of organization of governments, whether so-called "capitalist," meaning speculative, or "Communist," meaning super-capitalistic, bars the way to governments rendering those basic services to their citizenry. Dishonestly manipulated monetary systems share with other dishonest devices the responsibility for the breakdown of government services.

## FATAL FALLACY OF SUPPOSED "LAW OF SUPPLY & DEMAND" BLOCKS SERVICES TO NATIONS

The fundamental barrier to the rendering by governments of services to their citizenry that are axiomatically basic is the acceptance of the so-called *"Law of Supply & Demand"* as the cornerstone of their economies. This supposed "law" denies to all com-

330

modities, whether material or labor, other than a monetary base that now is usually gold, any intrinsic value. In practise, this "law" finds expression in its converse: *"It is primarily scarcity that gives value to commodities, both raw and fabricated, and to labor."* This means that it matters not that a bushel of wheat makes fifty loaves of bread, or that a worker can produce food, clothing or shelter. Their value is assured only if the immediately available supply is less than the immediate demand. The same "law" is applied to the control, or "management," of money.

The utter absurdity of this so-called "law of supply and demand," especially as applied to the necessities of life, is manifest in the classical textbook example of its operation:

"Two men are stranded on a desert island. Only one of them has sufficient food for survival. In view of the greater demand than supply of the food, its value, or its price, will rise."

Only an imbecile, or a professor of economics who has prostituted himself to his masters, could fail to recognize that the individual who possessed only enough food for his own survival would be trading in his life if he were so idiotic as to trade for profit the substance that he needed for his survival. He might share his hoard with his fellow man as a matter of charity, but he certainly would not, if he had any wits, do it as a matter of "good business." Nevertheless, that is exactly the course that our United States is pursuing currently, under the dictates of the conspirators, to serve their interests.

Therein lies the fallacy of "internationalism" and one of the roots of its failure when honestly motivated. It is the basic function of sound government to insure the survival of its own people, first, last and always. It must repudiate the thinly disguised commercialism and power-play of religion and "philanthropy," and be motivated by the rule that "charity begins at home," especially when the nation faces dire emergency, to which it has been reduced by substituting religious platitudes for the Constitution.

### "LAW OF SUPPLY & DEMAND," AS APPLIED TO NECESSITIES, IS A MENACE

Interaction of immediate supply and immediate demand in the marketplace implies speculative manipulation of prices. As applied to the staple products that are the raw materials of the necessities of life, it implies elimination of reserves. For reserves are viewed by speculators as excess supply, and consequently depress the market price. Drop in commodity prices means elimination of the marginal producer whose cost of production is higher than the market price. Elimination of the marginal producer, in turn, means a drop of employment and consequent drop in consumption. The drop in consumption, or demand, means a further drop in price, and further reduction in production, employment and consumption. This creates a vicious cycle which reaches stability only when there is less produced than the consumers require. At this point, the downward cycle is reversed and replaced by an equally vicious upward spiral of price and production, until there once again prevails a faltering demand relative to the supply stimulated by rising prices and profits. Absence of stability of commodity prices precludes the building up of adequate, long-term reserves, requisite for national survival.

This situation is well illustrated by the market in wheat during the interval between World War I and World War II. After the Armistice, growers of wheat and other grains around the world hastened to expand their production to maximum capacity in order to feed a hungry, clamoring world. Lakes and swamps, that were the natural habitat of birds that live on insects that destroy crops, and provide the reservoirs that maintain the table level of water, were drained, ploughed up and planted with wheat and other grain. Vegetation that anchors soil in arid regions and deserts and prevents their conversion into dust bowls was ploughed up for dry farming of grain.

American farming produced, in 1919, a larger crop of wheat than in any year in the following decade. It mounted, according to the Department of Agriculture, to 952,100,000 bushels. (185:407) The crop commanded the average price of $2.338, the highest in the two following decades. (186:539) The intensive farming brought about a steady drop in the table level of water under the land, that in the Plain States amounted to a drop of 100 feet, and converted them into a dust bowl. By 1933, American farming produced 552,200,000 bushels of wheat, or about 45% of the 1919 bumper crop; and in the following year the yield dropped to the lowest in our recent history, 526,100,000 bushels. (185:407) The greatly reduced supply of wheat in 1933 commanded the lowest price of the two decades, an average of 32.9 cents, or little more than 14% of the price it had commanded in 1919, when the crop was largest. (186:539) Kansas farmers, in 1933, were paid seven cents (7¢) a bushel for their wheat at harvest time.

## SPECULATION & MANIPULATION NOT "SUPPLY & DEMAND" DETERMINE PRICES

The agricultural market presented such a stark contradiction to the so-called "Law of Supply & Demand," the maximum production and over-supply of 1919 commanding the maximum price, and the low production and extremely short supply of 1933 commanding a minimum price, that the "New" Deal Brain Trust "economists" felt obliged to seek an explanation. Apparently, the economists lacked the intelligence to solve the problem. A "genius" from the poultry division of Cornell University, a Professor Warren, however, offered a "solution" that was adequately befuddling to be classed as a "gem" of the pseudoscience of economics. He gave a mathematic expression to the situation that was sufficiently absurd as to be classified as "abstruse" and regarded by his fellow "scientists" as a "solution." He pontificated that the proper expression for the "Law of Supply and Demand" is not that price varies inversely with the supply and directly with the demand. The proper formula, he "learnedly" declared, is that price varies with the ratio of the supply and demand of a commodity relative to the supply and demand of gold.

The supply of gold, even in those years when its production dropped to the lowest level, exceeded its demand for technoligic use, filling teeth and jewelry, by more than 95% of the then current production. Though the total amount of gold produced in the history of man would not fill a structure forty feet wide, forty feet long and forty feet high, its stable properties ensure at all times a supply of gold that exceeds its technologic and ornamental uses and demand. Despite its uneconomic use in coinage, the bulk of the world's gold is taken out of one hole in the ground and buried in another, as at Fort Knox. For practical purposes, gold is in constant oversupply relative to its essential, technologic uses. The ratio of supply and demand of gold is purely a matter of manipulation and speculation. This reduces the "abstruse" formula of the "learned" Prof. Warren to the commonly recognized fact that it is primarily speculation that determines the prices of commodities.

This brings us to the vital question:
*"Shall speculation and manipulation of the supply of gold be permitted to bar governments from performing their basic functions and reduce nations to starvation?"*

The answer is, quite obviously and emphatically: *"No!"* Our government was established by our progenitors and is supported by ourselves in the expectation that it will enable us to survive, individually and as a nation. Power has been delegated to persons in our midst for that purpose. It is quite as important as insuring and protecting us from invasion and physical threat, that our Government insure that there shall at all times be available for us, for purchase at reasonably stable prices, the raw, staple materials of the necessities of life; and that if we are willing to work for it, we shall have the wherewithal to purchase those necessities. It is rightly the function of our government to protect us against the vagaries of Nature, and to take advantage of her bountiful moods to provide us with enough staples to tide us over her niggardly moods. It is beyond the scope of private enterprise to insure adequate supplies of those necessities at a stable price, thereby stabilizing the purchasing power of our money in terms of those necessities and avoiding the privations and hardships of inflation, of excessive increases in those prices. Private enterprise is compelled, of necessity, to raise prices speculatively, in times of shortage to compensate for the expense involved in tying up funds in times of plenty for carrying reserves and surpluses until times of need. But the people as a whole, operating through their government, empowered to spread and average the cost involved over long periods of time, can be expected to maintain stability of money in purchasing power in terms of those necessities. This can be done exactly as is now done with a single commodity, gold: by defining the dollar in terms of the staple commodities, by widening its currency base to include those commodities as well as gold. This is the obvious solution of the monetary problem. It will insure personal and national survival, and frustrate the conspirators' scheme to loot and enslave us.

The problem of storage of commodities presented no insurmountable problem to Joseph and primitive man. They stored their grain in the desert in earthen jars. (172:I:107) It should present no difficulties to modern technology.

## "ONLY SEVEN PERSONS IN THE WORLD UNDERSTAND MONEY" WE ARE TOLD

The conspirators' propagandists in the field of money and finance, their prostituted so-called "authorities," professors of the "social sciences" and economic advisers, are called on to maintain a constant flow of false ideas on the subject of money and finance in the various channels of mass communication. This flow of lies and fallacies is greatly intensified during the weeks, months and often years prior to a planned especially immense steal. The prestige of their propagandists is enhanced, even beyond that emanating from the professorial and/or financial roles, by the intensively broadcast myth that "there are only seven men in the world who understand money." The conspirators omit a very important clause from this propaganda of theirs, to wit: "...who 'understand' money as we wish it misunderstood for our own profit."

## ALL BUT IDIOTS UNDERSTAND TOO WELL THE MEANING OF MONEY & ITS USES

Few of us fail to learn in childhood what "money" means: tokens that vary in substance, content and value, and are accepted in exchange for the things that we need or want. We know too well, from experience, that if money is not accepted in exchange for our needs, it has no value for us. We have learned that the only things that gives value, or serves as "security," for money are those items that we need or desire. We have personally learned from our experience the wisdom of Pharaoh's steward, Joseph, who rightly valued necessities above gold; and the folly of King Midas, who valued gold above food and converted to gold everything he touched, but starved to death. In rare instances in the past, recognition of this truth about money has been forced on our government, as in the case of the State of Massachusetts Bay.

Money, however, like love, "is a many-sided thing." For the usurer, the moneylender and the banker, money is a device for gaining profits by taking advantage of the needs of others, and for extortion. For the conspirator, the politician or the ruler or head of a state, money is not merely the medium of exchange. For them money is a device for exercise of power over others, and money that serves merely as a medium of exchange is unsatisfactory. Their purposes can only be served by money that can be manipulated by themselves in both value and volume to enable them to control the acts and fortunes of others. With those objectives in mind, they undertake to befuddle, indoctrinate and propagandize us into the belief that the obvious facts about money with which we have been acquainted since childhood are untrue and not to be trusted.

## MONEY USED AS MEDIUM OF EXCHANGE IS COMPARABLE TO HATCHECK

For the bulk of mankind, money has much the same role as a hatcheck. It is a device that can be exchanged for something that one needs that has been placed in storage. The number of tokens available must, obviously, equal the number of items exchanged. Anyone who would attempt to run a hatchecking establishment on the plan of having fewer tokens than hats that are checked would promptly be adjudged insane.

Our economy is operated, by the conspirators, however, on the basis that there must be less money (and credit) available to the nations than the value of all items that are exchanged; and that they must be kept in scarce supply by manipulation in order to "maintain the value of money." In other words, the conspirators undertake, and are empowered by their usurped power, to juggle the supply of money to maintain their profit therefrom by the supposed interaction of supply and demand, which means, in effect, maintaining it scarce. In order to provide themselves with enough loot from monetary dealings and manipulations, the conspirators force the nation to operate its government, commerce and industry with less money than the value of the items to be changed. This is no less insane than the operation of the hatchecking establishment with fewer hatchecks than there are hats to be checked, for the supposed purpose of "maintaining the value of hatchecks."

No matter how convenient are the devices of money, currency and credit for the exchange of commodities, they are not necessities, except for banker, moneylender and usurers. However, in modern society those media of exchange have become such essential conveniences that it is the duty of peoples to provide them through their governments in order to permit of more ready and widespread exchange of commodities and services.

## FRAMERS OF CONSTITUTION ERRED BECAUSE OF BIAS CREATED BY BOARD OF TRADE

The framers of the Constitution, as has been related, viewed the subject of money and the issue of currency with eyes jaundiced by their ugly experiences with the Board of Trade. As a consequence, they were lacking in perspective and foresight. They rejected empowering the government to provide for the issuance of currency, other than metallic coins of silver and gold, or the establishment of banks and financial institutions for the provision of media of exchange. They feared that giving Congress the power to do so would result in the same abuses as those perpetrated by the Board of Trade, and would lead to its gouging and oppressing the nation. (67) This attitude indicated their lack of faith in the Congress that they undertook to create. Either as a matter of shortsightedness, or possibly design, they disregarded the fact that the Board of Trade was in effect a private agency of King George and not responsible to public opinion as they planned to have Congress; and that granting the power of the purse, the power to issue currency, to private bankers would not eliminate the danger of monopoly and the abuses that they feared, but would actually aggravate them. Even the Board of Trade in all of its viciousness embodied some elements of responsibility to King, nation and the Church that is completely lacking in private control of the nation's power of the purse authorized by the Constitution. The sole, incredible, restriction on the monetary and financial activities of the private banker is voluntary restriction and control of his cupidity and greed, and competition therein between moneylenders. Bankers and moneylenders, however, are notoriously interested primarily in making money and increasing their wealth. For this they must eschew, in their official capacity, benevolence and philanthropy, and usually common decency and fairness, except under the pressure of competition. History has amply proved that in granting the power to issue currency, the real power of the purse, to private bankers, the framers of the Constitution plunged the nation from the frying pan into the fire.

## FRAMERS OF THE CONSTITUTION DISREGARDED SIGNIFICANCE OF POWER OF THE PURSE

The framers of the Constitution disregarded the fact that the issue of currency, the power of the purse, is inextricably tied in with the purposes stated in the Declaration of Independence and the Constitution; and that those purposes can not be carried out unless that power is guided and controlled by a number of motives and principles. Currency must be stable in terms of purchasing power, particularly for the raw materials of the necessities of life, and a reliable medium of exchange and saving. It must serve solely as a medium of exchange and not as a medium of control, manipulation, piracy and looting for the selective enrichment of a self-appointed chosen few, unscrupulous predatory persons, as does our private, so-called "Federal" Reserve System and its subsidiary agencies. To honestly and properly serve the nation, the monetary and banking systems must be free of self-biased control and manipulation and permit money and currency to expand with the wealth of the nation and its needs. This the framers of the Constitution failed to provide for and incorporate into it.

## FRAMERS OF CONSTITUTION IGNORED SOUNDEST LESSON TAUGHT BY THE BIBLE

In the matter of money, the framers of the Constitution disregarded the soundest lesson taught by the Bible, the story of Pharaoh's steward, Joseph; that wealth is not gold, or money, but is the raw materials of the necessities of life. Had they heeded that lesson, they would have been led to the same type of solution arrived at, in 1780, by the shrewd Yankee politicians of Massachusetts Bay. They would have spared the nation endless misery and looting.

## OBVIOUSLY INDICATED SOLUTION OF MONETARY PROBLEM

Since money is meaningless and valueless unless it will purchase, at least the necessities of life, it is obvious that the security behind money must be available supplies of the raw materials of the necessities of life that it is properly the function of government to assure. The government can do this only by maintaining reserves of staple products and by assuring employment that will enable individuals to obtain the earnings wherewith to purchase them. An economy of scarcity precludes the setting up of surpluses and reserves that alone can assure immediate availability of the raw materials essential for personal and national existence. It is a function of government, therefore, to eliminate the barrier constituted by speculation, inherent in a "supply and demand" economy, in essential staple commodities, to stimulate the maximal production thereof permitted by Nature's vagaries, and to provide for their continuous storage.

## CONSPIRATORS' "GOLD STANDARD" POINTS WAY TO ELIMINATION OF SPECULATION

Ironically, the operation of the conspirators' mythical "Gold Standard" offers an obvious method of stabilizing the value of other, needed and useful commodities. It has established and stabilized the monetary value of gold, a commodity that is a non-essential and costly burden on the economy. It did so in the face of constant and extreme overproduction of gold, by dictating the purchase of all that was produced and tendered, at a fixed price per ounce. Obviously, the same device can be applied successfully to essential commodities.

## IMMEDIATE WIDENING OF MONETARY BASE CAN AVERT DANGEROUS BRIGANDAGE

Immediate widening of the monetary base by the inclusion of staple commodities is the only measure that can avert the planned disastrous looting by the conspirators of the U.S. and the world in their current "Gold Corner." It must be accompanied by the termination of their thievish monopoly of monetary control through their "Federal" Reserve and IMF frauds and their control of other banks of issue around the world; elimination of the tax exemption of themselves and their confederates; an end to their "foreign aid" piracy and their power to dictate and precipitate domestic strife and foreign wars, both of which arise from their usurped power of the purse. This is the most critical issue facing the nation and the world. We are now at the crossroads. If we resolve this issue now, we have a chance to restore the properly amended Constitution as the basic law of the land; and to attain the Republic that was faultily designed to establish but failed to accomplish because of failure to retain for the nation the power of its purse. The rest of the world will benefit therefrom in the same measure as does the U.S. because their governments will of necessity, and for their own advantage, follow suit.

Amendment of our Constitution to give Congress the power to establish such a monetary base, to control the creation and issue of media of exchange, and to charter and control banks is essential for effecting this remedy and reform. Only such an amendment can make possible for us the attainment of the avowed purpose of our Constitution and Bill of Rights: "freedom of life, liberty and pursuit of happiness." Only the adoption of a staple product currency base will enable the setting up of maximal reserves in times of plenty, to provide against times of drought and need, as was wisely done even by primitive man, as exemplified by Biblical Joseph. The value of a bushel of wheat will then be measured in terms of the fifty loaves of bread that it will provide, instead of in the terms of what the speculator chooses to offer for it.

## STAPLE PRODUCT DOLLAR WILL MAKE POSSIBLE TRUE FREEDOM OF EMPLOYMENT

Money based on staple products will make it possible for the government to create freedom of employment to enable its citizenry to obtain the wherewithal to purchase the necessities of ilfe and other needs. True freedom of employment is as non-existent in our so-called "capitalist" land as it is in the super-capitalist, so-called "Commun-

337

ist," lands that accept the tenets of the Weishaupt-Marx "socialism." For in both, employment is ruled by the "law of supply and demand." Its operation is most clearly expressed in its converse: "Human beings and their labor must be scarce to have value." Creation and maintenance of scarcity of humans and their skills, is the purpose of the conspirators' Population Institutes and of their Labor Baron agents and unions. It is the height of irony that this antisocial doctrine and practise has been labelled with the tag "Socialism;" and has been established as the basic tenet from which no "Liberal" may dissent.

Labors "leaders" make the self-serving allegation, in which they are staunchly supported by "Liberal" sycophants, that there can be no freedom of employment, that their role in creating and maintaining a scarcity of workers in their respective trade union monopolies is essential because "sixty wealthiest families and their corporations" control all the machinery of production. How absurdly nonsensical is this pretense of theirs can be discerned from a consideration of what is the basic machinery of production. Labor is not the basic machinery of production. For labor engaged in tearing down a building, for example, is not engaged in production. Nor is unthinking labor, as in the instance of the ape that constantly engages in labors but produces nothing, a basic machinery of production. Human intelligence that creatively directs labor, however, is a basic machinery of production, though the Weishaupt-Marx indoctrinated "Liberals" refuse to recognize it as such.

## FALLACIES OF "NEW" DEAL AND ITS COMMUNIST BASIS

Therein rests a basic fallacy of the pseudo-science of Weishaupt and Marx, and of their "Socialist" and Communist followers. They have started with the false premise: wealth that was then extant was the limit of all possible wealth; that therefore, it must be "distributed" to provide for those who have little or nothing. They have failed to recognize that the distribution of existent wealth held by a minority merely serves to "remedy" poverty by making everyone poor. Such forced distribution of wealth serves to enrich and make dictators those individuals who undertake to enforce the distribution; and their role is no different than that of individuals who fraudulently and ruthlessly loot nations by tithes, tributes, taxes, graft, wars and the control and manipulation of money, as the conspirators are doing through their "Federal" Reserve. Those bogus "liberals" ignore the timeless adage: "Money is the root of all evil;" that the control of money which they aim to usurp is the very device that creates the ills that they pretend to desire to remedy; and their cure can only be effected by an honest and unmanipulable monetary system, not by their quack remedies that in no wise differ from those of the bogus "capitalism" that they pretend to oppose.

They ignore the amply proved fact that want can be relieved effectively and lastingly only by increased production, and that this, in turn, is dependent upon free exercise of human ingenuity. They heed not the fact that numerous new forms of wealth are being created continually by human ingenuity left free to exercise itself. When Weishaupt's disciple, Karl Marx, asserted that the limit of wealth had been reached and that therefore it must be distributed, there

338

existed none of the numerous devices on which is based a major part of the presently existent wealth, including: the auto, the telephone, the radio, the linotype, electric motors, electric lighting, plant hybridization, the harvester, railroads, plastics, petrochemicals, electronics, synthetic textiles and numerous others that have belied the dictum that the limit of worldly wealth had been reached. There had also been refuted, in some parts of the world, the Malthusian nonsense, that food production can not keep pace with population growth, by the development of new methods of agriculture by human ingenuity that has been responsible for periodic overproduction, relative to immediate needs.

Both history and the present scene make it obvious that no "sixty families" or thousand corporations can, or do, monopolize human ingenuity. Consequently that basic machinery of production can not be monopolized. Only the products of human ingenuity can be monopolized. And that can be accomplished only through private monopolistic control of the monetary and financial systems. This makes its obvious that the only remedy for monopoly is the cure and prevention of monetary and financial monopoly. But both Communism and our so-called "capitalism" do the very reverse. They foster the financial and monetary monopoly that are largely, if not entirely, responsible for the major ailments of society, by making money a monopolized medium of control instead of a free and unfettered medium of exchange that expands with the growth of wealth.

## LAND & ELEMENTS, TOOLS OF INGENUITY, UN-MONOPOLIZED IN U.S.A.

The other basic machinery of production, land and the elements with which human ingenuity works, in contrast with the Soviets and many other lands, are largely un-monopolized in our U.S.A. Less than 5% of our land is owned by our "sixty families" and thousand wealthiest corporations, even now in spite of the piracy and land-grabbing of the conspirators through their "blockbusting" slum creation and urban looting program that they have launched and mockingly labelled "slum clearance and urban redevelopment." (79:75) The largest owner of land in our U.S. is the people, through Federal, State and local governments. Thus with respect to this machinery of production, and its availability to the individual citizen, the U.S. is one of the most socialist countries in the world, with well over 50% of the land owned by the government. It is this situation that makes it feasible to create true freedom of employment and a job for every man who is willing to work, provided that stability of price is given staple products by their incorporation into the monetary base, in the same manner as gold.

## TRUE FREEDOM OF EMPLOYMENT READILY ATTAINABLE IN U.S.

To attain the freedom of employment that the conspirators and their racketeering Labor Barons abhor and dread, as a menace to their dictatorial power and to their power to levy a private tax on all workers for the right to earn a living, (which the Constitution was intended to grant at no cost, as a basic freedom but is denied them by the usurpers) requires in addition to the adoption of an monetary system merely a change of policy with respect to the land and resources owned by the people. At present this enormously valuable

339

asset is carried on the nation's balance sheet as a liability. And in its present treatment, it is a liability. For though it is rightly the property of all the people, it is given away to corporations and individuals, for homesteading to those who are willing to gamble on being able to develop and hold out on it, or for such developments as the building of railroads. Some of the land is leased out for grazing, and for mining. Land for drilling for oil and gas is leased to private entrepreneurs for a nominal charge per acre prior to production, and thereafter for a percentage of production. It is this last procedure that should apply to all the people's lands and resources, as is done with Crown lands by the British. With the incorporation of staple products in the monetary base, thus converting them to liquid wealth, it would become possible to lease the lands to persons in return for a percentage of the production of those commodities, as in the instance of oil lands. For the purpose of stimulating utilization of the land and national wealth, loans should be made to supply capital to the entrepreneurs for instituting production, repayable in a percentage of the production; and national insurance should be provided against the hazards of production, to protect both the entrepreneurs and the nation.

## A(GRICULTURAL) A(LOTTMENT) A(DMINISTRATION) WAS "NEW DEAL" FRAUD

This procedure that is so obviously sound and rational, would supplant the wholly irrational plan instituted by the conspirators' "New Deal" and currently applied, for the pretended purpose of helping the producers and the nation, that actually has been intended and serves to do exactly the reverse: to help the conspirators in their speculative and subversive operations. The A(gricultural A(llotment A(dministration, as drawn up by Bernard Baruch's Hentz & Co. "economist" agent, Svirinas Wagel, on behalf of the conspirators and their commodity stockpiling schemes, seconded by their "Federal" Reserve conspiracy, are used by them to convert the nation's and the world's real assets into liabilities. Their enforced continuance of their scarcity economy brigandage, enables them to urge the acceptance of their fraudulent currency, "based on wind," as the only "stable" basis of wealth. They are the chief devices of their piracy and racketeering, and perpetuation of a hand-to-mouth marginal existence, or poverty, for the bulk of mankind.

The supplanting of the world's present scarcity economy, whether so-called "capitalist" or super-capitalist, or Communist, by an economy of plenty based on an honest currency system, as outlined, would make possible the creation of true freedom of employment that is requisite for the creation of government providing "freedom of life" blueprinted in our Constitution. Unless forced, its adoption will be fought by the conspirators and their Communist, Labor Baron and speculator confererates, with every weapon at their command. The producer would no longer be at the mercy of the speculator in disposing of his production of staple products; but would be in the same position as is the producer of gold, who is empowered to demand of the Treasury a fixed amount of money for his production and originally was free to purchase it back from the Treasury for the same amount of money plus a moderate seignorage charge. The worker would no longer find it necessary to pay to the conspirators, through their Labor Barons, or so-called "leaders," a special private tax, in the form of union dues, for the privilege of working and be otherwise beholden to them. He would be free to accept employment at a wage that he regards as commensurate with his productive ability, or else to create employment for himself, with the help of the nation, in the production of any one of the many staple products that are the raw materials of the necessities of life, on land and with financing provided by the nation. Thus both leeches on the nation's economy, the "labor leader" and the speculator, would find their rackets wiped out, and would be forced to make an honest living for themselves, or starve.

## COMMUNIST "SOLVES" PROBLEM OF POVERTY BY MAKING EVERYONE POOR, EXCEPT RULERS

The fraud of Communism and its pretended "distribution of wealth" and its "solution" of the problem of poverty by making everyone poor except the ringleaders and conspirators, would become ultratransparent when the possession of wealth by some would not preclude everyone from obtaining all the money for which he is willing to work, money of such stability that its value could not be impaired. The Communist scarcity economy in which scarcity is maintained for the pretended purpose of averting unemployment because of mythical "over-production," would be recognized as a schemed device for forcing enslaved subjects into a treadmill existence for the preservation of the conspirators' predatory power.

## HONEST, STAPLE PRODUCT MONETARY BASE WOULD SERVE TO PRESERVE WORLD PEACE

An honest, staple product currency system would not only solve nations' domestic problems, but would go far toward the elimination of those wars that are the consequence of want and starvation. Though there would still remain the problem of wars waged by men driven to quest for domination and power by their madness, as is the case with the conspirators, they would find it infinitely more difficult and mayhaps impossible to stir up a martial spirit among a rich, well-nourished and contended people. It is not difficult to foresee the international repercussions of such an honest, staple product monetary base. If any one nation in the world would undertake to purchase all wheat offered anywhere in the world at a price of $2.50 per bushel, every other nation would be forced to set the same price for its wheat growers, or else do without bread. This stability and uniformity of price would ensure the same wage level in all countries producing wheat.

To be sure, not all nations can produce wheat. But few viable nations, that have a reason for existence other than tribal rivalries, lack some resources for the production of some staple product, the value of which would be likewise stabilized. The value of production, thus established, would inevitably assure the same wage level in all lands, and a free exchange of the staple products, raw materials of the necessities of life; and would ultimately assure an optimum living standard, and a measure of contentment around the world. The only social problem that it will fail to solve are those presented by such insane conspirators who seek to control and loot nations and the world. An awakened and informed public, who refuse to be deluded by bogus "benefactors" and "philanthropists" would give them short shift.

341

## IMF BYPASSED STAPLE COMMODITIES IN ABSURD
## QUEST FOR "NEW" MONETARY RESERVE

The conspirators' conscious and deliberate avoidance of the only possible, rational solution of the monetary problem is manifest in the proceedings of their International Monetary Fund meeting held under the direction of David Rockefeller, at Rio de Janeiro in the week of September 25, 1967. Its objective was announced to be the idiotic purpose of "creating 'new' monetary reserves." And it was personally "monitored" by Rockefeller, the man who proclaims himself, through his pressagents, to be "the most important banker in the world;" and who is in fact the worldwide top racketeer in international banking.

It was eminently fitting that international banking czar, David Rockefeller, opened the meeting with a memorial lecture in praise and honor of Per Jacobsson, for his service to the conspirators as managing director, until his death, of their international piracy agency, the IMF. (295:5) Per Jacobsson's complicity in the Kreuger Match fraud was regarded by the conspirators as the highest qualification for his appointment as director of their IMF swindle. That was a greater reward than Krueger himself enjoyed for his services to them, death, which was represented as being caused by his "jumping" out of a plane over the Atlantic Ocean.

## ROCKEFELLER'S IMF ACQUIESCED IN SDR TO
## DELAY OFFICIAL U. S. "BANKRUPTCY"

Under David Rockefeller's personal direction, the conspirators' IMF turned out an accomplishment that perfectly fits the purposes of their swindle. Their IMF agents ignored the only real reserve for money, those commodities that folks must have for their survival and wish to purchase with their money, and chose one that is based on less than "wind." They decreed as a supposed extension of monetary reserves something based on international "agreement" that they amusingly labelled *"Special Drawing Rights."* The SDR are nothing more than a permit that may be given by the conspirators, through their IMF to the U.S., Great Britain and some other countries, provided that other nations agree, to borrow more foreign currencies against the gold that they have put into the IMF, before being adjudged bankrupt under its rules and the "Gold Standard" on which they are based. In other words the SDR device that was acclaimed as a "solution" of the problem, by the conspirators and media of mass communication, is merely a device to permit some nations to go further into debt before being plunged into fraudulent bankruptcy, under the rules established for the IMF by the conspirators and their agents.

Under the terms laid down by the conspirators at that Conference, however, neither the U.S. or Great Britain may be allowed this dubious "privilege" unless they correct the "imbalance of payments" into which the U.S., in particular, has been plunged by their frauds. The irony of the situation is that the nations that dun the U.S. on behalf of the conspirators, are the very nations that owe it tens of billions of dollars on World War I and II and postwar debts that will never be repaid because they have been fraudulently cancelled, in large part, in a deal made with those nations by the conspirators in return for a "kickback" to themselves of sums that exceed the usual 10% payoffs

342

previously demanded by their "philanthropic" Special Work Inc. Even more ironic is the fact that our payment imbalance arises in part from the stationing of our troops in some of those lands for their security.

## CONSPIRATORS' RIGGED IMF DEAL MEANS HIGHER PROFITS FROM U.S. "BANKRUPTCY"

The deal that the conspirators effected for themselves at the Conference is delaying for a period of the bankruptcy of the U.S. that they have engineered during the past half century. The delay was designed to gain for themselves enough time to arrange to have Congress pass a bill, with the duped acquiescence of the American "peasants," that will revoke the 25% reserve of their gold that must be held by their "Federal" Reserve against the currency which they have issued, amounting to more than $10 billion in gold. With that provision of their "Federal" Reserve Act revoked, the conspirators will be able to transfer that gold to their dummy "foreign" accounts. And this will tremendously increase their profits from the upward revaluation of their gold after their "Gold Corner" had been fully consummated

## DEVALUATION OF POUND STERLING ILLUSTRATED EFFECTIVENESS OF CONSPIRACY

The devaluation of the British pound sterling in November, 1967, was another of the continuous round, in nation after nation, of demonstrations of the effectiveness of the conspirators quack bundle of "remedies" for financial ills, in precipitating inflation, looting and collapse of nations. It precipitated a wild scramble for gold in France and other nations that permit private gold ownership; and a flight from the pound into commodities and merchandise in Britain, that inevitably presaged further inflation and devaluations. These are products of the mythical "Gold Standard" that, ironically, was launched by England a century and a half earlier.

The devaluation of the pound materially assisted the conspirators in tightening their "Gold Corner" noose around the U.S. and the dollar. Much of the gold purchases attributed to France, it leaked out, were made for Americans defying our laws. Whether any of the purchases were made by the conspirators personally was not revealed. The bulk of the gold involved, the press reported, never left this country. It was merely transferred from the Assay Office in New York to the nearby New York Federal Reserve Bank, "earmarked" and stored there under the watchful eyes of the conspirators from their Chase Manhattan Bank on the opposite side of Pine Street. (372)

## CONGRESS RELEASE OF CONSPIRATORS' GOLD BALANCE DEMANDED BY PRES. JOHNSON

Pres. Johnson's January, 1968, message on the State of the Nation required passage of the law demanded by David Rockefeller of Pres. Kennedy six years earlier, releasing the balance of the conspirator's golden loot from their domestic to their "foreign accounts." Congress had shown its subservience to the conspirators by passing a bill, signed by the President on February 6, 1966, permitting a merger of their banks, Manufacturers Hanover Trust Co., First Security National Bank & Trust Co. and the Continental Illinois National Bank nullifying a 1963 Supreme Court decision that ruled, wisely and cor-

343

"WITHDRAWN" GOLD DOES NOT LEAVE COUNTRY. IT IS STORED IN FEDERAL RESERVE BANK (N.Y.) GOLD ROOM "EARMARKED"

Despite alarm about "gold withdrawals," on balance, no gold has left our country in the past three decades. Purchases of gold in the world markets for the "F"R conspirators have been made, steadily, at the expense of American taxpayers. There is more gold held here now than ever. But it has been stolen from the Treasury and the public by the conspirators under the Roosevelt "Gold Order." The Treasury has owned no gold since then; and we American "peasants" are barred from owning gold anywhere on earth. "Withdrawn" gold is merely transferred from one room to another in the conspirators' "Feder-al" Reserve Bank, as illustrated; or transferred several thousand feet, from the U.S. Assay Office on Front St. to the "Federal" Reserve Bank of New York, on Pine St. New York City. Seizure of this gold stolen from us by the conspirators as well as that "earmarked" and allegedly belonging to "foreign lands" that owe our country for World War I & World War II war and post-war debts many times the value of the gold and have defaulted on their debts to us, is legally justified. And it would save the dollar, our fortunes and our Republic.

U.S. News & World Report

rectly, that the Clayton (Antitrust) Act applied to bank mergers as monplies in restraint of trade. The conspirators' Congressional pawns acknowledged that mergers "substantially lessen competition." But they decreed that the conspirators and their banks shall be permitted to violate the Clayton Act and to *establish monopolies in restraint of trade if there are other "outweighing factors."* (178) Obviously, the conspirators' predatory objectives are the "outweighing factors" approved by Congress. Under the circumstances, its is not surprising that Congress hastened to pass the law releasing the looted gold by mid March, 1968, amid a "gold rush" staged, at the conspirators' instance, on European and world markets. Interests identified with the conspirators' are known to have made $100 million gold purchases in single contracts in the British and French markets, on which the gold bullion price was pushed up to more than $44 per ounce, and in coins, over $90.

## CONSPIRATORS USE THEIR "BIG 7" AGENTS AND IMF TO DUPE U.S. "PEASANTS

Following the demonstrations designed to justify the gold release, the conspirators' international agents assembled in Washington's "Federal" Reserve Building to hoodwink the nation by announcing that they had reduced the U.S. to the status of "second rate" nations that they had looted, by establishing a dual market for the dollar, by way of gold, in which the "official" exchange rate is mocked by an officially sanctioned "black market." It is safe to predict that the "remedy" will soon prove to be worse than the ailment it was pretended to "cure." (403) It is notable that though the conspirators' agents recommended that U.S. taxes be raised and expenditures reduced, they carefully refrained from advising discontinuance of "foreign (Rockefeller) aid" looting though its freshly voted total exceeds our trade imbalance. That would imply betrayal of the conspirator bosses. Nor did they recommend the other, obvious remedy: repayment to the U.S. by the foreign countries, that they represented, of their World War I and II war debts or seizure of the gold held by the conspirators in their name, and the abandonment by the U.S. of any further gold purchases. These measures would remedy the situation promptly and lastingly, at the expense of the loot of the conspirators and of their overseas confederates, especially of the absent partners of the conspirators, Soviet Russia and Communist China. The deal was negotiated, or rigged, by the conspirators' domestic agents, their "Federal" Reserve Chairman William M. Martin and Secretary of the Treasury Henry H. Fowler.

The acts of Congress have cleared the way for the conspirators to make more direct and free of restrictions their stranglehold on national and personal credit and finance through their "Federal" Reserve fraud. This means that Congress has established an additional legal barrier to an honest currency system that will serve the needs and interests of the nation. *It stresses the need for amendment of the Constitution that will give the Government control of currency and banking under conditions that will make the system automatic and place it beyond "management" and manipulation even by Congress itself.*

## REP. WRIGHT PATMAN, "FOE" OF "FEDERAL" RESERVE, "CHARMED" BY DAVID ROCKEFELLER

Illustrative of the "opposition" to the conspirators and their "Federal" Reserve fraud is the attitude of Rep. Wright Patman, the Democrat from Texarkana, Texas, of the Committee on Currency and Banking of the House. As has been noted, though some of the bills introduced by him appear to hit at some of the elements of "Federal" Reserve fraud, others fall completely in line with the interests of the conspirators advocated by their dummy "committees" that profitably serve their interests; and all of them imply content with the "F"R and its frauds. Sincere opponents of both, who in the past have regarded Patman as one of their leaders, rightly suspect him of defecting from their ranks.

An explanation of Patman's defection is to be found in his adherence, for an unexplained reason, to the ranks of supporters and admirers of banking czar David Rockefeller, whose attitude and acts epitomize all that is vicious in the "F"R fraud. Patman has gone out of his way to express his loyalty to David Rockefeller, in an interview given *Newsweek*, as follows:

"He's a brave man. Not all bankers are bad just because they are big." (352)

It has been this author's experience that whenever the "purity, nobility, benevolence, altruism and philanthropy" of Rockefellers is questioned, Patman bristles and throws a tantrum. When this author had occasion to phone Patman at his Texas home to inquire into the fate of one of his defeated banking bills, he was quite affable — until mention of Rockefeller involvement in the "F"R caused him to rudely interrupt the conversation by slamming up his receiver and disconnecting. One wonders about the exact manner in which Rockefeller has "charmed" that "militant foe of the 'Federal' Reserve," and the correctness of his colleagues' suspicions.

## MINOR MEMBER NATIONS OF THE IMF DEMANDED "STABILIZATION" OF COMMODITY PRICES

At the end of the IMF Rio de Janeiro conference, after its boss, David Rockefeller, had relaxed his control of it and left for other parts, the minor member nations took over from the "Big Ten" and "arrived at a moment of truth" with respect to the fraud and humbug of the SDR "solution" of the monetary and exchange problems. In what was characterized as "a revolt" (against the piracy projected by the conspirators), they moved that there be appointed a committee to consider *the stabilization of commodity prices, an honest currency base that would eliminate looting by speculative manipulation.* (299) In short, they made a move in the direction of adopting the only rational currency base, the necessities that money must purchase if it is to have value. It is the "moment of truth" arrived at by all nations in times of shortage and stress, as instanced by the adoption by the U.S. during the depression of the Wallace "Ever-Normal Granary" scheme that was a perversion of a commodity base intended to insure setting up of commodity reserves while insuring profits to speculators.

The conspirators, by their Rio de Janeiro parliamentary maneuver of appointing one of their rigged "committees" to report at a future date, averted an upset of their "Gold Corner" scheme for despoiling of the U.S. and the world. It was a clear demonstration of the effectiveness of "internationalism" as a treacherous device for betraying the nation and the world.

## BASIC PRINCIPLE FOR SOLUTION: PATRIOTISM AND END OF TREASON

Patriotism and service to our national interests, these are the requisites for a solution of our monetary problems. The financial "internationalism" of the conspirators that has betrayed the U.S. into its present status is earmarked by both thievery and treason. This is clearly revealed by their treatment of gold mining in the U.S. while dictating the purchase of gold for them by the taxpayers at the price of $35 an ounce, the American bid that for decades has alone maintained that price, in the world market. American gold mines were ordered shut down during World War II, on the ground that gold is "unessential," and barriers set up against its resumption; and requisite machinery therefor was ordered shipped to Communist Russia. If gold is an essential for our existence as their "Gold Standard" implies, is this not arrant treason? In the words of the conspirators' kinsman, Sen. Harry Shippe Truman, speaking of them and their activities: "Yes, it is treason. You cannot translate it in any other way." (15:3)

Treason in the field of finance is proving quite as effective as in the military field in endangering the survival of our Republic. The Rockefeller-Eaton financing of Communist Russian industry in January, 1967, with the funds of our taxpayers, furnished the North Vietnamese with tanks, plane, arms and munitions with which to slaughter our GIs one year later, in cities throughout South Vietnam and at Khesanh. Reinforcements by reservists ordered in mid-February 1968, seriously depleted our domestic strategic reserve and makes us vulnerable to attack both from within and without. (373) We must act promptly and forcefully, or face the possibility of overthrow of our Republic by the conspirators and their confederates.

It is imperative for survival that all treason shall be penalized to the full limit of the law, no matter what the status of the culprit: "philanthropist," Communist, priest, minister, rabbi, politician, judge, teacher, professor, "social" worker, Negro, public official or private individual or group. Failure to enforce observance of law and order and use by the culprits and the garden run of criminals, for the purpose of overthrow of our Republic, of the provisions of the Constitution, including the Amendments, written for the protection of loyal and law-abiding citizens, has brought us to the verge of anarchy.

The riots that have plagued our cities in the past half decade are nothing less than guerrilla warfare by the criminal and subversive elements. Justification of them by politicians, as by the National Advisory Commission on Civil Disorders, with or without suggestions that bribes and rewards be given the culprits, stamps responsible persons as more treasonous than the culprits themselves. (374) For it stamps them as sympathizers and inciters of the subversive and criminal elements, and agents provoca-

346

teurs of the most pernicious form of civil war that can benefit only our enemies.

Now, truly, is time for all brave men to come to the aid of their country.

CHAPTER XXIV
## WHAT ONE CAN DO TO SAVE ONE'S MEANS FROM THE CONSPIRATORS' THIEVERY

Your life savings and total wealth are the loot that the thievish conspirators aim to steal by wiping them out. Though they may be trifling from the viewpoint of the conspirators, in the aggregate the savings and property of 200 million Americans and billions of humans around the world constitute a fabulous total of loot. The conspirators' pathologic greed reinforces their psychopathic fear that so long as anyone other than themselves has any possessions and independence, there may arise a person more ruthless and criminal than themselves who might loot them as they have looted the world. Therefore it has become an absolute necessity for everyone who wishes to survive their "Gold Corner" plot with holdings, financial independence and liberty intact, to consider the ways and means of escaping their looting.

In order to avert ruin by the conspirators, one must clearly keep in mind their thievish devices. Their principal looting devices are inflation engineered through their control of their "Federal" Reserve and the Treasury; taxation through the agencies of governments, which they control; the confiscation of property, both direct by misuse of the powers of eminent domain, and indirect, by such devices as rent control and price control; manipulation of markets through their control of their "Federal" Reserve; and control of wages through their Labor Barons and their unions, and through their cunningly named "minimal wage acts" which are in reality employment control devices. One must seek to put oneself in the same type of holdings that the conspirators themselves hold so as to "be in the same boat with them" to outride the storm. Attention should be given to the experiences of the natives of the various lands that the conspirators have looted in the past, using the same devices that are being applied to our country, including France, England, Russia, China, and especially, Germany.

## MEASURES THAT ONE CAN ADOPT TO PRESERVE ONE'S ASSETS

1. Contract as much debt as one can manage to comfortably carry for a number of years. By preference, these debts should be long-term and standing, such as long term mortgages, fixed term

bank loans, fixed stock margins and others. This follows the pattern of the conspirators in their bank rackets, including the long-term certificates of deposit at fixed interest rates that they are vigorously touting, the quarter of a billion long-term issues of their Chase Manhattan Bank, and others. But one should be prepared for their use of their "Federal" Reserve and their governmental agencies to change the rules of the game whenever it suits their purpose and facilitates their looting. One should hold a reserve against such debts, an ace in the hole.

2. Reserves and savings should be held in the form of readily liquifiable holdings of which the best available are holdings of silver coins still in circulation and gold coin collections or objects obtained at no premium over their currency value. These should be safely stored, may be insured and, in some instances, may even be used as collateral for loans. It matters not that in so doing one foregoes interest payments on the sums involved. For, the interest payment offered by banks on savings, plus storage expenses involved, are a small fraction of the losses sustained by the annual devaluation of the dollar, and loss of its purchasing power, which amounts to about 20% a year. Thus the silver dollars which this author put in storage in the years 1964 to 1966, and urged his friends to put aside, have risen in value more than 100% on the basis of their silver content, and considerably more in numismatic value. As the "Federal" Reserve paper dollar's value is progressively destroyed by the conspirators, the value of the silver coins rises. The same is true of silver bricks and silver dust which will be available to the public in exchange for silver certificates until June 24, 1968. As of that date, Congress has nullified the contract of the Treasury to redeem them with silver of 99.99% fineness, because fraudulent manipulations of our silver supply by our Government will have exhausted the silver available for the redemption. The conspirators' "Federal" Reserve played an active role in exhausting the Treasury's supply of silver by offering to supply silver certificates to those desiring to withdraw hundred or thousand ounce silver bars from the Assay Office. The "F"R discontinued this practise only when the Treasury raised the price of the silver that it sold and permitted the silver market to find its level. Then, insiders in the bank put silver coins and certificates aside for themselves, to sell at a profit.

Incidentally, this author was informed at the U.S. Assay Office in New York that the $3 million of the rare and highly valuable uncirculated Carson City minted silver dollars prized by numismatists because of low mintage, that the Treasury refused to permit the public to withdraw, on the pretense that they were to be used for sale at auction where they would command a high premium that "would be used for charitable purposes," had been given to the conspirators' Chase Manhattan Bank. The conspirators evidently regarded themselves as the most worthy objects of charity of the nation.

A word of warning is in order with regard to gold and gold coins, as reserves. The conspirators have made it a criminal offense, a felony, in most countries around the world for anyone other than themselves to hold more than a limited amount of gold bullion or coins, or to import or export gold. In the U.S. a limited amount of gold ore or bars, of the value of several hundred dollars, gold coins constituting a numismatic collection in which none of the coins must be dated prior to 1933, gold jewelry and gold fillings in one's teeth, may be held under the law. Any other gold holdings, at home or abroad, make their owners felons subject to confiscation of the gold, fine and/or imprisonment. Whether the conspirators themselves will be subjected to the same penalties for their gold holdings in caves underlying their homes, and in vaults here and abroad is open to serious question. They do not believe in punishing themselves. After all, Kings and Emperors can do no wrong!

In Great Britain, the laws imposed by the conspirators on gold holders at the behest of their Labor government, are even more restrictive. Not even gold numismatic collections are legal. Any Englishmen who holds coins issued later than 1838, or more than two of them, is a "felon."

The silver coins that still remain available are readily distinguished from the clad copper coins by the latter's gleam and the copper color visible on their edge. The silver quarters and dimes which still remain in circulation but are rapidly disappearing and are due to be melted down by the Treasury, both exceeded their face value when the price of silver rose above $1.38. Silver at $2.75 an ounce doubles their face value. It is probable that the dime will rise to a higher premium for its numismatic value because more young collectors can afford dimes than quarters.

3. Investment may be safely made in reasonably purchased stocks, preferably in companies that have large natural resources and low labor costs. Invest surplus funds that leave enough in one's purse to meet the steadily rising taxes that the conspirators will impose. Investments may also be made with relative safety in bonds or debentures of such companies that are convertible into stock, on a favorable basis. Care must be taken to select well-managed, profitable companies, preferably those engaged in essential activities and automated. Or, for persons experienced in such enterprises, direct investments may be made in them, either alone or with experienced and reliable partners. The enterprises in the categories in question include companies engaged in the production and marketing of oil, minerals, metals, lumber, paper, production and marketing of agricultural and food products and others of the same categories.

Most highly desirable are investments that receive preferential tax treatment, including oil royalties that are allowed 27 1/2% depletion charges as well as chargeoff of cost of drilling and intangible items such as exploration; ranching, mining and agriculture that are entitled to varied allowances before taxes; and mergers of these types of companies that are prosperous with others of the same categories that have had huge losses that will serve as a tax shelter for the profits of the former. Debentures in these companies that are convertible into stock of the companies offer the advantage of an income from the interest payments plus the hedge against inflation and devaluation of the dollar that is offered by the rise in monetary value of the assets of the company, which rise with the fall of the dollar, reflected in the rise of the price of the company's stock. It is not uncommon for convertible bonds and debentures of par value of a thousand dollars to rise, in pace with the stock of the company, to values of several thousand dollars. And it is often possible to obtain interest returns on funds invested in them considerably higher than the prevailing interest rates offered by banks.

Examples of oil royalties that are available to the public in small and relatively inexpensive units are Saskatchewan Gulf Security Tidewater Royalty, Cedar Point Field Trust and Conwest Partnership Participating Units.

4. One of the soundest hedges against inflation is the purchase at reasonable prices of bare land in sections of the country such as California, Arizona and Florida, in which population and industrial growth are rapid and taxes are low. Provision must be made, in this instance, for meeting comfortably the taxes as they come due. It should be borne in mind in planning these land purchases that taxes are certain to rise in times of monetary devaluation and inflation. It should also be recognized that the moneys paid in property taxes are deductible from gross income for income tax calculations; and that whereas moneys paid in income tax will never be recovered, moneys paid out for property taxes may be, and often are when property is wisely purchased, recovered in profitable sales. The capital tax, so-called "capital gains" tax, is much lower than the normal income tax. Reforestation of bare land offers additional tax advantages in addition to the enhanced asset value offered thereby.

5. Works of art and antiques are the trickiest and least dependable hedges against inflation. As luxuries, the market for them almost invariably becomes depressed in times of need, of wild inflation and/or depression. Whether they rise in value with the restoration of prosperity is as often as not dictated by whims and fashions; and their disposal is dependent upon access to some ready market and purchasers for them that may prove costly. In the past half century, in the U.S., Russia, Germany, Austria, Great Britain and France, costly works of art and antiques went begging during the immediate post-war periods and depressions. With the return of prosperity, prices of some of them began to soar, while others that had been in vogue and demand in earlier periods became unmarketable, or dropped sharply in price because of changing tastes. Even experts in the field, who have not at their command the capability of creating fashions and demand, may sustain serious losses. In any event, the time to buy works of art and antiques is during periods of stress and depression when people need the proceeds for the purchase of necessities of life.

6. Jewelry, rare metals and gems, unless they are purchased at prices that represent little premium over the value of the metals and gems therein, generally respond in value to the same pressure as works of art and antiques. But they have the advantage over the latter in that they are portable and can be stored easily.

## TYPES OF "INVESTMENTS" THAT MUST BE AVOIDED OR GUARDED AGAINST

There are certain types of so-called "investments" that must be assiduously avoided or guarded against to avoid looting by the conspirators through devaluation and inflation. These include any investment that has a fixed repayable face value, that remain outstanding for prolonged periods of time, exceeding a few days or months; or that, on reseizure or foreclosure, may involve one in undesirable types of investments. Among these are:

1. Government bonds because their interest and capital are payable in dollars that steadily depreciate in purchasing power to the point of worthlessness when the conspiracy comes to its termination.

2. Industrial bonds that are not convertible into stock of companies of the type above noted, unless extremely depressed, and subject to foreclosure of good assets.

3. Savings either in the form of notes or of savings accounts. They are repayable in money that steadily grows more worthless.

4. Insurance and annuities. Both are repayable solely in dollars, no matter how worthless. The premiums paid over and above the rate for mere life, or term insurance, that are fraudulently represented by the insurance companies and their agents as "savings" merely intensify the looting. For they are in reality a fraudulent device for reducing the amount of insurance carried by the company. This one can readily determine when one goes to the insurance company to withdraw the "savings." The policyholder is required to pay interest on the amount of the so-called "savings" that is withdrawn, *and the face value of the insurance policy carried by the company is reduced by that sum.* Insurance that must be carried, such as fire insurance, should be steadily increased in pace with the inflation. *Persons with funds tied up in insurance and annuities should borrow on them the maximum allowable and invest the borrowed funds in investments of the desirable type* noted.

5. Pensions, like insurance and annuities, will fare much the same, will become valueless; and *should be treated in the same manner.*

6. Savings and Loan Association deposits will fare probably worse than savings accounts. *They should be treated in the same manner.*

7. Mortgages, like bonds, are repayable in dollars, no matter how depreciated. They should be avoided, *or treated in the same manner.*

8. Developed property, other than the home in which one lives, is the most dangerous type of investment in times of inflation. Governments seek the support of the masses and, especially in times of inflation, collaborate with them in looting the property holders. Rent controls are invariably imposed to bar the landlord from raising his rent to meet the increased costs. He is forced to bear the expense of the conspirators' subsidy of tenants. Taxes, wages, supplies and maintenance rise with fulminating rapidity to the point where the landlord is faced with steadily increasing losses, cannot maintain his property or even pay his taxes. In this manner the conspirators confiscate and steal his property after harassing

351

him endlessly. *Developed property should be assiduously avoided in periods of violent inflation* because the danger of the investment being wiped out far exceeds the potential of profit before the devaluation of the dollar has run its course.

Exception can be made in all these types of investments and contracts, if the value of the dollars that one will receive in payment is defined in terms of staple commodities, such as weights of silver. But therein lies danger. Investments and contracts stipulated on the basis of a dollar of fixed gold value, as was the practise prior to the "New" Deal thievery of the conspirators, were nullified by un-Constitutional and thoroughly dishonest decisions handed down by the corrupt and venal Supreme Court "Justices." History might repeat itself in respect to any contracts undertaken to fix the value of the dollar in terms of staples, until such time as a staple product currency base is established by unequivocal amendment. of our Constitution. Leases requiring payment of a base, minimal rental plus a percentage of earnings offer a measure of safety.

※ ※ ※ ※ ※ ※

As this goes to press, the obvious and anticipated consequence of the "two price system" for gold connivingly decreed by the conspirators, with its implication of devaluation and black market, is developing. On May 21, 1968 it was announced that for purposes of manipulation of the price of gold that had once again risen over $42 an ounce, we "peasants" will be permitted, once again, to purchase and hold gold. This presages a rise in gold prices well above that level and eventual explosive inflation and dollar devaluation—unless a patriotic majority in Congress decrees reseizure of the gold stolen from us by the conspirators through their "Federal" Reserve.

BIBLIOGRAPHY

Duplications: 88:49;95:84;260:255;319:243;365:356;369:92;371:
99;387:132;405:179.

1. J. Laurence Laughlin: The Federal Reserve Act. The
   McMillan Co., N.Y. 1933.
2. Lord Beveridge: Power & Influence. Beechhurst Press,
   N.Y. 1955.
3. John K. Winkler: John D. A Portrait In Oil. Vanguard
   Press. N.Y 1929.
4. F. A. Vanderlip & B. Sparks: From Farm Boy To Financier.
   Appleton Century. N.Y. 1935:
5. R. S. Baker: Life & Letters Of Woodrow Wilson. Doubleday
   Page. N.Y. 1927.
6. Wm. F. McCombs: Making Woodrow Wilson President.
   Fairview Publishing Co. N.Y. 1921.
7. E. M. Josephson: The Strange Death Of F.D.R. Chedney
   Press, N.Y. 1948 & 1959.
8. W. F. Fletcher: George Harvey, "A Passionate Patriot."
   Houghton Mifflin. Boston. 1929.
9. H. P. Willis: Federal Reserve. Doubleday Page & Co.
   Garden City. 1915
10. Carter Glass: An Adventure In Constructive Finance.
    Doubleday Page & Co. 1927.
11. J. P. Tumulty: Woodrow Wilson As I Knew Him. Doubleday
    Page. N.Y. 1929.
12 .Mary A. (Peck) Hulbert: The Woodrow Wilson I Knew.
    Liberty. N.Y. 12/20/24-2/21/25.
13. C. Seymour: The Intimate Paper Of Col. House. Ernest Benn
    Ltd. London. 1926.
14. Council On Foreign Relation: Annual Report, 1948-9. N.Y. 1949.
15. E. M. Josephson: Rockefeller "Internationalist." Chedney
    Press, N.Y. 1952.
16. John D. Rockefeller: Random Reminiscences. Doubleday
    Page & Co. N.Y. 1909.
17. J. A. Morris: Those Rockefeller Boys. Harper Bros. N.Y. 1953.
18. R. B. Fosdick: John D. Rockefeller Jr. A Portrait. Harper &
    Bros. N.Y. 1956.
19. Col. R. McCormick: Rockefeller Profits from the Marshall·Plan.
    Chicago Tribune 12/13/48.
20. C. H. Grattan: Why We Fought. Vanguard Press. N.Y. 1929.
21. Brewing & Liquor Interests & German Bolshevik Propaganda
    Vol. II, 1913. Senate Document 62.65 Congress, 2nd Session.
    Government Printing Office, Washington. 1919
22. N. A. Rockefeller: Purpose & Policy. Foreign Affairs 36:3:370.
    N.Y. 1960.
23. Cordell Hull. Memoirs of Cordell Hull. MacMillan, N.Y. 1948.
24. E. W. Kemmerer: The ABC Of The Federal Reserve System.
    Princeton U. Press, 1938.
25. Federal Reserve Act As Amended through October 1, 1961.
26. Walter Winchell. Los Angeles Times, May 23, 1961.
27. Board of Governors, FRS. The Federal Reserve System.
    Washington, 1954.
28. John Winkler. The First Billion. Vanguard Press. N.Y. 1934.
29. E. M. Josephson. Roosevelt's Communist Manifesto, Chedney
    Press, N.Y. 1955.
30. U. S. Department of Commerce Reports, 1928-32. Govt. Print.
    Office, Washington.
31. Annual Report Of Federal Deposit Insurance Corp. for 1934,
353

Washington.

32. H. E. Barnes: The Struggle Against The Historical Blackout, 6 ed. Stoneybrook. 1948.
33. James Farley: Jim Farley's Story. The Roosevelt Years. McGraw Hill. N.Y. 1948.
34. Jerry Voorhis: Confessions Of A Congressman. Doubleday & Co. Garden City. 1947.
35. Elizabeth Bentley. Out Of Bondage. Devin Adair. N.Y. 1951.
36. Earl Browder: The Road To Teheran. International Publisher, N.Y. 1944.
37. Nelson A. Rockefeller: Partners In Progress. Simon & & Schuster. N.Y. 1951.
38. Personal communication. N.Y. Federal Reserve information service.
39. R. & D. Harkness: Where Are Those Rampaging New Dealers? N.Y. Times; 6:88, 5/22/60.
40. David Rockefeller: Unused Resources & Economic Waste. U. of Chicago Press 1941.
41. David Rockefeller: Letter To Pres. Kennedy. Life, 7/6/62:30.
42. David Rockefeller: Report Of Commission On Money & Credit. Prentice Hall, Englewood, 1961.
43. The Rockefeller Dynasty, Generations Of Tainted Money Fakery. Vigilant Press 15 Beekman St. New York. 1932.
44. J. W. Hanks & R. Stucki: Money, Banking & National Income. A. A. Knopf, N.Y. 1956.
45. The Bullion Report of June 8, 1810. Parliament. London, 1810.
46. Louis Fischer: Oil Imperialism. International Publishers. N.Y. 1926.
47. Board of Governors of FRS: 48th Annual Report. Washington. 1961.
48. H. E. Barnes: Perpetual War For Perpetual Peace. Caxton Printers. Caldwell. 1953.
49. Raymond Fosdick: Chronicle Of A Generation. Harper & Bros. N.Y. 1958.
50. Earl Browder: Road To Teheran. International Publishers. N.Y. 1944.
51. R. McCormick: Rockefeller Profits From The Marshall Plan. Editorial 12/13/48.
52. Bank For International Settlement: Report for 1944.
53. Int'l Bank For Reconstruct. & Developm. Report For 1954-5.
54. Samuel Crowther: Patriot. London. 8/31/54.
55. Wm. Manchester: A Rockefeller Family Portrait. Little Brown & Co. Boston. 1958.
56. E. M. Josephson: Your Life Is Their Toy- Rackets Social Service & Medical Chedney Press, N.Y. 1940.
57. E. M. Josephson: The Truth About Milk. Reprinted from 56. Chedney Press, N.Y. 1940.
58. E. M. Josephson: The Unheeded Teaching Of Jesus. Chedney Press. N.Y. 1959.
58. U. S. Senate Com. on the Judiciary, 84 Congress: Harry Dexter White Papers, Interlocking Subversion in Govt. Depts. Part 30, Aug. 30, 1955. Govt. Print. Dept. Washington, 1955.
60. Who's Who. vol. 28.
61. Lauchlin Currie: The Supply & Control Of Money In The U.S. Harvard U. Press Cambridge. 1934.
62. D. C. Bruce: Congressional Record. Sept. 12, 1962: 18137.
63. D. C. Bruce: Is Katanga On The Auction Block. U.S. Govt. Printing Office. 1962.
64. A. N. Field: The Bretton Woods Plot. P.O. Box 103, Nelson, New Zealand. 1957.
65. Ludwell Denny: We Fight For Oil. Knopf, N.Y. 1928.
66. J. A. Morris: Nelson Rockefeller, A Biography. Harper & Bros. N.Y. 1960.

67. Hamilton, Madison etc.: The Federalist.
68. B. Franklin: Political, Miscellaneous & Philosophical Pieces. J. Johnson, 72 St. Paul's Church Yard. 1779.
69. Bancroft: History Of The Colonization Of The U.S. v.2, Part 3. Little Brown. Boston. 1841.
70. B. Franklin: Autobiography, edited by John Bigelow. Putman, N.Y. 1904.
71. B. Franklin: A Modest Inquiry Into The Nature & Necessity Of A Paper Currency. Philadelphia, 1729.
72. Burke McCarty: The Suppressed Truth About The Assassination Of Abraham Lincoln. Chedney Press, N.Y. 1962.
73. R. Owen: Congressional Record, April 25, 1916.
74. W. A. Swanberg: Jim Fisk, Longman, Green & Co. Ltd. London. 1960.
75. C. H. & H. Adams: Erie & Other Essays. Boston. 1871.
76. House of Representatives: Gold Panic Report No. 31. Washington, 1870.
77. Allan Nevins: John D. Rockefeller. Scribner. N.Y. 1940.
78. Paul de Kruif: Seven Iron Men. Harcourt Brace & Co. N.Y. 1929.
79. E. M. Josephson: The Truth About Rockefeller, "Public Enemy No. 1," Studies In Criminal Psychopathy. Chedney Press. N.Y. 1964.
80. Grand Duke Alexander: Once A Grand Duke. Garden City Pub. Co. Garden City, 1932.
81. "Coin" Harvey: Coin's Financial School. Coin Publishing. Chicago. 1894.
82. Infoplan: Editor & Publisher. N.Y. Jan. 9, 1965.
83. J. F. Kennedy: Profiles In Courage. Harper. N.Y. 1956.
84. E. M. Josephson: Rackets, Social Service & Medical. Chedney Press. 1936.
85. J. Robinson: Proofs Of A Conspiracy. Cadell & Davies. London. 1797.
86. Adam Weishaupt: Das verbesserten System der Illuminaten. 1787.
87. W. G. Carr: The Red Fog Over America, Natl. Fed. Christ. Laymen. Willowdale. 1957.
89. W. Patman: Tax Exempt Foundations. Report to H.R. 87 Congress. Washington. 1962.
90. Jules Abels: The Rockefeller Billions. MacMillan. N.Y. 1965.
91. C. A. Willoughby: Shanghai Conspiracy. Dutton. N.Y. 1952
92. K. Oberman: Joseph Weydemeyer, Pioneer Of American Socialism. Internatl. Pub. 1947.
93. J. D. Rockefeller IV: Student Gripes As Heard By Son Of Famous Family. Life 6/20/60.
94. Lait & Mortimer: USA Confidential. Crown Publishers. N.Y. 1952.
96. Sumner Welles: Roosevelt & The Far East. Harpers Magazine, Feb. 1951.
97. J. M. Blum: From The Morgenthau Diaries. Houghton, Mifflin Co. Boston 1959.
98. Post, Delancey & Darby: Basic Constitutional Cases. Oxford U. Press. N.Y. 1948.
99. J. D. Rockefeller Jr.: The Christian Church, What Of its Future? Protestant Council, N.Y. 1945.
100. Hoffman Nickerson: The American Rich. Doubleday Doran. N.Y. 1930.
101. Anthony Kubek: Morgenthau Diary. (Germany) Report to U.S. Senate. Govt. Print. Office. 1965.
102. Public Administration Clearing House: A Directory. Chicago. 1954.
103. Internal Security Subcommittee, 87th Congress: Institute Of Pacific Relations. Govt. Print. Off. 1952.

104. IPR correspondence in posession of this author.
105. Correspondence of IPR seized by Senate Int. Secur. Com.; unpublished.
106. AP.: Rockefeller Recalls Hiss Case. N.Y. Times 1/11/64:10:4
    UPI: "U.S. Sat On Hiss Case For Three Years," Rocky. Journal American, N.Y. 1/10/64.
    AP: ' FBI Told Me Of Hiss Case In 1945!" Rocky. Daily News. N.Y. 1/11/64.
107. F. Utley: The China Story. Henry Regnery. Chicago. 195.
108. S. Marley: IPR Axis. Plain Talk. Dec. 1946.
109. Congressional Record. March 30, 1950.
110. Elizabeth Bentley: Out Of Bondage. Devin Adair. N.Y. 1951.
111. Rockefeller Foundation 1935 Report, N.Y.
112. J. J. McCloy: Proposes Foundation Pattern For Europe's Giving. N.Y. Times. 8/6/65.
113. M. Klemme: The Inside Story Of The *Unrra*, Lifetime Edition. N.Y. 1949.
114. E. Castle: Billions, Blunder & Baloney. Devin Adair. N.Y. 1955.
115. E. M. Josephson: Rockefeller's Chicken War. Chedney Press. 1964.
116. House Un-American Committee: Appendix IX. Govt. Print. Office. Washington. 1944.
117. U. S. Senate Com. On Appropriations, Subcom. On Armed Services, Banking & Currency: Occupation Money Transactions. Govt. Print. Off. Washington, 1947.
118. G. R. Jordan: From Major Jordan's Diaries. Harcourt & Brace. N.Y. 1952.
119. W. Chambers: Winess. Random House. N.Y. 1952.
120. G. L. Kirk & W. R. Sharp: Uniting Today For Tomorrow. The United Nations In War & Peace. Foreign Policy Ass. N.Y. October, 1942.
121. E. J. Kahn Jr.: Profiles, Resources & Responsibilities. New Yorker. N.Y. 1/9/65.
122. E. J. Kahn Jr.: Profiles, Resources & Responsibilities. New Yorker. N.Y. 1/16/65.
123. Peter Tompkins: The Murder Of Admiral Darlan. Simon Schuster. N.Y. 196.
124. David Rockefeller: Who's Who In The East. Marquis, Chicago. 1963.
125. Time: Banking Man At The Top. Times Inc. N.Y. 9/7/62.
126. Alden Hatch: Bernard, Prince Of The Netherlands. Doubleday & Co. N.Y. 1962.
127. Bouscaren & Ellis: Canon Law. Bruce Publishing Co. Milwaukee, 1957.
128. Stimson & Bundy: On Active Service In Peace & War. Harper & Bros. 1947
129. N. Y. Herald Tribune: Obit column. N.Y. October 3, 1965.
131. Lyle Stuart: The Walter Winchell Story. Boars Head Books, N.Y. 1953.
132. E. M. Josephson: Rockefeller Confesses Treason, Chedney Press. 1964.
133. Nelson A. Rockefeller: The Future of Federalism. Harvard U. Press. Cambridge. 1962.
134. E. A. Nason: Foreign Aid & Foreign Policy. Council On Foreign Relations. N.Y. 1964.
135. Kwame Nkrumah: Neocolonialism—The Last Stage Of Imperialism. T. A. Nelson & Sons. London. 1965
137. Treasury Dept. Daily Statement, United States Treasury. Washington, 1965.
138. Id. 6/30/64.
139. E. M. Josephson: We Finance Rockefeller Interest's Theft Of Suez & Mideast Oilfields, Chedney Press, N.Y. Jan. 1957.
140. J. F. Kennedy: Why England Slept. Wilfrid Funk Inc. N.Y. 1940.

141. N.Y. Federal Reserve Bank: Personal Communication.
142. E. M. Josephson: Rockefeller's Chicken War Chedney Press. 1964.
143. U.S. News & World Report: Washington, Sept. 23, 1963,p. 88.
144. International Basic Economy Corp. Annual Report, 1964.
145. N.Y. Times: Supply Of Money Climbs Sharply. Rebounds To $160.5 Billion. After Decline in May. N.Y. June 25, 1965 p. 36.
146. E. L. Dale Jr.: Supply Of Money In World Drops. N.Y. Times 8/8/65:35.
147. R. Frost: Gold Stock Falls by $350 Million. N.Y. Times, July 2. 1965.
148. V. Riesel: Inside Labor, New Kind Of Partnership. Journal American, N.Y. 11/18/65:15.
149. J. Desmond: Nelson Rockefeller, A Political Biography. MacMillan Co. N.Y. 1964.
150. B. Biossat: Lindsay, Rockefeller Friendlier. World Telegram & Sun. N.Y. 12/9/65.
151. E. L. Dale Jr.: New Money Unit Gaining Support N.Y. Times. 11/30/65:3.
152. D. Jason: A Grain Reserve Urged By Grange. Farm Leader Notes Decline In Supply Of Major Crops. N.Y. Times, 11/9/65.
153. P. Healy: Grain To India In Food Crisis. Daily News, N.Y. 12/10/65:26.
154. T. Lambert: U.S. Food For India, Month By Month. Herald Tribune. N.Y. 11/3/65.
155. E. S. Mason: Foreign Aid & Foreign Policy. Council On Foreign Relations, N.Y. 1964.
156. Herald Tribune: U.S. To Sell All Types Of Wheat. N.Y. 12/16/65:52.
157. J. W. Finney: Wide Starvation In Decade Is Seen. N.Y. Times. 12/2/65.
158. T. Lewis: Capitol Stuff. N.Y. Daily News, 12/8/65:4.
159. E. L. Dale Jr.: Martin Testified He Asked Johnson To Back Rate Raise. N.Y. Times, 12/14/65:1.
160. T. Wicker: Johnson & Rate Rise. N.Y. Times. 12/8/65.
161. M. J. Rossant: What Role For The Federal Reserve. N.Y. Times 12/3/65.
162. J. W. Finney: An Irked U.S. Bars Ghana Food Plea. N.Y. Times 11/24/65.
163. W. E. Stone: Liberty Amendment Committee of U.S.A. 6413 Franklin Av. Los Angeles 28 Calif.
164. 83 Congress: Com. To Investigate Tax Exempt Foundations. Govt. Printing Off. Washington, 1954.
165. E. Pace: Foundation Curb by States Urged. Ending Tax Exemption By U.S. Can't Halt All Abuses, Russell Sage Study Says. N.Y. Times 12/14/65.
166. M. R. Fremont-Smith: Foundations & Government. Russell Sage Found. N.Y. 1965.
167. J. Monahan & K. Gilmore: The Great Deception. Farrar Straus & Co. N.Y. 1963.
168. Trial Of John Surratt: In Criminal Court For D. C. Govt. Printing Off. 1867.
169. H. Haskell: New Deal In Ancient Rome. A. A. Knopf. N.Y. 1939.
170. Personal Communication.
171. P. Bakewell Jr.: What We Are Using For Money. D. Van Nostrand. N.Y. 1952.
172. Views Of The Biblical World. Jordan Publications Inc. N.Y. 1959:1:107.
173. R. Braley: Blast Hits New U.S. Refinery In Bonn. Daily News. N.Y. 1/19/66.
174. E. M. Josephson: Advertisement Demanding Legal Action Against Strike N.Y Times. 1/12/66.
175. Louisiana State Legislature:Report By Joint Legislative Com-

mittee To Investigate The Rigging Of Voting Machines. Baton Rouge. 1960.
176. J. D. Rockefeller III; Time Is Running Out. N.Y. Herald Tribune. 1/13/66:11.
177. Group Insists It Will See TWU in Court. Journal American. 1/13/66.
178. Senate Approves Bank Merger; Hanover Affected. N.Y. Times 2/9/6.
179. Text of President's (Kennedy's) Call For Atlantic Unity N.Y. Times. 7/5/62.
180. John Davenport: International Money, Fortune. N.Y. January 1966.
181. Reuters Dispatch: China Boasts Of Oil, Daily News. N.Y. 1/3/66.
182. Rockefeller Nephew Explains Switch. N.Y Times 2/2/66.
183. Fowler Warns On Viet Dollar Drain. N.Y. Times 2/15/66:2.
184. H. E. Heinemann: Personality: Conciliatory Force In Banking. N.Y. Times 2/3/66.
185. Chicago Daily News Almanac. 1946.
186. World Almanac. N.Y. World Telegram 1940.
187. L. A. Emaleh & J. B. Samuel: Jewish Cemetery, 9th & Spruce St. Philadelphia. 1962.
188. .E M. Josephson: Roosevelt's Communist Manifesto. Chedney Press. 1955.
189. C. E. Miner: The Ratification Of The Federal Constitution By The State Of New York. Columbia U. 1921.
190. D. Bobbe: The Boyhood Of Alexander Hamilton. Am. Heritage. Vol., No. 4 N.Y. 1955.
191. F. Pick: Broadcast On Fay Henle Radio Program, Sta. WOR. N.Y. 4/13/66.
192. Board Of Governors, FRS: Banking Studies. Washington. 1941.
193. C. G. Bowers: The Tragic Era. Riverside Press, Cambridge. 1922.
194. 4 Wheat. (1819).
195. 8 Wall. 603 (1870)
196. 12 Wall. 457 (1871)
197. Post et al: Basic Constitution Cases. Oxford Press. N.Y.1948.
198. International Basic Economy Corp. Annual Report, 1965.
199. Father Chiniquy: Fifty Years In The Church Of Rome. R. Banks & Son London. 1885.
200. S. Diamond: A Casual View Of America. The Home Letters Of Salamon de Rothschild, 1859-61. Stanford U. Press. Stanford. 1961.
201. The Economist: Putting A Rothschild Myth To Rest. N.Y. Times. 6/27/65
202. Military Order Of The Loyal Legion: Bulletin. N.Y. June, 1959.
203. W. P. Overholser: A Short Review & Analysis Of Money In The U.S. Libertyville, Ind. 1936.
204. E. Pound: America, Roosevelt & The Causes Of The Present War. London. 1951.
205. E. Pound: Gold & Work. London 1951.
206. E. M. Josephson: The Gold Standard Myth 1933.
207. S. Birmingham: Our Crowd. Harper & Row. N.Y. 1966.
208. AP: Martin Assailed For "Cooling Off" Inflation At Expense Of Builders. N.Y. Times. 8/1/66:37:6.
209. G. A. Dondero, M. C.: UNESCO—Communism & Modern Art. Debate. 84th Congress reprinted by Chedney Press, N.Y. 1968.
210. W. Patman: On H. R. 10595. Congressional Record. Washington, 7/12/67.
211. G. R. C. Davis: Magna Carta. Trustees Of The British Museum. London. 1965.
212. R. Alden: City Gets Funds To Collect Taxes. N.Y. Times

9/21/66.
213. W. Patman: Investigation Of Problems of Small Business. Govt. Print. Off. 1962.
214. F. Pick: 1966 Pick's Currency Yearbook. Pick Publishing. N.Y 1966.
215. Rampart Report On S.E. Asia. Rampart Magazine. Los Angeles. 1966.
216. J. Cassidy & L. Abelman: JFK So Closely Guarded Only A "Why" Gets Through. Sunday Daily News, N.Y. 11/10/63:5:4.
217. J. E. Haley: A Texan Looks At Lyndon. Palo Dura Press, Canyon, Texas. 1964.
218. S. Alsop: Was John F. Kennedy A Great Man? Sat. Evening Post. Phila. 12/3/66.
219. W. Wolfe: The Courts Must Curb Culture. Sat. Evening Post. Phila. 12/3/66.
220. Sen. John F. Kennedy: On Sending GIs To Vietnam. Congress. Record, 1954- 2904; 4672-82;5120;10003-6. Govt. Print. Off. Washington. 1954.
221. Lindsay Says U.S. Has Missed Diplomatic Chances To End War. N.Y. Times. 11/27/66.
222. C. Glass: An Adventure In Constructive Finance. Doubleday. Page & Co.
223. Wm. Guy Carr: The Red Fog Over America. Willowdale, 1957.
224. R. B. Fosdick: Chronicle Of A Generation. Harper & Bros. N.Y. 1958.
225. S. H. Schanberg: Chase Bank To Seek Lottery Agencies. N.Y. Times 1/6/67:37.
226. R. E. Beddingfield: Personality: Eaton's Son Made It On His Own. N.Y. Times. 1/22/67:F 3:3.
227. State Times: Joint Legislative Committee To Investigate The Rigging·Of Voting Machines. Baton Rouge, La. Nov. 3, 1960.
228. W. H. Joe Cooper: What You Should Know About...Rigging Machines. Lillian B. Enterprises Inc. 2176 Alaska St. Baton Rouge, La. 1961.
229. S. Alsop: The Rockefeller Nobody Knows. Sat. Evening Post. Sept. 1959.
230. High Court Acts In Rape Case Of Negro. N.Y. Times. 1/24/67.
231. Saigon Catholics Stage A Protest. Militant Youths Condemn "Sellout" Peace Efforts. N.Y. Times. 2/26/67.
232. P. Tompkins: Italy Betrayed. Simon & Schuster. 1966.
233. F. Capell: The Strange Death of Marilyn Monroe. Herald of Freedom. N.Y. 1964.
234. Wiretap Probe Names 2nd Man. World Journal Tribune. N.Y. 12/17/66.
235. H. Bigart: Kennedy Defends View On Abortion. N.Y. Times. 2/23/67:1:2.
236. J. R. Sikes: Kennedy Predicts Abortion Reforms. N.Y. Times. 2/18/67:1:4.
237. AP: Pope Warns Jesuits On Obedience. N.Y. Times 11/16/67.
238. AP: Jesuits "Lying," Says Cushing. Daily News. 1/27/67:11:1.
239. S. Birmingham: Ladies Home J. Phila. March 1967.
240. H. Fairlee: New Kennedy Controversy: Harvard & Politics. World Journal Tribune. 1/22/67:24.
241. David Tappan: A discourse In The Chapel At Harvard College. June 19, 1798, To The Graduating Class On The Influence Of Illuminati on Religion And The French Revolution. Cambridge, 1798.
242. Personal report from guests.
243. Wm. Rodgers: Rockefeller's Follies. Stein & Day. N.Y. 1966.
244. Frances Bolton: Correspondence in possession of author.
245. P. L. Montgomery: Chase Convenes Big Parley In Rio. N.Y. Times. 3/13/67.
246. Gore Vidal: "The Holy Family." Esquire. N.Y. April 1967.

247. E. L. Madden: Rockefeller Race Cost $5 Million. N.Y. Times. 1/30/66:42:1
248. E. Spagnol: Charge Rocky Team Election Loans Illegal. Daily News. N.Y. 2/24/67:14:1.
249. V. Riesel: Rocky Dinner Party: Groundwork For 68? World Journal Tribune. N.Y. 12/20/66:26:6.
250. V. Riesel: The Governor Takes Another Giant Step. World Journal Tribune N.Y. 3/21/67:27.
251. J. Ortega y Gasset: The Revolt Of The Masses. W. W. Norton, N.Y. 1932.
252. C. Egan: Kennedy Hits Rocky On Power Plant. World Journal Tribune. N.Y. 3/20/67.
253. P. Milliones: Kennedy Assails State On Power. N.Y. Times 3/21/67:1.
254. T. O'Hara: RFK, Rocky Seek Pact On Power. World Journal Tribune. N.Y. 3/21/67:1.
255. Republicans For Better Government: The Shocking Facts About Winthrop Rockefeller. P.O. Box 450. Pine Bluff, Ark. 1966.
256. E. M. Josephson: Slaves For Sale. N.Y. Amsterdam News, 10/29/66:8:1.
257. J. Axler: Lynda At Wedding, But Missed Star Role. Daily News. N.Y. 4/2/67.
258. J. Herber: XXVth Amendment President Plan Has Been Passed. N.Y. Times. 2/11/67:1.
259. 11 Seized In Berlin In Reported Plot To Kill Humphrey. N.Y. Times. 4/6/67:1.
261. Wall St. Journal: Most Free-World Gold Is In U.S. But Half Is Not Ours. 4/11/67:1:6.
262. L. Silberman & R. Janssen: Gold Drain Plug. Wall St. Jour. N.Y. 4/11/67:1:6.
263. J. Deaver: Business In Brief. Chase Manhattan Bank. 4/1/67.
264. R. Dietsch: LBJ To Ask Congress To Free Gold. World Journal Tribune 4/17/67.
265. C. Kirk: Billion Dollar Dynasty. Sunday News. Sec. II:1. N.Y. 12/18/66.
266. E. L. Dale Jr.: U.S. Discount Rate Is Reduced To 4% To Loosen Credit. N.Y. Times. 4/7/67:1:8.
267. H. E. Heinemann: Chase Bank Defends S. Africa Loans. N.Y. Times 3/29/67:61.
268. Ronan Says Area Faces Crisis Over Jet Ports. N.Y. Times. 4/27/67.
269. Roosa A Rockefeller Trustee. N.Y. Times. 4/24/67.
270. R. E. Bedingfield: Eaton Joins Rockefeller To Spur Trade With Reds. N.Y. Times. 1/16/67:1:7.
271. Liberty Lobby: Consular Treaty Ratification: The Inside Story. Liberty Lowdown, Washington. April 1967. #50.
272. D. Houston: Eight Years In Wilson's Cabinet. Doubleday Page. Garden City. 1926.
273. Fr. John LaFarge Institute: Prospectus. c/o America, 106 W. 56 St. N.Y.
274. Rockefeller Lugs His Baggage Here. N.Y. Times, 11/14/48.
275. N. Sheehan: Armament Sales. U.S. Principal Supplier to World. N.Y. Times. 7/19/67.
276. N. Sheehan: U.S. Arms Sale Spurred By Large Field Force & Complex Credit System. N.Y. Times. 7/20/67.
277. N. Sheehan: American Does Brisk Business In Surplus Weapons. N.Y. Times. 7/21/67.
278. N. Sheehan: 16 Concerns Get Major Share Of U.S. Arms Sale Loans. N.Y. Times. 7/21/67.
279. U.S. Arms Salesman, Henry John Kuss Jr. N.Y. Times. 7/19/67:2.
280. Private Arms Dealer, Samuel Cummings. N.Y. Times. 7/21/67.

281. E. W. Kenworthy: Arms Sale Loans Fought In Senate. N.Y. Times. 8/9/67:1:4.
282. E. W. Kenworthy: Senate Defeats Move To Block Arms Sale Loans. N.Y. Times 8/10/67.
283. E. W. Kenworthy: Senate Vote Bars Loans To Nations Shipping To Hanoi. Dirksen Plan To Prohibit Help In Communist Trade Defeated 51-35. N.Y. Times 8/11/67.
284. Rockefeller Foundation-Directory Of Fellowship Awards 1917-50. N.Y. 1951.
285. Gunnar Myrdal: An American Dilemma. McGraw Hill. N.Y. 1964.
286. Reuter: Kills & Eats Family. Daily News. N.Y. Aug. 13, 1967.
287. Sean O'Callaghan: The Slave Trade Today. Crown Publishers. N.Y. 1961.
288. T. H. Hamilton: U.N Commission To Consider Report On World Slave Trade. N.Y. Times. 3/20/67.
289. D. A. Schmidt: Saudi Arabian Slavery Persists Despite Ban By Feisal, in 1962. N.Y. Times. 3/28/67.
290. D. A. Schmidt: British Group Finds Evidence Of An Increase In Human Slavery Since the End Of World War II, N.Y. Times. 4/6/67.
291. Negro Riots Called Part Of Black Plot. Daily News. N.Y. 9/19/67:24.
292. G. Dugan: Religious Bodies Stress Race Issue. N.Y. Times. 9/2/67:16.
293. New York Rebuilds Its Capital. Fortune Magazine. N.Y..
294. E. B. Fisk: A Tax On Profits Of Churches Urged By Episcopalian Group. N.Y. Times. 7/20/67.
295. Creation of New Monetary Reserves Slated At IMF Session This Week. Wall Street Journal. 9/25/67.
296. John Doe: Report From the Iron Mountain: On The Possibility & Desirability Of Peace. Dial Press. N.Y. 1967.
297. W. D. Smith: Martin Stresses Need For Tax Rise. N.Y. Times, 11/16/67:69:5.
298. A. L. Malabre Jr.: The New Confusion, More Analysts Question. "New Economics." Wall St. Jour. 11/7/67.
299. IMF Takes Up Commodity Price Props. Hand Drawing Rights, Veto Issue To Panel. Wall St. Jour., 9/29/67:8.
300. Gold & Its Relation To Dollars. N.Y. Times. 11/25/67:57.
301. N.Y. Times, David Rockefeller eulogizes Per Jacobsson. 10/19/67.
302. Pentagon Awards 75 Fuel Contracts Totaling $305 Million. Wall St. Jour. 12/4/67.
303. I. Seda & H. Greenberg: Behind the Egyptian Sphinx. Chilton. N.Y. 1960.
304. E. M. Josephson: A Poor Rockefeller Dies. Chedney Press. N.Y. 1960.
305. N.Y. Times:
306. J. P. Fried: "College Town" Is Rising On Fringe Of Lincoln Center. N.Y. Times. 12/4/67:49.
307. State Tax Aid Faces Probe As Gangster's Partner. Daily News. 9/29/67:22.
308. Colon Quits His Tax Post. Indicted In L.I. Tax Deal. 12/5/67:2.
309. E. Perlmutter: Ex-FBI Agent Links State Liquor Aid To Mafia. N.Y. Times 11/30/67.
310. Reuters: Capuchins Lose Appeal. Post, N.Y. 10/31/67.
311. James Clancy: Governor's Midtown Offices, The Unofficial State Capitol. N.Y. Times. 11/25/67:41.
312. A. Mulligan: Addicts Steal $10 Millon Per Day For Habit. N.Y. Times. 12/14/67.
313. Drugs Top Cars In '66 Profitability, U.S. Survey Shows. N.Y. Times. 12/13/67:65.
314. Six Narcotic Agents Arrested. N.Y. Times. 12/13/67:1.

315. Post: More Arrests Are Due In Cop Drug Scandal. N.Y. Times. 12/13/67:5.
316. T. Poster: Probe Told Of Airport Sabotage, Daily News. N.Y. 12/14/67.
317. B. Welles: India To Get Contraceptives Under New U.S. Aid Plan. N.Y. Times 9/15/67:1.
318. Reuters:Kills & Eats Family, Daily News. N.Y. 8/14/67.
320. R. Leon: Silver. Significance Of Its Rise & Fall. N.Y. 1/12/31.
321. W. Edwards: Has Lauchlin Currie Finally Learned Truth About Communism? Chicago Tribune Press Service. Human Events. Washington, 1967.
322. S. W. Baron: The Russian Jews Under Tsars & Soviets. MacMillan. N.Y. 1964.
323. E. L. Dale Jr.: Federal Reserve May Face Audit. Threat To Independence Seen N.Y. Times. 9/14/67.
324. B. E. Calame: Foundation Twist—Now Families Create Organization To Cut Their Liability For Taxes. Wall St. Jour. 8/28/67.
325. A. Wood: Ducks Query On Tax Dodge In Foundations. Daily News. N.Y. 11/8/67.
326. E. E. Asbury. Tax Dodges Laid To Foundations. N.Y. Times 8/19/67:54:3.
327. C. Glutzner: Foundations Get $981,863 Tax Bill. N.Y. Times. 3/27/67.
328. Council On Foundations Elects Chief Executives. N.Y. Times, 3/7/67.
329. H. Taubman: Ford, Rockefeller Foundations Adjusting To Changing World. N.Y. Times. 1/30/67.
330. A Foundation Hires Clark Kerr. Daily News. N.Y. 1967.
331. J. Hamill: Strange Career Of Mr. Hoover Under Two Flags. Wm. Faro Inc. N.Y. 1931.
332. D. Wharton: The Roosevelt Omnibus. A. A. Knopf. N.Y. 1934.
333. N. Rockefeller: Excerpts From Rockefeller's 10th State Of The State Message To Legislature. N.Y. Times 1/4/68:26.
334. J. C. Grew: Turbulent Era. Hammond, Hammond & Co. London. 1953.
335. S. H. Schanberg: Governor Opens Session; Says Vital Needs Demand A Tax Rise Of $500 Million. N.Y. Times 1/4/58:1.
336. T. J. Fleming: Fordham Is Trying To Be Catholic, With A Small "c". N.Y. Times Magazine. 12/10/67.
337. J. A. Lucas: The Drug Scene. Americans Are Found To Be Increasingly Oriented To A Wide Variety Of Drugs. Usage By Youth Grows Most. N.Y. Times. 1/8/68.
338. Lincoln: Kennedy & Johnson.
339. N.Y. Amsterdam News: Vote For Rockefeller. 10/29/66.
340. AP: Jesuits To Fight For Negroes. Daily News. N.Y. 11/6/67:4:1.
341. Union Leader Urges Sainthood For Kennedy. World Telegram & Sun. N.Y. 12/24/64.
342. J. A. Lucas: The Drug Scene: Dependence Grows. N.Y. Times. 1/8/68.
   R. D. Lyons: Science's Knowledge On Misuse Of Drugs Lags. N.Y. Times. 1/9/68.
   M. Arnold: The Scene. A Growing Number Of America's Elite Are "Turning On." Some See Insight, Others Sexuality. N.Y. Times 1/10/68.
   J. Kefner: The Drug Scene: Many Students Now Regard Marijuana As A Part Of Growing Up. N.Y. Times 1/11/68.
   M. Waldron: The Drug Scene: Nations Illegal Traffic Is Valued Up To $400 Million Annually. New York Called Distribution Area. N.Y. Times. 1/12/68.
343. S. Alsop: The Rockefeller No One Knows. Evening Post Sept. 1959.

344. D. Hudson: Factors Influencing The Nursing Shortage. Atlanta. 1966.
345. N. Sheehan: Pentagon To Sell $5 Billion Arms Abroad In 3 Years. N.Y. Times 1/5/68.
346. U.S. Senate: Civil & Criminal Disorders. Hearing 90th Congress. Govt. Print. Off. 1967.
347. R. Wright: Black Power. Harper & Bros. N.Y. 1954.
348. House Of Lords: Slavery In Africa & Asia. Hansard. O.R. v. 225, No. 104. 7/14/60.
349. P. P. Kennedy: Group Urges UN To Halt Slavery, N.Y. Times 12/4/66.
350. W. H. Ferry, Ed.: Students & Society. Report On A Confecence Center For The Study Of Democratic Institutions. Santa Barbara. 1967.
351. Speaking Freely- Interview, TV Guide 12/17/67 A-21.
352. David Rockefeller, Banker's Banker. Newsweek. 4/3/67:72.
353. V. Teasdale: Oil For The Lamps Of China.
354. E. M. Josephson: A Poor Rockefeller Dies. Chedney Press. 19.
355. E. M. Josephson: Roosevelt's Un-Constitutional Gold Order. N.Y. Times. 10/11/33:22:5.
356. American Council Of Christian Laymen: How Red Is The Federal Council Of Churches. Madison, Wis. 1949.
357. J. Crafton. Drug Raiders Nab 33 At Stony Brook, Post. N.Y. 1/17/68.
358. C. Haberman: Says L. I. Dean Tipped Kids On Raid. Post. N.Y. 1/31/68.
359. H. Dudar: Stony Brook Quizzed On Big Pill Theft. Post. N.Y. 1/25/68.
360. F. Mazza & J. McNamara: College's Chief Says One In Five Use Drugs. Daily News. N.Y. 2/2/68.
361. S. H. Schanberg: Governor Backs Albany Project. Answers Levitt Criticism Of South Mall's Soaring Costs. N.Y. Times. 1/3/68.
362. AP: A Rockefeller May Bid For West Virginia Post. N.Y. Times. 2/1/68.
363. David Rockefeller: Speaking Freely. WNBC Community Affairs Dept. N.Y. 11/20/67.
364. C. H. George, Ed.: Revolution. Five Centuries Of Europe In Conflict. Dell Publishing Inc. N.Y. 1962.
366. S. Rowland Jr.: Crucifixions Reported In Asia. N.Y. Times. 7/17/56:51.
367. Schuster: Thirteen For Christ.
368. Fr. Ryan: Personal Interview.
370. AP: Rosy Forecast In India. Daily News. N.Y. 1/13/68.
372. Gold & Its Relation To Dollars. N.Y. Times 11/25/67:67.
373. N. Sheehan: The Strategic Reserve. Serious Depletion Feared As A Result Of Decision To Bolster Vietnam Force. N.Y. Times 2/15/68.
374. J. Herbers: Riot Study Is Said To Express Alarm. N.Y. Times. 2/18/68:1:7.
375. Pope Pius XII: Sertum Laetitiae. Encyclical Letter To The Church In The U.S. A translation. Natl. Catholic Welfare Conference. Washington. 1954.
376. C. B. Dall: F.D.R. My Exploited Father-In-Law. Christian Crusade Pub. Tulsa. 1967.
377. GATT To Examine U.S. Policy Issue. N.Y. Times. 2/19/68:59:2.
378. K. Bloch: Dead Giveaway Foreign Aid Has Done More Harm Than Good. Barrons. N.Y. 2/9/68:1.
379. K. Gross & C. Pelleck: Leary & Garelik Feud Linked To Shakeup. Post. N.Y. 1/17/68.
380. Wm. Allen: Rockefeller, Giant Dwarf Symbol. Institute For Public Service N.Y. 1930.
381. W. Patman: HR11.

382. P. E. Sutton: Sees Viet Vets Using War Skills In Protests. Daily News. 2/23/68:1.
383. Pentagon Explains GIs Get Pep Pills To Diet & Survive. N.Y. Times. 3/7/68.
384. See 341.
385. A. Kubek. Ed.: Morgenthau Diary (China) Govt. Print. Off. 1965.
386. E. M. Josephson: Rockefeller's Brazilian Coffee Deal. Wake Up American, Feb. 1954. Chedney Press. N.Y.
388. J. Stack: Rocky Discloses FBI "Had Goods" on Hiss. Union Leader. Manchester. 1/10/64:1:1.
389. AP: Rockefeller Recalls Hiss Case. N.Y. Times 1/11/64.
390. UPI: U.S. Sat On Hiss Case For Three Years, Rocky. N.Y. Journ Amer. 1/10/64:1.
391. AP: "FBI Told Me Of Hiss Back In 1945," Rocky. N.Y. Daily News. 1/11/64:1.
392. Nelson Rockefeller, ghosted by Prof. H. A. Kissinger: Policy & The People. Foreign Affairs. January 1968.
393. Rocky's Next Item: Viet. Post. N.Y. 3/2/68.
394. E. P. Pasmowski: Bilderberger Meetings. Their Strategic Position Within The National Power Structure. Antioch College Master's Thesis. 1967.
395. A. Tully: CIA, The Inside Story. Wm. Morrow & Co. N.Y. 1962.
396. F. Lewis III: Top Of The News. v. 9, p. 331. Oct. 17, 1967.
397. R. Witkin: Rockefeller Urged By GOP Leaders To Get Into Race. N.Y. Times. 3/11/68.
398. R. Mathieu: GOP Summit Bids Rocky Act. GOP Bigs Put Pressure On R. Daily News. 3/11/68:1.
399. C. G. Fraser: 6 Narcotic Agents Seized As Sellers. N.Y Times. 12/13/67.
400. Editorial. Nongovernmental. Indianapolis News 2/29/68.
401. Pifer: Carnegie Corporation Report. N.Y. 1968.
402. 11 Seized In Report Plot To Kill Humphrey. N.Y. Times 4/6/67.
403. H. E. Heinemann: 7 Nations Back Dual Gold Price, Bar Selling To Private Buyers N.Y. Times. 3/18/68:1.
404. E. M. Josephson: Letter to Lefkowitz Demanding Rockefeller Prosecution For Openly Acknowledged Corruption. (79:203) Chedney Press. N.Y. 1960.
406. J. Resnick: The Loser. N.Y. Times 3/18/68:49.
407. A. Wiley: Conference Of European & American Leaders. Cong. Record. App: A 1199f Washington. 2/19/57.
408. B. Javits: The Bilderberger Meetings. Cong. Rec.: 7685. Washington. 4/11/64.
409. J. Monahan & K. O. Gilmore: The Great Deception. Farrar Straus & Co. N.Y. 1963.
410. *Rockefeller Urges Water Fluoridation.* World Telegram & Sun. 1/17/58.
411. Editorial: On Trade With The Enemy. Daily News. N.Y. 1/17/67.
412. W. Patman: Control of Commercial Banks & Interlocks Among Financial Institutions. Com. On. Bank. & Cur. 7/3/67.
413. W. Hoge & Wm. Rudy Jr.: I Can Defeat Any Democrat. Rocky. Post, N.Y. 4/11/68.
414. D. Lawrence: Nation's Disorder: Guerilla Warfare. Column, N.Y. 4/12/68:4.
415. Paul Scott: Reds Offer A Role For Negroes. Column. N.Y. 4/12/68.
416. Nat'l. Planning Ass.: The Case Study Of IBEC. N.Y. 1968.
417. Fluoridation Of Water. Gov't. Print. Off. 1954.

370

www.ingramcontent.com/pod-product-compliance
Lightning Source LLC
Chambersburg PA
CBHW070540270326
41926CB00013B/2158